A Southern Living Book

Copyright © 1975 by Oxmoor House, Inc.
Book Division of The Progressive Farmer Company
P.O. Box 2463
Birmingham, Alabama 35202

All rights reserved. No part of this book may be reproduced in any form or by any means without the prior written permission of the Publisher, excepting brief quotes used in connection with reviews written specifically for inclusion in a magazine or newspaper.

Library of Congress Catalog Card Number: 75-17097

Manufactured in the United States of America

Fifth Printing, 1978

For The Love Of Cooking

Cover Art & Illustrations: Thomas Ford
Photography: Taylor Lewis
Editor: Karen Phillips

CONTENTS

Appetizers, Snacks, and Sandwiches	3	Fish and Shellfish	169
Beverages	23	Meats	193
Breads	35	Pies and Pastry	243
Cakes and Frostings	59	Poultry and Dressing	267
Candies and Confections	81	Salads and Salad Dressing	295
Casseroles	91	Sauces	333
Cookies and Small Cakes	117	Soups, Stews, and Chowders	343
Desserts	137	Vegetables	361
Eggs and Grains	157	Index	401

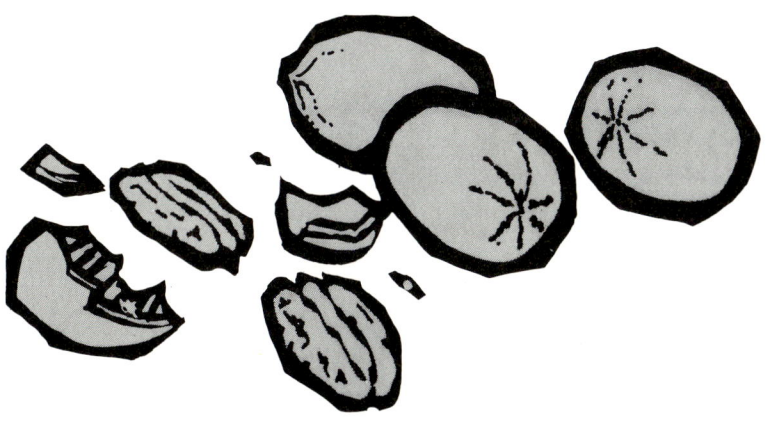

* Asterisks indicate budget recipes.

INTRODUCTION

When we were children we drew straws to see who would cook and who would wash the dishes, and invariably my sister Myrtle drew the smallest straw. I think I would have done anything to get out of washing dishes, and maybe that's one of the reasons I started to cook so early. At a very young age, I began collecting recipes and putting them in scrapbooks made from old catalogs from men's tailoring shops. One of the best of those recipes, for a devil's food cake, turned up recently in such a scrapbook; Big Sis (Mamma's younger sister) developed the recipe with raisins, dates, and pecans in the filling, and she put a white frosting on top. I wonder how many other recipes I might have stuck in something because I was always pasting things in catalogs.

Mamma was much more interested in planting than in cooking—we always laughed and said she could stick a broom handle in the ground and it would root. She usually managed to have a year-round garden because she was scared to use a pressure cooker. Since she refused to use a pressure cooker there was no way she could save out-of-season vegetables. My four sisters and I started helping her with the cooking, which gave us all experience at a very early age. By the time most of us had reached the age of twelve, we were able to take over and do the entire meal.

I remember once when Mamma was sick and I was old enough to be halfway competent in the pinch and dab method of cooking (that is, without a recipe), we decided to make some sausage with garlic like our German neighbors had. Well, we ended up with about four times as much garlic as we needed. We were stuck with eighty pounds of sausage—the whole year's supply of homemade sausage—bound up in that heavy garlic flavor.

I think simplicity is really the keynote to the kind of cooking that I learned from Mamma. She made soups—not many varieties and never any cream soups that I can remember—it was just good old, hearty beef soup or plain vegetable soup.

Mamma used to raise her own garlic; she would put the fresh green garlic strips in her delicious beans—boiled beans. She would add a little chili powder to them, and they were a real treat. Sometimes ground beef was added to make chili beans.

You couldn't beat Mamma's yeast rolls. We would come in from school and as soon as we hit the front porch, we could smell those rolls. We would drop our books, run to the kitchen, and eat so many that she would have hardly any left for the meal. Mamma's sourdough biscuits were awfully good, too. I couldn't possibly give you the recipe because she couldn't give it herself. Once she had her sourdough starter, she dropped the ball into a jar of buttermilk. This is unlike today's recipes for sourdough, but it worked.

Since we're on the subject of breads, I have a story that my Dad told on himself and Uncle Harry. Before either of them were married, they were going up to Lubbock, Texas, on the train to work on a ranch. The conductor came in about noon to see if they wanted to buy any sandwiches. Being as countrified as they were, neither of them had heard the term "sandwich," and they didn't know what sandwiches were. They said, "Well, hell no, we don't want any sandwiches. Just bring us some meat and bread." I guess as long as he lived, Daddy never ate what he called a sandwich. He might have had two slices of bread around some meat, but he still didn't call it a sandwich.

Mamma thought that a meal was incomplete without some kind of dessert. I can remember visiting her one time when she was about eighty; she brought out a dessert that looked green or red (I've forgotten exactly what color) in bowls, but it had a yellow cast to it. I asked her what it was and she told me it was Jello. I said, "I know, but what's this yellow stuff in it?"

She said, "Well, I just put butter in it to make it richer." When we were growing up, there was an abundance of eggs and cream and butter since we had our own cow and hogs, and Mamma thought that anything rich was good. She was never stingy with the butter or eggs in her cooking, but I don't think butter and Jello will ever catch on.

When I won a prize (third place) for my yeast bread, I think I knew that cooking, in some capacity, would be my career interest. Cooking had been so much a part of my life that I hadn't really thought about making it a career before. This recognition not only gave me a trip to a 4-H short course in San Antonio, but it gave me the confidence I needed to pursue cooking.

If my early experiences taught me anything, they made me aware that one does not have to be bound precisely by a recipe. Be flexible enough to try new flavorings in some of your recipes; for example, you may substitute a different flavoring for the vanilla in one of your cakes. I'm not advocating substitutions for basic ingredients, only that you experiment with the spices or seasonings.

All of us know there is great satisfaction in getting compliments for our cooking. The more encouragement you get from your family, the more you will feel like trying new things. Don't hesitate to ask how the family liked a meal or a recipe; they may like the food but forget to tell you.

Cooking can be a joy, but you must be willing to make some sacrifices, face a few failures, and start all over again. Most importantly, take time with your cooking; take as many pains in making a batch of cookies or a loaf of bread as you would in stitching a needlepoint pillow.

Lena E. Sturges

Food Editor

Southern Living Magazine

For The Love of Cooking

Appetizers, Snacks, and Sandwiches

Appetizers and snacks have been around for a very long time, but the names probably originated in the twentieth century. Sandwiches, on the other hand, have been around for several centuries; history tells us that the fourth Earl of Sandwich made the English people sandwich minded and gave the world a luncheon dish. Even today, a soup and sandwich midday meal is enjoyed around the world.

Appetizers, which are not meant to be a meal, are those dainty sandwiches, dips, spreads, and cheese balls that are generally served at cocktail parties. When entertaining large groups, the hostess prepares a variety of such hors d'oeuvres to stimulate appetites for the meal that follows; appetizers should not be too filling.

Snacks, on the other hand, may consist of a simple piece of fruit, a small sandwich, a handful of peanuts, or quite possibly some of the foods made from recipes in this chapter.

Ham, cheese, and seafoods are three foods used in abundance in Southern dishes, and they find special favor when used to prepare appetizers, snacks, and sandwiches.

Hot Burger-Cheese Sandwiches

1 pound ground round beef
1 clove garlic, minced
1 small onion, chopped
Salt and pepper to taste
½ teaspoon chili powder
1 (4-ounce) can roasted, peeled, diced green chiles
1 (8-ounce) can tomato sauce
¼ pound shredded pasteurized process cheese
10 small French rolls

Brown beef lightly; add garlic, onion, salt, pepper, and chili powder. Sauté until onions are transparent. Add the chiles and tomato sauce and simmer for 5 minutes, uncovered. Add cheese, mix well, and cool. Cut rolls part way through and scoop out centers. Fill centers with meat mixture. Place rolls on cookie sheet, cover with foil, and heat at 375° for about 20 minutes. Remove the foil and cook for an additional 5 minutes. Yield: 10 sandwiches.

Beefy Spread Sandwiches

2 cups finely chopped, cooked beef
½ cup chopped celery
1 teaspoon caraway seeds
½ teaspoon salt
2 tablespoons minced onion
½ cup mayonnaise
8 to 10 sourdough buns
Chopped cabbage

Mix all but last 2 ingredients. Spread on sourdough buns; add cabbage at the last minute. Yield: 8 to 10 sandwiches.

*Cheese and Egg Sandwich Filling

 2 cups (½ pound) shredded Cheddar cheese
 4 hard-cooked eggs, finely chopped
 ½ cup commercial sour cream
 ¼ cup chopped sweet pickle or drained sweet pickle relish
 1 teaspoon prepared mustard
 1 tablespoon chopped parsley
 ½ teaspoon salt
  Dash pepper

Combine all ingredients and blend. Yield: 3 cups filling.

Cheese Salad Sandwich Filling

 2 cups shredded Swiss cheese
 ½ cup chopped tomato
 3 tablespoons chopped stuffed olives
 2 tablespoons chopped green pepper
 ½ cup mayonnaise
  Salt to taste

Combine cheese, tomato, olives, green pepper, mayonnaise, and salt; mix well and put in covered container. Chill in refrigerator. Yield: 2 cups.

Cheese and Turkey Melt

 18 slices white bread
 8 eggs, beaten
  Butter
 12 slices Cheddar cheese
 24 slices cooked turkey breast
 12 slices tomato

Dip each slice of bread in eggs; cook in butter on preheated griddle until lightly browned. Cover each of 12 slices bread with 1 slice cheese, 2 slices turkey, and 1 slice tomato. Continue grilling the bread slices slowly in butter until cheese melts. Stack 2 slices together and top with remaining bread. Serve hot. Yield: 6 sandwiches.

*Cream Cheese Sandwich Filling

 1 (3-ounce) package cream cheese, softened
 1 teaspoon grated onion and juice
 1 teaspoon minced parsley
 2 tablespoons grated cucumber, drained well
 2 teaspoons lemon juice
  Dash salt
  Dash paprika

Combine ingredients and mix well. Spread between well-trimmed slices of sandwich bread. Sandwiches will keep several days if properly wrapped and refrigerated. Yield: 1 cup.

Note: Filling mixed with small amount of cream makes a nice dip.

*Crunchy Chicken Sandwiches

 1 (5-ounce) can chicken spread
 ½ cup finely chopped celery
 ¼ cup chopped sweet pickles
 1 tablespoon mayonnaise
  Salt and pepper to taste
 8 to 12 slices bread

Combine chicken spread, celery, pickles, mayonnaise, and seasonings. Spread on bread. Yield: filling for 4 to 6 sandwiches.

*Cucumber-Cheese Sandwiches

 2 (3-ounce) packages cream cheese, softened
 1 medium-size cucumber, pared and chopped
 1 small onion, chopped
  Salt to taste
 2 drops hot sauce
  Mayonnaise
  Rounds of thin bread, buttered

Mash cream cheese with a fork. Put cucumber and onion through blender and blend until smooth. Stir into cream cheese; add salt, hot sauce, and enough mayonnaise to make mixture of spreading consistency. Spread on bread rounds. Cover with damp cloth; place in refrigerator until time to serve. Garnish as desired. Yield: spread for about 30 tea sandwiches.

appetizers, snacks and sandwiches 5

*Cucumber Sandwiches

1 (3-ounce) package cream cheese, softened
1 medium-size cucumber, peeled, grated, and drained
1 tablespoon grated onion
1 tablespoon commercial sour cream
Salt and pepper to taste
Green food coloring (optional)
Bread slices

Combine all ingredients for filling and stir until smooth. Spread on thin slices of bread, cover with another slice, and cut into desired shapes. Yield: ¾ cup filling.

Grilled Crab Sandwich

1 pound cooked crabmeat, fresh or frozen
3 hard-cooked eggs, chopped
½ cup chopped celery
¼ cup relish
Mayonnaise (enough to moisten all ingredients)
Onion salt to taste
Garlic salt to taste
Salt and pepper to taste
18 slices bread
9 slices Cheddar cheese
Butter

Toss together the crabmeat, eggs, celery, relish, and mayonnaise. Add seasonings. Spread the crab filling on 9 slices of bread. Add a slice of cheese to the sandwich before closing it. Butter both sides of the sandwich and grill until golden brown. Yield: 9 sandwiches.

*Hot Corned Beef Sandwiches

1 (12-ounce) can corned beef
1 cup finely chopped celery
3 tablespoons hot dog relish
2 tablespoons chopped pimiento
⅓ cup mayonnaise
Seasoned pepper to taste
10 hot dog or hamburger buns

Chop corned beef; stir in celery, relish, pimiento, and mayonnaise. Add seasoned pepper. Fill buns with mixture and put on baking sheet (place hot dog buns filled-side up). Cover with foil; heat at 300° about 35 minutes. Yield: 10 sandwiches.

*Ham Salad Sandwiches

1 cup ground cooked ham
4 tablespoons finely minced green pepper
2 teaspoons prepared mustard
4 tablespoons mayonnaise
2 tablespoons finely minced onion
Bread slices, buttered

Mix together all ingredients for filling and chill. Bring to room temperature before spreading on bread. Top with another slice of bread and cut into desired shapes. Yield: 1½ cups.

Ham 'n Cheese French Toast

4 slices ham
4 slices cheese
8 slices day-old raisin bread
2 eggs, beaten
½ cup milk
½ teaspoon salt
1 teaspoon dry mustard
Butter or margarine

Place 1 slice of ham and 1 cheese slice between 2 slices raisin bread. Combine eggs, milk, salt, and mustard in a bowl. Heat butter on griddle; dip each sandwich in egg mixture and cook on hot griddle until bread is lightly browned on both sides and cheese has melted. Yield: 4 sandwiches.

appetizers, snacks and sandwiches

Shrimp Party Sandwiches

1 (8-ounce) package cream cheese, softened
Juice of 1 large lemon
1 small onion, grated
1 stalk celery, minced
Salt to taste
1 pound cooked shrimp
Rounds of buttered bread

Mash cream cheese; add lemon juice, onion, celery, and salt. Stir in shrimp, which has been broken into bits. Let stand at least 1 hour before spreading between bread rounds. Yield: 25 servings.

Hot Sardine-Egg Sandwiches

3 (3¼- to 4-ounce) cans sardines in oil
2 cups pasteurized process cheese spread
3 English muffins or 6 slices bread
6 eggs
1 tablespoon lemon juice

Put sardines in covered baking dish and heat at 350°. Heat cheese spread. Split and toast muffins, or toast bread slices; arrange on serving platter. Poach eggs. Put drained sardines on muffins and sprinkle with lemon juice. Add 1 poached egg to each sandwich and top with the hot cheese spread. Yield: 6 servings.

*Liverwurst and Egg Sandwich

1 (4¾-ounce) can liverwurst spread
1 tablespoon mayonnaise
2 hard-cooked eggs, chopped
¼ cup chopped green pepper
2 tablespoons butter, softened
8 slices rye bread

Combine liverwurst spread, mayonnaise, eggs, and green pepper; blend well. Butter 4 slices rye bread; spread with liverwurst mixture, and top with remaining bread. Yield: 4 sandwiches.

Po' Boy Sandwich

Small loaf French bread
Hot mustard or mayonnaise, or both
Swiss cheese
Sliced onion
Sliced ham
Sliced tomato
Shredded lettuce
Salami

Split a loaf of French bread. Spread French bread on one side with mustard or mayonnaise, or both. Make layers of the remaining ingredients as desired. Spread top slice of bread with mustard or mayonnaise and cover filling. Yield: 1 sandwich.

The Trail Driver

1 cup smoke-flavored barbecue sauce
12 ounces cooked roast beef, thinly sliced
6 enriched poppy-seed hamburger buns, split
Butter
6 tablespoons creamy coleslaw
12 onion rings, thinly sliced
18 dill pickle slices

Simmer barbecue sauce for 10 minutes. Add beef; simmer 30 minutes longer. Toast and butter buns. Place beef mixture on bun bottoms. Spread coleslaw on each; top with 2 onion rings and 3 dill pickle slices. Cover with bun top. Yield: 6 sandwiches.

Lemon Butter Party Sandwiches

Juice of 2 lemons
Grated rind of 2 lemons
1 cup sugar
2 tablespoons butter
2 eggs, well beaten
Rounds of thin white sandwich bread (cut with biscuit cutter)
1 (3-ounce) package cream cheese, softened

Combine juice, rind, sugar, butter, and eggs in top of double boiler. Cook over simmer-

appetizers, snacks and sandwiches

ing water, stirring constantly, until mixture is smooth and thick. Cool.

Spread bread with cream cheese. Then add a layer of the lemon butter to half the slices, and cover with rounds spread with cream cheese.

Package for freezing. Let thaw about 15 minutes before serving. These sandwiches may be stored for 2 weeks. Yield: 45 sandwiches.

Tuna-Cheese Soufflé Sandwiches

    8   slices white bread
    1   (17-ounce) can peas, well drained
    1   (7-ounce) can tuna fish, drained and flaked
    1   (4-ounce) can mushroom stems and pieces, drained
    1   (2-ounce) jar pimientos, drained and chopped
    ⅓   cup mayonnaise
    ¼   cup chopped onion
    ½   teaspoon dillweed
    ½   teaspoon grated lemon rind
    ½   teaspoon salt
    1   (10¾-ounce) can condensed Cheddar cheese soup
    2   eggs, beaten

Place 4 bread slices in greased 8-inch square pan. Combine remaining ingredients except soup and eggs; spread evenly over bread in pan. Cut remaining bread in half diagonally and arrange over tuna fish mixture. Blend together soup and eggs; pour over sandwiches. Bake at 350° for 45 to 50 minutes, or until set and lightly browned. Serve hot. Yield: 4 servings.

Little Hero Sandwiches

    1   (7-ounce) can tuna fish, drained and flaked
    ½   cup finely diced celery
    1   (4-ounce) jar pimientos, chopped
    2   tablespoons mayonnaise
    6   French rolls, split
        Frosting

Combine tuna fish, celery, pimiento (including liquid), and mayonnaise; blend well. Spread bottom half of rolls with Frosting; then spread with tuna fish filling. Place top of roll over filling and spread with the remaining Frosting. Yield: 6 sandwiches.

Frosting:

    2   cups crumbled blue cheese
    2   (3-ounce) packages cream cheese, softened
    1   (4-ounce) jar pimientos, chopped

Combine all ingredients; blend to a smooth paste. Yield: frosting for 6 sandwiches.

Miniature Pizzas

    1   (8-ounce) can tomato sauce
    1   (6-ounce) can tomato paste
    1   teaspoon salt
    1   tablespoon oregano
    2   cloves garlic, minced
    3   (10-ounce) packaged refrigerated biscuits
        Salad oil
    ¾   pound shredded Mozzarella cheese
        Toppers (anchovy filets, sardines, mushrooms, olives)
        Grated Parmesan cheese

Combine tomato sauce, tomato paste, salt, oregano, and garlic. Separate biscuits; place on baking sheet. Using a flour-dusted custard cup, flatten each biscuit in center to form a 3½-inch circle. Leave rim. Brush biscuits lightly with oil. Pour 1 rounded teaspoonful of tomato mixture in each biscuit and top with 1 tablespoon of mozzarella cheese. Arrange Toppers on cheese. Sprinkle with Parmesan cheese. Bake at 425° for 10 to 15 minutes. Serve hot. Yield: 30 miniature pizzas.

*Mini-Reuben Corned Beef Spread

Softened butter
24 *slices party-sized rye bread*
Prepared mustard
1 *(3½-ounce) can corned beef spread*
½ *cup drained sauerkraut*
12 *slices Swiss cheese, cut to fit bread slices*

Butter 1 side of each bread slice. Spread other side of 12 slices with mustard, then with corned beef spread. Top each of these with 2 teaspoons of sauerkraut and 1 cheese slice. Top with remaining bread, buttered-side up. Grill in small amount of butter on both sides until golden brown. Yield: 12 mini-reubens.

*Tuna Canapé Spread

1 *(7-ounce) can tuna fish in vegetable oil*
⅓ *cup finely chopped celery*
1 *tablespoon minced onion*
3 *tablespoons mayonnaise*
1 *tablespoon lemon juice*
½ *teaspoon Worcestershire sauce*

Combine tuna fish, celery, and onion. Blend together mayonnaise, lemon juice, and Worcestershire sauce; add to tuna fish mixture. Toss lightly. Yield: enough for 16 canapés or 3 to 4 sandwiches.
Variations:
   1) Add 2 tablespoons chopped pimiento-stuffed olives and ¼ teaspoon curry powder.
   2) Add 1 tablespoon mustard pickle relish.
   3) Add 2 tablespoons chopped green pepper and ¼ teaspoon ground dill.

*Crunchy Cottage Cheese Spread

2 *cups creamed cottage cheese*
¼ *cup mayonnaise or salad dressing*
¼ *cup finely chopped pared cucumber, drained*
¼ *cup finely chopped green pepper*
¼ *cup finely chopped celery*
½ *teaspoon seasoned salt*

Combine all ingredients; mix well. Cover and chill at least 1 hour. Yield: 2½ cups spread.

Blue-Cheddar Appetizer Spread

1 *pound blue cheese, crumbled*
½ *pound shredded natural Cheddar cheese*
¼ *cup softened butter or margarine*
½ *cup sherry*
Dash hot sauce

Place cheeses in mixing bowl; add butter and blend well. Gradually add sherry and hot sauce. Beat (preferably with an electric mixer) until smooth and creamy. Keep covered in refrigerator; bring to room temperature before spreading. Yield: 4½ cups.

Cheese-Beer Spread

1 *(12-ounce) can beer*
1½ *pounds shredded sharp Cheddar cheese*
¼ *pound blue cheese, crumbled*
¼ *teaspoon salt*
1 *teaspoon dry mustard*
2 *tablespoons shortening, softened*
1 *teaspoon Worcestershire sauce*
⅛ *teaspoon hot sauce*
2 *teaspoons grated onion*

Open beer; let stand at room temperature while preparing cheese. Mix ingredients, adding enough beer to make a spreading consistency. Let mixture ripen in refrigerator for 8 hours. Bring to room temperature before spreading. Yield: 1¾ pounds.

appetizers, snacks and sandwiches

Tangy Blue Cheese Spread

   ½ *cup butter, softened*
   ¼ *teaspoon salt*
   ½ *teaspoon paprika*
   ⅛ *to ¼ cup prepared horseradish*
   ¼ *cup crumbled blue cheese*

Combine butter, salt, and paprika; blend well. Add horseradish and blue cheese. Mix well; add more seasonings, if desired. Yield: ¾ cup.

Sherry-Cheese Spread

   1 *pound sharp Cheddar cheese, shredded*
   2 *tablespoons butter or margarine, softened*
   1 *teaspoon sugar*
   ½ *teaspoon salt*
      Dash cayenne pepper
   ⅓ *to ½ cup dry sherry*

Let cheese stand at room temperature at least 10 minutes after shredding. Cream butter; blend in cheese, sugar, salt, and cayenne pepper. Gradually add sherry, mixing well. Put in a covered container and refrigerate until ready to serve. Serve with crackers or corn chips. Yield: about 2 cups.

Guacamole Spread

   1 *small chili pepper*
   1 *medium-size onion*
   1 *clove garlic*
   1 *small tomato, peeled*
   2 *avocados*
   1 *teaspoon lemon or lime juice*
   ½ *teaspoon salt*
      Dash pepper

Chop chili pepper, onion, garlic, and tomato very fine; mash together thoroughly. Cut each avocado into halves and remove seed and skin. Mash with chili mixture. Blend in lemon or lime juice, salt, and pepper. Serve with crackers, corn chips, or celery stalks. Yield: about 1½ cups spread.

Guacamole Cocktail Spread

   1 *large avocado*
   1 *tablespoon grated onion*
   1 *tablespoon chili sauce*
      Dash cayenne pepper
   1 *clove garlic, grated*
   ½ *teaspoon or more salt*

Cut avocado in half lengthwise and remove pit. Scoop out inside of avocado, and mix with other ingredients. Adjust seasonings and stuff the avocado halves with this mixture. Chill and serve with whole wheat bread or tortilla chips. Yield: 12 servings.

*Chopped Liver Spread

   ½ *pound beef liver*
   2 *medium-size onions*
   6 *hard-cooked eggs*
   ½ *teaspoon salt*
   ⅛ *teaspoon pepper*
   3 *tablespoons melted butter*
      Parsley

Simmer liver until tender in water to cover. Drain. Put liver and onions through food grinder. Combine liver and onions with 5 chopped eggs. Season with salt and pepper. Add butter, mix well, and pack into a loaf pan. Chill. Turn onto chilled platter, and garnish with sliced hard-cooked egg and parsley. Serve as a luncheon meat or spread on toast or crackers. Yield: 2 cups.

Blue Cheese Spread

   1 *(4-ounce) package blue cheese, Roquefort, or Gorgonzola*
   1 *(3-ounce) package cream cheese*
   3 *tablespoons brandy*

Break up and mash blue cheese, Roquefort, or Gorgonzola. Mix in cream cheese until smooth. Add brandy. Mix well, and chill. Serve with crackers, pumpernickel and rye rounds, or apple and pear slices. Yield: ½ cup.

Sausage Balls

    1 *pound highly seasoned bulk sausage*
3½ *cups commercial biscuit mix*
    1 *(10-ounce) package shredded cheese*

Combine all ingredients with hands. Shape loosely into small balls and bake at 350° for 15 to 20 minutes. Yield: 100 cocktail-size balls.

Cheese Ball

1 *pound Cheddar cheese*
1 *cup walnuts*
2 *(3-ounce) packages cream cheese, softened*
¼ *teaspoon garlic powder*
1 *tablespoon Worcestershire sauce*
2 *tablespoons instant minced onion*
1 *tablespoon chili powder*

Grind Cheddar cheese and walnuts together. Blend in cream cheese, garlic powder, Worcestershire sauce, and onion. Shape into a ball about 4 inches in diameter. Roll ball in chili powder and refrigerate until well chilled (best made day before serving). Yield: 1-pound cheese ball.

Party Cheese Ball

2 *(8-ounce) packages cream cheese*
1 *(8-ounce) package Cheddar cheese, shredded*
1 *tablespoon chopped pimiento*
1 *tablespoon chopped green pepper*
1 *tablespoon finely chopped onion*
1 *teaspoon lemon juice*
2 *teaspoons Worcestershire sauce*
Dash cayenne pepper
Dash salt
Pecans, finely chopped

Cream cheeses together until well blended. Add other ingredients except pecans; mix well. Shape into a ball and roll in pecans. Wrap and refrigerate for 24 hours. Serve with crackers or chips. Yield: one (1½-pound) cheese ball.

*Zippy Cheese Ball Appetizers

2 *(3-ounce) packages cream cheese, softened*
1 *tablespoon horseradish*
1 *teaspoon milk (optional)*
¼ *cup finely chopped dried beef*
½ *cup crushed potato chips*
½ *cup finely chopped fresh parsley*

Blend cheese and horseradish until smooth. (If mixture is too stiff, add milk.) Add beef and potato chips, and blend thoroughly; chill until stiff. Shape into 24 to 26 small balls. Roll balls in parsley and serve on toothpicks. Yield: about 2 dozen cheese balls.

Merry Cheese Ball

1 *(26-ounce) ball Gouda cheese*
1 *(4½-ounce) can deviled ham*
¼ *cup grated onion*
½ *cup commercial sour cream*

Cut top off cheese. Scoop out cheese, leaving a ¼-inch shell. Cut top edge of cheese shell in scallops. Shred scooped-out cheese. Combine cheese, ham, onion, and sour cream and mix well. Fill shell with cheese spread. Chill until serving time. Serve with crackers, potato chips, or rye bread. Yield: 1 cheese ball.

*Cheese-and-Beef Log

1 *(8-ounce) package cream cheese*
2 *(4½-ounce) cans deviled ham*
2 *tablespoons horseradish*
¼ *cup butter*
1 *tablespoon prepared mustard*
1 *(3-ounce) package chipped beef, cut up*

Mix cheese, ham, horseradish, butter, and mustard. Spread beef on a large piece of waxed paper. Spread cheese mixture over beef. Roll up paper the long way. Store in refrigerator overnight. Serve with crackers or rounds of rye bread. Yield: 10 to 12 servings.

appetizers, snacks and sandwiches 11

Cheese Logs

    1 (8-ounce) package cream cheese
    ½ pound blue cheese
    ¼ cup margarine, softened
    1 tablespoon chives
    ¼ cup cooking sherry
    Chopped walnuts

Mix all ingredients except walnuts and chill until firm enough to handle. Form into logs and roll in chopped walnuts. Yield: two 10-inch logs.

*Cheese Hounds

    10 wieners
    10 strips Cheddar cheese
    10 slices bacon
    10 wiener buns

Slit wieners lengthwise to make pockets. Stuff each pocket with a strip of cheese. Wrap each wiener with a slice of bacon and fasten ends with toothpicks. Broil 4 to 5 inches from heat, turning frequently, for 5 minutes or until bacon is crisp. Serve in buns. Yield: 10 sandwiches.

Cheese and Egg Appetizer

    2 (3-ounce) packages cream cheese, softened
    4 hard-cooked eggs, grated
    ¼ teaspoon garlic powder
    ½ teaspoon salt
    2 tablespoons dry Rhine wine
    ⅛ teaspoon hot sauce
    ½ teaspoon vinegar
    Yellow food coloring
    Bacon bits

Combine first 7 ingredients and blend well. Divide mixture. Add food coloring to one-third of mixture to make it resemble an egg yolk. Shape "yolk" and remaining two-thirds of cheese-egg mixture around it into shape of an egg. Roll in bacon bits. Chill and serve with assortment of crackers. Yield: 2 cups.

Beer Cheese

    1 pound Cheddar cheese, shredded
    1 pound Swiss cheese, shredded
    1 clove garlic, mashed
    1 tablespoon dry mustard
    2 teaspoons Worcestershire sauce
    1 cup beer

Combine all ingredients and mix well. Store in covered jar and serve with crackers. Yield: 2½ cups.

Cheese Straws

    1½ cups all-purpose flour
    ½ cup shortening
    4 tablespoons ice water
    1 cup shredded Cheddar cheese
    Whole pecans
    Salt and cayenne pepper to taste

Mix first 3 ingredients as you would pie pastry; roll thin, and sprinkle half of the dough with a third of the cheese. Fold over and roll thin again. Repeat 3 times, adding cheese and folding. The fourth time, cut dough into strips and place a whole pecan in the center of each strip. Sprinkle salt and red pepper over all and bake at 400° for about 8 to 10 minutes. Watch carefully as they burn easily. Yield: 36 cheese straws.

Parmesan Puffs

    2 egg whites
    ⅛ teaspoon salt
    1 cup pitted, coarsely chopped ripe olives
    ¼ cup mayonnaise
    2 tablespoons finely chopped onion
    2 to 3 drops hot sauce
    36 small toast rounds
    Grated Parmesan cheese

Beat egg whites with salt until stiff. Fold in olives, mayonnaise, onion, and hot sauce. Pile onto toast rounds and sprinkle with cheese. Bake at 400° for about 10 to 12 minutes, or until topping is puffed and lightly brown. Serve hot. Yield: 36 puffs.

appetizers, snacks and sandwiches

Cheese Puffs

  1 *sandwich loaf bread, unsliced*
  1 *cup butter or margarine*
  1 *pound shredded sharp Cheddar cheese*
      Garlic salt or garlic powder
      Worcestershire sauce to taste
      Hot sauce to taste

Slice bread into 3 slices lengthwise and cut into cubes. Put butter and cheese into large bowl of mixer and beat well. Add garlic salt or powder, Worcestershire sauce, and hot sauce.

Frost bread cubes with butter-cheese mixture. After all sides of bread cubes have been frosted, place cubes in plastic bags and store in the freezer until ready to serve.

To serve, place frozen cubes on cookie sheet and bake at 450° for about 5 minutes. Yield: 150 puffs.

Corned Beef Spread Puff

  1 *egg white*
  ¼ *cup shredded sharp Cheddar cheese*
  ⅛ *teaspoon salt*
  ⅛ *teaspoon paprika*
  ¼ *cup mayonnaise*
 24 *melba rounds*
  1 *(4½-ounce) can corned beef spread*

Whip or beat egg white until stiff; fold in cheese, salt, paprika, and mayonnaise. Spread melba rounds with corned beef spread. Top with egg white mixture and broil until puffs are golden brown, about 5 minutes. Serve hot. Yield: 24 puffs.

*Wieners in Butter and Beer Sauce

  ¼ *cup butter*
  1 *(12-ounce) bottle beer*
  1 *large onion, thinly sliced*
  1 *(1-pound) package all-meat wieners*
 10 *wiener buns*

Melt butter in saucepan; add beer and onion. Cover and cook over low heat for 30 minutes. Transfer saucepan to grill; heat wieners on grill. While they grill, use tongs to dip them into beer sauce 4 or 5 times at 5-minute intervals. Serve wieners in buns; spoon cooked onion and sauce over wieners. Yield: 10 sandwiches.

Western Burgers

  3 *pounds ground steak*
  ½ *cup cooking wine*
  1 *teaspoon salt*
  ⅛ *teaspoon freshly ground black pepper*
  ½ *cup margarine*
 12 *hamburger buns (split)*
  1 *large Spanish onion, sliced*
  ¼ *cup chili sauce*

Combine meat, wine, salt, and pepper. Mix well and form into 12 patties. Broil patties for 3 minutes on each side (longer if you want them well done). Butter buns and toast them. Serve a patty on bun with an onion slice and chili sauce. Yield: 6 servings.

*Tuna Cheesies

  1 *cup shredded pasteurized process American cheese*
  ¼ *cup margarine, softened*
  1 *(7-ounce) can tuna fish, drained and flaked*
  2 *tablespoons lemon juice*
 1⅓ *tablespoons grated onion*
  1 *teaspoon Worcestershire sauce*
  ½ *teaspoon paprika*
  3 *drops hot sauce*
 30 *melba toast rounds*

Cream the cheese and margarine. Add tuna fish, lemon juice, onion, Worcestershire sauce, paprika, and hot sauce. Mix thoroughly. Spread each toast round with 2 teaspoonfuls of tuna mixture. Place on baking sheet. Broil for 3 to 5 minutes or until lightly browned. Yield: 30 servings.

appetizers, snacks and sandwiches

*Peanut Butter Sticks

    6 *slices bread*
  ⅓ *cup salad oil*
  ⅓ *cup smooth peanut butter*

Remove crusts from bread and place them on cookie sheet. Cut each bread slice into 4 or 5 sticks and place on cookie sheet. Bake crusts and sticks at 200° for 1 hour, or until bread is dry.

    Make bread crumbs by rolling crusts. Mix oil and peanut butter and coat the toasted sticks with mixture. Roll each stick in fine bread crumbs and place them on wire rack to dry. Yield: 24 to 30 sticks.

Bacon-Cheese Special

  8 *slices bacon*
  4 *hamburger buns, split and buttered*
  2 *eggs, well beaten*
  2 *cups (8-ounces) shredded Swiss cheese*
  1 *teaspoon lemon juice*
  ½ *teaspoon salt*
  ½ *teaspoon paprika*
  ½ *teaspoon Worcestershire sauce*
  ⅛ *teaspoon pepper*
      Dash garlic salt
      Dash celery salt

Cut bacon slices in half and partially fry; drain. Place buns on baking sheet; toast under broiler until lightly brown. Combine eggs, cheese, lemon juice, salt, paprika, Worcestershire sauce, pepper, garlic and celery salts in a mixing bowl. Divide cheese mixture equally over buns; top with 2 pieces bacon. Broil until the cheese is lightly browned and the bacon is crisp. Yield: 8 sandwiches.

Cheese Wafers

  2 *cups shredded sharp Cheddar cheese*
  1 *cup margarine, softened*
  2 *cups all-purpose flour*
  2 *cups crispy rice cereal*
      Cayenne pepper to taste (optional)

Cream the cheese and margarine, using electric mixer. Blend in flour slowly. Stir in rice cereal and cayenne pepper, if desired. Drop batter by teaspoonfuls onto ungreased cookie sheet and flatten with back of spoon or fork to make round wafers. Bake at 375° for 10 minutes. Store in airtight container to keep crisp. Yield: 36 wafers.

*Tamale Teasers

  1 *(8-ounce) can tomato sauce*
  1 *(10¾-ounce) can condensed cheese soup*
  1 *tablespoon instant minced onion*
  1 *teaspoon Worcestershire sauce*
  ½ *teaspoon dry mustard*
  2 *(15½-ounce) cans tamales, unwrapped and cut into 2-inch pieces*

Combine tomato sauce, cheese soup, onion, Worcestershire sauce, and mustard; place over low heat. Heat tamale pieces and add to tomato-cheese mixture. Serve hot. Yield: 12 servings.

*Crispy Crust Franks

  8 *frankfurters, split lengthwise*
  ½ *cup mayonnaise*
  1 *(5-ounce) package potato chips, crushed*

Brush frankfurters with mayonnaise; roll in potato chips. Broil until golden brown. Yield: 8 servings.

Zippy Stuffed Celery Sticks

  1 *cup (8-ounce carton) cottage cheese*
  ¼ *cup blue or Roquefort cheese*
  1 *teaspoon salt*
  2 *teaspoons ground dillseed or 2 teaspoons caraway seeds*
  24 *(3-inch) stalks celery*
      Minced fresh parsley

Blend cottage cheese with blue or Roquefort cheese. Add salt and dillseed or caraway seeds. Mix well. Stuff lightly into stalks of celery. Garnish with parsley. Yield: 24 sticks.

Hot Crabmeat Canapés

 1 (6½-ounce) can crabmeat, drained and flaked
 6 tablespoons mayonnaise
 ½ teaspoon salt
 ¼ teaspoon pepper
 ¼ teaspoon rosemary leaves
 24 thin triangle-shaped crackers
 Sharp Cheddar cheese, shredded

Combine first 5 ingredients and mix well. Spread about 1 teaspoonful of mixture on each cracker. Sprinkle with shredded cheese. Place under broiler until cheese melts and browns slightly. Serve immediately. Yield: 24 canapés.

Appetizer Clams Casino

 3 slices bacon, chopped
 1 small onion, chopped
 1 small stalk celery, chopped
 1 teaspoon lemon juice
 1 teaspoon salt
 ⅛ teaspoon pepper
 6 drops Worcestershire sauce
 4 drops hot sauce
 ¼ teaspoon seafood seasoning
 1 pint shucked soft-shell clams, drained

Fry bacon until partially cooked. Add onion and celery; cook until tender. Add lemon juice and seasonings. Arrange clams in well-greased, shallow baking pan; spread bacon mixture over clams. Bake at 400° for 10 minutes or until edges of clams begin to curl. Serve hot. Yield: 6 to 8 servings.

Chili Dandy Dip

 1 (4½-ounce) can chopped ripe olives
 1 cup commercial sour cream
 ¼ cup chili sauce
 ½ teaspoon seasoned salt
 ⅛ teaspoon Worcestershire sauce

Combine all ingredients and mix well. Yield: about 1½ cups.

Clam Chip Dip

 Thin sliver of garlic
 2 (3-ounce) packages cream cheese
 1 (8-ounce) can minced clams, drained
 1 to 2 tablespoons clam broth
 1 teaspoon lemon juice
 1 teaspoon Worcestershire sauce
 ½ teaspoon salt
 Dash pepper

Put all ingredients into blender and blend until smooth. Yield: 1 cup.

*Tasty Black-Eyed Pea Dip

 ½ pound dried black-eyed peas
 2 cups water
 1¼ teaspoons salt
 ⅓ cup diced lean ham
 ½ teaspoon red food coloring
 1 (4-ounce) can green chiles
 1 cup tomato juice
 ½ cup chopped onion
 ⅛ teaspoon garlic powder
 ½ (8-ounce) jar pasteurized process cheese spread
 ¼ teaspoon hot sauce

Wash peas; cover with water and allow to soak overnight. Drain peas and cover with 2 cups water in a heavy saucepan; bring to a boil. Lower temperature, cover pan, and simmer for 30 minutes. Add salt and ham, and simmer 25 to 30 minutes longer; add red food coloring. Drain peas, reserving liquid.

Drain and chop chiles, reserving 2 tablespoons liquid. Place peas, chiles, reserved juice from chiles, tomato juice, onion, and garlic powder in blender container; blend to make a puree. (If a blender is not available, put mixture through a food mill.) Add a small amount of liquid reserved from peas, if needed, to obtain desired consistency.

Spoon mixture into top of double boiler; add cheese spread and pepper sauce. Cook over medium heat until cheese melts. Serve warm with crackers or corn chips. Yield: 10 to 12 servings.

appetizers, snacks and sandwiches 15

Clam Appetizer Dip

  1 *clove garlic*
  2 *(3-ounce) packages cream cheese*
  1 *teaspoon lemon juice*
  1 *teaspoon Worcestershire sauce*
½ *teaspoon salt*
    Dash pepper
  1 *(8-ounce) can minced clams, drained*
  1 *teaspoon clam broth*

Rub a small mixing bowl with the garlic clove which has been halved. Place all remaining ingredients in the bowl; blend well. Cover and store in refrigerator to mellow flavors and remove from refrigerator to soften before serving. Serve as a dip for crackers, potato chips, or raw cauliflower buds. Yield: 1 cup.

Note: If a thinner dip is desired, more clam broth may be added.

*Chili-Cheese Dip

  1 *(16-ounce) jar pasteurized process cheese spread*
  1 *(16-ounce) can chili without beans*
  1 *to 2 tablespoons instant potato flakes (optional)*

Melt cheese in saucepan over low heat, stirring constantly. Blend in chili and heat thoroughly. To obtain a thicker dip, sprinkle potato flakes into mixture and cook for a few minutes. More potato flakes can be added, if desired. Yield: 4 cups.

Anchovy-Cheese Dip

  1 *(8-ounce) package cream cheese, softened*
  1 *tablespoon anchovy paste*
  1 *tablespoon chopped chives*
  2 *tablespoons minced, stuffed green olives*
  1 *teaspoon lemon juice*
¼ *teaspoon Worcestershire sauce*
  1 *tablespoon milk*

Combine all ingredients; beat on medium speed of electric mixer until light and fluffy. Chill until ready to serve. Serve with corn chips or crackers. Yield: 2 cups.

French Fried Shrimp with Coral Dip

Prepare frozen breaded shrimp (either fantail or round) according to package directions. Serve hot with Coral Dip.

Coral Dip:

  1 *cup mayonnaise*
⅓ *cup chili sauce*
  2 *tablespoons vinegar*
½ *teaspoon salt*
¼ *teaspoon sugar*
    Pepper to taste
⅛ *teaspoon onion salt (optional)*
  2 *tablespoons commercial sour cream (optional)*

Blend all ingredients together. Serve in a bowl as a dip for French fried shrimp. Yield: about 1½ cups.

*Curried Cottage Cheese Dip

  1 *cup cottage cheese*
¼ *cup sweet pickle relish, drained*
¼ *teaspoon curry powder*
  1 *teaspoon grated onion*
    Paprika

Sieve cottage cheese; combine with remaining ingredients except paprika. Mix well. Cover; refrigerate for about 1 hour. Garnish with paprika before serving. Yield: about 1 cup.

*Cucumber Dip

  1 *(3-ounce) package cream cheese*
  2 *tablespoons mayonnaise*
  1 *tablespoon grated cucumber*
    Dash each of Worcestershire sauce, paprika, salt, celery salt, onion salt

Soften cream cheese and blend in mayonnaise. Add cucumber and juice. Stir in seasonings and chill until time to serve. Yield: 1 cup.

appetizers, snacks and sandwiches

Cottage Cheese Dip

    2 cups cottage cheese
    2 to 3 tablespoons milk or commercial sour cream
    ¼ teaspoon grated onion
    2 teaspoons lemon juice
    ¼ teaspoon salt

Sieve or mash cottage cheese. Add remaining ingredients and mix well. Yield: 2 cups basic dip.
Variations:
    Clam Dip: Add 1 (8-ounce) can of well-drained minced clams to 2 cups basic dip. Add 2 to 3 teaspoons clam juice for good dipping consistency. Garnish with strips of pimiento.
    Blue Cheese Dip: Add 2 ounces crumbled blue cheese to 2 cups basic dip. Mix well with electric mixer, if possible. Garnish with chopped chives or parsley.
    Herring Dip: Add ¼ cup finely chopped pickled herring (mix in blender until smooth) to 2 cups basic dip. Garnish with a dash of paprika.
    Smoky Cheese Dip: Add 4 ounces shredded smoky-flavored pasteurized processed cheese food to 2 cups basic dip. Beat with an electric mixer or in blender. Garlic-flavored processed cheese may also be used.

*Spicy Tuna Dip

    ½ cup commercial sour cream
    1 (7-ounce) can tuna fish
    1 tablespoon prepared horseradish
    1 teaspoon Worcestershire sauce
    1 (8-ounce) package cream cheese, broken into pieces
    ½ small onion, sliced
    1 clove garlic
    ½ teaspoon salt
    Dash pepper
    ½ teaspoon Ac'cent

Place all ingredients in blender container. Blend only until smooth. Chill for several hours. Serve with crisp crackers. Yield: 3 cups.

*Tuna Dip

    2 (7-ounce) cans tuna fish
    ½ cup mayonnaise
    1 tablespoon minced onion
    1 tablespoon lemon juice
    ½ cup finely diced celery
    1 cup commercial sour cream

Blend tuna fish, mayonnaise, onion, lemon juice, and celery. Stir in sour cream. Serve with potato chips, crackers, celery, or carrot sticks. Yield: 3½ cups.
    Tuna Dogs: Omit sour cream in Tuna Dip. Split 6 hot dog buns and spread tuna mixture on bottom halves. Place under broiler heat until brown, about 5 minutes. Butter and brown top halves of buns at same time. Close sandwiches. Yield: 6 tuna dogs.
    Tuna heros: Omit sour cream in Tuna Dip. Split 3 hero rolls and spread tuna mixture on bottom halves. Cover with tomato slices, onion slices, and dill pickle slices. Close sandwiches with top halves of buns. Yield: 3 tuna heros.

*Tuna Cream Dip

    1 (7-ounce) can tuna fish, drained and flaked
    1 tablespoon prepared horseradish
    1½ teaspoons onion salt
    1 teaspoon Worcestershire sauce
    1 cup commercial sour cream
    2 teaspoons chopped parsley

Combine tuna fish, horseradish, onion salt, and Worcestershire sauce; fold in sour cream. Chill. Garnish with parsley. Yield: 1½ cups dip.

appetizers, snacks and sandwiches

*Peanut Butter-Cheese Dip

½ cup chopped onion
1 cup chopped green pepper
1 clove garlic, crushed
2 tablespoons peanut oil
2 tomatoes, peeled and chopped
¾ cup tomato juice
½ teaspoon ground thyme
¼ teaspoon ground oregano
½ bay leaf
½ pound Cheddar cheese, shredded
¾ cup smooth peanut butter
½ teaspoon salt
⅛ teaspoon pepper
Corn chips or potato chips

Cook onion, green pepper, and garlic in oil until tender but not browned. Add tomatoes, tomato juice, thyme, oregano, and bay leaf; cover and cook over low heat for 10 minutes. Stir once or twice. Put mixture in top of double boiler and add cheese, peanut butter, salt, and pepper. Cook and stir over boiling water until cheese is melted and mixture is blended. Transfer to chafing dish and keep warm. Serve with corn chips. Yield: 1 quart dip.

Shrimp Dip

1 hard-cooked egg
1 small clove garlic
1 pound cooked shrimp
1 tablespoon creole or horseradish mustard
2 teaspoons paprika
2 teaspoons Worcestershire sauce
Dash hot sauce
1½ tablespoons vinegar
1½ tablespoons chopped parsley
1 tablespoon grated onion
Mayonnaise
Salt and pepper to taste

Grind egg, garlic, and shrimp in food grinder or put in blender. Combine with remaining ingredients and blend well, adding enough mayonnaise to make mixture the right "dipping" consistency. Refrigerate for 12 hours before serving. Yield: 15 to 25 servings.

Indonesian Shrimp Dip

1 cup commercial sour cream
¼ teaspoon coriander
¼ teaspoon ground cumin
¼ teaspoon ground cinnamon
½ teaspoon curry powder
2 tablespoons chopped onion
1 teaspoon soy sauce
2 tablespoons peeled tomatoes, finely chopped
¼ cup cooked, chopped shrimp
Potato chips

Blend sour cream, coriander, cumin, cinnamon, and curry powder by hand or in blender. Stir in onion and soy sauce. Add tomatoes and shrimp. Blend well. Chill 1 hour. Serve with potato chips. Yield: about 1¼ cups dip.

Green Dragon Dip

1 ripe avocado
1 (3-ounce) package cream cheese
3 tablespoons mayonnaise or salad dressing
Few drops lemon juice or vinegar
¼ teaspoon seasoned salt
⅛ teaspoon pepper
Grated onion (optional)

Peel, pit, and mash avocado. Mix with remaining ingredients and blend well. Add onion, if desired. Chill before serving. Yield: 1 cup.

Smoked Oyster Dip

1 (3¾-ounce) can smoked oysters
2 (8-ounce) cartons cottage cheese
1 (8-ounce) package cream cheese, softened
1 teaspoon garlic salt
Paprika

Put oysters, cheeses, and garlic salt in blender; blend until smooth. Sprinkle with paprika before serving with crackers or potato chips. Dip freezes well; thaw at room temperature and mix thoroughly before serving. Yield: 3½ cups.

*Hot Bean Dip

  1   (28-ounce) can pork and beans
  ¾   cup shredded Cheddar cheese
  1   teaspoon garlic salt
  2   teaspoons chili powder
  ½   teaspoon salt
  2   teaspoons hot sauce
  2   teaspoons Worcestershire sauce
  2   teaspoons vinegar
  6   slices bacon, cooked crisp and drained

Put pork and beans through blender and add remaining ingredients except bacon. Heat in double boiler or chafing dish. Crumble bacon and sprinkle on top; serve with chips. Yield: 3½ cups.

*Zippy Dip

  1   (8-ounce) package sandwich spread
  ½   cup commercial sour cream
  2   teaspoons prepared horseradish

Combine sandwich spread, sour cream, and horseradish; mix well and chill until time to serve. Good with corn or potato chips. Yield: 1⅓ cups.

Party Mix

  ½   pound salted Spanish peanuts
  ½   pound salted mixed nuts
  3¾ cups slim pretzels
  3   cups bite-size shredded wheat squares
  5½ cups doughnut-shaped oat cereal
  4   cups bite-size rice cereal squares
  1   cup butter, melted
  1   tablespoon Worcestershire sauce
  1½ teaspoons garlic salt
  1½ teaspoons seasoned salt

Combine peanuts, nuts, pretzels, and cereals in a large roaster. Add butter, Worcestershire sauce, garlic salt, and seasoned salt; mix together thoroughly. Bake at 250° for 2 hours, stirring gently with a wooden spoon every 15 minutes. Store in sealed airtight jars. Yield: about 4 quarts.

Rumaki

  1½ cups water
  ½   cup soy sauce
  3   cloves garlic, minced
  ¾   teaspoon ground ginger
  ½   pound chicken livers
  3   tablespoons butter or margarine
  2   (5-ounce) cans water chestnuts
  ½   pound bacon

Prepare sauce by combining water, soy sauce, garlic, and ginger. Cook chicken livers slowly in butter for 5 minutes; remove and cut into quarters. Slice water chestnuts in half. Marinate liver and water chestnuts in sauce for 1 hour. Drain on paper towels. Cut bacon slices in half and wrap each piece of bacon around a portion of liver and water chestnut. Fasten with a toothpick. Broil about 3 inches from heat, turning until browned; or bake at 400° for 20 to 25 minutes. Yield: about 36 appetizers.

Bacon-Beef Roll-Ups

  2   pounds beef round steak, sliced ¼ inch thick
  ½   pound bacon, sliced
  1   large onion, chopped
  2   tablespoons vegetable oil
  1   (15-ounce) can tomato sauce
  1¼ cups water, divided
  2   teaspoons cornstarch

Pound beef with mallet to tenderize; cut into strips measuring about 1 x 5 inches. Top each strip with 1 slice of bacon and 1 tablespoon onion. Roll up, and secure with a toothpick.
Heat oil in skillet; add roll-ups, turning to brown. Stir in tomato sauce and 1 cup water. Cover; simmer for 1½ hours or until tender. Remove rollups. Stir 1 tablespoon water into cornstarch until smooth; then stir in remaining water. Blend cornstarch into mixture in pan. Cook and stir until thickened. Pour sauce over roll-ups. Serve with toothpicks. Yield: 5 to 6 servings.

Little Links in Oriental Sauce

1 cup firmly packed brown sugar
3 tablespoons all-purpose flour
2 teaspoons dry mustard
1 cup pineapple juice
½ cup vinegar
1½ teaspoons soy sauce
2 (1-pound) packages cocktail wieners
2 (1-pound) packages smoked cocktail sausages

Combine brown sugar, flour, and mustard in saucepan. Add pineapple juice, vinegar, and soy sauce. Heat to boiling, stirring constantly. Boil for 1 minute. Stir in wieners and sausages. Cook slowly for 5 minutes or until heated through. Keep warm over low heat in chafing dish. Serve with toothpicks. Yield: 64 appetizers.

Curried Beef Nuggets

2 pounds ground beef
½ cup finely chopped onion
1 clove garlic, finely chopped
½ cup corn flakes, crushed
1½ teaspoons salt
1 cup milk
⅓ cup finely chopped peanuts
2 tablespoons vegetable oil
½ cup finely chopped onion
1½ teaspoons curry powder
1 tablespoon all-purpose flour
1 teaspoon salt
1½ cups apple juice
¼ cup flaked coconut

Combine beef, ½ cup onion, garlic, corn flakes, 1½ teaspoons salt, milk, and peanuts. Shape into 60 walnut-size balls. Brown in oil. Remove meatballs. Pour off drippings and measure back 1 tablespoonful. Add ½ cup onion and cook for 5 minutes. Stir in curry powder, flour, and 1 teaspoon salt. Add apple juice. Mix well and cook, stirring constantly, until thickened. Return meatballs to gravy, cover, and simmer for 15 minutes. Serve topped with coconut. Yield: 60 nuggets.

*Celery Fingers

1 cup minced celery
1 tablespoon finely chopped nuts
1 tablespoon finely chopped olives
1 tablespoon mayonnaise
⅛ teaspoon salt
1/16 teaspoon ground black pepper
¼ teaspoon paprika
4 thin slices bread
Butter or margarine

Combine first 7 ingredients. Mix well. Remove crust from bread. Spread bread thinly with butter and then with celery mixture. Cut bread into 1-inch strips. Yield: 12 fingers.

*Ham Mousse-Pâté

1 tablespoon unflavored gelatin
1 cup orange juice
¾ cup beef bouillon, made with bouillon cube
1½ cups minced ham (canned luncheon meat may be used, but add any country ham or ham fat to give it flavor)
⅓ cup salad dressing or mayonnaise
2 tablespoons lemon juice or vinegar
½ cup dill pickle relish
Mayonnaise

Soften the gelatin in some of the orange juice. Heat the beef broth to boiling; add gelatin to dissolve. Add remaining orange juice.

Grind the ham or mash the luncheon meat to a puree consistency. Add the salad dressing or mayonnaise, lemon juice or vinegar, and dill pickle relish. Check seasoning, adding salt if necessary.

Pour the dissolved gelatin over ham mixture, adding additional seasoning if needed. Turn into a lightly greased 1-quart mold. Chill until firm. Unmold and garnish with mayonnaise piped on with a pastry tube. Yield: 25 servings.

Suggestion: Accent with sliced pickles or olives and parsley. Arrange pâté on a lettuce-lined tray, and garnish with groupings of marinated cooked vegetables (canned may be used).

Easy Chicken Liver Pâté

1 *pound fresh chicken livers*
½ *cup sherry*
½ *cup butter*
Salt, pepper, rosemary, and thyme to taste

Put chicken livers in a saucepan and add enough sherry to cover. Simmer over low heat just until done. Put livers into blender container; add butter and seasonings. Blend at high speed. Pour into ramekins for serving. Yield: about 3 cups.

Liver Pâté

1 *pound chicken livers*
1 *medium-size onion, quartered*
6 *tablespoons butter or margarine*
4 *hard-cooked eggs*
Mayonnaise
Salt and pepper to taste
Hot sauce to taste (optional)

Sauté chicken livers and onion in butter until livers are done. Grind livers, onion, and eggs in food grinder, or put through a food mill. Add mayonnaise to consistency desired. Add salt, pepper, and hot sauce, if desired; mix well. Keep refrigerated until ready to serve. Serve on crackers for canapés or between slices of whole wheat bread for sandwiches. Yield: about 2 cups.

Chicken Liver Pâté

1 *cup chicken broth, divided*
1 *(5¾-ounce) can pitted ripe olives, drained, liquid reserved*
1 *pound chicken livers*
2 *envelopes unflavored gelatin*
1 *teaspoon onion powder*
2 *tablespoons parsley flakes*
½ *teaspoon salt*
⅛ *teaspoon white pepper*
⅛ *teaspoon ground nutmeg*
⅛ *teaspoon thyme*
¼ *cup buttermilk*
1 *tablespoon prepared mustard*
2 *tablespoons brandy (optional)*

Place ½ cup chicken broth, ½ cup olive liquid, and chicken livers in saucepan; bring to boil. Lower heat and simmer 5 to 8 minutes or until livers are tender. Sprinkle gelatin over ½ cup chicken broth in blender container. Add chicken livers, olives, liquid, and all remaining ingredients to blender. Blend until mixture is smooth. Pour liver mixture into a 1-quart mold. Chill for 4 to 5 hours or until firm. Unmold and place on flat platter. Yield: 1 pound.

Ham Pinwheels

¼ *pound Roquefort cheese, crumbled*
¼ *cup cream cheese, softened*
¼ *cup butter or margarine, softened*
4 *slices boiled ham, about ⅛ inch thick*
2½ *dozen round, buttery crackers*

Combine cheeses and butter. Blend until smooth. Spread on ham slices. Roll up as for jelly roll; wrap in waxed paper and chill in the refrigerator. Keeps well for several days. Slice as needed to top crackers. Yield: about 2½ dozen.

Beef Fondue

1½ *pounds beef tenderloin, ¾ inch thick*
Fresh parsley
Peanut oil

Cut beef into cubes and arrange on platter with a parsley border. Heat oil on top of stove to 400°; pour into fondue pot to depth of 2 inches. Place pot on table and keep hot over canned heat. Spear meat with fondue fork or skewer and hold in hot oil until browned as desired. Dip in desired sauce. Yield: 4 to 6 servings.
Variations:
Chicken Fondue: Cut 3 whole chicken breasts (boned and skinned) into ½-inch cubes. Cook chicken in hot peanut oil until lightly browned, ½ to 1 minute.
Shrimp Fondue: Cook 2 pounds medium-size shrimp (shelled and deveined) in hot peanut oil until lightly browned, about ½ to 1 minute.

Teriyaki Steak for Fondue

1 pound sirloin steak
2/3 cup soy sauce
1/4 cup white wine
2 tablespoons sugar
1/2 tablespoon ground ginger
1 clove garlic, minced
Vegetable oil

Cut steak into 3/4-inch cubes. Combine next 5 ingredients and put into a glass dish. Add steak, cover, and marinate for at least 30 to 40 minutes. Spear meat with fondue fork and cook in hot oil until browned as desired. Yield: 4 to 6 servings.

Tangy Meatballs

1 pound ground beef
1 egg, slightly beaten
1/4 cup chili sauce
1/4 cup finely chopped onion
1 teaspoon salt
1/4 teaspoon freshly ground black pepper
1 1/2 cups cheese cracker crumbs, divided
Vegetable oil

Combine beef, egg, chili sauce, onion, salt, and pepper with 1 cup cracker crumbs. Mix thoroughly. Shape into tiny meatballs and roll in remaining 1/2 cup cracker crumbs. Sauté meatballs for 5 minutes in 1/2 inch of hot oil, turning to brown all sides. Remove to a chafing dish and serve with toothpicks. Yield: about 30 meatballs.

Party Meatballs

2 pounds lean ground beef
2 eggs
1/2 teaspoon salt
1/4 teaspoon pepper
1 (12-ounce) jar chili sauce
1 teaspoon lemon juice
1 (10-ounce) jar grape jelly

Mix beef, eggs, salt, and pepper; shape into very small balls. Combine chili sauce, lemon juice, and jelly and place in a large 13- x 9- x 2-inch pan. Add uncooked meatballs and bake, covered, at 350° for 1 1/2 hours. Remove cover from pan the last 30 minutes of baking. Transfer to chafing dish and serve hot with toothpicks. Yield: 30 to 40 meatballs.

Smoky Peanuts

1/3 cup liquid smoke
1/3 cup water
2 cups salted peanuts
3 tablespoons butter or margarine
Salt to taste

Combine liquid smoke and water in small saucepan; heat to boiling. Spread nuts in a shallow pan; pour smoke-water mixture over nuts and let stand for 1 hour. Drain off liquid; spread nuts in pan and roast at 250° for 1 hour. Toss nuts with butter and salt. Yield: 1 pound nuts.

Hot Chili Nuts

1 pound shelled raw peanuts
4 tablespoons peanut oil
3 teaspoons chili powder
3/4 teaspoon paprika
1 teaspoon salt
1/2 teaspoon cayene pepper

Brown the nuts in hot oil (substitute butter, if desired). Combine the chili powder, paprika, salt, and pepper. Sprinkle over peanuts and stir until well coated. Amounts of flavorings may be altered to taste; these are very hot. Yield: 1 pound nuts.

Beverages

The South is a hospitable place in which to live or visit, and we often need to serve a refreshing beverage. We have included a variety of drinks from which to choose, both alcoholic and nonalcoholic. Your choice will depend on the occasion.

Many servers have experimented with various fruits to produce their own punch. The early colonists did some experimenting themselves; they got tired of drinking the same old apple cider (made from homegrown apples) or berry punch (made from blackberries) and decided to vary the taste by adding other fruits. With the variety of fruits grown in the South, fruit punches seem to be a favorite; they may be served hot or cold.

Champagne Punch

1½ cups sugar
2 cups lemon juice
Block of ice
2 (⅘-quart) bottles dry Sauterne, chilled
1 (⅘-quart) bottle champagne, chilled
½ cup Cointreau (optional)
½ cup brandy (optional)
1 lemon, unpeeled, sliced into thin cartwheels
1½ cups sliced fresh strawberries

Stir sugar into lemon juice until dissolved; chill thoroughly. Just before serving, pour over ice in punch bowl. Gently stir in Sauterne and champagne; add Cointreau and brandy, if desired. Garnish with lemon and strawberry slices. Yield: 3¼ quarts.

Cranberry-Champagne Punch

6 cups cranberry juice cocktail
2 cups orange juice
½ cup lemon juice
2 (⅘-quart) bottles champagne

Combine cranberry, orange, and lemon juices. Chill well. To serve, pour chilled fruit juices into punch bowl and add champagne. Yield: about 20 servings.

Cranberry Christmas Punch

1 (3-ounce) package cherry-flavored gelatin
1 cup boiling water
1 (6-ounce) can frozen lemonade, undiluted
3 cups cold water
1 (32-ounce) bottle cranberry juice cocktail
Ice ring or cubes
1 (28-ounce) bottle ginger ale, chilled

Dissolve cherry gelatin in boiling water. Stir in lemonade; add cold water and cranberry juice cocktail. Pour punch over ice. Pour in ginger ale. Yield: 25 servings.

Sparkling Cranberry Punch

1 (32-ounce) bottle cranberry juice cocktail
1 (6-ounce) can frozen orange juice, undiluted
1 (6-ounce) can frozen lemon juice, undiluted
2 cups water
Ice ring or cubes
2 (10-ounce) bottles ginger ale, chilled
Orange slices

Combine fruit juices and water in punch bowl. Just before serving, add ice. Holding bottle on rim of bowl, carefully pour in ginger ale. Garnish with orange slices. Yield: about 18 servings.

Cranberry Brunch Float

6 cups orange juice
1 pint cranberry sherbet

Pour orange juice in chilled fruit juice glasses. Add a small scoop of cranberry sherbet to each glass and serve at once. Yield: 6 servings.

Cranberry Punch

2 cups cranberry juice cocktail
1 cup orange juice
½ cup pineapple juice
4 tablespoons sugar
1 to 2 cups water
Juice of 2 lemons

Combine all ingredients. Chill and serve. Yield: 4 to 6 servings.

Frozen Daiquiri

3 ounces light rum
1½ tablespoons lime juice
1 tablespoon sugar
2 cups crushed ice

Combine all ingredients in blender. Cover and blend for about 50 seconds. As mixture freezes around blades, stop motor and quickly push crust downward with rubber spatula. Continue to blend until it reaches the desired consistency. Yield: 2 servings.

Lime Delight

4 cups strong tea, cooled
Juice of 1 lime
3 tablespoons maraschino cherry juice
2 tablespoons sugar
Lime peel
Cherries

Combine tea, lime juice, cherry juice, and sugar. Pour over ice cubes in tall glasses. Garnish with a twist of lime peel and a cherry. Yield: 4 to 6 servings.

Limeade

⅓ to ½ cup sugar
1 cup water
Juice of 6 limes
Finely crushed ice
Carbonated or plain water
Orange slices or mint sprigs

Combine sugar and water in saucepan; place over heat and stir until sugar dissolves; cool. Add lime juice to sugar syrup; divide mixture among 6 tall glasses. Fill to top with crushed ice. Pour in carbonated or plain water; stir. Garnish with orange slices or mint sprigs. Yield: 6 servings.

Backyard Cooler

½ cup hot tea
½ to ¾ cup sugar
1 (12-ounce) can apricot nectar, chilled
1 cup orange juice
½ cup lemon juice
Ice cubes
1 (10-ounce) bottle ginger ale, chilled (optional)

Combine tea and sugar in a large pitcher; stir until sugar dissolves. Add remaining ingredients and stir briskly. Yield: 1 to 1¼ quarts.

Old-Fashioned Lemonade

1 cup sugar
1 cup water
Rind of 2 lemons, cut in strips
1 cup lemon juice
4 cups ice water
Green maraschino cherries

Combine sugar, water, and lemon rind in a saucepan; stir over low heat until sugar dissolves. Remove rind; chill syrup. Add lemon juice and ice water. Pour over ice cubes in which green maraschino cherries have been frozen. Yield: 6 servings.

*Spicy Lemon Tingle

½ cup sugar
⅛ teaspoon ground allspice
⅛ teaspoon ground cloves
⅛ teaspoon ground cinnamon
¼ teaspoon ground ginger
⅛ teaspoon salt
2 cups water
⅔ cup lemon juice
1 cup orange juice
2 cups ice water
Lemon or orange slices

Combine sugar, spices, salt, and water; boil for 5 minutes. Chill thoroughly to allow flavors to mellow. Strain through cheesecloth, if desired. Combine with fruit juices and ice water; pour into ice-filled glasses and garnish with lemon or orange slices. Yield: about 1½ quarts.

Fruit Punch Cooler

3 (6-ounce) cans frozen limeade, undiluted
3 (6-ounce) cans frozen lemonade, undiluted
4 quarts water
1 (32-ounce) bottle grapefruit juice, chilled
2 (28-ounce) bottles ginger ale, chilled
Sugar to taste
Green food coloring
Lime slices
Sliced strawberries

Pour limeade and lemonade into punch bowl. Stir in water. Add grapefruit juice and ginger ale. Add sugar and a few drops of green food coloring for desired shade of green. Add ice cubes, lime slices, and strawberries. Serve at once. Yield: 8 quarts.

*Fruit Punch

1 (12-ounce) package strawberry-flavored gelatin
2 cups boiling water
6 cups cold water
1 (46-ounce) can pineapple juice and water to make ½ gallon
1 (12-ounce) can frozen orange juice and water to make ½ gallon
Ice ring or cubes

Dissolve gelatin in boiling water. Stir in cold water and cool. Combine with pineapple juice and water and with orange juice and water. Chill. Put in punch bowl; add ice and serve cold. Yield: 1½ gallons.

*Citrus Punch

1 quart water
1¼ cups sugar
Rind of 4 lemons
1 cup lemon juice
1½ cups grapefruit juice
⅔ cup lime juice
3 cups orange juice
1 (10-ounce) bottle ginger ale
Block of ice

Combine water, sugar, and lemon rind in a large saucepan. Bring to a boil for 2 minutes. Remove rind and cool the syrup. Add fruit juices. Add ginger ale and mix well. Pour over ice in punch bowl. Yield: 3 quarts.

Planters Punch

⅓ cup grenadine syrup
1 (6-ounce) can frozen lemonade, undiluted
1 teaspoon almond flavoring
2 quarts strong tea, cooled
Pineapple wedges
Lemon slices
Cherries

Stir grenadine syrup, lemonade, and flavoring into the cool tea. Serve in tall glasses with ice. Garnish with pineapple wedge, lemon slice, and cherry. Yield: 8 servings.

Tangy Orange-Cranberry Punch

 1/3 *cup sugar*
 2 *cups orange juice, chilled*
 1/4 *cup lemon juice, chilled*
 6 *cups cranberry juice cocktail, chilled*
 1 *(12-ounce) can pineapple juice, chilled*
 1 *(28-ounce) bottle lemon-lime carbonated beverage, chilled (optional)*
  Block of ice or ice ring
  Fresh orange and lemon half-cartwheels

Combine sugar and orange juice until sugar is dissolved. Add remaining fruit juices and chill until ready to serve. Add carbonated beverage, if desired. Pour over ice in punch bowl; garnish with orange and lemon slices. Yield: 2½ to 3¼ quarts.

*Orange-Grape Harvest Punch

 2 *cups boiling water*
 8 *teaspoons tea*
 1½ *cups sugar*
 3 *cups orange juice*
 1 *cup lemon juice*
 2 *cups grape juice*
 2 *quarts boiling water*
  Orange and lemon slices

Pour boiling water over tea. Steep 5 minutes; strain. Dissolve sugar in warm liquid. Add fruit juices and boiling water. Garnish with orange and lemon slices. Serve hot. Yield: 30 (½-cup) servings.

Orange-Lime Fizz

 2 *cups orange juice, divided*
 ½ *cup granulated sugar*
 12 *sprigs of mint, cut up*
 4 *tablespoons lime juice*
 1 *(10-ounce) bottle carbonated water*

Heat 1 cup orange juice to boiling point. Add to sugar and mint. Cool, covered; then strain, and add rest of orange juice and lime juice. Just before serving, add carbonated water and ice. Yield: 4 (½-cup) servings.

Tropical Pineapple Punch

 1 *(4/5-quart) bottle Sauterne, or other white table wine, chilled (optional)*
 3 *cups canned pineapple juice, chilled*
 2 *cups orange juice, chilled*
 1/3 *cup lemon juice*
 ½ *cup sugar*
 ½ *teaspoon ground ginger*
  Block of ice or ice ring
 1 *(28-ounce) bottle lemon-lime carbonated beverage, chilled*

Combine wine, if desired, fruit juices, and sugar in a punch bowl; stir until sugar is dissolved. Dissolve ginger in a little juice mixture; stir into contents of punch bowl. Add a block of ice or ice ring. Pour in carbonated beverage. Serve at once. Yield: 3 quarts.

Pineapple Tea Fizz

 8 *teaspoons black tea leaves*
 3 *cups boiling water*
 2/3 *cup orange juice*
 1/3 *cup lemon juice*
 2/3 *cup sweetened pineapple juice*
 1 *(28-ounce) bottle ginger ale, chilled*
 ¼ *teaspoon mint flavoring*

Place tea leaves in a heated container. Pour boiling water over leaves; cover and steep for 5 minutes. Pour off tea immediately. Combine hot tea with remaining ingredients and mix well. Pour over cracked ice in tall glasses. Yield: 8 servings.

Strawberry Punch

 3 *(6-ounce) cans frozen orange juice, thawed*
 3 *(6-ounce) cans frozen pink lemonade, thawed*
 1 *(28-ounce) bottle ginger ale, chilled*
 2 *(10-ounce) packages frozen strawberries with syrup*

Add cold water to orange juice and lemonade as directed on cans; stir in ginger ale and frozen strawberries. Add ice cubes. Yield: 32 servings.

Strawberry-Lemon Freeze

1½ pints vanilla ice cream
1 (10-ounce) package frozen strawberries
¾ cup lemon juice
2 cups crushed ice

Combine ice cream, frozen strawberries (broken up), and lemon juice in electric blender. Blend until smooth. Pour two-thirds of mixture into large bowl. Add ice to remaining mixture in blender; blend until ice is well mixed with ice cream. Combine with mixture in bowl. Serve in chilled 8- to 10-ounce glasses with straws. Yield: 5 to 6 servings.

Banana-Strawberry Float

¾ cup mashed bananas
¾ cup mashed strawberries
¾ cup sugar
Dash salt
5 cups milk, chilled
1 pint vanilla ice cream
6 whole strawberries

Blend mashed bananas and strawberries with sugar and salt. Add milk and stir to blend. Pour into 6 tall cold glasses and top with ice cream. Garnish with whole strawberries. Yield: 6 servings.

✓ Summertime Cooler

3 cups sugar
2 quarts water
2 (29-ounce) cans apricot nectar
1 (46-ounce) can pineapple juice
4 cups orange juice
Juice of 3 lemons
6 cups strong tea
1 (1-pound) can crushed pineapple
2 (28-ounce) bottles ginger ale, chilled
Block of ice

Combine sugar and water; heat until sugar is dissolved. Cool. Stir in remaining ingredients and serve over ice in punch bowl. Yield: 2 gallons.

Punch for a Crowd

2 (46-ounce) cans pineapple juice
2⅔ cups orange juice
1⅓ cups lemon juice
⅔ cup lime juice
2 cups sugar
Block of ice or ice ring
2 (28-ounce) bottles ginger ale, chilled
2 (28-ounce) bottles carbonated water, chilled

Combine fruit juices and sugar; chill thoroughly. Pour over ice in punch bowl. Pour ginger ale and carbonated water slowly down the side of the bowl. Yield: about 8 quarts.

Three-Fruit Punch

2 (6-ounce) cans frozen orange juice, undiluted
2 (6-ounce) cans frozen lemon juice, undiluted
6 cups water
1 (46-ounce) can pineapple juice
1 cup sugar
2 (10-ounce) bottles ginger ale, chilled

Combine orange and lemon juices, add water and pineapple juice, and stir in sugar. Ladle into wide-topped freezer containers, leaving 1 inch headspace. Cover tightly and freeze.

To serve, partially thaw fruit juice mixture at room temperature, about 5 hours. Place in punch bowl. Stir with a fork to break up ice chunks. Add ginger ale. Yield: about 25 (6-ounce) servings.

Ruby Red Frost

   2 *pints raspberry sherbet, divided*
1¼ *cups sugar*
1½ *cups lemon juice*
   1 *cup orange juice*
      Block of ice
   1 *(32-ounce) bottle cranberry juice cocktail, chilled*
   2 *(28-ounce) bottles ginger ale, chilled*

Soften 1 pint sherbet; scoop by spoonfuls into pitcher. Add sugar, lemon, and orange juices; let stand a few minutes, stirring frequently, until sherbet melts. Pour over block of ice in punch bowl along with cranberry juice and ginger ale. Float scoops of remaining pint of sherbet on top. Yield: 3¾ quarts or 30 punch cup servings.

South Seas Sparkler

   2 *cups pineapple-grapefruit juice drink, divided*
 ½ *cup sugar*
24 *fresh or dried mint leaves*
 ¼ *cup lemon or lime juice*
   1 *(10-ounce) bottle sparkling water*
      Strawberries
      Pineapple chunks

Bring 1 cup pineapple-grapefruit juice drink to a boil; stir in sugar and mint. Remove from heat and cover. Let steep until cool; then strain. Stir in remaining juice drink and lemon or lime juice. Chill. When ready to serve, add sparkling water. Pour into 4 tall, ice-filled glasses with frosty rims. Garnish with a strawberry and pineapple chunk on a toothpick. Yield: 4 servings.

Hot and Ready Chocolate

   2 *(1-ounce) squares unsweetened chocolate*
 ⅓ *cup cold milk*
 ⅛ *teaspoon vanilla extract*
      Dash salt
1⅔ *cups hot milk*
 ⅓ *cup sugar*
      Dash ground cinnamon

Cut chocolate into small pieces. Put into the blender along with cold milk, vanilla, and salt. Cover and run at low speed until the chocolate is grated to fine bits. Stop the blender and use rubber spatula to push down any ingredients that may be on the sides of the container. Add hot milk and sugar. Cover and mix at low speed until chocolate is dissolved. Serve hot, topped with ground cinnamon. Yield: 3 cups.

Hot Tarry Chocolate

   2 *(1-ounce) squares unsweetened chocolate, cut into small pieces*
 ½ *cup hot water*
 ¼ *cup sugar*
 ¼ *cup light molasses*
   1 *quart milk*
      Pinch salt
      Whipping cream, whipped (optional)

Heat chocolate and water together in saucepan, stirring constantly until chocolate is melted; stir until mixture forms a smooth paste. Add sugar, molasses, milk, and salt; heat slowly, but do not let mixture boil. Serve hot, topped with whipped cream, if desired. Yield: 6 servings.

*Pink Buttermilk

   2 *cups buttermilk, chilled*
   2 *cups tomato-vegetable juice, chilled*
   1 *teaspoon Worcestershire sauce*
 ½ *teaspoon salt*
      Dash hot sauce

Combine all ingredients and pour into tall chilled glasses. Yield: 4 to 6 servings.

*Buttermilk Lemonade

    1 *quart buttermilk, chilled*
    ½ *cup lemon juice*
    2 *tablespoons sugar*
    2 *teaspoons vanilla extract*

Combine chilled buttermilk, lemon juice, sugar, and vanilla. Stir or shake mixture until well blended. Serve very cold in chilled glasses. Yield: 6 servings.

*Palm Springs Cooler

    3 *cups milk*
    3 *tablespoons sugar*
       Finely crushed ice
  1½ *cups orange juice*
    2 *teaspoons grated orange rind*
       Mint leaves
       Orange slices

Combine milk and sugar in shaker or blender and mix well with finely crushed ice. Add orange juice and rind and mix vigorously. Pour into glasses and garnish with mint and orange slices. Yield: 6 servings.

*Fruit Shake Cooler

    1 *(12-ounce) can apricot nectar*
    1 *(6-ounce) can frozen orange juice, thawed, undiluted*
  1¾ *cups pineapple juice*
   ⅓ *cup lemon juice*
    1 *cup sugar*
    1 *cup instant nonfat dry milk powder*
    1 *cup water*
    2 *quarts ginger ale, chilled*
       Orange and lemon slices

Mix apricot nectar, orange, pineapple, and lemon juices with sugar. Stir until dissolved. Pour into refrigerator trays and freeze to a mush. Beat nonfat dry milk and water until very stiff; add frozen juices and beat until well mixed. Return to trays and freeze. When ready to serve, spoon into a punch bowl and pour in ginger ale. Garnish with sliced fruit. Yield: 4 quarts.

*Strawberry Cooler

    1 *pint fresh strawberries, cleaned and sliced*
  ⅓ to ½ *cup sugar*
   ¼ *cup orange juice*
   ½ *cup pineapple juice*
    1 *quart milk*
    1 *pint pineapple sherbet*

Mash strawberries, stir in sugar. Add orange and pineapple juices; blend in milk. Pour into 4 chilled tall glasses. Top each with a scoop of sherbet. Yield: 4 servings.

  Note: Frozen strawberries may be substituted for fresh ones; use one 10-ounce package and omit sugar.

*Spiced Coffee Vienna

    3 *cups coffee (extra strong and very hot)*
    2 *cinnamon sticks*
    4 *whole cloves*
    4 *allspice berries*
       Whipping cream, whipped
       Ground nutmeg
       Sugar

Pour coffee over cinnamon sticks, cloves, and allspice. Allow to stand over low heat for 10 to 15 minutes. Strain; pour into glasses and top with whipped cream sprinkled with nutmeg. Serve with sugar. Yield: 6 servings.

Cafe Mexicano

    4 *teaspoons chocolate syrup*
   ½ *cup whipping cream*
   ¾ *teaspoon ground cinnamon, divided*
   ½ *teaspoon ground nutmeg*
    1 *tablespoon sugar*
  1½ *cups strong hot coffee*

Put 1 teaspoon chocolate syrup in each of 4 small cups. Combine cream, ¼ teaspoon cinnamon, nutmeg, and sugar; whip. Stir remaining ½ teaspoon cinnamon into hot coffee. Pour coffee into cups. Stir to blend with syrup. Top with dollops of spiced whipped cream. Yield: 4 servings.

Luscious Coffee Frosted

½ cup instant nonfat dry milk powder
½ cup ice water
¼ cup sugar
2 tablespoons instant coffee powder
1 pint coffee ice cream, slightly softened

Chill beater blades and small bowl of electric mixer. Measure nonfat dry milk into chilled bowl; add ice water and blend. Beat at high speed until soft peaks form, about 5 minutes. Combine sugar and instant coffee; add to milk mixture slowly, continuing to beat. Turn to low speed. Add ice cream, about ½ cup at a time, beating after each addition until blended. Serve at once in chilled glasses. Yield: 3 or 4 servings.

Cafe Brûlot

1 (4-inch) cinnamon stick
12 whole cloves
Peel of 2 oranges, cut in thin slivers
Peel of 2 lemons, cut in thin slivers
6 lumps sugar
8 ounces brandy
2 ounces curaçao
1 quart strong, black coffee

Using a ladle, mash cinnamon, cloves, orange and lemon peel, and sugar lumps in brûlot bowl or chafing dish. Add brandy and curaçao and mix well. Carefully ignite brandy and mix until sugar is dissolved. Gradually add black coffee and continue mixing until flame flickers out. Serve hot in brûlot or demitasse cups. Yield: 10 to 12 servings.

Spanish Egg Chocolate

2 (1-ounce) squares unsweetened chocolate
2 cups milk
½ cup sugar
1½ teaspoons ground cinnamon
Dash ground cloves
1 teaspoon vanilla extract
1 egg

Heat chocolate and milk in top of double boiler. Beat with rotary beater until creamy. Blend in sugar, spices, and vanilla. Slightly beat the egg and pour into hot chocolate. Whip to a froth and serve at once. Yield: 4 servings.

Eggnog Deluxe

12 egg yolks
1¾ cups sugar
1 teaspoon vanilla extract
½ teaspoon ground nutmeg
¾ cup light rum
1½ pints brandy
1 quart milk
1½ quarts whipping cream
12 egg whites
6 tablespoons sugar
Ground nutmeg (optional)

Beat egg yolks until light. Gradually add sugar, vanilla, and nutmeg; beat well. Place in punch bowl. Add rum gradually, stirring constantly. Add brandy and continue to stir until well blended. Let this mixture stand in a cold place overnight, stirring occasionally. The next day, add milk and cream, a small amount at a time. Beat egg whites with 6 tablespoons sugar. Fold into eggnog mixture. Sprinkle each serving with nutmeg, if desired. Yield: 40 servings.

Eggnog for Thirty

24 egg yolks
2 cups sugar
1 quart bourbon
1 pint brandy
1 quart whipping cream
2 quarts milk
1 quart vanilla ice cream
24 egg whites, stiffly beaten

Beat egg yolks and sugar until thick and lemon colored. Add bourbon and brandy and stir thoroughly. Blend in cream and milk and continue stirring. Add ice cream and mix well. Add stiffly beaten egg whites. Chill for at least 30 minutes before serving. Yield: 30 servings.

Eight-Egg Nog

   8 egg yolks
1¼ cups sugar, divided
   1 cup whiskey
 ¼ cup water
   8 egg whites, stiffly beaten
 ⅛ teaspoon salt
   1 quart whipping cream, whipped

Whip egg yolks with ¾ cup sugar until light and lemon colored. Pour whiskey over yolks and set aside. Make a syrup of ½ cup sugar and water; cook until mixture spins a thread. Pour hot syrup over stiffly beaten egg whites, to which salt has been added. Gently fold yolks and whites together; fold in whipped cream. The flavor of the eggnog is improved if allowed to sit for an hour before serving. Yield: 20 servings.

Orange Eggnog

   6 eggs
 ¼ cup sugar
 ¼ teaspoon ground cinnamon
 ¼ teaspoon ground ginger
 ¼ teaspoon ground cloves
   2 quarts orange juice, chilled
 ½ cup lemon juice
   1 quart vanilla ice cream
   1 (28-ounce) bottle ginger ale, chilled

Beat eggs until lemon colored; add sugar and spices. Stir in orange and lemon juices. Put ice cream in punch bowl and cut into small pieces. Pour in juice mixture and ginger ale. Yield: 20 to 25 servings.

*Chocolate Banana Nog

   2 ripe bananas, mashed
   1 quart milk
 ½ cup chocolate syrup
 ⅛ teaspoon salt
Banana slices (optional)

Mix all ingredients together using rotary beater or blender. Pour into tall glasses. Garnish with banana slices, if desired. Yield: 6 servings.

Note: Dairy chocolate milk may be substituted for white milk and chocolate syrup.

Hot Almond Eggnog

   6 egg yolks
 ¾ teaspoon salt
 ½ cup sugar
   6 cups milk, scalded
   1 tablespoon almond flavoring
   1 tablespoon vanilla extract
   6 egg whites
Whipping cream, whipped (optional)
Slivered almonds (optional)

Beat egg yolks until light. Add salt and sugar; blend. Add hot milk, almond flavoring, and vanilla. Beat egg whites until stiff; fold into hot mixture. Pour into cups. Garnish with dollops of whipped cream and slivered almonds, if desired. Yield: 6 servings.

Holiday Eggnog

10 egg yolks
 ¾ cup sugar
   1 pint rye whiskey
   1 quart whipping cream
10 egg whites, stiffly beaten
Ground nutmeg

Beat egg yolks and sugar. Add whiskey slowly, stirring constantly. Continue stirring and add cream, then the stiffly beaten egg whites. Chill and top each serving with nutmeg. Yield: 20 to 25 servings.

George Whitfield's Eggnog

12 egg yolks
12 ounces bourbon
12 tablespoons sugar, divided
12 egg whites
1 pint whipping cream
1 tablespoon powdered sugar

Beat egg yolks until thick and lemon colored. Slowly add bourbon, beating constantly. Slowly add 8 tablespoons sugar and continue beating until mixture is smooth.

Whip egg whites until stiff but not dry, adding 4 tablespoons sugar a small amount at a time. Put beaten egg whites in chilled punch bowl. Whip cream, adding powdered sugar. Put whipped cream on top of beaten egg whites. Pour the egg yolk mixture over this and carefully fold all ingredients together. Yield: 20 servings.

Mulled Wine

½ cup white or firmly packed light brown sugar
1½ cups water
1 stick cinnamon
¾ teaspoon whole cloves
Rind of ½ small lemon
Red Burgundy

Make a spiced syrup by combining sugar, water, cinnamon, cloves, and lemon rind in a saucepan. Simmer for 15 minutes. Strain and discard rind and spices. Cool; store, covered, until ready to use.

To serve, preheat glasses by rinsing in very hot water. Pour in about 1 ounce of spiced syrup, then add 3 ounces of red Burgundy. Yield: 12 servings.

*Banana Milk Smoothee

1 cup milk
1 medium-size ripe banana
1 thin slice lemon with peel
1 cup cracked ice
Ground nutmeg

Combine all ingredients except nutmeg in blender. Cover and process at high speed until ice is melted and all ingredients are thoroughly blended. Serve topped with ground nutmeg. Yield: 2 cups.

*Hot Spiced Afternoon Tea

4 quarts water
1 teaspoon whole cloves
1 stick cinnamon
15 tea bags or 5 tablespoons loose tea
1¼ cups sugar
1 cup orange juice
¾ cup lemon juice

Bring water to a boil; add spices and bring to a full rolling boil. Remove from heat. Add tea bags or loose tea and steep for 4 minutes. Strain; add sugar and stir until dissolved. Pour in fruit juices. Keep hot, or reheat over low heat, but do not boil. Yield: enough spiced tea for 30 punch cups.

*New Twist Iced Tea Cooler

4 tea bags or 4 teaspoons loose tea
1 cup boiling water
1 cup light corn syrup or honey
4 cups cold water
1 cup lemon juice
1 cup orange juice
1 (28-ounce) bottle ginger ale, chilled
Lemon slices

Steep tea in boiling water for 3 minutes; strain, if loose tea is used. Blend into corn syrup or honey; add water and fruit juices. Chill thoroughly. When ready to serve, add ginger ale and pour into tall, ice-filled glasses. Garnish with lemon slices. Yield: 2½ quarts.

Chocolate Peppermint Shakes

    1   quart milk
  1/3   cup chocolate syrup
  1/4   cup whipping cream
  1/4   teaspoon oil of peppermint
       Chocolate ice cream
    5   peppermint candy canes

Combine milk, chocolate syrup, and cream in shaker; shake well or beat with rotary beater until ingredients are well blended. Add oil of peppermint. Shake well and pour into 5 tall, chilled glasses.
    Top each with a large scoop of chocolate ice cream. Add 1 candy cane to a glass. Yield: 5 servings.

Vegetable-Clam Juice Cocktail

    4   cups tomato-vegetable juice
    4   cups bottled clam juice
  1/4   cup lemon juice
    1   teaspoon Worcestershire sauce
  1/4   teaspoon salt
       White pepper
       Celery sticks

Combine all ingredients in large pitcher and chill. Serve in old-fashioned glasses and garnish with a celery stick for stirring. Yield: 10 servings.

*Orange Milk Shake

    2   cups milk
  1/2   pint vanilla ice cream
  1/2   cup frozen orange juice, undiluted
       Orange slices

Combine milk, ice cream, and orange juice in electric blender. Cover and blend at high speed until smooth and fluffy, about 15 seconds. Pour into 4 tall, chilled glasses. Garnish with orange slices and serve immediately. Yield: 4 servings.

Hot Tom and Jerry

    2   egg yolks
    2   tablespoons sugar
  1/2   teaspoon ground cinnamon
  1/8   teaspoon ground cloves
    2   egg whites
       Bourbon
       Hot milk or water

Beat egg yolks; add sugar, cinnamon, and cloves. Beat egg whites and fold into yolk mixture. In each cup or mug place a heaping tablespoon of the egg mixture and 1 jigger of bourbon; then fill the mugs with either hot milk or hot water. Yield: 6 cups.

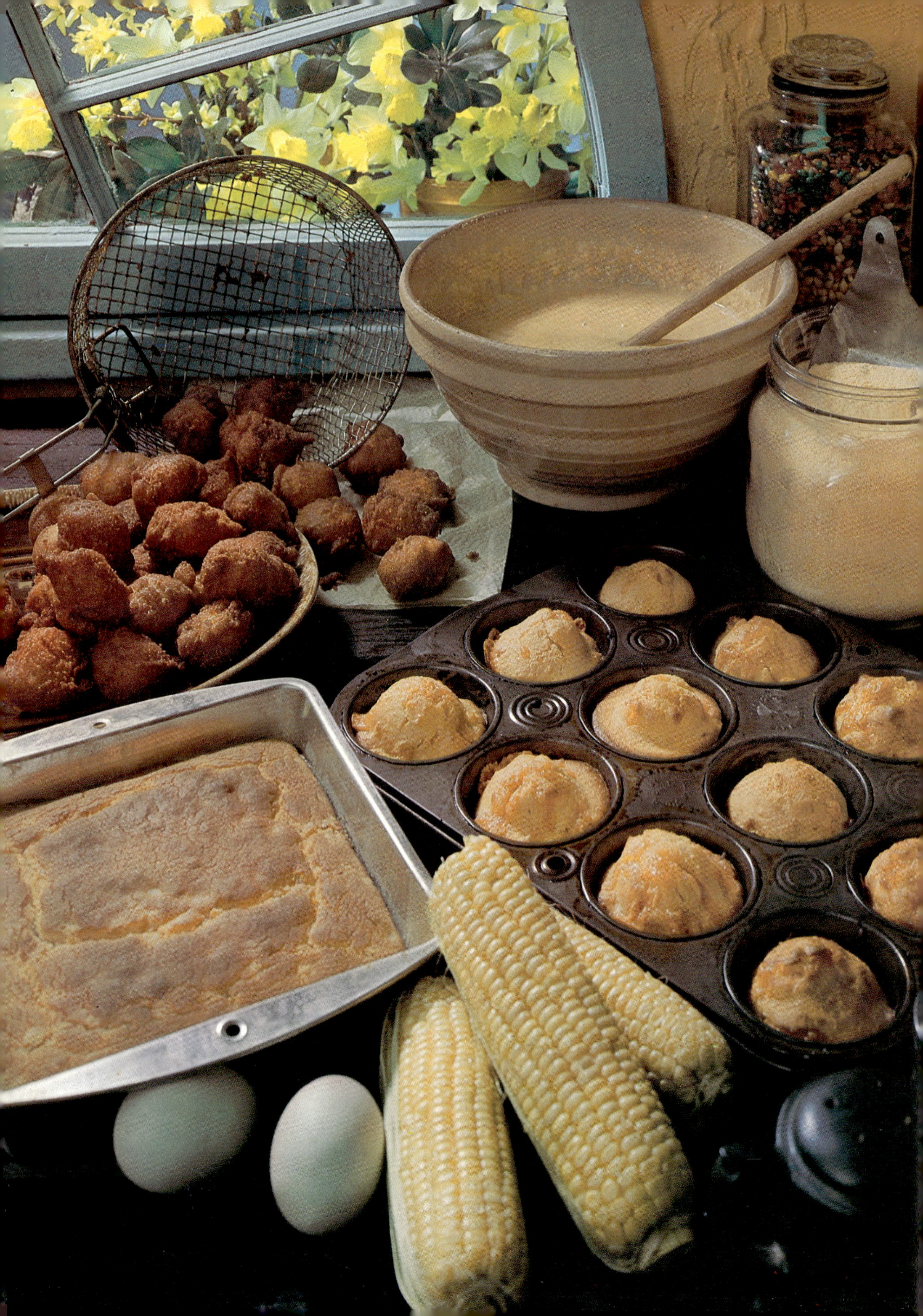

Breads

We've come a long way in our methods of baking breads. Few people today cook their corn pones in ashes, and it would be hard to find a cook who makes her yeast bread by getting up at 7 A.M. on hot sunny days to "take 1 teacup full of morning's milk, scald with 1 teacup of boiling water . . . put in hot place in sun by 8 or 9 . . . keep it moved to hotter place . . . if you see bubbles, don't stir no more . . ." The directions go on and on with the final admonition, "you will lose it if it comes on a cloud, rains much."

Despite dependence on the fickle fates of fire and weather, the art of bread making has survived, probably because of one irresistible element—the aroma of oven-baked bread. This one delight is possibly responsible for so many modern-day cooks returning to homemade breads.

Yeast breads and corn breads are big items in the Southern diet. Corn bread is an essential with vegetables; biscuits a favorite with any meal; and fresh hot rolls, coffee cakes, or loaf breads delicious treats between meals as well as with meals. Besides all these enticing assets, bread making is fun.

Deluxe Corn Bread

1¼ *cups cornmeal*
¾ *cup all-purpose flour*
¼ *cup sugar*
1 *tablespoon baking powder*
½ *teaspoon salt*
1 *egg*
1 *cup milk*
¼ *cup vegetable oil*

Combine cornmeal, flour, sugar, baking powder, and salt. Add egg, milk, and oil. Beat with rotary beater just until smooth, about 1 minute. Bake in greased 8-inch square baking pan at 425° for 20 to 25 minutes. Yield: 9 servings.

Muffins: Mix corn bread batter as directed. Fill greased muffin tins two-thirds full. Bake at 425° for 15 to 20 minutes. Yield: 12 medium-size muffins.

Corn Sticks: Pour corn bread batter into hot, well-greased corn stick pans. Bake at 425° for 15 to 20 minutes. Yield: 14 to 16 corn sticks.

*Buttermilk Corn Bread

1 *cup cornmeal*
½ *cup all-purpose flour*
1 *teaspoon salt*
1 *teaspoon baking powder*
½ *teaspoon soda*
1 *cup buttermilk*
1 *egg, beaten*
¼ *cup melted shortening*

Combine dry ingredients and mix well. Combine buttermilk, beaten egg, and melted shortening and add to dry mixture. Stir well and spoon into hot, greased 9-inch square baking pan or corn stick pan. Bake at 450° for about 15 to 20 minutes or until bread is browned. Yield: 6 to 8 servings.

*Country Corn Bread

- 1½ cups cornmeal
- ¾ cup all-purpose flour
- 1 teaspoon salt
- 2½ teaspoons baking powder
- 2 eggs, beaten
- 1½ cups milk
- 6 tablespoons shortening

Combine cornmeal, flour, salt, and baking powder. Combine beaten eggs and milk and stir into cornmeal mixture. Mix well. Spoon shortening into a 10-inch skillet and place in 400° oven. As soon as shortening is very hot, coat sides of skillet and stir remaining shortening into corn bread mixture. Spoon mixture into hot skillet and bake at 400° for about 20 to 25 minutes or until golden brown. Yield: 6 to 8 servings.

*Tennessee Corn Bread

- 1 cup all-purpose flour
- 1 cup cornmeal
- 4 teaspoons baking powder
- 1 teaspoon salt
- 1 egg
- ¼ cup salad oil
- ¾ to 1 cup milk

Combine flour, cornmeal, baking powder, and salt. Add egg, oil, and milk; beat well. Grease an 8-inch square baking pan and heat in 450° oven until hot. Pour batter into pan and bake at 450° for 20 to 25 minutes. Yield: 6 to 8 servings.

*Florida Hoe Cake

- 1 cup cornmeal
- ½ cup all-purpose flour
- 1 teaspoon salt
- Water

Combine cornmeal, flour, and salt. Add water until consistency of pancake batter. Pour onto hot griddle; grill as you would pancakes. Yield: 4 to 6 servings.

Jalapeño Corn Bread

- 1 cup cornmeal
- ½ teaspoon salt
- ½ teaspoon soda
- 1 cup cream-style corn
- 2 eggs, slightly beaten
- 1 (4-ounce) can green chili peppers, finely chopped
- ⅔ cup buttermilk
- ⅓ cup melted shortening
- 1 cup shredded sharp Cheddar cheese

Combine all ingredients, except cheese, in a bowl. Mix well and pour half the batter into a hot, greased 9-inch baking pan. Sprinkle cheese on top and cover with remaining batter. Bake at 375° for 30 to 40 minutes. Yield: 6 to 9 servings.

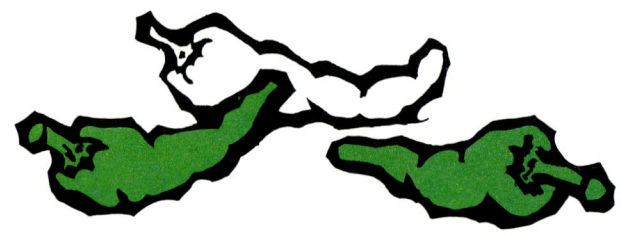

Mexican Corn Bread

- 1 pound ground beef
- Salt to taste
- 1 cup cornmeal
- ½ teaspoon salt
- 1 small onion, grated
- ½ pound Cheddar cheese, shredded
- 4 jalapeño peppers, chopped (optional)
- 3 eggs, beaten
- 1 cup milk
- 1 (17-ounce) can cream-style corn

Season beef with salt and sauté in heavy skillet; drain. Set aside. Combine cornmeal, ½ teaspoon salt, onion, cheese, and peppers, if desired, in a large bowl; mix well. Stir eggs into milk; add to dry mixture and stir just to moisten. Add corn and blend well.

Spoon half the batter into a greased 2-quart casserole; place beef over batter and top with remaining batter. Bake at 350° for 45 minutes or until done. Yield: 6 to 8 servings.

*Southern Corn Pones

1 cup cornmeal
1 teaspoon salt
¼ teaspoon plus a pinch of soda
1 tablespoon melted shortening
Buttermilk

Combine cornmeal, salt, soda, and shortening in a bowl. Add just enough buttermilk to make the mixture thin enough to shape into pones. Place in a greased iron pan and bake at 450° about 10 minutes or until the bottom browns. Place under broiler to brown the top. Don't bake too long before putting under broiler or bread will dry out. Yield: 3 or 4 servings.

*Hush Puppies with Onions

1¾ cups cornmeal
4 tablespoons all-purpose flour
1 teaspoon baking powder
1 teaspoon salt
6 tablespoons chopped onion
1 egg, beaten
2 cups boiling water
Salad oil

Combine dry ingredients, onion, and egg; add boiling water, stirring constantly until mixture is smooth. Add more water if necessary. Drop by teaspoonfuls into deep hot oil. Cook until golden brown; drain on paper towels. Yield: 8 to 10 servings.

*Florida Hush Puppies

½ cup all-purpose flour
2 teaspoons baking powder
1 tablespoon sugar
½ teaspoon salt
1½ cups cornmeal
1 small onion, finely chopped (optional)
1 egg, beaten
¾ cup milk
Shortening

Combine dry ingredients. Add onion, egg, and milk to dry ingredients, stirring lightly. Drop a teaspoon of batter for each hush puppy into deep hot shortening (360°), frying only a few at a time. Fry until the hush puppies are a golden brown. Drain on paper towels. Yield: 2 dozen hush puppies.

*Corn Kernel Corn Bread

¾ cup all-purpose flour
1 cup cornmeal
4 teaspoons baking powder
1 teaspoon salt
¼ cup sugar
2 eggs, well beaten
1 cup milk
3 tablespoons margarine, melted
1 cup fresh cooked or canned yellow cream-style corn

Combine flour, cornmeal, baking powder, salt, and sugar. Combine eggs, milk, melted margarine, and corn. Add to the flour mixture and stir until well blended. Pour into a well-greased 9-inch square baking pan and bake at 475° for 20 to 25 minutes or until tester comes out clean. Yield: 6 to 8 servings.

*Southern Corn Dodgers

1 cup cornmeal (not self-rising)
3 cups boiling water
2 eggs, beaten
1 teaspoon sugar
¼ teaspoon salt
1 small onion, diced
Shortening

Pour cornmeal slowly into boiling water; cook about 3 minutes, stirring constantly. Set aside to cool. Add eggs, sugar, salt, and diced onion to cornmeal. Mix well and drop by spoonfuls into deep hot shortening. Fry until golden brown. Drain on paper towels. Yield: about 6 servings.

*Hot Water Corn Bread

    2 cups white cornmeal
    3 cups boiling water
    1 teaspoon salt
    1 tablespoon butter

Scald cornmeal with boiling water; add salt and butter. Mixture will be very stiff. Spread in a heavy, greased 9-inch square baking pan or corn stick pans; bake at 400° about 30 minutes. Put under broiler to brown, if desired. Yield: 8 to 10 servings.

*Whole Wheat Biscuits

    1 cup whole wheat flour
  ⅞ cup all-purpose flour
    1 tablespoon baking powder
  ¾ teaspoon salt
  ¼ to ⅓ cup shortening
  ¾ cup water or milk

Combine dry ingredients and mix well. Cut in shortening and add water or milk to make a soft dough. Place dough on a lightly floured surface and pat or roll until ½- or ¾-inch thick; or knead gently, and roll to the desired thickness. Cut with a 2-inch cutter and place on greased baking sheets. Bake at 450° for about 15 minutes. Yield: about 16 (2-inch) biscuits.

Easy Buttermilk Biscuits

 2½ cups all-purpose flour
    3 teaspoons baking powder
    1 teaspoon salt
  ½ teaspoon soda
  ⅓ cup melted butter
    1 cup buttermilk

Combine flour, baking powder, salt, and soda. Add butter and buttermilk and stir to form a sticky dough. Knead a few times on a floured surface to make a smooth ball. Roll out to ½-inch thickness. Cut with a 2-inch cutter and place on greased baking sheets. Bake at 450° for 10 to 12 minutes. Yield: 16 (2-inch) biscuits.

Cheese Biscuits

    2 cups all-purpose flour
    4 teaspoons baking powder
    1 teaspoon salt
  ½ cup shortening
    1 cup shredded sharp Cheddar cheese
  ⅔ cup buttermilk

Combine flour, baking powder, and salt; cut in shortening. Add cheese and gradually stir in buttermilk. Turn dough out onto a lightly floured surface and roll thin. Cut into small biscuits and place on greased baking sheets. Bake at 400° for 8 to 10 minutes. Yield: 18 small biscuits.

*Baking Powder Biscuits

    2 cups all-purpose flour
    3 teaspoons baking powder
  ½ teaspoon salt
  ⅓ cup shortening
  ¾ to 1 cup milk

Combine flour, baking powder, and salt, and sift into a mixing bowl. Cut shortening into sifted dry ingredients with a pastry blender or two knives, until the mixture resembles coarse meal. Pour in milk, smaller amount first, and stir with a fork until dough is mixed but rough-looking. Add remaining milk if necessary. Work quickly.

Pat dough about ½ inch thick on a lightly floured surface. The less flour you work into biscuits, the lighter your biscuits will be. Cut dough with floured cutter and place on an ungreased baking sheet. Bake at 450° for 15 minutes. Yield: about 18 biscuits.

*Stir 'n' Roll Biscuits

    2 cups all-purpose flour
    1 teaspoon salt
    3 teaspoons baking powder
  ⅔ cup milk
  ⅓ cup salad oil

Sift dry ingredients into a large mixing bowl. Pour milk and oil into measuring cup. Do not stir, but pour all at once into flour. Mix dough with a fork until mixture leaves sides of bowl and forms a ball. Turn onto a large square of waxed paper and roll to thickness of ½ inch or less. Cut with a 2-inch cutter and place on an ungreased baking sheet. Bake at 475° for 10 to 12 minutes. Yield: 12 to 14 (2-inch) biscuits.

Quick Apricot Coffee Cake

2 *cups corn flakes, crushed*
1 *cup sugar, divided*
¼ *cup melted butter or margarine, divided*
1½ *cups commercial biscuit mix*
½ *teaspoon ground nutmeg*
½ *cup milk*
1 *egg, beaten*
1 *cup dried apricots, cooked, drained, and cut into quarters*

Combine crushed corn flakes, ½ cup sugar, and 2 tablespoons butter; mix well. Sprinkle half of mixture evenly over bottom of a greased 9-inch square baking pan.

Combine biscuit mix, remaining ½ cup sugar, remaining 2 tablespoons butter, nutmeg, milk, and egg; mix well. Stir in apricots. Spoon batter over mixture in pan. Sprinkle remaining cornflake mixture over top. Bake at 375° for 30 to 35 minutes or until done. Yield: 9 servings.

Skillet Cheese Bread

½ *cup vegetable shortening (not oil)*
2 *beaten eggs*
1 *cup milk*
3 *cups commercial biscuit mix*
2 *cups shredded pasteurized process American cheese*
2 *tablespoons poppy seeds*
2 *teaspoons dried minced onion*

Melt shortening in electric skillet. Combine eggs, milk, and melted shortening in mixing bowl; add to biscuit mix. Stir in cheese, poppy seeds, and onion. Stir just until dry ingredients are moistened. Line electric skillet with a double layer of waxed paper and spread dough in skillet. Bake at 300° for 25 minutes. Turn out of skillet and serve. Yield: 12 to 16 servings.

Basil Cheese Bread

3 *cups commercial biscuit mix*
½ *cup finely shredded sharp Cheddar cheese*
1 *tablespoon sugar*
1¼ *cups milk*
1 *tablespoon salad oil*
1 *egg, slightly beaten*
1 *teaspoon chervil*
1 *teaspoon sweet basil, crushed*

Combine biscuit mix, cheese, and sugar in a large mixing bowl. Stir milk, oil, egg, chervil, and basil together until well blended. Add to cheese mixture all at once. Stir until just blended. Turn into a heavily greased 9- x 5- x 3-inch loaf pan.

Bake at 350° for 45 to 50 minutes, or until the crust is golden and the bread tests done. Turn onto a wire rack to cool slightly. Serve while loaf is still warm. Yield: 1 loaf.

*Chewy Dumplings

2 *cups all-purpose flour*
½ *teaspoon salt*
2 *tablespoons salad oil*
Ice water
Chicken broth

Mix flour, salt, and oil. Add enough ice water to make a soft dough. Knead lightly on a floured surface. Roll about ¼ inch thick; cut into strips. Drop strips, one at a time, into boiling chicken broth. Cover tightly and simmer for 15 minutes. Yield: 4 servings.

Molasses Muffins

1¼ cups butter or margarine, softened
1 cup sugar
4 eggs
½ cup molasses
2 teaspoons soda
1 cup buttermilk
4 cups all-purpose flour
½ teaspoon ground cinnamon
¼ teaspoon ground ginger
1 cup chopped nuts
1 cup seedless raisins

Cream butter and sugar. Add eggs, one at a time, beating well after each addition; add molasses. Combine soda and buttermilk; add to molasses mixture, blending well. Combine flour and spices; add to molasses mixture, and mix well. Stir in nuts and raisins. Fill greased and floured muffin tins two-thirds full and bake at 400° for 15 minutes. Yield: 3½ dozen muffins.

Note: If you do not want to bake all the muffins at one time, unused batter may be kept about 2 weeks in a tightly covered container in refrigerator.

*Oatmeal Muffins

1¼ cups boiling water
½ teaspoon salt
1 cup oats, quick-cooking or regular, uncooked
½ cup butter or margarine, softened
1 cup firmly packed brown sugar
1 cup sugar
2 eggs
1⅓ cups self-rising flour
1 teaspoon ground cinnamon
1½ cups flaked coconut

Combine water, salt, and oats; let stand 20 minutes. Cream butter and sugar; add eggs and beat well. Combine flour and cinnamon; stir into creamed mixture. Add coconut and oat mixture; stir well.

Fill greased or paper-lined muffin tins two-thirds full. Bake at 350° for 25 minutes or until done. Yield: 2 dozen muffins.

*Banana Bran Muffins

1 cup whole bran cereal
1 cup sour milk or buttermilk
2 tablespoons margarine
4 tablespoons sugar
1 egg, beaten
1½ cups all-purpose flour
½ teaspoon soda
1 teaspoon baking powder
1 teaspoon ground cinnamon
¾ cup mashed ripe bananas

Soak bran in milk a few minutes. Cream margarine and sugar until smooth; add egg and beat well. Combine dry ingredients and add to creamed mixture alternately with sour milk-bran mixture. Stir in bananas and mix just to blend. Do not beat. Spoon into well-greased muffin tins. Bake at 400° about 12 to 15 minutes. Yield: 15 muffins.

*Whole Wheat Muffins

2 cups whole wheat flour
¼ cup sugar
1 teaspoon salt
4 teaspoons baking powder
1 cup milk
1 egg, well beaten
1 to 3 tablespoons butter, melted

Combine dry ingredients; add milk gradually, then egg and butter. Spoon into greased muffin tins and bake at 400° for 20 minutes. Yield: 12 muffins.

Cheese Corn Muffins

½ cup all-purpose flour
2½ teaspoons baking powder
¾ teaspoon salt
1 tablespoon sugar
½ cup yellow cornmeal
1 cup shredded Cheddar cheese
1 egg
¾ cup milk
2 tablespoons melted shortening

Combine flour, baking powder, salt, and sugar. Stir in cornmeal and cheese. Make a well in the center of mixture. Add egg, milk, and shortening. Stir just to moisten dry ingredients. Fill greased muffin tins two-thirds full; bake at 400° for 20 to 25 minutes or until golden brown. Yield: 8 muffins.

*Sweet Potato Muffins

- 2 cups all-purpose flour
- 2 teaspoons baking powder
- ½ teaspoon soda
- 1 teaspoon salt
- 1 teaspoon ground cinnamon
- ½ teaspoon ground cloves
- 1 egg
- ⅔ cup firmly packed brown sugar
- ½ cup melted shortening
- 1 cup buttermilk
- 2 cups lightly packed shredded raw sweet potato

Combine flour, baking powder, soda, salt, cinnamon, and cloves. Beat egg in a second bowl and add sugar, shortening, and buttermilk. Make a well in the center of the dry ingredients. Pour in the liquid mixture and mix by hand just until ingredients are well moistened. Stir in shredded sweet potatoes. Bake in muffin tins at 350° for 20 minutes. Yield: 18 muffins.

*Corn Muffins

- 1 cup cornmeal
- ½ cup all-purpose flour
- 1 tablespoon baking powder
- 1 teaspoon salt
- 1 tablespoon sugar
- 1 cup niblet corn, drained
- ¾ cup milk
- 1 egg, slightly beaten
- 2 tablespoons butter or margarine

Combine dry ingredients; add corn and mix well. Add milk, egg, and butter and blend well. Pour into greased muffin tins and bake at 450° about 20 minutes. Yield: 12 muffins.

Butterfly Orange Muffins

- 2 cups self-rising flour
- 3 tablespoons sugar
- 1 egg, beaten
- 1 cup milk
- 3 tablespoons melted shortening or oil
- 1 tablespoon grated orange rind
- 24 mandarin orange sections, drained

Combine flour and sugar in a large mixing bowl. Combine egg, milk, shortening, orange rind; add all at once to flour mixture, stirring only until flour is moistened. Fill greased muffin tins two-thirds full. Place 2 orange sections on each muffin in opposite directions to form a butterfly. Bake at 425° for 20 to 25 minutes or until golden brown. Yield: 12 muffins.

*Blueberry Muffins

- 2 cups all-purpose flour
- ⅓ cup sugar
- 3 teaspoons baking powder
- 1 teaspoon salt
- 3 tablespoons softened shortening
- 1 egg
- 1 cup milk
- 1 cup blueberries

Combine dry ingredients. Cut in shortening with a pastry blender. Add egg and milk, stirring just until all flour is moistened. Drain blueberries well if canned; fold into batter. Fill greased muffin tins two-thirds full. Bake at 400° for 20 to 25 minutes. Yield: 12 muffins.

*Lost Bread

- 1 (1-pound) loaf day-old French bread
- 2 eggs, well beaten
- ¼ cup milk
- Shortening or butter
- Powdered sugar

Slice bread in 1-inch thick slices. Combine eggs and milk. Dip bread slices in egg mixture; brown on both sides in hot shortening. Drain on absorbent paper. Dust lightly with powdered sugar. Yield: 4 to 6 servings.

Basic Crêpes

2 cups all-purpose flour
½ teaspoon salt
4 large eggs
1 cup cold milk
1 cup cold water
4 tablespoons butter, melted
Salad oil

Combine flour, salt, and eggs; blend well. Blend in milk, water, and melted butter. Mix well. Refrigerate batter for at least 2 hours, allowing flour particles to swell and soften so that the crêpes are light in texture.

Lightly brush the bottom of a 6- or 7-inch crêpe pan or heavy skillet with salad oil and heat pan over medium heat until just hot, not smoking. Pour a scant ¼ cup of batter in pan and *quickly* tilt pan in all directions to coat bottom of pan in a thin film. Cook about 1 minute. Lift edge of crêpe to test for doneness. The crêpe is ready for flipping when it can be shaken loose from the bottom of pan. Flip the crêpe and cook for about ½ minute on other side; this is rarely more than a spotty brown and is used as side on which filling is placed. Crêpes may be made in advance, stacked between layers of waxed paper to prevent them from sticking, and frozen. To thaw, heat in a covered dish at 300°. Yield: about 22 crêpes.

*Banana Breakfast Loaf

2 cups all-purpose flour
⅔ cup sugar
1 tablespoon baking powder
1 teaspoon salt
3 tablespoons melted shortening or salad oil
⅓ cup milk
3 eggs, beaten
1 cup mashed ripe bananas
½ cup chopped nuts

Combine all ingredients in a large mixing bowl; beat at medium speed of electric mixer for 30 seconds or 75 strokes by hand, scraping sides and bottom of bowl often. Pour into a greased 9- x 5- x 3-inch loaf pan.

Bake at 350° for 55 to 60 minutes or until a toothpick inserted in center comes out clean. Cool on wire rack for 10 minutes before removing from pan; cool thoroughly before slicing. Yield: 1 loaf.

Chocolate Surprise Doughnuts

4½ cups all-purpose flour, divided
2 packages active dry yeast
1 teaspoon grated lemon rind
1 cup milk
½ cup sugar
2 teaspoons salt
¼ cup salad oil
2 eggs
¾ cup semisweet chocolate morsels
Oil
Sugar or cinnamon-sugar mixture

Combine 2 cups flour, yeast, and lemon rind. Heat milk, sugar, salt, and oil over low heat only until warm, stirring to blend. Add to flour mixture and beat until smooth, about 2 minutes on medium speed of electric mixer or 300 strokes by hand.

Blend in eggs. Add 1 cup flour and beat 1 minute on medium speed or 150 strokes by hand. Stir in remaining flour to make a moderately stiff dough. Turn out onto a lightly floured surface and knead until smooth and satiny, about 8 to 10 minutes. Shape dough into ball and place in lightly greased bowl, turning to grease all sides. Cover and let rise in a warm place (80° to 85°) until doubled in bulk, about 1½ hours. Punch down. Let rest 10 minutes.

Divide dough into 36 equal pieces. Flatten each piece and place 6 chocolate morsels in center of each; shape into balls, sealing edges securely. Let rise, sealed side down, in warm place until doubled in bulk, about 30 minutes.

Deep fry doughnuts balls in hot oil (375°) for 6 to 8 minutes, turning once. Drain. Coat with sugar or cinnamon-sugar mixture. Yield: 3 dozen doughnuts.

breads

*Drop Doughnuts

  2 *packages active dry yeast*
  ½ *cup very warm water*
  ¾ *cup milk, scalded*
  ¼ *cup sugar*
  1 *teaspoon salt*
  ½ *teaspoon ground mace*
  ½ *teaspoon ground nutmeg*
  About 3½ *cups all-purpose flour, divided*
  2 *eggs*
  ⅓ *cup softened shortening*
    Oil
    Sugar

Add yeast to very warm water; let stand. Pour milk over sugar, salt, and spices in a large bowl. Stir until dissolved and slightly cooled. Add half the flour and beat until smooth. Beat in eggs and yeast mixture. Blend in shortening and remaining flour; beat until smooth.

Scrape batter from sides of bowl. Cover; let rise in a warm place until doubled in bulk, about 30 minutes. Punch dough down and let rest while oil is heating (350° to 375°).

Drop batter by teaspoonfuls into hot oil. Turn when edges show color, frying until golden brown, about 1½ minutes on each side. Drain on absorbent paper. Roll in sugar while still warm. Yield: about 5 dozen doughnuts.

Japanese Doughnuts

  1 *cup butter or margarine*
  1 *cup sugar*
  4 *eggs*
  4 *cups all-purpose flour*
  3 *tablespoons baking powder*
  ¼ *teaspoon salt*
  1 *teaspoon ground cinnamon*
  ½ *teaspoon ground nutmeg*
  1 *cup milk*
  ½ *cup chopped nuts*
  ½ *cup chopped seedless raisins*
    Salad oil

Cream butter and sugar. Add eggs, one at a time, beating well after each addition. Combine dry ingredients; gradually stir into creamed mixture alternately with milk. Stir in nuts and raisins.

Drop small spoonfuls of dough into deep hot oil and fry until golden brown. Drain on paper towels. Yield: 4 dozen doughnuts.

*Pumpkin Doughnuts

  4½ *cups all-purpose flour*
  4 *teaspoons baking powder*
  ¾ *teaspoon salt*
  1 *cup sugar*
  1 *teaspoon ground nutmeg*
  1¼ *cups milk*
  1 *egg, slightly beaten*
  2 *tablespoons melted butter or margarine*
  ½ *teaspoon vanilla extract*
  ¾ *cup cooked pumpkin*
    Shortening
    Sugar (optional)

Combine dry ingredients. Combine remaining ingredients except shortening and sugar and mix well. Add to dry mixture and stir just until blended. Roll dough about ¼ inch thick on a well-floured surface. Cut with doughnut cutter. Fry in deep hot shortening until brown; drain on paper towels. Dust with sugar, if desired. Yield: about 2 dozen (2½-inch) doughnuts.

Doughnut Wonder Balls

    2 tablespoons shortening
  ½ cup sugar
    4 slices bread, crusts removed
    1 egg, beaten
  ⅔ cup milk
1¾ cups all-purpose flour
    2 teaspoons baking powder
  ½ teaspoon salt
  ½ teaspoon ground nutmeg
      Salad oil

Cream shortening and sugar. Cut bread into cubes and combine with egg and milk; add to creamed mixture, blending well. Stir in flour, baking powder, salt, and nutmeg. Chill dough for 1 hour.

Remove one-fourth of dough at a time from refrigerator; roll about ½ inch thick on a lightly floured surface. Cut with a 1½-inch cutter and fry in hot oil (365°). Drain on paper towels. Yield: 8 to 10 servings.

Cinnamon Buns

  ¾ cup light corn syrup
  ¼ cup butter or margarine
  ¼ cup firmly packed brown sugar
    3 cups all-purpose flour
    4 teaspoons baking powder
1½ teaspoons salt
  ½ cup shortening
    1 cup milk
      Filling

Combine corn syrup, butter, and brown sugar in a saucepan; bring to a boil over medium heat and boil for 1 minute. Pour into a 9-inch square baking pan.

Combine flour, baking powder, and salt; cut in shortening. Add milk to make a soft dough. Turn out onto a floured surface. Roll into a rectangle ¼ inch thick. Spread Filling over dough. Roll in jelly roll fashion. Cut into 1-inch slices and place cut side up in syrup that was poured in baking pan. Bake at 350° for 30 to 40 minutes. Yield: 1 dozen buns.

Filling:

  ¼ cup light corn syrup
    2 tablespoons melted butter
  ¼ cup firmly packed brown sugar
    2 teaspoons ground cinnamon
  ½ cup seedless raisins
  ½ cup chopped nuts

Combine corn syrup and melted butter; spread over surface of dough. Sprinkle with brown sugar, cinnamon, raisins, and nuts.

Banana Bran Nut Bread

  ¼ cup shortening
  ½ cup sugar
    1 egg
    1 cup whole bran cereal
1½ cups all-purpose flour
    2 teaspoons baking powder
  ½ teaspoon salt
  ½ teaspoon soda
  ½ cup chopped nuts
1½ cups mashed bananas
    2 tablespoons water
    1 teaspoon vanilla extract

Cream shortening and sugar. Add egg and beat well. Add bran cereal and mix thoroughly. Combine flour, baking powder, salt, and soda; add nuts.

Combine bananas and water. Add to bran mixture alternately with flour mixture. Stir in vanilla. Pour into a greased 9- x 5- x 3-inch loaf pan and bake at 350° for 1 hour. Yield: 1 loaf.

*Carrot-Orange Bread

    2 cups all-purpose flour
  ¾ cup sugar
1½ teaspoons baking powder
  ½ teaspoon soda
    1 teaspoon salt
    2 tablespoons salad oil
    1 cup finely grated carrots
    3 tablespoons wheat germ (optional)
    1 teaspoon grated orange rind
    1 egg
  ¾ cup orange juice

Combine flour, sugar, baking powder, soda, and salt in a large mixing bowl. Make a well in center of dry mixture and stir in remaining ingredients. Mix with a fork until just blended (do not beat). Spoon into a greased and floured 9- x 5- x 3-inch loaf pan and bake at 350° for 30 to 35 minutes. Yield: 1 loaf.

Pumpkin Bread

 3 *cups sugar*
 1 *cup salad oil*
 4 *eggs, beaten*
 1 *(1-pound) can pumpkin*
3½ *cups all-purpose flour*
 1 *teaspoon baking powder*
 2 *teaspoons soda*
 2 *teaspoons salt*
 ½ *teaspoon ground cloves*
 1 *teaspoon ground cinnamon*
 1 *teaspoon ground nutmeg*
 1 *teaspoon ground allspice*
 ⅔ *cup water*

Combine sugar, oil, and beaten eggs. Add pumpkin and mix well. Combine dry ingredients and add to pumpkin mixture. Add water, beat thoroughly, and pour into two greased 9- x 5- x 3-inch loaf pans. Bake at 350° for 1 hour. Yield: 2 loaves.

Pineapple Nut Bread

1¾ *cups all-purpose flour*
 2 *teaspoons baking powder*
 ½ *teaspoon salt*
 ¼ *teaspoon soda*
 ½ *cup seedless raisins*
 ¾ *cup chopped nuts*
 ¾ *cup firmly packed brown sugar*
 3 *tablespoons softened butter or margarine*
 2 *eggs*
 1 *(8¼-ounce) can crushed pineapple*
 2 *tablespoons sugar*
 ½ *teaspoon ground cinnamon*

Combine flour, baking powder, salt, and soda in a large bowl. Rinse raisins in hot water and drain well; add raisins and nuts to dry ingredients. Cream sugar, butter, and eggs until fluffy. Stir in half the flour mixture, the undrained pineapple, then remaining flour, beating just until smooth after each addition. Pour into a greased 9- x 5- x 3-inch loaf pan. Combine sugar and cinnamon; sprinkle over top of batter. Bake at 350° for 60 to 70 minutes. Yield: 1 loaf.

Apricot Nut Bread

1½ *cups all-purpose flour*
 2 *teaspoons baking powder*
 ½ *teaspoon salt*
 ¼ *teaspoon soda*
 ½ *cup sugar*
 ½ *cup dried apricots, chopped*
 ½ *cup chopped walnuts or pecans*
 1 *tablespoon grated orange rind*
 1 *egg*
 ¾ *cup milk*
 ¼ *cup salad oil*

Combine flour, baking powder, salt, and soda. Mix in sugar, apricots, and nuts. Add orange rind, egg, milk, and salad oil; stir until blended. Pour into a greased 8½- x 4½-inch loaf pan. Bake at 350° for 45 minutes or until bread tests done. Cool 10 minutes; remove from pan and cool on wire rack. Yield: 1 loaf.

*Onion Rolls

 1 *(14½-ounce) package commercial hot roll mix*
 ½ *cup instant minced onion*
 1 *cup water*
 3 *tablespoons melted butter or margarine*

Prepare hot roll mix according to package directions. Combine onion and water; set aside for 5 minutes; drain.

 Roll dough ½ inch thick on a lightly floured surface. Brush with butter; sprinkle with onion. Roll dough in jelly roll fashion. Cut into ½-inch thick slices; place on a baking sheet. Cover and let rise; bake according to package directions. Yield: 20 rolls.

Cheesy Biscuit Finger Rolls

    2 *(8-ounce) packages refrigerated buttermilk or country-style biscuits*
    4 *ounces pasteurized process American or Cheddar cheese*
    2 *tablespoons butter or margarine, melted*
  ½ *teaspoon Worcestershire sauce*
  ¼ *teaspoon garlic salt*
  ½ *cup finely crushed potato chips*

Separate each can of biscuit dough into 10 biscuits. Pat out each to about a 3½-inch oval. Cut cheese into 20 strips (3 x ¼ x ¼ inches). Place one strip of cheese on each biscuit. Wrap dough around cheese strip, pressing all edges to seal. Place rolls in two rows in a greased 8- or 9-inch square baking pan. Combine butter, Worcestershire sauce, and garlic salt; brush over tops of rolls. Sprinkle with potato chips; gently press into rolls. Bake at 400° for 18 to 22 minutes, or until golden brown. Serve warm. Yield: 20 rolls.

Tips: To reheat, wrap rolls loosely in foil and bake at 400° for 8 to 10 minutes until warm. To make ahead, prepare, cover, and chill up to 2 hours before baking; bake as directed above.

*Buttermilk Puffs

    2 *cups all-purpose flour*
  ¼ *cup sugar*
    1 *teaspoon baking powder*
  ½ *teaspoon soda*
    1 *teaspoon ground nutmeg*
    1 *teaspoon salt*
  ¾ *cup buttermilk*
  ¼ *cup salad oil*
    1 *egg*
       Oil
       Sifted powdered sugar

Combine dry ingredients. Stir in buttermilk, oil, and egg; with a fork beat until smooth. Drop by teaspoonfuls (too-large puffs will not cook through) into hot cooking oil (375°). Drain well on absorbent paper. Roll warm puffs in sifted powdered sugar. Yield: 6 to 8 servings.

Cheese Spoonbread

    2 *cups milk*
    2 *tablespoons butter or margarine*
1⅓ *cups self-rising cornmeal*
    2 *egg yolks, beaten*
1½ *cups (6 ounces) shredded Cheddar cheese*
    2 *egg whites, stiffly beaten*

Scald milk; add butter. Stir in cornmeal and cook over medium heat until mixture thickens and becomes smooth, about 1 minute. Remove from heat and blend in beaten egg yolks and shredded cheese.

Fold in stiffly beaten egg whites. Turn into a well-greased 1½-quart casserole. Bake at 375° about 35 minutes. Yield: 6 to 8 servings.

*Plain Spoonbread

    3 *cups milk, divided*
    1 *cup cornmeal*
    2 *rounded tablespoons vegetable shortening*
    1 *teaspoon salt*
    1 *teaspoon baking powder*
    4 *egg yolks, well beaten*
    4 *egg whites, stiffly beaten*

Pour 1 cup milk over cornmeal in a medium-size bowl. Scald 2 cups milk over medium heat. When milk begins to boil, add cornmeal mixture. Cook for 10 minutes, stirring constantly. The mixture should become very thick. Add shortening, salt, and baking powder. Remove from heat; add well-beaten egg yolks and fold in stiffly beaten egg whites. Pour into a greased 1½-quart casserole. (At this point the batter may be chilled until ready to be cooked.) Bake at 375° for 50 minutes. Serve at once. Yield: 6 servings.

Soufflé Pancakes

    6 *egg yolks*
  ⅓ *cup commercial buttermilk pancake mix*
  ⅓ *cup commercial sour cream*
  ½ *teaspoon salt*
    6 *egg whites*
       Melted butter
       Maple syrup, honey, or favorite fruit sauce

breads 47

Beat egg yolks until thick and lemon colored. Add pancake mix, sour cream, and salt; blend well. Beat egg whites until stiff but not dry; carefully fold into batter.

Drop by tablespoonfuls onto a hot, well-greased griddle. Cook until golden brown on one side; turn and brown other side. Serve hot with butter; top with maple syrup, honey, or favorite fruit sauce. Yield: 6 servings.

German Apple Pancakes

    4   egg yolks
    ½   cup sifted cake flour
    ½   teaspoon salt
    ¼   cup sugar
    ½   cup milk
    ½   teaspoon grated lemon rind
    1   tablespoon lemon juice
    1   medium-size apple, coarsely grated
    2   tablespoons butter
    ½   cup commercial sour cream
        Canned apple slices (optional)

Beat egg yolks until light and fluffy. Combine flour, salt, and sugar. Add alternately with milk to egg mixture; mix well. Stir in lemon rind and juice. Fold in grated apple. Melt butter in 10-inch iron or ovenproof skillet. Pour in batter and bake at 400° for 10 minutes. Reduce heat to 350° and bake an additional 15 minutes. Loosen sides and bottom of pancake immediately with spatula. Spread sour cream over half the pancake. Fold over other half of pancake like an omelet. Remove to hot platter. Serve with canned apple slices, if desired. Yield: 4 servings.

Eggcellent Pancakes

    ¾   cup commercial buttermilk pancake mix
    ¼   teaspoon salt
    6   egg yolks
    ¾   cup commercial sour cream
    6   egg whites
        Butter

Combine pancake mix and salt. Beat egg yolks until thick and lemon colored. Add beaten yolks and sour cream to dry mixture; stir until batter is fairly smooth. Beat egg whites until stiff; fold into batter.

For each pancake, pour about ¼ cup batter onto hot, lightly greased griddle. Turn pancakes when tops are covered with bubbles and edges look cooked. Turn only once. Spread pancakes with butter. Yield: 12 pancakes.

Pecan Waffles

    2   cups all-purpose flour
    3   teaspoons baking powder
    ¼   teaspoon salt
    ¾   cup chopped pecans
    2   egg yolks
    1½   cups milk
    6   tablespoons shortening, melted
    2   egg whites

Combine dry ingredients and add pecans. Beat egg yolks until light; combine with milk and melted shortening and add to dry ingredients, mixing just until smooth. Beat egg whites until stiff; fold into batter. Bake in hot waffle iron. Yield: 6 to 8 waffles.

*Cornmeal Waffles

    1   cup self-rising cornmeal
    1   cup all-purpose flour
    2   tablespoons sugar
    2   egg yolks
    1   to 1½ cups milk
    ⅓   cup melted shortening or salad oil
    2   egg whites

Combine cornmeal, flour, and sugar. Beat egg yolks slightly. Blend egg yolks, 1 cup milk, and melted shortening. Add to dry ingredients and mix lightly. Add more milk if needed to form a thin batter. Beat egg whites until stiff peaks form; fold into batter. Bake in hot waffle iron. Yield: 4 servings.

Date Nut Bread

 1 *pound pitted dates, chopped*
 1 *teaspoon soda*
 1½ *cups boiling water*
 2 *tablespoons softened butter or margarine*
 1½ *cups sugar*
 2 *eggs, beaten*
 ¼ *teaspoon salt*
 1 *teaspoon vanilla extract*
 3½ *cups all-purpose flour*
 1 *cup chopped walnuts or pecans*

Put chopped dates in a large mixing bowl. Sprinkle soda over dates and pour boiling water over all. Stir well and let sit until cool. Cream butter and sugar until light; add eggs, salt, and vanilla and beat well. Add to dates and beat vigorously. Stir in flour, a small amount at a time. Stir in nuts. Spoon batter into two greased 8-inch loaf pans and bake at 300° for 1 hour. Yield: 2 loaves.

Cheese Bread

 1 *cup milk*
 1 *tablespoon sugar*
 1 *teaspoon salt*
 ½ *package dry yeast*
 ¼ *cup very warm water*
  About 3 cups all-purpose flour, divided
 1½ *cups finely shredded sharp Cheddar cheese*
  Melted margarine

Scald milk; stir in sugar and salt. Cool to lukewarm. Dissolve yeast in warm water; add milk mixture. Stir in 2 cups flour; mix well. Add cheese and remaining flour, mixing until thoroughly blended. Knead until smooth and satiny on a floured surface. Place dough in a greased bowl; brush with margarine. Cover and let rise in a warm place until doubled in bulk.

Knead lightly; roll out to a rectangle. Roll in jelly roll fashion; seal ends with edge of hand and fold ends under loaf. Place in a greased 9- x 5- x 3-inch loaf pan. Brush with margarine; cover and let rise until doubled in bulk. Bake at 375° for 50 minutes. Turn out of pan immediately. Yield: 1 loaf.

*Batterway Cheese and Herb Bread

 1 *cup warm water (110° to 115°)*
 1 *package active dry yeast*
 1 *egg, beaten*
  About 3 cups all-purpose flour
 2 *tablespoons sugar*
 1 *teaspoon salt*
 3 *tablespoons softened shortening*
 ½ *teaspoon basil*
 ½ *teaspoon oregano*
  Topping

Pour water into large mixing bowl; add yeast. Let stand a few minutes; stir until yeast dissolves and blend in egg. Combine flour, sugar, salt, shortening, basil, and oregano; add half of this mixture to liquid. Beat until smooth, about 2 minutes on medium speed of electric mixer or 300 strokes by hand. Add remaining flour mixture and stir until flour disappears and batter is smooth, about 150 strokes. Scrape batter down from sides of bowl. Cover and let rise in a warm place until doubled in bulk, about 30 minutes.

Stir batter down in 20 to 25 strokes. Place in a greased 13- x 9- x 2-inch pan (two 8- or 9-inch square pans may be used). Spread Topping evenly over the batter. Grease fingers and press down in several places through topping, almost to the bottom of the pan. Tap the pan on the table. Let rise in warm place until doubled in bulk, 20 to 30 minutes. Bake at 375° for 30 to 35 minutes or until golden brown. Remove from pan and serve warm. Yield: 10 to 12 servings.

 Topping:

 ½ *pound shredded Cheddar Cheese*
 ¼ *cup minced onion*
 ½ *teaspoon oregano*
 ½ *teaspoon basil*

Combine all ingredients; blend well. Spread mixture evenly over batter.

Note: This bread may be made the day before and reheated in foil. Like all yeast breads, it freezes beautifully.

*Cheese Crown

   2 cups all-purpose flour
   3 teaspoons baking powder
   1 teaspoon salt
   ⅓ cup shortening
   ⅔ to ¾ cup milk
   ¼ cup sharp commercial cheese spread

Combine flour, baking powder, and salt. Cut in shortening until mixture is crumbly. Add milk to make a soft dough. Turn out onto a lightly floured surface and knead gently for 30 seconds. Roll out into an 18- x 12-inch rectangle. Spread evenly with cheese spread and roll in jelly roll fashion. Form into a ring on a lightly greased baking sheet. With scissors, cut through ring almost to center in slices about 1 inch thick. Turn each slice slightly, lifting every other one to center or ring. Bake at 450° about 15 minutes. Yield: 1 ring.

Dutch Batter Bread

   1 package active dry yeast
   1¼ cups very warm (not hot) water
   2 tablespoons softened shortening
   2 teaspoons salt
   2 tablespoons sugar
   3 cups all-purpose flour, divided
   ⅛ teaspoon ground cardamom
   ¼ cup currants
   3 tablespoons chopped citron
   3 tablespoons chopped candied cherries
   Butter or margarine

Dissolve yeast in warm water in large bowl. Add shortening, salt, sugar, and half the flour. Beat 2 minutes, medium speed on mixer or 300 vigorous strokes by hand. Scrape sides and bottom of bowl frequently. Add remaining flour, cardamom, and fruit; blend in thoroughly with spoon. Scrape batter from sides of bowl. Cover with cloth and let rise in a warm place (85°) until doubled in bulk, about 30 minutes. If kitchen is cool, place dough on a rack over a bowl of hot water and cover completely (bowl and dough) with a towel. Be sure dough does not rise more than ¾ inch from top of bowl or bread will fall.

Stir batter down by beating about 25 strokes. Divide batter in half and spread evenly in 2 greased 1-pound coffee or candy cans. Batter will be sticky. Smooth out tops of loaves by flouring hand and patting loaves into shape. Again let rise in warm place (85°) until batter is within ¾ inch from top of cans, about 40 minutes. Bake at 375° for about 40 minutes or until brown.

To test loaf, tap the top crust; it should sound hollow. Remove immediately from pan. Place on wire rack to cool. Brush top with butter. Do not place in direct draft. Cool before cutting. Yield: 2 loaves.

*Yeast Corn Bread

   2 cups skim milk
   2 tablespoons sugar
   2 teaspoons salt
   2 tablespoons vegetable shortening
   1 package active dry yeast
   ¼ cup very warm water
   About 6 cups all-purpose flour, divided
   2 cups yellow cornmeal

Heat milk to steaming and pour over sugar, salt, and shortening; stir until shortening is melted. Cool to lukewarm. Dissolve yeast in very warm water; add to milk mixture. Add enough flour to make a stiff batter. Stir out all lumps and beat vigorously until batter is smooth. Cover bowl with a damp cloth and let rise in a warm place until doubled in bulk.

Add cornmeal and enough flour to make a dough that can be kneaded without sticking to either the hands or floured surface. Knead until velvety and smooth. Place dough in a well-greased mixing bowl. Cover and let stand in a warm place to rise. Knead on a lightly floured surface. Shape into 4 loaves and put in well-greased loaf pans. Cover the loaf pans and let rise until doubled in bulk. Bake at 325° for 40 to 45 minutes. Remove from pans immediately. Yield: 4 loaves.

*Danish Pastry

Butter Dough:

    ⅓ *cup all-purpose flour*
1½ *cups butter*

Blend flour and butter with pastry blender to make a dough. Chill.

Yeast Dough:

  2 *packages dry yeast*
  ¼ *cup very warm water*
  1 *cup cold milk*
  1 *egg*
  ¼ *cup sugar*
3½ *cups all-purpose flour*

Dissolve yeast in very warm water. Stir in cold milk, egg, and sugar. Gradually add the flour, beating until smooth and glossy.

Turn dough out onto a floured surface. Roll out to 14 inches square. Spread chilled Butter Dough over half the Yeast Dough, leaving a 1-inch border. Fold the unspread half over the buttered half. Roll out fairly thin. Fold into thirds. Chill for 10 to 15 minutes. Roll out and repeat the preceding step three times. Cover and chill for 30 minutes.

Roll dough into a 20-inch square and shape into envelopes, combs, or crescents as directed below. Place on ungreased baking sheets. Allow to rise at room temperature (not too hot) about 1 hour. Brush with beaten egg. Bake at 450° about 8 to 10 minutes or until golden brown

Envelopes: Cut dough into 4-inch squares. Drop a teaspoon of filling in the center. Fold corners toward the center and pinch edges. Yield 25 pastries.

Combs: Cut dough into four 5- x 20-inch strips. On each strip place filling lengthwise down the middle and fold sides over. Cut each strip into 4-inch pieces and make 4 slashes about a third of the way through on one side. Brush with water; dip in sugar mixed with almonds. Yield: 20 pastries.

Crescents: Cut dough into fourteen 3- x 5-inch strips. Cut each strip diagonally, forming two triangles. Place filling on base of triangle and roll up. Yield: 28 pastries.

Filling:
    Applesauce, almond paste, custard, and fruit preserves are suitable fillings.

Almond Paste:

¼ *pound ground almonds*
½ *cup sugar*
1 *egg*

Mix almonds and sugar and add beaten egg. Yield: enough for 10 combs.

Custard:

½ *cup milk*
1 *egg yolk*
1 *tablespoon all-purpose flour*
1 *tablespoon sugar*
½ *teaspoon vanilla extract*

Mix milk, egg yolk, flour, and sugar in top of double boiler. Cook until thickened, stirring constantly. Remove from heat; add vanilla. Yield: enough for 10 envelopes.

*Basic Sweet Dough

  2 *cups all-purpose flour*
  ½ *cup sugar*
  2 *packages active dry yeast*
  2 *teaspoons salt*
1¼ *cups milk*
  ¼ *cup butter or margarine*
  2 *eggs*
  About 3 *cups all-purpose flour*

Combine 2 cups flour, sugar, yeast, and salt in a large bowl; mix thoroughly. Combine milk and butter in a small saucepan. Heat over low heat until liquid is warm (butter does not need to melt). Gradually add to dry ingredients and beat 2 minutes at medium speed of electric mixer, scraping bowl often. Add eggs and beat well.

Beat in additional flour to make a soft dough (do this with a wooden spoon if you do not have a heavy-duty mixer). Turn out onto a lightly floured surface; knead until smooth and elastic, about 10 minutes. Place in a greased bowl, turning to oil top. Cover and let rise in a warm place, free from draft, until doubled in bulk, about 1 hour.

Punch dough down and let rest about 10 minutes. Shape into tea rings, coffeecakes, cinnamon rolls, kolaches, or sweet rolls. Place in greased pans and let rise until doubled in bulk, about 1 hour. Bake coffeecakes and small loaves at 350° for 30 minutes; 25 minutes for pan rolls. Yield: enough dough for 3 coffeecakes or about 3½ dozen rolls.

Cinnamon Loaf: Divide Basic Sweet Dough into halves. Roll each half about ½ inch thick and brush with melted butter. Combine 1 cup sugar and 2 teaspoons ground cinnamon; spread over each piece of dough. Roll in jelly roll fashion and place in greased loaf pans to rise. Bake at 350° about 30 minutes. Yield: 2 loaves.

Cinnamon Rolls: Divide Basic Sweet Dough into halves. Roll each half into a rectangle about ½ inch thick and brush with melted butter. Combine 1½ cups sugar, ⅔ cup seedless raisins, and 2 teaspoons ground cinnamon. Sprinkle half of this mixture over each piece of dough. Roll in jelly roll fashion to make 18-inch rolls. Seal edges firmly. Cut each roll into 1½-inch slices and place, cut side down, in greased pans. Cover; Let rise in a warm place until doubled in bulk, about 1 hour. Bake at 350° about 25 minutes or until done. Remove from pans and cool on wire racks. Serve plain or frost with a mixture of 1 cup powdered sugar mixed with about 3 tablespoons milk. Yield: 3 to 4 dozen rolls.

Kolaches: Divide Basic Sweet Dough into halves. Roll each half about ½ inch thick on a floured surface. Cut circles with a 2½-inch cutter. Place about 2 inches apart on greased baking sheets. Cover; let rise in a warm place until doubled in bulk, about 1 hour. Press an indentation in center of each bun, leaving a rim about ¼ inch wide. Fill with preserves. Bake at 350° about 20 minutes. Yield: about 3 dozen kolaches.

Stickies: Work with ½ recipe of Basic Sweet Dough. After dough has risen the first time, punch down and shape into 18 balls. Place ½ teaspoon butter in 18 muffin tins; add about 1 teaspoon white or brown sugar and 1 tablespoon finely chopped pecans. Place balls of dough in tins; cover and let rise until doubled in bulk. Bake at 350° about 20 minutes. Yield: 18 muffins.

Christmas Küchen

½ cup milk
1 cup sugar
1 teaspoon salt
1 cup butter or margarine
1 package active dry yeast
½ cup very warm water
4 eggs, well beaten
1 tablespoon grated lemon rind
About 4 cups all-purpose flour, divided
¼ cup slivered candied cherries
¼ cup cubed candied pineapple
¼ cup diced citron
¼ cup diced candied lemon peel
Powdered sugar

Heat milk until bubbles form around edge of pan. Add sugar, salt, and butter; stir until sugar is dissolved and butter is melted. Let cool to lukewarm. Meanwhile, sprinkle yeast over very warm water in large bowl; stir until dissolved. Add milk mixture, eggs, grated lemon rind, and half the flour; beat with spoon until smooth. Stir in remaining flour and beat vigorously for 2 minutes.

Cover with damp towel; let rise in a warm place (85°), free from draft, until light and bubbly, about 1 hour; stir down with spoon. Stir in fruit. Pour into a lightly greased 10-inch tube pan. Cover with damp towel; let rise until doubled in bulk, about 1½ hours.

Bake at 350° for 45 minutes or until golden brown. Let cool in pan on wire rack. Loosen from pan and invert onto serving plate. Sprinkle with powdered sugar. Yield: 1 loaf.

*Sweet Brioche

¼ cup milk
1 package active dry yeast
¼ cup very warm water
⅓ cup sugar
¼ teaspoon salt
About 2⅓ cups all-purpose flour
⅓ cup butter or margarine, softened
1 egg
1 egg yolk
1 teaspoon grated lemon rind
Melted margarine
1 egg white, lightly beaten (optional)

Scald milk; cool to lukewarm. Sprinkle yeast into very warm water; stir until dissolved. Add lukewarm milk, sugar, salt, and half the flour; beat until smooth. Beat in softened butter; add egg and egg yolk and mix well. Add remaining flour and lemon rind; stir to mix; then beat 5 minutes with spoon. Brush batter with melted margarine. Cover; let rise in a warm place, free from draft, until doubled in bulk, about 1 hour. Cover with foil or with waxed paper and damp towel; chill overnight.

Turn out onto a lightly floured surface. Shape as directed below. Cover and let rise in warm place, free from draft, until doubled in bulk. Brush with lightly beaten egg white, if desired. Bake as follows:

Traditional Brioche—Small (Les Petites Brioches): Turn dough out onto a lightly floured surface; cut off one-fourth and set aside. Shape remaining dough into 1½-inch balls. Place one ball in each greased brioche mold or muffin cup. Make a deep dent with finger in center of each. Shape remaining dough into same number of smaller balls; place 1 ball in each indentation. Brush tops with melted margarine. Cover and let rise. Brush with egg white; bake at 375° for 15 minutes or until done. Yield: 14 to 18 muffins.

Creole Style: Shape dough into 12-inch long roll; cut into 10 or 12 equal pieces. Shape each piece into a 5-inch roll with tapered ends. With a sharp knife, make 3-inch long, lengthwise cut down center of each, about ¼ inch deep. Cover and let rise. Brush with egg white and sprinkle with sugar. Bake at 375° about 15 or 20 minutes. Yield: 10 to 12 rolls.

Luncheon Braid: Divide dough into thirds; form each third into a roll 18 to 20 inches long. Braid the 3 strips together; pinch ends to seal. Place on large greased baking sheet. Cover and let rise; brush with egg white, if desired. Bake at 375° for 25 minutes or until golden brown. Serve warm as is, cut into thick slices, or cool and add powdered sugar frosting. Yield: 1 large braid.

Coffee Bran Kuchen

2½ cups all-purpose flour
3 teaspoons baking powder
Few grains salt
2 cups firmly packed brown sugar
1 cup all-bran cereal
½ cup vegetable shortening
½ cup butter or margarine
½ cup strong coffee
½ cup evaporated milk
⅛ teaspoon soda
2 eggs, beaten
1 teaspoon ground cinnamon
Whole pecans

Combine flour, baking powder, salt, brown sugar, and cereal. Cut in shortening and butter with two knives or pastry blender. Reserve 1 cup of this mixture for topping. Combine coffee, evaporated milk, and soda; add to remaining flour mixture, mixing well. Add beaten eggs. Spoon into two greased and floured 9-inch round cakepans, filling half full. Add cinnamon to topping mixture; sprinkle over batter. Scatter whole pecans on top. Bake at 375° for 25 to 30 minutes. Yield: 2 (9-inch) layers.

Basic Yeast Dough

  2 *cups milk*
  1 *cup sugar*
  1 *teaspoon salt*
 ½ *cup melted butter*
  3 *eggs, well beaten*
  2 *packages active dry yeast*
     About 6 cups all-purpose flour

Scald milk, sugar, salt, and butter together in a saucepan. Pour into large bowl and let stand until lukewarm. Blend in eggs and yeast; stir until yeast is dissolved. Stir in enough flour to make a soft dough; cover and set aside for 20 minutes. Turn out onto a floured surface and knead until dough is not sticky. Yield: enough dough for 2 Stollen and 1 large twist.

Stollen:

 ½ *cup diced citron*
  2 *tablespoons candied cherries, slivered*
  2 *tablespoons cubed candied pineapple*
 ¼ *cup chopped walnuts*
 ½ *Basic Yeast Dough recipe*
     Melted butter
     Powdered sugar

Knead citron, cherries, pineapple, and walnuts into basic dough. Divide dough into halves and pat each half into oval shape. Brush melted butter over tops. Fold over pocketbook-style. Shape into crescents and place on greased baking sheet. Let rise until doubled in bulk. Bake at 350° about 45 minutes. Cool on wire racks. Sprinkle with powdered sugar. Yield: 2 loaves.

Bohemian Twist:

 ½ *Basic Yeast Dough recipe*
 ½ *cup seedless raisins*
 ½ *cup chopped blanched almonds*
  2 *tablespoons candied orange peel*
  2 *tablespoons lemon peel*
     Melted butter
     Butter Icing

Punch dough down and turn out onto a floured surface. Knead in raisins, almonds, orange and lemon peel. Divide dough into 4 ropes about 12 inches long. Join ends at top; twist a pair of ropes together and repeat with remaining 2 ropes. Press the twists together, side by side. Place on greased baking sheet; let rise until doubled in bulk. Brush with melted butter. Bake at 350° about 55 to 60 minutes. Cool. Spread with Butter Icing. Yield: 1 large twist.

Butter Icing:

  4 *cups powdered sugar*
  4 *tablespoons cream*
  1 *teaspoon vanilla extract*
     Almonds and cherry halves (optional)

Combine sugar, cream, and vanilla; spread over bread. Decorate with blanched almonds and cherry halves.

*Pumpernickel

 ¾ *cup cornmeal*
1½ *cups cold water*
1½ *cups boiling water*
1½ *tablespoons salt*
  2 *tablespoons sugar*
  2 *tablespoons shortening*
  1 *tablespoon caraway seeds*
  1 *package active dry yeast*
 ¼ *cup very warm water*
  2 *cups mashed potatoes*
  4 *cups rye flour*
4¼ *cups all-purpose flour*

Place cornmeal in a 2-quart saucepan and stir in cold water. Add boiling water and cook, stirring constantly, for 2 minutes. Add salt, sugar, shortening, and caraway seeds; let stand until lukewarm.

    Dissolve yeast in warm water and add to cornmeal mixture along with potatoes; stir well. Add rye flour and white flour, a small amount at a time. Knead until smooth, using cornmeal on the surface. Place in greased bowl; turn to grease all sides. Let rise until doubled in bulk. Knead again.

    Put in three greased 9- x 5- x 3-inch loaf pans. Let rise until doubled in bulk. Bake at 375° for 45 minutes to 1 hour. Yield: 3 loaves.

*Onion Bread

    1 *package active dry yeast*
    1 *cup very warm (not hot) water*
    2 *teaspoons sugar*
    2 *teaspoons salt, divided*
    3 *cups all-purpose flour, divided*
    2 *tablespoons melted butter or margarine*
    ½ *cup coarsely chopped onion*
    2 *teaspoons paprika*

Sprinkle yeast into very warm water; stir until dissolved. Add sugar, 1 teaspoon salt, and 2 cups flour. Stir to blend; then beat thoroughly. Stir in ½ cup additional flour. Turn dough out onto a surface dusted with ¼ cup flour. Knead until smooth and satiny, 5 to 7 minutes, adding remaining flour as needed.

Shape dough into a smooth ball. Put into greased bowl; cover and let rise until doubled in bulk, about 1 hour. Punch dough down. Divide into halves; cover and let rest for 5 minutes.

Pat dough into two greased 9-inch round cakepans or shape into two flat rounds ½ inch thick on greased baking sheet. Brush tops with with melted butter and sprinkle evenly with onions. With thumb or fingertips, punch onions down into dough so entire surface looks dented. Let rise until doubled in bulk, about 45 minutes. Sprinkle each loaf with remaining ½ teaspoon salt and dust generously with paprika. Bake at 450° for 20 to 25 minutes. Serve hot or cold. Yield: 2 (9-inch) loaves.

Old-Fashioned Raisin Bread

    1 *package active dry yeast*
    ¼ *cup sugar*
    1½ *cups warm buttermilk*
    2 *eggs, slightly beaten*
    ½ *cup melted butter or margarine*
    5 *to* 5½ *cups all-purpose flour*
    1½ *teaspoons salt*
    ½ *teaspoon soda*
    1 *cup seedless raisins*
    Melted butter

Add yeast and sugar to buttermilk and stir until yeast is dissolved. Combine eggs and ½ cup melted butter; stir into yeast mixture. Combine dry ingredients and add by thirds to yeast mixture, beating well after each addition.

Turn dough out onto a lightly floured surface; knead until smooth and elastic, working in more flour as needed. Knead in raisins. Place dough in greased bowl; brush with melted butter and let rise until doubled in bulk, about 1 hour.

Punch dough down and turn out onto a floured surface. Divide dough in half and let rest 15 to 20 minutes. Shape into loaves and place in two 9- x 5- x 3-inch loaf pans. Let rise until doubled in bulk. Bake at 400° for 25 to 30 minutes. Yield: 2 loaves.

*Sally Lunn

    About 4 *cups all-purpose flour, divided*
    ⅓ *cup sugar*
    1 *teaspoon salt*
    1 *package active dry yeast*
    ½ *cup milk*
    ½ *cup water*
    ½ *cup margarine*
    3 *eggs, at room temperature*

Thoroughly mix 1¼ cups flour, sugar, salt, and undissolved yeast in a large bowl. Combine milk, water, and margarine in a saucepan. Heat over low heat until mixture is warm (margarine does not need to melt).

Gradually add liquid to dry ingredients and beat 2 minutes on medium speed of electric mixer, scraping bowl occasionally. Add eggs and 1 cup flour, or enough additional flour to make a stiff batter.

Cover bowl; let rise in a warm place, free from draft, until doubled in bulk, about 1 hour. Stir batter down and beat well, about ½ minute. Turn into a large, well-greased and floured loaf pan (or a 9-inch tube pan). Cover; let rise in a warm place, free from draft, until mixture is doubled in bulk, about 1 hour.

Bake at 325° for 45 to 50 minutes or until done. Remove from pan and cool on a wire rack. Yield: 1 loaf.

*Orange-Cinnamon Yeast Rolls

  1 *cup sugar*
  2 *teaspoons ground cinnamon*
  2 *tablespoons grated orange rind*
  3 *tablespoons orange juice*
 ¼ *cup butter or margarine*
  1 *package active dry yeast*
 ¾ *cup very warm water*
2½ *cups commercial biscuit mix*

Combine sugar, cinnamon, orange rind and juice, and butter in a saucepan. Bring to a boil, stirring constantly; cook 2 minutes. Cool.

Dissolve yeast in very warm water; stir in biscuit mix, beating vigorously. Turn dough out onto a floured surface; knead about 20 times or until smooth.

Roll dough into an 8- x 16-inch rectangle. Spread two-thirds of cooled syrup over dough, spreading to within ½ inch of edges. Roll dough in jelly roll fashion, beginning at long side. Seal by pinching edges of roll together. Cut roll into 1-inch slices.

Spoon remaining syrup into greased muffin tins; set rolls in tins. Cover; let rise in a warm place until doubled in bulk. Bake at 350° for 25 to 30 minutes. Yield: 12 rolls.

*Refrigerator Rolls

 ¾ *cup hot water*
 ½ *cup sugar*
  1 *tablespoon salt*
  3 *tablespoons margarine*
  2 *packages active dry yeast*
  1 *cup very warm water (105° to 115°)*
  1 *egg, beaten*
     About 5¼ cups all-purpose flour, divided

Combine hot water, sugar, salt, and margarine; cool to lukewarm. Dissolve yeast in very warm water in a large warm bowl; stir in sugar mixture, egg, and half the flour, beating until smooth. Stir in enough remaining flour to make a soft dough.

Turn out onto a lightly floured surface and knead until smooth and elastic, about 10 minutes. Place dough in greased bowl, turning to grease top. Cover tightly with waxed paper or aluminum foil. Chill until doubled in bulk or until needed.

To bake, punch dough down and cut off amount needed. Shape into rolls as desired and let rise 1 hour. Bake at 375° for 15 to 20 minutes. Yield: about 2½ dozen rolls.

Note: Dough may be kept 4 to 5 days in refrigerator at about 40° to 45°.

*Sweet Potato Yeast Rolls

  1 *cup milk*
 ½ *cup sugar*
1½ *teaspoons salt*
 ¼ *teaspoon ground mace*
 ⅓ *cup butter or margarine*
  2 *cups cooked, mashed red-skin sweet potatoes*
  1 *teaspoon lemon juice*
  1 *package active dry yeast*
 ¼ *cup very warm water*
  1 *egg, slightly beaten*
     About 4½ cups all-purpose flour, divided
     Melted butter

Scald milk; add sugar, salt, mace, and butter. Stir until butter is melted. Pour over potatoes, add lemon juice, and beat until smooth. Cool to lukewarm. Dissolve yeast in very warm water; add to potato mixture along with beaten egg and mix well. Stir in 2 cups flour and beat on medium speed of electric mixer for 3 minutes. Add remaining flour and beat with a spoon.

Turn out onto a floured surface and knead until smooth. Place in a greased bowl, turning to grease top of dough, cover, and let rise until doubled in bulk. Knead lightly on a floured surface; shape into rolls. Place in greased baking pans, cover, and let rise until doubled in bulk. Bake at 400° for 20 minutes. Brush tops with melted butter. Yield: about 5 dozen rolls.

Note: To make brown-and-serve rolls, bake for 20 minutes at 300°; cool completely. Place in moisture-vaporproof containers, seal, and freeze. To brown for serving, remove wrapper, place on greased sheets, and bake at 400° for 10 minutes.

*Sixty-Minute Rolls

1½ cups very warm milk
1 package active dry yeast
2 tablespoons vegetable shortening
1 beaten egg
2 tablespoons sugar
1 teaspoon salt
About 4 cups all-purpose flour (not self-rising)

Heat milk; sprinkle yeast over top of milk and allow to dissolve. Add shortening, egg, sugar, salt, and flour and mix well. Cover and let rise for 15 minutes. Punch down, cover, and let rise 15 minutes longer.

Shape into rolls and place in greased pans. Cover pans and let rolls rise 15 minutes. Bake at 400° for 15 minutes or until rolls are brown. Yield: 3 dozen rolls.

Pecan Yeast Rolls

2 packages active dry yeast
¼ cup very warm water
1 cup milk
¼ cup shortening
⅓ cup sugar
1 teaspoon salt
½ teaspoon grated lemon rind
2 eggs, beaten
About 5 cups all-purpose flour, divided
⅓ cup melted butter or margarine
1 cup firmly packed light brown sugar
1 cup chopped pecans
108 pecan halves

Dissolve yeast in very warm water. Scald milk and add shortening, sugar, salt, and lemon rind. Cool to lukewarm. Stir in beaten eggs and dissolved yeast. Add half the flour and beat thoroughly. Add remaining flour and mix well. Turn out onto a lightly floured surface and knead lightly. Place in a greased bowl; cover and set in a warm place. Allow dough to rise until doubled in bulk. When light, punch down and turn out onto a floured surface. Roll dough into a large rectangle about ½ inch thick. Spread with melted butter, brown sugar, and chopped pecans. Roll in jelly roll fashion and cut in ¾-inch slices. Grease muffin tins and place 3 pecan halves in bottom of each cup; put a slice of the roll on top, cut side down. Allow to rise again until doubled in bulk. Bake at 400° for 15 to 18 minutes. Yield: 3 dozen rolls.

*Sweet Potato Rolls

1 cup cooked mashed sweet potatoes
3 tablespoons melted butter or margarine
1 package active dry yeast
½ cup very warm water
1 egg
1 teaspoon salt
3 tablespoons sugar
About 5 cups all-purpose flour
¾ cup warm water
Melted butter or margarine

Blend sweet potatoes and 3 tablespoons melted butter. Dissolve yeast in ½ cup very warm water; add to potatoes. Add egg, salt, and sugar; blend well. Add flour alternately with ¾ cup warm water. Turn out onto a well-floured surface and knead until smooth. Place in greased bowl, turning to grease top; cover. Allow to rise for 2 hours.

Place dough on a floured surface and roll to desired thickness; cut into shapes desired. Brush tops of rolls with melted butter. Place on greased baking sheets and allow to rise for 1 hour. Bake at 425° for 15 to 20 minutes. Yield: 2½ dozen rolls.

*Yeast White Bread

About 6½ cups all-purpose flour, divided
1 package active dry yeast
1 cup milk
1 cup water
2 tablespoons sugar
2 tablespoons salad oil
1 tablespoon salt
Salad oil

Combine 2 cups flour and yeast. Heat milk, water, sugar, 2 tablespoons oil, and salt over low heat only until warm, stirring to blend. Add liquid ingredients to flour mixture and beat until smooth, about 2 minutes on medium speed of electric mixer or

300 strokes by hand. Add 1 cup flour and beat 1 minute on medium speed or 150 strokes by hand. Stir in more flour to make a moderately stiff dough.

Turn out onto a lightly floured surface and knead until smooth and satiny, about 8 to 10 minutes. Shape into ball and place in a lightly greased bowl, turning once to grease all sides. Cover and let rise in a warm place (80° to 85°) until doubled in bulk, about 1½ hours. Punch down. Divide dough in half; shape each into a ball. Let rest 10 minutes.

To shape loaves, roll dough into rectangle 9 inches wide. Starting at 9-inch end, roll in jelly roll fashion. Seal seam. With side of hand, press ends to seal. Fold ends under loaf; place seam side down in two greased 8½- x 4½- x 3-inch loaf pans; brush with oil. Let rise in a warm place until doubled in bulk, about 1 hour. Bake at 400° for 30 to 35 minutes or until done. Remove from pans immediately and brush with oil. Yield: 2 loaves.

*Old-Country Tomato Bread

1 package active dry yeast
1 cup very warm water
1 tablespoon shortening
2 tablespoons sugar
1 teaspoon salt
1 cup tomato juice, scalded
4 cups all-purpose flour, divided
Melted butter

Dissolve yeast in very warm water and set aside. Cream shortening, sugar, and salt until smooth; add tomato juice and mix well. Cool to lukewarm and add to yeast, stirring well. Gradually add half the flour, beating well. Add the remainder of the flour; mix well.

Turn dough out onto a lightly floured surface and knead at least 5 minutes. Place in greased bowl; turn dough once to grease all sides. Cover with clean cloth and let rise in a warm place for 2 hours.

Turn dough out onto a lightly floured surface and shape into 1 large loaf or 2 small loaves. Place in greased loaf pans and brush top with melted butter. Cover and let rise until doubled in bulk.

Bake at 400° for 15 minutes; lower heat and bake at 375° for 45 minutes. Yield: 1 large loaf or 2 small loaves.

Swedish Rye Bread

2 packages active dry yeast
¼ cup very warm water
½ cup light molasses
⅓ cup butter
1¾ cups beer
2 teaspoons salt
1 tablespoon caraway seed
3 cups rye flour
About 3 cups all-purpose flour
2 tablespoons melted butter

Dissolve yeast in very warm water. Combine molasses and butter in saucepan and heat until butter has melted; stir in beer. Add dissolved yeast, salt, and caraway seed. Add rye flour and mix well. Stir in enough white flour to make a soft dough. Brush top of dough with melted butter, cover bowl, and let dough rise until doubled in bulk.

Punch dough down, turn out onto a floured surface, and knead thoroughly for about 7 or 8 minutes. Stir in white flour as needed, but be careful not to add too much. Shape into two loaves and place in greased loaf pans. Cover and let rise until doubled in bulk. Bake at 350° for 35 to 45 minutes or until loaves sound hollow when tapped. Yield: 2 loaves.

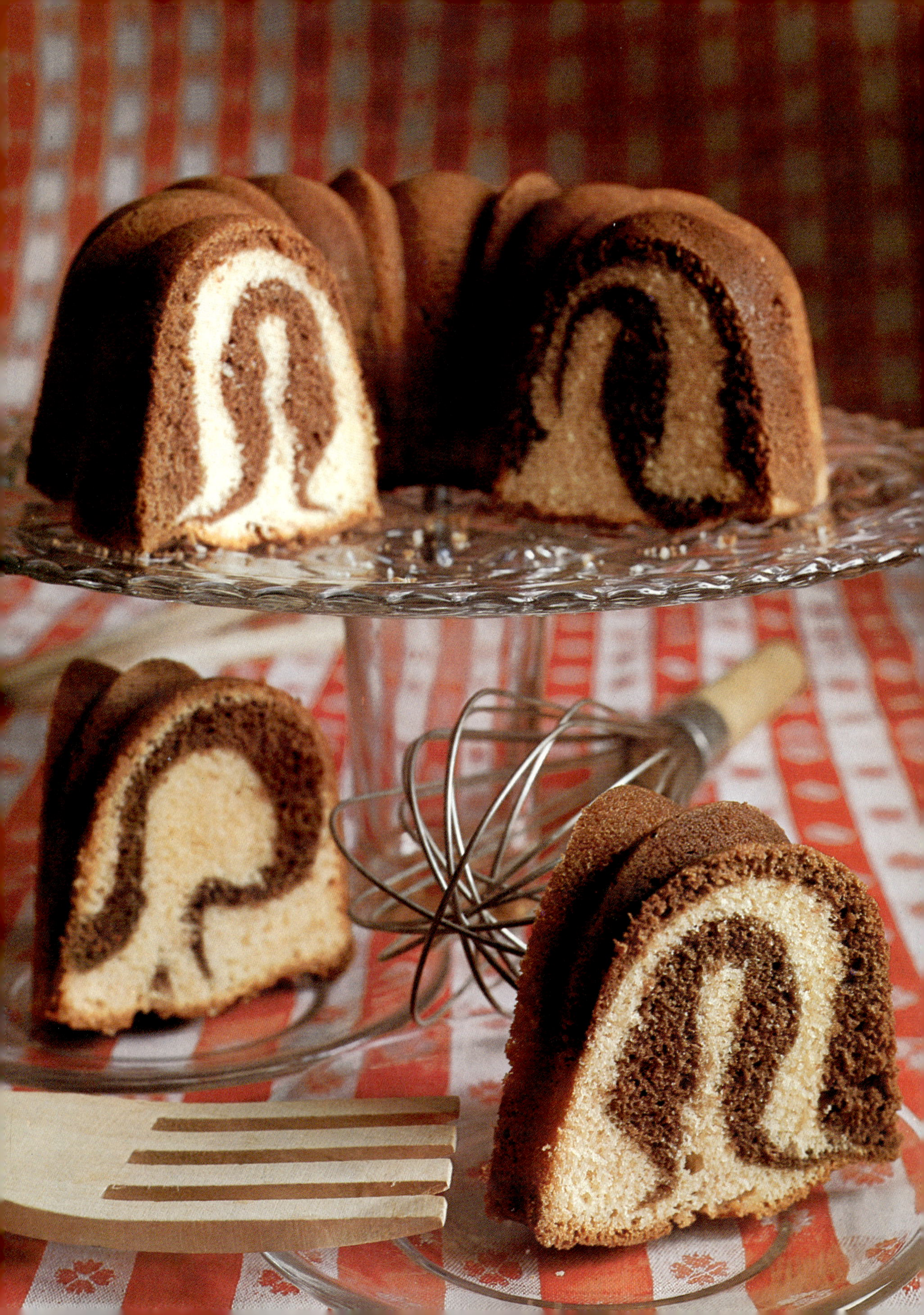

Cakes and Frostings

Many of our cake recipes came over with the first settlers from England. When they tried to duplicate the "receipts" from home, some of the ingredients were not available and substitutions were made. The result? A new recipe, one that the cook could name for herself or a friend or famous person.

Our first cakes were "pound" cakes, and all ingredients were weighed and added by the pound rather than by cupfuls or spoonfuls as we now make them.

Pecans, one of the most prolific nuts grown in the South, are added to many cakes. Use is also made of almonds and walnuts, as well as peanuts.

There doesn't have to be a particular reason for baking a cake, but there are in this chapter special recipes for birthdays, weddings, and holiday events. You'll also find cakes to suit other occasions including a few you will want to make "just because."

Sour Cream Coffee Cake

  1 *cup butter or margarine*
1½ *cups sugar*
  1 *cup commercial sour cream*
  2 *eggs, well beaten*
  1 *teaspoon vanilla extract*
  2 *cups all-purpose flour*
  1 *teaspoon baking powder*
  ¼ *teaspoon salt*
  ½ *teaspoon soda*
  1 *cup finely chopped nuts*
1½ *teaspoons sugar*
2½ *teaspoons ground cinnamon*

Cream butter, sugar, and sour cream; add eggs and vanilla and beat well. Combine dry ingredients and add to creamed mixture; beat well. Thoroughly grease a 10-inch tube pan.

Make topping by combining nuts, sugar, and cinnamon. Put a third of topping mixture in bottom of tube pan; alternate layers of batter and topping and end with batter. Bake at 350° for 45 minutes. Yield: 1 (10-inch) cake.

*Molasses Pound Cake

  3 *sticks (1½ cups) butter or margarine, softened*
1¼ *cups firmly packed brown sugar*
  6 *eggs*
  5 *cups sifted cake flour*
  1 *tablespoon ground cinnamon*
1½ *tablespoons ground ginger*
  1 *teaspoon ground nutmeg*
  ½ *teaspoon salt*
1½ *teaspoons soda*
  2 *cups light molasses*
  ½ *cup milk*

Cream butter and sugar until light and fluffy. Add eggs, one at a time, beating well after each addition. Combine flour, spices, and salt; dissolve soda in molasses. Add dry ingredients to creamed mixture alternately with molasses and milk. Spoon into 3 (8-inch) loaf pans that have been greased and floured, and bake at 325° for 35 to 45 minutes or until cake tests done. Cool in pan for 5 minutes; then turn out on cake rack to cool. Yield: 3 (8-inch) loaf cakes.

Berry Patch Coffee Cake

  1 *cup sugar*
  1 *(8-ounce) package cream cheese, softened*
 ½ *cup vegetable shortening or margarine*
  2 *eggs*
  1 *teaspoon vanilla extract*
1¾ *cups all-purpose flour*
  1 *teaspoon baking powder*
 ½ *teaspoon soda*
 ¼ *teaspoon salt*
 ¼ *cup milk*
 ½ *cup red raspberry, blackberry, or cherry preserves*
 ½ *to ¾ teaspoon ground cinnamon*
 ½ *cup coarsely chopped pecans*

Combine sugar, cream cheese, and shortening, mixing until well blended. Add eggs, one at a time, mixing well after each addition. Blend in vanilla. Combine dry ingredients; add alternately to creamed mixture with milk, mixing well after each addition. Pour into a greased and floured 13- x 9- x 2-inch pan or two 9-inch pans. Dot with preserves and sprinkle with cinnamon and pecans. Cut through batter with a knife several times for marbled effect. Bake at 350° for 35 to 40 minutes or until a toothpick inserted in the center comes out clean. Yield: 10 servings.

Elizabeth's Easy Coffee Cake

  1 *cup butter or margarine*
1¼ *cups sugar*
  2 *eggs*
  1 *cup commercial sour cream*
  2 *cups all-purpose flour*
 ½ *teaspoon soda*
1½ *teaspoons baking powder*
  1 *teaspoon vanilla extract*
 ¾ *cup finely chopped walnuts*
  1 *teaspoon ground cinnamon*
  2 *tablespoons sugar*

Cream butter and sugar in large bowl of electric mixer. Add eggs, one at a time, beating well after each addition. When mixture is light and fluffy, blend in sour cream. Sift flour, measure, then sift with soda and baking powder. Blend into batter and add vanilla.

Grease and lightly flour a 9-inch tube pan. Pour in half the batter. Combine nuts, cinnamon, and sugar and sprinkle half the mixture over batter; spoon in remaining batter and top with rest of nut mixture. Place in a cold oven; set temperature at 350° and bake about 55 minutes, or until cake tests done. (If preferred, dough may be divided and baked in 3 round 8- or 9-inch foil pans, with baking time approximately 25 minutes.) May be served warm from pan or inverted quickly while hot. Yield: 8 to 10 servings.

Christmas Nut Fruitcake

  1 *(8-ounce) package dates, chopped*
1½ *pounds light seedless raisins*
  1 *pound candied cherries, cut into halves*
 ½ *pound candied pineapple, chopped*
  3 *tablespoons flaked coconut*
1½ *cups bourbon*
 ¾ *pound butter*
  3 *cups sugar*
  9 *eggs*
  6 *cups all-purpose flour*
  3 *teaspoons baking powder*
  3 *teaspoons ground nutmeg (optional)*
 ¼ *teaspoon almond extract*
  1 *pound pecans, chopped*

Soak fruit and coconut overnight in bourbon. The following day, cream butter and sugar. Add eggs, one at a time, beating well after each addition. Combine dry ingredients; add to creamed mixture. Stir in almond extract, fruit and bourbon, and pecans, stirring lightly. Nuts may be dusted with a part of the flour mixture to keep them from sinking.

Put batter into pans (three 9-inch loafpans or a very large tube pan) that have been greased and lined with buttered brown paper. Bake at 250° for approximately 3 hours. Yield: 3 (9-inch) loaves or 1 large cake.

*German Streusel Coffee Cake

½ cup milk
2 tablespoons sugar
¼ cup butter or margarine
1 teaspoon salt
1 package dry yeast
¼ cup very warm water
1 egg
2 to 2¼ cups all-purpose flour
½ cup all-purpose flour
½ cup sugar
1 teaspoon ground cinnamon
¼ cup butter or margarine

Scald milk; pour into large mixing bowl. Add 2 tablespoons sugar, ¼ cup butter, and salt, and cool to lukewarm. Dissolve yeast in water; add yeast mixture and egg to milk mixture and stir well. Add 2 to 2¼ cups flour gradually, beating well after each addition. Cover and let rise until doubled in bulk (about 1 hour). Spread in a greased 13- x 9- x 2-inch pan.

Combine ½ cup flour, ½ cup sugar, and cinnamon. With a fork or pastry blender, cut in ¼ cup butter. Sprinkle over the mixture in pan. Let rise until doubled in bulk (30 to 45 minutes). Bake at 375° for 20 to 25 minutes. Yield: 1 coffee cake.

Date Cake

4 cups chopped pecans
1 cup sugar
5 egg yolks, slightly beaten
1 cup all-purpose flour
1 teaspoon baking powder
¼ teaspoon salt
1 pound pitted dates, chopped
1 teaspoon vanilla extract
5 egg whites, stiffly beaten

Place pecans and sugar in a large bowl; add egg yolks and mix well. Mix flour, baking powder, salt, and dates in another bowl. Combine mixtures from the 2 bowls; add vanilla and stir well. Fold in egg whites. Place mixture in an 8- or 9-inch tube pan and bake at 325° for 1 to 1¼ hours, or until cake tests done. Yield: 1 (3-pound) cake.

Dump Cake

1 (22-ounce) can cherry pie filling
1 (8¼-ounce) can crushed pineapple, undrained
1 (18½-ounce) package yellow cake mix
1 cup margarine, melted
1 (3½-ounce) can flaked coconut (optional)
1 cup pecans

Spoon pie filling evenly into bottom of a 13- x 9- x 2-inch pan. Spread pineapple over cherry pie filling. Sprinkle dry cake mix over pineapple. Pour margarine evenly over all. Sprinkle with coconut and pecans. Bake at 325° about 1 hour. Yield: 1 (13- x 9- x 2-inch) cake.

Date and Applesauce Cake

½ cup butter or margarine
1 cup firmly packed light brown sugar
2 eggs
2 cups all-purpose flour
2 teaspoons baking powder
½ teaspoon ground cinnamon
½ teaspoon ground nutmeg
¼ teaspoon ground cloves
1 cup chopped dates
1 cup seedless raisins
1 cup chopped nuts
2 teaspoons soda
1½ cups applesauce
1 teaspoon vanilla extract

Cream butter; add brown sugar and continue beating until mixture is light and fluffy. Add eggs, one at a time, beating well after each addition. Combine flour, baking powder, and spices. Sprinkle about ½ cup of flour mixture over dates, raisins, and nuts; stir until coated.

Add soda to applesauce; then add to creamed mixture alternately with flour mixture. Add vanilla; stir in date, raisin, and nut mixture and stir well. Spoon into a greased and floured 9-inch tube pan. Bake at 325° for 1 hour or until cake tests done. Yield: 1 (9-inch) cake.

Date-Nut Loaf Cake

 1 *cup butter*
 2 *cups sugar*
 4 *eggs*
 3 *cups all-purpose flour*
 ¼ *teaspoon salt*
 1 *teaspoon soda*
 2 *tablespoons orange juice*
 ½ *cup buttermilk*
 1 *cup chopped dates*
 1 *cup chopped nuts*
 1 *cup grated or flaked coconut*
  Orange Sauce

Cream butter and sugar together until light and fluffy. Add eggs, one at a time, beating well after each addition. Combine flour and salt and set aside. Add soda and orange juice to buttermilk.

Add dry ingredients to creamed mixture alternately with buttermilk, beginning and ending with flour mixture. Stir in dates, nuts, and coconut. Spoon mixture into a greased 10-inch tube pan and bake at 350° for 1 to 1¼ hours, or until cake tests done. Remove from pan and drizzle with Orange Sauce while cake is still hot. Yield: 1 (10-inch) cake.

Orange Sauce:

 2 *tablespoons grated orange rind*
 2 *cups powdered sugar*
 1 *cup orange juice*

Mix well together and spoon over Date-Nut Loaf Cake while it is still hot.

Light Fruitcake

 2 *cups all-purpose flour*
 2 *teaspoons baking powder*
 ½ *teaspoon salt*
 1 *pound coarsely chopped candied pineapple*
 1 *pound candied cherries*
 1½ *pounds coarsely chopped pitted dates*
 4 *eggs*
 1 *cup sugar*
 2 *pounds (8 cups) pecan halves*

Combine flour, baking powder, and salt. Add fruits and mix well to coat with flour. Beat eggs until light and fluffy. Gradually beat in sugar. Add fruit-flour mixture and nuts; mix well with hands. Grease two 9-inch spring-form pans (or 1 tube pan and assorted molds, as desired). Line pans with greased brown paper. Divide mixture between pans and press firmly into pans. Bake at 275° about 1 hour and 15 minutes or until cakes test done. Let cakes stand in pans about 10 minutes; turn out on cake racks and remove brown paper. Cool well before wrapping for storage. Yield: 2 (9-inch) cakes.

Kentucky Fruitcake

 1 *cup butter or margarine*
 1½ *cups sugar*
 5 *large egg yolks*
 1½ *cups all-purpose flour*
 ¼ *teaspoon soda*
 2 *teaspoons ground nutmeg*
 ⅛ *teaspoon salt*
 1 *teaspoon cream of tartar*
 ¼ *cup bourbon*
 1½ *cups chopped seedless raisins*
 4 *cups coarsely ground pecans*
 ¼ *cup all-purpose flour*
 5 *egg whites, stiffly beaten*
  Pecan halves (optional)
  Candied cherries (optional)

Cream butter and sugar; add egg yolks and beat well. Combine dry ingredients and add alternately to creamed mixture with the bourbon. Dredge raisins and pecans with ¼ cup flour and add to mixture. Fold in egg whites. Pour batter into a well-greased and floured 10-inch tube pan. Decorate top with pecan halves and candied cherries, if desired. Bake at 325° for 1 hour and 15 minutes or until cake tests done. Let stand in pan for 30 minutes on cake rack; remove from pan and put on waxed paper-covered cake rack to cool. Store in airtight container. Yield: 1 (10-inch) cake.

Mardi Gras Fruitcake

   1 *cup butter*
   1 *(8-ounce) package cream cheese*
1½ *cups sugar*
1½ *teaspoons vanilla extract*
   4 *eggs*
2¼ *cups all-purpose flour*
   2 *teaspoons baking powder*
   1 *cup chopped candied cherries*
   1 *cup chopped candied pineapple*
   1 *cup chopped nuts*
 ¼ *cup all-purpose flour*

Cream butter and cream cheese together until smooth; add sugar and continue beating until mixture is fluffy. Stir in vanilla. Add eggs, one at a time, beating well after each addition. Combine 2¼ cups flour and baking powder; add to creamed mixture and mix well.

Combine candied fruits and nuts; coat with ¼ cup flour; then add to creamed mixture. Stir well and spoon into 1 greased Bundt pan or two 9- x 5- x 3-inch loaf pans and bake at 325° for 70 to 80 minutes. Yield: 1 Bundt cake or 2 (9- x 5- x 3-inch) cakes.

Easy-Do Fruitcake

 1 *pound (4 cups) chopped pecans*
 1 *pound candied cherries, chopped*
 1 *pound pitted dates, chopped*
 4 *(3½-ounce) cans flaked coconut*
 2 *(14- or 15-ounce) cans sweetened condensed milk*

Place all ingredients in very large mixing bowl and mix well with hands. Spoon mixture into two 9- x 5- x 3-inch loaf pans that have been lined with greased brown paper (this is very important). Bake at 250° for 1½ hours. Cool on cake rack before removing from pans. Fruitcake improves with age. Yield: 2 (9- x 5- x 3-inch) cakes.

Favorite Fruitcake

   1 *cup chopped pecans*
 ¾ *cup chopped dates*
 ½ *cup chopped cherries*
 ½ *cup chopped candied pineapple*
2½ *cups flaked coconut*
   1 *cup sweetened condensed milk*
      Pecan halves, cherry halves, pineapple halves

Combine all ingredients; put into small loaf pan that has been well greased and floured or lined with waxed paper. Over the top, alternate pecan, cherry, and pineapple halves for decoration. Bake at 325° for 50 minutes or until slightly brown. Cool slightly; then invert on waxed paper and do not lift pan until cake drops down. Leave cake on paper until cold and firm; this takes several hours. Yield: 1 small loaf.

Mississippi Mud Cake

   1 *cup butter or margarine*
 ½ *cup cocoa*
   2 *cups sugar*
   4 *eggs, slightly beaten*
1½ *cups all-purpose flour*
      Dash salt
1½ *cups chopped nuts*
   1 *teaspoon vanilla extract*
      Miniature marshmallows
      Chocolate Frosting

Melt butter and cocoa together. Remove from heat and stir in sugar and eggs; mix well. Add flour, salt, nuts, and vanilla; mix well. Spoon batter into a greased 13- x 9- x 2-inch pan and bake 350° for 35 to 45 minutes. Sprinkle marshmallows on top of warm cake; cover with Chocolate Frosting. Yield: 1 (13- x 9- x 2-inch) cake.

Chocolate Frosting:

   1 *(1-pound) box powdered sugar*
 ½ *cup whole milk*
 ⅓ *cup cocoa*
 ¼ *cup softened butter or margarine*

Combine sugar, milk, cocoa, and butter. Mix until smooth and spread on hot cake.

Lady Baltimore Cake

  3 *cups sifted cake flour*
  3 *teaspoons baking powder*
½ *teaspoon salt*
¾ *cup shortening*
  2 *cups sugar*
½ *cup milk*
½ *cup water*
  1 *teaspoon vanilla extract*
  6 *egg whites*
     Lady Baltimore Filling
     Seven Minute Frosting

Combine flour, baking powder, and salt. Cream shortening with sugar until fluffy. Combine milk, water, and vanilla. Add combined dry ingredients to creamed mixture alternately with liquids. Beat egg whites until stiff but not dry. Fold whites into batter. Pour batter into 3 greased 9-inch layer cakepans and bake at 350° for 25 minutes. Cool. Spread Lady Baltimore Filling between layers and cover top and sides with Seven Minute Frosting. Yield: 1 (9-inch) cake.

Lady Baltimore Filling:

1½ *cups sugar*
  6 *tablespoons water*
⅛ *teaspoon cream of tartar*
  2 *egg whites, stiffly beaten*
  1 *teaspoon vanilla extract*
  1 *cup chopped seedless raisins*
1½ *cups chopped nuts*
  1 *cup chopped figs*
½ *teaspoon lemon extract*

Combine sugar, water, and cream of tartar in heavy saucepan. Cook syrup (without stirring) to 238°, or until a small amount forms a soft ball when dropped in cold water. Pour one-third of the syrup in a fine stream over egg whites, beating constantly.

Cook remainder of syrup to 248° or until a small amount forms a firm ball when dropped into cold water. Remove from heat; pour half of the remaining syrup in a fine stream into the egg white mixture, beating constantly. Cook remaining syrup to 268° or the hard-ball stage. Remove from heat and pour rest of syrup in a fine stream into the mixture, beating thoroughly.

Add vanilla and beat until thick enough to spread. Add raisins, nuts, figs, and lemon and mix carefully. Spread between layers of Lady Baltimore Cake.

Seven Minute Frosting:

  3 *tablespoons water*
  1 *egg white*
  1 *tablespoon corn syrup or ⅛ teaspoon cream of tartar*
  1 *cup of sugar*
⅛ *teaspoon salt*
  1 *teaspoon vanilla extract*

Heat water to boiling in lower part of double boiler. Water in lower part should surround upper part. Place 3 tablespoons water, egg white, syrup or cream of tartar, sugar, and salt in upper part of double boiler. Beat the mixture with a rotary egg beater or electric beater, rapidly at first, then steadily and continuously for about 7 minutes. Keep water boiling in lower part of double boiler during the beating. Remove from heat, pour out hot water, and fill with cold water; then replace upper part of double boiler. Let stand for 5 minutes. Add flavoring and stir. Use as icing on top and sides of Lady Baltimore Cake.

Cola Cake

  2 *cups sugar*
  2 *cups all-purpose flour*
½ *cup butter*
½ *cup vegetable shortening*
  3 *tablespoons cocoa*
  1 *cup cola drink*
½ *cup buttermilk*
  1 *teaspoon soda*
  2 *eggs, beaten*
  1 *teaspoon vanilla extract*
1½ *cups small marshmallows*
     Cola Topping

Mix cake by hand; do not use electric mixer. Combine sugar and flour in a large bowl. Combine butter, shortening, cocoa, and cola and heat until butter is melted;

pour over flour mixture and stir well. Add buttermilk, soda, eggs, vanilla, and marshmallows. Mix well and spoon into 2 well-greased 13- x 9- x 2-inch pans. Marshmallows will tend to gather in one section. Distribute throughout pan. Bake at 350° for 45 minutes or until cake tests done. Spread with Cola Topping while cake is still hot. Yield: 12 servings.

Cola Topping:

- ½ cup butter
- 6 tablespoons cola drink
- 3 tablespoons cocoa
- 1 (1-pound) box powdered sugar
- 1 teaspoon vanilla extract
- 1 cup chopped pecans

About 5 minutes before cake is done, combine butter, cola, and cocoa and bring to a boil. Stir in other ingredients and pour over hot cake while it is still in the pan. Topping will be very thin, but will thicken as it cools on cake. Leave cake in pan until completely cooled. Yield: enough for 1 (13- x 9- x 2-inch) cake.

*Marble Cake

- ⅔ cup butter or margarine
- 2 cups sugar
- 4 eggs, well beaten
- 3 cups all-purpose flour
- 4 teaspoons baking powder
- ½ teaspoon salt
- 1 cup milk
- 1 square unsweetened chocolate, melted
- 1 teaspoon vanilla extract

Cream butter and sugar until light and fluffy; add eggs and mix well. Sift flour, baking powder, and salt; add to creamed mixture alternately with milk. Put one-third of batter into a bowl and add chocolate. Add vanilla to the remaining white batter. Drop white batter, then chocolate batter, by teaspoonfuls into a well-greased 10-inch tube pan or Bundt pan. Bake at 350° for 1 hour. Cool for 1 hour before removing from pan. Yield: 1 (10-inch) cake.

Orange-Nut Butter Cake

- ¾ cup butter, softened
- 1 cup sugar
- 1 tablespoon freshly grated orange rind
- 1 teaspoon vanilla extract
- 3 eggs
- 1 cup orange marmalade
- 3 cups all-purpose flour
- 1½ teaspoons soda
- 1 teaspoon salt
- ½ cup orange juice
- ½ cup evaporated milk
- 1 cup chopped nuts
- Whipped Orange Topping

Cream butter thoroughly. Add sugar, orange rind, and vanilla. Beat until mixture is light and fluffy. Add eggs, one at a time, beating well after each addition. Blend in marmalade. Combine flour, soda, and salt. Add to creamed mixture alternately with combined orange juice and evaporated milk. Stir in nuts and blend. Spoon into well-buttered 10-inch tube pan, and bake at 350° for 55 to 60 minutes. Cool in pan for 10 minutes. Serve warm or cooled with Topping. Yield: 1 (10-inch) tube cake.

Whipped Orange Topping:

- 1 cup whipping cream
- 2 tablespoons sugar
- 1 tablespoon grated orange rind
- Orange sections

Beat cream until stiff. Add sugar and grated orange rind. Blend. Swirl mixture over top surface of cooled cake. Garnish with orange sections. Yield: about 1 cup.

Oldtime Fudge Cake

    2/3 cup softened butter or margarine
 1 3/4 cups sugar
     2 eggs
     1 teaspoon vanilla extract
 2 1/2 squares unsweetened chocolate, melted and cooled
 2 1/2 cups sifted cake flour
 1 1/4 teaspoons soda
  1/2 teaspoon salt
 1 1/4 cups ice water

Cream together butter and sugar until light and fluffy. Add eggs and beat well. Stir in vanilla and blend in chocolate. Combine dry ingredients and add to creamed mixture alternately with ice water, beating well after each addition. Spoon batter into 2 waxed paper-lined and greased 9-inch layer cakepans, and bake at 350° for 30 to 35 minutes, or until cake tests done. Frost as desired. Yield: 1 (9-inch) cake.

Double Fudge Cake

     4 squares unsweetened chocolate
 1 1/4 cups milk
  3/4 cup firmly packed brown sugar
 2 1/4 cups all-purpose flour
     1 teaspoon soda
  1/2 teaspoon salt
  2/3 cup shortening
     1 cup sugar
     3 eggs
     1 teaspoon vanilla extract
         Fudge Frosting

Cut chocolate into small pieces and melt in milk in top of double boiler. Blend with a rotary beater. Add brown sugar and stir until smooth. Set aside to cool. Sift together flour, soda, and salt.

    Cream shortening: gradually add sugar and continue to cream until light and fluffy. Add eggs, one at a time, beating well after each addition. Add vanilla and blend. Add flour mixture and chocolate mixture slowly; blend well. Bake in 3 greased 8-inch cakepans at 350° for 25 to 30 minutes, or until cake tests done. Cool and frost with Fudge Frosting. Yield: 3 (8-inch) layers.

Fudge Frosting:

     2 cups sugar
  1/8 teaspoon salt
     2 squares unsweetened chocolate, cut into small pieces
     1 cup evaporated milk
     2 tablespoons butter or margarine
     1 teaspoon vanilla extract

Combine sugar, salt, chocolate, and milk in a saucepan. Cook until a few drops will form a soft ball when dropped into cool water. Remove from heat and add butter and vanilla. Let cool to lukewarm; then beat to spreading consistency. Yield: enough for 3 (8-inch) layers.

Chocolate Cream Cake

     1 (8-ounce) package cream cheese, softened
     1 (3-ounce) package cream cheese, softened
     1 cup butter
     2 (1-pound) boxes powdered sugar
     1 (4-ounce) package sweet cooking chocolate
  1/4 cup water
  1/4 cup shortening
     3 eggs
 2 1/4 cups all-purpose flour
     1 teaspoon soda
     1 teaspoon salt
     1 cup buttermilk
     1 teaspoon vanilla

Put cream cheese and butter in large mixing bowl. Beat until light and fluffy. Stir in powdered sugar gradually and beat well. Melt chocolate in water in top of a double boiler and stir into sugar mixture.

    Divide sugar mixture into two parts. Reserve one part for the frosting. To the other half, add shortening and eggs and beat well. Combine flour, soda, and salt, and add to egg-sugar mixture alternately with buttermilk. Stir in vanilla and mix well. Spoon batter evenly into 3 greased 9-inch layer cakepans, and bake at 350° for 35 minutes, or until cake tests done. After cake has cooled, put layers together with reserved sugar mixture. Yield: 3 (9-inch) layers.

Different Chocolate Cake

 1⅓ cups boiling water
 1 cup oats, regular or quick-cooking, uncooked
 ½ cup butter
 1 cup sugar
 1 cup firmly packed brown sugar
 1 teaspoon vanilla extract
 2 eggs
 1½ cups all-purpose flour
 ½ teaspoon salt
 1 teaspoon soda
 3 tablespoons cocoa
  German Chocolate Frosting

Pour boiling water over oats. Cover and let stand for 10 minutes. Uncover, stir, and let stand 10 minutes more. Beat butter until fluffy; add sugars and vanilla and mix well. Add eggs and oats mixture, and mix well. Combine flour, salt, soda, cocoa, and add to creamed mixture. Mix well and pour into 2 greased and floured 8-inch cakepans. Bake at 350° about 30 minutes. Cool for 10 minutes before frosting with German Chocolate Frosting. Yield: 2 (8-inch) layers.

German Chocolate Frosting:

 1 *cup evaporated milk*
 1 *cup sugar*
 1 *teaspoon vanilla extract*
 3 *egg yolks, beaten*
 ½ *cup butter*
 1 *cup chopped pecans*
 1 *cup flaked coconut*

Mix all ingredients except nuts and coconut in saucepan and cook over low heat for 12 minutes, stirring constantly. Add nuts and coconut and beat until mixture is of spreading consistency. Yield: enough icing for a 2-layer cake.

Sour Cream Cheesecake

 2 eggs
 ½ cup sugar
 2 teaspoons vanilla extract
 1½ cups commercial sour cream
 2 (8-ounce) packages cream cheese, softened
 2 tablespoons butter, melted
 1 (9-inch) Crumb Crust
 1 (22-ounce) can cherry pie filling (optional)

Blend eggs, sugar, vanilla, and sour cream for 15 seconds in blender. Continue blending and gradually add cream cheese that has been cut into pieces. Add butter; blend well. Pour cheese mixture into a 9-inch piepan prepared with Crumb Crust. Bake at 325° for 35 minutes or until set in center. Filling will be very soft but will firm up as cake cools. Top with cherry pie filling, if desired; chill thoroughly before serving. Yield: 8 servings.

Crumb Crust:

 15 *graham cracker squares, crushed*
 ½ *cup sugar*
 ½ *teaspoon ground cinnamon*
 ¼ *cup butter, melted*

Combine all ingredients. Press into a buttered 9-inch piepan. Bake at 400° for 6 minutes. Cool before filling. Yield: 1 (9-inch) pie shell.

*Nutmeg Cake

¼ cup butter
¼ cup vegetable shortening
1¼ cups sugar
3 eggs
2 cups all-purpose flour
1 teaspoon baking powder
1 teaspoon soda
2½ teaspoons ground nutmeg
Dash salt
¼ teaspoon ground cinnamon
¼ teaspoon ground ginger
¼ teaspoon ground lemon rind
1 cup buttermilk
¼ teaspoon brandy extract

Beat butter and shortening until smooth; add sugar and continue beating until well mixed. Add eggs and beat until light and fluffy.

Combine dry ingredients and add to creamed mixture alternately with buttermilk and brandy extract (combined), beating well after each addition. Spoon batter into a greased 8- or 9-inch tube pan and bake at 350° for about 50 minutes. Yield: 1 (8- or 9- inch) cake.

Man on the Moon Cake

3 eggs
½ cup cooking oil
2 cups all-purpose flour
¼ teaspoon salt
1 teaspoon soda
2 teaspoons ground cinnamon
2 cups sugar
2 teaspoons vanilla extract
4 cups chopped pared apples
1 cup chopped walnuts
Lunar Landing Topping

Beat eggs and oil until foamy. Combine flour, salt, soda, and cinnamon; add to egg mixture. Add remaining ingredients, except Topping, and mix well. Pour into greased 13- x 9- x 2-inch baking pan. Bake at 350° for 35 to 40 minutes or until cake tests done.

Remove from oven and spread with Lunar Landing Topping. Cool before cutting. Yield: 1 (13- x 9- x 2-inch) cake.

Lunar Landing Topping:

1 (3-ounce) package cream cheese, softened
1 teaspoon vanilla extract
1½ cups sifted powdered sugar
¼ cup butter or margarine, softened
Few drops of milk (optional)

Blend ingredients until creamy. If necessary, add a few drops of milk for spreading consistency. Spread on hot cake. Yield: 1½ cups.

*Gingerbread

½ cup butter
1 cup sugar
1 cup dark molasses
2 egg yolks, beaten
3 cups cake flour
1 teaspoon salt
1 teaspoon soda
2 teaspoons ground ginger
2 teaspoons ground cinnamon
1 cup buttermilk
2 egg whites, stiffly beaten
Hard Sauce

Cream butter; add sugar, and cream until light and smooth. Add molasses and egg yolks and mix thoroughly. Sift flour; measure. Sift flour again with salt, soda, and spices. Add flour mixture alternately with buttermilk to molasses mixture. Fold in egg whites. Turn batter into well-greased and floured 9-inch tube pan. Bake at 350° for 30 to 40 minutes. Serve hot; top with Hard Sauce. Yield: 1 (9-inch) gingerbread cake.

Hard Sauce:

½ cup (1 stick) butter
1½ cups sifted powdered sugar
1 egg yolk
2 teaspoons grated lemon rind
1 egg white, stiffly beaten

Cream butter and sugar. Add egg yolk, beating constantly. Blend in lemon rind. Fold in egg white; chill. Yield: 2 cups.

cakes and frostings

*Plantation Gingerbread

- 2¾ cups all-purpose flour
- 2 teaspoons baking powder
- 2 teaspoons ground ginger
- 2 teaspoons ground cinnamon
- ¼ teaspoon ground cloves
- ½ teaspoon soda
- 4 tablespoons cocoa
- ½ teaspoon salt
- 1 cup shortening
- 1 cup sugar
- 1 cup molasses
- 2 eggs, well beaten
- 1 cup milk

Combine dry ingredients; set aside. Cream shortening; add sugar and beat until light and fluffy. Stir in molasses; add eggs and beat well. Add dry ingredients alternately with milk beating well after each addition. Spoon into a well-greased 10-inch square pan and bake at 350° about 50 minutes, or until bread tests done. Yield: 10 to 12 servings.

Orange Rum Cake

- 1 cup margarine
- 1 cup sugar
- 2 eggs
- Grated rind 2 large oranges
- Grated rind 1 lemon
- 2½ cups all-purpose flour
- 2 teaspoons baking powder
- 1 teaspoon soda
- ½ teaspoon salt
- 1 cup buttermilk
- 1 cup chopped pecans
- Orange Glaze

Beat margarine until light and fluffy; add sugar and beat well. Add eggs and grated rinds and beat until mixture is very light. Combine dry ingredients and add to creamed mixture alternately with buttermilk, beginning and ending with dry ingredients. Stir in pecans. Spoon mixture into a well-greased 10-inch tube pan. Bake at 350° for 1 hour or until cake tests done. Leave in pan and pour glaze over top of cake. Cake should be covered and left in pan for several days before serving. Yield: 1 (10-inch) tube cake.

Orange Glaze:

- Juice 2 large oranges
- Juice 1 lemon
- 1 cup sugar
- 2 tablespoons rum

Mix all ingredients and bring to a boil. Pour over hot Orange Rum Cake. Yield: about ¾ cup.

Orange Slice Cake

- 1 cup butter or margarine
- 2 cups sugar
- 4 eggs
- 1 teaspoon soda
- 1½ cups buttermilk
- 4 cups all-purpose flour
- 1 pound chopped dates
- 1 pound candy orange slices, chopped
- 2 cups chopped nuts
- 1 (3½-ounce) can flaked coconut
- Glaze

Cream butter and sugar until smooth. Add eggs, one at a time, beating well after each addition. Dissolve soda in buttermilk and add to creamed mixture. Place flour in large bowl; add dates, orange slices, and nuts. Stir to coat each piece. Add flour mixture and coconut to creamed mixture. Bake in a greased 9- or 10-inch tube pan at 250° for 3 hours and 15 minutes. Remove from oven; pour hot Glaze over top of cake and let cake sit in pan overnight: Yield: 1 (9- or 10- inch) tube cake.

Glaze:

- 1 cup firmly packed brown sugar
- ½ (6-ounce) can frozen orange juice, undiluted

Combine sugar and orange juice; heat and pour over hot cake. Yield: enough glaze for 1 (9- or 10-inch) tube cake.

Kentucky Jam Cake

½ cup butter
2 cups sugar
3 eggs
3 cups all-purpose flour
1 teaspoon soda
¼ teaspoon each of ground cloves, ground cinnamon, and ground allspice (optional)
⅓ cup cocoa
½ cup buttermilk
About ⅓ cup coffee
2 cups strawberry jam
Kentucky Jam Cake Frosting

Cream butter and sugar until light and fluffy. Add eggs, one at a time, beating well after each addition. Combine dry ingredients; add alternately to creamed mixture with buttermilk and coffee. Stir in jam. Bake in 3 greased 8-inch layer pans at 325° for 25 minutes or until cake tests done. Do not overbake. Cool and frost. Yield: 3 (8-inch) layers.

Kentucky Jam Cake Frosting:

½ cup butter
2⅓ cups sugar
4 eggs
1 cup milk
1½ cups seedless raisins
2 cups chopped candied cherries
2 cups chopped pecans
1½ cups flaked coconut

Cream butter and sugar until light and fluffy; add eggs and beat well. Add milk and cook in top of double boiler until thick, stirring constantly. Add all fruits, nuts, and coconut, and cook a few minutes longer. Spread this mixture between layers and on top and sides of cake. Yield: enough for 3 (8-inch) layers.

*Oatmeal Cake

1¼ cups boiling water
1 cup oats, quick-cooking or regular, uncooked
½ cup butter or margarine
1 cup firmly packed brown sugar
1 cup white sugar
2 eggs
1⅓ cups all-purpose flour
1 teaspoon ground cinnamon
1 teaspoon soda
1 teaspoon salt
Topping

Mix boiling water and oats and let stand for 20 minutes. Cream together butter and sugars. Add eggs and beat well. Add oats mixture. Add dry ingredients and mix well. Bake in a greased 13- x 9- x 2-inch pan at 275° for 35 to 45 minutes. While cake is still warm, spread with topping and return to oven for about 5 minutes. Yield: 1 (13- x 9- x 2-inch) cake.

Topping:

1 cup firmly packed light brown sugar
½ cup butter or margarine
¼ cup cream
1 cup coconut

Mix all ingredients and spread on warm cake.

*Peanut Butter Cake

½ cup shortening
1 cup peanut butter
1 cup sugar
2 eggs, well beaten
1½ cups all-purpose flour
½ teaspoon salt
3 teaspoons baking powder
1 cup milk
½ teaspoon vanilla extract
Caramel Frosting

Cream shortening; gradually add peanut butter and cream until smooth. Add sugar and cream until mixture is light and fluffy. Add eggs and mix well.

Combine all dry ingredients and add to creamed mixture alternately with milk. Stir in vanilla. Spoon mixture into 2 greased 9-inch layer cakepans and bake at 375° for 25 minutes, or until cake pulls away from sides of pan. Cool and frost with Caramel Frosting. Yield: 2 (9-inch) layers.

Caramel Frosting:

- 2 cups firmly packed brown sugar
- 2 tablespoons butter or margarine
- 6 tablespoons whipping cream
- 1 cup powdered sugar

Combine brown sugar, butter, and cream. Cook until bubbles form around edges of pan. Remove from heat, add powdered sugar, and beat well. Cool before spreading on cake. Yield: enough for top and sides of 2 (9-inch) layers.

Christmas Pecan Cake

- 2 cups (1 pound) butter or margarine
- 2 cups sugar
- 6 eggs
- 1 tablespoon lemon juice
- 1 teaspoon grated lemon rind
- 1 tablespoon vanilla extract
- 4 cups chopped pecans
- 1½ cups golden raisins
- 3 cups all-purpose flour, divided
- ¼ teaspoon salt
- 1 teaspoon baking powder

Cream butter and sugar until fluffy. Beat in eggs, one at a time. Add lemon juice, rind, and vanilla. Mix nuts and raisins with ¼ cup flour. Sift remaining dry ingredients. Alternately fold nuts and raisins and dry ingredients into creamed mixture. Spoon into a greased, waxed paper-lined 10-inch tube pan; bake at 300° about 1 hour and 50 minutes. Cool; then remove from pan. Yield: 1 (10-inch) cake.

Variation: For a sweeter, more moist cake, pour a syrup of ¼ cup each of orange juice, lemon juice, and sugar over cake while hot. Pan may be lined with aluminum foil. Flavor improves in the freezer.

Symphony Cake

- ¾ cup vegetable shortening
- 1½ cups sugar
- 3 eggs, well beaten
- 1¾ cups all-purpose flour
- 1 teaspoon baking powder
- ½ teaspoon soda
- ½ teaspoon salt
- ¾ teaspoon ground nutmeg
- 1 teaspoon ground cinnamon
- 2 tablespoons cocoa
- ¾ cup sour milk
- 1 teaspoon vanilla extract
- 1 teaspoon lemon extract
- ½ cup coarsely ground toasted pecans or almonds

Cream shortening and sugar until mixture is fluffy. Blend in eggs. Combine flour, baking powder, soda, salt, spices, and cocoa; add to creamed mixture alternately with sour milk. Blend in vanilla and lemon extracts and the nuts. Pour into 2 round 8- or 9-inch, well-greased and floured layer pans. Bake at 350° for 30 minutes. Cool and ice with a caramel or fudge frosting. Yield: 2 (8- or 9-inch) layers.

*Silver Cake

- 1 cup shortening
- 2 cups sugar
- 3½ cups all-purpose flour
- ½ teaspoon soda
- 2 teaspoons baking powder
- ¼ teaspoon salt
- 1 cup buttermilk
- 1 teaspoon vanilla extract
- 6 egg whites, stiffly beaten

Cream shortening and sugar until light and fluffy. Sift together flour, soda, baking powder, and salt. Combine buttermilk and vanilla. Add dry mixture to creamed mixture alternately with buttermilk, beating well after each addition. Fold in egg whites. Spoon in batter into 3 greased 8-inch cakepans or a greased Bundt pan. Bake layers at 350° for 25 to 30 minutes or 50 minutes for the Bundt cake. Yield: 3 (8-inch) layers.

cakes and frostings

Apple Dapple Cake

    3 eggs
1½ cups salad oil
    2 cups sugar
    3 cups all-purpose flour
    1 teaspoon salt
    1 teaspoon soda
    2 teaspoons vanilla extract
    3 cups chopped apples
1½ cups chopped pecans
    Topping

Mix eggs, oil, and sugar, and blend well. Combine flour, salt, and soda; add to egg mixture. Add vanilla, apples, and nuts. Pour into a greased 8- or 9-inch tube pan. Bake at 350° for 1 hour. While cake is still hot, pour hot Topping over it in the pan and let cool. When completely cool, remove cake from pan. Yield: 1 (8- or 9-inch) cake.

Topping:

    1 cup firmly packed brown sugar
   ¼ cup milk
   ½ cup margarine

Combine all ingredients and cook for 2½ minutes. Pour immediately over cake in pan.

Applesauce Cake

    1 cup butter
    3 eggs
    2 cups sugar
    2 teaspoons vanilla extract
    1 (16-ounce) can applesauce
    3 cups all-purpose flour
   ¼ teaspoon salt
1½ teaspoons soda
    1 teaspoon ground cinnamon
    1 cup chopped pecans
    1 cup seedless raisins

Cream butter, eggs, and sugar together. Add vanilla and applesauce; beat well. Combine dry ingredients; add to applesauce mixture. Mix together and add pecans and raisins. Mix well. Bake in 3 greased and floured 9-inch round cakepans at 325° for 25 to 30 minutes or until cake tests done. Frost as desired. Yield: 3 (9-inch) layers.

Apple Loaf Cake

    3 cups all-purpose flour
   ½ teaspoon ground cinnamon
   ½ teaspoon ground nutmeg
    2 teaspoons soda
    1 cup seedless raisins
    1 cup chopped dates
    2 cups sugar
   ⅔ cup vegetable oil
    2 eggs
    1 cup cold coffee
    2 cups peeled, chopped apples
    1 cup chopped pecans

Combine flour, cinnamon, nutmeg, and soda; add raisins and dates, and set aside. Cream sugar and vegetable oil; add eggs, one at a time, beating well after each addition. Stir in coffee, apples, and pecans and mix well. Add raisin-date mixture and mix well. Grease and flour two 9- x 5- x 3-inch loaf pans. Fill each pan two-thirds full, and bake at 350° for 1 to 1¼ hours. Yield: 2 (9- x 5- x 3-inch) loaf cakes.

Strawberry Cream Roll

    4 eggs
    1 teaspoon vanilla extract
    1 cup sugar
    1 cup sifted cake flour
   ¾ teaspoon baking powder
   ¼ teaspoon salt
    Powdered sugar
    1 cup whipping cream, whipped and sweetened
    2 cups strawberries, sliced and sweetened

Beat eggs and vanilla until thick and lemon colored. Gradually beat in sugar and continue beating until mixture is fluffy and thick. Sift together the flour, baking powder, and salt; fold into egg mixture. Pour into a 15- x 10- x 1-inch jelly roll pan which has been lined with aluminum foil and lightly greased. Bake at 375° for 12 to 15 minutes or until a very light brown. Do not overbake.

Turn out on a large sheet of aluminum foil which has been sprinkled with powdered sugar. Peel off the foil in which cake was cooked. Trim off crisp edges. Working very quickly, roll up in sugar-sprinkled aluminum foil. Let stand for about 15 to 20 minutes. Unroll and spread with whipped cream and strawberries. Reroll and chill for at least 1 hour in refrigerator before serving. Yield: about 10 servings.

Banana Nut Layer Cake

2/3 cup shortening
1 3/4 cups sugar
3 eggs
2 1/4 cups all-purpose flour
1 teaspoon soda
1/4 teaspoon salt
1 teaspoon baking powder
1/2 cup milk
1 1/2 cups mashed ripe bananas
3/4 cup chopped pecans
1 teaspoon vanilla extract
Caramel Frosting

Measure the first 8 ingredients into mixing bowl. Beat for 2 minutes on low speed. Add bananas, nuts, and vanilla and beat for another 2 minutes. Pour into three 9-inch cakepans that have been lined with waxed paper. Bake at 350° about 25 minutes. When done, place on wire rack to cool for 5 minutes before turning out of pans. When completely cool, frost cake with Caramel Frosting. Yield: 1 (9-inch) 3-layer cake.

Caramel Frosting:

3 1/4 cups sugar, divided
1/4 cup water
1 cup milk
1/2 cup butter
1/8 teaspoon soda
1 teaspoon vanilla extract
1/2 cup chopped pecans

Put 1/4 cup sugar in heavy skillet. Place over low heat and cook until brown, stirring constantly. Gradually add water to make thin syrup. Stir in 3 cups sugar, milk, butter, and soda; boil briskly and stir for 10 minutes. Cook, beating constantly, until a few drops will form a soft ball when dropped into cold water; cool in water, beating constantly. Add vanilla and nuts. Spread between layers and on top and sides of cake. Yield: enough frosting for a 3-layer cake.

Sour Cream Banana Cake

1/4 cup shortening
1 1/3 cups sugar
2 eggs
1 teaspoon vanilla extract
2 cups all-purpose flour
1 teaspoon baking powder
1 teaspoon soda
3/4 teaspoon salt
1 cup commercial sour cream
1 cup mashed bananas
1/2 cup chopped pecans (optional)
Cream Cheese Frosting

Cream shortening and sugar until light and fluffy. Add eggs and vanilla; blend thoroughly.

Combine flour, baking powder, soda, and salt; add to creamed mixture alternately with sour cream, beginning and ending with dry ingredients. Add bananas and pecans, mixing until just blended.

Spoon batter into a greased and floured 13- x 9- x 2-inch pan. Bake at 350° for 40 to 45 minutes. Cool and frost with Cream Cheese Frosting. Yield: 1 (13- x 9- x 2-inch) cake.

Cream Cheese Frosting:

1 (8-ounce) package cream cheese, softened
1/4 cup melted margarine
1 teaspoon vanilla extract
1 (1-pound) box powdered sugar

Combine all ingredients and blend well. Yield: frosting for 1 (13- x 9- x 2-inch) cake.

Bohemian Cake

    2 cups sugar
    ½ cup firmly packed brown sugar
    1 cup vegetable shortening
    4 eggs
    2½ cups all-purpose flour
    1 teaspoon baking powder
    Dash salt
    1 cup milk
    1 cup chopped pecans or walnuts*
    1 cup flaked coconut
    1 teaspoon vanilla extract

Cream sugars and shortening until light and fluffy. Add eggs, one at a time, beating well after each addition. Mix dry ingredients and add alternately with milk. Add nuts, coconut, and vanilla. Spoon into a greased tube pan and bake at 325° for 1 to 1½ hours or until cake tests done. Yield: 1 cake.

*Nuts may be blended in blender with milk, if desired.

Chocolate Nut Cake

    1 cup butter
    2 cups sugar
    5 eggs
    2 (2-ounce) squares unsweetened chocolate, melted
    1 teaspoon vanilla extract
    2½ cups all-purpose flour
    ½ teaspoon salt
    1 teaspoon soda
    1 cup commercial sour cream
    1 cup chopped walnuts or pecans

Cream butter and sugar until light and fluffy. Add eggs, one at a time, beating thoroughly after each addition. Add chocolate and vanilla and mix thoroughly. Add dry ingredients alternately with sour cream. Add nuts, beating until smooth after each addition. Turn into a greased, waxed paper-lined, 10-inch tube pan. Bake at 325° for 1 hour or until cake tests done. May be frozen without icing. Yield: 1 (10-inch) cake.

Chocolate Oatmeal Cake

    1 cup oats, regular or quick-cooking, uncooked
    1½ cups boiling water
    ½ cup shortening
    1½ cups sugar
    2 eggs
    1 cup all-purpose flour
    1 teaspoon soda
    ½ cup cocoa
    ½ teaspoon salt
    1 teaspoon vanilla extract
    1 cup chopped nuts (optional)

Mix oats with boiling water and let cool. Cream shortening, sugar, and eggs until light and fluffy. Add oatmeal to creamed mixture along with mixture of dry ingredients. Stir in vanilla, and beat until smooth. Add nuts, if desired. Spoon mixture into a greased 13- x 9- x 2-inch pan, and bake at 350° for 35 to 40 minutes or until cake pulls away from sides of pan. Yield: 1 (13- x 9- x 2-inch) cake.

Western Fudge Cake

    1½ teaspoons soda
    ¾ teaspoon salt
    3 cups sifted cake flour
    3 (1-ounce) squares unsweetened chocolate
    ¾ cup butter, softened
    2¼ cups sugar
    1½ teaspoons vanilla extract
    3 eggs
    1½ cups ice water
    Date Cream Filling
    Chocolate Frosting

Add soda and salt to sifted flour and resift 3 times. Melt chocolate. Set aside flour mixture and chocolate.

Cream butter. Add sugar slowly while continuing to cream constantly until light and fluffy. Add vanilla. Add eggs, 1 at a time, beating well after each addition. Add melted chocolate, cooled to lukewarm. Add flour mixture alternately with ice water (ice cubes removed), beginning and ending with flour mixture.

Divide batter among 3 8-inch round cakepans lined with waxed paper. With spatula or knife, level batter. Then cut through batter several times, being very careful not to touch bottom. Bake at 350° for 30 to 35 minutes or until done. Turn the layers onto a rack, remove paper liners, and allow to cool.

Put layers together with Date Cream Filling. Do not spread filling too close to edge of layers; leave about ¼-inch space around edges. This will fill in as the layers are piled on top of one another. Cover cake with cake cover and let stand for 1 hour or so. If some of filling has run out, press back into position with cake knife. Then cover with Chocolate Frosting. Yield: 1 (8-inch) layer cake.

Date Cream Filling:

 1 cup milk
 ½ cup chopped dates
 ¼ cup sugar
 1 tablespoon all-purpose flour
 Dash salt
 1 egg, beaten
 ½ cup chopped nuts
 1 teaspoon vanilla extract

Heat milk and dates in saucepan over low heat until warm. Mix sugar, flour, and salt together. To dry ingredients add egg and enough of the warm milk to make smooth. Pour flour mixture into milk in saucepan, stirring constantly. Cook over low heat, stirring constantly, until thick and smooth. Remove from heat and add chopped nuts and vanilla. Turn into bowl to cool, or place boiler in pan of ice water to cool. Yield: enough for a 3-layer cake.

Chocolate Frosting:

 1 cup half-and-half
 2 cups sugar
 2 (1-ounce) squares unsweetened chocolate, broken into pieces

Measure half-and-half into saucepan first. Pour sugar in center. Stir gently so that no sugar gets on sides of pan. Add chocolate. Start heating and bring to boil. Stir mixture, being careful to prevent scorching until boiling point is reached. Cook to the soft-ball stage, or 238° on candy thermometer.

Cool and beat until creamy and of spreading consistency. Work fast. If frosting gets too thick, add 1 or 2 drops of half-and-half and beat until smooth. Yield: enough for top and sides of a 3-layer cake.

Chantilly Cake

 1 angel food cake ring
 5 or 6 tablespoons sugar
 ½ teaspoon vanilla extract
 1 (10-ounce) package frozen strawberries, thawed, or 2 cups crushed fresh strawberries
 1 (8¼-ounce) can crushed pineapple, drained
 12 large marshmallows, cut into small pieces
 ½ pint whipping cream, stiffly whipped
 Toasted coconut

Cut angel food cake in 2 layers. Add sugar, vanilla, strawberries, pineapple, and marshmallows to whipped cream. Mix well; then cover bottom and top layers of cake with mixture. Sprinkle top and sides generously with coconut. Keep in refrigerator. Yield: 8 to 10 servings.

Banana Nut Cake

 ½ cup softened butter or margarine
 1½ cups sugar
 2 eggs, lightly beaten
 4 tablespoons buttermilk
 1 teaspoon vanilla extract
 1 cup mashed ripe bananas
 1½ cups all-purpose flour
 1 teaspoon salt
 1 teaspoon soda
 ½ teaspoon baking powder
 1 cup chopped nuts

Cream butter and sugar until light and fluffy. Add eggs, buttermilk, and vanilla and beat well. Stir in bananas. Combine dry ingredients with creamed mixture. Stir in nuts. Bake in a greased 9- x 5- x 4-inch loaf pan at 375° for 50 to 60 minutes. Yield: 1 (9- x 5- x 4-inch) cake.

*Sauerkraut Chocolate Cake

- 2/3 cup softened butter or margarine
- 1 1/2 cups sugar
- 3 eggs
- 2 1/4 cups all-purpose flour
- 1/2 cup cocoa
- 1 teaspoon baking powder
- 1 teaspoon soda
- 1/4 teaspoon salt
- 1 cup water
- 1 1/2 teaspoons vanilla extract
- 2/3 cup rinsed, drained, and chopped sauerkraut
- Mocha Whipped Cream Frosting or Chocolate Cream Cheese Frosting

Cream butter and sugar until light and fluffy. Add eggs, one at a time, beating well after each addition. Combine dry ingredients and add to creamed mixture alternately with water. Add vanilla. Beat well; then stir in sauerkraut.

Bake in 2 greased and floured 8-inch cakepans at 350° for 30 minutes or until cake tests done. Cool.

Frost with Mocha Whipped Cream Frosting or Chocolate Cream Cheese Frosting. Yield: 2 (8-inch) layers.

Mocha Whipped Cream Frosting:

- 1 1/2 cups whipping cream
- 3 tablespoons sugar
- 1 tablespoon dry instant coffee
- 2 teaspoons cocoa
- 1 1/2 teaspoons vanilla extract

Combine all ingredients and beat until soft peaks form. Yield: enough for 2 (8-inch) layers.

Chocolate Cream Cheese Frosting:

- 2 (4-ounce) packages sweet cooking chocolate
- 2 (3-ounce) packages cream cheese, softened
- 2 tablespoons half-and-half
- 2 cups sifted powdered sugar
- 1/4 teaspoon salt
- 1 teaspoon vanilla extract

Melt chocolate over hot water. Cool slightly; then blend in cream cheese and half-and-half. Add sugar gradually. Then add salt and vanilla. Yield: enough for 2 (8-inch) layers.

Sweet Chocolate Cake

- 4 squares semisweet chocolate
- 1/2 cup boiling water
- 1 cup butter or margarine
- 2 cups sugar
- 4 egg yolks, unbeaten
- 1 teaspoon vanilla extract
- 2 1/4 cups all-purpose flour
- 1 teaspoon soda
- 1/2 teaspoon salt
- 1 cup buttermilk
- 4 egg whites, stiffly beaten
- Date Pecan Filling
- Easy Chocolate Frosting

Melt chocolate in boiling water; cool. Cream butter and sugar until light and fluffy; add egg yolks, one at a time, beating well after each addition. Add vanilla and chocolate; mix until blended. Combine dry ingredients. Add to creamed mixture alternately with buttermilk, beating after each addition until batter is smooth. Fold in stiffly beaten egg whites.

Spoon batter into three 8- or 9-inch layer cakepans, which have been lined on bottoms with waxed paper. Bake at 350° for 35 to 40 minutes. Cool. Spread Date Pecan Filling between layers and frost outside with Easy Chocolate Frosting. Yield: 1 (8- or 9-inch) cake.

Date Pecan Filling:

- 1 cup sugar
- 1/2 cup half-and-half
- Dash salt
- 1/2 cup chopped dates
- 1/2 cup chopped pecans
- 1/2 teaspoon vanilla extract

Combine sugar, half-and-half, and salt and bring to a boil. Add dates and pecans; boil until mixture is thick and dates are blended. Add vanilla. Cool. Spread between layers of Sweet Chocolate Cake.

Easy Chocolate Frosting:

½ cup butter or margarine
⅓ cup cocoa
¼ teaspoon salt
2 cups sugar
⅔ cup (5⅓-ounces) evaporated milk
1 teaspoon vanilla extract

Melt butter slowly in heavy saucepan. Combine cocoa, salt, and sugar; add to butter along with the evaporated milk. Boil for 3 minutes; add vanilla and cool. Beat to spreading consistency. Use as icing for Sweet Chocolate Cake.

Tutti-Frutti Cake

½ cup butter or margarine
1 cup sugar
2 eggs, well beaten
1 teaspoon vanilla extract
1 tablespoon vinegar
1½ cups all-purpose flour
2 tablespoons cocoa
½ cup buttermilk
1 teaspoon soda
½ cup chopped dates
½ cup chopped pecans
Tutti-Frutti Filling

Cream butter and sugar until light and fluffy; add eggs, vanilla, and vinegar. Combine flour and cocoa. Add to creamed mixture alternately with buttermilk to which soda has been added. Mix well. Stir in dates and pecans. Bake in 2 greased 8-inch layer cakepans at 350° for 25 to 30 minutes. After cake has cooled, put layers together with Filling. Yield: 2 (8-inch) layers.

Tutti-Frutti Filling:

1 cup sugar
1 (8¼-ounce) can crushed pineapple
1 cup whipped cream

Add sugar to pineapple. Cook until mixture is very thick and pineapple is transparent. Cool. Stir cooled mixture into whipped cream. Spread between layers and on top of cake.

Variation: If desired, use only ½ cup whipped cream. Spread cream between the 2 layers, and cover top and sides with chocolate frosting.

Pineapple Ambrosia Upside-Down Cake

¼ cup butter
⅓ cup firmly packed brown sugar
1 (20-ounce) can pineapple slices, drained
7 maraschino cherries
6 walnut halves
1¼ cups all-purpose flour
2 teaspoons baking powder
¾ teaspoon salt
2⅔ tablespoons shortening
2⅔ tablespoons butter
1 teaspoon grated orange rind
1 teaspoon vanilla extract
⅔ cup sugar
1 egg
½ cup milk
⅓ cup flaked coconut
Whipped cream (optional)

Melt butter in 9- or 10-inch round cakepan or heavy skillet. Sprinkle with brown sugar. Line bottom of pan with 7 pineapple slices and sides of pan with halved pineapple slices, rounded-side down. Center whole pineapple slices with cherries and place walnut halves between slices. Set aside and keep warm while preparing batter.

Combine flour, baking powder, and salt. Blend together shortening, butter, orange rind, and vanilla until soft; slowly add sugar, beating well. Beat in egg thoroughly. Add dry ingredients alternately with milk, mixing until smooth. Stir in coconut. Spoon batter over pineapple in pan. Bake at 350° for 55 to 60 minutes. Remove from oven; let cake stand for 5 to 10 minutes before inverting on serving plate. Serve warm. May be topped with whipped cream, if desired. Yield: 8 servings.

Berry-Glazed Cheesecake

- 2 (8-ounce) packages cream cheese
- 2 cups small-curd cottage cheese, sieved
- 1½ cups sugar
- 2 teaspoons vanilla extract
- ½ teaspoon salt
- 6 eggs, separated
- ⅓ cup all-purpose flour
- Graham Cracker Crust
- Berry Glaze

Mix together cream cheese and cottage cheese until smooth; add sugar, vanilla, and salt. Gradually beat in egg yolks. Gradually blend in flour. Beat egg whites until soft peaks form; fold into cheese mixture. Pour into 9-inch tube pan that has been prepared with a Graham Cracker Crust and chilled.

Bake at 350° for 1 hour and 15 minutes. Turn off heat, open oven door, and let cake cool in oven to room temperature. (It is normal for cake to sink slightly in center.) Chill cake before topping with Berry Glaze. Yield: 1 (9-inch) tube cake.

Graham Cracker Crust:

- 2 cups graham cracker crumbs
- ¼ cup sugar
- ½ cup butter or margarine, melted

Combine all ingredients until well blended; press onto bottom and sides of 9-inch tube pan. Chill.

Berry Glaze:

- 1 pint strawberries, frozen or fresh
- ¾ cup sugar
- ¾ cup water, divided
- 2 tablespoons lemon juice
- 2 tablespoons cornstarch

Mash ½ pint berries and combine with sugar, ½ cup water, and lemon juice; bring to boil. Mix cornstarch with ¼ cup water and add to fruit mixture. Cook, stirring constantly, until mixture thickens. Strain and cool. Top cheesecake with remaining berries. Pour sauce over cake to glaze. Yield: 1⅓ cups.

Cheesecake

- 3 (8-ounce) packages cream cheese, at room temperature
- 4 eggs, separated
- 1 cup sugar, divided
- 1 teaspoon vanilla extract
- 16 graham crackers, crushed
- ¼ cup butter, melted
- 1 pint commercial sour cream

Combine cream cheese, egg yolks, ¾ cup sugar, and vanilla. Beat until smooth. Beat egg whites stiff; fold into cream cheese mixture. Combine ¾ of graham cracker crumbs and butter. Cover bottom of greased 9-inch tube pan with crumb mixture. Pour cake mixture on top of crumbs and bake at 350° for 40 to 50 minutes, or until slightly brown. Remove from oven. Combine sour cream and remaining sugar. Slowly pour this topping over cake. Sprinkle remaining cracker crumbs on top; bake at 450° for 5 minutes. Allow cake to cool completely. Refrigerate for 12 hours before serving. Yield: 1 (9-inch) tube cake.

Apple-Coconut Coffee Cakes

- ½ cup butter or margarine
- ¾ cup sugar
- 2 eggs
- 1 cup all-purpose flour
- 1½ teaspoons baking powder
- ¼ teaspoon salt
- ½ cup milk or half-and-half
- ½ cup flaked coconut
- ½ teaspoon vanilla extract
- 4 (about 4 cups) tart apples, cut into slices ¼ inch thick
- ¾ teaspoon ground cinnamon
- ½ cup sugar

Cream butter and sugar until smooth. Add eggs, one at a time, beating well after each addition. Combine flour, baking powder, and salt, and add to creamed mixture alternately with milk or half-and-half, beating well after each addition. Stir in coconut and vanilla.

Spread half the batter in a 9-inch round, well-greased cakepan. Spread a layer of ap-

cakes and frostings

ple slices over batter; add the rest of the batter and top with remaining apple slices. Combine cinnamon and ½ cup sugar; sprinkle over apples. Bake at 375° for 35 to 40 minutes or until cake tests done. Serve plain or with sweetened whipped cream. Yield: 6 servings.

Apple Coffee Cake

  ½ *cup shortening*
  1 *cup sugar*
  1 *teaspoon salt*
  1 *teaspoon vanilla extract*
  2 *eggs*
2½ *cups all-purpose flour*
  1 *teaspoon soda*
  1 *teaspoon baking powder*
  1 *cup commercial sour cream*
  2 *cups peeled, chopped, cooking apples*
  ½ *cup chopped nuts*
  ½ *cup firmly packed brown sugar*
  1 *teaspoon ground cinnamon*
  4 *tablespoons melted margarine*

Cream together shortening and 1 cup sugar. Add salt and vanilla and mix well. Add eggs and beat well. Combine flour, soda, and baking powder; add to creamed mixture alternately with sour cream. Stir in apples. Spoon batter into a greased 13- x 9- x 2-inch pan; sprinkle nuts evenly over batter. Combine brown sugar, cinnamon, and margarine and pour over top. Bake at 350° for 25 minutes. Yield: 12 servings.

*Red Velvet Cake

2½ *cups sifted cake flour*
  ½ *teaspoon salt*
  3 *tablespoons quick chocolate-flavored drink mix*
  ½ *cup shortening*
1½ *cups sugar*
  2 *eggs*
  2 *ounces red food coloring*
  1 *teaspoon vanilla extract*
  1 *cup buttermilk*
  1 *tablespoon white vinegar*
  1 *teaspoon soda*
Mystery Icing

Combine flour, salt, and chocolate-flavored mix. Cream together the shortening and sugar. When mixture is well creamed, beat in eggs one at a time. Blend well and add food coloring and vanilla. Mix buttermilk, vinegar, and soda. Add alternately with dry ingredients to the creamed mixture. Blend at low speed on electric mixer after each addition.

Grease and line two 9- x 1½-inch round cakepans (cake rises high). Pour in batter and bake at 350° about 30 minutes or until done. Remove from pans and cool on wire racks before frosting. Yield: 2 (9- x 1½-inch) layers.

Mystery Icing:

  4 *tablespoons all-purpose flour*
  1 *cup milk*
  1 *cup sugar*
  ½ *cup butter*
  ½ *cup vegetable shortening*
     Dash of salt
  ¼ *teaspoon vanilla extract, or more if desired*

Blend the flour and milk. Cook until mixture thickens to consistency of cream. Cool, but don't chill. Cream sugar, butter, and shortening, adding salt and vanilla. Add the slightly cooked flour mixture and continue beating until very fluffy. Yield: icing for a 2-layer cake.

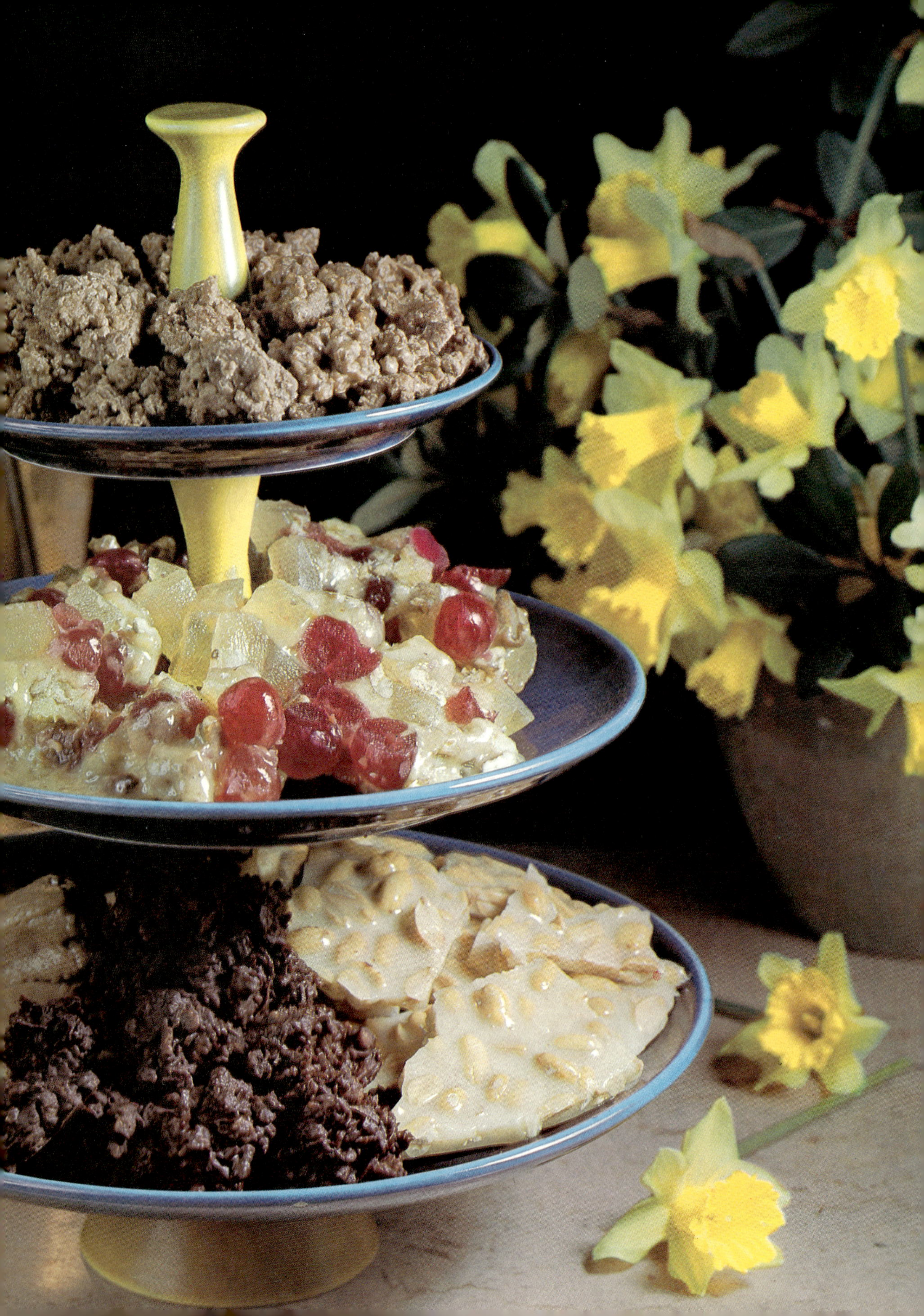

Candies and Confections

Columbus brought sugar to the New World in the late 15th century; later it was one of the early imports to the American Colonies. At first, the druggist made candy which was eaten for healing purposes as well as for taste. The first real candy was made in stick form.

Peanuts and pecans are favorite nuts in candy recipes. They add a special flavor all their own and are especially favored for Christmas giving. Pralines, those old-time favorites of New Orleans, find favor with all members of the family at any season of the year.

All of us treasure memories of the candies we loved as children: divinity fudge, peanut brittle, taffy, and many others. Children today enjoy these tried and true recipes as much as their parents did.

Apples-On-A-Stick

    8 *medium-size red apples*
    3 *cups sugar*
  ½ *cup light corn syrup*
  ½ *cup water*
    1 *drop oil of cinnamon*
    1 *teaspoon red food coloring*

Wash and dry apples; remove stems. Insert wooden skewers into stem ends of apples. Combine sugar, corn syrup, and water in a heavy deep saucepan. Cook over medium heat, stirring constantly, until mixture boils. Then cook without stirring to the soft crack stage (285°), or until a small amount separates into threads which are hard (but not brittle) when tested in very cold water. Remove from heat; add flavoring and coloring, and stir only enough to mix. Hold each apple by skewer end and quickly twirl in syrup, tilting pan to cover apple with syrup. Remove from syrup; allow excess to drip off; then twirl to spread syrup smoothly over apple. Place on lightly buttered baking sheet to cool. Store in cool place. Yield: 8 servings.

*Ripple Divinity

    3 *cups sugar*
  ½ *cup water*
  ½ *cup white corn syrup*
    2 *egg whites, stiffly beaten*
    1 *teaspoon vanilla extract*
    1 *cup chocolate pieces*

Combine sugar, water, and corn syrup in a 2-quart saucepan. Cook over high heat to boiling stage: reduce heat and continue cooking until mixture reaches 240°. Slowly pour one-third of the mixture over the egg whites, beating constantly. Cook remaining syrup to 265°; then gradually add to first mixture. Beat until mixture will hold its shape when dropped from a spoon. Add vanilla and fold in chocolate pieces. (Since the mixture is warm, the chocolate pieces will partially melt and give a rippled appearance to the divinity.) Drop from teaspoonfuls onto a greased baking sheet. Yield: about 4 dozen.

Note: Black walnuts or shredded coconut may be substituted for chocolate pieces, if desired.

Almond Paste

¼ cup water or orange juice
½ cup sugar
1 cup blanched almonds, divided
⅛ teaspoon almond extract (optional)

Combine water or orange juice, sugar, and ½ cup of the almonds in blender. Blend until smooth on high speed; add half the remaining almonds and blend again. Add remaining nuts and blend well. Stop motor and scrape sides of container when necessary. Add almond extract, if desired. Yield: 1½ cups.

Note: Almond Paste is the basis for miniature candy fruits called marzipan. To prepare these, mix 1 beaten egg white, 1 cup of almond paste, and 1 to 2 cups of powdered sugar to make a dough stiff enough to handle. Refrigerate overnight. Shape into miniature fruits and vegetables; color with food coloring.

*Molasses Coconut Chews

¼ cup molasses
¾ cup light corn syrup
1 tablespoon cider vinegar
2 tablespoons butter
2 cups flaked coconut
1 teaspoon vanilla extract
Few grains salt

Combine molasses, corn syrup, vinegar, and butter. Cook the mixture slowly, stirring occasionally, until the temperature reaches 240° (or when a small quantity dropped into cold water forms a soft ball). Remove from heat; add coconut, vanilla, and salt. Using two forks, quickly drop small clusters onto greased surface. Cool and store. Yield: 28 clusters.

Chocolate Crunchies

1 (6-ounce) package semisweet chocolate pieces
½ cup flaked coconut
1 cup crisp rice cereal or corn flakes
½ cup chopped nuts
1 teaspoon vanilla extract

Melt chocolate pieces in top of double boiler over hot water. Remove from heat; stir in coconut, cereal or corn flakes, nuts, and vanilla. Mix well. Drop by teaspoonfuls onto waxed paper. Chill until firm. Yield: 24 crunchies.

Old-Fashioned Chocolate Fudge

3 cups sugar
¾ cup milk
3 tablespoons margarine
2 tablespoons light or dark corn syrup
2 ounces unsweetened chocolate
1 teaspoon vanilla extract
1 cup coarsely chopped walnuts (optional)

Combine sugar, milk, margarine, corn syrup, and chocolate in a heavy 3-quart saucepan. Cook over medium heat, stirring constantly, until mixture boils. Then cook, stirring occasionally, until temperature reaches 238°, or until a small amount of mixture dropped into very cold water forms a soft ball. Remove from heat. Add vanilla. Cool to lukewarm (110°). Beat until fudge begins to thicken and lose its gloss. Stir in nuts. Quickly pour into greased 8- x 8- x 2-inch cakepan. Cut into squares when cold. Yield: 2 pounds fudge.

Caramel Fudge Roll

 ⅔ cup undiluted evaporated milk
1⅔ cups sugar
 ½ teaspoon salt
1½ cups miniature marshmallows
1½ cups caramel chips
 1 teaspoon vanilla extract
 ½ cup chopped nuts
 Additional chopped nuts

Combine milk, sugar, and salt in saucepan. Bring to a boil over low heat; then cook for 5 minutes, stirring constantly.

Remove from heat. Add marshmallows, caramel chips, vanilla, and nuts. Stir until marshmallows melt. Pour mixture on waxed paper. Shape into a roll as fudge cools, then roll in additional chopped nuts. Slice. Yield: about 1½ pounds.

10-Minute Fudge

 3 (1-ounce) squares unsweetened chocolate
 4 tablespoons margarine
4½ cups powdered sugar
 ⅓ cup instant nonfat dry milk powder
 ½ cup light or dark corn syrup
 1 tablespoon water
 1 teaspoon vanilla extract
 ½ cup chopped nuts (optional)

Melt chocolate and margarine in top of 2-quart double boiler. Sift together powdered sugar and dry milk. Stir corn syrup, water, and vanilla into chocolate mixture. Stir in sugar and dry milk in 2 additions. Continue stirring until mixture is well blended and smooth. Remove from heat; stir in nuts. Turn into greased 8-inch square pan. Cool. Cut into squares. Yield: 1¾ pounds fudge.

*Fudgies

 2 cups sugar
 ½ cup cocoa
 ½ cup butter or margarine
 ½ cup skim milk
 ¼ teaspoon salt
 1 teaspoon vanilla extract
 ½ cup peanut butter
 2 to 2½ cups uncooked rolled wheat or oat cereal
 ¾ cup seedless raisins or flaked coconut (optional)

Mix sugar and cocoa in saucepan. Add butter, milk, and salt. Bring to a boil, and boil for 1 minute. Remove from heat; cool until almost cold. Add remaining ingredients. Spoon level tablespoonfuls onto waxed paper and allow to set for 30 minutes. Yield: 50 cookies.

Minted Walnuts

 2 cups toasted walnuts
 1 cup sugar
 Few grains salt
 ⅓ cup water
 ⅓ teaspoon mint flavoring

Measure walnuts and set aside. Combine sugar, salt, and water in saucepan; bring to a boil and boil for 2 minutes. Remove from heat and stir in mint flavoring. Add walnuts and stir until syrup looks milky. Pour out and separate the nuts quickly. Yield: 2 cups.

Pecan Brittle

 1 pound sugar
 1 pound butter
 1 pound pecans (halves or pieces)

Combine sugar and butter in heavy saucepan. Bring to a boil and cook until mixture is golden brown, stirring constantly, but not beating. Remove from heat and stir in pecans. Spread very thin in shallow buttered pans. Break into pieces after brittle has cooled. Yield: about 1½ pounds.

candies and confections

Heavenly Delight

  3 *cups sugar*
  1 *cup light corn syrup*
1½ *cups cream or undiluted evaporated milk*
1½ *pounds chopped candied cherries*
1½ *pounds chopped candied pineapple*
  ½ *pound chopped walnuts*
  ½ *pound chopped pecans*
  ½ *pound chopped Brazil nuts*
     Candied pineapple or nuts (optional)

Cook sugar, corn syrup, and cream or milk to the hard-ball stage. Beat until mixture is almost ready to lose glossiness. Add candied fruit and nuts. Press into buttered or waxed paper-lined pans. Garnish the top with pineaple or nuts, if desired. Keep in refrigerator until hard. Cut into slices after 24 hours. Store in refrigerator until ready to use. Yield: 5½ pounds.

Divinity

2 *cups sugar*
½ *cup white corn syrup*
½ *cup water*
   Dash of salt
2 *egg whites, stiffly beaten*
1 *teaspoon vanilla extract*
¾ *cup broken pecans*

Combine sugar, corn syrup, water, and salt in a saucepan over low heat. Stir until sugar is dissolved; then cook without stirring to 250°. Remove from heat and pour into egg whites, beating constantly. Continue beating until mixture loses its gloss. Add vanilla and pecans; drop quickly from tip of spoon onto waxed paper, or spread in greased pan; cut into squares when cold. Yield: 18 to 24 pieces.

Filbert Sweetmeats

4 *cups filberts*
2 *egg whites*
1 *cup sugar*
   Dash salt
½ *cup butter or margarine*

In a large shallow baking pan, toast filberts at 325° for 15 minutes, stirring occasionally. Meanwhile, beat egg whites until foamy; gradually add sugar and salt, beating until stiff. Fold in toasted filberts. Melt butter in baking pan in which filberts were toasted; spread nut mixture in pan and bake at 325° for 30 to 40 minutes, or until nuts are slightly browned and butter is absorbed. Stir nuts thoroughly every 10 minutes during baking. Yield: 2 quarts.

Walnut Clusters

1⅔ *cups sugar*
 ⅓ *cup evaporated milk*
 ½ *teaspoon salt*
1½ *cups marshmallows*
1½ *cups butterscotch bits*
  1 *teaspoon vanilla extract*
  2 *cups coarsely chopped walnuts*

Combine sugar, evaporated milk, and salt in saucepan. Bring to a boil over medium heat and cook for 5 minutes (start counting time when mixture begins to bubble around sides of pan). Stir constantly. Remove from heat and stir in marshmallows, butterscotch bits, vanilla, and walnuts. Stir vigorously for 1 minute. Working very fast, drop by teaspoonfuls onto waxed paper. Yield: about 2½ pounds.

Orange Pecans

2 *cups sugar*
¾ *cup orange juice*
1 *tablespoon grated orange rind*
3 *cups pecan halves*

Put sugar and orange juice in a large saucepan and cook to soft-ball stage (236° to 240°). Turn off heat, and add orange rind and pecans. Stir with wooden spoon until mixture turns cream color, about 5 to 7 minutes. Pour onto waxed paper or cookie sheet. When cool enough to handle, break apart. Yield: 1 pound.

Date Nut Fondant

   2/3 cup sweetened condensed milk
   1 teaspoon vanilla extract
   4 cups sifted powdered sugar
   1 cup finely chopped nuts
   1/2 cup finely chopped pitted dried dates
     Pecan halves

Blend together condensed milk and vanilla in a large mixing bowl. Gradually stir in sugar. Blend in nuts and dates. Turn into an 8- x 8- x 2-inch pan and press evenly on bottom. Refrigerate until firm. With sharp knife, cut into 1-inch squares. Top each piece with a pecan half. Yield: about 1½ pounds.

Glazed Nuts

   2 2/3 cups firmly packed brown sugar
   1/2 cup water
   1/3 cup blanched almonds
   1/3 cup pecan halves
   1/3 cup walnut halves

Mix sugar and water in 3-quart heavy saucepan. Put over medium heat. Stir to dissolve sugar. Crystals that form on sides of pan should be removed with a dampened pastry brush or cloth wrapped around tines of fork. Boil without stirring, until mixture foams—about 212°. Add nuts. Continue to boil, without stirring, to 270° or to the soft crack stage.

Pour nuts into a large sieve; drain quickly. Turn onto a buttered cookie sheet. Using forks, separate nuts at once. When cool, serve or store. Yield: 1 cup.

Raisin Peanut Clusters

   1/2 cup light molasses
   1/2 cup light corn syrup
   1 teaspoon cider vinegar
   3 tablespoons butter
   2 cups raw shelled peanuts
   1 cup seedless raisins

Combine molasses, corn syrup, and vinegar; cook slowly, stirring occasionally, to 250° (or when a small quantity dropped into cold water forms a hard ball). Remove from heat; add butter; mix well. Combine nuts and raisins; add to molasses mixture. Drop by teaspoonfuls onto a greased baking sheet. If mixture begins to harden, reheat. Yield: about 28 clusters.

*Molasses Peanut Crunch

   1 cup light molasses
   1 cup sugar
   2 tablespoons shortening
   1/8 teaspoon soda
   2½ cups chopped peanuts

Combine molasses, sugar, and shortening; cook slowly, stirring constantly, until temperature reaches 252° (or when a small quantity dropped into cold water forms a hard ball). Remove from heat; add soda; stir until bubbling stops. Add nuts. Pour into greased shallow pan. Cool slightly; cut in small squares or bars. Wrap in waxed paper. Yield: about 1¾ pounds.

candies and confections

Peanut Brittle

  1 cup light or dark corn syrup
  1 cup sugar
  ¼ cup water
  2 tablespoons margarine
  1½ cups salted peanuts
  1 teaspoon soda

Combine corn syrup, sugar, water, and margarine in a heavy 2-quart saucepan. Cook over medium heat, stirring constantly, until sugar is dissolved and mixture comes to boil. Continue cooking, without stirring, until temperature reaches 280°, or until a small amount of mixture dropped into very cold water separates into threads which are hard but not brittle.

Gradually stir in salted peanuts so mixture continues to boil. Cook, stirring frequently, until temperature reaches 300°, or until small amount of mixture dropped into very cold water separates into threads which are hard and brittle. Remove from heat. Add soda; blend quickly, but thoroughly. Immediately turn onto heavily greased baking sheet. Spread mixture evenly to edges of baking sheet with a greased metal spatula. Cool. Break into pieces. Yield: 1½ pounds.

Dixie Peanut Brittle

  ½ cup water
  2 cups sugar
  ½ cup light corn syrup
  1½ cups raw shelled peanuts
  2 tablespoons butter
  1 teaspoon salt
  1 teaspoon soda

Cook water, sugar, and syrup until it spins a thread. Add peanuts and cook until they begin to pop. Add butter, salt, and soda. Pour onto large cookie sheet. Cool, and break into pieces. Yield: about 1½ pounds.

Chocolate-Covered Peanut Balls

  2 sticks margarine
  1 cup peanut butter
  1 (1-pound) box powdered sugar
  2 cups finely crushed graham crackers
  1 cup flaked coconut
  1 cup chopped nuts
  1 (6-ounce) package chocolate bits
  1 (4-ounce) stick paraffin

Melt margarine; stir in peanut butter and powdered sugar, and mix well. Add graham crackers, coconut, and nuts. Roll into small balls.

Melt chocolate bits and paraffin in top of a double boiler. Dip balls in chocolate mixture and set on racks to cool. Yield: about 6 dozen.

Chocolate Peanut Logs

  1 pound powdered sugar
  1 cup flaked coconut
  1 cup chopped toasted peanuts
  1 teaspoon vanilla extract
  1 cup graham cracker crumbs
  ½ cup crunchy peanut butter
  1 cup peanut oil
  ½ (4-ounce) block of paraffin
  1 (12-ounce) package semisweet chocolate chips

Thoroughly mix all ingredients except paraffin and chocolate chips. After all ingredients have been well mixed, roll into logs about 1½ inches long, or into round balls about the size of a quarter.

Melt paraffin and chocolate chips in top

candies and confections

of a double boiler. Work quickly and dip logs into hot chocolate-paraffin mixture and place on waxed paper to dry. Two toothpicks or a wide 4-pronged fork can be used effectively for dipping logs. Yield: about 3 dozen.

*Quick Peanut Butter Fudge

⅓ cup margarine
½ cup light corn syrup
¾ cup peanut butter
½ teaspoon salt
1 teaspoon vanilla extract
4½ cups sifted powdered sugar
¾ cup chopped nuts

Combine margarine, corn syrup, peanut butter, salt, and vanilla in large bowl. Stir in powdered sugar gradually. Turn onto board and knead until well blended and smooth. Add nuts gradually, pressing and kneading into candy. Press out with hands or rolling pin into a square ½ inch thick. Cut into serving pieces. Yield: 2 pounds fudge.

Penuche

2 cups firmly packed brown sugar
¾ cup sugar
¾ cup milk
⅛ teaspoon salt
2½ tablespoons butter or margarine, softened
1 teaspoon vanilla extract
½ cup chopped walnuts or pecans (optional)

Combine both sugars, milk, and salt in thick saucepan. Place over moderate heat, stirring until sugar dissolves. Wipe sugar crystals from sides of pan as necessary; cook without stirring until candy reaches 238° or soft-ball stage. Remove from heat. Add butter; without stirring, cool to 110° or lukewarm.

Add vanilla and nuts. Stir continuously until thick and creamy. Turn into buttered 9- x 5-inch pan at once. When firm, cut into squares. Yield: 1¼ pounds penuche.

Southern Pralines

2 cups sugar
¾ teaspoon soda
1 cup half-and-half
1½ tablespoons butter
2 cups pecan halves

Combine sugar and soda in a deep 3-quart saucepan. Mix well with wooden spoon. Then add half-and-half. Stir carefully to keep sugar crystals in lower part of pan. All crystals should be dissolved when candy boils. This makes it smooth and creamy.

Bring to boil over medium heat, stirring occasionally to prevent scorching. When mixture starts to boil, reduce the heat and continue stirring to keep it from boiling over. Mixture caramelizes slightly as it cooks. Cook until candy forms soft ball when tested in cold water. Test several times.

Remove pan from heat and add butter immediately. Measure accurately—too much butter may keep pralines from forming. Add pecan halves, and beat mixture with metal spoon until thick enough to drop from spoon. Drop candy on waxed paper or buttered aluminum foil. Yield: 30 (1½-inch) pralines.

Louisiana Yam Pralines

3 cups sugar
1 cup half-and-half
1¼ cups mashed, cooked yams, fresh or canned
Dash salt
1 cup firmly packed brown sugar
2 cups broken pecans

Combine sugar, half-and-half, yams, and salt; mix well. Cook over medium heat until mixture reaches soft-ball stage (224° to 225°), stirring occasionally. Melt brown sugar over medium heat. When yam mixture reaches 227°, add brown sugar and pecans; mix well. Remove from heat and drop from a spoon onto well-greased baking sheets. Let cool until crystallized. Yield: 20 (3-inch) pralines.

Pralines

- 1 (1-pound) box brown sugar
- 3 cups broken pecan meats
- ¼ cup butter or margarine
- ⅓ cup water
- 1 teaspoon vanilla extract

Combine brown sugar, pecans, butter, and water in heavy saucepan. Cook to 240° or soft-ball stage. Remove from heat; add vanilla and stir until mixture begins to lose its gloss. Drop small portions onto waxed paper. Work fast, keeping the saucepan over a warm surface while dropping the pralines. Yield: 2 pounds.

Pecan Pralines

- 2 cups firmly packed brown sugar
- 1 tablespoon butter
- 4 tablespoons water
- ½ pound chopped pecans

Mix sugar, butter, and water and bring to a boil. Add pecans and let boil until mixture begins to bubble. Remove from heat and stir constantly until the syrup thickens and begins to sugar. Drop by teaspoonfuls onto buttered platter. Yield: 12 pralines.

Plantation Pralines

- 3 cups firmly packed brown sugar
- ¾ cup sugar
- ¼ teaspoon cream of tartar
- ⅛ teaspoon salt
- 1 cup milk
- 2 tablespoons margarine, softened
- 1 teaspoon vanilla extract
- 2½ cups pecan halves

Combine sugars, cream of tartar, and salt in thick saucepan. Stir milk into mixture. Place over moderate heat, stirring gently, until sugar dissolves. Wipe sugar crystals from sides of pan as necessary; cook without stirring to 236°-238° or soft-ball stage. Remove from heat; cool to 220°.

Add margarine, vanilla, and pecans. Stir continuously until creamy. Drop from large spoon onto buttered surface or waxed paper. Store in airtight container with waxed paper between layers. Yield: 1½ to 2 dozen pralines.

*Molasses Taffy

- 1 (15-ounce) can sweetened condensed milk
- ½ cup light molasses
- ⅛ teaspoon salt

Blend together sweetened condensed milk, molasses, and salt in heavy saucepan. Cook over medium heat, stirring constantly, to 235° or until a little dropped into very cold water forms a semifirm ball which holds its shape when taken from water. Remove from heat at once. Pour onto large, buttered platter or into buttered 8- x 8- x 2-inch pan. Let stand until cool enough to handle. Pull taffy between buttered fingers until shiny and light colored. Twist into rope about ¾ inch thick. Cut into 1-inch pieces with kitchen scissors. Yield: ¾ pound.

*Vanilla Taffy

- 1 cup sugar
- ¾ cup light corn syrup
- ½ cup water
- ¼ teaspoon cream of tartar
- 1 teaspoon vanilla extract
- 1 tablespoon margarine

Combine sugar, corn syrup, water, and cream of tartar in saucepan. Bring to a boil over medium heat, stirring constantly until sugar dissolves. Continue cooking without stirring to hard-ball stage (266°) or until a small amount of mixture forms a hard ball when tested in very cold water.

Remove from heat; stir in vanilla and margarine. Pour into a greased, 8-inch square pan; let stand until cool enough to handle. Pull candy with fingers until it has a satinlike finish and milky white color. Pull into long strips ¾ inch in diameter. Cut into 1-inch pieces with scissors. Wrap in waxed paper. Yield: about ½ pound.

Bourbon Balls

3 cups vanilla wafers, rolled to a dust
3 tablespoons corn syrup
1 cup powdered sugar
½ cup cocoa
1 cup finely chopped pecans
½ cup bourbon
Powdered sugar, cocoa, or coconut

Mix all ingredients together. Shape into small balls (about ½ inch in diameter). Roll balls in powdered sugar, cocoa, or finely shredded coconut. Rum may be substituted for bourbon. Yield: about 50 balls.

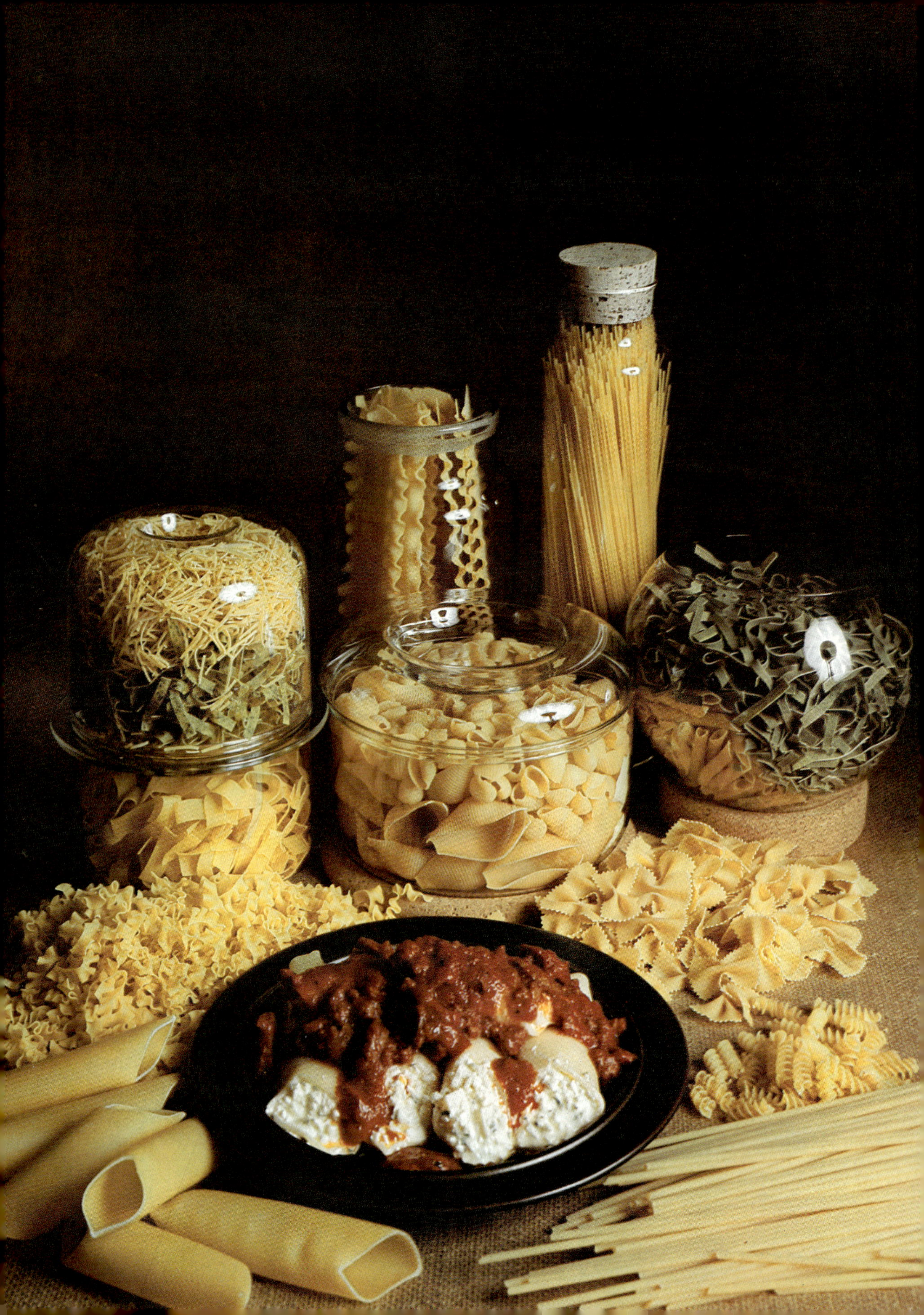

Casseroles

Casseroles . . . what would we do without them! The reputation of the early casserole was not very good, probably because of the cook's practice of combining all leftovers to make a new dish for the family. A very thrifty idea, no doubt, but it did not meet with great favor at the dinner table.

Today our casseroles are all made with fresh ingredients, except for those recipes using leftover or cooked meat or poultry. The homemaker finds the casserole a challenge to make and a timesaving endeavor as well. She can prepare the dish, put it in the refrigerator, and save mixing time when she gets ready to cook it. Also, many casseroles can be frozen for at least a month if carefully wrapped.

A casserole with vegetables, plus a green or congealed salad, and a fruit dessert, will make a complete meal. Pick a recipe with ingredients your family will like; your choice is limitless.

Creole Rice Casserole

- 4 slices bacon
- 1 medium onion, chopped
- ½ cup chopped green pepper
- 1 cup uncooked regular rice
- 1 pound ground lean beef
- 1 clove garlic, minced
- 1¾ cups water
- 1 cup commercial spaghetti sauce or 1 (8-ounce) can tomato sauce
- ⅔ cup raisins
- 2 teaspoons salt
- 2 teaspoons chili powder
- 2½ cups shredded Cheddar cheese

Fry bacon until crisp, drain on absorbent paper, and crumble.

Drain all but 2 tablespoons drippings from skillet; add onion and pepper and cook until tender. Add rice and cook until golden, stirring constantly. Add ground beef and garlic, and cook until meat turns grey. Add water, spaghetti sauce, raisins, salt, and chili powder. Heat to a boil; then cover skillet and reduce heat. Simmer for 20 minutes.

Put half of rice mixture into 2-quart casserole. Sprinkle with half the cheese and half the crumbled bacon. Add remainder of rice mixture, bacon, and cheese. Bake at 450° about 15 minutes. Yield: 8 servings.

Creamed Fresh Corn

- 1½ cups fresh corn cut from cob
- 2 strips bacon
- ¼ teaspoon sugar
- Salt and pepper to taste
- ¾ cup whipping cream

Cut kernels from ears of corn; scrape out milk with back of knife. Cook bacon; drain, crumble, and set aside.

Measure 1½ tablespoons bacon drippings into skillet. Add corn; cook and stir until every kernel is coated. Add sugar, salt, and pepper and cook slowly stirring constantly, until corn is golden brown. Add cream, stir well, and cook just until cream is hot. Stir in crumbled bacon before serving. Yield: 2 servings.

*Spanish Delight Casserole

1 large onion, chopped
1 green pepper, chopped
3 stalks celery, chopped
1 tablespoon salad oil
1 pound lean ground beef
1 teaspoon salt
2 (8-ounce) cans tomato sauce
1 (4-ounce) can mushroom stems and pieces
1 (8¾-ounce) can whole kernel corn
2 tablespoons chili powder
2 or 3 drops hot sauce
1 (8-ounce) package noodles
Cheddar cheese strips

Sauté onion, pepper, and celery in hot salad oil. Add meat and salt, and cook until meat turns grey. Add tomato sauce, mushrooms, corn, chili powder, and hot sauce; simmer for 30 minutes, stirring occasionally.

Cook noodles according to package directions; drain. Add noodles to meat mixture. Spoon mixture into a 3-quart casserole dish and cool. Seal securely and freeze.

To serve, remove from freezer and thaw. Add cheese strips and bake at 350° until heated thoroughly and cheese is melted. Yield: 6 to 8 servings.

*Sweet Potato and Marshmallow Casserole

2 cups cooked, mashed sweet potatoes
¼ cup melted margarine
¼ cup light or dark corn syrup
¼ cup orange juice
2 tablespoons milk
¼ teaspoon salt
¼ teaspoon ground nutmeg
Miniature marshmallows

Combine sweet potatoes, margarine, corn syrup, orange juice, milk, salt, and nutmeg; mix well. Spoon into a greased 1-quart casserole. Arrange marshmallows on top. Bake at 375° for 25 to 30 minutes, or until casserole is bubbly and marshmallows are lightly browned. Yield: about 6 servings.

*Quenelle De Grits

½ cup instant grits
2 cups boiling water
1 teaspoon salt
1 tablespoon instant minced onion
¾ teaspoon dried parsley
1 egg, beaten
1 cup all-purpose flour
4 cups salted water, chicken broth, or consommé
2 tablespoons melted butter
¼ cup grated Parmesan cheese

Slowly stir grits into boiling, salted water with onion and parsley. Cook, uncovered, for 3 to 5 minutes, stirring occasionally. Stir in beaten egg and flour, and blend well. Drop from tablespoon into simmering salted water, chicken broth, or consommé; poach for 10 minutes. Remove from liquid with slotted spoon and drain on paper towels. Place in a flat baking dish; top with melted butter and Parmesan cheese. Broil for 5 minutes or until lightly browned. Serve at once. Yield: 6 servings.

Crab and Shrimp au Gratin

4 tablespoons all-purpose flour
⅓ teaspoon salt
⅓ teaspoon black pepper
2 cups milk, divided
⅓ cup pasteurized process cheese spread
⅛ teaspoon hot sauce
2 (4-ounce) cans shrimp, drained
1 (4-ounce) can crabmeat, drained
1 cup shredded Cheddar cheese
Cooked rice

Combine flour, salt, pepper, and 1 cup milk; stir until mixture is smooth.

Combine cheese spread and remaining milk in top of double boiler: cook over hot water until cheese has melted. Add flour mixture and hot sauce to cheese mixture; stir until smooth and thickened. Add shrimp and crabmeat. Pour into a greased 1½-quart casserole and top with shredded cheese. Bake at 350° for 20 minutes. Serve over rice. Yield: 4 servings.

Golden Shrimp Casserole

    5 slices bread, cut into ½-inch cubes
    ¼ cup melted butter or margarine
    ½ cup sliced mushrooms
    2 cups peeled, cooked, deveined shrimp
    2 cups shredded pasteurized process American cheese
    3 eggs, beaten
    2 cups milk
    ½ teaspoon salt
       Dash pepper
       Dash paprika

Brown bread cubes in butter; remove from skillet and set aside. Cook mushrooms in butter for about 10 minutes. In a greased 1½-quart casserole, alternate layers of bread cubes, mushrooms, shrimp, and cheese.

Combine eggs, milk, and seasonings; pour over layers. Place casserole in a pan of hot water, and bake at 350° for about 1 hour and 15 minutes. Yield: 6 servings.

Happy Accident Shrimp Casserole

    2 cups cooked rice
    2 cups cooked shrimp
    3 tablespoons minced onion
    1 (8½-ounce) can green peas, with liquid
       Dash pepper
  1½ teaspoons Worcestershire sauce
    1 (1⅜-ounce) package green onion dip mix
    1 cup mayonnaise
   ¾ to 1 cup packaged herb-flavored dressing
    3 tablespoons melted butter or margarine

Combine all ingredients except dressing and butter. Spoon mixture into a 1½ quart ungreased casserole dish. Stir dressing into melted butter and sprinkle over casserole. Bake, uncovered, at 350° for 30 minutes. Remove from oven and cover casserole dish for a few minutes before serving. Yield: 4 to 6 servings.

*Sherry Tuna Scallop

    1 (5½-ounce) package scalloped potato mix
    1 cup chopped onion
    3 tablespoons margarine, melted
    3 tablespoons all-purpose flour
       Salt and pepper
    1 cup cooking sherry
    2 (7-ounce) cans tuna, drained
    ½ cup shredded Cheddar cheese
    ½ cup mayonnaise
       Dash hot sauce
    1 teaspoon prepared mustard
       Paprika

Prepare potatoes as directed on package; add onion. Bake 20 minutes. Combine margarine, flour, and salt and pepper to taste; stir over low heat until bubbly. Add sherry, stirring constantly until mixture is smooth and thick. Fold in tuna. Pour tuna mixture over potatoes; stir to blend together. Combine cheese, mayonnaise, hot sauce, and mustard. Spread over tuna and potato mixture. Bake at 350° for 10 to 20 minutes. Sprinkle lightly with paprika. Yield: 6 servings.

*Tuna Bake

    ¼ cup finely chopped onion
    ¼ cup finely chopped green pepper
    2 tablespoons salad oil
    1 (3-ounce) can chow mein noodles
    1 (7-ounce) can tuna, drained and flaked
    1 (2-ounce) jar pimientos, drained and chopped
    ¼ cup finely chopped celery
    1 (10¾-ounce) can condensed golden mushroom soup
    ¼ cup milk
    ½ teaspoon salt
    ¼ teaspoon pepper

Sauté onion and green pepper in salad oil. Combine remaining ingredients; add onion and green pepper, and mix well. Place in a greased 1½-quart casserole. Cover and bake at 375° for 25 minutes. Remove cover; bake an additional 10 minutes. Yield: 4 servings.

*Skillet Macaroni and Cheese

¼ cup butter or margarine
1 cup chopped onion
1 tablespoon all-purpose flour
1½ teaspoons salt
¼ teaspoon oregano
1 (7- or 8-ounce) package elbow macaroni
3½ cups milk
2 cups shredded Cheddar cheese
Parsley

Melt butter in skillet; add onion and sauté until tender. Stir in flour, salt, and oregano; add macaroni and milk. Cover and bring to boil; reduce heat and simmer 15 minutes or until macaroni is tender, stirring occasionally. Add cheese and stir until cheese is melted (do not boil). Garnish with parsley. Yield: 6 to 8 servings.

Macaroni and Cheese

7 or 8 ounces elbow macaroni
3 tablespoons butter or margarine, divided
½ cup fine dry bread crumbs
1 tablespoon grated onion
1 tablespoon all-purpose flour
¾ teaspoon salt
⅓ teaspoon black pepper
¼ teaspoon dry mustard
2 cups milk
½ pound pasteurized process sharp American cheese, shredded
Paprika

Cook macaroni as directed on package; drain. Preheat frypan or electric skillet to 300°. Melt 2 tablespoons butter; add bread crumbs and brown, stirring constantly. Remove bread crumbs from skillet. Add remaining butter and melt. Set temperature at 240° and sauté onion. Blend in flour, salt, pepper, and mustard. Add milk gradually, stirring until smooth. Stir in three-fourths of the cheese. Turn dial to "off." Fold in drained macaroni, and mix lightly with a fork. Top with remaining cheese and bread crumbs. Sprinkle with paprika. Cover; open vent in skillet top and cook at simmering until bubbly and hot. Yield: 4 to 6 servings.

Hearty Bacon Casserole

1 pound sliced bacon
½ cup chopped onion
1 (8-ounce) package macaroni, cooked (5 cups cooked macaroni)
¾ cup shredded sharp cheese
1 (10¾-ounce) can condensed tomato soup
1 cup milk

Reserve 4 slices of bacon. Cut remaining bacon crosswise into ½-inch slices with a pair of kitchen shears. Fry bacon pieces until crisp; remove from pan. Cook onion in 2 tablespoons drippings until soft. Combine onion, crisp bacon, macaroni, cheese, soup, and milk. Mix lightly and pour into a greased 2-quart casserole. Place the reserved slices of bacon on top and bake at 375° for 25 to 30 minutes. Yield: 4 servings.

Ham and Asparagus Casserole

1 (10-ounce) package frozen cut asparagus
2 cups diced cooked ham
¼ cup shredded pasteurized process American cheese
2 tablespoons quick-cooking tapioca
2 tablespoons chopped green pepper
2 tablespoons chopped onion
1 tablespoons minced parsley
1 tablespoon lemon juice
2 hard-cooked eggs, sliced
½ cup milk
1 (10¾-ounce) can condensed cream of mushroom soup
2 tablespoons melted butter or margarine
½ cup coarse dry bread crumbs

Cook asparagus until tender. Drain thoroughly and arrange in an ungreased 1½-quart casserole. Combine ham, cheese, tapioca, green pepper, onion, parsley, and lemon juice. Cover asparagus with half of the ham mixture, then egg slices; top with remaining ham mixture. Combine milk with mushroom soup and pour over casserole. Mix melted butter with bread crumbs. Sprinkle over the top. Bake at 375° for 25 to 30 minutes or until crumbs are lightly browned. Yield: 5 to 6 servings.

*Ham and Egg Casserole

  1 *teaspoon chopped onion*
 ¼ *cup chopped green pepper*
 ¼ *cup butter, melted*
 ¼ *cup all-purpose flour*
 ½ *teaspoon salt*
 ⅛ *teaspoon pepper*
  1 *cup milk*
1½ *cups cubed cooked ham*
  4 *hard-cooked eggs, sliced*
  1 *cup condensed cream of mushroom soup*
  2 *cups buttered bread crumbs*

Sauté onion and green pepper in butter. Blend in flour, salt, and pepper. Add milk; heat and stir until smooth. Add ham. Layer ham mixture and egg slices in a 2-quart casserole. Repeat layers. Spread mushroom soup over casserole. Top with bread crumbs. Bake at 350° for 30 minutes. Yield: 6 to 8 servings.

Cheddar Chops Casserole

6 *pork chops, 1 inch thick*
2 *cups thin onion slices*
1 *cup chopped green pepper*
1 *cup uncooked regular white rice*
2 *cups water*
1 *teaspoon salt*
1 *(16-ounce) can tomatoes*
½ *cup water*
1 *teaspoon salt*
¼ *teaspoon black pepper*
6 *thin slices (about ½ pound) Cheddar cheese*

Trim fat from pork chops. Fry fat out in a large skillet. Add chops and brown slowly on both sides. Remove chops from skillet, and add onions and green pepper to skillet. Cook about 15 minutes or until onions are tender.

Cook rice in boiling salted water according to package directions. Place cooked rice in bottom of a greased shallow 9- x 11- x 2-inch baking dish. Top with onions and green pepper; arrange browned chops on top. Spoon tomatoes over chops; add ½ cup water, 1 teaspoon salt, and pepper. Cover dish with a lid or aluminum foil. Bake at 350° for 1 hour. Uncover, and add water if mixture has cooked dry. Lower oven temperature to 300°. Place slices of cheese on top of pork chops and bake at 300° for about 15 minutes or until cheese melts. Yield: 6 servings.

Vegetable-Pork Chop Casserole

2 *(16-ounce) cans green beans, drained*
2 *onions, sliced*
2 *potatoes, sliced*
1 *(17-ounce) can tomatoes*
   Salt and pepper
6 *pork chops*

Layer beans, onion, and potatoes in 13- x 9- x 2-inch pan. Repeat layers. Pour tomatoes over top; sprinkle with salt and pepper to taste. Place pork chops over tomatoes. Bake at 400° for 1 hour. After 30 minutes of cooking, baste meat and vegetables well. Yield: 6 servings.

*Ground Beef in Sour Cream

½ *pound egg noodles*
1 *pound ground beef*
¾ *teaspoon salt*
¼ *teaspoon pepper*
1 *green pepper, minced*
1 *tablespoon butter or margarine*
½ *cup commercial sour cream*
½ *cup cottage cheese*
2 *tablespoons chopped chives*
2 *tablespoons chopped parsley*
2 *tablespoons butter or margarine*

Cook noodles according to package directions; drain and set aside. Mix beef, salt, pepper, and green pepper; cook in butter until meat turns grey.

Combine noodles, sour cream, cottage cheese, chives, and parsley. In a greased 3-quart casserole, place a layer of the noodle mixture, then a layer of meat mixture. Alternate layers, with noodle layer on top. Dot with butter or margarine. Bake at 325° about 20 minutes. Yield: 4 to 6 servings.

*Baked Beef and Rice

1½ pounds ground beef
1 cup uncooked regular rice
1 small onion, chopped
2 tablespoons shortening
1½ teaspoons salt
½ teaspoon pepper
1 teaspoon paprika
1 (2-ounce) bottle stuffed olives, sliced
2 cups tomato juice
1½ cups boiling water
½ cup shredded Cheddar cheese

Brown ground beef, rice, and onion in shortening. Pour off drippings. Add salt, pepper, and paprika. Add sliced olives, tomato juice, and boiling water. Place in an ungreased 1½-quart baking dish. Cover tightly and bake at 300° for 1 hour. Uncover, sprinkle with cheese, and continue baking about 10 minutes or until cheese is melted. Yield: 6 servings.

*Meatball Casserole

1 pound ground beef
¼ cup chopped onion
¼ cup chopped green pepper
¼ teaspoon pepper
1 teaspoon salt
1 cup cracker crumbs
1 egg
1 cup milk
1 (10¾-ounce) can condensed cream of mushroom soup
⅓ cup all-purpose flour
1 tablespoon salad oil
½ cup chili sauce

Combine first 7 ingredients in a large mixing bowl. Add milk to soup and stir well. Add half this mixture to meat mixture and mix well. Form meat into balls; dip in flour and brown on all sides in hot oil. Place meatballs in a 2-quart casserole dish. Combine chili sauce and remaining soup mixture; pour over meatballs. (If you plan to freeze casserole, cool, cover, and freeze at this stage.) Bake at 350° for 30 minutes. Yield: 6 servings.

*Mañana Beef Dinner

2 pounds ground beef
1½ cups chopped onion
1½ cups chopped celery
1 medium-size green pepper, chopped
1 (10¾-ounce) can condensed tomato soup
1 (8-ounce) can tomato sauce
1 clove garlic, minced
2 to 3 teaspoons chili powder
1½ teaspoons salt
⅛ teaspoon pepper
1 (5-ounce) package instant mashed potato puffs
½ cup shredded Cheddar cheese

Brown ground beef, onion, celery, and green pepper; stir until vegetables are tender. Pour off drippings. Add soup, tomato sauce, garlic, chili powder, salt, and pepper. Pour into an ungreased 2½-quart casserole. Bake at 400° for 30 minutes. Prepare potatoes as directed on package. Spoon potatoes around edge of beef mixture; sprinkle with shredded cheese. Bake 10 minutes longer. Yield: 8 servings.

*Italian Meat Casserole

1 pound ground beef
½ cup chopped onion
1 clove garlic, minced
½ to 1 teaspoon oregano
½ teaspoon salt
1 (10¾-ounce) can condensed tomato soup
⅓ cup water
1 (5-ounce) package noodles, cooked and drained
1 cup shredded Cheddar cheese

Brown beef in skillet with onion, garlic, oregano, and salt. Combine in an ungreased 1½-quart casserole with soup, water, and cooked noodles. Sprinkle cheese over top, and bake at 350° for 30 minutes or until cheese is melted. Yield: 4 or 5 servings.

Mexican Casserole

2 pounds ground chuck
1 cup chopped onion
1 (12-ounce) can whole kernel corn, drained
1 (10¾-ounce) can condensed cream of celery soup
1 (10¾-ounce) can condensed cream of mushroom soup
1 cup commercial sour cream
Dash hot sauce
Salt and pepper
1 cup taco-flavored corn chips, divided
3 cups cooked noodles

Brown chuck and onion lightly. Add next 6 ingredients and half the corn chips. Mix well. Stir in noodles. Pour into a 2-quart casserole. Top with remaining corn chips. Cool in refrigerator; then freeze. When ready to serve, thaw overnight in the refrigerator and bake at 350° for 45 minutes. Yield: 6 servings.

*German Meat Casserole

3 large potatoes, thinly sliced
5 carrots, quartered
1 small onion, diced
2 tablespoons butter or margarine
1 pound lean ground beef
1 tablespoon catsup
1 (10¾-ounce) can condensed cream of mushroom soup
1 (4-ounce) can button mushrooms, drained
2 tablespoons butter or margarine
1 (3½-ounce) can French fried onion rings

Parboil potatoes and carrots for 20 minutes. Sauté onion in 2 tablespoons butter or margarine; add beef and cook until it turns gray. Alternate layers of beef-onion mixture and vegetables in a greased 2½-quart casserole. Combine catsup and soup and pour over casserole. Sauté mushrooms in 2 tablespoons butter or margarine and place on top of casserole. Sprinkle onion rings over mushrooms. Bake at 350° about 20 minutes or until onion rings are brown and crisp. Yield: 6 servings.

*Enchilada Casserole

2 pounds lean ground beef
3 small onions, chopped
Dash garlic powder
1 (4-ounce) can green chiles, chopped
1 dozen tortillas
1 (10-ounce) can enchilada sauce
½ pound shredded Cheddar cheese
1 (10¾-ounce) can condensed cream of mushroom soup

Combine ground beef, chopped onions, garlic powder, and chopped green chiles in a skillet. Simmer for about 20 minutes, stirring occasionally.

Dip 3 tortillas in enchilada sauce and place in the bottom of a shallow greased casserole. Add one-fourth of the meat mixture, spreading to form a thin layer. Add one-fourth of the shredded cheese, then one-fourth of the soup. Continue layers of tortillas, meat, cheese, and soup until all ingredients have been used. Pour any remaining enchilada sauce over the top. Bake at 450° for 20 minutes. Yield: 8 servings.

*Favorite Casserole

12 slices bacon, diced
2 pounds ground beef
1 medium onion, chopped
2 (5-ounce) packages noodles, cooked and drained
2 (10¾-ounce) cans condensed tomato soup
2 (10¾-ounce) cans condensed cream of mushroom soup
1 (1-pound) can English peas, drained
1 cup buttered cracker crumbs
1½ cups shredded sharp Cheddar cheese

Fry bacon, ground beef, and onion together until lightly browned. Drain off drippings. Mix noodles with ground beef mixture, soups, and peas. Place in two 3½-quart casseroles. Top with cracker crumbs and add cheese for topping. Bake at 300° to 325° for 45 minutes. One casserole may be frozen for later use. Yield: 10 to 12 servings.

*Hamburger-Corn Casserole

- 1½ pounds lean ground beef
- 1 cup chopped onion
- 1 (12-ounce) can whole kernel corn, drained
- 1 (10¾-ounce) can condensed cream of chicken soup
- 1 (10¾-ounce) can condensed cream of mushroom soup
- 1 cup commercial sour cream
- ¼ cup chopped pimiento
- ¾ teaspoon salt
- ½ teaspoon monosodium glutamate
- ¼ teaspoon pepper
- 3 cups cooked noodles, drained
- 3 tablespoons melted butter or margarine
- 1 cup soft bread crumbs

Lightly brown ground beef; add onion and cook until tender but not brown. Add drained corn, soups, sour cream, pimiento, salt, monosodium glutamate, and pepper. Mix well; then stir in noodles. Taste and add more seasoning if needed.

Put into ungreased 2½-quart casserole, seal, and freeze. To serve, thaw and add melted butter to bread crumbs and sprinkle over top of casserole. Bake at 350° for 30 minutes or until hot. Yield: 10 servings.

*Beef and Squash Casserole

- 4 cups cooked yellow crookneck squash
- 1 pound lean ground beef
- ½ cup chopped onion
- 1 tablespoon margarine
- 2 cups cooked rice
- 1 teaspoon salt
- 1 (10¾-ounce) can condensed cream of mushroom soup
- 2 cups buttered bread crumbs

Drain cooked squash. Brown ground beef and onion in margarine and add to cooked rice. Season with salt. Place half of squash in an ungreased 2- to 2½-quart baking dish. Cover squash with beef mixture. Add a second layer of squash. Cover with soup and sprinkle with bread crumbs. Bake at 350° for 35 to 40 minutes. Yield: 8 servings.

*Beef-Corn Casserole

- 1 pound lean ground beef
- 3 tablespoons butter or margarine
- Seasoned salt to taste
- 1 cup uncooked regular rice
- 1 cup whole kernel corn
- ½ cup chopped onion
- ½ cup minced green pepper
- 1 tablespoon Worcestershire sauce
- 1 teaspoon prepared mustard
- 1 teaspoon sugar
- ½ teaspoon paprika
- 2 cups cooked tomatoes
- ½ cup buttered bread crumbs
- ½ cup chopped pimiento
- 3 slices bacon

Lightly brown beef in butter; add seasoned salt to taste. Remove beef from skillet and place in a greased 2-quart casserole; add rice, corn, onion, and green pepper and mix well. Combine Worcestershire sauce, mustard, sugar, paprika, and tomatoes. Add more salt, if needed. Pour tomato mixture over beef mixture. Top with bread crumbs, pimiento, and bacon. Bake, uncovered, at 350° for 30 to 40 minutes. Yield: 6 servings.

Beef-Noodle Casserole

- 3 pounds lean ground beef
- 2 eggs, beaten
- 1½ cups uncooked oats (regular or quick-cooking)
- 1 clove garlic, crushed
- 1 medium onion, minced
- 1½ teaspoons basil
- 2 teaspoons oregano
- 2 teaspoons salt
- ½ teaspoon pepper
- ½ cup shortening
- 6 cups water
- 1 (10¾-ounce) can condensed tomato soup
- 2 (8-ounce) cans tomato sauce
- 2 beef bouillon cubes
- 1 bay leaf
- 2 (5-ounce) packages thin noodles

Combine ground beef, eggs, oats, garlic, onion, basil, oregano, salt, and pepper in a large bowl. Mix well; form into 48 meatballs. Brown meatballs in hot shortening and set aside. Combine water, tomato soup, tomato sauce, bouillon cubes, and bay leaf in large heavy Dutch oven. Add noodles; bring mixture to a boil. Lower heat and simmer, uncovered, about 30 to 45 minutes, stirring occasionally. Serve meatballs over the noodles. Yield: 12 servings.

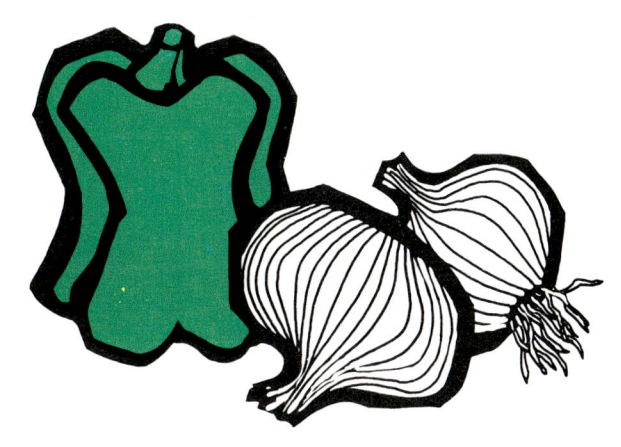

*Hamburger-Noodle Bake

2 tablespoons butter or margarine
1 pound lean ground beef
1 clove garlic, minced (optional)
1 teaspoon salt
Dash pepper
1 teaspoon sugar
2 (8-ounce) cans tomato sauce
1 (5-ounce) package noodles
6 scallions, chopped
1 (3-ounce) package cream cheese
1 cup commercial sour cream
½ cup shredded pasteurized process American cheese

Melt butter in skillet; add hamburger and brown. Add garlic, salt, pepper, sugar, and tomato sauce. Cover and cook slowly for 15 to 20 minutes. Cook noodles according to package directions; drain.

Put a layer of drained noodles in the bottom of a 2-quart baking dish. Mix chopped scallions, cream cheese, and sour cream and spread half this mixture and repeat layers. Sprinkle top with cheese, and bake uncovered at 350° for 20 minutes or until cheese is bubbly. Yield: 8 servings.

*Ground Beef Casserole

1 pound ground beef
1 clove garlic, minced
1 teaspoon salt
1 teaspoon sugar
⅛ teaspoon pepper
2 (15-ounce) cans tomato sauce
1 (5-ounce) package small noodles
5 scallions or green onions
1 (3-ounce) package cream cheese
1 cup commercial sour cream
½ cup shredded Cheddar cheese

Brown beef and pour off excess drippings. Add garlic, salt, sugar, pepper, and tomato sauce. Cover and simmer about 15 minutes.

Cook noodles and drain. Finely chop scallions, including tops; mix with cream cheese and sour cream. In a buttered 13- x 9- x 2-inch casserole place a layer of noodles, meat sauce, sour cream mixture, and shredded cheese; repeat, ending with cheese. Bake at 350° about 20 minutes. Yield: 8 servings.

*Beef-Zucchini Casserole

1½ pounds zucchini squash
1 pound lean ground beef
½ cup chopped onions
1 teaspoon seasoned salt or garlic salt
1 teaspoon ground oregano
2 cups cooked regular rice
1 pint small curd creamed cottage cheese
1 (10¾-ounce) can condensed cream of mushroom soup
Buttered bread crumbs or cracker crumbs

Cut or slice squash (do not peel) into 1-inch pieces and cook in boiling salted water until barely tender. Drain well. Brown beef and onion; drain off excess fat. Add seasonings and cooked rice to beef mixture. Place half of squash in a 3-quart casserole; spread beef mixture over squash. Cover with cottage cheese, then with the rest of the squash. Spread mushroom soup over all. Sprinkle crumbs over top. Bake at 350° for 35 to 40 minutes. Yield: 6 to 8 servings.

*South's Favorite Casserole

12 slices bacon, diced
2 pounds ground beef
1 medium onion, chopped
2 (5-ounce) packages noodles, cooked and drained
2 (10¾-ounce) cans condensed tomato soup
2 (10½-ounce) cans condensed cream of mushroom soup
1 (16-ounce) can English peas, drained
1 cup buttered cracker crumbs
1½ cups shredded sharp Cheddar cheese

Fry bacon, ground beef, and onion until lightly browned. Drain off all excess fat. Mix noodles with beef mixture, soups, and peas. Place in two 3½-quart casseroles. Top with cracker crumbs that have been lightly sautéed in melted butter, and sprinkle cheese over all. Bake at 300° to 325° for 45 minutes. One casserole may be frozen for later use. Yield: 10 to 12 servings.

Johnny Marzetti

6 medium-size onions, chopped
1½ pounds ground chuck
1½ teaspoons salt
¼ teaspoon garlic salt
⅛ teaspoon pepper
¼ cup butter or margarine
1 pound shell macaroni
¼ cup butter or margarine
4 cups shredded sharp Cheddar cheese, divided
2 (8-ounce) cans tomato sauce
2 (3-ounce) cans mushroom pieces
¼ cup Burgundy

Sauté onion, ground chuck, salt, garlic salt, and pepper in ¼ cup butter for about 15 minutes, stirring often with fork to prevent meat mixture from sticking.
Cook macaroni according to directions on package; drain. Toss macaroni with ¼ cup butter and place in two 2-quart casseroles. Add 2½ cups cheese to meat mixture, and stir until cheese melts. Add 1 can tomato sauce and the mushrooms, and mix well. Pour mixture over macaroni, and top with the other can of tomato sauce and remaining cheese. Cool quickly. Wrap for freezing, or bake at 350° for 40 to 60 minutes. Pour wine on top before serving. Yield: 8 servings.

To thaw frozen casserole: The day before serving, remove casserole from freezer and thaw in refrigerator. Bake according to previous directions.

*Chili Con Carne Casserole

1 pound ground beef
1 tablespoon shortening
1 (1-pound) can kidney beans, undrained
1 (10¾-ounce) can condensed tomato soup
1 teaspoon salt
2 teaspoons chili powder
¼ cup instant minced onion

Brown meat in shortening. Add kidney beans, tomato soup, salt, chili powder, and instant minced onion. Mix well. Turn into an ungreased 1-quart casserole. Bake at 350° for 40 minutes. Serve hot as a main dish. Yield: 6 servings.

Lamb Risotto Casserole

½ lemon
4 thick lamb chops
¾ cup uncooked brown rice
1 (10½-ounce) can consommé
2 carrots, julienned
10 small pearl onions
1 cup Sauterne
¼ teaspoon marjoram
⅛ teaspoon oregano
½ teaspoon salt
Dash black pepper

Squeeze lemon over chops; set aside. Meanwhile, put brown rice, consommé, carrots, onions, and Sauterne in a large casserole or baking dish. Arrange lamb chops on top.
Cover and bake at 350° for 30 minutes. Remove from oven, add seasonings, and stir. Return to oven and bake 30 minutes longer. Yield: 4 servings.

casseroles 101

Liver and Rice Casserole

  1 *pound sliced liver, cut into 1-inch squares*
¼ *cup chopped green pepper*
½ *cup chopped celery*
  1 *medium-size onion, diced*
  2 *tablespoons shortening*
  1 *(8-ounce) can tomato sauce*
  1 *(16-ounce) can tomatoes*
1½ *teaspoons salt*
½ *teaspoon pepper*
⅛ *teaspoon thyme*
  3 *cups cooked regular rice*
½ *cup shredded sharp Cheddar cheese*

Cook liver, green pepper, celery, and onion in shortening until liver is very lightly browned and vegetables are tender. Pour off drippings. Add tomato sauce, tomatoes, salt, pepper, thyme, and rice. Pour into a greased 1½-quart casserole. Sprinkle shredded cheese over the top and bake at 350° for 20 to 30 minutes. Yield: 4 to 5 servings.

*Individual Turkey Casseroles

⅓ *cup butter*
¼ *cup all-purpose flour*
1½ *teaspoons salt*
⅛ *teaspoon pepper*
1½ *teaspoons curry powder*
½ *teaspoon ground ginger*
  3 *cups milk*
  1 *tablespoon soy sauce*
  1 *(1-pound) can Chinese vegetables, drained*
  2 *cups sliced cooked turkey chunks*
  2 *cups cooked rice*
  1 *(3-ounce) can chow mein noodles*

Melt butter in saucepan. Blend in flour, salt, pepper, curry powder, and ginger. Add milk and soy sauce; cook, stirring constantly, until sauce is thickened and smooth. Fold in vegetables and turkey. Place an equal amount of rice in six 10-ounce individual casseroles; top each with an equal amount of turkey mixture and noodles. Bake at 375° until hot and bubbly, about 15 minutes. Yield: 6 servings.

*Chicken-Corn Bread Casserole

  4 *cups crumbled corn bread*
¼ *cup chopped green pepper*
¼ *cup chopped onion*
¼ *cup chopped celery*
1½ *cups coarsely chopped cooked chicken*
  1 *(10¾-ounce) can condensed cream of chicken soup*
1½ *cups chicken broth*

Combine corn bread, green pepper, onion, and celery; mix well. Place half of mixture in a 2-quart baking dish. Spread chicken over corn bread layer.

Combine soup and chicken broth; pour over chicken. Place remaining corn bread mixture over chicken; press mixture down. Set aside 20 minutes. Bake at 350° for 45 minutes. Yield: 8 to 10 servings.

*Chicken Enchilada Casserole

  1 *(4- to 5-pound) chicken*
  1 *large onion, diced*
  2 *cups chicken broth*
Salt and pepper to taste
Crushed garlic (optional)
  2 *(3- or 4-ounce) cans chopped green chiles*
  1 *(10¾-ounce) can cream of mushroom soup*
  1 *(10¾-ounce) can cream of celery soup*
1½ *to 2 dozen tortillas*
  1 *pound shredded Cheddar cheese*

Simmer chicken until tender. Remove from water, cool, and remove meat from bones. Cut in small pieces. Reserve broth in which chicken was cooked.

Cook onion until slightly wilted in a small amount of fat removed from cooled chicken broth. Add chicken broth, salt, pepper, garlic, and chopped chicken. Add chopped chiles, mushroom and celery soups and heat thoroughly.

Cut tortillas in quarters or leave whole. In a 4- to 6-quart casserole dish arrange layers of tortillas, chicken mixture, and shredded cheese. Cover; bake at 325° for 35 minutes. Yield: 8 to 12 servings.

*Party Chicken Casserole

1 chicken (3½ to 5 pounds), disjointed
1 onion, sliced
1 teaspoon salt
1 bay leaf
3 or 4 peppercorns
1 (6-ounce) can sliced mushrooms, with liquid
1 cup evaporated milk (undiluted)
½ cup butter or margarine
½ cup all-purpose flour
1 teaspoon salt
½ teaspoon turmeric
Dash pepper
¼ teaspoon oregano
½ cup shredded pasteurized process American cheese, divided
½ cup slivered or whole blanched almonds
½ cup slivered toasted almonds

Cover chicken and onion with water in large saucepan. Add salt, bay leaf, and peppercorns, and bring slowly to a boil. Reduce heat and simmer for 1 hour or until chicken is tender. Cool chicken in broth; then remove skin and bones. Cut chicken into bite-size pieces. Strain and reserve broth.

Measure liquid from drained mushrooms; add enough chicken broth to make 3 cups. Add evaporated milk. Melt butter or margarine; blend in flour, 1 teaspoon salt, turmeric, and pepper. Add chicken broth mixture and cook over low heat, stirring constantly, until thickened. Add oregano and ¼ cup cheese; then stir until cheese melts. Add mushrooms, chicken, and ½ cup blanched almonds. Put into a 3-quart casserole, and sprinkle with toasted slivered almonds and remaining cheese. Bake at 350° until top is golden brown and sauce is bubbly. Yield: 6 to 8 servings.

*Chicken-Noodle-Almond Casserole

4 large chicken breasts
2 (10¾-ounce) cans condensed cream of chicken soup
½ soup can chicken broth
4 to 5 stalks celery, chopped
¼ green pepper, chopped
¼ medium onion, chopped
1 tablespoon butter or margarine
1 (4-ounce) can mushrooms, with liquid
8 onion tops, cut into ½-inch pieces
3 tablespoons cooking sherry
1 (5-ounce) package noodles, cooked and drained
¼ to ½ cup slivered almonds
Buttered bread crumbs
Paprika

Cook chicken breasts; drain, cool, and cut into bite-size pieces. Heat soup and broth together and set aside. Cook celery, green pepper, and onion in butter until almost tender. Combine soup, cooked vegetables, mushrooms, onion tops, and cooking sherry.

Place a layer of cooked noodles and a layer of chopped chicken in a 2-quart casserole; cover with soup mixture and sprinkle with almonds. Repeat layers until all ingredients have been used. Cover top with buttered bread crumbs and sprinkle with paprika. Bake at 350° about 30 minutes or until mixture bubbles. Yield: 8 servings.

Sherried Chicken

3 whole chicken breasts, cut in half
Salt and pepper
¼ cup melted butter or margarine
1 (10¾-ounce) can condensed cream of chicken soup
½ cup sherry or Sauterne
½ cup sliced water chestnuts
1 (4-ounce) can sliced mushrooms, drained and sauteed
2 tablespoons chopped green pepper
¼ teaspoon thyme
Hot cooked rice (optional)

Sprinkle chicken breasts with salt and pepper; brown slowly in butter. Place chicken breasts in a shallow baking dish; reserve drippings.

Add soup to drippings; slowly add wine, and stir until smooth. Add remaining ingredients except rice, and heat to boiling; pour over chicken. Cover and bake at 350° for 25 minutes. Uncover; bake 25 additional minutes or until tender. Serve over rice. Yield: 6 servings.

Chicken-Wild Rice Casserole

 3 *pounds chicken pieces*
 5 *cups water, divided*
 ½ *cup dry sherry*
 1 *medium onion, quartered*
 ½ *teaspoon curry powder*
 2 *teaspoons salt*
 1 *stalk celery with leaves*
 1 *pound fresh mushrooms, sliced*
 ¼ *cup butter or margarine*
 2 *(6-ounce) packages long grain and wild rice*
 1 *(10¾-ounce) can condensed cream of mushroom soup*
 1 *cup commercial sour cream*

Combine chicken, 2 cups water, sherry, onion, curry, salt, and celery; simmer 1 hour. Cool; remove chicken. Strain and reserve broth. Remove skin, and bone chicken; cut into bite-size pieces. Set aside.

Sauté mushrooms in butter; drain and set aside. Cook rice in reserved chicken broth and remaining water until tender; do not drain. Combine soup, sour cream, chicken, rice, and mushrooms. Pour into a 4-quart casserole; bake at 350° for 1 hour. (Casserole will be soupy, but will thicken as it cooks.)

To freeze, pour unbaked chicken mixture into a 4-quart casserole lined with heavy-duty aluminum foil. Cool; seal foil packet securely, label, and freeze. Remove foil packet from casserole dish; store in freezer. To serve, place frozen block in a 4-quart casserole and thaw overnight in refrigerator. Fold foil back and bake at 350° for 1 hour. Yield: 10 servings.

*Swiss-Chicken Casserole

 4 *cups diced cooked chicken*
 2 *cups diced celery*
 2 *cups toasted bread cubes*
 1 *cup salad dressing or mayonnaise*
 ½ *cup milk*
 ¼ *cup chopped onion*
 1 *teaspoon salt*
  Dash pepper
 1 *(8-ounce) package Swiss cheese, cut in thin strips*
 ¼ *cup slivered almonds*

Combine all ingredients except almonds. Spoon into a greased 2-quart casserole; sprinkle with almonds. Cover and bake at 350° for 30 to 40 minutes. Yield: 6 servings.

Note: This casserole can be made the day before serving. Omit baking, and refrigerate overnight; then bake, covered, at 350° for 50 minutes. Uncover and continue baking 10 minutes.

*Chicken Spaghetti

 1 *(3-to 4-pound) hen*
 1 *(12-ounce) package thin spaghetti*
 1 *green pepper, chopped*
 1 *medium onion, chopped*
 ½ *cup celery, chopped*
 ½ *cup sliced, pitted olives*
 ½ *cup sliced green olives*
 2 *tablespoons margarine*
 1 *tablespoon sherry*
 2 *(10¾-ounce) can condensed cream of mushroom soup*
 1 *cup chicken broth*
 ½ *cup grated Parmesan cheese*

Cook hen until tender; bone and cut into bite-size pieces. Cook spaghetti according to package directions; drain and set aside.

Sauté green pepper, onion, celery, and olives in margarine and set aside.

Mix sherry with soup. Stir in cooked spaghetti. Add enough chicken broth to make a smooth consistency. Add the sautèed ingredients and the cooked chicken. Put into a greased 2½-quart casserole dish. Sprinkle Parmesan cheese on top. Bake at 350° for 20 minutes. Yield: 8 to 10 servings.

Chicken-Shrimp Tetrazzini

    2 *whole (4 half) chicken breasts*
    1 *(5-ounce) package vermicelli*
    1 *small onion, chopped*
    1 *clove garlic, chopped*
  ½ *green pepper, chopped*
    1 *cup chopped celery*
  ¼ *cup margarine*
    1 *teaspoon chopped parsley*
    1 *tablespoon Worcestershire sauce*
    1 *(4½-ounce) can shrimp*
    1 *(10¾-ounce) can condensed cream of mushroom soup*
    1 *(8-ounce) can tomato sauce*
       Shredded Cheddar cheese

Put chicken in pan, cover with water, and cook until tender; cool. Remove meat from bones and cut into bite-size pieces. Cook vermicelli for half the time given on package directions.

Sauté onion, garlic, green pepper, and celery in margarine. Add parsley and Worcestershire sauce. Stir in chicken, vermicelli, shrimp, soup, and tomato sauce. Cool and spoon into a 2½-quart casserole; seal and freeze. To serve, thaw in refrigerator overnight. Top with shredded Cheddar cheese and bake at 325° for 45 minutes to 1 hour. Yield: 4 to 6 servings.

*Continental Chicken Casserole

    3 *tablespoons butter or margarine*
    6 *tablespoons all-purpose flour*
    2 *cups chicken broth*
    1 *cup half-and-half*
    1 *teaspoon prepared mustard*
  ½ *teaspoon salt*
      Dash pepper
  ⅛ *teaspoon ground allspice*
  ⅛ *teaspoon ground nutmeg*
  ½ *teaspoon sugar*
  ⅛ *teaspoon cayenne pepper*
  ½ *teaspoon paprika*
  ½ *teaspoon seasoned salt*
  ¼ *cup dry sherry*
    4 *hard-cooked eggs, cubed*
    4 *cups cooked chicken, chopped*
      Buttered bread crumbs

Melt butter in saucepan and stir in flour until smooth. Over low heat, slowly blend in broth, then half-and-half. Cook over medium heat until thick, stirring constantly. Combine all seasonings; then blend into sauce. Stir in wine; fold in eggs and chicken. Turn into buttered 3-quart casserole, top with crumbs, and bake at 350° for 30 minutes. (Leftover turkey may be substituted for chicken.) Yield: 10 to 12 servings.

*Chicken Noodle Casserole

    1 *(10¾-ounce) can condensed cream of chicken soup*
  ⅓ *cup commercial sour cream*
  ⅓ *cup water*
    1 *cup (5-ounce can) diced cooked chicken*
    2 *tablespoons chopped pimiento*
    1 *tablespoon sherry*
    2 *cups (about 5 ounces uncooked) cooked noodles*
      Water chestnuts, sliced
      Paprika

Combine all ingredients except water chestnuts and paprika in a 1½-quart casserole. Bake at 350° for 30 minutes. About halfway through the cooking, cover top with water chestnuts and sprinkle with paprika. (Cream of mushroom soup may be substituted for cream of chicken soup. If so, cover the top with sliced mushrooms instead of water chestnuts.) Yield: 4 servings.

*Chicken-Green Noodle Casserole

    1 *(3½-pound) chicken*
    1 *cup chopped green pepper*
    1 *cup chopped onion*
    1 *cup chopped celery*
  ½ *cup melted margarine*
  ½ *pound pasteurized process American cheese, cut into cubes*
    1 *(6-ounce) can sliced mushrooms*
    1 *(10¾-ounce) can cream of mushroom soup*
    1 *(5-ounce) package green noodles*
    1 *cup cheese crackers, crushed*

Put chicken in large saucepan. Cover with water and simmer until chicken is done. Reserve stock. Cool chicken, remove meat from bones, and cut into bite-size pieces.

Sauté green pepper, onion, and celery in margarine until tender. Add cheese and stir gently until cheese is melted. Add mushrooms and chicken, blending well; then stir in soup. Mix well.

Boil noodles in chicken stock. Drain and combine with chicken mixture. Put into a greased 2-quart casserole and top with crushed cheese crackers. Cool; seal and freeze. To serve, thaw and heat. Yield: 8 servings.

*Company Casserole

    8 hard-cooked eggs
    ¼ cup melted butter
    ½ teaspoon Worcestershire sauce
    ¼ teaspoon prepared mustard
    1 teaspoon finely chopped parsley
    1 teaspoon chopped chives
    ⅓ cup finely chopped cooked ham
    3 tablespoons butter
    3 tablespoons all-purpose flour
    1 cup chicken broth
    ¾ cup milk
       Dash salt and pepper
    1 cup shredded pasteurized process American
       cheese

Cut hard-cooked eggs in half lengthwise; remove and mash yolks. Mix yolks with ¼ cup melted butter, Worcestershire sauce, mustard, parsley, chives, and ham. Fill whites with this mixture.

Arrange filled egg halves in a greased, flat 1½-to 2-quart baking dish.

Melt butter in saucepan; blend in flour and cook until bubbly. Add chicken broth, milk, and seasonings. Cook over low heat, stirring constantly, until mixture is smooth and thickened throughout. Pour sauce over egg halves. Sprinkle with shredded cheese. Bake at 350° for 20 minutes or until cheese is melted. Yield: 4 to 6 servings.

*True Grits Casserole

Prepare 4 servings of grits, but do not add salt to the cooking water. Cook only 15 minutes, or half the prescribed cooking time. Stir in about ¼ cup butter, melted. Turn into a greased 1-quart casserole and mix in the following:

    ¼ pound sharp Cheddar cheese, shredded
    ½ cup shredded beef or chopped ham
    1 teaspoon Worcesterhire sauce
       Dash garlic salt
       Freshly ground black pepper

After mixing, place a large dollop of butter on top. Bake for 15 to 20 minutes at 350° Serve as a main dish for lunch or dinner or for brunch with scrambled eggs. Yield: 4 servings.

*Southern Grits Casserole

    1½ cups regular grits
     4 cups boiling water
    1½ teaspoons salt
     ½ teaspoon grated orange rind
     6 tablespoons butter or margarine
    1½ cups orange juice
     5 eggs, slightly beaten
        Orange slices
        Sugar

Pour grits into boiling water; add salt and orange rind. Stir grits constantly until mixture is thickened but not dry. Remove from heat; add margarine and orange juice, stirring until well blended. Gently stir in eggs. Spoon into a 2½-quart casserole, and bake at 350° for 55 minutes or until knife comes out clean when inserted 1 inch from middle of casserole. Garnish with fresh orange slices and sprinkle with sugar. Yield: 6 to 8 servings.

Baked Eggs New Orleans

2 teaspoons instant minced onion
1 tablespoon water
2 tablespoons finely chopped green pepper
2 tablespoons finely chopped celery
¼ cup butter or margarine
¼ cup all-purpose flour
½ teaspoon salt
1⅓ cups half-and-half
¼ cup Chablis or other white dinner wine
1 cup cleaned, cooked shrimp
6 eggs
Salt and pepper
Buttered bread crumbs

Measure instant minced onion into water. Cook green pepper and celery in butter until tender-crisp; add onion and cook until vegetables are soft but not browned. Blend in flour and ½ teaspoon salt. Slowly stir in half-and-half; cook and stir until mixture boils and thickens. Stir in wine and cook a few minutes longer.

Add shrimp and spoon into 6 (6-ounce) custard cups or individual baking dishes. Break an egg into each filled cup; sprinkle with salt, pepper, and crumbs. Bake at 350° just until eggs are set but still soft, about 15 minutes. Yield: 6 servings.

*Baked Deviled Egg Casserole

6 hard-cooked eggs
2 teaspoons prepared mustard
3 tablespoons commercial sour cream
¼ teaspoon salt
2 tablespoons margarine
½ cup chopped green pepper
⅓ cup chopped onion
¼ cup chopped pimiento
1 (10¾-ounce) can condensed cream of mushroom soup
¾ cup commercial sour cream
½ cup shredded Cheddar cheese

Cut eggs in half lengthwise; remove yolks. Mash together the yolks, mustard, 3 tablespoons sour cream, and salt. Fill whites with yolk mixture.

Melt margarine in large skillet; sauté green pepper and onion until tender. Remove from heat; stir in pimiento, soup, and ¾ cup sour cream. Place half the soup mixture in a 1½-quart shallow baking dish; arrange eggs, cut side up in single layer in dish. Pour remaining soup mixture over top; sprinkle with cheese. Bake at 350° for 20 minutes or until heated through. Casserole may be assembled in advance; refrigerate until ready to bake. Yield: 12 servings.

Egg Casserole

6 hard-cooked eggs
¼ cup finely chopped celery
1 tablespoon mayonnaise
1 teaspoon prepared mustard
6 slices cooked ham
1 (10¾-ounce) can condensed cream of mushroom soup
⅓ cup milk
½ cup shredded Cheddar cheese
¼ cup crushed potato chips
Sliced olives

Slice eggs in half and remove yolks. Mash yolks and combine with celery, mayonnaise, and mustard. Refill whites with yolk mixture; put halves together again. Wrap each egg in ham slice and place in shallow baking dish. Combine soup and milk; pour over ham rolls. Sprinkle with cheese and potato chips. Top with sliced olives. Bake at 350° for 30 minutes. Yield: 6 servings

*Hominy and Tomato Casserole

1 (16-ounce) can tomatoes
1 (29-ounce) can hominy, drained
1 tablespoon butter
¼ cup cubed pasteurized process cheese spread
Salt and pepper

Combine tomatoes, hominy, butter, and cheese. Season to taste with salt and pepper. Pour into a well-greased 2-quart baking dish. Bake at 400° for 45 minutes. Yield: 8 servings.

Sweet Potato-Nuts Casserole

    3 *cups cooked mashed sweet potatoes*
  ½ *cup sugar*
  2 *eggs, beaten*
  ½ *teaspoon salt*
  ¼ *cup margarine, melted*
  ½ *cup milk*
1½ *teaspoons vanilla extract*
  ½ *cup firmly packed brown sugar*
  ⅓ *cup all-purpose flour*
  1 *cup chopped nuts*
  3 *tablespoons margarine, melted*

Combine potatoes, sugar, eggs, salt, ¼ cup margarine, milk, and vanilla. Spoon into an ungreased 1- to 1½-quart baking dish. Combine brown sugar, flour, nuts, and 3 tablespoons margarine; spread over sweet potato mixture. Bake at 350° for 35 minutes. Yield: 8 servings.

*Potato Patch Casserole

  1 *pound ground beef*
  ½ *cup chopped onion*
  1 *egg, beaten*
  ¼ *cup bread crumbs*
  1 *teaspoon salt*
  ¼ *teaspoon black pepper*
  ¼ *teaspoon celery salt*
     Salad oil
  5 *cups sliced potatoes*
  1 *(10-ounce) package frozen peas and carrots, partially thawed*
  1 *teaspoon salt*
     Dash pepper
1½ *cups milk*
  1 *(1½-ounce) package white sauce mix*
  ½ *pound pasteurized process American cheese, cubed*

Combine ground beef, onion, egg, bread crumbs, and seasonings. Mix well. Shape into 10 meatballs; brown in salad oil. Combine potatoes, peas and carrots, salt, and pepper. Gradually add milk to sauce mix and bring to a boil, stirring constantly. Reduce heat and cook until thickened; stir in cheese and heat until melted. Arrange meatballs in greased shallow 3-quart casserole dish. Add potato mixture; cover with cheese sauce. Bake at 375° for 45 minutes or until potatoes are done. Yield: 5 to 6 servings.

*Sweet Potato Casserole

  2 *cups cooked, mashed sweet potatoes*
  ½ *cup light or dark corn syrup*
  1 *teaspoon grated lemon rind*
  1 *teaspoon salt*
     Dash ground nutmeg
     Dash pepper
  3 *egg yolks, well beaten*
  3 *egg whites, stiffly beaten*

Combine sweet potatoes, corn syrup, lemon rind, salt, nutmeg, pepper, and egg yolks. Fold in stiffly beaten egg whites. Spoon into an ungreased 1½-quart baking dish. Set dish in a pan and fill pan with hot water almost to top of dish. Bake at 350° until knife inserted in center of casserole comes out clean, about 1¼ hours. Yield: 6 servings.

Scalloped Potatoes and Ham

  1 *(10¾-ounce) can condensed cream of celery soup*
  ½ *cup milk*
     Generous dash pepper
  1 *teaspoon salt*
  3 *cups thinly sliced potatoes*
1½ *cups diced cooked ham*
  ½ *cup thinly sliced onion*
  ½ *cup shredded Cheddar cheese*
     Paprika

Combine soup, milk, pepper, and salt. Set aside. Place a layer of sliced potatoes in a 1½-quart ungreased casserole. Add a layer of ham, then a layer of onion slices; repeat until all have been used. Pour soup mixture over all. Cover and bake at 375° for 1 hour. Uncover, sprinkle shredded cheese on top, and add a dash of paprika. Bake an additional 15 minutes or until potatoes are tender. Yield: 4 servings.

Rice-Broccoli Casserole

½ cup chopped onion
½ cup chopped celery
2 tablespoons shortening
1 cup uncooked regular rice
1 (10-ounce) package frozen chopped broccoli
1 (10¾-ounce) can condensed cream of mushroom soup
1 (10¾-ounce) can condensed cream of chicken soup
1 (4-ounce) jar cheese spread

Sauté onion and celery in shortening until soft. Cook rice and broccoli separately. Mix all ingredients together in a 2-quart greased baking dish. Bake at 375° for 10 minutes before serving. (This may be prepared in advance and stored in refrigerator; bring to room temperature before baking.) Yield: 6 servings.

*Baked Ratatouille Casserole

2 large onions, sliced
2 large cloves garlic, minced
1 medium eggplant, cut in ½-inch cubes
6 medium zucchini, thickly sliced
2 green peppers, seeded and cut in chunks
4 large tomatoes, cut in chunks
2 teaspoons salt
1 teaspoon basil
½ cup minced parsley
4 tablespoons olive oil
Salt to taste

Layer onions, garlic, eggplant, zucchini, peppers, and tomatoes in a 3- to 4-quart ungreased casserole. Sprinkle a little of the salt, basil, and parsley between each layer. Drizzle olive oil over the top layer. Cover and bake at 350° for 3 hours. Baste the top occasionally with some of the liquid. If it becomes soupy, uncover during the last hour of baking to let the juices cook down.

Mix gently after removing from the oven. Add salt to taste. This may be served hot, cold, or reheated, and is good to serve as a buffet dish for a crowd. Yield: 12 to 15 generous servings.

*Royal Zucchini Parmesan

1 pound ground beef
2 medium-size onions, chopped
2 tablespoons salad oil
1 (16-ounce) can tomatoes
1 (8-ounce) can tomato sauce
1 (6-ounce) can tomato paste
1 green pepper, chopped
1 cup shredded Cheddar cheese
½ teaspoon oregano
1 teaspoon salt
¼ teaspoon pepper
¼ teaspoon garlic salt
4 medium-size zucchini, cut into ¼-inch slices
½ cup grated Parmesan cheese

Sauté beef and onion in salad oil until meat is brown and crumbly. Add tomatoes, sauce, paste, and green pepper. Simmer for 10 minutes, stirring occasionally. Blend in Cheddar cheese, oregano, salt, pepper, and garlic salt; add zucchini. Simmer another 10 minutes. Put into an ungreased 3-quart casserole and sprinkle with Parmesan cheese. Bake at 350° for 45 minutes. Yield: 6 to 8 servings.

*Eggplant Casserole

2 large eggplants
¾ cup soft bread crumbs
2 teaspoons grated onion
2 tablespoons catsup
1 teaspoon salt
⅛ teaspoon pepper
Dash Worcestershire sauce
2 beaten eggs
2 tablespoons butter or margarine
2 tablespoons all-purpose flour
¾ cup milk
1 cup cubed Cheddar cheese

Boil peeled and sliced eggplant in water until well cooked. Drain, mash, and mix with bread crumbs, onion, catsup, salt, pepper, Worcestershire sauce, and eggs. Melt butter, stir in flour, and add milk. Cook until mixture thickens. Add to eggplant mixture. Place in a greased 1½-quart casserole, sprinkle with cheese, and bake at 350° for 30 to 40 minutes. Eggplant should be browned slightly and cheese well melted before removing from the oven. Yield: 6 servings.

To freeze, mix all ingredients except cheese and freeze in plastic freezer containers. Add cheese when ready to bake the casserole.

*Eggplant Meat Casserole

- 1 pound ground beef
- Salt and pepper
- 2 tablespoons salad oil
- 1 medium-size eggplant
- 1/3 cup all-purpose flour
- 1/4 cup olive oil
- 2 (8-ounce) cans tomato sauce
- 1/2 teaspoon oregano
- 1 tablespoon Parmesan cheese
- 1 cup shredded Cheddar cheese

Shape ground beef into patties; season with salt and pepper. Brown in hot oil. Slice unpeeled eggplant into thick slices. Season with salt and pepper, coat with flour, and brown in olive oil. Place cooked eggplant slices in a shallow baking dish. Top each with a browned meat patty. Cover with tomato sauce. Sprinkle oregano and Parmesan cheese over all. Top with shredded Cheddar cheese. Bake at 300° for 35 minutes. Yield: 6 servings.

*Okra and Cheese Casserole

- 4 medium-size tomatoes, peeled and sliced
- 1/2 pound okra, cut in 1/4-inch slices
- 1/2 cup chopped onion
- 1 teaspoon salt
- 1/4 teaspoon black pepper
- 1 pound Cheddar cheese, cut in cubes

Arrange all ingredients in layers in 1 1/2-quart greased casserole. Start with sliced tomatoes, then okra, onion, and salt and pepper; top with cheese. Cover and bake at 325° for about 40 minutes. Yield: 8 servings.

*Corn and Tomato Casserole

- 1/4 cup butter or margarine
- 1/4 cup all-purpose flour
- 1 cup milk
- 1/2 teaspoon salt
- 1/8 teaspoon pepper
- 1/2 teaspoon onion salt
- 2 cups drained canned whole kernel corn
- 1 cup drained canned tomatoes
- 1 teaspoon rosemary
- 2 tablespoons butter or margarine, melted
- 1/2 cup bread crumbs

Melt 1/4 cup butter; stir in flour. Remove from heat and stir in milk. Cook until mixture thickens, stirring constantly. Add salt, pepper, onion salt, and corn. Combine tomatoes and crushed rosemary; stir into milk mixture. Spoon mixture into a 1 1/2-quart greased casserole. Combine 2 tablespoons melted butter and 1/2 cup bread crumbs; spread over vegetable mixture, and bake at 350° for 45 minutes or until browned. Yield: 6 servings.

Corn-Cheese Casserole

- 18 double saltine crackers, crushed
- 1 teaspoon dry mustard
- 1 teaspoon salt
- 3 eggs, separated
- 1 cup milk, scalded
- 1/4 teaspoon hot sauce
- 1 1/2 cups shredded Cheddar cheese
- 1 tablespoon butter, melted
- 1 (17-ounce) can cream-style corn
- Paprika

Combine cracker crumbs, mustard, and salt; set aside. Beat egg yolks well; gradually stir in scalded milk and hot sauce. Add crumb mixture, cheese, butter, and corn. Beat egg whites until stiff but not dry; fold into mixture. Pour into an ungreased 1 1/2-quart casserole dish. Bake at 325° for about 40 minutes or until golden brown and slightly firm to touch. Sprinkle with paprika before serving. Yield: 8 servings.

*Scalloped Rutabaga and Apple Casserole

    1 *large rutabaga, peeled and diced*
    1 *tablespoon butter or margarine*
1½ *cups peeled, sliced apples*
 ¼ *cup firmly packed brown sugar*
      Dash ground cinnamon
 ⅓ *cup all-purpose flour*
 ⅓ *cup firmly packed brown sugar*
    2 *tablespoons butter or margarine*

Cook rutabaga in small amount of boiling salted water until tender. Drain and mash; add 1 tablespoon butter. Toss sliced apples with ¼ cup brown sugar and cinnamon. Arrange alternate layers of mashed rutabaga and sliced apples in a greased 2-quart casserole, beginning and ending with rutabaga. Combine flour, ⅓ cup brown sugar, and 2 tablespoons butter. Mix until crumbly and sprinkle over top of casserole. Bake at 350° for 1 hour. Yield: 6 to 8 servings.

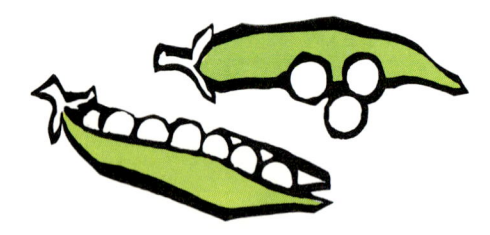

*Black-eyed Pea Casserole

    3 *cups cooked dried black-eyed peas*
1½ *tablespoons hot sauce*
    1 *(8-ounce) can tomato sauce*
    2 *tablespoons prepared mustard*
    1 *teaspoon pepper*
      Salt to taste
    2 *medium onions, sliced*
 ½ *cup catsup*
    4 *medium-size sausage patties*

Combine black-eyed peas, hot sauce, tomato sauce, mustard, pepper, and salt. Spoon into a greased 1½-quart baking dish. Place onion slices, catsup, and sausage on top. Bake, uncovered, at 350° for 1 hour or until sausage is brown. Yield: 4 to 6 servings.

*Ranch-Style Lentil Casserole

1 *teaspoon salt*
5 *cups boiling water*
1 *(12-ounce) package lentils*
1 *pound ground beef*
½ *cup salad oil*
1 *(1⅜-ounce) package onion soup mix*
1 *cup catsup*
1 *teaspoon prepared mustard*
1 *teaspoon vinegar*
1 *cup water*

Add salt to 5 cups boiling water; add lentils and cook for 20 to 30 minutes.

Brown beef in oil; drain off excess oil and transfer meat to a 2½-quart ungreased casserole. Stir in remaining ingredients; cover and bake at 400° for 30 minutes. To freeze, cool and seal securely. Yield: 8 to 10 servings.

*Squash-Cheese Casserole

    3 *pounds small yellow squash*
    1 *small green pepper, minced*
 ¼ *cup minced onion*
    4 *tablespoons margarine*
    2 *teaspoons sugar (optional)*
    1 *cup whole milk*
    4 *slices dry toasted bread*
1½ *cups shredded sharp Cheddar cheese, divided*
    3 *eggs, beaten*
      Few drops hot sauce

Slice squash; combine with green pepper and onion in boiling salted water. Cook until squash is tender. Remove from heat and drain. Add margarine and sugar, and stir until melted.

Combine milk, crumbled toasted bread, 1 cup shredded cheese, eggs, and hot sauce. Add to squash mixture and mix well. Divide mixture evenly between two 2-quart casseroles or put all into an ungreased 4-quart dish. Sprinkle ½ cup shredded cheese over top, cover, and bake at 350° for about 20 minutes. Yield: 10 servings.

Texas Bean Casserole

2 (16-ounce) cans pork and beans with tomato sauce
1½ cups cooked cubed beef
⅓ cup cooked or canned whole kernel corn
¼ cup chopped green pepper
¼ cup chopped onion
2 teaspoons chili powder
2 slices pasteurized process American cheese, cut into strips

Combine all ingredients except cheese in a greased 1½-quart casserole. Bake at 375° for 30 minutes. Arrange strips of cheese in crisscross fashion over beans; bake until cheese melts. Yield: 4 to 6 servings.

Lima Bean and Mushroom Casserole

1 onion, coarsely chopped
6 tablespoons butter or margarine, divided
2 (10-ounce) packages frozen lima beans
1 tablespoon sugar
½ teaspoon salt
¼ teaspoon pepper
1 (8-ounce) can sliced mushrooms
1 tablespoon water
3 tablespoons all-purpose flour
3 cups half-and-half or milk
¼ cup dry sherry
2 egg yolks, lightly beaten
½ teaspoon salt
½ teaspoon pepper
¼ cup shredded pasteurized process American cheese

Sauté onion in 2 tablespoons butter until limp; add beans. Cover and cook 5 minutes. Use a fork to separate beans. Add sugar, salt, pepper, mushrooms, and water. Cover again and cook until beans are tender.
   Melt remaining butter in a separate pan. Add flour and cook until bubbly. Add cream and cook, stirring frequently, until sauce begins to thicken. Remove from heat; add sherry, egg yolks, salt, and pepper. Combine with lima beans and mushrooms. Pour into an ungreased 1½-quart casserole and sprinkle with cheese.
   Cool, wrap, and freeze. To serve, bake for 1 hour at 350°. To serve without freezing, cut baking time to 35 minutes. Yield: 6 to 8 servings.

Beans Hawaiian Style

¼ pound cooked ham, cut into pieces
1 (21-ounce) can pork and beans
½ teaspoon dry mustard
¼ cup firmly packed brown sugar
1 tablespoon chopped onion
1 cup drained pineapple chunks

Combine all ingredients and put into a greased 1½-quart casserole dish. Cover and bake at 350° for 1 hour. Yield: 4 to 6 servings.

Sausage-Bean Casserole

½ pound dried lima beans
1 pint hot water
2 teaspoons salt
1 (20-ounce) can tomatoes
2 pounds sausage links
2 tablespoons water
1 small onion, sliced
1 tablespoon all-purpose flour
1 teaspoon dry mustard
1 tablespoon sugar
Dash pepper

Cover beans with water and soak overnight. Drain. Add hot water and salt and cook until just tender, about 1 hour. Add tomatoes and continue cooking for 1 hour. Place sausage links and 2 tablespoons water in a cold frying pan. Cover and cook slowly for 8 to 10 minutes. Remove cover and brown the links. Remove links; pour off all but 2 tablespoons drippings. Brown onion in drippings. Blend in flour and add remaining ingredients. Combine with beans. Add sausage links to mixture and simmer for 10 minutes. Yield: 8 to 10 servings.

*Baked Beans Deluxe

 6 slices bacon
 ¼ cup chopped onion
    Bacon drippings
 2 (16-ounce) cans pork and beans
 ½ cup catsup
 ¼ cup dark corn syrup
 1 teaspoon dry mustard
 ½ teaspoon chili powder
    Dash hot sauce
 ½ teaspoon Worcestershire sauce

Fry bacon until crisp; drain on absorbent paper. Sauté onion in bacon drippings. Combine all ingredients except bacon in a greased 1½-quart casserole and mix well. Top with bacon. Bake at 350° for 45 minutes. Yield: 6 to 8 servings.

Ham, Macaroni, and Broccoli Casserole

 3 tablespoons butter or margarine
 ¼ cup all-purpose flour
 ½ teaspoon salt
    Dash white pepper
 ½ teaspoon dry mustard
 1 tablespoon grated onion
 3 cups milk
 ⅔ cup shredded American or Cheddar cheese
 8 ounces elbow macaroni
 ¾ cup cubed cooked ham
 1 (10-ounce) package frozen broccoli spears, cooked and cut in 1-inch pieces
    Grated Parmesan cheese

Melt butter in large saucepan; blend in flour, salt, pepper, dry mustard, and onion. Gradually add milk, stirring constantly, and cook until sauce is thickened. Remove from heat and blend in ⅔ cup cheese, stirring until cheese is melted.
 Meanwhile, cook macaroni in boiling salted water until tender; drain. Add macaroni, ham, and broccoli to cheese sauce. Spoon mixture into a lightly greased 2-quart casserole. Sprinkle with Parmesan cheese. Bake at 375° for about 20 minutes or until sauce is bubbly and cheese is melted. Yield: 4 to 6 servings.

*Ham and Spaghetti Casserole

 3 tablespoons butter or margarine
 ¼ cup all-purpose flour
 ½ teaspoon salt
 ½ teaspoon white pepper
 3 cups milk
 1 cup shredded pasteurized process American cheese
 1 cup cubed cooked ham
 1 (7-ounce) package spaghetti, cooked and drained
    Sliced hard-cooked eggs (optional)

Melt butter in large saucepan; blend in flour, salt, and white pepper. Gradually add milk, stirring until thickened. Remove from heat and blend in cheese; add ham and cooked spaghetti. Stir well, and spoon into a greased 2-quart casserole.
 Cover and bake at 375° about 15 minutes or until mixture is thoroughly heated. Garnish with sliced hard-cooked eggs, if desired. Yield: 8 servings.

*Caballero Casserole

 2 (15-ounce) cans tamales
 2 (12-ounce) cans whole kernel corn with sweet peppers
 1 (14-ounce) can pizza sauce
    Cheese Olive Topping

Cut each tamale into 6 slices and place half in bottom of a 13- x 9- x 2-inch pan. Spread with 1 can corn; top with remaining tamale slices and corn. Pour pizza sauce over all. Spoon Cheese Olive Topping over casserole. Bake at 400° for 30 minutes. Yield: 8 servings.

Cheese Olive Topping:

 ½ cup all-purpose flour
 ¾ cup cornmeal
 1 (0.5-ounce) envelope cheese sauce mix
 1½ teaspoons baking powder
 1 teaspoon salt
 1 egg, slightly beaten
 ¾ cup milk
 ¼ cup salad oil
 2 tablespoons chopped ripe olives

In a large mixing bowl combine flour, cornmeal, cheese sauce mix, baking powder, and salt; add remaining ingredients. Stir until dough is formed. Spoon over casserole.

*Tasty Casserole

1 pound ground beef
2 medium onions, minced
1 clove garlic, minced (optional)
2 teaspoons salt
¼ teaspoon black pepper
5 tablespoons butter or margarine
1 cup canned English peas with liquid
1 (16-ounce) can tomatoes
3 cups cooked regular rice
½ cup shredded Cheddar cheese

Brown the beef, onion, garlic, salt, and pepper in butter. Combine peas, tomatoes, rice, and cheese in a large mixing bowl. Add the browned beef and onion, stirring well with a fork. Spoon into a 2-quart casserole. Freeze until ready to bake or bake immediately at 350° about 45 minutes or until brown. Yield: 8 to 10 servings.

Pork and Mushroom Casserole

3 slices bacon
⅓ cup diced onion
½ cup canned mushrooms, liquid reserved
1 pound pork tenderloin
1 teaspoon salt
⅛ teaspoon pepper
1 egg, beaten
1 cup sifted bread crumbs
¼ cup mushroom liquid

Dice bacon and fry in skillet. Remove bacon. Brown onion and mushrooms in drippings. Remove and combine with bacon. Cut pork into pieces ½ inch thick. Season with salt and pepper. Dip in egg and crumbs. Brown in remaining bacon drippings. Fill a 1-quart casserole with alternate layers of meat and vegetables. Add ¼ cup mushroom liquid. Cover. Bake at 350° for 30 minutes. Yield: 4 servings.

*Joseph Harris Cheese Casserole

8 to 10 slices bread
1 pound semi-sharp cheese, shredded
4 eggs
2 cups milk
Salt and pepper to taste
1 teaspoon dry mustard

Remove crusts from bread. Spread half of cheese in bottom of a greased 11- x 7-inch pan. Cover cheese with slices of bread; cut to fit so that entire cheese layer is covered. Sprinkle remainder of cheese.

Beat eggs. Add milk, salt, pepper, and mustard, and pour over cheese and bread mixture. Cover and refrigerate several hours or overnight. Bake, covered, at 325° for 45 minutes. Yield: 6 to 8 servings.

Elegant Cheese Puff

1 cup all-purpose flour
½ teaspoon salt
½ teaspoon pepper
1½ cups commercial sour cream
¼ cup grated Parmesan cheese
5 egg yolks
5 egg whites
1 tablespoon grated Parmesan cheese
Melted butter
Grated Parmesan cheese

Preheat oven to 350°. Set a 1½-quart well-greased casserole in a shallow baking pan; place in oven. Pour boiling water around casserole to a depth of at least 1 inch; let casserole heat while preparing cheese puff.

Combine flour, salt, and pepper. Add sour cream and ¼ cup Parmesan cheese; mix thoroughly. Add unbeaten egg yolks, and beat until ivory colored. Beat egg whites until stiff but not dry. Fold into sour cream mixture gently but thoroughly. Pour into hot casserole. Sprinkle with 1 tablespoon Parmesan cheese.

Bake at 350° about 1 hour or until a knife blade inserted halfway between center and outside edge comes out clean. Serve immediately with melted butter and additional Parmesan cheese. Yield: 4 to 5 servings.

Crab and Cheese Casserole

   5 *ounces (2½ cups) medium noodles, uncooked*
  ¼ *cup butter or margarine*
  2 *tablespoons minced onion*
  ½ *cup finely diced celery*
  ¼ *cup all-purpose flour*
  ½ *teaspoon dry mustard*
  1 *teaspoon salt*
  ⅛ *teaspoon pepper*
  2 *cups milk*
  1 *tablespoon lemon juice*
  1 *(7½-ounce) can crabmeat*
  2 *cups creamed cottage cheese*
  ½ *cup buttered bread crumbs*

Cook noodles in boiling salted water just until tender; drain and rinse thoroughly with cold water, and drain again.

Melt butter in a saucepan over low heat; add onion and celery and cook until tender but not brown. Add flour and seasonings and blend well. Add milk, stirring constantly, and cook until thick and bubbly. Add lemon juice, stirring briskly.

Combine noodles, sauce, crabmeat (free of cartilage), and cottage cheese. Pour into a 2-quart buttered casserole and sprinkle buttered crumbs around the top. Bake at 350° for 30 to 40 minutes or until mixture is thoroughly heated and the crumbs are slightly browned. Yield: 6 servings.

Asparagus Pinwheel Casserole

  1⅔ *cups evaporated milk*
  ½ *teaspoon salt*
  1½ *teaspoons dry mustard*
  1 *tablespoon steak sauce*
  2 *cups shredded pasteurized process American cheese*
  3 *cups cooked spaghetti*
  1 *(7-ounce) can tuna, drained*
  ¾ *pound fresh asparagus, cooked*
      Parsley

Combine evaporated milk, salt, mustard, and steak sauce in saucepan; simmer over low heat until just below boiling point (about 2 minutes). Add cheese. Stir over low heat about 1 minute until cheese melts. Add spaghetti and tuna to cheese sauce. Mix well. Arrange layers of spaghetti mixture and asparagus in greased 2-quart casserole dish. Arrange pieces of asparagus in a spoke pattern on top of casserole. Bake at 350° for 30 minutes. Garnish with parsley. Yield: 4 to 6 servings.

Asparagus Casserole

  1 *(19-ounce) can asparagus spears*
  3 *tablespoons melted butter, divided*
  2 *tablespoons cornstarch*
  3 *tablespoons milk*
  1 *(4-ounce) jar pimientos, chopped*
  2 *hard-cooked eggs, chopped*
  ¾ *cup shredded Cheddar cheese*
  12 *round buttery crackers, crumbled*
  1 *cup blanched slivered almonds*

Drain asparagus and reserve liquid. Combine 1 tablespoon butter, cornstarch, asparagus liquid, and milk; cook until thick.

In a lightly greased baking dish, place a layer of each of the following: asparagus, pimiento, eggs, cheese, cracker crumbs, and sauce. Repeat layers until all ingredients are used. Spread almonds over top and drizzle with remaining butter. Bake, uncovered, at 400° for 30 minutes. Yield: 6 servings.

Asparagus, Peas, & Mushroom Casserole

  2 *(10-ounce) packages frozen asparagus spears*
  2 *(10-ounce) packages frozen peas*
  1 *(10¾-ounce) can cream of mushroom soup*
  ¾ *cup shredded sharp Cheddar cheese*
  2 *tablespoons melted butter or margarine*
  1 *cup soft bread crumbs*

Heat asparagus to boiling in a small amount of salted water; drain. Repeat process with peas. Arrange half of the asparagus in a greased 2-quart casserole. Gently mix peas, soup, and cheese in a bowl. Spoon half the mixture over asparagus layer. Add remaining asparagus; top with remaining peas. Stir melted butter into crumbs and sprinkle over top of casserole. Bake at 350° for 30 minutes. Yield: 8 servings.

Green Pea and Asparagus Casserole

- 2 (10-ounce) packages frozen green peas
- 1 (10¾-ounce) can condensed cream of mushroom soup
- ½ cup water
- 1 (2-ounce) jar chopped pimiento
- 1½ cups shredded Cheddar cheese, divided
- 2 (10½-ounce) cans asparagus tips, drained

Cook peas according to package directions until tender; drain. Combine soup and water; gently mix in peas, pimientos, and cheese, reserving some cheese for topping. Line bottom of a lightly greased 3-quart casserole with asparagus. Pour soup mixture over asparagus and sprinkle remaining cheese on top. Bake at 350° until bubbly, about 20 minutes. Yield: 8 to 10 servings.

Giralda Rice

- ½ cup salad oil, divided
- 1 medium eggplant
- 1 teaspoon salt
- 4 large tomatoes, peeled
- 2 cloves garlic, minced
- 1 medium onion, chopped
- 1½ cups uncooked regular rice
- 1 (10½-ounce) can minced clams
- 2 to 2½ cups chicken stock or broth
- 2 medium green peppers, chopped
- ½ cup sliced pimiento-stuffed olives
- 2½ pounds raw shrimp, shelled, cleaned, and coarsely chopped
- ⅛ teaspoon pepper
- 4 ounces Swiss or Gruyère cheese, shredded
- ½ cup small pimiento-stuffed olives

Heat about ⅓ cup oil in large skillet. Cut unpeeled eggplant into ½-inch slices and sauté in hot oil just until tender. Remove and drain on paper towels. Sprinkle with salt.

Chop 2 tomatoes and slice remaining 2 tomatoes. Heat remaining oil in same skillet; add garlic, onion, and rice. Stir over medium heat until rice turns opaque. Drain clams and reserve juice. Add enough chicken broth to juice to make 3 cups; add to rice, along with green pepper and chopped tomatoes. Bring to a boil; stir; then cover and simmer 15 to 20 minutes or until rice is just tender. Mix in drained clams, olives, shrimp, and pepper. Cover and simmer 5 minutes or until shrimp turn pink.

Spoon into a shallow 3½-quart ovenproof serving dish. Overlap slices of eggplant and tomato around edge of dish and sprinkle with cheese. Place whole olives in center. Broil 6 inches from source of heat for 8 to 10 minutes or until cheese melts and browns slightly. Yield: 8 servings.

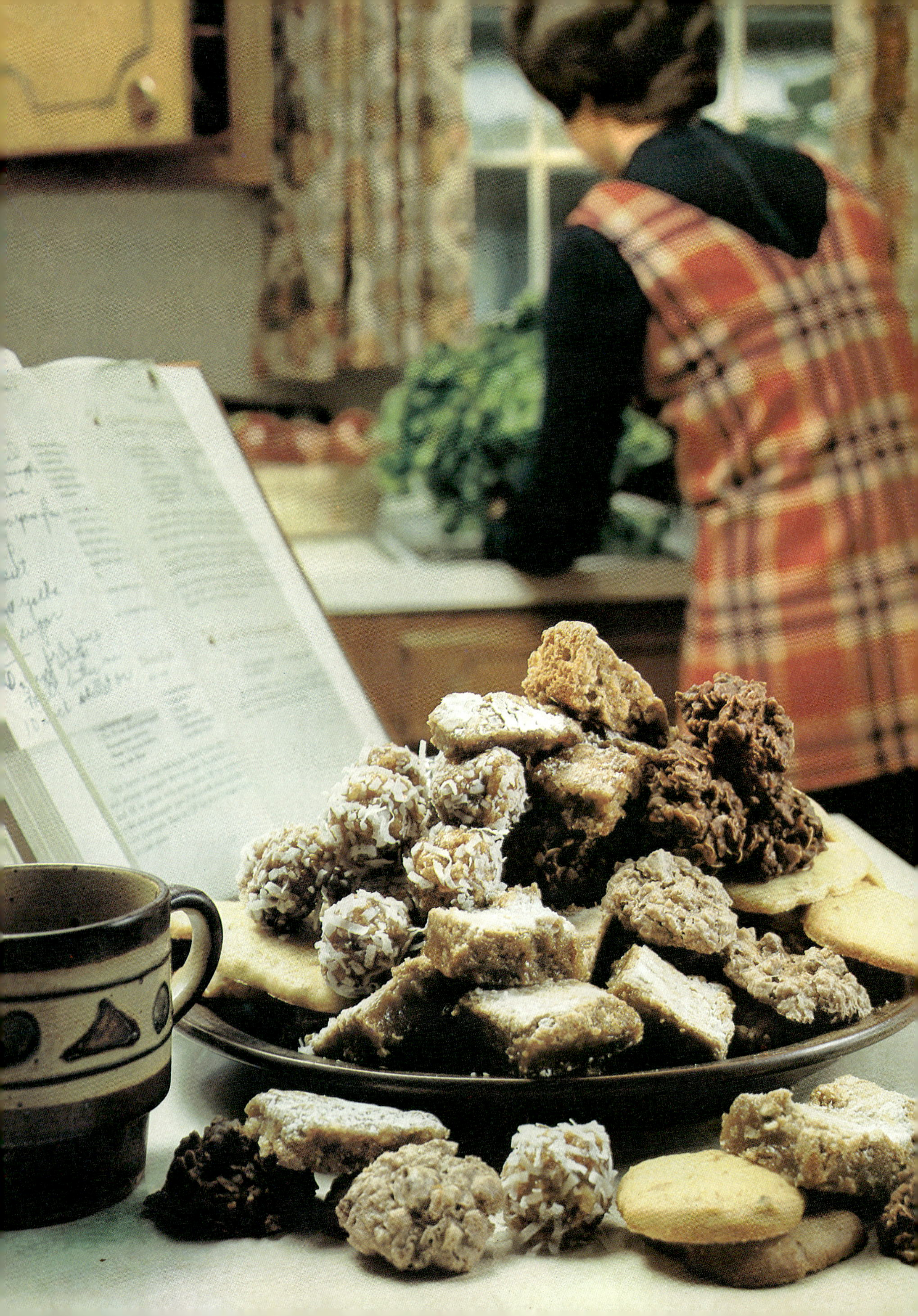

Cookies and Small Cakes

Happiness shows in the eyes of a small child at the mention of homemade cookies. Gingerbread men have always been favorites of boys and girls (and a few adults), and no child has ever been known to turn down a sugar cookie or a tea cake. In fact, children seem to prefer the plainer cookies.

There are a number of recipes for cookies which would be appropriate to serve at the most formal occasions or at any kind of party. Many of these cookies can be prepared days ahead of time and stored in the freezer until time for the party.

You'll find some of your old-time favorites in this group as well as some of the newer recipes for cookies of almost every flavor, shape, and texture.

Oldtime Jumbles

    1 *cup butter or margarine*
1¼ *cups sugar*
    2 *eggs*
    4 *cups all-purpose flour*
1½ *teaspoons baking powder*
    1 *teaspoon salt*
    1 *teaspoon ground nutmeg*
    2 *tablespoons fruit juice*
    Powdered sugar
    Egg white (optional)
    Chopped nuts, shredded coconut, cinnamon sugar (optional)

Cream butter until consistency of mayonnaise. Add sugar slowly, continuing to cream. Add eggs, one at a time, beating well after each addition. Combine flour, baking powder, salt, and nutmeg and stir in gradually. Add fruit juice a little at a time until it is all used.

Roll out ½ inch thick on surface dusted with powdered sugar. Cut with large round cutter or doughnut cutter. Bake on lightly greased cookie sheets at 375° for 15 minutes or until delicately browned. If desired, the cookies may be brushed with slightly beaten egg white and sprinkled with chopped nuts, shredded coconut, or cinnamon sugar before baking. Yield: about 3 dozen.

*Peanut Brittle Delights

    1 *(5½-ounce) stick piecrust mix*
  ¾ *cup firmly packed brown sugar*
    1 *egg, slightly beaten*
  ½ *teaspoon vanilla extract*
  ¾ *cup chopped peanuts, divided*

Mix piecrust mix according to package directions, but do not roll out. Cut in the brown sugar until mixture resembles coarse crumbs. Add egg, vanilla, and ¼ cup peanuts. Spread mixture on well-greased and floured cookie sheet to form a 12-inch square. Press remaining ½ cup peanuts into dough. Bake at 350° for 15 to 20 minutes. Loosen edges as soon as removed from oven. Cool on sheet and cut into 2-inch squares. Yield: 3 dozen squares.

*Gingerbread Men

- 1½ cups whipping cream
- 2½ cups firmly packed brown sugar
- 1½ cups dark or light molasses
- 1 tablespoon ground ginger
- 2 tablespoons soda
- 9 cups all-purpose flour

Whip cream; add sugar, molasses, ginger, and soda. Stir and beat for 10 minutes. Add flour and work until smooth. Cover and put in a cool place overnight. Roll out portions on lightly floured surface and cut in desired shapes. Brush flour from cookies —even a trace of flour on gingerbread spoils the looks. Lightly brush each cookie with water. Bake at 250° for 15 minutes. Scraps of dough may be cut in strips, baked, and decorated. Yield: about 3 dozen.

Best Brownies

- ⅔ cup vegetable oil
- 4 squares unsweetened chocolate
- 2 cups sugar
- 1 teaspoon vanilla extract
- 1½ cups all-purpose flour
- 4 eggs
- 1 cup chopped pecans
- About ¼ cup sifted powdered sugar

Place vegetable oil and chocolate squares in an ovenproof bowl and put in oven preheated to 350°. Leave in oven about 10 minutes for chocolate to melt; pour into a large mixing bowl. Beat in sugar and vanilla until mixture is smooth. Add flour and mix well. Add eggs, one at a time, beating well after each addition. Add chopped pecans and spoon batter into a greased and floured 13- x 9- x 2-inch pan. Bake at 350° for 25 minutes or until cake pulls away from sides of pan. Dust the top with sifted powdered sugar while the cake is still warm. Cut into squares and cover securely with foil or plastic wrap. These are hardy travelers and are really better the next day. Yield: about 4 dozen.

Brownies Deluxe

- 1 cup margarine
- 3 squares unsweetened chocolate
- 4 eggs, beaten
- 2 cups sugar
- 1½ cups all-purpose flour
- 1 teaspoon baking powder
- 1 cup chopped pecans
- 2 teaspoons vanilla extract
- 4 cups miniature marshmallows
- Deluxe Icing

Melt margarine and chocolate in top of double boiler; set aside. Combine eggs and sugar, beating well; add flour and baking powder, mixing well. Add chocolate mixture, pecans, and vanilla. Pour into two greased 13- x 9- x 2-inch pans and bake at 325° for 30 minutes. Remove brownies from oven and cover top with marshmallows. Brownies may need to go back in oven long enough for marshmallows to melt. Frost with Deluxe Icing. Yield: about 6 dozen. (Note: Begin to prepare icing a few minutes before brownies are done so both will be hot at the same time.)

Deluxe Icing:

- 1 cup sugar
- ¾ cup evaporated milk
- ½ cup margarine
- 2 squares unsweetened chocolate
- 1 (1-pound) box powdered sugar
- 1 teaspoon vanilla extract

Combine sugar, milk, margarine, and chocolate; cook over medium heat until soft ball stage (about 236°). Add powdered sugar and vanilla. Beat well. Spread icing over marshmallows. Cool brownies and cut into squares. Yield: icing for 6 dozen brownies.

Upside-Down Coconut Brownies

⅔ cup all-purpose flour
½ teaspoon baking powder
¼ teaspoon salt
2 eggs
1 cup sugar
⅓ cup melted butter or shortening
⅔ cup flaked coconut
2 tablespoons melted unsweetened chocolate

Combine flour, baking powder, and salt; set aside. Beat eggs in electric mixer and gradually add the sugar. Blend well. Stir in the melted butter and then add the flour mixture.

Pour about one-fourth of the dough into a small bowl and stir in the coconut. Pour the melted chocolate into the remaining batter and blend well. Pour chocolate batter into a well-greased 8- x 8- x 2-inch pan. Spread the coconut mixture evenly over chocolate layer in the pan.

Bake at 350° for about 35 minutes or until done. Let cool in the pan before cutting into 1-inch squares. Yield: 30 brownies.

Choco-Nut Brownies

½ cup all-purpose flour
½ teaspoon baking powder
¼ teaspoon salt
¼ cup margarine
2 squares unsweetened chocolate
¼ cup peanut butter
1 cup firmly packed brown sugar
1 egg, well beaten
1 teaspoon vanilla extract
½ cup chopped peanuts

Combine flour, baking powder, and salt. Melt margarine, chocolate, and peanut butter in saucepan over low heat. Add sugar to egg; beat well. Stir in peanut butter mixture and vanilla. Mix in dry ingredients, then nuts. Turn into greased 8- x 8- x 2-inch baking pan. Bake at 350° until done, about 30 minutes. Yield: 16 (2-inch) squares.

Butterscotch Brownies

1 cup sifted cake flour
1 teaspoon baking powder
½ teaspoon salt
1 cup firmly packed brown sugar
¼ cup corn oil
1 egg
½ cup chopped nuts
1 teaspoon vanilla extract

Grease an 8- x 8- x 2-inch baking pan. Combine cake flour, baking powder, and salt. Cream sugar and corn oil; add egg and beat well. Mix in nuts and vanilla. Fold in dry ingredients. Pour into prepared pan. Bake at 350° about 30 minutes. Cut into squares while warm. Yield: 16 squares.

Fruit and Nut Bars

½ cup butter or margarine, softened
1 cup firmly packed brown sugar
1 egg yolk
1 teaspoon vanilla extract
1¾ cups all-purpose flour
¼ teaspoon salt
¼ teaspoon soda
1 egg white
2 tablespoons sugar
½ teaspoon ground cinnamon
¼ teaspoon ground nutmeg
⅛ teaspoon ground cloves
½ cup diced mixed candied fruits
1 cup coarsely chopped pecans

Cream butter and brown sugar until light and fluffy. Beat egg yolk and vanilla together and add to creamed mixture. Combine flour, salt, and soda; add to creamed mixture and mix well. Dough will be crumbly. Pat dough into lightly greased 13- x 9- x 2-inch pan.

Beat egg white; gradually beat in the 2 tablespoons sugar. Stir in remaining ingredients. Spread this fruit and nut topping over dough; bake at 350° for 20 minutes or until light golden brown. Cool and cut into bars. Yield: 4 dozen bars.

cookies and small cakes

Fruit 'n Nut Squares

   2 *eggs*
   1 *cup powdered sugar*
   3 *tablespoons shortening, melted*
  ¾ *cup all-purpose flour*
1½ *teaspoons baking powder*
   1 *teaspoon salt*
   1 *teaspoon grated lemon peel*
   1 *cup chopped pecans*
1¼ *cups dried apricots, diced*
  ½ *cup dark, seedless raisins*
     Powdered sugar (optional)

Beat eggs in large mixing bowl until foamy; gradually beat in sugar. Blend in shortening. Combine flour, baking powder, and salt; stir into egg mixture. Mix in lemon peel, pecans, and fruits. Spread batter evenly in a greased 8-inch square pan; bake at 325° for 45 minutes. Cool in pan and cut into squares. (Sprinkle with powdered sugar before cutting, if desired.) Yield: 16 squares.

Apricot Sticks

⅔ *cup shortening*
½ *cup sugar*
2 *egg yolks*
1 *teaspoon grated lemon rind*
1 *teaspoon lemon juice*
½ *teaspoon salt*
¼ *teaspoon soda*
1 *cup all-purpose flour*
1 *(12-ounce) jar apricot jam*
2 *egg whites*
¼ *cup sugar*
½ *cup chopped nuts*
  Powdered sugar

Cream shortening and sugar together. Add egg yolks, lemon rind and juice, salt, soda, and flour. Mix thoroughly (this will be a very stiff dough). Spread in a 13- x 9- x 2-inch greased pan and then spread jam over dough. Beat egg whites until stiff but not dry. Add sugar and nuts. Spread this mixture over the jam. Bake at 350° for 45 minutes. Let cool; cut in pieces and sprinkle with powdered sugar. Yield: 3 dozen.

Orange Slice Bars

2 *cups firmly packed brown sugar*
4 *eggs*
2 *tablespoons orange juice*
1 *pound candy orange slices*
1 *to 2 cups chopped nuts*
2 *cups all-purpose flour, divided*
½ *teaspoon salt*
½ *teaspoon baking powder*
1 *teaspoon ground cinnamon*
1 *teaspoon vanilla extract*
1 *teaspoon lemon extract*
  Powdered sugar

Beat brown sugar, eggs, and orange juice until light and fluffy. Cut up oranges slices and combine with chopped nuts. Measure flour; remove ¼ cup to dust orange slices and nuts. Sift remainder of flour with salt, baking powder, and cinnamon and add to egg mixture. Stir in vanilla and lemon. Add orange slices and nuts and mix well.

    Spread mixture in a 15- x 10- x 1-inch pan or in a 13- x 9- x 2-inch pan which has been greased and lined with oiled brown paper. Bake at 250° for 1½ hours for the 13-inch pan and about 1 hour for the 15-inch pan. Place pan of water on oven rack below cake. When cake is partially cooled, cut into bars and roll in powdered sugar. Yield: about 4 dozen bars.

Marzipan Bars

First Layer:

½ *cup butter or margarine*
½ *cup firmly packed brown sugar*
1 *teaspoon vanilla extract*
¼ *teaspoon salt*
1½ *cups all-purpose flour*
¾ *cup red raspberry jelly*

Cream butter or margarine until light and fluffy; gradually add sugar and beat until fluffy. Stir in vanilla and salt. Gradually add flour. Batter will be very stiff. Pat dough into bottom of a 13- x 9- x 2-inch pan. Spread with jelly.

bars and squares 121

Second layer:

   1 *(8-ounce) can almond paste*
   ½ *cup sugar*
   3 *eggs*
   1 *teaspoon vanilla extract*

Beat almond paste and sugar until smooth. Add eggs, one at a time, beating well after each addition. Stir in vanilla. Spread mixture evenly over first layer in pan. Bake at 350° for 20 minutes. Remove from oven and cool before adding third layer.

Third Layer:

   2 *tablespoons butter or margarine*
 1½ *cups powdered sugar*
   2 *tablespoons milk*
   1 *teaspoon vanilla extract*
   1 *(1-ounce) square unsweetened chocolate, melted and cooled*
   ¼ *cup toasted slivered almonds*

Cream butter in small mixing bowl; add sugar, milk, vanilla, and chocolate. Spread over second layer; sprinkle top with almonds. Cut into squares and store tightly covered. These cookies freeze well. Yield: about 4 dozen bars.

Date Sticks

   1 *cup chopped dates*
   1 *cup chopped nuts*
   1 *cup all-purpose flour*
   ¼ *teaspoon salt*
   ½ *teaspoon ground nutmeg*
   2 *large eggs*
   1 *cup sugar*
      Powdered sugar

Mix dates, nuts, flour, salt, and nutmeg. Combine well to coat dates and nuts with flour. Beat eggs well; add 1 cup sugar and continue beating until well mixed. Stir in flour mixture and mix well; batter will be stiff. Spread in a well-greased and floured 11- x 7-inch pan or 9-inch cakepan.

Bake at 350° for 20 to 25 minutes. Sprinkle with powdered sugar while hot. Cut into bars when cool. Yield: 3 dozen bars.

Date Nut Bar Cookies

   ¼ *cup butter or margarine*
   1 *cup firmly packed brown sugar*
   1 *egg*
   ½ *cup all-purpose flour*
   ¼ *teaspoon salt*
   ¼ *teaspoon baking powder*
   1 *teaspoon vanilla extract*
   1 *(8-ounce) package dates, chopped*
   1 *cup chopped nuts*

Cream butter and sugar; add egg and beat well. Combine flour, salt, and baking powder and add to creamed mixture; add vanilla and beat well. Stir in dates and nuts and mix well. Spoon batter into a greased 8-inch square cakepan, and bake at 350° for 20 to 30 minutes. Cool; then cut into bars. Yield: about 16 bars.

Coconut Pecan Bars

   2 *cups all-purpose flour*
   1 *teaspoon baking powder*
   1 *teaspoon salt*
   1 *cup butter or margarine*
   2 *cups firmly packed brown sugar*
   2 *eggs*
   2 *teaspoons vanilla extract*
   1 *(3½-ounce) can flaked coconut*
   1 *cup chopped pecans*
      Powdered sugar

Combine flour, baking powder, and salt; set aside. Cream butter well, and add brown sugar, eggs, and vanilla; beat until smooth and creamy. Add dry ingredients; mix well. Stir in coconut and pecans. Spread in buttered 15- x 10- x 1-inch jelly roll pan. Bake at 350° about 25 minutes. Cool. Sprinkle with powdered sugar and cut into bars. Yield: 3½ dozen bars.

*Coconut Cherry Bars

    1 *cup butter or margarine*
1¼ *cups sugar*
    1 *egg*
    1 *teaspoon vanilla extract*
2⅓ *cups all-purpose flour*
1½ *teaspoons baking powder*
   ½ *teaspoon salt*
   ½ *cup chopped nuts*
   ½ *cup chopped maraschino cherries*
   ⅔ *cup flaked coconut*
    1 *(6-ounce) package semisweet chocolate pieces*

Cream butter and sugar. Blend in egg and vanilla. Combine flour, baking powder, and salt, and stir into creamed mixture. Add nuts, cherries, coconut, and chocolate bits. Spread dough in a greased 13- x 9- x 2-inch pan, and bake at 375° for 25 minutes. Cool slightly; then cut into bars. Yield: about 40 bars.

Coconut Bars

   ¾ *cup self-rising cornmeal*
    1 *cup firmly packed light brown sugar*
    1 *cup flaked coconut*
   ½ *cup chopped pecans*
    2 *eggs, beaten*
   ¼ *cup melted butter*

Grease and line an 8-inch square pan with waxed paper. Combine the cornmeal, sugar, coconut, and chopped pecans. Blend together eggs and melted butter. Add all at once to cornmeal mixture, stirring until blended. Pour into pan and bake at 350° for 30 to 35 minutes or until brown around edges. Cool. Remove from pan, remove waxed paper, and cut into 1- x 2-inch bars. Yield: 16 bars.

Molasses Date-Nut Bars

   ¼ *cup shortening*
   ½ *cup sugar*
    1 *egg*
   ½ *molasses*
    2 *cups all-purpose flour*
   ¼ *teaspoon salt*
   ¼ *teaspoon soda*
1½ *teaspoons baking powder*
   ½ *cup milk*
    1 *cup chopped nuts*
    1 *cup chopped dates*

Cream together shortening and sugar. Add egg and beat well; add molasses and beat. Combine flour, salt, soda, and baking powder. Add dry ingredients alternately with milk to creamed mixture. Add chopped nuts and dates. Line 2 greased 8- x 8- x 2-inch pans with greased waxed paper. Pour in batter. Bake at 350° for 25 to 27 minutes. Cool 5 minutes; remove from pans and cut into squares. Yield: 32 squares.

*Lemon Squares

    1 *cup butter or margarine*
   ½ *cup powdered sugar*
    2 *cups all-purpose flour*
   ⅛ *teaspoon salt*
    4 *eggs*
    2 *cups sugar*
    6 *tablespoons all-purpose flour*
    6 *tablespoons lemon juice*
    1 *tablespoon grated lemon*
Powdered sugar

Combine butter, powdered sugar, 2 cups flour, and salt. Mix with a pastry blender until mixture is well blended. Pat evenly into a 15- x 10- x 1-inch jelly roll pan and bake at 350° for 20 minutes.

  Beat eggs slightly. Stir in sugar, flour, lemon juice, and lemon rind. Mix well and spread over baked crust. Bake at 350° for 25 minutes. Remove from oven and sift powdered sugar over top. Let cool; then cut into squares. Yield: about 3 dozen.

Taffy Bars

½ cup shortening
⅓ cup light molasses
¾ cup firmly packed brown sugar
1 egg
1¼ cups all-purpose flour
½ teaspoon salt
¼ teaspoon soda
½ cup chopped walnuts

Combine shortening and molasses in small saucepan; heat to boiling. Remove from heat and stir in brown sugar. Beat egg; add molasses mixture and beat until fluffy. Sift dry ingredients together; add to molasses mixture along with chopped nuts. Blend well. Spoon into greased 9- x 9- x 2-inch pan and bake at 350° for 20 minutes. Cut into bars. Yield: 6 servings.

Penuche Bars

4 eggs
1 (1-pound) box light or dark brown sugar
1 teaspoon vanilla extract
2 cups all-purpose flour
1 teaspoon baking powder
2 cups chopped pecans or walnuts

Beat eggs slightly; add brown sugar and vanilla and put in top of double boiler. Cook over simmering water, stirring constantly, until mixture thickens slightly. Cool. Combine flour and baking powder, stir in pecans, and add to cooled egg mixture. Spread in a greased 15- x 10- x 1-inch jelly roll pan. Bake at 325° for 12 to 15 minutes or until cake tests done. Cool and cut into squares or strips. Yield: about 7½ dozen squares.

*Butterscotch Bars

¾ cup butter or margarine, softened
1 cup sugar
2 eggs
1 teaspoon vanilla extract
2 cups all-purpose flour
1 teaspoon salt
1 teaspoon soda
2 teaspoons ground cinnamon
2 (6-ounce) packages butterscotch pieces

Cream butter and sugar until light and fluffy. Add eggs, one at a time, beating well after each addition. Add vanilla. Combine flour, salt, soda, and cinnamon; add to creamed mixture, mixing until batter is smooth. Stir in butterscotch pieces. Spread mixture in a lightly greased 15- x 10- x 1-inch jelly roll pan. Bake at 350° for 25 to 30 minutes. Cut into bars while warm. Yield: 5 dozen bars.

"Hello Dolly" Cookies

½ cup margarine, melted
1 cup graham cracker crumbs
1 cup pecans, chopped
1 cup chocolate chips
1 cup flaked coconut
1 (15-ounce) can sweetened condensed milk

Mix ingredients in the order given. Bake in a buttered 8-inch square pan at 350° for 45 minutes. Let cookies cool; then cut into squares to serve. Yield: 4 dozen squares.

Chocolate-Toffee Squares

- 1 cup butter or margarine, softened
- 1 cup firmly packed light brown sugar
- 1 egg
- 1 teaspoon vanilla extract
- ¼ teaspoon salt
- 2 cups all-purpose flour
- 1 (6-ounce) package semisweet chocolate pieces
- ¾ cup coarsely chopped walnuts (optional)

Cream butter and sugar until light and fluffy. Add egg, vanilla, and salt; stir until well blended. Add flour and stir just to blend. Put batter into greased 13- x 9- x 2-inch pan and bake at 350° for 25 minutes or until golden brown. Remove from oven; sprinkle with chocolate pieces. When chocolate is soft, spread evenly over top. Sprinkle with walnuts. Cut into squares while warm. Let cool in pan. Yield: 32 squares.

Baked Chocolate Fudge Squares

- ½ cup butter
- 3 ounces unsweetened chocolate
- 2 cups sugar
- 3 eggs
- 1 cup coarsely chopped walnuts
- 1½ cups all-purpose flour
- 1 teaspoon vanilla extract
- Powdered sugar

Combine butter and chocolate; melt over low heat. Add sugar and beat well. Add eggs one at a time, beating well after each addition. Add nuts, flour, and vanilla. Spread in a greased 11- x 7-inch pan. Bake at 350° for 30 minutes. Cool; cut in squares. Sprinkle with powdered sugar. Yield: 15 squares.

*Lemon Bars Deluxe

- 2¼ cups all-purpose flour, divided
- ½ cup powdered sugar
- 1 cup margarine, softened
- 4 eggs, beaten
- 2 cups sugar
- ⅓ cup lemon juice
- ½ teaspoon baking powder
- Powdered sugar

Sift together 2 cups flour and ½ cup powdered sugar. Cut in margarine until mixture clings together; press into a greased 13- x 9- x 2-inch pan. Bake at 350° for 25 to 30 minutes or until lightly browned.

Combine eggs, sugar, and lemon juice; beat well. Sift together ¼ cup flour and baking powder; stir into egg mixture. Pour over baked crust. Bake at 350° for 25 to 30 minutes or until lightly browned. Sprinkle with powdered sugar. Cool; cut into bars. Yield: 3 dozen bars.

*Sesame Seed Wafers

- 1 (2¼-ounce) jar sesame seeds
- 6 tablespoons butter or margarine, softened
- 1 cup firmly packed dark brown sugar
- 1 large egg, well beaten
- ½ cup all-purpose flour
- ¼ teaspoon baking powder
- ⅛ teaspoon salt
- 1 teaspoon vanilla extract

Toast sesame seeds in a heavy skillet, stirring constantly over low heat for about 20 minutes or until golden brown; cool. Cream butter and sugar until fluffy. Add egg and blend well. Combine flour, baking powder, and salt; add to creamed mixture. Add vanilla and sesame seeds.

Using an iced tea spoon, drop level amounts of dough 2 inches apart onto greased cookie sheets. Bake at 350° for 8 minutes; cool for 1 minute before removing from cookie sheet. Let wafers finish cooling on a wire rack and place in an airtight container. These keep fresh for several weeks. Yield: about 6 dozen.

Holiday Fruit Cookies

- 1 pound candied cherries
- 1 pound candied pineapple
- 5 (8-ounce) packages dates
- 1 pound (4 cups) shelled pecans
- 3 cups all-purpose flour
- ½ teaspoon soda
- ½ teaspoon salt
- ½ cup butter or margarine
- 1½ cups sugar
- 3 eggs, well beaten
- 1 teaspoon vanilla extract
- 1 teaspoon lemon extract
- 2 teaspoon ground cinnamon

Cut fruit in small pieces; leave pecans in halves. Combine flour, soda, and salt and sift over fruit and pecans. Cream butter and sugar until light; add beaten eggs and mix well. Stir in vanilla, lemon, and cinnamon. Stir in fruit-nut mixture. Drop by teaspoonfuls onto greased cookie sheets and bake at 300° for 10 to 15 minutes and watch carefully. Yield: 12½ dozen small cookies.

Fruit Cookies

- 6 cups chopped nuts
- 1 pound pitted dates, chopped
- 1 pound candied cherries, chopped
- 1 pound candied pineapple, chopped
- ¾ cup all-purpose flour
- ½ cup butter or margarine
- 1 cup firmly packed brown sugar
- 4 eggs
- 2¼ cups all-purpose flour
- 3 teaspoons soda
- 1 teaspoon ground cinnamon (optional)
- 1 teaspoon ground nutmeg (optional)
- 1 teaspoon ground cloves (optional)
- 1 teaspoon salt
- 3 tablespoons milk
- ½ cup bourbon

Place chopped nuts and fruits in a large bowl. Stir in ¾ cup flour to coat all pieces; set aside.

Cream butter and brown sugar until smooth. Add eggs, one at a time, beating well after each addition.

Combine flour, soda, spices, and salt; add to creamed mixture. Add milk and bourbon and stir well. Stir in fruits and nuts. Drop by teaspoonfuls onto greased cookie sheets, and bake at 325° for about 10 minutes or until cookies are lightly browned. Remove from cookie sheets and cool on brown paper. These cookies freeze and keep well. Yield: 10 to 12 dozen.

Smackeroons

- 2 egg whites
- ⅛ teaspoon salt
- 1 cup firmly packed light brown sugar
- 1 teaspoon vanilla extract
- 2 cups corn flakes
- 1 cup flaked coconut
- ½ cup chopped walnuts

Beat egg whites and salt until stiff. Gradually beat in sugar. Add vanilla; then stir in remaining ingredients. Drop by tablespoonfuls onto well-greased cookie sheets. Bake at 350° for about 12 minutes. Remove from cookie sheets at once. Yield: about 3 dozen cookies.

Date Nut Cookies

- 1 cup butter or margarine
- 1½ cups firmly packed brown sugar
- 3 eggs, well beaten
- 2 cups all-purpose flour
- ½ teaspoon soda
- ¼ teaspoon salt
- 1 cup finely chopped pecans or walnuts
- 1 (8-ounce) package dates, chopped

Cream butter and sugar until smooth and fluffy. Add eggs and beat until smooth. Combine flour, soda, and salt; add to creamed mixture. Stir in nuts and dates. Drop by teaspoonfuls onto well-greased cookie sheets. Bake at 350° about 15 minutes. These cookies are very brittle. For a more cakelike cookie, use a 1 pound package of chopped dates and bake a little longer. Yield: 5 dozen cookies.

Jumbo Raisin Cookies

    4   cups all-purpose flour
    1   teaspoon baking powder
    1   teaspoon soda
    2   teaspoons salt
 1½ teaspoons ground cinnamon
  ¼ teaspoon ground nutmeg
  ¼ teaspoon ground allspice
    1   cup water
    2   cups seedless raisins
    1   cup shortening
    2   cups sugar
    3   eggs
    1   teaspoon vanilla extract
    1   cup chopped nuts

Sift together first 7 ingredients. Add water to raisins and boil for 5 minutes or until liquid is decreased to ½ cup. Cool. Cream shortening, add sugar, and blend well. Add eggs, one at a time, to creamed mixture, beating well after each addition. Add vanilla, nuts, and cooled raisin mixture. Add sifted dry ingredients and blend well. Drop by teaspoonfuls onto greased cookie sheets. Bake at 400° for 12 to 15 minutes. Yield: 5 dozen cookies.

Sour Cream Nut Cookies

  ½ cup butter
  ½ cup shortening
    2   cups firmly packed brown sugar
    2   eggs
    1   teaspoon vanilla extract
 4⅓ cups all-purpose flour
    1   teaspoon soda
    2   teaspoons baking powder
  ½ teaspoon salt
    1   cup commercial sour cream
    1   cup chopped black walnuts

Cream butter, shortening, and sugar together and beat well. Add eggs and beat until light and fluffy. Add vanilla. Combine flour, soda, baking powder, and salt and add to creamed mixture alternately with sour cream. Add nuts. Drop by teaspoonfuls onto greased cookie sheets. Bake at 400° for 10 to 12 minutes. Yield: 5 dozen.

Sour Cream Cookies

  ½ cup margarine
    1   cup firmly packed brown sugar
  ½ cup commercial sour cream
    1   egg, well beaten
    2   cups all-purpose flour
  ½ teaspoon baking powder
  ¼ teaspoon soda
  ¼ teaspoon salt
  ¼ teaspoon ground nutmeg
  ½ cup chopped nuts or raisins

Cream margarine, sugar, and sour cream until smooth. Stir in beaten egg and mix well. Combine dry ingredients and stir into creamed mixture. Add chopped nuts. Drop by heaping teaspoonfuls 2 inches apart onto greased cookie sheets. Bake at 350° for 8 to 10 minutes. Yield: 3 dozen.

Molasses Oatmeal Cookies

    1   cup all-purpose flour
  ¼ teaspoon soda
    1   teaspoon salt
 1½ teaspoons baking powder
    1   teaspoon ground ginger
    1   teaspoon ground cinnamon
    1   teaspoon ground nutmeg
    2   cups oats (regular or quick-cooking)
  ½ cup shortening
  ½ cup sugar
  ½ cup light molasses
    1   teaspoon vanilla extract
    1   egg
    2   tablespoons milk
  ½ cup seedless raisins
  ½ cup chopped nuts

Combine flour, soda, salt, baking powder, and spices; stir in oats and set aside. Cream shortening and sugar; add molasses and vanilla and beat in egg. Add milk, raisins, and nuts to creamed mixture. Stir in flour mixture and drop by tablespoonfuls onto ungreased cookie sheets. Bake at 375° for 10 to 12 minutes. Cool and store in tightly covered container. Yield: 4½ dozen cookies.

drop cookies 127

Cream shortening and sugars until light and fluffy. Add eggs and beat well. Combine flour, soda, salt, and baking powder and stir into creamed mixture. Add oats, vanilla, and chocolate pieces and mix well. Drop by teaspoonfuls onto lightly greased baking sheets and bake at 350° for 10 to 15 minutes. Yield: about 12 dozen.

*Cottage Cheese Cookies

- ½ cup butter, softened
- 1 cup firmly packed brown sugar
- 1 egg
- 1¾ cups all-purpose flour
- ½ teaspoon soda
- ½ teaspoon salt
- ¼ teaspoon ground cloves
- ¼ teaspoon ground nutmeg
- ½ teaspoon ground cinnamon
- ⅓ cup cottage cheese

Cream butter and sugar until light and fluffy; add egg and beat well. Combine dry ingredients; alternately add dry ingredients and cottage cheese to creamed mixture. Drop by teaspoonfuls onto greased cookie sheets; bake at 375° for about 12 minutes. Yield: about 3 dozen cookies.

*Coconut Puffs

- 3 egg whites
- 2 tablespoons all-purpose flour
- 1 cup sugar
- Dash salt
- 1½ cups flaked coconut
- 1 teaspoon vanilla extract
- ¼ teaspoon almond extract

Place egg whites in top of double boiler; beat until stiff but not dry. Combine flour, sugar, and salt; add to beaten egg whites, beating constantly. Cook over gently boiling water for about 2 minutes, beating constantly. Remove from hot water; add remaining ingredients. Drop from teaspoon onto well-greased cookie sheets. Bake at 325° about 20 minutes. Yield: 3 dozen cookies.

*Oatmeal Delights

- 1 cup shortening
- 1 cup sugar
- 1 cup firmly packed brown sugar
- 2 eggs
- 2 cups all-purpose flour
- 1 teaspoon soda
- ½ teaspoon salt
- ½ teaspoon baking powder
- 2 cups oats (regular or quick-cooking)
- 1 teaspoon vanilla extract
- 1 (6-ounce) package semisweet chocolate pieces

Coconut Macaroon Cookies

 1 cup shortening
 2 cups firmly packed brown sugar
 2 eggs, well beaten
 1½ cups all-purpose flour
 ¼ teaspoon baking powder
 ½ teaspoon salt
 ½ teaspoon soda
 2 cups flaked coconut
 2 cups rolled oats (regular or quick-cooking)
 ½ cup chopped pecans

Cream shortening and sugar until light and fluffy. Add eggs and mix well. Combine flour, baking powder, salt, and soda and add to creamed mixture, mixing well. Add coconut, oats, and pecans. Drop by teaspoonfuls onto lightly greased cookie sheets. Bake at 375° for 10 to 12 minutes. Yield: 4 dozen.

*Meringue Cookies

 2 egg whites (at room temperature)
 ⅛ teaspoon salt
 ⅛ teaspoon cream of tartar
 1 teaspoon vanilla extract
 ¾ cup sugar
 1 (6-ounce) package semisweet chocolate pieces
 ¼ cup chopped pecans

Beat egg whites, salt, cream of tartar, and vanilla until soft peaks form. Add sugar gradually, and beat until the mixture is stiff. Fold in the chocolate pieces and pecans (preferably using a plastic spatula).

Cover cookie sheets with heavy brown paper. Drop meringue mixture by teaspoonfuls into small mounds. Bake at 300° for about 25 minutes, reducing heat to 250° if cookies begin to show signs of browning.

Meringues should be creamy white and crisp-dry when done.

Let the meringues cool and store in sealed tin container in refrigerator. For best results, make these meringues on a bright clear day. Yield: about 6 dozen (1-inch) cookies.

*Crisp Coconut Cookies

 ¾ cup shortening
 ¾ cup sugar
 ½ cup firmly packed brown sugar
 1 teaspoon vanilla extract
 1 egg, beaten
 2 cups all-purpose flour
 1 teaspoon soda
 1 teaspoon baking powder
 ½ teaspoon salt
 1 cup rolled oats (regular or quick-cooking)
 1 cup flaked coconut
 ½ cup chopped pecans

Cream shortening and sugars until fluffy; stir in vanilla and beaten egg. Combine other ingredients and stir into creamed mixture. Dough will be very stiff. Drop by teaspoonfuls onto lightly greased cookie sheets. Bake at 375° for 12 to 15 minutes or until lightly browned. Cool a few minutes on cookie sheet before removing to cooling racks. Yield: about 5 dozen.

Orange Oatmeal Cookies

 2 cups all-purpose flour
 4 teaspoons baking powder
 1 teaspoon salt
 1 teaspoon ground cinnamon
 1 teaspoon ground nutmeg
 ½ teaspoon ground allspice
 ¼ teaspoon ground cloves
 1 cup shortening
 1 cup sugar
 1 cup firmly packed light brown sugar
 2 eggs
 3 tablespoons frozen orange juice concentrate, thawed and undiluted
 3 tablespoons grated orange rind
 3 cups quick-cooking oats, uncooked
 Semisweet chocolate pieces or raisins (optional)

Combine flour, baking powder, salt, and spices; set aside. Cream shortening and sugars until light and fluffy; beat in eggs one at a time. Add orange juice concentrate to creamed mixture. Blend in dry ingredients and stir in orange rind and oats. Drop level tablespoons of batter 2 inches apart onto greased cookie sheets. Make faces with chocolate pieces or raisins, if desired. Bake at 375° for 10 to 12 minutes. Yield: 4 dozen cookies.

Fruitcake Cookies

½ cup shortening
1 cup firmly packed brown sugar
1 egg
¼ cup buttermilk
1¾ cups all-purpose flour
¼ teaspoon soda
½ teaspoon salt
½ cup chopped pecans
1 cup chopped dates
1 cup chopped candied cherries
Pecan halves

Thoroughly mix shortening, sugar, and egg. Stir in buttermilk. Combine dry ingredients and add. Stir in pecans, dates, and cherries. Chill. Drop by teaspoonfuls 2 inches apart onto greased cookie sheets. Top with pecan halves. Bake at 400° for 8 to 10 minutes. Yield: 4 dozen.

Holiday Lizzies

½ cup sugar
⅓ cup butter or margarine
2 eggs, well beaten
1½ cups all-purpose flour
1½ teaspoons soda
1½ tablespoons milk
1 pound candied cherries, chopped
1 pound dates, chopped
1 pound chopped pecans
1 pound candied pineapple, chopped
¼ cup whiskey

Cream together sugar, butter, and eggs. Combine flour and soda and add to creamed mixture; stir in milk. Add rest of ingredients and mix well. Drop by teaspoonfuls onto greased cookie sheets; bake at 325° for 12 to 15 minutes. Yield: 80 or 90 cookies.

*Favorite Sugar Cookies

2 eggs
⅔ cup salad oil
2 teaspoons vanilla extract
1 teaspoon grated lemon peel
¾ cup sugar
About 2¼ cups sifted all-purpose flour
2 teaspoons baking powder
½ teaspoon salt
Sugar
¼ teaspoon ground cinnamon

Beat eggs with fork until well blended. Stir in oil, vanilla, and lemon peel. Blend in sugar until mixture thickens. Combine flour, baking powder, and salt; stir into egg mixture. Drop by teaspoonfuls about 2 inches apart onto ungreased cookie sheets. Gently press each cookie flat with the bottom of a glass that has been lightly oiled. Sprinkle each cookie with sugar and cinnamon. Bake at 400° for 8 to 10 minutes. Remove immediately from cookie sheets. Yield: 3 dozen (3-inch) cookies.

Salted Peanut Cookies

½ cup soft butter or margarine
1¼ cups firmly packed brown sugar
1 egg
1½ cups all-purpose flour
½ teaspoon baking powder
¾ teaspoon soda
½ teaspoon salt
¼ cup milk
¾ cup salted peanuts, chopped
1½ cups crisp rice cereal

Cream butter or margarine until light and fluffy; gradually add sugar and continue beating until fluffy. Add egg and beat well. Combine flour, baking powder, soda, and salt; add to creamed mixture alternately with milk, and mix well. Stir in nuts and cereal. Drop by teaspoonfuls onto greased cookie sheets and bake at 375° for about 8 minutes. Let cookies cool for about 2 minutes before removing from cookie sheets. Yield: about 6 dozen.

Rocky Road Cookies

2 cups all-purpose flour
1 cup sugar
1 tablespoon baking powder
1 teaspoon salt
½ cup shortening, softened
2 squares unsweetened chocolate, melted
2 eggs
½ cup milk
1 teaspoon rum extract
½ cup chopped nuts
Chocolate Marshmallow Frosting

Combine flour, sugar, baking powder, and salt in mixing bowl. Add shortening, chocolate, eggs, milk, and flavoring. Mix until well blended and smooth. Stir in nuts. Drop by teaspoonfuls onto greased cookie sheets. Bake at 350° for 15 to 20 minutes. Cool. Frost with Chocolate Marshmallow Frosting. Yield: 4 dozen cookies.

Chocolate Marshmallow Frosting:

1 square unsweetened chocolate
⅓ cup milk
2 cups powdered sugar
1 cup miniature marshmallows

Melt chocolate in milk in top of double boiler over simmering water; stir until smooth. Remove from heat and beat in sugar, ½ cup at a time, mixing thoroughly after each addition. Cool slightly; fold in marshmallows. Frost cookies. Yield: frosting for 4 dozen cookies.

*Peanut Butter Cookies

2 cups all-purpose flour
1½ teaspoons baking powder
½ teaspoon soda
⅛ teaspoon salt
1 cup peanut butter
½ cup margarine
1 cup white sugar
1 cup firmly packed brown sugar
2 eggs
½ cup milk
1 teaspoon vanilla extract

Combine first 4 ingredients. Cream peanut butter, margarine, and sugars. Add eggs; beat until fluffy. Stir in dry ingredients alternately with milk. Add vanilla. Drop by teaspoonfuls onto ungreased cookie sheets. Bake at 350° for 18 minutes. Yield: 6 dozen.

Orange Date Cookies

¾ cup shortening
¼ cup butter or margarine
1½ cups firmly packed brown sugar
2 eggs, beaten
¼ cup orange juice
1 tablespoon grated fresh orange rind
1 teaspoon vanilla extract
1 cup sour milk
3½ cups all-purpose flour
2 teaspoons baking powder
1 teaspoon soda
¼ teaspoon salt
1 cup chopped dates
1 cup chopped pecans
Orange Glaze

Cream together shortening, butter, and sugar. Beat in eggs, juice, rind, vanilla, and sour milk. Combine dry ingredients; add to creamed mixture. Stir in dates and nuts. Drop from a teaspoon onto lightly greased cookie sheets; bake at 350° for 15 minutes. Cool; spread with Orange Glaze. Yield: about 5 dozen.

Orange Glaze:

1 teaspoon grated fresh orange rind
3 tablespoons or more orange juice
2 cups sifted powdered sugar

Add rind and enough juice to sugar to make a stiff spreadable topping.

Chocolate-Nut Puffs

    1   (6-ounce) package semisweet chocolate pieces
    2   egg whites
   1/8 teaspoon salt
   1/2 cup sugar
   1/2 teaspoon vanilla extract
   1/2 teaspoon vinegar
   3/4 cup chopped nuts

Melt chocolate over warm water. Beat egg whites with salt until foamy; gradually add sugar. Beat until stiff peaks form; beat in vanilla and vinegar. Fold in melted chocolate and nuts. Drop by teaspoonfuls, about 1 inch apart, onto greased cookie sheets. Bake at 350° for 10 minutes. Yield: 3 dozen.

*Corn Flake Macaroons

    3   egg whites
    1   cup sugar
   1/4 teaspoon almond extract
   1/4 teaspoon vanilla extract
   1 1/2 cups flaked coconut
    3   cups corn flakes

Beat egg whites until stiff but not dry; gradually add sugar. Add flavorings, and fold in coconut and corn flakes. Drop by teaspoonfuls onto well-greased cookie sheets. Bake at 300° about 20 minutes. Remove from cookie sheets as soon as taken from oven. Yield: about 2 1/2 dozen cookies.

*Peanut-Oatmeal Cookies

    1   cup all-purpose flour
    2   teaspoons baking powder
   1/2 teaspoon salt
   1/3 cup firmly packed brown sugar
   1/2 cup shortening, softened
   1/2 cup peanut butter
    1   egg
    1   teaspoon vanilla extract
   1/2 cup dark corn syrup
   1 1/2 cups uncooked regular oats

Combine flour, baking powder, and salt in a bowl. Add next 5 ingredients and about half the syrup; beat until smooth, about 2 minutes. Fold in remaining syrup and oats. Drop by teaspoonfuls onto greased baking sheets. Bake at 375° for 10 to 12 minutes. Yield: 3 1/2 dozen.

Pecan Cookies

    1   cup shortening
    1   cup firmly packed brown sugar
    1   cup sugar
    2   eggs
   1/2 teaspoon salt
    1   teaspoon baking powder
    1   teaspoon soda
    2   cups all-purpose flour
    2   cups oats, regular or quick-cooking, uncooked
    2   cups coarsely chopped pecans
    1   teaspoon vanilla extract

Cream shortening and sugars; add eggs. Add salt, baking powder, soda, and flour; blend well. Add oats, pecans, and vanilla. Drop by teaspoonfuls onto greased cookie sheets. Bake at 375° for 10 to 12 minutes. Yield: about 5 dozen cookies.

Crisp Buttery Cookies

    1   cup shortening
    1   cup sugar
   1/2 cup firmly packed brown sugar
    2   eggs
   2 1/3 cups all-purpose flour
    1   teaspoon soda
    1   teaspoon salt
    1   teaspoon vanilla extract
    1   teaspoon butter flavoring
   1 1/2 cups chopped pecans

Cream together shortening and sugars. Add eggs one at a time, beating well after each addition. Combine flour, soda, and salt; add to creamed mixture and mix. Add flavorings and stir in nuts. Drop by spoonfuls onto ungreased cookie sheets. Bake at 350° for 10 to 12 minutes. Yield: 7 to 8 dozen.

132 cookies and small cakes

*Chocolate Chip Cookies

½ cup butter or margarine
6 tablespoons sugar
6 tablespoons firmly packed brown sugar
1 egg
½ teaspoon vanilla extract
¼ teaspoon water
1 cup plus 2 tablespoons all-purpose flour
½ teaspoon soda
½ teaspoon salt
½ cup chopped nuts
1 (6-ounce) package semisweet chocolate pieces

Cream together butter and sugars. Beat in egg; add vanilla and water. Combine flour, soda, and salt; stir into creamed mixture. Add nuts and semisweet chocolate pieces; mix well. Drop by well-rounded half teaspoonfuls onto greased cookie sheets. Bake at 375° for 10 to 12 minutes. Yield: about 50 cookies.

Yum Yum Cookies

1 cup shortening
1½ cups sugar
3 eggs
3 cups all-purpose flour
1 teaspoon soda
1 teaspoon ground cinnamon
¼ teaspoon salt
1 tablespoon water
1 (8-ounce) package dates, chopped
1 cup chopped nuts

Blend shortening with sugar until light and fluffy. Add eggs, one at a time, beating well after each addition. Combine dry ingredients and add to sugar mixture. Add water to dates and add with nuts to flour mixture. Drop by teaspoonfuls onto greased cookie sheets. Bake at 375° for 12 to 15 minutes. Yield: 6 dozen cookies.

*Yogurt Cookies

½ cup butter, softened
2 cups sugar
3 eggs, beaten
½ cup yogurt
2 teaspoons ground nutmeg, divided
1½ teaspoons vanilla extract
¼ teaspoon salt
3 cups all-purpose flour
1 teaspoon soda
1 tablespoon sugar

Cream butter and 2 cups sugar until light and fluffy. Add eggs, yogurt, 1 teaspoon nutmeg, vanilla, salt, flour, and soda. Beat until smooth. Refrigerate dough for 1 hour.
Drop by teaspoonfuls onto greased cookie sheets. Combine 1 teaspoon nutmeg and 1 tablespoon sugar; sprinkle over cookies. Bake at 400° for 8 to 10 minutes. Cookies will look soft. Remove from cookie sheets immediately. Yield: 8 dozen.

*Sour Cream Twists

1 cup butter
½ cup sugar
1 cup commercial sour cream
1 teaspoon soda
3 cups all-purpose flour
Powdered sugar

Cream butter and sugar until smooth. Gradually stir in sour cream, mixing well. Add soda mixed with small amount of flour. Gradually work in remaining flour.
Turn dough out onto floured surface and work until smooth. Divide dough into 40 equal parts and roll out each piece into a strip. Shape into twists. Place on greased baking sheet. Bake at 475° about 19 minutes or until lightly golden. Dust with powdered sugar. Yield: 40 twists.

Almond Cakes

 2½ cups all-purpose flour
  1 teaspoon baking powder
 ¼ teaspoon salt
 ¾ cup sugar
 ⅔ cup salad oil
  1 egg yolk
  1 tablespoon orange juice
  2 teaspoons almond extract
  1 teaspoon vanilla extract
  1 egg white
  1 egg, slightly beaten
  1 tablespoon water
 ⅓ cup blanched almonds, slightly toasted

Combine flour, baking powder, and salt. Combine sugar and salad oil in large mixing bowl; beat in egg yolk. Mixture will look curdled. Beat in orange juice, almond, and vanilla. Stir in half the dry ingredients. Beat egg white until stiff but not dry; fold into batter. Add remaining dry ingredients, kneading slightly with fingers to make a smooth dough. Shape in 1-inch balls; place on ungreased cookie sheet. Press with bottom of flat glass.

Brush each cookie lightly with beaten egg and water. Press almond in center of each cookie. Bake at 350° about 12 minutes or until lightly browned. Yield: about 3 dozen cookies.

Koulourakia (Cookie Twists)

  1 cup butter, softened
 2¼ cups sugar
 10 eggs
  4 teaspoons vanilla extract
  4 teaspoons baking powder
 8½ to 9½ cups all-purpose flour
  1 egg, slightly beaten

Cream butter and sugar until light and fluffy. Add 10 eggs, one at a time, beating well after each addition; add vanilla.

Combine baking powder and flour; add enough flour to creamed mixture to make a pliable dough. Shape into twists. Brush tops of cookies with beaten egg. Bake on ungreased cookie sheets at 375° for 20 to 25 minutes. Yield: 10 dozen cookies.

*Coconut Jumbles

 ½ cup butter or margarine, softened
 ¼ cup sugar
  1 egg, beaten
 1¼ cups all-purpose flour
 ½ teaspoon baking powder
 ⅛ teaspoon salt
  1 teaspoon vanilla extract
  1 egg white, slightly beaten
Shredded coconut

Cream butter; add sugar gradually, continuing to cream. Add egg; blend well. Combine flour, baking powder, and salt; add to creamed mixture, beating well. Stir in vanilla.

Roll out dough about ⅛ inch thick on a lightly floured surface; cut with doughnut cutter. Brush tops with egg white; sprinkle with coconut. Bake at 400° for 8 minutes or until a delicate brown. Yield: about 4 dozen.

*Crisp Rolled Molasses Cookies

  1 cup shortening
  1 cup sugar
  2 teaspoons ground ginger
 ½ teaspoon salt
  1 egg, beaten
  1 teaspoon soda
  1 cup dark molasses
 2½ cups all-purpose flour, divided

Cream shortening, sugar, ginger, and salt. Add egg; mix well. Combine soda and molasses; stir until frothy, and add to creamed mixture. Add 2 cups flour; turn onto a floured surface and add enough of the remaining flour to make a dough that can be rolled.

Using a small amount of dough at a time, roll to ⅛-inch thickness; cut with a floured 3-inch cutter. Place on greased baking sheets; bake at 375° for 15 minutes. These cookies keep well in a covered container. Yield: about 4 dozen.

Sour Cream-Nutmeg Sugar Cookies

4½ cups all-purpose flour
1 teaspoon salt
1 teaspoon soda
1 teaspoon baking powder
½ teaspoon ground nutmeg
1 cup butter
1½ cups sugar
2 eggs
1 cup commercial sour cream
1½ teaspoons vanilla extract
Sugar

Combine flour, salt, soda, baking powder, and nutmeg. Cream butter with sugar until fluffy; add eggs, one at a time, beating well after each addition. Add dry ingredients to creamed mixture alternately with sour cream, mixing until smooth after each addition. Blend in vanilla. Wrap in waxed paper and chill until firm enough to roll. Roll out on floured surface to about ¼ inch thickness; cut with large cookie cutter and place on ungreased baking sheets. Sprinkle with sugar; bake at 375° for 12 minutes or until browned. Yield: about 5 dozen.

*Powdered Sugar Cookies

1½ cups sifted powdered sugar
1 cup butter
1 egg
1 teaspoon vanilla extract
½ teaspoon almond extract
2½ cups all-purpose flour
1 teaspoon cream of tartar
1 teaspoon soda

Cream sugar and butter; add egg and flavorings; mix thoroughly. Combine dry ingredients and stir into creamed mixture. Refrigerate 2 to 3 hours. Divide dough in half and roll out on lightly floured surface. Roll thin, but leave dough thick enough to pick up the design in the cookie cutters. Dip cutters in flour before each cutting. Cut as many cookies from each rolling as possible. The least amount of working with the dough gives the best cookies. Place on lightly greased baking sheet.
Bake at 375° for 7 or 8 minutes or until cookies are delicately golden. Yield: about 4 dozen cookies.

*Orange Sugar Cookies

½ cup butter or margarine
1 cup sugar, divided
2 eggs
1 tablespoon frozen orange juice concentrate, thawed and undiluted
3 tablespoons grated orange rind, divided
2 cups all-purpose flour
2 teaspoons baking powder

Cream butter and ½ cup sugar until light and fluffy. Add eggs, one at a time, beating well after each addition. Blend in orange juice concentrate and 1 tablespoon grated orange rind. Combine flour and baking powder; blend into creamed mixture.

Wrap dough in waxed paper and refrigerate for 3 hours. Roll out on lightly floured surface to ¼-inch thickness. Cut with a 2-inch cookie cutter. Place on greased cookie sheets. Combine ½ cup sugar and 2 tablespoons grated orange rind; sprinkle mixture over cookies. Bake at 375° for 8 to 10 minutes. Yield: 5 dozen cookies.

Coffee Crescents

    1 *cup butter or margarine, softened*
    2 *cups sugar, divided*
        Juice of 1 orange
  ½ *teaspoon orange extract*
    3 *cups all-purpose flour*
  ½ *teaspoon soda*
    1 *teaspoon baking powder*
  ½ *cup honey*
  ¾ *cup brewed coffee*
    1 *cup chopped nuts*

Cream butter and 1 cup sugar until light and fluffy. Add orange juice and orange extract. Combine flour, soda, and baking powder; add gradually to creamed mixture. Chill dough 1 hour. Roll out to ¼-inch thickness on floured surface. Cut with crescent-shaped cookie cutter; place on greased cookie sheets. Bake at 350° for 8 minutes or until delicately browned. Cool.

Combine remaining 1 cup sugar, honey, and coffee in saucepan; bring to a boil and simmer 5 minutes. Dip the cooled cookies in honey mixture and sprinkle them with nuts. Place on cake racks to drain. Yield: about 4 dozen cookies.

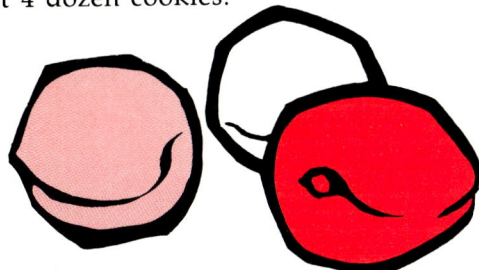

Brown Sugar Refrigerator Cookies

    2 *eggs*
    1 *cup butter or margarine, softened*
    2 *cups firmly packed brown sugar*
    1 *teaspoon vanilla extract*
3½ *cups all-purpose flour*
  ½ *teaspoon salt*
    1 *teaspoon soda*
    1 *cup finely chopped nuts*

Combine eggs, butter, sugar, and vanilla in large mixing bowl. Cream until smooth. Combine flour, salt, and soda; add to creamed mixture and blend well. Stir in nuts.

Roll dough into small rolls; wrap in waxed paper, and put in refrigerator to chill overnight. Slice very thinly and place on lightly greased cookie sheets. Bake at 350° for 12 to 15 minutes. Yield: 5 to 7 dozen.

*Sugar Cookies

    1 *cup butter or margarine*
1½ *cups powdered sugar*
    1 *egg*
    1 *teaspoon vanilla extract*
1½ *teaspoons soda*
    1 *teaspoon cream of tartar*
2½ *cups all-purpose flour*

Cream butter and sugar until light and fluffy. Add egg, vanilla, soda, and cream of tartar; blend in flour. Cover and chill for 2 hours. Roll out and cut in desired shapes. Bake at 350° for about 15 to 20 minutes. Yield: 3 dozen.

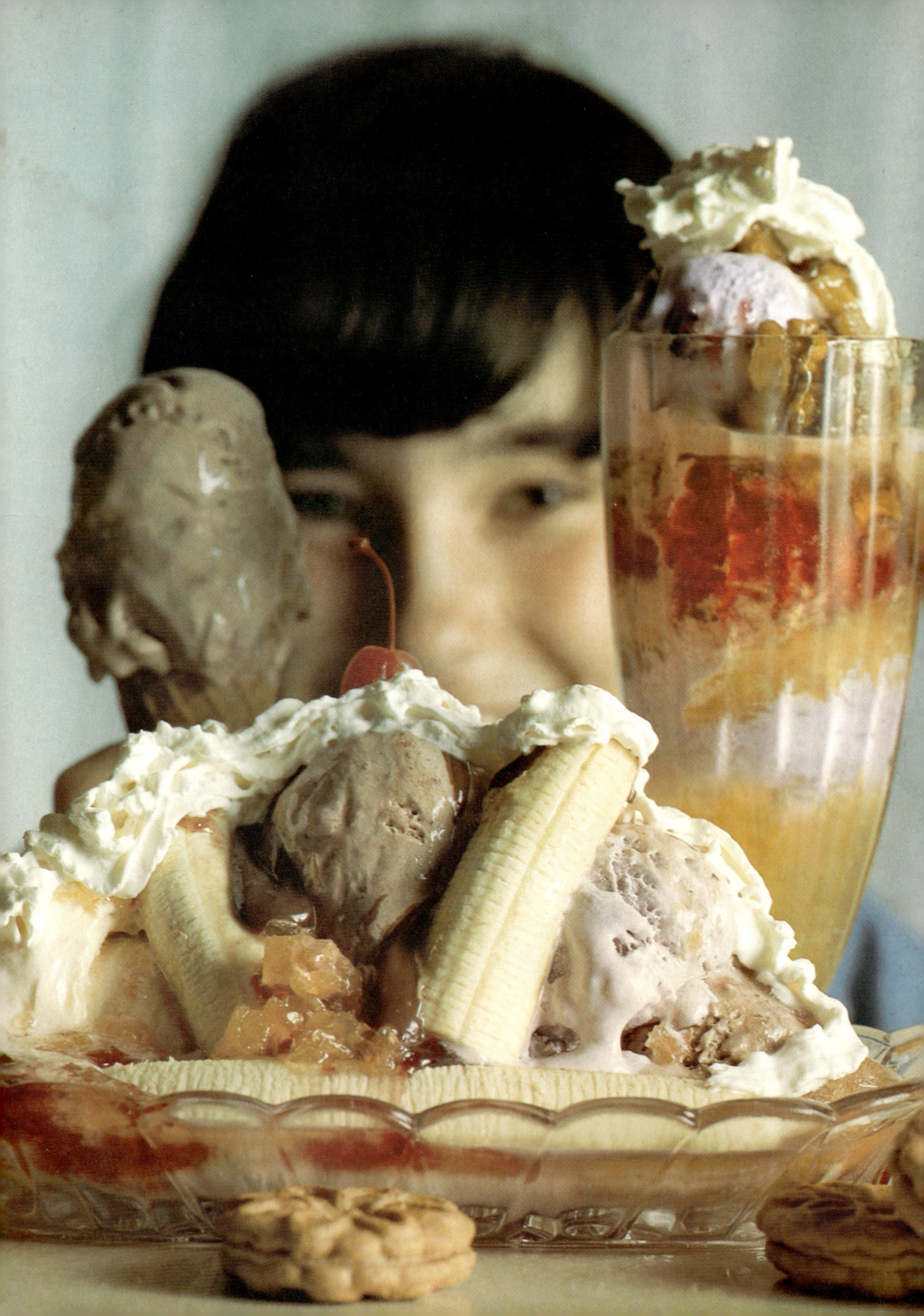

Desserts

Such favorite Southern desserts as homemade ice cream, bread pudding, sherbets of all flavors, and baked apples are included in this chapter. All are easy to prepare, delightful to look at, and even better to eat, as both family and company will readily testify. Either served as an end-of-the-meal treat or even as a midnight snack, the following desserts are guaranteed to satisfy the sweet tooths of old and young alike.

Chocolate Custard Ice Cream

1 *cup sugar*
2 *tablespoons all-purpose flour*
¼ *teaspoon salt*
4 *cups half-and-half, divided*
2 *squares unsweetened chocolate, melted*
2 *eggs, slightly beaten*
1½ *teaspoons vanilla extract*

Combine sugar, flour, and salt in a 1-quart saucepan or in top of double boiler. Stir in 2 cups cream and melted chocolate. Cook over low heat, stirring constantly, until thickened. Cook an additional 2 minutes. Add a small amount of the mixture to the eggs; return eggs to pan. Cook, stirring constantly, for 1 minute. Remove from heat. Stir in the remaining 2 cups cream and the vanilla. Chill thoroughly. Freeze. Yield: 1½ quarts.

Chocolate Ice Cream

2 *squares chocolate*
2 *cups milk*
1 *cup sugar*
Dash salt
1½ *teaspoons vanilla extract*
1 *cup half-and-half*
1 *cup whipping cream*

Melt chocolate in milk in top of double boiler. Stir in sugar and salt. Remove from heat and beat until cool and fluffy. Add vanilla and half-and-half. Fold in cream. Pour into half-gallon freezer can.

Freeze in hand-turned or motor-driven freezer, using a mixture of 8 parts crushed ice to 1 part ice cream salt. When ice cream is frozen, tip freezer to drain off all water. Before opening can, wipe lid carefully. Scrape ice cream off dasher and pack firmly in can. Cover with double thickness of waxed paper and replace lid (fitted with cork or paper plug). Repack with a mixture of 4 parts crushed ice to 1 part ice cream salt. Cover with paper or heavy cloth. Let stand 1½ to 2 hours to ripen. Yield: ½ gallon.

Old-Fashioned Custard Ice Cream

1½ *cups sugar*
¼ *cup all-purpose flour*
½ *teaspoon salt*
1 *quart milk*
4 *eggs, beaten*
1 *quart whipping cream*
3 *tablespoons vanilla extract*
Bottled chocolate, butterscotch, and nut toppings

Combine sugar, flour, and salt. Gradually stir in milk. Cook over a low heat, stirring until thickened. Stir small amount of hot mixture into beaten eggs. Return to the hot mixture. Cook 2 minutes over low heat, stirring constantly. Chill. Stir in cream and vanilla. Freeze in ice cream freezer. Offer a choice of toppings. Yield: 2½ quarts.

*Banana-Orange Ice Cream

¾ cup evaporated milk
½ cup mashed bananas
2 tablespoons lemon juice
½ cup fresh orange juice
⅔ cup sugar
Dash salt
2 tablespoons lemon juice

Put evaporated milk in ice tray of refrigerator; chill until ice crystals begin to form around edges. Meanwhile, mix together the bananas, lemon juice, orange juice, sugar, and salt; stir until sugar is dissolved. Let stand.

Put ice-cold milk into a cold 1-quart bowl. Whip with cold beater until milk is fluffy. Add 2 tablespoons lemon juice; continue whipping until stiff. Add banana mixture gradually, beating at low speed until blended. Put into 1-quart ice tray; freeze, without stirring, at coldest temperature until firm. Yield: 1 quart.

*Quick Pineapple Milk Sherbet

1 (15¼-ounce) can crushed pineapple
½ cup sugar
Dash salt
1 teaspoon grated lemon peel
2 tablespoons lemon juice
1 teaspoon vanilla extract
2 cups milk

Drain pineapple. There should be about 1½ cups fruit and 1 cup syrup. To the syrup add sugar, salt, lemon peel, lemon juice, and vanilla; stir until sugar is dissolved. Stir gradually into milk. Freeze in refrigerator tray at coldest temperature until firm around edges and slushy in center. (Chill mixing bowl, beaters, and drained pineapple at same time.)

Put sherbet into the chilled bowl; break up with a fork and beat slowly, just until fluffy. Fold in drained pineapple, return to tray, and freeze until firm but not hard. Turn refrigerator to medium cold setting to "ripen" sherbet until serving time. Yield: 1 quart or 6 servings.

Orange-Pineapple Sherbet

2 (15-ounce) cans sweetened condensed milk
2 (8¼-ounce) cans crushed pineapple
5 or 6 (10-ounce) bottles orange soda

Insert dasher in can of electric or hand freezer. Add sweetened condensed milk and pineapple. Add enough orange soda to fill can three-fourths full or slightly higher.

Position can in bucket; put on cover. Freeze mixture, using 2½ cups rock salt or 1½ cups table salt and 20 pounds ice. Alternate layers of ice and salt until mixture is level with top of can. Reserve some ice and salt to add during freezing. Yield: 1 gallon.

Variations: Substitute frozen strawberries for pineapple and strawberry soda water for orange; or use pineapple with citrus-flavored low-calorie beverage.

*Pineapple-Lemon Ice Cream

2 cups crushed pineapple
1½ cups sugar
Juice of 6 lemons
1 (15-ounce) can sweetened condensed milk
1 (13-ounce) can evaporated milk
Whole milk

Combine pineapple and sugar; heat and stir until sugar is dissolved. Cool. Add lemon juice to cooled mixture. Stir in sweetened condensed milk and evaporated milk, and mix well. Put mixture in bucket of 1-gallon freezer. Add whole milk to fill bucket about two-thirds full. Freeze until firm. Yield: 1 gallon.

Easy Peach Ice Cream

4 pounds ripe peaches
½ to ¾ cup sugar
Dash salt
1 teaspoon vanilla extract
½ cup sugar
2 cups milk
2 cups whipping cream

ice cream and sherbets 139

Pare and slice peaches. Stir in sugar and salt, and let sit in refrigerator until sugar is dissolved. Combine vanilla, sugar, milk, and cream. Partly freeze until mushy; remove dasher and stir in peaches. Continue freezing until firm. Yield: 9 servings.

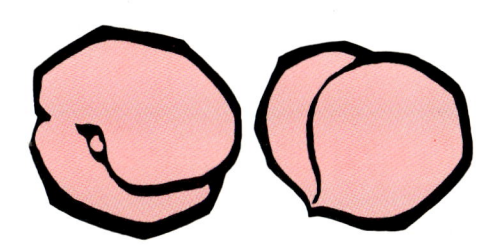

*Peach Ice Cream

10 egg yolks
3 cups sugar
½ teaspoon salt
1 teaspoon vanilla extract
1 (13-ounce) can evaporated milk
1 quart fresh peaches, mashed
4 envelopes unflavored gelatin
¼ cup water
2 cups milk
Milk

Put egg yolks, sugar, salt, and vanilla in large mixer bowl. Beat at high speed until mixture is very thick. Add evaporated milk and peaches and mix well. Sprinkle gelatin over water to soften. Add to 2 cups milk and heat at low temperature until gelatin is dissolved.

Combine peach and gelatin mixtures and put in freezer can immediately. Add additional milk if needed, and start freezing at once. All ingredients except gelatin may be refrigerated ahead of time. Yield: 1 gallon.

Tia Maria Marble Ice Cream

¼ to ½ cup Tia Maria
1 quart vanilla ice cream

Swirl Tia Maria into slightly softened ice cream. Return to freezer until serving time.
Serve in small scoops. Yield: 8 to 10 servings.

Butter Pecan Ice Cream

1 cup firmly packed light brown sugar
½ cup water
Dash salt
2 eggs, beaten
2 tablespoons butter or margarine
1 cup milk
1 teaspoon vanilla extract
1 cup whipping cream
½ cup finely chopped toasted pecans

Combine sugar, water, and salt in top of double boiler. Cook until sugar is melted. Pour a small amount over beaten eggs and return eggs to sugar mixture. Stir and cook over hot, not boiling, water until thickened. Add butter. Cool; then add milk and vanilla. Beat cream until thick and fold into cooled mixture. Stir in pecans. Freeze in half-gallon freezer until firm. Yield: 6 servings.

*Strawberry Ice Cream

1 pint fresh strawberries or 1 (10-ounce) package frozen strawberries
⅔ cup sugar
⅛ teaspoon salt
1 tablespoon lemon juice
1 cup evaporated milk

Wash, drain, and hull fresh strawberries; thaw frozen ones. Put into a bowl and mash thoroughly with bottom of a glass or bottle. Add sugar, salt, and lemon juice. Stir in evaporated milk. Freeze in hand-turned or motor-driven freezer, using a mixture of 8 parts crushed ice to 1 part ice cream salt.

When ice cream is frozen, tip freezer to drain off water. Wipe lid carefully. Open can; scrape ice cream off dasher and pack firmly in can. Replace lid (fitted with cork or paper plug). Repack with a mixture of 3 parts crushed ice to 1 part ice cream salt. Cover with paper or heavy cloth. Let stand 1½ to 2 hours to ripen. Yield: about 1½ pints.

Marshmallow-Vanilla Ice Cream

30 large marshmallows
½ cup milk
4 eggs, beaten
½ cup sugar
1 tablespoon vanilla extract
1 (15-ounce) can sweetened condensed milk
1 pint whipping cream
Whole milk

Melt marshmallows in ½ cup milk in top of a double boiler over simmering water. Remove from heat and stir into eggs to which sugar has been added. Stir in vanilla and sweetened condensed milk. Put mixture in bucket of a 1 gallon freezer. Add whipping cream and enough whole milk to fill freezer two-thirds full. Freeze until firm. Remove dasher, pack freezer wih ice and salt, and let sit at least 1 hour before serving. Yield: 1 gallon.

Rich Strawberry Ice Cream

1 quart fresh strawberries
¾ to 1 cup sugar
2 cups half-and-half
2 cups whipping cream
Dash salt

Wash and hull strawberries; put through a food mill. Add sugar and let stand for several hours. Combine with half-and-half, whipping cream, and salt. Freeze until firm. Yield: 9 servings.

*Vanilla Ice Cream

⅓ cup corn syrup
2 tablespoons cornstarch
¾ cup sugar
½ teaspoon salt
3 cups milk
2 eggs, slightly beaten
2 teaspoons vanilla extract
1 cup half-and-half

Combine corn syrup, cornstarch, sugar, salt, and milk in top of double boiler. Mix in eggs. Cook over boiling water, stirring constantly, until mixture is slightly thickened, about 5 minutes. Chill. Add vanilla and half-and-half.

With electric freezer, follow manufacturer's directions. With crank freezer, pour chilled custard mixture into can, filling no more than two-thirds full. Pack tub with alternate layers of crushed ice and rock salt, using 8 parts ice to 1 part salt. Turn crank slowly, increasing speed and turning until crank no longer turns easily. Remove dasher. Pack ice cream; cover. Repack tub with ice and salt, using 4 parts ice to 1 part salt. Let stand 2 hours. Yield: about 2 quarts.

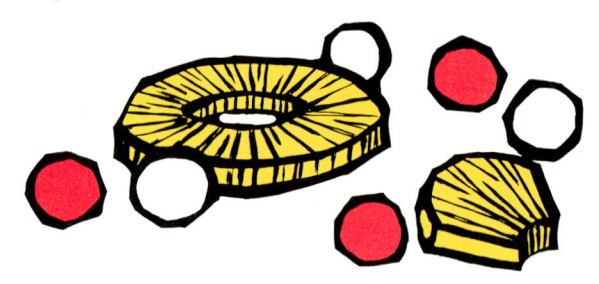

*Baked Custard

4 eggs, slightly beaten
½ cup sugar
¼ teaspoon salt
3 cups milk, scalded
1½ teaspoons vanilla extract
Ground nutmeg

Combine eggs, sugar, and salt and stir until well blended. Slowly pour milk into egg mixture, stirring constantly. Add vanilla. Pour into six (5-ounce) custard cups or a 1½-quart casserole. Sprinkle with nutmeg. Set in a large baking pan and pour hot water into pan to within ½ inch of top of custard.

Bake at 325° until a knife inserted halfway between center and outside edge comes out clean (35 to 40 minutes for individual custard cups and 45 to 50 minutes for casserole). Remove promptly from oven and cool. Serve hot or cold. Yield: 6 servings.

*Coconut Noodle Custard

  1 *(5-ounce) package noodles*
  3 *eggs, well beaten*
 ¾ *cup sugar*
     Pinch salt
  2 *teaspoons vanilla extract*
  2 *cups milk*
  1 *cup flaked coconut*
     Whipped cream (optional)

Cook noodles according to package directions. Drain in colander and rinse well with boiling water. Beat eggs until light and fluffy. Gradually add sugar and beat well. Stir in salt, vanilla, milk, and coconut. Stir in drained noodles. Turn into greased 1½-quart casserole dish. Set dish in a pan of hot water and bake at 325° about 1 hour or until custard is firm in center. May be served plain or with whipped cream. Yield: 8 servings.

*Baked Peach Custard

  1 *cup sliced cling peaches*
  1 *tablespoon softened butter or margarine*
 ¼ *teaspoon vanilla extract*
  2 *tablespoons sugar*
  1 *tablespoon all-purpose flour*
     Dash salt
  1 *egg yolk*
  3 *tablespoons evaporated milk*
  1 *egg white, stiffly beaten*

Grease two 6-ounce custard cups and set aside. Drain peaches and reserve liquid. Divide drained peaches between custard cups. Put butter and vanilla in a small bowl. Combine sugar, flour, and salt; add a small amount at a time to butter and vanilla, beating well after each addition. Add egg yolk; beat well.
    Combine evaporated milk and 3 tablespoons peach juice and stir into butter mixture. Fold in stiffly beaten egg white. Spoon mixture over peaches. Set custard cups in a pan holding about ½-inch hot water. Bake on center rack of oven at 325° for 25 to 35 minutes or until top is light brown. Yield: 2 servings.

*Banana Pudding

 ½ *cup sugar*
 ¼ *cup all-purpose flour*
 ¼ *teaspoon salt*
  2 *cups scalded milk*
  2 *egg yolks*
  1 *teaspoon vanilla extract*
     About 25 vanilla wafers
  4 *bananas, sliced*
  2 *egg whites*
 ¼ *cup sugar*

Put ½ cup sugar, flour, and salt into top of double boiler. Mix well; then stir in milk. Cook over simmering water for about 15 minutes, stirring constantly. Beat egg yolks well and combine with custard; cook 2 minutes longer. Add vanilla. Line a 1-quart baking dish with vanilla wafers. Add a layer of sliced bananas. Top with custard. Repeat layers, if necessary. Beat egg whites until stiff. Gradually add sugar. Spread meringue over pudding and bake at 350° about 12 to 15 minutes. Yield: 6 servings.

Date Pudding

  1 *(1-pound) package pitted dates*
  1 *teaspoon soda*
  1 *cup boiling water*
  1 *cup sugar*
  2 *tablespoons butter or margarine*
  1 *egg, well-beaten*
1¼ *cups all-purpose flour*
 ¼ *teaspoon baking powder*
  1 *cup chopped nuts*
     Whipped cream

Cut dates in small pieces and put in a bowl. Sprinkle soda over top of dates and pour boiling water over all. Let stand while mixing the other ingredients.
    Cream sugar and butter; add well-beaten egg and mix well. Combine flour and baking powder and stir into creamed mixture. Stir in date mixture and nuts. Spoon batter into a greased 13- x 9- x 2-inch pan and bake at 325° about 30 minutes. Serve with whipped cream. May be wrapped and frozen. Yield: 12 servings.

Double Chocolate Pudding Cups

- 1 cup canned chocolate syrup
- 1 cup boiling water
- ½ teaspoon almond extract
- 1½ cups all-purpose flour
- ½ cup sugar
- 3 tablespoons cocoa
- 2 teaspoons baking powder
- ½ teaspoon salt
- 1 egg, beaten
- ½ cup milk
- 3 tablespoons melted shortening or oil
- 1 teaspoon vanilla extract
- 2 tablespoons slivered blanched almonds

Set out 8 individual custard cups. Preheat oven to 425°.

Blend chocolate syrup, water, and almond extract; pour ¼ cup into each custard cup. Set aside.

Combine flour, sugar, cocoa, baking powder, and salt into a medium-size mixing bowl. Blend egg, milk, shortening or oil, and vanilla. Add liquid all at once to flour mixture, stirring until well blended. Drop heaping tablespoonfuls over chocolate sauce in custard cups. Sprinkle with almonds. Bake at 425° for 18 to 20 minutes, or until cake tester inserted in center comes out clean. Serve warm. Yield: 8 servings.

Chocolate Fudge Pudding

- 1¼ cups sugar, divided
- 2 tablespoons margarine
- ½ cup milk
- 1 cup all-purpose flour
- 2 teaspoons baking powder
- ¼ teaspoon salt
- 2 tablespoons cocoa
- ½ cup chopped walnuts
- ⅓ cup cocoa
- ½ cup firmly packed brown sugar
- 1½ cups boiling water

Cream ¾ cup sugar and margarine until light and fluffy; stir in milk. Combine flour, baking powder, salt, and 2 tablespoons cocoa; add to creamed mixture and blend until smooth. Fold in walnuts. Spread in a greased 9-inch square pan.

Combine ½ cup sugar, ⅓ cup cocoa, and brown sugar; blend well. Sprinkle over batter. Pour boiling water over entire mixture. Bake at 350° for 35 to 40 minutes. Yield: 8 servings.

*Rice Pudding

- 3 cups cooked rice
- 3 cups milk
- ½ cup sugar
- 3 tablespoons butter or margarine
- 1 teaspoon vanilla extract

Combine rice, milk, sugar, and butter. Cook over medium heat until thickened, about 30 minutes, stirring often. Add vanilla. Pour into serving dish. Serve hot or cold. Yield: 6 servings.

Strawberry Smoothie: Follow directions above until pudding is slightly thickened; to 3 beaten egg yolks add enough pudding mixture to blend. Stir egg yolks into remaining pudding mixture. Cook 1 minute or until pudding is thickened. Spoon into individual dessert dishes. Chill. *Strawberry Topping:* Beat 3 egg whites until frothy. Add ¾ cup strawberry (or cherry, pineapple, raspberry) preserves; continue beating until whites are stiff. Top chilled pudding with meringue whip; spoon 1 teaspoon preserves on top of whip.

Mocha Rice Pudding: To milk in recipe for Rice Pudding add 2 teaspoons instant coffee. Prepare according to directions given. Cool. Fold ¾ cup marshmallow cream into pudding. Spoon into dessert dishes. Top with marshmallow cream and chocolate syrup.

Caramel Rice Pudding: prepare recipe for Rice Pudding. Pour ½ cup sugar into a loafpan. Cook over very low heat, stirring constantly, until sugar melts and turns a golden color. Tilt pan frequently as sugar melts to coat sides thoroughly. Remove from heat. Pour Rice Pudding into loafpan. Cover and bake at 350° for 30 minutes. Cool. Unmold onto serving dish. Serve plain or with whipped cream.

Pineapple Upside Down Bread Pudding

      2 eggs, beaten
     ½ cup sugar
      1 (20-ounce) can pineapple tidbits
     ½ cup juice, drained from pineapple
      2 quarts soft bread cubes
     ⅓ cup butter or margarine
     ½ cup firmly packed brown sugar
      6 maraschino cherries, chopped

Combine beaten eggs and sugar. Drain pineapple and set aside. Measure ½ cup juice and add to eggs and sugar; add bread cubes.

Melt butter or margarine in electric skillet set at 250°. Remove 3 tablespoons of the melted butter and add to bread cube mixture. Combine brown sugar with butter remaining in skillet and spread evenly over bottom of skillet. Sprinkle chopped cherries over sugar mixture and arrange pineapple tidbits over cherries. Pour bread mixture over fruit in skillet.

Cover skillet and bake at 250° about 35 minutes, or until pudding is set and lightly browned on the bottom. Remove cover and continue baking about 15 minutes longer. Disconnect the skillet.

Place a platter or large cake plate over skillet and invert skillet so pudding falls out, upside down, onto plate. Yield: 9 servings.

*Bread Pudding

      6 eggs
      2 cups sugar
      2 teaspoons salt
      1 quart milk
      1 tablespoon vanilla extract
      3 drops yellow food coloring (optional)
    1½ cups stale bread cubes
     ½ cup seedless raisins
      1 tablespoon all-purpose flour
     ½ teaspoon ground nutmeg
      2 tablespoons butter

Beat eggs, sugar, and salt until mixture is lemon colored. Add milk, vanilla, and food coloring. Place bread cubes and raisins which have been coated with flour in the bottom of an oiled 13- x 9- x 2-inch pan. Sprinkle with nutmeg; then pour in milk mixture. Dot with butter and bake at 350° for 30 to 35 minutes. Serve with or without custard sauce. Yield: 16 to 20 servings.

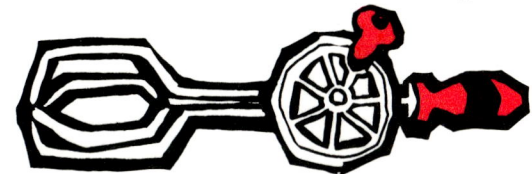

Bread Pudding with Whiskey Sauce

      1 (1-pound) loaf French bread or 6 cups
          broken bread slices
      1 quart milk
      3 eggs, slightly beaten
      2 cups sugar
      2 tablespoons vanilla extract
      1 cup seedless raisins
      3 tablespoons melted margarine
     Whiskey Sauce

Break bread into small chunks and put in a large bowl. Add milk and let soak about 10 minutes; crush with hands until well mixed. Add eggs, sugar, vanilla, and raisins.

Melt margarine in a 13- x 9- x 2-inch pan. Spoon pudding mixture into pan; bake at 325° for 30 to 45 minutes, or until very firm. Let mixture cool; then cut into cubes. Spoon cubes into dessert dishes and cover with Whiskey Sauce. Pudding may be put under broiler if dessert dishes are ovenproof. Yield: 6 to 8 servings.

Whiskey Sauce:

     ½ cup butter or margarine
      1 cup sugar
      1 egg, beaten
     Whiskey to taste

Put butter and sugar in top of double boiler and cook until very hot and sugar has dissolved. Add beaten egg and whip very fast to prevent mixture from curdling. Let cool and add whiskey to taste. Serve over bread pudding. Yield: about ½ cup.

*Old-Fashioned Bread Pudding

- 4 slices buttered toast, cut in quarters
- 1/3 cup seedless raisins
- 2 eggs, slightly beaten
- 5 teaspoons sugar, divided
- 1/8 teaspoon salt
- 1 cup milk
- 1 cup boiling water
- 1 teaspoon vanilla extract
- 1/4 teaspoon ground cinnamon

Place toast in a greased 1½-quart casserole; sprinkle with raisins. Combine eggs, 4 teaspoons sugar, salt, milk, water, and vanilla; pour over toast. Let stand 10 minutes; sprinkle with cinnamon and remaining sugar. Bake at 350° for 30 to 40 minutes or until knife inserted in center comes out clean. Yield: 4 to 6 servings.

Apricot Rice Pudding

- 1½ cups cooked regular rice
- ½ cup shredded coconut
- 1½ cups apricot nectar
- ½ cup water
- 2/3 cup sugar, divided
- ½ teaspoon salt
- 3 eggs, separated
- 1 teaspoon grated lemon rind
- 1 teaspoon vanilla extract
- ¼ teaspoon almond extract
- ½ cup apricot preserves

Mix rice and coconut in 10- x 6- x 2-inch baking dish. Blend apricot nectar, water, 1/3 cup sugar, and salt in small saucepan and bring to a boil. Combine egg yolks, lemon rind, and flavorings; beat slightly. Gradually stir in hot apricot nectar. Pour over rice and coconut. Set in pan of hot water. Bake at 350° about 45 minutes or until set. Cool slightly. Spread top with apricot preserves. Beat egg whites until soft peaks form. Gradually add remaining sugar and beat until egg whites stand in stiff peaks. Spread meringue over pudding. Return to oven and bake 15 minutes longer or until lightly browned. Cut into squares and serve warm or cold as desired. Yield: 8 servings.

*Butterscotch Rice Pudding

- 1 (3¾-ounce) package butterscotch pudding and pie filling mix
- 1½ cups milk
- 2 eggs, separated
- 2 cups cooked regular rice
- 1 teaspoon vanilla extract
- 2 tablespoons firmly packed brown sugar

Combine pudding mix, milk, and egg yolks. Cook over medium heat, stirring constantly until thickened. Add rice and vanilla. Cool. Beat egg whites until soft peaks form; add brown sugar gradually, beating until whites stand in stiff peaks. Fold into pudding. Spoon into serving dishes. Chill. Yield: 6 servings.

Chantilly Raisin Rice Pudding

- 2/3 cup seedless raisins
- 2½ cups half-and-half
- 2 eggs
- 1/8 teaspoon ground nutmeg
- 1/8 teaspoon salt
- 3 tablespoons sugar
- 1 tablespoon vanilla extract
- 1 cup cooked regular rice
- ¼ cup chopped toasted walnuts or pecans
- Sweetened whipped cream (optional)

Combine raisins and half-and-half and heat slowly. Meanwhile, beat eggs with nutmeg, salt, sugar, and vanilla. Combine with cooked rice. Stir in hot half-and-half and raisins. Turn into a 1-quart baking dish; set in shallow pan of hot water. Bake at 350° for 15 minutes. Sprinkle top with nuts and continue baking 10 to 15 minutes longer, until custard is barely set in center. Place pudding dish in pan of cold water to cool quickly and keep custard creamy. Serve warm or cold. May be topped with sweetened whipped cream if desired. Yield: 8 servings.

*Rice Pudding with Raisins

      4 eggs, beaten
    ¼ teaspoon salt
    ⅓ cup sugar
      2 teaspoons vanilla extract
  1½ teaspoons grated lemon peel
      3 cups milk
  1½ cups cooked regular rice
    ½ cup raisins

Combine eggs, salt, sugar, vanilla, and lemon peel in a greased 2-quart casserole. Combine milk and rice. Stir into egg mixture and add raisins. Set casserole in a pan of hot water filled to within 1 inch of the top of casserole. Bake, uncovered, at 300° for 1½ to 2 hours. After the first 30 minutes, insert spoon at edge of pudding and stir from bottom. Near end of baking time insert a silver knife in the center; if it comes out clean, pudding is done. Serve hot or cold. Yield: 6 to 8 servings.

Orange Sponge Pudding

      2 tablespoons butter or margarine
      1 cup sugar
      4 egg yolks
    ½ cup frozen orange juice concentrate
    ¼ teaspoon salt
      2 tablespoons all-purpose flour
      1 cup milk
      4 egg whites, beaten

Cream butter and sugar together until light and fluffy; add egg yolks and beat well. Add orange juice concentrate and salt, and stir to blend. Add flour, milk, and egg whites and mix well. Pour into 8 greased custard cups. Place cups in a pan of hot water and bake at 375° about 25 minutes. Serve chilled if desired. Yield: 8 servings.

Tappy Peach Pudding

      6 eggs
      3 cups milk
    ½ cup light molasses
    ½ cup sugar
      1 cup seedless raisins
    ½ cup chopped walnuts
      1 teaspoon lemon juice
    ½ teaspoon salt
      1 teaspoon ground cinnamon
    ½ teaspoon ground nutmeg
      2 cups cooked brown rice
      2 cups sliced fresh peaches

Beat eggs and add milk, molasses, sugar, raisins, walnuts, lemon juice, salt, cinnamon, and nutmeg; mix well. Stir in rice and peaches. Pour into a 2-quart casserole and mix well. Place casserole in large baking pan and add boiling water to a depth of 1 inch. Bake at 350° for 1 hour and 15 minutes (stir after 30 minutes) or until tip of knife inserted halfway between center and edge comes out clean. Cool 15 minutes before serving. Yield: 12 servings.

Rhubarb Surprise Pudding

      1 pound fresh rhubarb
  1½ cups sugar, divided
      3 tablespoons butter or margarine
    ½ cup all-bran cereal
    ¾ cup all-purpose flour
      1 teaspoon baking powder
    ¼ teaspoon salt
    ½ cup milk
  3½ teaspoons cornstarch
    ¼ teaspoon salt
    ½ cup boiling water

Cut rhubarb into small pieces and place in greased 8-inch square pan. Blend half the sugar with butter; add cereal. Sift flour with baking powder and salt; add to shortening mixture alternately with milk. Mix well. Spread batter evenly over the rhubarb. Combine remaining sugar with cornstarch and salt; sprinkle over batter. Pour boiling water over pudding and bake at 375° about 1 hour. Yield: 6 servings.

Persimmon Pudding

    1 *cup persimmon pulp*
    1 *cup sugar*
    1 *cup milk*
    2 *tablespoons butter*
    1 *teaspoon vanilla extract*
    1 *cup all-purpose flour*
1½ *teaspoons baking powder*
  ¼ *teaspoon salt*
  ¼ *teaspoon soda*

To prepare a cup of fresh persimmon pulp, force soft, ripe, peeled persimmons through a strainer or ricer. Mix together pulp, sugar, milk, butter, and vanilla.

Combine flour, baking powder, salt, and soda. Add to the persimmon mixture all at once and stir until batter is smooth. Pour into greased 1-quart mold which has a cover. Place covered mold in a steamer or large kettle with about 3 inches of boiling water. Cover kettle and steam 1 to 1¼ hours. It may be necessary to add more boiling water to keep up the level in the kettle. Unmold and serve hot with spiced hard sauce or whipped cream. Yield: 6 servings.

*Indian Pudding

    4 *cups milk*
  ⅓ *cup corn meal*
  ¾ *cup dark molasses*
  ¼ *cup butter or margarine*
    1 *teaspoon salt*
    1 *teaspoon ground ginger*
    3 *tablespoons sugar*
    1 *egg, well beaten*
  ½ *cup seedless raisins*
  ½ *teaspoon ground cinnamon*
    1 *cup milk*

Heat 4 cups milk in top of a double boiler. Stir in corn meal and cook 15 to 20 minutes or until mixture thickens. Add molasses and cook an additional 5 minutes. Remove from heat and stir in butter, salt, ginger, sugar, beaten egg, raisins, and cinnamon. Pour mixture into a well-greased 6-cup baking dish. Pour 1 cup milk over top of mixture. Bake at 325° for 1½ to 2 hours. Serve with vanilla ice cream, if desired. Yield: 8 servings.

Queen of Puddings

    2 *cups milk*
  ⅛ *teaspoon salt*
    1 *tablespoon butter or margarine*
    1 *teaspoon grated lemon rind*
    1 *teaspoon vanilla extract*
    2 *egg yolks, beaten*
1½ *cups vanilla wafer crumbs, finely rolled (about 35 cookies)*
  ¼ *cup red currant jelly*
    2 *egg whites*
  ¼ *cup sugar*

Heat milk with salt, butter or margarine, lemon rind, and vanilla. Add beaten egg yolks. Fold in vanilla wafer crumbs. Pour into 6 (6-ounce) greased glass baking dishes. Place dishes in a baking pan. Pour in water to 1-inch depth. Bake at 325° until set, about 35 to 40 minutes. Cool slightly. Dot surface of each pudding with red currant jelly. Beat egg whites until foamy. Gradually add sugar; beat until smooth and glossy. Spread on top of jelly. Return puddings to oven until meringue is set and lightly browned. Serve immediately. Yield: 6 servings.

French Strawberry Pudding

    1 *(12-ounce) box vanilla wafers*
  ½ *cup butter or margarine*
1½ *cups powdered sugar*
    1 *teaspoon vanilla extract*
    2 *eggs*
    1 *cup whipping cream or 1 (2-ounce) envelope whipped topping mix, prepared*
    1 *(10-ounce) package frozen sweetened strawberries, thawed*
    1 *cup chopped pecans*

Crumble wafers into fine crumbs. Put half the crumbs in bottom of a 13- x 9- x 2-inch pan. Whip butter, sugar, vanilla, and eggs together until light and creamy. Spread over crumb mixture in pan. Whip the cream or topping mix and spread over butter mixture. Spread strawberries over whipped cream. Mix chopped pecans and remaining wafer crumbs. Sprinkle over strawberries. Chill overnight in refrigerator, or put into freezer until firm but not frozen. Yield: 8 servings.

Baked Apples and Figs

  6 *dried figs*
    Boiling water
  6 *baking apples*
 ¼ *cup chopped nuts*
  6 *tablespoons butter, divided*
  1 *cup sugar, divided*
 ½ *cup hot water*

Cover figs with boiling water and let stand 10 minutes; drain. Snip off stems and chop coarsely. Wash and core apples, leaving a large cavity. Place apples in baking dish. Stuff apples with figs and nuts; add 1 tablespoon butter and 1 teaspoon sugar to each apple. Add remaining sugar to water and pour around apples. Cover baking dish and bake at 350° for 40 to 50 minutes or until apples are almost done; uncover. Turn heat to 500° and finish baking, basting frequently to glaze them. Yield: 6 servings.

Note: To prevent apples from bursting, pare top third of apple before baking; or pare a strip around the middle of each one; or prick the skin in several places with a fork.

Cinnamon Baked Apples

 4 to 6 *baking apples*
    Ground cinnamon
  1 *cup maple-blended syrup*
 ½ *cup boiling water*
    Ice Cream Sauce

Core apples; remove about 1 inch of skin from stem end of each apple. Sprinkle each with a dash of cinnamon. Place stem end down in baking dish, and add syrup and water. Bake at 400° for 45 minutes, basting every 15 minutes. Invert apples and continue to cook and baste for 15 to 30 minutes or until apples are soft. Allow to cool, basting occasionally. Serve with Ice Cream Sauce. Yield: 4 to 6 servings.

   Ice Cream Sauce:

  1 *egg*
 ¼ *cup sugar*
    Dash salt
 ¼ *cup melted butter*
1½ *teaspoons vanilla extract*
 ½ *cup cold milk*
  1 *(2-ounce) package dessert topping mix*

Beat egg until thick and light; add sugar and salt, beating constantly. Gradually beat in butter and vanilla. Combine milk and dessert topping in a small bowl; blend; then beat until mixture stands in soft peaks. Fold into egg mixture. Serve on warm cake, baked apples, or other fruit. Yield: 2½ cups.

*Southern Fried Apples

  1 *teaspoon bacon drippings*
10 *large cooking apples*
  1 *cup sugar*

Heat bacon drippings in a heavy skillet or Dutch oven with a lid. Wash apples, but do not pare; cut into quarters and remove core. Cut quarters into ¼-inch slices. Put apples in skillet and sprinkle with sugar. Cover and cook over low heat until apples are soft. Uncover and let simmer, stirring frequently and gently, until most of the liquid is absorbed. May be served as a vegetable or as a dessert, either hot or cold. Yield: 8 servings.

*Marshmallow Apple Crisp

    4 cups peeled, sliced apples
  ¼ cup water
  ¾ cup all-purpose flour
  ½ cup sugar
    1 teaspoon ground cinnamon
  ¼ teaspoon salt
  ½ cup margarine
  ½ cup miniature marshmallows

Place apples and water in an 8-inch square baking dish. Combine flour, sugar, cinnamon, and salt; cut in margarine until mixture is like coarse crumbs. Sprinkle over apples. Bake at 350° for 35 to 40 minutes or until apples are tender. Sprinkle with marshmallows. Broil until lightly browned. Yield: 6 servings.

Apple Brown Betty

    1 cup sugar
  ¼ teaspoon ground cloves
  ¼ teaspoon ground cinnamon
  ¼ teaspoon ground nutmeg
  ¼ teaspoon salt
    3 cups soft bread crumbs, divided
    4 large tart apples, thinly sliced
  ¼ cup melted butter or margarine
    Whipped cream (optional)

Combine sugar, spices, and salt; set aside. Sprinkle ¾ cup bread crumbs in bottom of a greased 2-quart casserole; add a layer of apples and sprinkle with one-third of sugar mixture. Repeat crumb, apple, sugar layers 2 times. Sprinkle remaining ¾ cup bread crumbs on top. Pour melted butter over crumbs. Bake at 350° about 30 minutes or until apples are soft. Serve warm; top with whipped cream. Yield: 6 servings.

*Ambrosia

    2 tablespoons sugar
    4 medium oranges, peeled and sectioned
  ½ cup flaked coconut, divided
    Whipped cream (optional)

Sprinkle sugar over orange sections. Stir to mix. Place half of sections in bowl and sprinkle with half the coconut. Add remaining orange sections and coconut. Cover dish and set in refrigerator until time to serve. Top with whipped cream, if desired. Yield: 6 servings.

Baked Bananas

    6 bananas
  ¼ cup melted butter or margarine
  ¼ cup orange marmalade
    Lemon juice

Peel bananas and brush with butter. Spread with thin coating of orange marmalade and sprinkle with lemon juice. Wrap each banana in heavy-duty aluminum foil. Cook on grill over moderate heat for 15 minutes. Serve as dessert or appetizer. Yield: 6 servings.

Mocha Date Dessert

    1 envelope (1 tablespoon) unflavored gelatin
  ¼ cup cold water
    1 cup strong, hot coffee
  ⅓ cup sugar
    2 tablespoons instant cocoa
  ¼ teaspoon salt
    1 cup pitted dates, sliced
  ¼ cup chopped walnuts
  ½ cup whipping cream, whipped
  ½ teaspoon vanilla extract
    Whipped cream
    Dates
    Peanut butter
    Sugar

Sprinkle gelatin on cold water. Add coffee; stir until gelatin dissolves. Combine sugar, cocoa, and salt; add to gelatin mixture and stir until dissolved. Chill until consistency of unbeaten egg whites; fold in dates, nuts, whipped cream, and vanilla extract. Pour into 3-cup mold; chill until set. Unmold; garnish with whipped cream and additional dates stuffed with peanut butter and rolled in granulated sugar. Yield: 8 servings.

miscellaneous 149

Chocolate Soufflé

    3 (3-ounce) squares unsweetened chocolate
1¼ cups milk
2½ tablespoons cornstarch
 ¾ cup sugar
 ¼ cup cold milk
1½ teaspoons vanilla extract
 ½ teaspoon salt
  6 eggs, separated

Preheat oven to 350°. Butter a 1½-quart soufflé dish and dust with sugar. Set dish in shallow baking pan and place in oven. Pouring boiling water around dish to depth of at least 1 inch.

Melt chocolate with 1¼ cups milk in top of double boiler placed over simmering water. Blend cornstarch and sugar in heavy saucepan. Stir in ¼ cup cold milk to make a smooth mixture. Add hot chocolate mixture gradually, stirring constantly. Cook and stir over low heat until sauce is smooth and thickened. Remove from heat; stir in vanilla.

Add salt to egg whites and beat until stiff and glossy, but not dry. Beat egg yolks until thick and lemon colored. Fold egg yolks into chocolate sauce. Fold mixture into beaten egg whites, adding about one-fourth of mixture at a time. (A rubber spatula is excellent for folding.) Fold gently but thoroughly. Pour mixture into hot soufflé dish. Bake at 350° for 1 to 1¼ hours. Serve at once. Yield: 6 servings.

Sherry Fruit Cup

  2 (10-ounce) packages frozen mixed fruit, thawed
 ¼ cup powdered sugar
  2 tablespoons Cointreau
 ⅓ cup sherry

Cover fruit with sugar. Combine Cointreau and sherry and pour over fruit. Cover and chill for 2 to 3 hours to blend flavors. Yield: 6 servings.

Chocolate Angel Food Dessert

  2 (6-ounce) packages chocolate chips
  4 egg yolks, beaten
Pinch of salt
  1 teaspoon vanilla extract
  4 egg whites
  2 tablespoons sugar
  1 pint whipping cream, whipped
  1 cup chopped pecans
  1 angel food cake, sliced
Whipped cream (optional)

Melt chocolate chips in top of double boiler over simmering water (do not let water boil). Slowly add beaten egg yolks to chocolate and stir well. Add salt and vanilla. Remove from heat. Beat egg whites until stiff, add sugar, and fold into chocolate mixture. Fold in whipped cream and pecans. Set aside.

Line the bottom of a 13- x 9- x 2-inch pan with slices of angel food cake. Save half the slices for second layer. Pour chocolate mixture over layer, cover with remaining slices, and pour chocolate mixture over top. Chill 6 hours or longer. Top with whipped cream, if desired. Yield: 12 to 16 servings.

Chocolate Bavarian

  1 envelope unflavored gelatin
  2 tablespoons cold water
1¾ cups milk
  2 ounces unsweetened chocolate
 ½ cup sugar
Dash salt
1½ teaspoons vanilla extract
 ¼ teaspoon almond extract (optional)
  1 cup whipping cream, whipped

Soak gelatin in cold water. Scald milk in top of a double boiler; add chocolate, sugar, and salt and stir until chocolate is melted. Stir in softened gelatin, and stir until gelatin dissolves. Remove from heat, add vanilla and almond extract, and chill thoroughly. Whip until fluffy, and fold in whipped cream. Spoon into a 3-cup mold and chill thoroughly. Serve with whipped cream, if desired. Yield: 8 servings.

Apple Pudding Soufflé

 1 *cup finely chopped, peeled apples*
 ¼ *cup butter or margarine*
 3 *cups ½-inch bread cubes*
 2 *cups milk, scalded*
 ½ *cup sugar*
 ½ *cup seedless raisins*
 1 *teaspoon grated lemon rind*
 1 *teaspoon vanilla extract*
 ¼ *teaspoon salt*
 3 *eggs, separated*
  Ground nutmeg
  Custard Sauce

Sauté apples in butter until tender but not brown; add bread cubes and brown lightly. Combine apples and bread cubes with milk, sugar, raisins, lemon rind, vanilla, and salt; add well-beaten egg yolks and blend well. Beat egg whites until they hold soft peaks. Fold whites into bread mixture. Pour into a 2-quart casserole. Sprinkle top with nutmeg.
 Set casserole dish into pan of hot water. Bake at 350° for 45 to 50 minutes, or until set. Serve hot or cold with Custard Sauce. Yield: 6 to 8 servings.

 Custard Sauce:

 2 *eggs, beaten slightly*
 3 *tablespoons sugar*
 ⅛ *teaspoon salt*
 1⅓ *cups milk, scalded*
 1½ *teaspoons vanilla extract*
 ¼ *teaspoon ground nutmeg or mace*

Combine eggs, sugar, and salt in heavy saucepan or top of double boiler; gradually stir in milk. Cook over very low heat if using a heavy saucepan, or over hot, not boiling, water if a double boiler is used; stir constantly until mixture thickens and coats a metal spoon. Cool quickly. Stir in vanilla and nutmeg. Serve with Apple Pudding Soufflé. Yield: 1½ cups sauce.

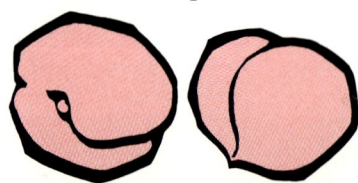

Cherry Delight Dessert

 6 *egg whites*
 ¾ *teaspoon cream of tartar*
 2 *cups sugar*
 2 *teaspoons vanilla extract*
 2 *cups broken salted crackers*
 ¾ *cup chopped English walnuts*
 4 *(¼-ounce) envelopes whipped topping mix*
 2 *(22-ounce) cans cherry pie filling*

Beat egg whites until foamy. Add cream of tartar and continue beating, adding sugar 2 tablespoons at a time; stir in vanilla, crackers, and walnuts. Spoon mixture into an oiled 13- x 9- x 2-inch pan and bake at 325° for 25 minutes. Let cool 1 hour before adding topping.
 Prepare topping as directed on package and spread over cooled mixture in pan. Cover with cherry pie filling and chill for at least 6 hours. This dessert will keep for several days in refrigerator. Yield: 16 servings.

Cherries in the Snow

 1½ *cups graham cracker crumbs*
 1 *tablespoon sugar*
 ¼ *cup melted butter*
 1 *envelope (1 tablespoon) unflavored gelatin*
 ¼ *cup cold water*
 ¼ *cup milk*
 1 *(8-ounce) package cream cheese*
 ½ *cup sifted powdered sugar*
 2 *teaspoons grated lemon peel*
 1 *(4-ounce) package whipped topping mix*
 1 *(22-ounce) can cherry pie filling*

Mix cracker crumbs, sugar, and butter. Press into bottom of 8-inch springform pan. Line sides with waxed paper.
 Soften gelatin in cold water. Heat milk, stir in gelatin, and heat until gelatin dissolves. Set aside.
 Beat cream cheese with powdered sugar until smooth. Add gelatin mixture and lemon peel; beat until well blended.
 Reconstitute prepared whipped topping mix according to package directions. Fold into the cream cheese mixture. Pour filling

Cherries á la Mode

1 pint lemon sherbet
1 pint vanilla ice cream
2 cups canned cherry pie filling, chilled
Whipped dessert topping

Put a scoop of lemon sherbet and one of vanilla ice cream in each of 4 dessert dishes. Top with chilled cherry pie filling. Garnish with whipped dessert topping. Yield: 4 servings.

*Pineapple Puff

1 envelope (1 tablespoon) unflavored gelatin
⅓ cup lemon juice
4 eggs, separated
¼ teaspoon salt
1⅓ cups sweetened condensed milk
1 (15¼-ounce) can crushed pineapple

Prepare a 1-quart soufflé dish or straight-sided baking dish with a 4-inch collar by folding a 20- to 22-inch length of aluminum foil in half lengthwise. Wrap foil around edge of dish and tie with string or fasten with tape.

To soften gelatin, sprinkle over lemon juice in top of double boiler; add slightly beaten egg yolks and salt. Cook over hot water, stirring until gelatin is dissolved (about 3 minutes). Stir in condensed milk and pineapple. Remove top of double boiler from heat; place in ice water. Stir mixture frequently until it mounds slightly when dropped from spoon.

Beat egg whites in a large bowl until stiff but not dry. Fold gelatin mixture into egg whites. Carefully pour mixture into prepared dish. Chill 4 to 5 hours or until firm. Remove foil collar before serving. Yield: 6 to 8 servings.

into springform pan and refrigerate until firm. Gently spread cherry pie filling on top and refrigerate until serving time (overnight, if possible). Cut into wedges to serve. Yield: 9 servings.

Unbaked Pineapple Soufflé

2 envelopes (2 tablespoons) unflavored gelatin
1 (20-ounce) can crushed pineapple
4 egg yolks
⅓ cup sugar
1 teaspoon salt
1 teaspoon vanilla extract
½ teaspoon almond extract
2 tablespoons lemon juice
4 egg whites, stiffly beaten
1 cup whipping cream

Soften gelatin in syrup drained from pineapple; dissolve over hot water. Beat egg yolks, sugar, salt, and flavorings until thick. Blend in gelatin, pineapple, and lemon juice. Cool until slightly thickened; then beat until fluffy. Fold in stiffly beaten egg whites and whipping cream. Wrap a 5-inch wide foil strip around a 4-cup soufflé dish. Tie with string so foil extends 3 inches above dish. Spoon in the pineapple mixture. Place in refrigerator and chill thoroughly.

Remove the foil collar; garnish with additional pineapple, if desired. Yield: 10 servings.

Coconut Torte

1 cup graham cracker crumbs
½ cup chopped flaked coconut
½ cup chopped English walnuts or pecans
4 egg whites
¼ teaspoon cream of tartar
¼ teaspoon salt
1 cup sugar
1 teaspoon vanilla extract
1 pint vanilla ice cream

Combine crumbs, coconut, and nuts. Beat egg whites, cream of tartar, and salt until soft peaks form; gradually add sugar and vanilla, beating until stiff peaks form and all sugar has dissolved.

Fold graham cracker mixture into egg white mixture. Spread in well-greased 9-inch piepan. Bake at 350° about 30 minutes. Cool. Cut in wedges, and top with ice cream. Yield: 6 servings.

Cherry Whirl

- ½ lemon, seeded and peeled
- 1 (4-ounce) bottle maraschino cherries and juice
- 2 envelopes (2 tablespoons) unflavored gelatin
- ⅓ cup sugar
- ½ cup hot pineapple juice
- ½ cup half-and-half
- 2 heaping cups crushed ice
- Whipped cream and cherries for garnish

Put all ingredients except cream and ice into blender container. Cover and blend until gelatin is dissolved and cherries liquefied. Turn off blender and scrape down sides. Then add cream and ice and blend until mixture begins to thicken. Pour at once into sherbet glasses, top with whipped cream, and garnish with cherries; serve at once. Yield: 6 to 8 servings.

Peaches-and-Cream Rice Dessert

- 3 cups cooked rice
- 3 cups milk
- ½ cup sugar
- ¼ teaspoon salt
- 4 eggs
- 1 teaspoon vanilla extract
- 1 (1-pound 13-ounce) can sliced peaches, drained
- 2 tablespoons sugar
- 1 cup commercial sour cream
- 1 cup firmly packed brown sugar
- 1 teaspoon ground cinnamon

Combine rice, milk, ½ cup sugar, and salt; bring to a boil over medium heat. Cook for 15 minutes, stirring frequently. Combine eggs and vanilla; blend some rice mixture into eggs. Gradually stir eggs into rice mixture. Cook 1 minute. Spoon into a greased ovenproof dish. Arrange peaches over pudding. Sprinkle with 2 tablespoons sugar. Broil until sugar melts (about 4 or 5 minutes). Watch carefully to prevent burning. Remove from oven and top with sour cream. Sprinkle with brown sugar and cinnamon. Yield: 6 servings.

Peach Crisp

- 6 or 7 large peaches, peeled and sliced
- Juice of 1 lemon
- ½ cup all-purpose flour
- ¾ cup oats, regular or quick-cooking, uncooked
- ½ cup firmly packed brown sugar
- ⅓ cup margarine
- Hard Sauce

Put peaches in a shallow 2-quart baking dish; sprinkle with lemon juice. Combine flour, oats, and brown sugar; cut in margarine with pastry blender. Press mixture over peaches. Bake at 325° for 30 minutes or until peaches are tender. Serve warm with Hard Sauce. Yield: 6 servings.

Hard Sauce:

- ½ cup butter
- ¾ cup powdered sugar
- ½ teaspoon vanilla extract
- 1 tablespoon hot water

Cream butter until smooth; gradually stir in sugar and vanilla. Stir in hot water a few drops at a time to prevent separation of sauce. Chill thoroughly. Serve over Peach Crisp. Yield: about 1 cup.

Peach Freeze

- 1 cup commercial sour cream
- ½ cup sugar
- 1 cup fresh pureed peaches
- ¾ cup vanilla wafer crumbs
- ½ cup butter, softened
- 2 cups powdered sugar
- 2 eggs
- 2 tablespoons vanilla wafer crumbs

Beat sour cream in mixing bowl about 5 minutes or until very fluffy. Continue to beat while gradually adding sugar. Mash peaches thoroughly or puree in a blender. Fold peaches into sour cream mixture. Spread ¾ cup crumbs over bottom of 8-inch square pan; cover with peach mixture and freeze until firm.

Cream butter; gradually add powdered

sugar and beat until light and fluffy. Add eggs one at a time, beating well after each addition. Spread over peach layer; sprinkle with 2 tablespoons crumbs; freeze. Yield: 9 servings.

Meringue au Chocolat

1 envelope unflavored gelatin
¼ cup water
2⅓ squares unsweetened chocolate
½ cup milk
Dash of salt
¼ cup sugar
¾ teaspoon vanilla extract
1 pint coffee, peppermint, or vanilla ice cream
1 (9-inch) baked Meringue-Pecan Shell, cooled
Whipped cream or prepared dessert topping mix
Chocolate curls

Soften gelatin in ¼ cup water. Combine chocolate with milk, salt, and sugar and melt over hot (not boiling) water. Remove from hot water; add gelatin and vanilla and stir until gelatin dissolves. Soften ice cream in mixing bowl. Add chocolate mixture and blend well with wire whip or beat at low speed of electric mixer until well blended, about 2 minutes. Pour into meringue shell. Chill about 3 hours. Serve with a dollop of whipped cream and decorate with chocolate curls. Yield: 6 to 8 servings.

Meringue-Pecan Shell:

Beat 2 egg whites until foamy. Add ⅛ teaspoon cream of tartar and beat until meringue is stiff but not dry. Gradually beat in ½ cup sugar. Fold in 1 cup chopped pecans. Spread mixture over bottom and sides of a buttered 9-inch piepan, or spoon part of meringue onto unglazed paper on a baking sheet. Form into a heart shape about ¼ inch thick and the size of the bottom of a 9-inch piepan. Build up sides with remaining meringue. Bake at 275° about 1 hour or until lightly browned and crisp. Cool before adding filling.

Fresh Blueberry Cream

1 pint fresh blueberries
¼ cup sugar
1 (8-ounce) carton cottage cheese, softened
1 (8-ounce) carton commercial sour cream
½ teaspoon grated lemon rind

Sprinkle blueberries with sugar. Combine cottage cheese with sour cream and lemon rind. Pile lightly into serving bowl. Place sugared blueberries in center. Serve as dessert. Yield: 6 servings.

Cottage Cheese Blintzes

¾ cup all-purpose flour
½ teaspoon salt
1½ cups milk
3 eggs, well beaten
Melted butter
Cottage Lemon Filling

Combine flour and salt; add alternately with milk to eggs, mixing well. Brush a heated 8-inch skillet with melted butter. Pour about 3 tablespoons batter into hot skillet; rotate pan to spread batter uniformly. Cook over medium heat on one side only until top is dry and blistered. Turn out onto clean cloth, cooked side up. Repeat until all batter is used.

Fill blintzes on cooked side with about 2 tablespoons Cottage Lemon Filling. Roll jelly roll fashion. Melt butter in large heavy skillet. Place blintzes folded side down; fry until golden brown; turn and fry other side. Yield: about 1½ dozen.

Cottage Lemon Filling:

2 cups dry cottage cheese
1 egg, slightly beaten
¼ cup commercial sour cream
¼ cup sugar
2 tablespoons butter, softened
2 teaspoons grated lemon rind
½ teaspoon vanilla extract

Beat cottage cheese and egg together; fold in sour cream, sugar, butter, lemon rind, and vanilla. Yield: about 3 cups.

Fresh Strawberries and Cream

2 cups sliced fresh strawberries
1 tablespoon sugar
¼ pound miniature marshmallows
1 cup commercial sour cream
6 whole strawberries

Combine sliced strawberries and sugar; let stand 10 minutes. Combine marshmallows and sour cream. Fold strawberries into sour cream mixture. Refrigerate at least 1 hour before serving. Serve in sherbet glasses topped with a whole strawberry. Yield: 6 servings.

Coeur a la Crème

2 (8-ounce) packages cream cheese, softened
1 pound creamed cottage cheese
1 cup whipping cream
¼ cup powdered sugar
Candied cherries
Sweetened strawberries

Beat cream cheese until smooth. Gradually add cottage cheese and continue beating until almost smooth. Add whipping cream and sugar and beat until blended.
Put a colander, lined with a double thickness of cheesecloth, in a low pan. Pour cheese mixture into colander; drain overnight in refrigerator to remove the whey.
Line individual molds or large heart-shaped gelatin mold with single thickness of cheesecloth; spoon and pack cheese mixture into molds and chill about 2 or 3 hours in refrigerator. Unmold and remove cheesecloth. Garnish with candied cherries; serve with sweetened strawberries. Yield: 12 servings.

Fruit Cocktail Mint Delight

1 (30-ounce) can fruit cocktail
½ cup mint jelly
1 (3-ounce) package lime-flavored gelatin
1 cup whipping cream
1 tablespoon powdered sugar
Dash of salt

Drain syrup from fruit cocktail; combine syrup with mint jelly. Simmer over medium heat until jelly is melted. Add lime gelatin and stir until gelatin is dissolved. Cool; then chill until gelatin is slightly set but not firm.
Whip cream with powdered sugar and salt. Whip gelatin until fluffy; fold in whipped cream. Add drained fruit cocktail and mix thoroughly. Place in freezing compartment of refrigerator in a bowl or freezer tray. Freeze 1 to 2 hours until mixture is softly frozen, stirring once or twice. Spoon into sherbet glasses. Yield: 6 servings.

Frosted Mint Delight

1 package unflavored gelatin
½ cup cold water
1 (15¼-ounce) can crushed pineapple, drained and liquid reserved
⅓ cup apple-mint jelly
½ pint whipping cream
2 teaspoons powdered sugar
Whipped cream
Fresh mint leaves
Mint extract

Soften gelatin in cold water. Heat ½ cup syrup from crushed pineapple and add to dissolved gelatin. Melt apple-mint jelly and combine with gelatin mixture, adding drained crushed pineapple at the same time. Refrigerate until it starts to thicken.
Fold in whipped cream which has been sweetened with powdered sugar. Pour into mold and let stand overnight in refrigerator.
Unmold and decorate with additional whipped cream and fresh mint leaves. To intensify the mint flavor, use a few drops of pure mint extract. Yield: 8 servings.

Hawaiian Parfait

1 quart vanilla ice cream
1 (13¼-ounce) can crushed pineapple, drained
1 pint orange sherbet
Chopped nuts
½ cup flaked coconut
Maraschino cherries, slivered

In each of 8 parfait glasses, arrange layers of vanilla ice cream, pineapple, orange sherbet, nuts, and more pineapple. Top each with a scoop of vanilla ice cream that has been rolled in coconut. Garnish with more pineapple and slivers of maraschino cherries. Yield: 8 servings.

Rice Florentine Dessert

1 cup uncooked regular rice
2 cups water
1 teaspoon salt
2 cups milk
2 tablespoons butter or margarine
½ cup sugar
¼ teaspoon each ground cinnamon, cloves, and nutmeg
½ cup sweet white wine
1 teaspoon vanilla extract
½ cup seedless raisins
½ cup currants
6 eggs, beaten
Powdered sugar

Combine rice, water, and salt. Bring to a boil, cover, and simmer 14 minutes or until liquid is absorbed. Add milk and continue cooking until thick and creamy, about 30 minutes, stirring occasionally. Stir in butter, sugar, spices, wine, vanilla, raisins, and currants. Stir a little hot rice into the eggs; fold eggs into rice mixture and cook 2 minutes longer. Turn into serving dishes; serve hot or cold sprinkled with powdered sugar. Yield: 10 servings.

Green Grapes in Cognac

3 pounds fresh seedless grapes
¾ cup honey
¾ cup Cognac
1 tablespoon lemon juice
1 to 2 cups commercial sour cream

Wash grapes and drain thoroughly; remove grapes from stem. Combine honey, Cognac, and lemon juice; toss grapes in this mixture. Chill at least 5 hours, stirring occasionally. Serve in chilled sherbet dishes; top with sour cream. Yield: 6 servings.

Butterscotch-Apricot Sundaes

¼ cup evaporated milk
2 tablespoons light corn syrup
Dash salt
1 (6-ounce) package butterscotch morsels
½ teaspoon vanilla extract
1 tablespoon butter or margarine
1 quart vanilla ice cream
1 (16-ounce) can apricot halves, drained and cut into pieces

Combine milk, corn syrup, and salt in saucepan; bring to a boil. Remove from heat and stir in butterscotch morsels until melted and smooth. Add vanilla and butter. Scoop ice cream into 8 individual sherbet dishes. Top each with apricots and warm butterscotch sauce. Yield: 8 servings.

Pineapple Cream

Juice of ½ lemon
¼ cup maraschino cherry juice
2 envelopes (2 tablespoons) unflavored gelatin
½ cup hot pineapple juice
⅓ cup sugar
2 heaping cups crushed ice
½ cup half-and-half
12 maraschino cherries

Put lemon juice, cherry juice, and gelatin in blender container. Add hot pineapple juice; cover and blend for 40 seconds. Add sugar; cover and blend for 2 seconds. Add crushed ice, half-and-half, and cherries; cover and continue to blend for about 30 seconds or until dessert begins to thicken. Yield: 6 servings.

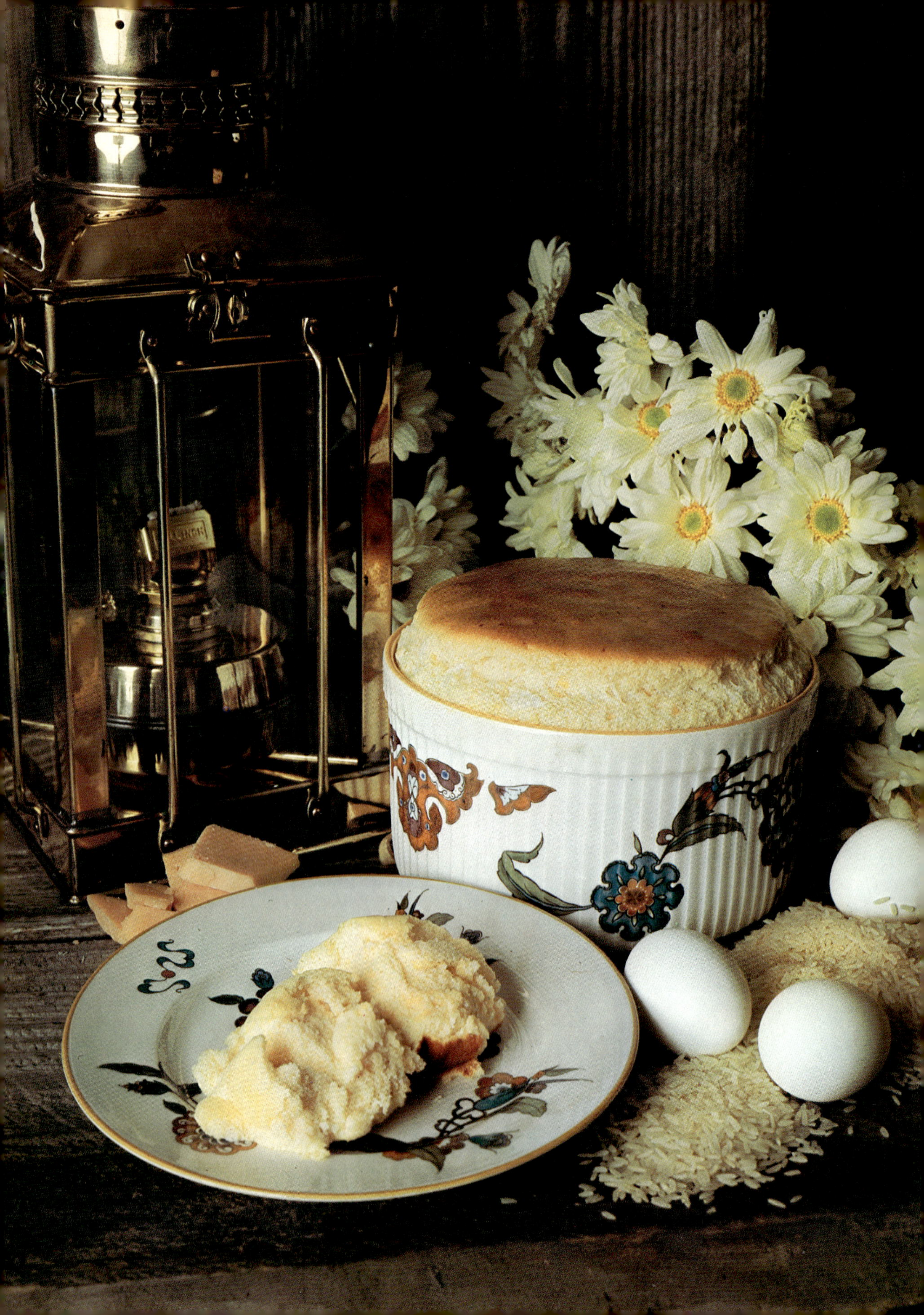

Eggs and Grains

Eggs are among the most useful and versatile of foods, and it would be difficult to make almost any recipe in this cookbook without using them. But dishes with eggs as a main ingredient rightfully deserve a section of their own, so together with grains they make up this special chapter.

Grains, too, are a common ingredient throughout the book, and since Southerners have a special fondness for grits and rice dishes, they are a part of this chapter. In fact, the majority of rice grown in the United States is grown in the Southland, where it is used in every imaginable way from soup to dessert.

Beefy Deviled Eggs

  6 hard-cooked eggs
  ¼ cup mayonnaise or salad dressing
  ¼ teaspoon dry mustard
  ½ cup finely chopped dried beef

Slice eggs in half lengthwise, and carefully remove yolks. Mash yolks, and add mayonnaise and mustard; stir in dried beef. Stuff egg whites. Yield: 6 servings.

French-Style Baked Eggs

  6 hard-cooked eggs, chopped
  1 (4½-ounce) can shrimp, drained
  ¾ cup half-and-half
  1 tablespoon chopped parsley
  ¼ teaspoon dry mustard
    Salt and pepper to taste
  1 cup shredded sharp pasteurized process cheese, divided
  4 buns, toasted

Combine eggs, shrimp, half-and-half, parsley, seasonings, and ½ cup cheese. Pour into an ungreased 1-quart casserole. Bake at 350° for 30 minutes. Sprinkle remaining cheese over top and heat 5 minutes. Serve on toasted buns. Yield: 4 servings.

Baked Eggs Creole

  1 tablespoon margarine
  1 small onion, sliced
  ½ cup green pepper strips
  2 tablespoons sliced mushrooms
  6 green olives, sliced
  ½ cup chicken broth
  1 cup canned drained tomato wedges
  1 teaspoon salt
  ½ teaspoon pepper
  1 whole clove
  ⅛ teaspoon marjoram
  4 eggs
    Green pepper rings (optional)
    Parsley (optional)

Melt margarine in skillet; add onion, green pepper, mushrooms, and olives; cook over low heat for 5 minutes. Add broth, tomatoes, salt, pepper, clove, and marjoram. Cover; cook for 5 minutes.

Place mixture in an ungreased baking dish. Press 4 nests in Creole mixture and break eggs individually into nests. Bake at 325° for 15 to 20 minutes or until eggs are set. Garnish with pepper rings and parsley, if desired. Serve immediately. Yield: 4 servings.

Variation: Use rich milk or thin cream instead of chicken broth.

Creamed Eggs Diable

1½ tablespoons instant minced onion
1 (8-ounce) can sliced mushrooms, undrained
1 cup thinly sliced celery
¼ cup butter or margarine
½ cup all-purpose flour
1½ cups half-and-half
⅓ cup Sauterne or other white dinner wine
1 pimiento, chopped
Deviled Eggs
Almond Crumbs

Combine instant minced onion with undrained mushrooms. Cook celery in ¼ cup butter until tender-crisp; add onion-mushroom mixture and cook gently for a few minutes. Mix flour into cream; blend into hot mixture. Cook and stir until mixture boils and begins to thicken. Add wine and cook a few minutes longer; stir in pimiento. Pour into a chafing dish or 1½- to 2-quart ungreased shallow baking dish; set Deviled Eggs into cream mixture, and sprinkle with Almond Crumbs. Keep hot in chafing dish or in 300° oven until time to serve. Yield: 6 servings.

Deviled Eggs:

6 hard-cooked eggs
½ teaspoon salt
½ teaspoon dry mustard
¼ cup mayonnaise
Parsley (optional)

Shell eggs and cut in half lengthwise. Remove yolks and mash or press through a sieve. Combine egg yolks with salt, mustard, and mayonnaise; refill egg whites with yolk mixture. Garnish each egg with a sprig of parsley, if desired.

Almond Crumbs:

1 cup soft stale bread crumbs
1 tablespoon melted butter or margarine
2 tablespoons sliced or slivered almonds

Combine bread crumbs, butter, and almonds. Toast to a golden brown in skillet over medium heat or at 375° in oven.

*Eggs Germaine

4 tablespoons butter or margarine, divided
¼ cup all-purpose flour
2 cups milk
1 teaspoon salt, divided
¼ teaspoon pepper
¼ teaspoon ground nutmeg
1 (10-ounce) package frozen chopped spinach
8 hard-cooked eggs
2 tablespoons grated Parmesan cheese
Hot toast points (optional)

Melt 2 tablespoons butter in skillet over low heat; blend in flour. Add milk and cook, stirring constantly, until thickened and bubbly. Add ½ teaspoon salt, pepper, and nutmeg; set sauce aside.

Cook spinach according to package directions; drain well and set aside.

Cut hard-cooked eggs in half lengthwise; remove yolks. Mash yolks; combine with spinach and ½ teaspoon salt. Stuff whites with spinach mixture, placing filled eggs in a 1½-quart shallow baking dish.

Pour sauce over eggs. Sprinkle with Parmesan cheese and dot with remaining butter. Broil for 5 minutes or until lightly browned. Serve over hot toast points, if desired. Yield: 5 to 6 servings.

*Curried Eggs in Rice Ring

6 tablespoons melted butter or margarine
6 tablespoons all-purpose flour
1½ teaspoons curry powder
1½ teaspoons salt
Grated rind of 1 orange
2¾ cups milk
⅓ cup orange juice
9 hard-cooked eggs, quartered
Hot cooked rice

Blend butter, flour, curry powder, salt, and orange rind in saucepan; cook until bubbly. Gradually add milk, stirring constantly. Bring mixture to a boil over medium heat; simmer, stirring constantly, until thickened. Stir in orange juice; add eggs and heat thoroughly. Arrange rice in a ring; spoon curried eggs in center. Yield: 6 servings.

Deviled Eggs with Cheese

6 hard-cooked eggs
¼ cup shredded sharp cheese
1 dill pickle, finely chopped
1 tablespoon grated onion
5 tablespoons mayonnaise
2 tablespoons prepared mustard
Paprika and parsley

Cut eggs in half; remove yolks and place in small mixing bowl. Mash egg yolks and blend with cheese, pickle, onion, mayonnaise, and mustard. Stuff egg whites with mixture and garnish with parsley and paprika. Yield: 12 servings.

Eggs Hussarde

2 large, thin slices ham, grilled
2 Holland rusks
¼ cup Marchand de Vin Sauce
2 slices tomatoes, grilled
2 eggs, soft poached
¾ cup Hollandaise Sauce
Paprika

Lay a large slice of grilled ham across each rusk and cover with Marchand de Vin Sauce. Add a slice of grilled tomato and then the egg. Top with Hollandaise Sauce, and sprinkle with paprika. Yield: 1 serving.

Marchand de Vin Sauce:

¾ cup butter
⅓ cup finely chopped fresh mushrooms
½ cup minced cooked ham
⅓ cup finely chopped shallots
½ cup finely chopped onion
2 tablespoons minced garlic
2 tablespoons all-purpose flour
½ teaspoon salt
⅛ teaspoon black pepper
Dash cayenne pepper
¾ cup beef stock
½ cup red wine

Melt butter in a 9-inch skillet; add mushrooms, ham, shallots, onion, and garlic. Sauté until lightly browned. Add flour, salt, black pepper, and cayenne pepper; cook until browned. Blend in beef stock and wine, and simmer over low heat for 35 to 45 minutes. Yield: 2 cups.

Hollandaise Sauce:

4 egg yolks
2 tablespoons lemon juice
½ pound butter, melted
¼ teaspoon salt
Dash pepper

Beat egg yolks in top of a double boiler. Stir in lemon juice. Cook very slowly over low heat, never letting water in bottom of pan come to a boil. Add butter, a small amount at a time, stirring constantly with a wooden spoon. Add salt and pepper; continue cooking until mixture has thickened. Yield: 1 cup.

Baked Eggs with Rice and Cheese Sauce

4 tablespoons butter or margarine
½ cup finely chopped green pepper
½ cup sliced fresh mushrooms
3 tablespoons all-purpose flour
1 teaspoon salt
⅛ teaspoon pepper
2 cups milk
1 cup shredded pasteurized process American cheese
3 cups cooked regular rice
8 eggs

Melt butter; add green pepper and mushrooms and cook until tender but not brown. Blend in flour, salt, and pepper. Add milk; cook, stirring constantly, until thickened and bubbly. Remove from heat and stir in cheese until it melts.

Combine 1½ cups of the sauce with the cooked rice. Spread the rice mixture evenly in a well-greased 13- x 9- x 2-inch shallow baking dish. Make 8 indentations with back of a spoon. Carefully break an egg into each indentation. Bake at 350° for 20 to 25 minutes or until eggs cook to desired doneness. Serve with remaining cheese and mushroom sauce. Yield: 8 servings.

Creole Eggs

    1 *(2-ounce) can mushroom pieces*
    3 *tablespoons chopped onion*
  ¼ *cup sliced celery*
  ¼ *cup chopped green pepper*
    2 *tablespoons all-purpose flour*
  ½ *cup water*
    1 *(10¾-ounce) can condensed tomato soup*
    1 *teaspoon salt*
  ¾ *teaspoon chili powder*
    6 *hard-cooked eggs, coarsely chopped*
    6 *slices toast or split, toasted English muffins*

Combine mushrooms, onion, celery, and pepper and cook in the mushroom liquid until vegetables are tender. Blend flour and water; stir into vegetables, and blend well. Add soup, salt, chili powder, and eggs. Blend well.

Heat thoroughly and serve hot on toast or on English muffins. Yield: 6 (½-cup) servings.

Poached Egg on Ham Toast

    2 *tablespoons margarine*
 1½ *teaspoons all-purpose flour*
    1 *teaspoon dry mustard*
 1½ *teaspoons prepared horseradish*
  ½ *cup milk*
    1 *cup ground, cooked ham*
    6 *slices bread*
    6 *poached eggs*

Melt margarine in a saucepan. Blend in flour, mustard, and horseradish. Add milk and cook until thickened, stirring constantly. Add ham and cook for an additional 2 minutes. Toast one side of bread under a preheated broiler. Spread untoasted side with ham mixture. Return to broiler for 2 minutes. To serve, top each slice of ham toast with a poached egg. Yield: 6 servings.

To Poach Eggs: Break each egg into a cup. Slip into a skillet or shallow pan two-thirds full of simmering, salted water (add ½ teaspoon salt for each 2 cups of water used). Be sure eggs are not crowded in the pan and that there is enough water to cover. Cover and cook gently to the desired degree of firmness. For soft poached eggs, cook for 3 to 5 minutes. Lift eggs from water with a slotted spoon and place immediately on hot ham toast.

Note: If egg whites appear thin and runny, ¾ teaspoon vinegar or lemon juice added to each cup of water will keep them from spreading.

Egg Croquettes with Mushroom Sauce

    3 *tablespoons butter or margarine*
    3 *tablespoons all-purpose flour*
  ¾ *cup milk*
  ½ *teaspoon salt*
      Dash paprika
    4 *hard-cooked eggs, chopped*
  ¼ *teaspoon grated onion*
    1 *tablespoon chopped parsley*
      Cracker crumbs
    1 *egg, slightly beaten*
      Deep hot oil
      Mushroom Sauce

Melt butter in top of a double boiler; add flour and stir until blended. Add milk, salt, and paprika and cook until mixture is thickened. Remove from heat and add hard-cooked eggs, onion, and parsley. Set aside to cool. When cold, shape into croquettes. Roll in cracker crumbs; dip in egg and again in crumbs. Fry in deep hot oil (365° to 380°) until golden brown, about 2 to 5 minutes. Serve with Mushroom Sauce. Yield: 6 servings.

Mushroom Sauce:

    2 *tablespoons butter or margarine*
  ½ *pound mushrooms, sliced*
    2 *tablespoons all-purpose flour*
    1 *cup chicken broth*
  ¼ *teaspoon salt*
  ⅛ *teaspoon pepper*

Melt butter; add mushrooms and cook about 5 minutes. Blend in flour. Add chicken broth gradually and cook until thickened, stirring constantly. Add seasonings and serve hot. Yield: 1¾ cups.

*Ten-Minute Omelet

    4   *eggs, separated*
  ¼   *teaspoon salt*
  ⅛   *teaspoon pepper*
    1   *tablespoon all-purpose flour*
    2   *tablespoons softened butter or margarine, divided*
    1   *tablespoon water*

Beat egg whites with salt until stiff but not dry. Beat egg yolks with pepper, flour, 1 tablespoon softened butter, and water until fluffy. Fold beaten yolks into beaten whites.

Heat the remaining butter in an 8- or 9-inch skillet until hot enough to sizzle a drop of water; pour eggs into skillet. Cover tightly. Reduce heat to low and cook 8 to 10 minutes on top of range until surface of omelet is dry when touched lightly with fingertip. Fold omelet in half and serve promptly. Yield: 2 to 3 servings.

*Plain Omelet

    3   *eggs*
    3   *tablespoons water*
  ⅜   *teaspoon salt*
  ⅛   *teaspoon pepper*
    1   *tablespoon butter, margarine, or oil*

Mix eggs, water, salt, and pepper with a whisk or three-tined fork until yolks and whites are blended. Meanwhile, heat butter, margarine, or oil in a 7- or 8-inch omelet pan or heavy skillet until it is just hot enough to sizzle a drop of water. Pour in egg mixture all at once. Mixture should begin to cook immediately at the outer edges. With a fork, lift cooked portions at the edges so uncooked portions flow underneath. Slide pan rapidly back and forth over the heat to keep mixture in motion and sliding freely to avoid sticking. When the mixture is set properly, it no longer flows freely and is moist and creamy on top. Let the omelet cook about 1 minute to brown the bottom slightly. Fold or roll, and serve promptly on a warm platter. The omelet should be tender and light, moist, and delicately brown on the bottom. Yield: 1 or 2 servings.

Herb Omelet: Add 1 teaspoon fresh snipped herbs or ½ teaspoon dry herbs to ingredients of Plain Omelet before cooking. Try basil, celery seeds, chives, dill, marjoram, mint, or parsley.

Poultry or Meat Omelet: Fold ½ cup finely diced or chopped cooked chicken, turkey, or duckling into the omelet mixture before cooking. Or add meat to 1 (10¾-ounce) can condensed cheese or cream of mushroom soup. Serve over your favorite omelet. Or try adding to the omelet mixture or soup, crisp crumbled bacon, cooked sausage, dried beef, smoked turkey, tuna fish, or shrimp.

Swiss Omelet: Add 3 tablespoons grated Swiss cheese (or your favorite cheese) to ingredients of Plain Omelet before cooking. Additional cheese may be sprinkled on top of the omelet before serving.

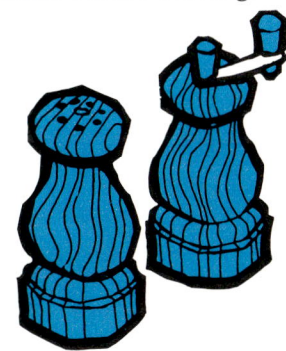

*Red Beet Eggs

    1   *(16-ounce) can beets*
    1   *cup vinegar*
  ¾   *cup sugar*
    1   *tablespoon salt*
    1   *tablespoon mixed pickling spices*
    6   *hard-cooked eggs*
    1   *medium-size onion, thinly sliced and separated into rings*

Drain beets, reserving liquid. Pour liquid into a glass jar or bowl; add vinegar, sugar, salt, and spices; stir until sugar dissolves. Add beets, eggs, and onion; cover.

Chill 2 hours or longer before serving. Serve drained eggs in one dish, beets and onions in another. Yield: 6 servings.

Cottage Cheese Scrambled Eggs

 9 *eggs*
 1 *cup cottage cheese*
 4 *tablespoons milk*
1½ *tablespoons chopped chives*
 ¾ *teaspoon salt*
 ¼ *teaspoon pepper*
 3 *tablespoons butter*

Beat eggs in a mixing bowl. Add cottage cheese, milk, chives, salt, and pepper; beat lightly until blended. Melt butter in skillet over low heat. Add eggs to skillet and cook slowly, turning portions of cooked egg with a spatula as they begin to thicken. Do not stir and do not overcook. As soon as eggs are cooked, remove from heat. Serve immediately. Yield: 6 servings.

Swiss Scrambled Eggs

 6 *eggs*
 ⅓ *cup milk*
 ¾ *teaspoon salt*
 ⅓ *teaspoon pepper*
 ¼ *pound Swiss cheese, diced*
  Butter

Combine eggs, milk, salt, and pepper; blend well with a fork. Stir in Swiss cheese. Heat a small amount of butter in a skillet. Add egg mixture and cook over medium heat.
 As eggs begin to set, lift cooked portions so that the thin uncooked portions can flow to the bottom. Cook until eggs are thickened but still moist, 3 to 5 minutes. Yield: 4 servings.

•Parsley Scrambled Eggs

 4 *eggs*
 4 *tablespoons cream*
 ½ *teaspoon salt*
 2 *tablespoons chopped parsley*
 2 *tablespoons butter or margarine*
 ½ *cup shredded sharp cheese*

Combine eggs, cream, and salt. Beat until fluffy; add parsley. Cook in butter in heavy frying pan over moderate heat until done. Turn once. For variety add shredded sharp cheese after turning. Serve at once. Yield: 4 servings.

*Scrambled Eggs

 4 *eggs*
 ¼ *cup milk or cream*
 ½ *teaspoon salt*
 ⅛ *teaspoon pepper*
 1 *tablespoon butter*

Mix eggs, milk, salt, and pepper with a fork. Heat butter in an 8-inch skillet over medium heat until just hot enough to sizzle a drop of water. Pour in egg mixture. As mixture begins to set at bottom and sides, gently lift cooked portions with a spatula so that the thin, uncooked part can flow to the bottom. Avoid constant stirring. Cook until eggs are thickened throughout but still moist, 3 to 5 minutes. Yield: 2 servings.

Cheese Stuffed Eggs

 2 *hard-cooked eggs*
 2 *tablespoons blue cheese, crumbled*
 ¼ *cup cream cheese, softened*
 1 *tablespoon parsley*

Cut eggs in half lengthwise and remove yolks. Combine yolks, cheeses, and parsley and mix until well blended. Stuff whites with mixture. Yield: 4 servings.

*Peanutty Stuffed Eggs

 3 *hard-cooked eggs*
 1 *tablespoon peanut butter*
1½ *teaspoons prepared mustard*

Cut eggs in half lenthwise. Carefully remove yolks and blend with peanut butter and mustard. Spoon mixture into whites. Cover and chill thoroughly. Yield: 3 servings.

Caper Stuffed Eggs

  4 hard-cooked eggs
  3 anchovy fillets, drained, or 2 teaspoons anchovy paste
  1 tablespoon drained capers
  4 ripe olives, pitted
  2 tablespoons mayonnaise
½ teaspoon anchovy liquid
     Pepper to taste
     About 2 teaspoons lemon juice
     Paprika
     Ripe olives, slivered

Cut eggs in half; mash yolks through a fine sieve. Grind anchovies, capers, and olives in food grinder or chop finely in a wooden bowl; combine with mayonnaise and sieved yolks. Add anchovy liquid, pepper, and lemon juice. Stuff eggs and sprinkle with paprika. Garnish with slivers of ripe olives. Yield: 8 servings.

*Grits Soufflé

2¼ cups milk
 ½ cup regular grits, uncooked
  1 teaspoon salt
 ½ cup butter or margarine
  4 egg yolks, beaten
 ¼ cup grated Parmesan cheese (better if freshly grated)
  6 egg whites (7 if large eggs are not used)
 ½ teaspoon cream of tartar

Heat the milk. Add grits and salt, and stir. Continue to cook and stir over low heat for 16 minutes. Add butter and stir until melted. Gradually add egg yolks and cheese. Cool for 10 minutes or so.

Meanwhile, beat egg whites until foamy, and add cream of tartar. Continue beating until whites are stiff but not dry. Beat one-fourth of the egg whites into the grits mixture. Fold in the remaining whites very carefully. Turn into a chilled soufflé dish. Bake at 350° for 30 to 40 minutes. Watch carefully. Do not overcook, or it will fall. Serve as a dinner vegetable, as a main dish for lunch, or with bacon for brunch. Yield: 4 to 6 servings.

*Cheese Grits Casserole

  2 cups boiling water
  1 teaspoon salt
  1 cup instant grits
  2 cups milk
 ¼ cup margarine
  4 ounces shredded sharp Cheddar cheese
     Paprika

Pour boiling water into a large saucepan. Add salt and grits and stir well. Add milk and margarine and mix well. Spoon into a greased 3-quart casserole and sprinkle shredded cheese on top. Bake at 350° for 20 to 30 minutes or until mixture thickens. Remove from oven and sprinkle generously with paprika. Serve hot. Yield: 8 servings.

*Chinese Rice

⅔ cup uncooked regular rice
  2 tablespoons vegetable oil
1½ teaspoons salt
1½ cups boiling water
  1 bouillon cube
  2 teaspoons soy sauce
  1 medium-size onion, chopped
  1 stalk celery, chopped
 ½ green pepper, chopped

Cook rice in hot oil over medium heat until golden brown. Add salt, water, bouillon cube, and soy sauce. Cover; simmer 20 minutes. Add onion, celery, and pepper. Cover tightly and simmer 10 minutes more. (It may be necessary to add a little more water.) All water should be absorbed at end of cooking time. Yield: 2 servings.

Olive-Rice Casserole

1 cup uncooked regular rice
1 cup diced Cheddar cheese
1 (3-ounce) jar sliced stuffed olives
1 cup drained cooked tomatoes
½ cup chopped onion
½ cup salad oil
1 cup water
Salt and pepper to taste

Combine all ingredients in a 2-quart baking dish. Bake, uncovered, at 350° for 1 hour. Yield: 4 to 6 servings.

Elegant Curried Rice

3 tablespoons butter or margarine
1 cup minced onion
1 cup chopped green pepper
½ cup currants
2 cups uncooked regular rice
1 teaspoon salt
½ teaspoon pepper
½ teaspoon curry powder
1 quart chicken broth

Melt butter in heavy skillet. Add onion, green pepper, and currants. Sauté until tender. Stir in rice and seasonings; brown slightly.
    Pour the chicken broth over rice and mix well. Bring to a boil. Cover with a tight-fitting lid, and simmer for 14 minutes. This rice mixture may also be put in a casserole, covered, and baked at 350° for 30 minutes. Yield: 8 servings.

Rice Amandine

1 cup uncooked regular rice
1 cup chopped green onions and tops
2 tablespoons butter or margarine, melted
2 cups chicken broth
1 teaspoon salt
½ cup slivered almonds

Cook rice and onions in butter until golden but not brown. Add broth and salt. Heat to boiling; stir; cover. Lower heat and simmer for 14 minutes or until rice is tender. Remove from heat and toss lightly with slivered almonds. Yield: 6 servings.

*Herb Fried Rice

1 cup chopped onions
3 tablespoons butter or margarine
3 cups cooked rice
1 teaspoon marjoram
½ teaspoon salt
⅛ teaspoon black pepper
¼ teaspoon cayenne pepper

Cook onions in butter until tender, but not browned. Add rice, marjoram, salt, pepper, and cayenne pepper. Continue cooking until the rice is thoroughly heated. Yield: 6 servings.

*Rice Soufflé

3 egg yolks, beaten
1 cup cold, cooked rice
½ cup whole milk
2 tablespoons melted butter
½ cup shredded Cheddar cheese
3 egg whites, stiffly beaten
Salt to taste

Add beaten egg yolks to cooked rice. Blend in milk, butter, and cheese. Stir well. Fold in stiffly beaten egg whites, adding a little salt. Spoon into a greased 1-quart glass casserole. Bake, uncovered, at 300° for 30 to 45 minutes or until soufflé is browned on top. Yield: 4 to 6 servings.

*Spanish Rice with Meat

1 pound ground beef
1 tablespoon shortening
1 cup diced onion
¾ cup diced green pepper
1 (4-ounce) can mushrooms with liquid (optional)
1 cup diced celery
¾ cup uncooked regular rice
2½ cups canned tomatoes
3 teaspoons salt
¼ teaspoon pepper

Brown meat in shortening. Add remaining ingredients and simmer until rice is tender, about 30 minutes. Yield: 6 to 8 servings.

Green Goddess Rice

3 cups chicken broth
1½ cups uncooked regular rice
¾ teaspoon salt
1 clove garlic, crushed
⅓ cup chopped parsley
¼ cup chopped green onions
2 tablespoons anchovy paste
3 tablespoons tarragon vinegar
Coarsely ground black pepper
1½ cups commercial sour cream

Combine broth, rice, and salt in a 3-quart saucepan. Heat to boiling; stir once; cover. Reduce heat and simmer for 14 minutes or until liquid is absorbed. Blend garlic, parsley, onion, anchovy paste, vinegar, and pepper into sour cream. Serve over rice. Yield: 6 to 8 servings.

Far East Fruited Rice

¼ cup butter or margarine
3 cups hot cooked rice
1 cup cooked cubed ham
1 cup cooked cubed chicken
1 cup pineapple tidbits
1 cup finely sliced green pepper
½ cup sliced water chestnuts
1 teaspoon salt
½ teaspoon pepper
2 tablespoons soy sauce
¼ teaspoon garlic powder
1 teaspoon onion powder

Stir butter into hot rice. Add ham, chicken, pineapple, and green pepper. Stir in water chestnuts and seasonings. Mix well and spoon into a greased 1½-quart casserole. Cover and bake at 350° for 30 minutes. Yield: 6 servings.

*Curried Rice

2 tablespoons butter or margarine
½ cup chopped onion
2 cups chicken broth
1 teaspoon salt
⅛ teaspoon pepper
1 teaspoon curry powder
Juice of 1 lemon
2 tablespoons parsley flakes
1 cup regular uncooked rice
Dash paprika (optional)

Melt butter in a 2-quart saucepan; add onion, cooking slowly until tender. Combine chicken broth, salt, pepper, curry powder, lemon juice, and parsley flakes; add to onion and bring to a boil. Add rice, cover, and cook over low heat for 20 minutes.

Remove from heat; set aside for 10 minutes. Garnish with paprika, if desired. Yield: 6 to 8 servings.

Beefeater Wild Rice

1 tablespoon chopped green onion
1 tablespoon chopped bacon
1 tablespoon slivered blanched or toasted almonds
1 tablespoon butter
1 cup cooked wild rice

Sauté green onion, bacon, and almonds in butter. When mixture is hot, add cooked wild rice. Stir rice in butter until blended with other ingredients. Yield: 4 servings.

*Green Rice

¾ cup thinly sliced green onions
3 tablespoons salad oil
1 cup uncooked regular rice
½ cup chopped green pepper
¼ cup chopped parsley
2 cups hot chicken stock
1 teaspoon salt
¼ teaspoon black pepper

Cook onion (use tops as well as white part) in salad oil until soft but not browned. Add remaining ingredients. Pour into a 1½-quart baking pan; cover with a tight lid or foil. Bake at 350° for 30 minutes or until rice is tender. Toss lightly with a fork before serving. Yield: 6 servings.

*Chili-Rice Dish

2 tablespoons margarine
1 pound lean pork shoulder, ground
½ cup chopped onion
1 clove garlic, minced (optional)
½ cup chopped green pepper
1 (16-ounce) can tomatoes
1 tablespoon chili powder
2 tablespoons flour
1 (17-ounce) can whole kernel corn
2 tablespoons chopped pimiento (optional)
Salt and pepper to taste
2½ to 3 cups hot, cooked rice

Melt margarine in a large saucepan over low heat. Add ground pork, onion, garlic, if desired, and green pepper. Sauté lightly until vegetables are limp and slightly browned. Add tomatoes and simmer gently for 30 minutes. Mix the chili powder and flour together. Add enough water to make a smooth paste. Add paste slowly to the hot mixture, stirring constantly until the mixture is thickened. Continue cooking for 15 minutes. Add corn and pimiento, if desired; season with salt and pepper. Let stand over low heat for about 5 minutes. Serve over a bed of hot rice. Yield: 4 to 5 servings.

Louisiana Chili Rice

5 slices bacon
2 cups uncooked regular rice
½ cup chopped onion
½ cup chopped green pepper
½ cup chopped celery
½ cup peanut butter
3 cups chicken broth
2 cups canned tomatoes
1½ teaspoons chili powder
2 teaspoons salt
¼ teaspoon pepper

Fry bacon until done; remove, drain, and set aside. Add rice, onion, green pepper, and celery to bacon drippings and saute until rice is golden and vegetables are tender. Slowly stir in peanut butter; add chicken broth, tomatoes, chili powder, salt, and pepper. Stir and blend well. Cover and cook over low heat, stirring occasionally, until rice is tender, about 20 minutes. Spoon into serving dish. Crumble bacon over top for garnish. Yield: 8 to 10 servings.

Romany Rice

3 cups cooked rice
2 green onions, finely chopped
1 (12-ounce) carton large curd cottage cheese
1 (8-ounce) carton commercial sour cream
¼ cup milk
¼ teaspoon hot sauce
½ teaspoon salt
½ cup grated Parmesan cheese

Combine rice and onion; set aside. Combine cottage cheese, sour cream, milk, hot sauce, and salt; stir into rice. Spoon mixture into a greased 1½-quart casserole, sprinkle with Parmesan cheese, and bake at 350° for 25 minutes. Yield: 8 to 10 servings.

*Delmonico Rice

3 cups cooked rice
⅓ cup chopped green pepper
3 hard-cooked eggs, chopped
1 (10¾-ounce) can cream of celery soup
1 cup milk
¼ teaspoon pepper
Buttered bread cubes
Sliced hard-cooked egg (optional)

Combine rice, green pepper, chopped eggs, soup, milk, and pepper. Pour into a greased casserole. Top with buttered bread cubes. Bake at 350° for 20 to 30 minutes. Garnish with sliced hard-cooked egg, if desired. Yield: 6 servings.

*Orange Rice

1 cup uncooked long grain rice
2 cups water
1 teaspoon salt
1 tablespoon grated orange rind
½ cup orange juice

Cook rice in boiling salted water. Add orange rind and juice. Drain and serve. Yield: 4 to 6 servings.

*Tarragon Rice

2 tablespoons butter or margarine
1 tablespoon chicken-flavored stock base or 2 chicken bouillon cubes
1 teaspoon tarragon
1 tablespoon lemon juice
3 cups hot cooked rice
Salt and pepper

Combine and heat butter, chicken flavoring, tarragon, and lemon juice. Pour over rice, add seasonings, and toss lightly. Yield: 6 servings.

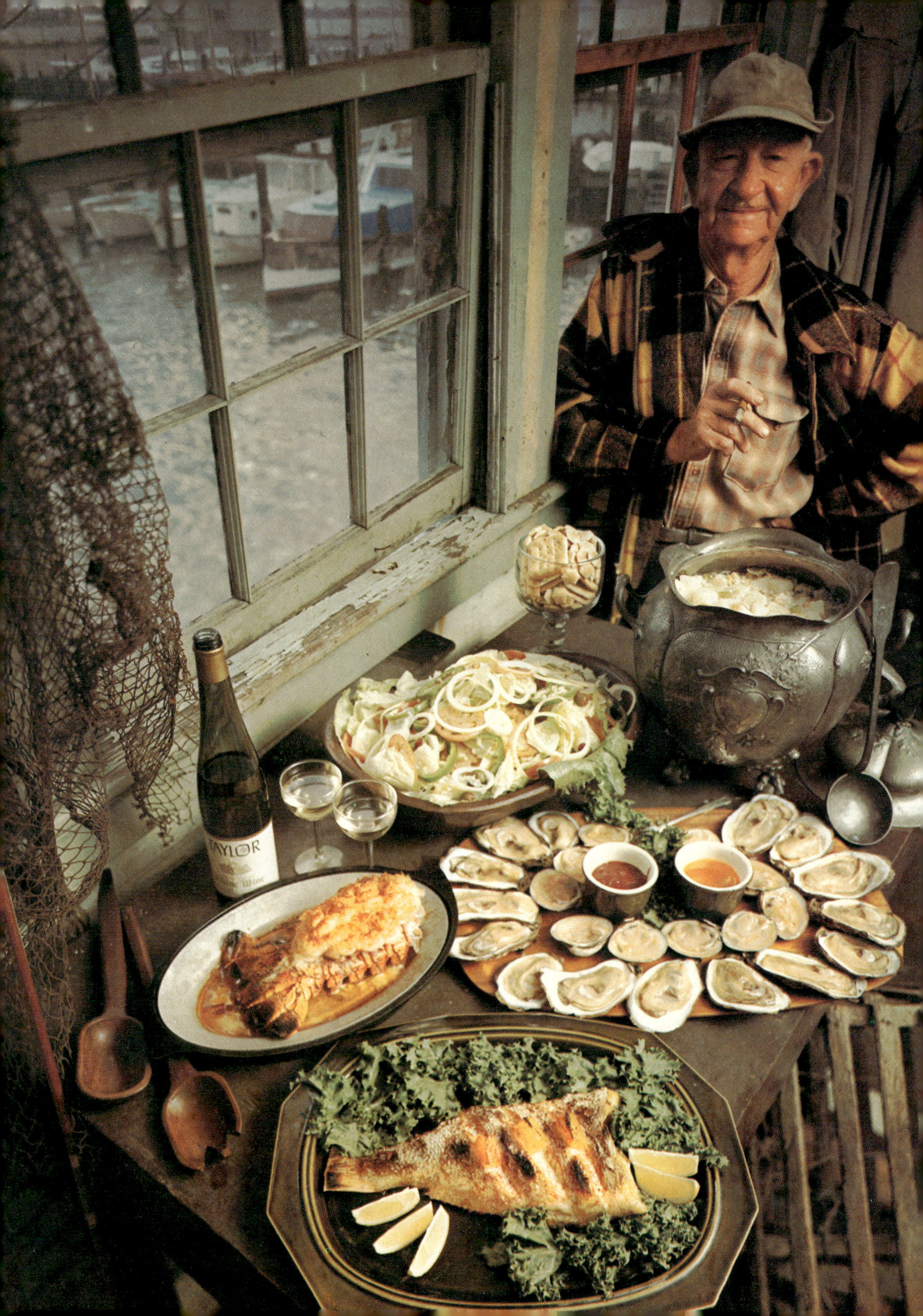
TAYLOR

Fish and Shellfish

The colonial settlers were both surprised and delighted with the abundance of fish and shellfish they found off our Eastern shores. Many of them had been able to get fresh foods from coastal waters near their former homes, and now their favorite recipes could be used to prepare delectable meals for their families in the new land.

Actually, our Southland has more shoreline than any other section of the country, and we are blessed with an abundance of lakes and streams that furnish fresh water fish to the lucky fishermen. Time-honored recipes such as Oysters Rockefeller and Shrimp Mull had their beginnings in Southern kitchens. And their fame has spread throughout the length and breadth of this land.

Fish and shellfish are staples in the appetizer field as well as in the field of main dishes. They blend well with pastas and rice and are coveted for use in casseroles and salads. With modern refrigeration, even inland homes are able to get quick-frozen fish which tastes just as it did when it came out of the water; as a result, more and more people are relying on fish and shellfish to meet their daily demands for protein foods.

*Smoky Broiled Catfish

6 *skinned, pan-dressed catfish, fresh or frozen*
⅓ *cup soy sauce*
3 *tablespoons vegetable oil*
1 *tablespoon liquid smoke*
1 *clove garlic, finely chopped*
½ *teaspoon ground ginger*
½ *teaspoon salt*
Lemon wedges

Thaw frozen fish; clean, wash, and dry fresh fish. Combine remaining ingredients except lemon wedges and mix thoroughly. Brush inside of fish with sauce. Place fish on a well-greased broiler pan; brush with sauce. Broil about 3 inches from source of heat for 4 to 6 minutes. Turn carefully and brush other side with sauce. Broil 4 to 6 minutes longer, basting occasionally, until fish flakes easily when tested with a fork. Serve with lemon wedges. Yield: 6 servings.

Cajun Catfish

6 *skinned, pan-dressed catfish, fresh or frozen*
½ *cup tomato sauce*
2 *(¾-ounce) packages cheese-garlic salad dressing mix*
2 *tablespoons vegetable oil*
2 *tablespoons chopped parsley*
2 *tablespoons grated Parmesan cheese*

Thaw frozen fish; clean, wash, and dry fresh fish. Combine remaining ingredients except cheese. Brush fish inside and out with sauce. Place in a well-greased 13- x 9- x 2-inch baking dish. Brush fish with remaining sauce and sprinkle with cheese. Let stand for 30 minutes. Bake at 350° for 25 to 35 minutes or until fish flakes easily when tested with a fork. Turn oven control to broil. Place fish about 3 inches from source of heat and broil for 1 to 2 minutes or until crisp and lightly browned. Yield: 6 servings.

Continental Catfish

    6 *skinned, pan-dressed catfish, fresh or frozen*
    1 *teaspoon salt*
       Dash pepper
    1 *cup chopped parsley*
  ¼ *cup butter or margarine, softened*
    1 *egg, beaten*
  ¼ *cup milk*
    1 *teaspoon salt*
  ¾ *cup dry bread crumbs*
  ½ *cup shredded Swiss cheese*
    3 *tablespoons melted shortening*

Thaw frozen fish; clean, wash, and dry fresh fish. Sprinkle inside and out with salt and pepper. Add parsley to butter and mix thoroughly. Spread inside of each fish with approximately 1 tablespoon parsley butter. Combine egg, milk, and salt. Combine bread crumbs and cheese. Dip fish in egg mixture and roll in crumb mixture. Place on a well-greased 15½- x 12-inch baking sheet. Sprinkle remaining crumb mixture over fish. Drizzle with melted shortening. Bake at 400° for 15 to 20 minutes or until fish flakes easily when tested with a fork. Yield: 6 servings.

Crispy Catfish

    6 *skinned, pan-dressed catfish*
  ½ *cup evaporated milk*
    1 *tablespoon salt*
       Dash pepper
    1 *cup all-purpose flour*
  ½ *cup cornmeal*
    2 *teaspoons paprika*
  12 *slices bacon*

Wash and dry fish. Combine milk, salt, and pepper. Combine flour, cornmeal, and paprika. Dip fish into milk mixture and roll in flour mixture; set aside. Fry bacon until crisp; drain. Fry fish in hot bacon drippings for 4 minutes. Turn very carefully and fry 4 to 6 minutes longer or until fish is brown and flakes easily when tested with a fork. Drain on paper towels. Serve with bacon. Yield: 6 servings.

*Dixieland Catfish

    6 *skinned, pan-dressed catfish, fresh or frozen*
  ½ *cup commercial French dressing, divided*
  12 *thin lemon slices, divided*
       Paprika

Thaw frozen fish; clean, wash, and dry fresh fish. Brush inside and out with French dressing. Cut 6 lemon slices in half. Place 2 halves in each body cavity. Place fish in a well-greased 13- x 9- x 2-inch baking dish. Place a lemon slice on each fish. Brush top of fish with remaining dressing; sprinkle with paprika. Bake at 350° for 30 to 35 minutes or until fish flakes easily when tested with a fork. Yield: 6 servings.

*Southern Fried Catfish

    4 *(1- to 1¼-pound) pan-dressed catfish*
    1 *cup buttermilk*
 1⅓ *cups cornmeal*
  ⅔ *cup all-purpose flour*
    1 *tablespoon salt*
    2 *teaspoons pepper*
       Oil

Dip each fish in buttermilk. Combine remaining ingredients and thoroughly coat fish with mixture. Fry fish in 1 inch hot oil (360°) for 6 to 10 minutes on each side, or until fish flakes easily when tested with a fork. Drain fish on paper towels; arrange on heated platter. Yield: 4 servings.

*Grilled Sesame Catfish

    6 *skinned, pan-dressed catfish, fresh or frozen*
  ½ *cup vegetable oil*
  ½ *cup sesame seeds*
    4 *tablespoons lemon juice*
    1 *teaspoon salt*
       Dash pepper

Thaw frozen fish; clean, wash, and dry fresh fish. Place in a well-greased hinged

fish and shellfish

wire grill. Combine remaining ingredients. Cook fish about 4 inches from moderately hot coals for 8 minutes. Baste with sauce. Turn and cook 7 to 10 minutes longer or until fish flakes easily when tested with a fork. Yield: 6 servings.

New Orleans Catfish

    2 *pounds catfish steaks, fresh or frozen*
  1/2 *teaspoon salt*
      Dash pepper
    2 *cups cooked rice*
    2 *tablespoons grated onion*
  1/2 *teaspoon curry powder*
    6 *thin lemon slices*
  1/4 *cup butter or margarine*
      Chopped parsley

Thaw frozen fish; clean, wash, and dry fresh fish. Cut into serving-size portions and place in a well-greased 13- x 9- x 2-inch baking dish. Sprinkle fish with salt and pepper. Combine rice, onion, and curry powder; spread over fish. Top with lemon slices and dot with butter; cover. Bake at 350° for 25 to 35 minutes or until fish flakes easily when tested with a fork. Remove cover the last few minutes of cooking to allow for slight browning. Sprinkle with parsley. Yield: 6 servings.

Bacon-Barbecued Fish

    2 *pounds small, pan-dressed fish*
    2 *tablespoons lemon juice*
    2 *teaspoons salt*
  1/4 *teaspoon pepper*
    1 *pound sliced bacon*

Clean fish; wash and dry thoroughly. Brush inside of fish with lemon juice and sprinkle with salt and pepper. Wrap each fish with a slice of bacon and place in a well-greased, hinged wire grill. Cook about 5 inches from moderately hot coals for 10 to 15 minutes. Turn and cook an additional 10 minutes or until bacon is crisp and fish flakes easily when tested with a fork. Yield: 4 to 6 servings.

*Savory Baked Fish

    1 *teaspoon instant minced onion*
  1/2 *teaspoon dry mustard*
  1/4 *teaspoon tarragon leaves, crushed*
 1/16 *teaspoon pepper*
    2 *teaspoons warm water*
 1 1/2 *pounds filet of whitefish, halibut, or cod*
      Salt to taste
    1 *teaspoon lemon juice*
  1/2 *cup mayonnaise*
      Paprika

Combine onion, mustard, tarragon, and pepper with warm water; let stand for 10 minutes for flavors to blend. Wipe fish and arrange in a greased baking dish. Sprinkle with salt. Add lemon juice and mayonnaise to tarragon mixture; spread over fish. Bake at 425° for 25 to 30 minutes or until lightly browned and fish flakes easily when tested with a fork. Garnish with paprika. Yield: 6 servings.

Baked Fish and Cheese

    1 *pound fish filets*
    6 *ounces pasteurized process American cheese, sliced*
  1/4 *cup chopped parsley*
    1 *teaspoon oregano or thyme*
  1/4 *cup salad oil*
    2 *medium-size onions, chopped*
    2 *tablespoons all-purpose flour*
  1/8 *teaspoon salt*
  1/8 *teaspoon pepper*
 1 1/2 *cups milk*

Alternate layers of fish and cheese in lightly greased oblong baking dish, ending with cheese. Sprinkle with parsley and oregano or thyme. Heat oil in skillet; add onions and cook until tender, stirring frequently. Blend in flour, salt, and pepper. Pour in milk; cook, stirring constantly, until thickened. Pour mixture over fish. Bake at 400° for 20 to 30 minutes or until fish flakes easily when tested with a fork. Yield: 4 servings.

Deviled Crabs

- 2 eggs, beaten
- ½ cup beef bouillon or half-and-half
- 2 tablespoons melted butter or margarine
- 1 tablespoon minced onion
- 1 teaspoon hot sauce
- 1 teaspoon prepared mustard
- ½ teaspoon salt
- ¼ teaspoon white pepper
- 2 cups chopped, cooked crabmeat
- 1 cup bread or cracker crumbs, divided
- Butter

Combine eggs, bouillon or half-and-half, melted butter, onion, and seasonings; mix well. Stir in crabmeat and half the cracker crumbs; mix well. Fill crab shells or ramekins with this mixture; top with remaining cracker crumbs, and dot with butter. Bake at 350° until crumbs are lightly browned. Yield: 6 servings.

Crab Burgers

- 1 (6½-ounce) can crabmeat
- 1 egg
- 2 hard-cooked eggs, chopped
- Dash cayenne pepper
- 1 teaspoon dry mustard
- 1 tablespoon chopped green pepper
- 2 tablespoons mayonnaise
- 2 tablespoons Worcestershire sauce
- 1 teaspoon chopped parsley
- 1 teaspoon minced onion
- 1 cup bread crumbs
- Salt and pepper to taste
- Cracker crumbs
- Butter

Combine all ingredients except cracker crumbs and butter. Mix well and form into cakes. Roll in cracker crumbs and fry in butter. Yield: 4 servings.

Gulf Deviled Crab

- 1 pound crabmeat
- 4 hard-cooked eggs, chopped
- 1 tablespoon Worcestershire sauce
- ½ teaspoon hot sauce
- ½ teaspoon pepper
- 2 cups cracker crumbs
- ½ cup butter, melted
- 12 crab shells

Break crabmeat into pieces; combine with remaining ingredients and spoon into crab shells. Bake at 375° about 10 minutes. Yield: 12 servings.

Crab Cakes

- 1 slice bread, crust removed
- 1 egg, beaten
- ½ teaspoon salt
- Dash pepper
- 2 tablespoons mayonnaise
- 1 tablespoon prepared mustard
- 1½ teaspoons Worcestershire sauce
- 1 pound fresh backfin lump crabmeat
- Salad oil

Soak bread in beaten egg; tear into small pieces and add seasonings, mayonnaise, mustard, Worcestershire sauce, and crabmeat. Try not to break up the lumps of crabmeat. Toss and carefully form into cakes the size of hamburgers; brown in hot oil. Yield: 6 large or 8 medium-size crab cakes.

Fried Soft-Shell Crabs

Buy dressed soft-shell crabs during the molting season (summer). They are available from most seafood markets, particularly along the coast.

Season with salt and pepper and fry in a mixture of half shortening and half butter until crisp.

You will find that the whole crab is delicious. Flippers and legs are like French fries.

Crab Imperial

- ½ fresh green pepper, finely diced
- 2 teaspoons finely diced pimiento
- 1 teaspoon dry mustard
- ¾ teaspoon salt
- ¼ teaspoon white pepper
- 1 egg
- ⅓ cup mayonnaise
- 2 tablespoons melted butter
- 1 pound fresh backfin lump crabmeat
- Mayonnaise
- Paprika

Combine all ingredients except mayonnaise and paprika. Be careful not to break up lumps of crabmeat; toss lightly. Divide mixture into four portions and place in separate casseroles or ramekins (large seashells or crab shells make attractive serving dishes). Coat each serving with a light topping of mayonnaise, and sprinkle with paprika. Bake at 300° about 20 minutes. Yield: 4 servings.

Crab Ravigote

- 1 pound crabmeat
- ¼ cup mayonnaise or salad dressing
- 2 tablespoons lemon juice
- 2 tablespoons chopped onion
- 2 tablespoons chopped sweet pickle relish
- 1 tablespoon chopped parsley
- 1 hard-cooked egg, chopped
- ¼ teaspoon salt
- Dash pepper
- Salad greens
- ¼ cup mayonnaise or salad dressing
- 2 tablespoons chopped stuffed olives
- ¼ teaspoon paprika
- Pimiento strips

Remove any shell or cartilage from crabmeat. Combine crabmeat with ¼ cup mayonnaise, lemon juice, onion, pickle relish, parsley, egg, and seasonings. Shape into a mound on salad greens. Combine ¼ cup mayonnaise with olives and paprika. Spread over crabmeat mixture. Chill. Garnish with pimiento strips. Yield: 6 servings.

Crabmeat Royale

- 1 pound crabmeat
- 1 (4-ounce) can mushrooms, drained
- ¼ cup butter or margarine
- 1 tablespoon chopped onion
- 1 teaspoon Worcestershire sauce
- ¼ cup dry sherry (optional)
- 3 tablespoons all-purpose flour
- 1 cup milk
- Salt and pepper to taste
- Shredded cheese

Remove any shell or cartilage from crabmeat. Sauté drained mushrooms in butter for about 5 minutes. Add onion and cook until onion is tender. Add crabmeat, Worcestershire sauce, and sherry, if desired.

Make a paste of flour and milk; add to crabmeat mixture and cook until sauce thickens. Add salt and pepper. Spoon mixture into a 1-quart baking dish or individual shells or ramekins. Sprinkle shredded cheese over the top. Bake at 350° for 5 minutes or until cheese melts and mixture is bubbly. Yield: 6 servings.

Corn and Crab Imperial

- ½ cup chopped onion
- 2 tablespoons butter, melted
- 2 tablespoons all-purpose flour
- ¼ cup milk
- 1 (17-ounce) can cream-style corn
- 1 (12-ounce) can whole kernel corn
- 2 teaspoons prepared mustard
- 1 teaspoon Worcestershire sauce
- ½ teaspoon salt
- ½ teaspoon celery salt
- Dash pepper
- 1 (6½-ounce) can crabmeat
- 2 hard-cooked eggs, chopped
- Patty shells or toast points

Sauté onion in butter. Add flour and stir well. Add milk, corn, mustard, Worcestershire sauce, salt, celery salt, and pepper; cook until thickened, stirring constantly. Add crabmeat and eggs; continue cooking until hot. Serve in patty shells or over toast points. Yield: 6 servings.

Crab-Stuffed Avocados

   1 *pound fresh or frozen crabmeat or 3 (6⅓-ounce) cans crabmeat*
   2 *tablespoons all-purpose flour*
  ¼ *teaspoon salt*
      Dash pepper
   2 *tablespoons melted shortening or oil*
   1 *cup milk*
  ¼ *teaspoon Worcestershire sauce*
   2 *tablespoons chopped stuffed olives*
   2 *tablespoons chopped pimiento*
   3 *ripe avocados*
  ¼ *cup shredded Cheddar cheese*

Thaw frozen crabmeat, or drain canned crabmeat. Remove any shell or cartilage from crabmeat. Blend flour, salt, and pepper into melted shortening. Add milk gradually and cook until thick and smooth, stirring constantly. Add Worcestershire sauce, olives, pimiento, and crabmeat. Cut avocados in half and remove the pit. Fill with crabmeat mixture and sprinkle cheese over the top. Place in a well-greased baking dish and bake at 350° for 20 to 25 minutes or until brown. Yield: 6 servings.

Crayfish or Shrimp Étouffée

   2 *onions, finely chopped*
 1½ *cups chopped celery*
   1 *small green pepper, chopped*
      Garlic, finely minced (optional)
  ½ *cup butter or margarine*
   1 *pound crayfish meat or shrimp, peeled and deveined*
  ½ *(10¾-ounce) can condensed cream of celery soup*
  ½ *(10¾-ounce) can condensed cream of mushroom soup*
   1 *bunch green onions, finely chopped*
   1 *bunch parsley, finely chopped*

Cook chopped onions, celery, green pepper, and garlic, if desired, in butter until softened. Add crayfish meat or shrimp and cook until almost done. Add cream of celery and mushroom soups, green onions, and parsley, and simmer for about 20 minutes. Serve hot. Yield: 4 servings.

Classic Jambalaya

 1½ *cups diced cooked ham*
   2 *tablespoons vegetable oil*
   1 *medium-size onion, sliced*
   1 *medium-size green pepper, chopped*
   1 *clove garlic, minced*
   1 *(14½-ounce) can whole tomatoes, undrained*
   1 *(6-ounce) can tomato paste*
 2½ *cups water*
  ¾ *cup uncooked regular rice*
   1 *bay leaf, crumbled*
  ½ *teaspoon salt*
  ¼ *teaspoon thyme*
  ⅛ *teaspoon cayenne pepper*
   1 *pound shrimp, cooked, peeled, and cleaned or 2 (6-ounce) cans shrimp, drained and rinsed*
  ¼ *cup minced parsley*

Lightly brown ham in oil in a large skillet or Dutch oven. Add onion, green pepper, and garlic; cook until tender. Add undrained tomatoes, tomato paste, water, rice, bay leaf, salt, thyme, and cayenne pepper. Cover; simmer 25 minutes, stirring occasionally. Add shrimp and parsley; simmer just until shrimp are heated through. Yield: 6 servings.

Crayfish Jambalaya

  ½ *cup margarine*
   2 *cups chopped white onion*
   1 *cup chopped celery*
  ½ *cup chopped green pepper*
   2 *cloves garlic, chopped*
   1 *fresh ripe tomato, chopped*
   2 *cups peeled crayfish tails*
  ½ *cup crayfish fat (from heads of parboiled crayfish)*
   3 *tablespoons chopped green onion*
   2 *bay leaves*
  ¼ *teaspoon thyme*
   1 *teaspoon Spanish paprika*
   2 *tablespoons chopped parsley*
   6 *cups water*
   3 *cups uncooked regular rice*
      Salt and pepper to taste
      Hot sauce (optional)

Melt margarine in large iron pot with a cover. Add onion, celery, green pepper, and garlic; cook until vegetables are transparent. Add chopped tomato, crayfish tails, and fat; cook 5 minutes. Add green onion, bay leaves, thyme, paprika, and parsley; cook 5 minutes more.

Add water, rice, salt, and pepper. Bring to a boil while stirring; cover and reduce heat to simmer. Cook for 15 minutes. Do not remove cover until rice is done. Remove bay leaves. Add hot sauce, if desired. Yield: 6 to 8 servings.

Note: If crayfish are not available, 2 cups peeled and deveined shrimp may be substituted. Delete crayfish fat from recipe if shrimp is used.

Lobster Newburg

¾ pound cooked lobster meat
¼ cup melted butter or margarine
2 tablespoons all-purpose flour
1 teaspoon salt
¼ teaspoon paprika
Dash cayenne pepper
1 pint whipping cream
2 egg yolks, beaten
2 tablespoons sherry
Toast points

Cut cooked lobster meat into ½-inch pieces. Combine melted butter, flour, and seasonings in a saucepan. Add cream gradually and cook over medium heat until thick and smooth, stirring constantly. Stir a little of the hot sauce into beaten egg yolks; add to remaining sauce, stirring constantly. Add lobster meat and heat. Remove from heat and slowly stir in sherry. Serve immediately on toast points. Yield: 6 servings.

Broiled Florida Lobster

2 boiled Florida lobsters
1 tablespoon melted butter or margarine
⅛ teaspoon white pepper
⅛ teaspoon paprika
¼ cup melted butter or margarine
1 tablespoon lemon juice

Split boiled lobsters. Place lobsters, opened as flat as possible, on a broiler pan. Brush lobster meat with 1 tablespoon melted butter. Sprinkle with pepper and paprika. Broil about 4 inches from source of heat for 5 minutes or until lightly browned. Make a sauce of ¼ cup melted butter and lemon juice; serve with lobster. Yield: 4 servings.

Gourmet Rock Lobster

3 (8-ounce) packages frozen rock lobster tails
Boiling salted water
6 tablespoons melted butter
2 tablespoons dry mustard
2 teaspoons Worcestershire sauce
Juice of 3 small limes
6 tablespoons mango chutney
½ cup finely chopped salted peanuts
Grated Parmesan cheese

Drop frozen lobster tails into boiling salted water. When water reboils, drain lobsters immediately and drench with cold water. Cut away underside membrane with scissors and carefully remove meat from shell. Remove intestinal vein from tail. Reserve shells. Cut up lobster meat, which will be translucent and only partly cooked, into small pieces.

Combine melted butter, mustard, Worcestershire sauce, and lime juice in a heavy skillet. Stir in chutney, lobster meat, and peanuts. Sauté very slowly until heated through and lobster is tender. Stuff shells with mixture; sprinkle lightly with Parmesan cheese and quickly brown under broiler for a few minutes. Yield: 6 servings.

Broiled Lobster

    2 *(1-pound) live lobsters*
    1 *tablespoon melted butter or margarine*
  ¼ *teaspoon salt*
      Dash white pepper
      Dash paprika
  ¼ *cup melted butter or margarine*
    1 *tablespoon lemon juice*

Kill each lobster by placing it on its back and inserting a sharp knife between the body shell and tail segment, cutting down to sever the spinal cord. Cut in half lengthwise. Remove the stomach (located just back of the head) and the intestinal vein (runs from the stomach to the tip of the tail). Do not discard the green liver and coral roe; they are delicious. Crack claws.

Place lobster, opened as flat as possible, on a broiler pan. Brush lobster meat with 1 tablespoon melted butter. Sprinkle with salt, pepper, and paprika. Broil about 4 inches from source of heat for 12 to 15 minutes or until lightly browned. Combine ¼ cup melted butter and lemon juice; serve with lobster. Yield: 2 servings.

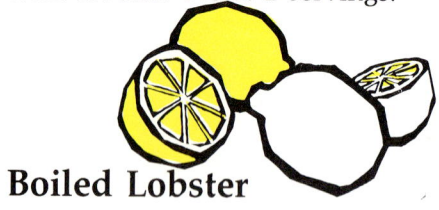

Boiled Lobster

    2 *(1-pound) live lobsters*
    3 *quarts boiling water*
    3 *tablespoons salt*
      Melted butter

Plunge lobsters headfirst into boiling salted water. Cover and return to boiling point. Simmer about 15 minutes; drain. Place lobster on its back; insert a sharp knife between body shell and tail segment, cutting down to sever the spinal cord. Cut in half lengthwise. Remove the stomach (located just back of the head) and the intestinal vein (runs from the stomach to the tip of the tail). Do not discard the green liver and coral roe; they are delicious. Crack claws. Serve lobster with melted butter. Yield: 2 servings.

Stuffed Flounder

    1 *(1½-pound) flounder*
    1 *cup bite-size pieces Alaskan king crab*
    2 *shallots, chopped*
  ½ *teaspoon chopped parsley*
    1 *tablespoon chopped green pepper*
  ½ *teaspoon Worcestershire sauce*
      Salt and pepper to taste
    1 *teaspoon grated Parmesan cheese*
    1 *egg yolk*
  ½ *cup whipping cream*
  ⅛ *teaspoon anisette*
  ⅛ *teaspoon Pernod*
      Lemon wedge

Clean and bone flounder. Combine crabmeat, shallots, parsley, green pepper, Worcestershire sauce, salt, pepper, and Parmesan cheese. Beat egg yolk with cream and add to mixture. Stir in anisette and Pernod and mix well. Stuff center cavity of flounder with mixture and bake at 350° about 25 minutes. Serve hot with a wedge of lemon. Yield: 1 serving.

Oyster Mario

    2 *dozen select oysters, in shells*
    1 *clove garlic*
    3 *tablespoons butter*
      Dash salt
      Dash pepper
    1 *cup bread crumbs*
    2 *tablespoons olive oil*
    2 *tablespoons chopped parsley*
  ½ *teaspoon oregano*
      Juice of 1 lemon

Scrub shells; rinse in cold water. Remove oysters from shells. Rub the half shell with garlic and butter; replace oyster. Sprinkle with salt and pepper. Combine bread crumbs, olive oil, parsley, and oregano. Sprinkle mixture on each oyster. Arrange in shallow baking dish; bake at 350° about 10 minutes or until edges of oysters curl. Serve very hot with lemon juice. Yield: 4 servings.

Panned Oysters

    6 to 8 *fresh oysters*
    1 *tablespoon butter*
    ¼ *teaspoon seafood seasoning (optional)*
    1 *tablespoon cooking sherry*
    Drawn butter

Sauté oysters in butter about 2 to 3 minutes or until edges begin to curl. Add seasoning and sherry; serve hot with drawn butter. Yield: 1 serving.

Low Country Oyster Loaf

    1 *(14-ounce) loaf French bread*
    ½ *cup butter or margarine*
    1 *tablespoon minced onion*
    ½ *teaspoon thyme*
    ½ *teaspoon basil*
    ½ *teaspoon paprika*
    Oyster Filling
    Parsley
    6 *lemon wedges*

Slice bread in half lengthwise; scoop out soft center of lower half and save for use in other dishes. Place both halves of loaf, cut side up, on a baking sheet.

Melt butter in a small saucepan; blend in onion, thyme, basil, and paprika. Brush two-thirds of butter mixture over cut sides of bread, covering completely. Bake at 350° for 15 minutes or until slightly toasted.

Fill lower half of bread with Oyster Filling; cover with top half and brush with remaining seasoned butter. Bake an additional 5 to 10 minutes. Cut into 6 diagonal pieces; garnish each piece with parsley and a wedge of lemon. Serve hot. Yield: 6 servings.

    Oyster Filling:

    1 *pint oysters, drained*
    1 *egg, well beaten*
    ½ *teaspoon salt*
    ¼ *teaspoon pepper*
    1¼ *cups finely crushed cracker crumbs*
    ¼ *cup melted butter or margarine*

Rinse oysters in cold water; drain. Mix egg, salt, and pepper in a small bowl. Dip oysters into egg mixture; coat with cracker crumbs. Sauté oysters in butter until golden brown.

Oyster Surprise

    1 *cup oysters, drained*
    4 *eggs*
    ½ *teaspoon salt*
    ⅛ *teaspoon white pepper*
    4 *tablespoons butter or margarine*
    1 *teaspoon anchovy paste*
    4 *slices hot buttered toast*

Dry oysters well on paper towel. Beat eggs; add salt and pepper. Melt butter in chafing dish over low heat; blend in anchovy paste. Stir in eggs; push eggs to edge of pan when they first begin to set.

Heat oysters in center of dish; eggs should be done when oysters are heated. Cover oysters with eggs. Serve on toast. Yield: 2 servings.

Oyster Soufflé

    1 *onion, finely chopped*
    ¼ *green pepper, minced*
    2 *tablespoons shortening*
    6 *egg yolks*
    1½ *cups fried oysters, chopped*
    ¾ *cup rice, cooked*
    1½ *cups milk*
    ⅜ *cup tomato sauce*
    1½ *tablespoons all-purpose flour*
    1½ *teaspoons Worcestershire sauce*
    Salt and pepper to taste
    6 *egg whites, beaten*

Sauté onion and green pepper in shortening in a saucepan. Stir in remaining ingredients except egg whites; heat. Remove from heat and add beaten egg whites. Pour into a lightly greased 1½-quart baking dish; bake at 350° until lightly browned on top. Yield: 4 to 6 servings.

Oysters Parmesan

 1 *cup oysters, drained*
 1 *tablespoon chopped onion*
 1 *cup milk, divided*
1½ *tablespoons shortening*
 2 *tablespoons all-purpose flour*
 ¼ *teaspoon salt*
  Dash pepper
 ¼ *teaspoon celery salt*
 ¼ *cup grated Parmesan cheese*
 1 *teaspoon chopped parsley*
 3 *hard rolls*
  Paprika

Combine oysters, onion, and ½ cup milk in a saucepan. Cook over medium heat for 15 minutes. Melt shortening and blend in flour, salt, pepper, and celery salt. Add remaining ½ cup milk and cook until thickened, stirring constantly. Add Parmesan cheese and parsley. Combine cheese sauce with oyster mixture and cook for an additional 5 minutes. Serve hot over split hard rolls. Sprinkle paprika over each serving. Yield: 3 servings.

Creole Oyster Pie

 1 *cup all-purpose flour*
 ¼ *teaspoon salt*
 ⅓ *cup vegetable shortening*
 1 *tablespoon cold water*
 1 *quart oysters, drained*
 1 *cup all-purpose flour*
 2 *teaspoons salt, divided*
 ¼ *teaspoon freshly ground black pepper*
 ⅛ *teaspoon ground mace*
 ¼ *teaspoon paprika*
 2 *slices bacon, diced*
 1 *small onion, minced*
 1 *tablespoon minced green pepper, divided*
 8 *to 10 drops hot sauce*
  Juice of 1 large lemon (about 2 tablespoons)
 1 *tablespoon minced parsley, fresh, frozen or dried*
 2 *tablespoons butter*

Blend 1 cup flour, ¼ teaspoon salt, shortening, and water in a large bowl. Roll to ¼-inch thickness on a lightly floured surface. Cut into six 2¾-inch rounds, using a regular size glass as a cutter. Remove center of each round with a 1-inch biscuit cutter. Set aside pastry rounds while preparing rest of recipe.

 Dry the drained oysters on paper. Roll in mixture of 1 cup flour, 1 teaspoon salt, pepper, mace, and paprika. Sauté bacon and onion until crisp and brown.

 Place a layer of oysters close together in a greased baking dish. Sprinkle half of bacon mixture over oysters. Add half of minced green pepper, hot sauce, 1 teaspoon salt, lemon juice, and parsley. Repeat layers. Dot with butter and place all the pastry rounds on top. Bake at 450° for 25 minutes or until pastry rounds are golden. Serve at once. Yield: 6 servings.

Corn and Oyster Scallop

 1 *quart oysters in liquor*
 2 *cups niblet corn, drained*
 ¼ *large onion, minced*
  Salt and pepper to taste
 ¼ *teaspoon ground nutmeg*
 ⅛ *teaspoon ground mace*
 3 *cups cracker crumbs, divided*
 ¼ *cup oyster liquor*
 ¼ *cup half-and-half*
 ¾ *cup dry Sauterne*
 ½ *cup butter or margarine*
  Tartar sauce
  Lemon wedges

Drain oysters, reserving liquor; remove shell particles. Strain liquor and reserve. Blend corn and onion in a mixing bowl; season with salt and pepper. Add nutmeg and mace and mix well.

 Spread 1 cup cracker crumbs in bottom of a greased 2-quart casserole. Cover with corn mixture; sprinkle with an additional 1 cup cracker crumbs. Arrange oysters over crumbs; sprinkle lightly with pepper and top with remaining crumbs.

 Blend oyster liquor, half-and-half, and wine; pour over all. Dot generously with butter. Bake at 350° for 20 minutes or until golden brown. Serve hot with tartar sauce and lemon wedges. Yield: 6 servings.

Fried Oysters

   3 *dozen large oysters*
     Salt and pepper to taste
   2 *cups cracker crumbs, finely crushed*
   2 *eggs, beaten*
     Shortening

Drain oysters and press between paper towels. Season oysters with salt and pepper. Dip in cracker crumbs, beaten eggs, and again in cracker crumbs. Fry in shortening until golden brown. Yield: 6 servings.

Scalloped Oysters

   2 *cups cracker crumbs*
  ½ *teaspoon salt*
     Dash pepper
  ½ *cup melted butter*
   1 *pint oysters, drained*
  ¼ *teaspoon Worcestershire sauce*
   1 *cup milk*

Combine cracker crumbs, salt, pepper, and butter; sprinkle one-third of this mixture in a greased 1-quart casserole and cover with a layer of oysters. Repeat layers, reserving a little of the crumb mixture for topping. Add Worcestershire sauce to milk; pour over casserole. Sprinkle remaining crumbs over top. Bake at 350° for 30 minutes or until brown. Yield: 6 servings.

Broiled Oysters

   8 *to 10 crab shells*
     Cracker crumbs
   1 *quart oysters*
   2 *tablespoons butter*
   1 *whole lemon, cut in pieces*
   1 *tablespoon Worcestershire sauce*
  ½ *teaspoon pepper*
   2 *tablespoons hot water*

Cover bottom of crab shells with cracker crumbs. Place oysters over the cracker crumbs. Combine remaining ingredients and heat. Place 1 teaspoon mixture over each shell of oysters and broil about 5 minutes. Yield: 8 to 10 servings.

*Salmon Croquettes with Celery Sauce

   1 *cup cooked grits*
   2 *cups flaked salmon*
   2 *tablespoons chopped onion*
   1 *teaspoon salt*
  ½ *teaspoon pepper*
   1 *tablespoon Worcestershire sauce*
     Bread crumbs
   2 *eggs, beaten*
     Shortening
   1 *(10¾-ounce) can condensed cream of celery soup*
  ¼ *cup milk*
     Pimiento strips

Combine grits, salmon, onion, salt, pepper, and Worcestershire sauce. Chill. Shape into 12 croquettes. Roll in bread crumbs; dip in egg and roll again in bread crumbs. Panfry in hot shortening until golden brown, turning only once.

  Heat soup and milk to make celery sauce; pour over croquettes. Garnish with pimiento strips. Yield: 6 servings.

Salmon Loaf

   2 *eggs*
   1 *(1-pound) can red salmon*
   3 *slices soft bread, cut into small cubes*
   1 *teaspoon salt*
  ¼ *cup butter, melted*
1½ *cups milk*

Beat eggs in a small bowl. Drain salmon, remove skin and bones, and flake. Add salmon, bread cubes, salt, and butter to eggs. Heat milk to lukewarm and add to salmon mixture. Mix thoroughly. Place in a greased 9- x 5- x 3-inch loaf pan. Bake 350° for 1 hour. Yield: 6 to 8 servings.

Salmon-Macaroni Casseroles

 1 *(1-pound) can macaroni in cheese sauce*
 1 *teaspoon prepared mustard*
 1 *(7 3/4 -ounce) can salmon, drained*
 2 *slices bread*
 2 *tablespoons melted butter or margarine*

Combine macaroni and mustard. Break salmon into chunks; gently stir in macaroni mixture. Place in three or four individual casseroles or ramekins. Cut bread slices into tiny cubes; sprinkle over casseroles. Dribble with melted butter. Bake at 375° about 20 minutes or until heated. Yield: 3 or 4 servings.

*Country Salmon and Cracker Pie

 1 *(1-pound) can red or pink salmon, liquid reserved*
  Milk
 1 *tablespoon instant minced onion*
 1 *teaspoon parsley flakes*
 1 *teaspoon salt*
 1/2 *teaspoon thyme*
 1/8 *teaspoon pepper*
 1 1/2 *cups (about 30 crackers) medium-coarse cracker crumbs*
 3 *tablespoons butter or margarine, divided*

Drain liquid from salmon into measuring cup. Add enough milk to liquid to make 1 cup. Turn salmon into bowl and flake. Add milk mixture, minced onion, parsley flakes, salt, thyme, and pepper; mix lightly and set aside.

Sprinkle a layer of cracker crumbs in bottom and around sides of buttered 9-inch pieplate. Spoon in salmon mixture. Dot with 1 tablespoon butter. Sprinkle remaining cracker crumbs over top. Dot with remaining butter. Bake at 400° for 10 to 15 minutes or until crackers have browned. Yield: 6 servings.

Shad Bake, Outdoor Style

Split several 2 1/2 - or 3-pound shad down the middle and fasten to wide planks which can be set up around a fire. The Indians fastened the fish to boards with leather thongs, but it is now customary to nail the fish to the boards. New boards should be well oiled, but at most of the old hunting and fishing clubs the same boards, well seasoned, are used again and again.

Build a good fire of oak or hickory. When it has burned down to coals, begin the long slow baking of the shad. Although shad sometime cook as long as 5 hours, 2 hours is usually sufficient.

During the cooking, baste the fish three times with the following mixture, which has been preheated: Juice of 2 lemons, 1/2 cup Worcestershire sauce, 2 tablespoons salt, 1 cup water, 1 cup melted butter or margarine, and cayenne and black pepper to taste. Since the fish is quite dry, this flavoring is important.

At a large shad bake, the cook daubs on the sauce using a broomstick with a cloth fastened to it. For home use, the usual method is acceptable. While the shad bakes, prepare the roe, but do not cook it until time to serve. Dip the roe in beaten egg, roll in cornmeal, and fry in bacon drippings. Serve with several slices of crisp bacon.

Properly cooked, shad has much more texture than is usually identified with baked fish and is slightly dry, like kippered herring.

Seafood Casserole

 4 *cups cooked shrimp, peeled and deveined*
 1 *(7-ounce) can lobster, flaked*
 1 *(6 1/2 -ounce) can crabmeat, flaked*
 2 1/2 *cups thinly sliced celery*
 2/3 *cup finely chopped onion*
 1 *cup mayonnaise*
 2 *teaspoons Worcestershire sauce*
 1 *teaspoon salt*
 1/2 *teaspoon pepper*
 1 1/2 *cups fine dry bread crumbs*
 1/3 *cup butter or margarine, melted*
 2 *slices lemon*
  Parsley

Cut shrimp in half lengthwise. Combine shrimp, lobster, and crabmeat; mix in celery, onion, mayonnaise, Worcestershire sauce, salt, and pepper. Spread mixture in 1½-quart casserole. Combine bread crumbs and butter; sprinkle over casserole. Bake at 350° for 30 to 35 minutes or until lightly browned. Garnish with lemon slices and parsley. Yield: 6 to 8 servings.

Shrimp and Olive Casserole

   3 tablespoons shortening
   3 tablespoons all-purpose flour
     Pepper
1½ cups milk
  ¼ teaspoon Worcestershire sauce
   1 cup diced celery
1¾ cups cooked or uncooked peeled shrimp
  ¾ cup sliced stuffed olives
   1 cup soft whole wheat bread crumbs or fresh bread cut into ¼-inch cubes

Blend shortening, flour and pepper. Gradually add milk, Worcestershire sauce and celery; blend well. Cook for 10 minutes; add shrimp and cook for 3 minutes. Combine olives and bread crumbs. Alternate layers of shrimp mixture and olive mixture in a greased 9- x 5- x 3-inch loaf pan or a 2-quart casserole. Bake at 400° for 15 minutes. Yield: 4 to 6 servings.

Shrimp Creole with Cheese Rice

  ¼ cup butter
   1 cup coarsely chopped onion
   1 cup diced celery
   1 small clove garlic, finely minced
   2 tablespoons all-purpose flour
   1 teaspoon salt
   1 teaspoon sugar
     Dash cayenne pepper
   1 teaspoon paprika
  ½ small bay leaf
   4 drops hot sauce
  ½ cup diced green pepper
   1 (1-pound) can tomatoes
   2 cups cooked, cleaned shrimp
     Cheese Rice

Melt butter in skillet. Add onion, celery, and garlic and cook slowly until tender but not brown. Add flour and seasonings; stir until blended. Stir in green pepper and tomatoes. Cook 10 minutes over low heat, stirring occasionally. Add shrimp and heat. Serve in casserole lined with Cheese Rice. Yield: 6 servings.

Cheese Rice:

   3 cups water
   1 tablespoon butter
   1 teaspoon salt
1½ cups uncooked regular rice
   2 cups (½ pound) shredded pasteurized process American cheese
   2 tablespoons finely chopped onion
   1 teaspoon prepared mustard

Bring water to boiling point; add butter, salt, and rice. Bring to boil, reduce heat to low, and cook, covered, until tender, about 20 to 25 minutes. Stir cheese, onion, and mustard into hot rice. Line hot 2-quart casserole with Cheese Rice and fill center with Shrimp Creole. Yield: 6 servings.

Broiled Barbecued Shrimp

   2 pounds fresh jumbo shrimp
  ¼ cup salad oil
  ⅓ cup chopped green onions
   1 cup chili sauce
  ⅓ cup lime juice
   2 tablespoons firmly packed brown sugar
   2 teaspoons prepared mustard
   2 tablespoons Worcestershire sauce
  ½ teaspoon salt

Peel and devein shrimp; set aside. Heat salad oil in a saucepan; add onion and sauté until tender but not brown. Add remaining ingredients except shrimp and simmer, covered, for 10 minutes.

While the sauce is cooking, arrange shrimp in foil-lined broiler pan. Pour sauce over shrimp. Broil, about 3 inches from source of heat, for 5 to 8 minutes. Remove shrimp to platter; pour sauce in separate bowl to serve with shrimp. Yield: 6 servings.

Creole Rice and Shrimp

1½ cups uncooked regular rice
2 tablespoons shortening
1 tablespoon all-purpose flour
1 green pepper, chopped
1 tablespoon minced onion
1 clove garlic, chopped
2 tablespoons tomato paste
Pinch cayenne pepper
1 cup cooked shrimp
1 cup water
Salt and pepper to taste

Cook rice according to package directions. Heat shortening in a heavy skillet; add flour and cook until light brown, stirring constantly. This is a roux, the shortening and flour foundation of most Creole dishes.

Add green pepper, onion, garlic, tomato paste, and cayenne pepper to the roux. Add shrimp, water, salt, and pepper. Cook slowly for 1 hour. Place rice in a 2-quart casserole; add shrimp mixture. Cover and bake at 350° for 25 to 30 minutes. Yield: 4 servings.

Broccoli-Shrimp Crisp

1 cup cooked shrimp
1 (10-ounce) package frozen broccoli spears
1 (10¾-ounce) can condensed cream of mushroom soup
¼ cup milk or water
½ cup shredded pasteurized process American cheese
1 cup toasted bread crumbs
2 tablespoons melted butter or margarine
2 hard-cooked eggs

Peel, devein, and cut shrimp in half. Cook broccoli according to package directions, until almost tender. Heat soup in saucepan with milk or water; stir until smooth. Stir in shrimp. Arrange layer of broccoli, soup mixture, and cheese in a baking dish. Sprinkle with bread crumbs and spoon melted butter over top. Bake at 350° for 20 minutes. Just before serving, slice hard-cooked eggs and arrange over casserole. Yield: 4 to 5 servings.

Shrimp De Jonghe Casserole

1 cup melted butter or margarine
2 cloves garlic, minced
⅓ cup chopped parsley
½ teaspoon paprika
Dash cayenne pepper
⅔ cup cooking sherry
2 cups soft bread crumbs
5 to 6 cups cleaned cooked shrimp
Chopped parsley

Combine melted butter, garlic, parsley, paprika, cayenne pepper, and cooking sherry; mix well. Add bread crumbs and toss. Place shrimp in an 13- x 9- x 2-inch baking dish. Spoon butter mixture over all and bake at 325° for 20 to 25 minutes or until crumbs are brown. Sprinkle with additional chopped parsley before serving. Yield: 6 to 8 servings.

Grilled Shrimp

2 pounds large fresh or frozen shrimp
¾ cup salad oil, divided
2 teaspoons salt, divided
4 tablespoons chopped parsley
½ teaspoon cayenne pepper
¼ teaspoon dry mustard
½ to 1 clove garlic

Peel and devein shrimp, leaving tails on. Place shrimp in a bowl with ¼ cup salad oil and 1 teaspoon salt. Chill for a few hours or overnight.

Mix chopped parsley, remaining salad oil, salt, cayenne pepper, and dry mustard. Crush garlic and stir into mixture. Cover and chill.

About an hour before cooking, combine the two mixtures; toss, and allow to marinate nearly an hour more. Remove shrimp and arrange on grill over very low fire; brush with sauce. Turn when shrimp begin to turn pink; brush again with sauce and finish grilling. Serve very hot. Yield: 6 to 8 servings.

Note: Half-inch wire mesh screening is excellent when placed over the grill or open fire for broiling small foods such as shrimp.

Shrimp De Jonghe

- 1 pound cooked, peeled, cleaned shrimp, fresh or frozen
- ¾ cup toasted dry bread crumbs
- ¼ cup chopped green onion and tops
- ¼ cup chopped parsley
- ¾ teaspoon crushed tarragon
- ¼ teaspoon crushed garlic
- ¼ teaspoon ground nutmeg
- ¼ teaspoon salt
- Dash pepper
- ½ cup butter or margarine, melted
- ¼ cup sherry

Thaw frozen shrimp. Combine bread crumbs, onion, parsley, and seasonings; add butter and sherry, mixing thoroughly. Combine crumb mixture and shrimp; toss lightly. Grease six 6-ounce custard cups; place about ⅔ cup shrimp mixture in each. Bake at 400° for 10 to 15 minutes or until lightly browned. Yield: 6 servings.

Shrimp à la King

- 1½ pounds boiled shrimp
- 2 cups Medium White Sauce
- ½ teaspoon celery salt
- 1 tablespoon minced pimiento
- Toasted bread shell (French loaf)

Peel and devein shrimp. Add Medium White Sauce, celery salt, and pimiento. Heat to boiling. Hollow out French loaf of bread. Toast in oven. Fill with shrimp mixture. Yield: 6 servings.

Medium White Sauce:

- 4 tablespoons butter or margarine
- 4 tablespoons all-purpose flour
- 2 cups milk
- Salt and pepper to taste

Melt butter in a saucepan. Remove from heat and blend in flour, a small amount at a time. Add milk gradually, stirring constantly. Return to heat and stir constantly until mixture thickens and bubbles. Add seasonings and cook for at least 5 minutes, stirring occasionally. Yield: about 2 cups.

Shrimp Creole

- ½ cup salad oil
- 1 cup sliced green pepper
- 2½ cups sliced onion
- 1 cup diced celery
- ½ cup chopped celery leaves
- ¼ cup chopped parsley
- 1 (1-pound) can tomatoes
- ½ cup chili sauce
- ½ cup seedless raisins
- ¾ cup slivered, blanched almonds
- ½ teaspoon thyme
- ½ teaspoon curry powder
- ½ teaspoon salt
- ½ teaspoon black pepper
- ½ teaspoon cayenne pepper
- 2 bay leaves
- 2½ pounds shrimp, cooked
- Cooked rice

Heat oil in a large skillet. Add green pepper, onion, celery, and celery leaves. Cook over low heat until onion is transparent, but not browned. Add remaining ingredients except shrimp and rice. Simmer gently for 1 hour, stirring occasionally to prevent sticking. Add cooked shrimp and heat through. Serve over rice. Yield: 12 servings.

Curry of Shrimp Suzanne

- ⅓ cup butter or margarine
- 3 tablespoons all-purpose flour
- 1 to 2 tablespoons curry powder
- ½ teaspoon salt
- ¼ teaspoon paprika
- Dash ground nutmeg
- 2 cups half-and-half
- 3 cups cleaned cooked shrimp
- 1 tablespoon finely chopped candied ginger
- 1 tablespoon lemon juice
- 1 teaspoon cooking sherry
- 1 teaspoon onion juice
- Dash Worcestershire sauce
- Salt to taste

Melt butter; blend in flour, curry powder, salt, paprika, and nutmeg. Gradually stir in cream; cook until mixture thickens, stirring constantly. Add remaining ingredients; heat through. Yield: 6 servings.

Curried Shrimp

¼ cup butter or margarine
¼ cup onion flakes, crushed
⅓ cup all-purpose flour
1 teaspoon salt
3 teaspoons curry powder
1 cup chicken stock
2 cups milk
1 teaspoon lemon juice
4 cups cooked shrimp

Melt butter; add crushed onion flakes and cook until softened. Stir in flour and seasonings. Add stock; cook until thickened, stirring constantly. Add milk, lemon juice, and shrimp. Heat thoroughly. Yield: 8 servings.

Shrimp Casserole to Freeze

2 tablespoons chopped onion
2 tablespoons butter or margarine
1 (10¾-ounce) can condensed golden mushroom soup
1 (10½-ounce) package frozen cooked shrimp
½ teaspoon salt
⅛ teaspoon pepper
1 cup water
1 cup quick-cooking rice, uncooked
1 (0.58-ounce) package instant sour cream mix
½ cup milk
1 teaspoon all-purpose flour
Chopped chives or parsley
2 tablespoons Madeira wine (optional)

Sauté onion in butter until transparent. Add soup, shrimp, salt, pepper, water, and rice. Bring to a boil; cover and simmer 5 minutes. Prepare the sour cream mix with milk according to package directions. Stir flour into sour cream; add to shrimp mixture and let simmer a few more minutes. Spoon into a casserole; cool. Seal securely and freeze.

To serve, thaw and bake at 350° until mixture bubbles. Garnish with chives or parsley; add wine just before serving, if desired. Yield: 6 servings.

Shrimp Bisque

¾ pound cooked shrimp
2 tablespoons chopped onion
2 tablespoons chopped celery
¼ cup butter or shortening, melted
2 tablespoons all-purpose flour
1 teaspoon salt
¼ teaspoon paprika
Dash pepper
4 cups milk
Chopped parsley

Grind shrimp. Cook onion and celery in butter until tender. Blend in flour and seasonings. Add milk gradually and cook until thickened, stirring constantly. Add shrimp; heat. Garnish with chopped parsley. Yield: 6 servings.

Marinated Hibachi Shrimp

2 cloves garlic, minced
1 cup finely chopped onion
1 teaspoon dried basil
1 teaspoon dried mustard
1 teaspoon salt
½ cup olive oil or salad oil
6 tablespoons lemon juice
2 pounds jumbo shrimp, cleaned and cooked

Combine all ingredients except shrimp. Pour over shrimp in a large jar or bowl that can be covered. Chill several hours or overnight.

When ready to cook, thread shrimp on metal or wooden skewers, allowing 5 shrimp per person. Grill about 5 minutes over coals, basting with marinade; turn once. Yield: 6 servings.

Shrimp Casserole

½ cup condensed cream of celery soup
¼ cup milk
1 heaping tablespoon grated onion
½ small green pepper, finely chopped
1 tablespoon Worcestershire sauce
Dash cayenne pepper
¼ teaspoon salt
Black pepper to taste
1 tablespoon lemon juice
1 tablespoon sherry
1 to 1½ cups boiled small shrimp
Mayonnaise
Cracker crumbs
Parmesan cheese
Paprika

Combine soup, milk, onion, green pepper, Worcestershire sauce, cayenne pepper, salt, pepper, lemon juice, and sherry. Add shrimp to the mixture and pour into a 1½-quart casserole. Coat top with mayonnaise; sprinkle with cracker crumbs, Parmesan cheese, and paprika. Bake at 325° for 40 minutes or until bubbly. Yield: 4 servings.

Shrimp Supreme

3 pounds shrimp, fresh or frozen
2 (4-ounce) cans sliced mushrooms, well drained
¾ cup melted butter or margarine
½ cup chopped parsley
4 tablespoons chopped onion
2 tablespoons lemon juice
2 tablespoons chili sauce
1 teaspoon salt
½ teaspoon garlic salt
Dash Worcestershire sauce
Dash hot sauce

Thaw frozen shrimp; peel and devein. Wash and drain on toweling. Divide shrimp into 6 portions and place on squares of heavy-duty aluminum foil. Place mushrooms on shrimp. Combine remaining ingredients; spoon over mushrooms. Fold foil and seal edges. Place on grill about 4 inches from moderately hot coals. Cook for 20 minutes or until tender. Yield: 6 servings.

Shrimp Tempura

2 small eggs (or 1 large)
1 cup milk
1⅛ cups all-purpose flour
½ teaspoon salt
Few drops hot sauce
2 teaspoons baking powder
3 pounds large shrimp, peeled, tails left intact
Salad oil
Commercial sweet and sour sauce

Beat eggs in small mixing bowl; stir in milk. Add flour, salt, and hot sauce; beat until blended. Add baking powder, and mix well. Dip shrimp into batter and fry in hot salad oil until golden brown, turning once. Drain on absorbent paper. Serve hot with sweet and sour sauce. Yield: 6 servings.

Shrimp Mull

¾ cup diced bacon
¼ cup butter or margarine
¾ cup chopped onion
2½ cups water
1 (1-pound) can tomatoes
1 can condensed tomato soup
½ lemon, thinly sliced
1 small clove garlic, minced
½ cup chopped celery
¾ cup catsup
1 drop hot sauce
2 teaspoons Worcestershire sauce
¼ teaspoon ground allspice
¼ teaspoon curry powder
½ teaspoon celery seeds
3 pounds frozen or raw shrimp, peeled
½ cup salted cracker crumbs
Cooked rice

Brown bacon in large kettle; drain. Add butter and onion; sauté until onion is golden. Add water, tomatoes, tomato soup, lemon, garlic, celery, catsup, hot sauce, Worcestershire sauce, and spices. Cover and simmer 2 hours. Add shrimp (thaw if frozen) and cook slowly for 20 minutes. Thicken with cracker crumbs. Serve over hot, cooked rice. Yield: 6 servings.

Filet of Sole Marguery

 24 *frozen peeled and deveined shrimp*
 15 *fresh mushrooms*
  1 *tablespoon melted butter*
  1 *(13-ounce) can evaporated milk*
  3 *cups half-and-half*
  2 *teaspoons salt*
  1 *teaspoon white pepper*
   About 1 tablespoon cornstarch
  3 *tablespoons cold water*
  1 *tablespoon monosodium glutamate (optional)*
 ⅔ *cup shredded Swiss or Gruyère cheese*
  1 *whole lemon, cut in quarters*
  2 *bay leaves*
  6 *filets of sole*
 ⅓ *cup dry Sauterne*
   Lemon wedges, parsley, or watercress

Place shrimp in lightly salted water; bring to boiling point. Drain; set aside. Select 6 whole mushrooms with good caps to use as garnish; set aside. Chop remaining mushrooms, stems and all, very coarsely. Sauté whole and chopped mushrooms in melted butter about 2 minutes. Set aside.

Pour evaporated milk and half-and-half into a heavy saucepan. Season with salt and white pepper. Scald, but do not allow to come to a boil. When scalding hot, thicken to the consistency of buttermilk with cornstarch mixed with cold water. Add monosodium glutamate, if desired, and shredded cheese; mix well. Cover pan and keep hot.

Pour boiling water to a depth of about 1 inch in a large skillet or shallow baking pan. Lightly salt; add lemon and bay leaves. Simmer, covered, about 5 minutes. Place filets in water to poach about 5 minutes or until fish flakes easily when tested with a fork. Carefully remove with spatula; drain and place on a heated platter.

Add Sauterne to the hot cream sauce. Fold chopped mushrooms into sauce and spoon over individual servings of filets. Place 4 of the cooked shrimp on each filet and cover with sauce. Place a whole mushroom cap in the center of each filet. Garnish with lemon wedges, parsley, or watercress. Yield: 6 servings.

Shrimp Rockefeller

 12 *slices bacon*
 2½ *cups cooked spinach, drained and chopped*
 1½ *cups minced onion*
 ½ *cup chopped parsley*
  2 *bay leaves, crumbled*
  1 *teaspoon celery salt*
  1 *cup butter or margarine*
  1 *cup fine dry bread crumbs*
  2 *pounds shrimp, peeled, deveined, and cooked*

Fry bacon until crisp; crumble. Combine bacon, cooked spinach, onion, parsley, bay leaves, and celery salt. Melt butter; add spinach mixture and cook, stirring constantly, until heated through. Stir in bread crumbs and let bubble 1 minute.

Grease eight 1-cup ramekins. Reserve 16 shrimp, and arrange remaining shrimp in ramekins; add spinach sauce. Top with reserved shrimp, 2 per serving. Bake at 400° for 5 to 10 minutes or until heated through. Yield: 8 servings.

*Shrimp Wiggle in Toast Cups

 4 *tablespoons butter*
 4 *tablespoons all-purpose flour*
 2 *cups milk*
 1 *teaspoon salt*
  Dash pepper
 1 *cup cooked shrimp*
 1 *cup cooked peas*
  Toast cups

Melt butter in a saucepan; remove pan from heat. Stir in flour until blended. Gradually add milk, stirring until smooth. Return pan to heat and cook, stirring constantly, until thickened. Add salt and pepper, shrimp, and peas. Continue cooking until shrimp and peas are heated through. Serve hot in Toast Cups. Yield: 4 (2-cup) servings.

Toast Cups:

 8 *slices sandwich bread*
  Softened butter or margarine

Trim crusts from bread slices; butter both sides. Press each slice into a muffin cup so that corners turn up. Toast at 375° about 10 minutes or until golden brown. If cups are made ahead of time, heat just before filling and serving. Yield: 8 Toast Cups.

Red Snapper Mozart

Salt and pepper to taste
Juice of 2 lemons
Worcestershire sauce
4 (8- to 10-ounce) filets of red snapper
Flour
Butter
Sauce

Combine salt, pepper, lemon juice, and Worcestershire sauce in a baking dish. Marinate red snapper in this mixture for 30 minutes. Remove fish and coat with flour. Melt butter in skillet; brown snapper slowly on both sides. Place browned filets in oven and bake at 375°. Total cooking time will be from 10 to 15 minutes. Serve topped with Sauce. Yield: 4 servings.

Sauce:

1 *cucumber*
3 *fresh tomatoes*
4 *tablespoons butter*
1 *clove garlic, minced*
Salt and pepper to taste
Juice of 1 lemon
Worcestershire sauce
1 *tablespoon freshly chopped parsley*

Peel, half, remove seeds, and dice cucumber into ¼-inch cubes. Peel, remove seeds, and dice tomato into ¼-inch cubes. Melt butter in a skillet; sauté cucumber, garlic, salt, and pepper for 5 minutes. Add tomatoes and sauté for 3 minutes more. Season with lemon juice and a dash of Worcestershire sauce. Serve over cooked red snapper filets. Sprinkle parsley over snapper just before serving.

Broiled Red Snapper

Clean snapper; remove head, if desired. Sprinkle fish on both sides with salt and pepper. Place on a well-greased broiler pan. Broil 3 inches from source of heat about 3 to 5 minutes or until fish is nicely browned but not dry. Turn carefully and broil other side. Cook until fish flakes easily when tested with a fork.

Baked Trout with Oyster Stuffing

1 *(3- or 4-pound) trout, dressed*
1½ *teaspoons salt*
Oyster Stuffing
4 *tablespoons butter, melted*

Clean, wash, and dry trout. Sprinkle inside and out with salt. Stuff fish loosely with Oyster Stuffing and sew the opening with needle and string, or close with skewers. Place fish in a greased baking pan. Brush with melted butter. Bake at 350° for 40 to 60 minutes or until fish flakes easily when tested with a fork. If fish seems dry while baking, baste occasionally with drippings or melted butter. Remove string or skewers and serve immediately on a hot platter either plain or with a sauce. Yield: 4 to 6 servings.

Oyster Stuffing:

1 *pint oysters*
½ *cup chopped celery*
½ *cup chopped onion*
4 *tablespoons butter*
4 *cups day-old bread cubes*
1 *teaspoon chopped parsley*
1 *teaspoon salt*
⅛ *teaspoon poultry seasoning*
⅛ *teaspoon pepper*

Drain oysters, reserving liquor, and chop. Sauté celery and onion in butter until tender. Combine oysters, celery and onion mixture, bread cubes, and seasonings; mix thoroughly. If stuffing seems dry, moisten with oyster liquor. Yield: enough stuffing for a 4-pound fish.

Barbecued Trout

6 medium-size dressed trout
Salt
⅓ cup dry sherry
⅓ cup melted butter
2 tablespoons lemon juice
6 slices bacon
2 teaspoons sesame seeds
¼ cup butter
1 tablespoon dry sherry
1 tablespoon lemon juice

Sprinkle cavity of trout with salt. Combine ⅓ cup sherry, melted butter, and 2 tablespoons lemon juice; pour over trout and marinate for 1 hour. Turn trout once in marinade. Remove trout and wrap strip of bacon around each. Cook over medium-hot coals until bacon is crisp. Baste 3 or 4 times with marinade; turn trout only once during cooking. Brown sesame seeds in ¼ cup butter; add 1 tablespoon sherry and 1 tablespoon lemon juice and serve over trout. Yield: 4 to 6 servings.

*Baked Trout and Cheese

1 pound trout filets
6 ounces pasteurized process American cheese, sliced
¼ cup chopped parsley
1 teaspoon ground oregano or thyme
¼ cup corn oil
2 medium-size onions, chopped
2 tablespoons all-purpose flour
⅛ teaspoon salt
⅛ teaspoon pepper
1½ cups milk

Alternate layers of fish and cheese in a lightly greased oblong baking dish, ending with cheese. Sprinkle with parsley and oregano or thyme. Heat corn oil in skillet; add onions and cook until tender, stirring frequently. Blend in flour, salt, and pepper. Pour in milk; cook, stirring constantly, until thickened. Pour over fish. Bake at 400° until fish flakes easily when tested with a fork, about 20 to 30 minutes. Yield: 4 servings.

*Barbecued Trout Filets

2 pounds trout filets
⅓ cup salad oil or bacon drippings, divided
1 tablespoon Worcestershire sauce
1 tablespoon prepared mustard
2 tablespoons firmly packed brown sugar
¼ cup tarragon vinegar
2 teaspoons salt
¾ cup catsup
Dash hot sauce
Paprika
1 large onion, thinly sliced

Place fish in a shallow baking pan greased with part of the salad oil or bacon drippings. Combine remaining oil with other ingredients except paprika and onion. Sprinkle fish with paprika, cover with sliced onion, and spread sauce mixture over all.

Place on lower rack of oven and bake at 450° for 10 minutes, basting and adding water if fish becomes dry. Brown under broiler for a few minutes just before serving. Yield: 6 servings.

*Trout Treat

½ small onion, grated
1 clove garlic, grated
2 tablespoons butter
½ cup vegetable oil
1 teaspoon Worcestershire sauce
½ teaspoon salt
½ teaspoon pepper
Juice of 3 lemon slices
1 (4- to 5-pound) lake trout

To make basting sauce, brown onion and garlic in butter. Combine vegetable oil, Worcestershire sauce, salt, pepper, and lemon juice in a small bowl. Add onion and garlic and stir well. Thread trout (head and tail removed) to the spit of a rotisserie and fasten securely. Broil over charcoal for 45 minutes. Baste frequently with sauce (every 6 or 7 minutes) while cooking. Yield: 6 servings.

Trout Veronique

6 (6-ounce) trout filets, skin removed
2 cups water
1 cup dry vermouth
Juice of 1 lemon
Salt and pepper to taste
Small bunch tiny white seedless grapes
3 cups Hollandaise Sauce

Place filets in a shallow baking dish; cover with water and vermouth. Sprinkle lemon juice over fish and season with salt and pepper. Bake at 350° about 10 to 12 minutes until fish is white and flaky. Remove from water-wine mixture and put aside in a warm place until needed.

When ready to serve, place fish on ovenproof plate. Cut tiny, white seedless grapes in half and place 10 to 12 halves on each portion of fish. Cover with scant ½ cup Hollandaise Sauce and glaze under broiler to set sauce. Yield: 6 servings.

Hollandaise Sauce:

6 egg yolks
1 pound butter, melted
Dash hot sauce
2 tablespoons tarragon vinegar
Juice of 1 small lemon

Beat egg yolks until creamy in top of double boiler over low heat. Continue beating and slowly add melted butter, then remaining ingredients. Remove to warm, not hot, place. Do not chill. Serve over trout. Yield: 3 cups.

Tuna Tetrazzini

½ (8-ounce) package spaghetti
2 (7-ounce) cans flaked tuna fish
¼ cup diced pimiento
¼ cup chopped green pepper
1 small onion, chopped
½ cup water
1 (10¾-ounce) can condensed cream of celery soup
1¾ cups shredded sharp cheese, divided
Salt and pepper to taste

Break spaghetti into pieces and cook in salted water until tender; drain. Combine tuna fish, pimiento, green pepper, and onion in a casserole.

Combine water and soup and add to tuna fish mixture. Add 1¼ cups cheese and the spaghetti; season to taste. Toss lightly until well mixed and coated with sauce. Sprinkle with remaining ½ cup cheese. Bake at 350° about 45 minutes. Yield: 4 servings.

*Egg and Tuna Toss

5 hard-cooked eggs, diced
1 (7-ounce) can tuna fish, drained and flaked
¼ teaspoon oregano
½ teaspoon onion salt
⅛ teaspoon garlic salt
½ cup mayonnaise
4 lettuce cups
Parsley (optional)
Pimiento strips (optional)

Combine eggs, tuna, seasonings, and mayonnaise; blend well. Serve in lettuce cups. Garnish with parsley and pimiento, if desired. Yield: 4 servings.

*Grilled Tuna Burgers

½ cup mayonnaise or salad dressing
1 tablespoon minced onion
1 tablespoon chili sauce
1 tablespoon prepared mustard
2 (7-ounce) cans tuna fish
6 hamburger buns
2 tablespoons softened butter or margarine

Combine mayonnaise, onion, chili sauce, and mustard; mix with tuna fish. Split hamburger buns; spread with butter. Pile tuna fish mixture on bottom halves. Place in a medium-hot broiler 3 inches below source of heat. Broil 7 to 10 minutes or until lightly browned and heated through. Place remaining halves, buttered side up, in broiler the last 2 or 3 minutes of broiling time. Close sandwiches. Yield: 6 servings.

*One-Dish Tuna Dinner

    14 small white onions, peeled
     1 teaspoon salt
     2 tablespoons butter or margarine
        Water
    1½ cups milk
     1 (10-ounce) package frozen peas
     3 tablespoons all-purpose flour
    ¼   cup cold water
     1 (7-ounce) can solid-pack tuna fish, drained
     1 cup commercial biscuit mix
    ⅓   cup milk

Combine onions, salt, butter, and enough water to cover onions. Cook, covered, over medium heat until onions are tender. Add 1½ cups milk and peas. Heat to boiling point.

Combine flour and ¼ cup water; blend. Add to onion mixture and cook, stirring constantly, until thickened. Break tuna fish into large pieces and add to onion mixture. Spoon into a greased 1½-quart casserole.

Combine biscuit mix and ⅓ cup milk; mix well. Turn out onto a lightly floured surface and knead 10 times. Roll out to ½-inch thickness and cut into 4 rounds. Place biscuit rounds over tuna fish mixture. Bake at 450° for 20 minutes or until biscuits are done. Yield: 4 servings.

Sweet-Sour Tuna

     2 tablespoons salad oil
     1 cup sliced onion
    1½ cups diced celery
    ⅛   teaspoon pepper
     1 (4-ounce) can mushrooms, drained
    1½ cups chicken stock
    ¼   cup unsulphured molasses
     2 tablespoons vinegar
     1 (1-pound) can bean sprouts, drained
     2 tablespoons cornstarch
     3 tablespoons soy sauce
     2 (7-ounce) cans tuna fish
        Cooked rice or noodles

Heat oil in a large skillet. Add onion, celery, and pepper; cook 2 minutes, stirring occasionally. Add drained mushrooms to chicken stock. Stir in molasses and vinegar. Add to onion mixture, along with bean sprouts. Cover and simmer for 10 minutes. Combine cornstarch and soy sauce, and quickly stir into hot mixture. Add tuna fish and mix well. Cook and stir carefully for 2 to 3 minutes more until thickened and heated through. Serve over hot fluffy rice or cooked noodles. Yield: 6 servings.

Tuna-Broccoli Almondine

     2 (10-ounce) packages frozen broccoli or 1¼ pounds fresh broccoli
     2 (7-ounce) cans tuna fish, drained and flaked
    ½   cup slivered almonds
    ¼   cup butter
    ¼   cup all-purpose flour
    ½   teaspoon salt
    ⅛   teaspoon pepper
        Dash ground nutmeg
     2 cups milk
     1 tablespoon cooking sherry
        Paprika

Cook broccoli until tender; drain and arrange in a greased 1½-quart casserole. Spread tuna fish evenly over broccoli. Sauté almonds in butter until lightly browned; remove from butter and drain on paper towels.

Blend flour, salt, pepper, and nutmeg into butter. Add milk and cook over low heat, stirring constantly, until sauce is smooth and thickened. Stir sherry into sauce and pour over tuna fish. Sprinkle with paprika. Bake at 350° for 25 minutes or until bubbly. Sprinkle browned almonds over top just before serving. Yield: 6 servings.

*Tuna-Water Chestnut Casserole

½ cup regular rice
1 (6-ounce) can water chestnuts, drained and sliced
2 stalks celery, diced
½ green pepper, diced
1 tablespoon dried minced onion
1 (10¾-ounce) can condensed cream of mushroom soup
2 tablespoons lemon juice
½ teaspoon salt
1 teaspoon Worcestershire sauce
1 teaspoon soy sauce
1 (7-ounce) can tuna fish, drained
Paprika

Cook rice according to package directions. While rice boils, combine remaining ingredients except tuna fish and paprika. Lightly stir in rice, then flaked tuna fish. Turn into a shallow 2-quart casserole and sprinkle with paprika. Cover and bake at 350° for 25 minutes. Yield: 4 to 5 servings.

Baked Redfish

2 (3-pound) redfish
Olive oil
Salt and pepper to taste
1 cup water
1 large onion, chopped
2 cups sliced small red tomatoes
3 bay leaves
2 lemons, sliced
3 fresh sweet basil leaves
½ cup white wine
Lemon slices
3 tablespoons minced fresh parsley
Hot cooked rice

Clean redfish thoroughly, but do not remove the heads. Rub fish inside and out with olive oil, salt, and pepper; place in flat baking pan. Add water, onion, tomatoes, bay leaves, lemons, basil, and wine. Bake uncovered at 350° for 1 hour, basting every 15 minutes. Garnish with lemon slices and parsley; serve with hot cooked rice. Yield: 8 servings.

Pompano en Papillote

1 (2-pound) pompano
1 bay leaf
½ lemon
1 stalk celery
Dash tarragon, chervil, and basil
⅛ teaspoon sherry
Ground nutmeg
Salt and pepper to taste
8 oysters
3 mushrooms, sliced
1 finely chopped shallot
4 finely chopped shrimp
1 cup fresh white lump crabmeat
1/16 teaspoon cognac
1/16 teaspoon Pernod
3 egg yolks, well beaten

Fillet pompano. Place enough water to cover fish in a large pan; add bay leaf, lemon, celery, tarragon, chervil, basil, sherry, nutmeg, salt, and pepper; simmer. To poach pompano in this liquid, wrap with cheesecloth and gently drop into simmering water. Bring just to the boiling point; remove pompano. Strain liquid and place in saucepan. Add oysters, mushrooms, shallots, shrimp, and crabmeat; boil approximately 1 minute; add cognac and Pernod. Stir in beaten egg yolks. Pour sauce over the filets, which have been placed in a paper bag. Seal bag and bake at 400° for 15 to 20 minutes. Remove from oven and serve immediately. Yield: 1 to 2 servings.

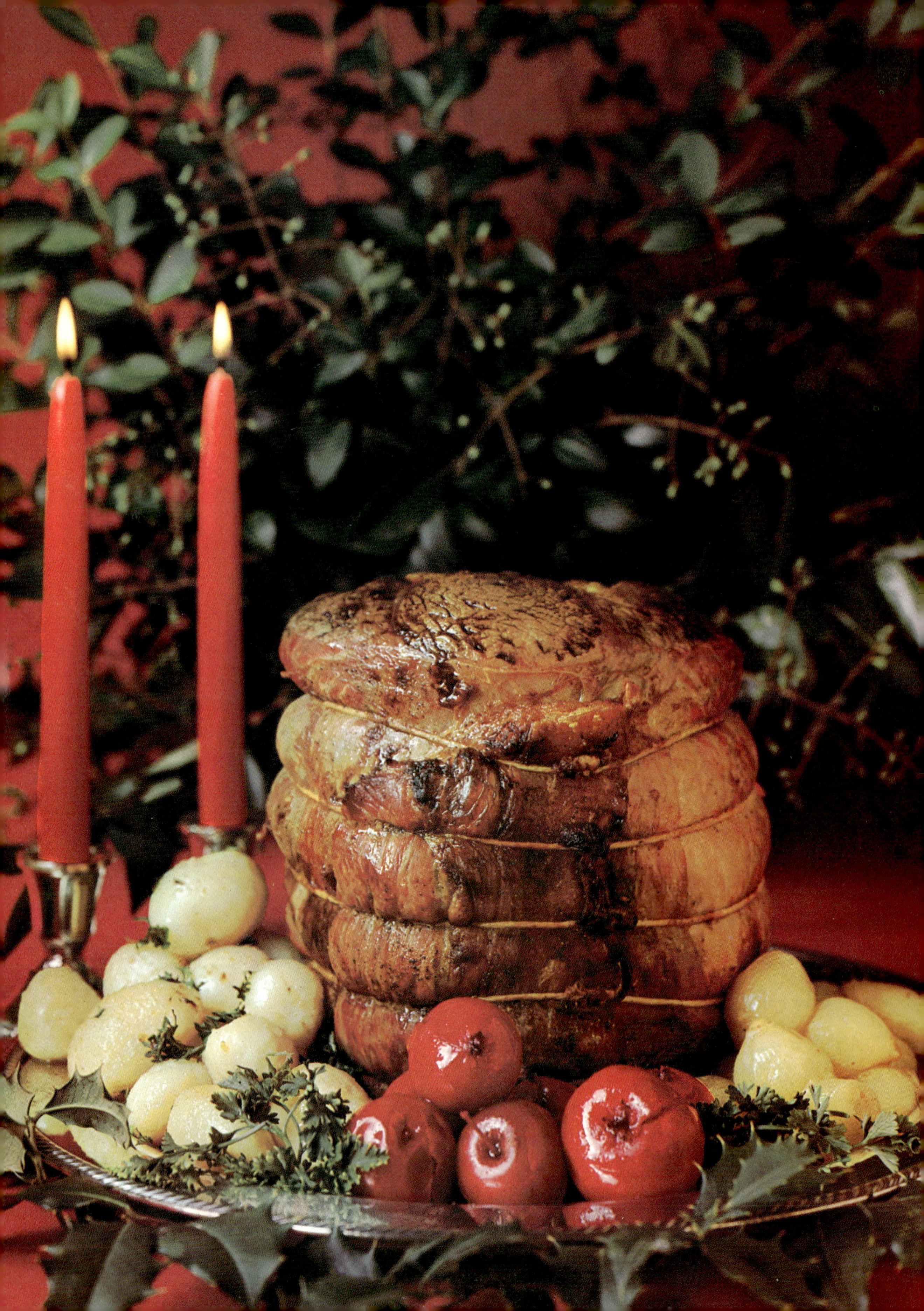

Meats

Beef, pork, lamb, frankfurters, game, and veal are all popular meats in the South and are served often. There are enough cuts and kinds of meat available at grocery stores so that a homemaker may prepare an infinite number of dishes. For Southerners, barbecuing is one of the most popular forms of cooking meats since the weather permits it almost year-round.

Meat is the most important element in our diet, and it ranks very high nutritionally because of its high protein content. It is included among the four food groups required for a balanced diet.

When you choose meat, remember that there are seven basic cuts which apply to all animals: leg, breast, rib, shoulder, loin, arm, and sirloin. One doesn't need to be an expert to select a good cut of meat.

*Rotisserie Bologna

- 2 to 3 pounds large bologna in one piece
- 2 tablespoons salad oil
- 1 small onion, grated
- ½ teaspoon garlic salt
- 1 tablespoon Worcestershire sauce
- ⅓ cup cider vinegar
- ¼ cup firmly packed brown sugar

Remove casing from bologna; score the meat into diamonds about ½ inch deep. Place bologna on rotisserie rod; fasten end clips securely. Combine remaining ingredients and blend well. Brush sauce generously over bologna. Grill for 30 minutes above gray coals, brushing with the sauce every 5 minutes. Remove from rod and cut into slices to serve. Yield: 6 to 8 servings.

Bonanza Steak Broil

- 2 chuck or blade steaks, cut about 2 inches thick
- Meat tenderizer (seasoned or unseasoned)
- ½ cup melted butter or margarine
- ¼ cup thick bottled meat sauce

Score fat edges of steaks about 2 inches apart. Sprinkle meat tenderizer evenly over both sides of meat (do not use salt). Pierce steaks deeply all over with a fork; let stand at room temperature for 1 hour.

Combine melted butter and meat sauce. Place steaks on grill; brush with sauce and cook for a few minutes. Turn steaks and brush other side. Cook until desired doneness, about 9 to 10 minutes each side for rare and 10 to 12 minutes for medium. Yield: 2 to 4 servings.

*Barbecue Meat Patties

- ½ cup catsup
- 1 (8-ounce) can tomato sauce
- ½ teaspoon salt
- Few grains pepper
- 1 teaspoon Worcestershire sauce
- Few drops hot sauce
- ⅛ teaspoon chili powder
- ½ onion, chopped
- 1 pound ground beef
- 1½ cups cracker crumbs

Combine first 8 ingredients. Add 1 cup of this sauce to meat along with cracker crumbs. Mix well. Shape into 8 patties; top with remaining sauce. Broil for 8 minutes or as desired. Yield: 4 to 8 servings.

Blue Cheese Hamburgers

1½ pounds ground beef
¾ cup oats, quick-cooking or regular, uncooked
½ teaspoon salt
Dash pepper
⅓ cup milk
½ cup crumbled blue cheese
6 hamburger buns

Combine thoroughly the ground beef, oats, salt, pepper, and milk. Shape into 12 thin patties. Shape blue cheese to form 6 thin rounds. Top 6 of the patties with blue cheese. Cover with remaining patties; pinch edges together to seal. Place on broiler rack. Broil 4 inches from source of heat for 7 minutes. Turn and broil 5 more minutes for medium doneness. Serve on hamburger buns. Yield: 6 servings.

Smoke-flavored Burgers

1 (8-ounce) can tomato sauce
¼ cup Worcestershire sauce
2 tablespoons butter or margarine
1 teaspoon sugar
1 teaspoon salt
½ teaspoon pepper
½ teaspoon instant coffee
¼ cup chopped onion
1 pound ground beef
Butter
4 hamburger buns

Soak wood chips in water for about 30 minutes. Combine first 7 ingredients in saucepan; heat to boiling. Stir together ¼ cup sauce mixture and the onion. Shape ground beef into 8 thin patties. Spread about 2 tablespoons onion mixture on half the patties. Top with remaining thin patties and seal edges. Arrange hot coals in bottom of grill. Drain chips; add to hot coals. Place patties on grill about 4 inches from coals; cover grill. Cook 7 to 10 minutes on each side. Brush patties with sauce; butter hamburger buns lightly. Place buns on grill when patties are turned. Serve patties in buns. Yield: 4 servings.

*Polynesian Hamburgers

1 pound ground beef
2 cups soft bread crumbs
¼ cup chopped onion
½ cup ice water
1 teaspoon seasoned salt
2 medium-size onions, cut into thick slices
2 tablespoons butter
¼ cup firmly packed brown sugar
2 tablespoons water
½ teaspoon dry mustard
¼ cup vinegar

Combine ground beef, bread crumbs, onion, water, and seasoned salt. Shape into 4 patties. Sauté onion in butter; remove. Brown hamburgers. Return onion to skillet. Combine remaining ingredients; add to hamburgers. Cover; bring to a boil. Reduce heat; simmer for 30 minutes. Yield: 4 servings.

Home on the Range Burgers

1½ pounds ground beef
1 clove garlic, minced
1 small onion, minced
1 tablespoon chili sauce
1 tablespoon prepared mustard
1 tablespoon Worcestershire sauce
2 eggs, beaten
1½ teaspoons seasoned meat tenderizer

Put beef into bowl; add minced vegetables, seasonings, and the eggs. Sprinkle with meat tenderizer. Blend mixture well with forks. Handling lightly, form into 4 large or 6 small patties. Cook in greased folding wire broiler or on a greased grill over charcoal fire, 3 to 5 inches from hot coals. Allow 3 to 6 minutes per side. Yield: 4 large or 6 smaller burgers.

Fondue Bourguignon

12 ounces tenderloin of beef tips, cut into bite-size pieces
½ to ¾ cup peanut oil
Hot Mustard, Red Cocktail Sauce

This dish is partially prepared before it is brought to the table. For serving, arrange tenderloin pieces and sauces on a large, sectioned serving platter. Heat the peanut oil in a fondue pot until it is very hot and bubbling. (Peanut oil is preferred as it is practically odorless and does not splatter badly.) Bring fondue pot to the table and place over alcohol burner (use wood alcohol only) or canned heat. Cook beef tips to desired doneness and dip in sauces listed below. Yield: 6 to 8 servings.

Hot Mustard Sauce:

¼ cup prepared hot mustard
¼ cup mayonnaise

Blend together well and serve in side dish. Yield: ½ cup.

Red Cocktail Sauce:

½ cup catsup
3 to 4 drops hot sauce
½ teaspoon lemon juice

Mix thoroughly, adding more lemon juice if desired. Yield: about ½ cup.

Burgundy Beef

2 pounds cubed lean beef
¼ cup all-purpose flour
1 tablespoon salt
¼ teaspoon pepper
¼ cup bacon drippings
1 cup water
1 cup Burgundy
6 carrots
6 small onions
1 (10-ounce) package frozen peas
6 medium-size potatoes, cooked, seasoned, and mashed
1 egg yolk, beaten
1 tablespoon half-and-half

Dredge beef cubes in flour seasoned with salt and pepper. Brown meat in bacon drippings; add water and Burgundy. Cover and simmer for 45 minutes. Pare carrots and peel onions; add to meat and simmer 45 minutes longer or until vegetables are tender.

Cook peas according to package directions and set aside. Cook potatoes; mash and season as desired. Add peas to meat mixture and put in a 3-quart casserole; flute potatoes around the edges of the dish. Brush with mixture of egg yolk and cream; cool and freeze. To serve, thaw and bake at 350° for 15 to 20 minutes or until potatoes are lightly browned. Yield: 6 servings.

Variation: This recipe can be frozen without the mashed potatoes, which can be added (fluted and brushed, as above) after the casserole has been partially heated.

*Florentine Beef with Rice

1 tablespoon salad oil
1 medium onion, coarsely chopped
½ medium-size green pepper, coarsely chopped
1 pound ground beef
2 (8-ounce) cans tomato sauce
½ cup catsup
1 tablespoon Worcestershire sauce
2 teaspoons salt
⅛ teaspoon black pepper
2 cups cooked rice
Green pepper, parsley or celery leaves (optional)
Shredded cheese (optional)

Heat oil in a heavy skillet. Add the onion, green pepper, and beef. Cook, stirring occasionally, until the beef is browned and the onion and green pepper are tender. Add more oil if the mixture begins to stick.

Stir in the tomato sauce, catsup, Worcestershire sauce, salt, and black pepper. Simmer about 15 minutes, stirring occasionally.

While the sauce is cooking, cook rice according to package directions. Just before serving, press hot rice into six 5-ounce custard cups (dip the molds in water before pressing in the rice). Unmold immediately onto serving platter.

Spoon the hot sauce around the mounds of rice. Serve immediately. If desired, garnish with green pepper, parsley, or celery leaves and sprinkle with shredded cheese. Yield: 6 servings.

*East Indian Beef

    2 cups bread cubes
    2 tablespoons butter or margarine, melted
  ¼ pound dried beef, cut into pieces
     Cold water
    3 tablespoons butter or margarine
    3 tablespoons all-purpose flour
    1 teaspoon curry powder
    2 cups milk
    2 (6-ounce) cans mushroom sauce
    1 cup shredded sharp cheese
    1 (8-ounce) package spaghetti, cooked

Toss bread cubes with 2 tablespoons melted butter. If dried beef is salty, soak in cold water for about 30 minutes. Drain.

Melt 3 tablespoons butter in saucepan or skillet. Sauté dried beef until lightly browned. Blend in flour and curry powder. Combine milk and mushroom sauce. Add all at once to dried beef mixture. Stir constantly until sauce thickens and boils, about 1 minute. Remove from heat. Blend in cheese, stirring until melted.

Arrange alternating layers of spaghetti and dried beef mixture in a greased 1½-quart shallow baking dish, ending with beef mixture. Top with bread cubes. Bake at 375° for 20 minutes or until mixture is bubbly. Yield: 6 servings.

Beef Bourguignon

    3 pounds sirloin strip steak, weighed after removing all fat and bone
  2½ cups Burgundy, divided
  ½ teaspoon garlic powder
  ¼ teaspoon thyme
  ½ bay leaf
  ¼ cup vegetable oil
    3 tablespoons all-purpose flour
    1 (10½-ounce) can condensed onion soup
  1½ cups water
    6 carrots, cut lengthwise into 1-inch pieces
    1 (8-ounce) can small onions
  ½ pound fresh mushrooms or 2 (4-ounce) cans button mushrooms
    2 tablespoons butter

Have the beef cut 1½ to 2 inches thick. Cut beef into cubes of 1½ x 1½ or 2 x 2 inches. Combine 2 cups Burgundy with garlic powder, thyme, and bay leaf. Pour this over the steak cubes, cover, and marinate for about 24 hours.

When ready to cook, drain steak, reserving marinade. Dry the beef on paper towels, heat oil in heavy skillet, and sear beef thoroughly.

Remove beef from oil with a slotted spoon and place in a large (2-quart) covered casserole. Mix flour with oil remaining in skillet (you may have to add a little more oil), and add the reserved Burgundy marinade, onion soup, and water.

Stirring constantly, cook until the mixture reaches a high boil. Pour the mixture over the steak, cover tightly, and cook at 300° for 2 hours. At the end of this time, the beef should be very tender. If not, cook a bit longer.

At this stage of the preparation, the beef-marinade mixture may be refrigerated for another 24 hours if desired. In the meantime, cook carrots in salted water, drain onions, and sauté fresh mushrooms in butter. If you are using canned mushrooms, drain them first.

When ready to prepare for dinner, be sure refrigerated beef has come to room temperature. Add vegetables and remaining ½ cup Burgundy to beef. Bake, covered, at 300° until Beef Bourguignon is heated thoroughly. Serve immediately. Yield: 6 servings.

*Corned Beef 'n Eggs

    1 (12-ounce) can corned beef, chilled
  ⅓ cup slivered green pepper
  ½ cup shredded pasteurized process American cheese
    8 eggs
  ⅓ cup milk
    2 tablespoons butter

Cut corned beef into ½-inch cubes. Combine with green pepper and cheese. Beat eggs slightly; add milk. Beat with fork until whites and yolks are blended. Melt butter in an electric skillet. When butter is sizzling, but not brown, add eggs and cook over gentle heat. When eggs are not yet set, add corned beef mixture, folding to distribute. Continue cooking until eggs are almost set, but still moist. Serve immediately. Yield: 5 to 6 servings.

Chef's Grilled Steak

   ½ *cup lemon juice*
   ¼ *cup salad oil*
   ½ *teaspoon salt*
   ½ *teaspoon celery salt*
   ½ *teaspoon pepper*
   ½ *teaspoon thyme*
   ½ *teaspoon oregano*
   ½ *teaspoon rosemary*
   1 *clove garlic, minced*
   ½ *cup chopped onion*
 2½ *pounds chuck steak, about ½ inch thick*

Combine first 10 ingredients. Place steak in flat container or heavy plastic bag. Add marinade and marinate steak in mixture for 3 hours, turning several times. Cook to desired doneness on grill over hot coals or broil in range. Baste with the marinade during broiling. Yield: 4 servings.

Beefburger Special

   1 *pound lean ground beef*
   ½ *cup shredded sharp Cheddar cheese*
   1 *tablespoon Worcestershire sauce*
   ½ *cup grated onion*
   ¼ *cup pickle relish*
   ½ *to 1 teaspoon salt*
   ½ *teaspoon pepper*
      Ice cubes
      Bacon slices (optional)

Combine beef, cheese, Worcestershire sauce, onion, relish, salt, and pepper; mix well. Divide into 6 portions and shape each hamburger around half an ice cube. If desired, wrap each with a bacon slice. Grill 4 inches from high heat on grill. Turn often to sear the meat. Cook about 5 to 7 minutes on each side. Yield: 6 servings.

*Hamburger Hash

   1 *pound ground beef*
   1 *cup chopped celery*
   2 *medium onions, chopped*
   ¾ *cup regular rice, uncooked*
   1 *(10½-ounce) can condensed cream of chicken soup*
   ¼ *cup soy sauce*
 1½ *cups warm water*
   ⅛ *teaspoon pepper*
   1 *(5-ounce) can chow mein noodles*

Combine first 8 ingredients in a 3-quart casserole dish. Cover and bake at 350° for 1½ hours. Sprinkle noodles over top of casserole and bake an additional 10 or 15 minutes. Yield: 6 to 8 servings.

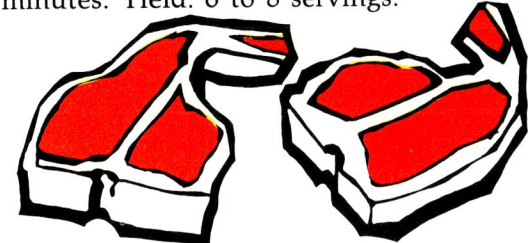

*Lemon Barbecued Chuck Steak

   1 *(about 4 pounds) chuck steak, cut 1½ inches thick*
   1 *teaspoon grated lemon rind*
   ⅔ *cup lemon juice*
   ⅓ *cup salad oil*
   2 *teaspoons monosodium glutamate*
 1½ *teaspoons salt*
   ⅛ *teaspoon pepper*
   1 *teaspoon Worcestershire sauce*
   1 *teaspoon prepared mustard*
   2 *green onion tops, sliced*

Score fat edges of meat. Place in shallow dish. Combine remaining ingredients; pour over steak. Let stand for 3 hours at room temperature or 6 hours in refrigerator, turning steak several times. Remove steak from marinade: with paper towels remove excess moisture. Cook over hot coals about 12 minutes on each side for rare or 15 minutes on each side for medium, brushing occasionally with marinade. Carve meat across grain in thin slices. Yield: 6 to 8 servings.

Country Steak a la Sonora

Garlic juice
8 *chuck steaks, cut ¼ to ½ inch thick*
Seasoned salt and pepper to taste
¼ *cup salad oil*
1 *onion, sliced*
2 *pounds tomatoes, cut into eighths*
1 *(8-ounce) can tomato sauce (optional)*
1 *(15-ounce) can tomato sauce*
¾ *teaspoon coriander*
1½ *teaspoons salt*
1 *(4-ounce) can green chiles, seeded and thinly sliced*

Sprinkle garlic juice on steaks and rub in; allow to sit for an hour. Sprinkle with seasoned salt and pepper. Sear steaks on both sides in hot oil. Remove from oil and place in 13- x 9- x 2-inch casserole.

Brown onion in oil until golden brown and transparent. Blend tomatoes, a few pieces at a time, in blender. If blender requires additional liquid to function, use 1 (8-ounce) can tomato sauce. Combine pureed tomatoes, the remaining can of tomato sauce, coriander, and 1½ teaspoons salt with browned onions; cook over medium heat for 10 minutes, stirring occasionally. Pour sauce over steaks in casserole. Dot top with chiles. Cover; bake at 350° for 30 minutes. Remove cover and bake 1 additional hour. Yield: 8 servings.

Sirloin Kabobs

5-*pound sirloin tip roast, cut into cubes*
¾ *cup soy sauce*
1 *cup corn oil*
1 *cup red wine*
1 *(6-ounce) can frozen orange juice concentrate*
½ *teaspoon garlic powder*
¼ *cup prepared mustard*
1 *teaspoon lemon-pepper marinade*
½ *teaspoon ground ginger*
¼ *cup Worcestershire sauce*
Onion cubes
Green pepper strips

Cut roast into cubes. For the marinade, combine other ingredients except onion and green pepper. Put cubed sirloin in a shallow pan and pour marinade over meat. Let meat remain in marinade for 24 hours. Drain and put meat, onion cubes, and green pepper strips on wet wooden skewers. Cook over low to medium heat on grill until meat has cooked to desired doneness. Yield: 12 to 18 servings.

Kabobs Kyoto

2 *pounds lean meat (beef, lamb, or pork)*
1 *(8¼-ounce) can pineapple tidbits, drained*
2 *green peppers, cut into 1-inch squares*
4 *ounces fresh mushrooms*
2 *tomatoes, cut into wedges*
½ *cup soy sauce*
½ *cup sherry*
¼ *cup catsup*
¼ *cup chopped onion*
2 *tablespoons sugar*
Juice and rind of ½ lemon
1 *clove garlic, crushed (optional)*

Cut meat into 1½-inch cubes. Thread meat onto skewers alternately with pineapple, green pepper, mushrooms, and tomatoes. Combine remaining ingredients to make marinade. Marinate kabobs for 1 hour. Cook 15 to 20 minutes on grill, basting and turning occasionally. Yield: 8 servings.

Beef Kabobs Waikiki

2 *pounds round steak, cut 2 inches thick*
1½ *teaspoons dry mustard*
¾ *teaspoon ground ginger*
⅛ *teaspoon freshly ground black pepper*
⅛ *teaspoon garlic powder*
6 *tablespoons soy sauce*
3 *tablespoons lemon juice*
3 *tablespoons salad oil*
8 *cherry tomatoes*
8 *wedges green pepper*
8 *whole fresh mushrooms*

Slice round steak into strips ¼ inch thick and place in shallow pan or dish. (Round steak may be chilled or partially frozen for ease in cutting the strips.) Combine mustard, ginger, pepper, and garlic powder. Mix soy sauce, lemon juice, and oil and add this mixture to the seasonings. Mix well. Pour marinade over steak strips and allow meat to marinate at least 4 hours.

Thread marinated steak strips on metal skewers, accordion-style, alternating cherry tomatoes, green pepper wedges, or whole mushrooms between every second fold.

Brush kabobs with marinade and place in broiler 4 inches from heat. Broil 3 minutes on first side. Turn, brush with marinade, and broil 3 to 4 minutes on second side. Yield: 4 to 6 servings.

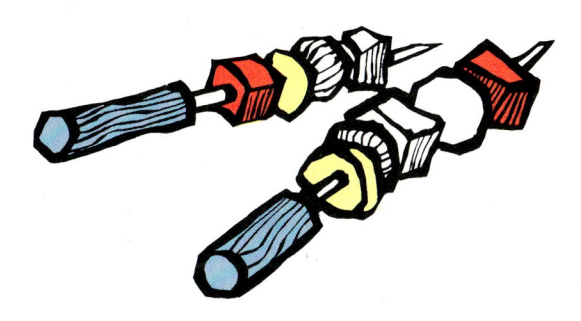

Beef Teriyaki Kabobs

½ pound sirloin tip steak
1 cup bottled Italian dressing
½ cup soy sauce
1 teaspoon grated fresh gingerroot
1 (8-ounce) jar mild jalapeño peppers

Cut beef into very thin strips using a sharp knife and cutting at an angle or across the grain of the meat. Combine next three ingredients for marinade. Put beef strips in this mixture and marinate for at least 1 hour before grilling.

To prepare kabobs, remove beef strips from marinade and drain. Place 1 or 2 peppers lengthwise on top of each marinated beef strip. Holding beef and pepper together, thread onto bamboo skewer. Place skewers on bottom rack of grill. Cook at medium heat for 5 to 8 minutes, basting with marinade during grilling. Do not overcook. Yield: 4 to 6 servings.

Shish Kabobs

1 (2-pound) sirloin steak, 1 inch thick
¼ cup lemon juice
¼ cup soy sauce
3 carrots, cut into 1-inch slices
2 onions
2 green peppers, cut into 1-inch squares
2 tomatoes, cut into wedges
½ pound bacon, cut into 5-inch strips

Cut steak into 1-inch cubes. Combine lemon juice and soy sauce; marinate meat cubes in this mixture for at least 4 hours in refrigerator. Parboil carrots about 5 minutes. Quarter onions and separate sections. Alternate meat, carrots, onions, green pepper, and tomatoes on skewers, weaving bacon strips over and under pieces of food. Grill 15 minutes or until done, basting and turning occasionally. Yield: 8 servings.

Charley-Bobs

4 pounds sirloin steak, 2 inches thick
1 (3-pound) slice center-cut ham, 2 inches thick

Cut sirloin steak and ham into 2-inch cubes. Alternate steak and ham on metal skewers; grill over medium heat to desired doneness. Yield: 8 servings.

*Cheeseburger Loaf

½ cup evaporated milk
1½ pounds ground beef
1½ teaspoons salt
1 tablespoon catsup
1 egg
1 cup cracker crumbs
2 teaspoons dry mustard
1 cup shredded cheese, divided

Combine all ingredients except cheese. Spread ½ cup cheese in bottom of greased 9- x 5- x 3-inch loafpan. Cover with half the meat mixture. Repeat with remaining cheese and meat mixture. Bake at 350° about 1 hour. Allow loaf to stand 10 minutes before removing from pan. Yield: 8 servings.

*Creole Meat Loaf

2 pounds ground beef
1 (15-ounce) can Spanish rice
2 eggs, slightly beaten
1 teaspoon salt
½ teaspoon hot sauce
4 slices pasteurized process American cheese
Sauce

Combine all ingredients except cheese and Sauce; mix well. Pack half of the mixture into a greased 9- x 5- x 3-inch loaf pan; cover with cheese slices and pack remaining meat on top. Bake at 350° for 1 hour. Serve with Sauce. Yield: 8 servings.

Sauce:

1 (8-ounce) can tomato sauce
¼ cup sweet pickle relish
¼ cup chopped onion
1 tablespoon firmly packed brown sugar
1 tablespoon vinegar
1 tablespoon Worcestershire sauce

Combine all ingredients; stir over medium heat until well blended. Serve over Creole Meat Loaf. Yield: 1½ cups sauce.

Cheese-Stuffed Meat Loaf

1 (8-ounce) package sliced pasteurized process American cheese, divided
2 eggs, slightly beaten
2 pounds ground beef
1 cup milk
1 cup oats, regular or quick-cooking, uncooked
¾ cup chopped onion
2 tablespoons finely chopped green pepper (optional)
2 teaspoons salt
¼ teaspoon pepper
1 tablespoon prepared mustard
1 teaspoon prepared horseradish

Cut cheese slices in half diagonally; save half of the cheese triangles for top of meat loaf. Finely chop remaining cheese slices and combine with remaining ingredients; mix thoroughly. Press meat into greased 9- x 5- x 3-inch loaf pan. Invert pan onto a foil-covered shallow baking pan and remove loaf; fold foil edges up around meat loaf to hold juices during baking. Bake at 375° about 1 hour or until meat is done. Two or three minutes before end of baking time, lay cheese slices in double thickness over top of loaf. Return to oven just long enough to soften cheese. Garnish as desired. Yield: 8 servings.

Mainly-Meat Loaf

1½ pounds ground beef
1 medium onion, chopped
½ cup seasoned tomato juice
¼ cup Worcestershire sauce
1 teaspoon salt
½ teaspoon pepper
½ pound whole mushrooms
1 teaspoon vegetable oil

Mix together beef, onion, tomato juice, Worcestershire, salt, and pepper. Remove stems from mushrooms. Set aside enough mushroom caps to cover top of meat-loaf. Slice remaining mushrooms and stems, and add to meat loaf. Put mixture into oblong baking dish. Place mushroom caps on top, and brush with oil. Bake at 325° for 90 minutes. Yield: 4 to 6 servings.

Hamburger and Sausage Loaf

1½ pounds ground lean beef
½ pound bulk pork sausage
1 onion, grated
1 egg
1 cup soft bread crumbs
½ cup milk
1 teaspoon salt
¼ teaspoon pepper
½ teaspoon ground nutmeg
½ teaspoon ground allspice

Combine all ingredients, mixing thoroughly. Shape into a loaf and bake at 350° for 1 hour and 15 minutes. Yield: 8 servings.

Layered Meat Loaf

 1 *medium onion, chopped*
 ¾ *cup diced celery*
 ¼ *cup shortening*
 3 *cups soft bread cubes*
 ½ *cup water*
 2 *eggs, beaten*
 ⅓ *cup diced green pepper*
 1 *tablespoon salt*
 1 *pound ground pork butt*
 1 *pound ground lean beef*
 ½ *cup tomato juice*
 2 *tablespoons melted butter*

To make dressing, brown onion and celery in melted shortening. Mix with bread cubes, water, eggs, green pepper, and salt. Grind beef and pork together; add half the dressing mixture to the meat mixture. Spread half the meat mixture in bottom of a 9- x 5- x 3-inch loaf pan. Spread with remainder of the dressing mix, and top with remainder of meat mixture. Bake at 350° for 1 hour and 15 minutes.

Baste loaf with a mixture of tomato juice and melted butter. Yield: 6 to 8 servings.

*Meat Loaf Delight

 2 *eggs*
 1 *cup cooked tomatoes or tomato juice*
 2 *tablespoons Worcestershire sauce*
 ½ *cup grated carrots*
 ½ *cup chopped celery*
 1 *cup chopped onion*
 1 *cup crushed corn flakes*
 1 *cup cracker crumbs*
 ⅓ *cup chopped green pepper*
 1 *teaspoon salt*
 ½ *teaspoon pepper*
 2 *pounds ground beef*
 ½ *cup evaporated milk*
 ½ *cup catsup*

Beat eggs and put in a very large bowl. Add tomatoes, Worcestershire sauce, carrots, celery, onion, crushed corn flakes, cracker crumbs, green pepper, salt, and pepper. Mix well; add ground beef and evaporated milk and mix thoroughly.

Pack mixture into two 9- x 5- x 3-inch loaf pans and spread catsup over top of meat. Bake at 350° for 1 hour. Yield: 12 to 16 servings.

Meat Loaf in the Round

 2 *pounds lean ground beef*
 1½ *cups shredded Cheddar cheese, divided*
 2 *cups soft bread crumbs*
 1 *egg, slightly beaten*
 ½ *cup chopped celery*
 ½ *cup chopped onion*
 1 *teaspoon Worcestershire sauce*
 1 *teaspoon salt*
 1 *teaspoon pepper*
 1 *(8-ounce) can tomato sauce*

Combine ground beef, 1 cup cheese, bread crumbs, egg, celery, onion, Worcestershire sauce, salt, and pepper. Mix well and shape into a ball. Place in a shallow 9-inch round pan and bake at 350° for 1 hour. Pour off drippings, and pour tomato sauce over meat. Sprinkle with ½ cup shredded cheese and bake an additional 15 minutes. Yield: 8 servings.

Frosted Meat Loaf

 3 *pounds ground beef*
 ⅓ *cup grated onion*
 1½ *cups soft bread crumbs*
 ¾ *cup strong coffee*
 2 *teaspoons salt*
 1 *tablespoon prepared mustard*
 1 *tablespoon Worcestershire sauce*
 ¼ *teaspoon hot sauce*
 3 *cups hot mashed potatoes*
  Cooked lima beans and carrots

Combine beef, onion, bread crumbs, coffee, and seasonings. Blend well. Pack lightly into a greased 10-inch ring mold. Bake at 350° for 40 minutes. Drain off any liquid. Invert ring on serving platter. Quickly "frost" with mashed potatoes. Brown under broiler if desired. Fill center with cooked vegetables. Serve at once. Yield: 6 to 8 servings.

Gourmet Meat Loaf

 1 *cup fresh or canned sliced mushrooms, drained*
 ½ *cup chopped onion*
 2 *tablespoons butter or margarine*
 ⅓ *cup commercial sour cream*
1½ *pounds ground beef*
 ¾ *cup regular or quick-cooking oats, uncooked*
 1 *egg*
 2 *teaspoons salt*
 ¼ *teaspoon pepper*
 1 *teaspoon Worcestershire sauce*
 ⅔ *cup milk*

For filling, lightly brown mushrooms and onion in butter in medium-size skillet. Remove from heat; stir in sour cream.

 For meat loaf, thoroughly combine all remaining ingredients. Place half of meat mixture in shallow baking pan. Shape to form an oval base. Lengthwise down the center make a shallow "well" for the filling. Spoon filling into "well."

 Shape remaining meat mixture over filling, making sure all filling is covered. Seal bottom and top meat mixtures together. Bake at 350° for 1 hour. Let stand 5 minutes before slicing. Yield: 6 servings.

Triple-Treat Meat Loaf

 1 *pound ground beef*
 1 *pound ground pork*
 1 *pound ground veal*
 ¼ *cup finely chopped onion*
 ¼ *cup finely chopped celery*
 1 *cup quick-cooking oats, uncooked*
 2 *teaspoons salt*
 ¼ *teaspoon pepper*
 2 *eggs, beaten*
 1 *cup milk*
 1 *tablespoon Worcestershire sauce*
 1 *cup chili sauce, divided*
 ¼ *cup dry bread crumbs*
 ¼ *cup Parmesan cheese*
 ¼ *cup chopped peanuts*
 2 *tablespoons brown sugar*
 2 *tablespoon fruit juice*
 1 *teaspoon prepared mustard*

Combine all the ground meat and mix thoroughly. Add onion, celery, oats, salt, and pepper. Add beaten egg to milk; add Worcestershire sauce and add to meat mixture; mix well. Form into 3 loaves and place in a greased 13- x 9- x 2-inch pan. Spread ½ cup chili sauce over 1 loaf and sprinkle on a topping made by combining dry bread crumbs and Parmesan cheese.

 Spread second loaf with ½ cup chili sauce and sprinkle with chopped peanuts. Top third loaf with a glaze made by combining brown sugar, fruit juice, and mustard. Bake, uncovered, at 350° for 1 hour. Yield: 6 to 9 servings.

Meat Loaf with Orange Slices

1½ *pounds ground chuck, or half beef and half veal*
 1 *(1-ounce) package instant oatmeal*
 ½ *cup half-and-half*
 1 *small onion, finely diced*
 3 *tablespoons minced green pepper*
 1 *tablespoon Worcestershire sauce*
 1 *teaspoon salt*
 ½ *teaspoon black pepper*
 2 *tablespoons catsup*
 1 *egg, slightly beaten*
Orange sections
Sauce

Combine all ingredients except the orange sections and sauce; mix well. Form into a loaf and place in a baking dish. Garnish the sides and top with orange sections. Make sauce and pour half over the loaf. Bake at 350° for 1 hour. Baste the loaf often with remaining half of sauce. Serve with pan drippings. Yield: 6 servings.

 Sauce:

 ½ *cup firmly packed brown sugar*
 3 *tablespoons tarragon vinegar, or enough to make a thin sauce*
 1 *teaspoon prepared mustard*
 2 *teaspoons Worcestershire sauce*

Blend all ingredients well.

Triple Meat Loaf with Mustard Sauce

2 cups ground baked ham
2¼ pounds lean ground beef
½ pound bulk pork sausage (hot)
1½ cups tomato juice
2 cups soft bread crumbs
½ cup minced celery
2 eggs
1 teaspoon coarsely ground black pepper
Salt to taste (scant)
Mustard Sauce

Combine all ingredients for meat loaf and mix until thoroughly blended. Pack into large greased loaf pan and bake at 350° for 1½ hours. Serve hot with Mustard Sauce. Yield: 10 servings.

Mustard Sauce:

½ cup mayonnaise
2 tablespoons prepared mustard
½ cup whipping cream, whipped
Salt to taste

Fold mayonnaise and mustard into whipped cream; add salt.

✓Meat Loaf with Zesty Topping

2 pounds lean ground beef
¾ cup milk
1½ cups soft bread crumbs
2 teaspoons salt
⅛ teaspoon pepper
1 medium carrot, grated
1 small onion, diced
2 eggs, beaten
¼ cup catsup
3 tablespoons firmly packed brown sugar
2 tablespoons prepared mustard

Put ground beef in a large bowl. Pour milk over bread crumbs and add to ground beef. Add salt, pepper, carrot, onion, and beaten eggs. Mix thoroughly and pack in a 9- x 5- x 3-inch loaf pan. Mix catsup, brown sugar, and mustard; spread over the meat loaf. Bake at 325° for 1½ hours. Yield: 8 servings.

Beef and Potato Loaf

4 cups thinly sliced potatoes
1 tablespoon chopped onion
1 teaspoon salt
⅛ teaspoon pepper
1 teaspoon parsley flakes (optional)
1 pound ground lean beef
¾ cup evaporated milk
½ cup cracker crumbs or rolled oats
¼ cup catsup or chili sauce
¼ cup chopped onion
1 teaspoon salt
⅛ teaspoon pepper

Arrange peeled, sliced potatoes in a 3-quart baking dish. Sprinkle with 1 tablespoon chopped onion and salt and pepper. Add parsley flakes if desired.

Mix ground beef, milk, cracker crumbs, catsup, ¼ cup chopped onion, 1 teaspoon salt, and ⅛ teaspoon pepper. Spread evenly over potatoes. Bake, covered, at 350° for 1 hour or until potatoes are tender. Yield: 4 to 6 servings.

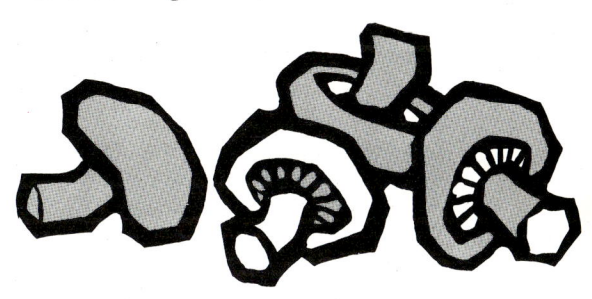

Meat Loaf

2 pounds ground lean beef
4 teaspoons salt
¼ teaspoon pepper
¼ teaspoon ground nutmeg
1 medium-size onion, minced
1 cup quick-cooking oats, uncooked
1 (1-pound) can tomatoes

Mix meat with seasonings, onion, and oats. Force tomatoes through coarse sieve; combine with meat mixture. Form into 1 large flat loaf or 2 small loaves in baking pan; crisscross top surface with a knife. Bake at 350° for 1 hour for small loaves and 1½ hours for large loaf. Yield: 8 servings.

*Favorite Meat Loaf

- 1½ pounds ground beef
- ¾ cup oats, quick-cooking or regular, uncooked
- 1½ teaspoons salt
- ¼ teaspoon pepper
- ¼ cup chopped onion
- 1 (8-ounce) can tomato sauce
- 1 egg, beaten

Combine beef, oats, salt, pepper, onion, tomato sauce, and egg; mix thoroughly. Pack firmly into an 8½- x 4½- x 2½-inch loafpan. Bake at 350° for about 1 hour. Let stand for 5 minutes before slicing. Yield: 8 servings.

*Deviled Meatballs

- 1 (10½-ounce) can condensed tomato soup divided
- 1 pound ground beef
- 1 egg, slightly beaten
- 3 tablespoons finely chopped onion
- 2 tablespoons fine dry bread crumbs
- 2 teaspoons prepared horseradish
- 1½ teaspoons prepared mustard
- 1½ teaspoons Worcestershire sauce
- 2 tablespoons shortening
- ½ cup water

Combine ¼ cup soup with beef, egg, onion, bread crumbs, horseradish, mustard, and Worcestershire sauce. Shape into balls about 1 inch in diameter. In skillet, brown meatballs in shortening. Stir in remaining soup and water. Cover; simmer 35 to 40 minutes, stirring occasionally. Yield: 4 servings.

French-Fried Liver

- 1 pound beef liver, sliced ½ inch thick
- ⅓ cup all-purpose flour
- 1 teaspoon salt
- ⅛ teaspoon pepper
- 2 pounds shortening
- Fiesta Sour Cream Dip

Cut liver into strips about ¼ inch wide and 3 inches long. Combine flour, salt, and pepper. Dredge liver strips in seasoned flour. Fry in shortening at 350° until brown, about 2 to 3 minutes. Drain on paper towels. Serve hot or cold with Fiesta Sour Cream Dip. Yield: about 6 servings.

Fiesta Sour Cream Dip:

- 1 cup commercial sour cream
- ½ teaspoon curry powder
- 1 teaspoon chopped parsley
- ¼ teaspoon hot pepper sauce
- ½ teaspoon salt

Combine sour cream, curry powder, parsley, hot sauce, and salt. Mix well. Refrigerate until ready to serve. Yield: about 1¼ cups.

*Saucy Meatballs

- 1½ pounds lean ground beef
- ¾ cup quick-cooking oats, uncooked
- ¼ cup chopped onion
- 1 teaspoon salt
- ¼ teaspoon black pepper
- ¼ teaspoon oregano
- 1 egg
- ½ cup milk
- Shortening

Sauce:

- ½ cup chopped onion
- ⅓ cup chopped green pepper
- 1 (1-pound) can tomatoes
- 1 (8-ounce) can tomato sauce
- ½ teaspoon salt
- ¼ teaspoon garlic salt or garlic powder
- Dash cayenne pepper
- ¼ teaspoon oregano
- 1 bay leaf
- Cooked noodles or rice

For meatballs, combine ground beef, oats, chopped onion, salt, pepper, oregano, egg, and milk. Shape to form 12 meatballs. Brown in just enough shortening to cover bottom of large skillet. Remove meatballs.

For sauce, lightly brown onion and green pepper in skillet. Add tomatoes, tomato sauce, salt, garlic salt, dash cayenne pepper, oregano, and bay leaf. Add meatballs to sauce, cover, and simmer about 30 minutes. Remove bay leaf. Serve with hot buttered noodles or cooked rice. Yield: 8 servings.

Liver Piquant

½ pound beef liver, sliced
½ teaspoon salt
  All-purpose flour
2 tablespoons butter
1 tablespoon all-purpose flour
½ cup water
1 teaspoon freshly squeezed lemon juice
4 stuffed olives, sliced
¼ cup canned mushrooms
½ teaspoon Worcestershire sauce
  Rice or potatoes

Dip slices of liver in salted flour and panfry in butter for 6 to 7 minutes or until browned. Do not overcook. Remove to hot plate. Stir 1 tablespoon flour into pan, add water, and stir until thickened. Add lemon juice, olives, mushrooms, and Worcestershire sauce and blend well. When thoroughly heated, serve as a gravy with the liver. Serve with rice or potatoes. Yield: 2 servings.

*Cheese Meatballs with Spaghetti Sauce

Sauce:

2 tablespoons olive oil
½ cup chopped onion
¼ cup chopped green pepper
1 clove garlic, minced
2 (6-ounce) cans tomato paste
3 cups water
2 teaspoons salt
¼ teaspoon pepper
2 teaspoons chili powder
¼ teaspoon oregano

Heat olive oil in large Dutch oven or frying pan. Add onion, green pepper, and garlic; cook slowly until onion is transparent. Blend in remaining sauce ingredients.

Cover and simmer gently over very low heat for 30 minutes. While sauce is cooking, prepare meatballs.

Meatballs:

1 pound ground beef
½ pound ground pork
1 cup grated Parmesan cheese
1 cup milk
1 egg
1 cup soft bread crumbs
½ cup chopped parsley
1 clove garlic, minced
2 teaspoons salt
¼ teaspoon pepper
½ teaspoon oregano
¼ cup butter
  Hot cooked spaghetti (optional)

Combine all ingredients except butter and mix well. Shape meat mixture into 24 balls about 1 to 2 inches in diameter. Melt butter in large frying pan. Brown meatballs slowly in butter over low heat. Place browned balls in hot cooked sauce; cover and cook an additional 30 minutes. Serve sauce over hot cooked and salted spaghetti, or plain as an entrée. Yield: 8 servings.

Sweet and Sour Meatballs

1 pound ground beef
1 teaspoon salt
¼ teaspoon pepper
  Salad oil
1 (20-ounce) can pineapple slices
½ cup sliced sweet pickles
1 tablespoon pickle juice
1 tablespoon cornstarch

Season ground beef with salt and pepper; form into meatballs about 1 inch in diameter. Brown meatballs slowly in heated salad oil. Drain pineapple slices, reserving juice. Combine pineapple juice, pickles, pickle juice, and cornstarch; add to meatballs. Cook and stir until sauce thickens and is clear. Add pineapple slices; cover and cook 5 minutes over medium heat. Yield: 4 servings.

Sherried Spaghetti and Meatballs

1 pound ground beef
½ cup chopped onion
1 teaspoon salt
¼ teaspoon pepper
2 tablespoons salad oil
1 cup sliced mushrooms
1 cup sliced celery
1 (12½-ounce) can condensed tomato soup
⅓ cup sherry
1 (12-ounce) package spaghetti

Combine beef, onion, salt, and pepper; mix well, and shape into 12 balls. Heat oil and add meatballs; cook until lightly browned on all sides. Add mushrooms, celery, and tomato soup. Cover and cook over low heat 30 minutes, stirring occasionally. Add sherry and continue cooking 10 minutes.

Cook spaghetti according to package directions. Drain; serve hot with meatballs and sauce. Yield: 6 to 8 servings.

Swedish Meatballs

1 cup soft bread crumbs
1 cup milk
⅓ cup finely chopped onion
2 tablespoons butter
1 pound ground beef
½ pound ground veal
½ pound ground pork
2 eggs
2½ teaspoons salt
¼ teaspoon pepper
¼ cup butter
2 tablespoons flour
2 cups half-and-half
½ teaspoon salt
½ teaspoon ground nutmeg (optional)

Soak bread crumbs in milk. In a small skillet sauté onions in 2 tablespoons butter until transparent but not brown. Mix bread crumbs and onions with meat, eggs, salt, and pepper; mix thoroughly. Shape into about 4 dozen meatballs. Melt ¼ cup butter in electric skillet. Add meatballs, set temperature at 325°, and cook until meatballs are brown on all sides. Remove meatballs and set aside.

Lower temperature to 240°; add flour to juices in skillet and blend well. Add cream, ½ teaspoon salt, and nutmeg. Transfer meatballs to skillet, cover, set temperature to "warm," and let stand until time to serve. Serve with noodles tossed with toasted sesame seeds. Yield: 8 servings.

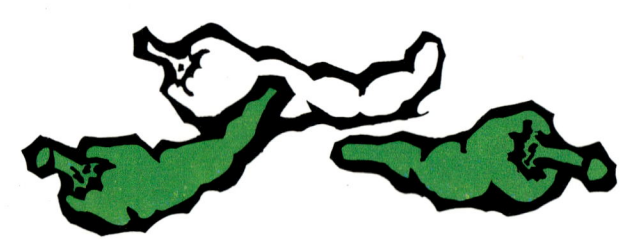

*Braised Short Ribs with Vegetables

2½ to 3 pounds beef short ribs
Salt and pepper to taste
¼ cup all-purpose flour
2 tablespoons shortening
1 medium onion, sliced
½ cup chopped celery leaves
2 sprigs parsley
1½ cups hot water or bouillon
6 medium carrots
8 small onions
6 medium potatoes
Flour for gravy

Cut short ribs into individual servings. Sprinkle with salt and pepper and roll in flour. Brown ribs in hot shortening in a heavy skillet or Dutch oven. Add onion, celery leaves, parsley, and liquid. Cover skillet and cook over low heat for 2 hours, adding more liquid if necessary. Add vegetables; sprinkle with salt and pepper to taste. Cover skillet and continue cooking for 30 minutes or until meat and vegetables are tender. Remove meat and vegetables to hot platter.

For gravy, skim any excess fat from liquid, and dilute liquid to preferred strength. Thicken by cooking with a smooth flour and water paste. Serve gravy over meat and potatoes. Yield: 6 servings.

Daube of Beef with Fruit (Hot Pot Roast)

- 4- to 4½-pound English-cut roast beef (or chuck, round, etc.), rolled
- ¾ cup Burgundy
- Fat from roast or 2 tablespoons salad oil
- 1½ teaspoons salt
- ¾ teaspoon ground pepper
- All-purpose flour
- ¾ cup chopped onion
- ¾ cup coarsely chopped celery
- ½ green pepper, cut in lengthwise strips
- 1 clove garlic, minced
- Hot water (about 3 cups)
- 1 tablespoon Worcestershire sauce
- ½ teaspoon tarragon leaves
- 1 tablespoon catsup
- 1 cup boiled dried prunes, pitted and chopped
- 1 cup diced raw apple, peeled
- 1 cup canned peaches, cut in bite-size pieces
- ¼ cup white raisins
- ½ cup syrup from cooked prunes
- ¼ cup juice from canned peaches
- 1 tablespoon flour mixed with 2 tablespoons cold water
- Salt and pepper to taste

Marinate the beef in the wine for about 3 hours, turning often. Drain the beef, pat it dry; reserve the marinade.

In a heavy Dutch oven type roaster, place any excess fat from roast in the pan and fry out to make 2 tablespoons of fat, or use oil. Heat the fat until it smokes. Sprinkle the roast with salt and pepper; then dredge it lightly on all sides with flour. Sear the roast in the hot fat, allowing it to brown on sides and ends. Push the roast to one side and stir in the onion, celery, green pepper, and garlic. Sauté the vegetables for 1 minute. Add about 3 cups hot water, or enough to come halfway up the side of the roast (lay roast lengthwise in pan). Add the Worcestershire sauce, tarragon leaves, and catsup. Add the reserved marinade. Cover; bake at 325° for 2½ hours, turning the roast and basting it about every 30 minutes.

Combine the fruits. Remove roast from oven; cut off the strings from roast and pull sides open a little to make pockets around the center. Spread the fruit over the roast and into the pockets. Carefully spoon some of the pan gravy over the fruits. Cover pan and return it to the oven. Roast for 50 to 60 minutes longer or until meat is fork tender. With two spatulas remove the roast to a heated platter. Skim off the fat from gravy and discard; put rest of gravy in skillet. Add the prune and peach juices and stir in the flour mixture. Boil gravy rapidly until it has thickened to desired consistency. Reseason with salt and pepper. Slice the meat and serve with hot gravy. Yield: 6 servings.

Deviled Pot Roast

- 1 (4- to 5-pound) boneless beef roast (chuck, shoulder, or rump)
- 2 cloves garlic, slivered
- ½ cup (about) small stuffed olives
- Sliced bacon (about ¼ pound)
- Salt and pepper
- All-purpose flour
- 5 tablespoons salad oil, divided
- 1 large onion, chopped
- ⅛ teaspoon thyme (optional)
- ⅛ teaspoon marjoram (optional)
- 1 (1-pound) can tomatoes

Cut slits about 1½ inches deep in meat and into these push a sliver of garlic and an olive wrapped in a small piece of bacon. Season with salt and pepper; dredge with flour. In heavy skillet heat 3 tablespoons oil and brown meat thoroughly on all sides.

Sauté onion in 2 tablespoons oil in Dutch oven large enough to accommodate the roast. Transfer browned meat to this pot; sprinkle with more salt, pepper, thyme, and marjoram (about ¼ teaspoon of each). Spoon tomatoes slowly over roast (so as not to disturb seasonings), cover tightly, and bake at 300° for about 3½ hours or until meat is quite tender. Baste the roast occasionally.

When meat is done, remove from pot and chill gravy thoroughly so fat may be skimmed from top. Reheat whole or sliced roast in the gravy. Good served hot or cold. Yield: 4 to 6 servings.

Pineapple Beef Short Ribs

 3 to 4 *pounds beef short ribs*
 1 *(20-ounce) can unsweetened pineapple chunks*
 4 *tablespoons molasses*
 2 *tablespoons cornstarch*
 1 *beef bouillon cube*
 1 *cup hot water*
 4 *tablespoons lemon juice*
 ½ *teaspoon salt*
 1½ *teaspoons prepared mustard with horseradish*

Cut ribs into serving portions and trim off excess fat. Place ribs in shallow baking dish; cover and bake at 350° for 1½ hours.

Drain pineapple, reserving ½ cup juice; set pineapple aside. Combine pineapple juice, molasses, and cornstarch in a saucepan. Dissolve bouillon cube in hot water; add to pineapple juice mixture along with lemon juice, salt, mustard, and pineapple chunks. Cook and stir over medium heat until thickened.

After ribs have cooked 1½ hours, pour sauce over ribs; wrap securely and freeze. To serve, thaw and reheat at 350° for 15 minutes or until bubbly. Yield: 6 servings.

*Marinated Chuck Roast

 1 *(3- to 5-pound) chuck roast*
 Meat tenderizer
 1 *tablespoon butter or margarine*
 1 *tablespoon sesame seeds*
 ½ *cup strong coffee*
 ½ *cup soy sauce*
 1 *tablespoon Worcestershire sauce*
 1 *tablespoon vinegar*
 1 *large onion, chopped finely*

Sprinkle meat with tenderizer and set aside. Melt butter; add sesame seed and brown slightly. Add coffee, soy sauce, Worcestershire sauce, vinegar, and onion. Pour over roast and let stand at room temperature for at least 12 hours. Turn meat often. Remove from marinade and grill, basting frequently with marinade. Cook to desired doneness. Yield: 6 to 8 servings.

*Mexican Dinner

 1 *onion, chopped*
 1 *tablespoon salad oil*
 2 *pounds ground beef*
 1 *teaspoon salt*
 ½ *teaspoon black pepper*
 2 *(8-ounce) cans tomato sauce*
 ½ *cup water*
 1 *(1¼-ounce) package chili mix*
 1 *(15-ounce) can ranch-style beans*
 1 *(6-ounce) package corn chips*
 6 *slices pasteurized process American cheese*

Sauté onion in oil until tender. Add ground beef and cook until meat is browned. Add salt, pepper, tomato sauce, water, and chili mix; simmer 10 minutes. Add beans; simmer 15 minutes. Press corn chips lightly into chili mixture. Cover with cheese slices; simmer until cheese softens but does not melt into sauce. Yield: 6 servings.

Beef and Beans Paprikash

 1 *pound (2 rounded cups) dried red kidney beans soaked in 6 cups water*
 1 *cup chopped onion*
 ¼ *cup salad oil*
 2 *pounds boneless beef*
 1 *large bay leaf*
 1 *clove garlic, minced*
 2 *teaspoons salt*
 2 *teaspoons paprika*
 1 *tablespoon tomato paste*
 2 *cups commercial sour cream*

Soak beans in 6 cups water at least 2 hours. Cook onion in oil until limp; remove. Add beef cut in ½-inch cubes. Brown on all sides over high heat, using about half the cubes at a time. Bring beans and soaking water to boiling point. Add onion and meat and other ingredients except sour cream. Cover and simmer about 2 hours or until meat and beans are tender. (This may be done the day before.)

Just before serving, bring beef and bean mixture to boiling point, adding small amount of water if too thick. Stir in sour cream. Allow to simmer 10 minutes. Serve hot. Yield: 10 servings.

*Beef Brisket

 4- to 5-pound well-trimmed boneless beef brisket
1½ teaspoons salt
½ cup catsup
¼ cup vinegar
½ medium onion, finely chopped (about ½ cup)
 1 tablespoon Worcestershire sauce
1½ teaspoons liquid smoke
 1 bay leaf, crushed
 ¼ teaspoon coarsely ground black pepper

Wipe beef dry; rub with salt. Place on 15- x 20-inch piece of double thickness heavy-duty aluminum foil. Combine remaining ingredients; pour over brisket. Wrap securely in foil. Place on grill 5 inches from medium coals. Cook 1½ hours or until tender, turning once. Cut diagonally across the grain into thin slices. Yield: 10 to 12 servings.

Savory Grilled Beef Roast

 1 (4- to 6-pound) rolled rib, standing rib, or top sirloin roast
Salt and pepper
 1 (10½-ounce) can condensed consommé
½ cup tomato juice or dry red wine
 1 clove garlic, crushed
 2 tablespoons minced onion
¼ teaspoon freshly ground pepper
 1 tablespoon Worcestershire sauce

Season roast with salt and pepper. Build fire at one side of grill. Using heavy-duty aluminum foil, make a pan about 1 inch larger all around than the roast to catch drippings; turn up edges of foil and miter corners to make pan sturdy. Place this pan beside the fire in the grill.

When the fire is ready, place roast on grill directly over pan. Insert meat thermometer in thickest part of roast. Cover grill with hood, and open damper; let meat roast for 45 minutes or longer.

Combine consommé, tomato juice, and seasonings. Lift hood and baste roast with sauce. Add damp hickory chips and a few charcoal briquets to fire if needed. Cover and continue roasting, basting once or twice more and adding hickory chips and briquets if needed. Roast will be done when meat thermometer registers 140° for rare, 160° for medium, and 170° for well done.

Remove roast to carving board or platter. Slip foil pan with drippings onto a cookie sheet for support. Combine drippings with any remaining basting sauce. Skim off excess fat; simmer sauce and add additional seasonings if needed. Serve sauce with roast. Yield: 6 servings.

Noisettes of Beef

 3 (3-ounce) prime filets of beef
Salt and pepper
 1 teaspoon butter
 1 teaspoon salad oil
 2 finely chopped shallots
 4 medium mushrooms, sliced
Chopped parsley, garlic, and leeks to taste
 2 tablespoons Beaujolais
Hot rice

Slice filets of beef, season with salt and pepper, and place in preheated skillet with butter and cooking oil. Brown on both sides and remove filets from pan. Into the same pan add the shallots, mushrooms, parsley, garlic, and leeks; sauté until tender. Add wine. There will be a small flame within the pan. Place beef filets on hot plate; pour sauce over filets and serve with rice. Yield: 2 servings.

Roast Sirloin of Beef (Rare)

 1 (5- to 6-pound) sirloin tip of beef
12 strips salt pork (¼ inch thick)
Beef suet
Salt and pepper

Lard the sirloin with strips of salt pork and wrap it in beef suet. Season with salt and pepper and bake at 325° (using a meat thermometer) in same manner as any other roast of beef. Allow 2½ to 3 hours for roast of this size. Yield: 8 servings.

Beef Almond Supreme

1 (2-pound) round steak, cut into cubes
⅓ cup butter or margarine
½ clove garlic, crushed
½ cup chopped onion
¼ cup chopped celery
⅓ cup all-purpose flour
1 teaspoon salt
⅛ teaspoon pepper
3 cups beef bouillon
1 teaspoon prepared mustard
½ cup chutney (optional)
¼ cup chopped or slivered almonds
Hot rice

Brown meat cubes on all sides in the butter. Add garlic, onion, and celery; cook 5 minutes longer.

Combine flour, salt, and pepper and stir into a small amount of the bouillon. Add to meat mixture. Slowly stir in the remaining bouillon, stirring constantly until mixture thickens. Add other ingredients except rice, cover pan, and simmer 45 minutes or until meat is tender. Serve over hot rice. Yield: 6 to 8 servings.

Oven Barbecued Round Steak

4 individual servings round steak
Salt, pepper, flour
3 tablespoons vegetable shortening
½ cup chopped onion
½ cup chopped celery
½ cup clove garlic, minced
3 tablespoons firmly packed brown sugar
2 teaspoons prepared mustard
2 tablespoons Worcestershire sauce
1 tablespoon vinegar
1 (10¾-ounce) can condensed tomato soup

Sprinkle steak with salt and pepper and coat with flour; pound thoroughly. Melt shortening in a Dutch oven or large, heavy skillet. Lightly brown onion, celery, and garlic; push to one side and brown steak. Combine remaining ingredients and add. Cover and cook over low heat or in a 325° oven for 2 hours or until tender. Yield: 4 servings.

*Grillades with Gravy

1 pound round steak
1 tablespoon shortening
2 tablespoons all-purpose flour
½ cup minced onion
½ cup chopped fresh tomatoes
1 tablespoon minced garlic
3 tablespoons minced parsley
Salt and pepper
1 tablespoon minced green pepper
Hot rice

Cut steak into 4 serving-size pieces. Fry until brown; then remove from shortening and set aside. Brown the flour in the same shortening and add minced onion. Let yellow slightly; then add tomatoes, garlic, parsley, salt, pepper, and green pepper. Put meat back into this gravy and add about 2 cups water (or enough to make 2 or more cups gravy). Cover and cook slowly until meat is tender, about 1½ to 2 hours. Serve with cooked rice. Yield: 4 servings.

Fruited Spiced Pot Roast

1 (3- to 5-pound) beef pot roast (chuck or rump)
2 tablespoons salad oil
2 cups water
3 tablespoons mixed pickling spices
1 cup dried prunes

Brown roast in hot oil in a heavy kettle. Add water and spices. Cover tightly and simmer 3 to 3½ hours or until fork-tender. Add prunes during last hour of cooking. Yield: 6 to 8 servings.

Enchiladas

2 dozen tortillas
½ pound shortening
1 quart Enchilada Sauce or gravy
2 to 3 cups finely chopped onions
1 pound Cheddar cheese, shredded
About 3 to 4 cups Enchilada Sauce or homemade chili
Grated cheese

Use tongs to dip tortillas, one at a time, in medium hot shortening. Leave long enough to soften tortilla, but do not cook until crisp. Dip tortilla immediately into Enchilada Sauce or gravy and leave until soft. (This step may be reversed, if you like.)

Place softened tortilla on a flat surface. Sprinkle with chopped onion and shredded cheese and roll as you would a jelly roll. Place in large flat pan with the flap of tortilla on bottom. When pan has been filled, cover with Enchilada Sauce or chili; sprinkle with grated cheese and place in oven preheated to 350°. Bake until cheese has melted and mixture is bubbly. Yield: 12 servings (2 enchiladas per person).

Enchilada Sauce:

- 1 *tablespoon salad oil*
- 1 *medium-size onion, chopped*
- 3 *cups tomato sauce or tomato puree*
- 2 *teaspoons chili powder*
- *Salt to taste*
- 1 *to 3 jalapeño peppers or green chiles, finely chopped*

Heat salad oil in skillet. Cook onion in oil until wilted. Add tomato sauce and chili powder and cook about 10 minutes. Add salt, peppers or chiles; keep mixture warm.

Oriental Celery Steak

- 1 *pound round steak or boneless chuck*
- 1½ *teaspoons salt, divided*
- ⅛ *teaspoon freshly ground black pepper*
- 3 *tablespoons all-purpose flour*
- ¼ *cup shortening or salad oil*
- 1 *medium green pepper*
- 1 *cup onion rings*
- 1½ *cups sliced celery*
- ¼ *teaspoon ground ginger*
- ¼ *teaspoon ground mustard*
- 1 *teaspoon turmeric*
- 1 *tablespoon freshly squeezed lemon juice*
- 1 *cup boiling water*
- *Mashed potatoes*

Cut meat into 2- x ½- x ¼-inch strips. Rub all sides with 1 teaspoon salt and the pepper. Roll in flour. Brown in hot shortening, adding more shortening as needed. Remove meat from skillet and keep warm while vegetables are being cooked.

Wash green pepper, remove seeds, and cut into strips ½ inch wide. Sauté pepper strips, onion, and celery for 8 minutes in pan in which meat was browned, adding more shortening if needed. Return meat to pan. Add remaining salt, spices, lemon juice, and water. Cover and simmer 10 minutes or until meat is tender. Serve over mashed potatoes. Yield: 6 servings.

Paprika Beef

- 1½ *pounds round steak*
- 1 *medium onion, thinly sliced*
- 1 *clove garlic, minced*
- ¼ *cup salad oil*
- ¼ *cup all-purpose flour*
- 1 *teaspoon salt*
- 1 *teaspoon pepper*
- 1 *(10½-ounce) can condensed beef consommé*
- 1 *tablespoon paprika*
- 3 *drops (or more) hot sauce*
- 1 *cup commercial sour cream*

Cut meat into serving-size pieces. Pound meat until slices are very thin; set aside. Cook onion and garlic in salad oil until wilted but not browned. Remove from skillet.

Combine flour, salt, and pepper; coat beef slices with flour mixture. Brown meat in hot oil. Return onion and garlic to skillet. Add consommé, paprika, and hot sauce and cook for 15 to 20 minutes or until meat is tender. Just before serving, add sour cream and heat. Do not boil after sour cream has been added. (To freeze, cool mixture before sour cream has been added. Add sour cream when mixture thaws.) Yield: 4 servings.

Chicken Fried Steak

1 pound round steak, ½ inch thick
Salt and pepper
1 egg, beaten
1 tablespoon milk
1 cup cracker meal
¼ cup salad oil

Cut steak into 3 or 4 pieces, add salt and pepper, and pound thoroughly. Mix egg and milk. Dip meat into egg mixture, then into cracker meal. Brown slowly on both sides in hot oil. Cover tightly; cook over very low heat 45 to 60 minutes or until tender. Yield: 2 servings.

Hot Tamale Pie

2 cups cornmeal*
3 cups boiling water
1 tablespoon salt
Dash of pepper
⅓ cup margarine
¼ cup all-purpose flour
1½ pounds lean ground beef
1 medium onion, chopped
1 clove garlic, minced
1½ teaspoons salt
⅛ teaspoon thyme
2 tablespoons chili powder
1 (1-pound) can tomatoes
1 (6-ounce) can tomato paste

Slowly stir cornmeal into boiling, salted water. Cook until thick; add pepper and set aside. Melt margarine in large, heavy skillet or Dutch oven. Stir in flour and cook until slightly browned. Add meat, onion, and garlic, and cook until meat is browned. Stir in salt, thyme, chili powder, tomatoes, and tomato paste. Simmer about 30 minutes or until mixture thickens.
 Spread a layer of the cornmeal mush mixture in a 3-quart casserole; top with a layer of meat sauce. Repeat layers, ending with mush mixture. Bake at 400° about 45 minutes. Yield: about 8 to 10 servings.

*Quick-cooking grits may be substituted for the cornmeal in making the mush for the dish.

Teriyaki Steak

½ cup soy sauce
¼ cup white wine
1 clove garlic, crushed
2 tablespoons brown sugar
½ teaspoon ground ginger
1 (2- to 3-pound) flank steak

Combine soy sauce, wine, garlic, brown sugar, and ginger to make a marinade. Place flank steak in a flat shallow dish and pour marinade over it. Cover and refrigerate overnight. The next day, cut steak into strips and string on skewers or put strips in hinged grill basket. Broil over medium heat on the grill until the desired doneness. Yield: 6 to 8 servings.

Hamburger Stroganoff

1 (6-ounce) package egg noodles
½ cup chopped onion
¼ cup margarine
1 pound ground round beef
1 tablespoon flour
½ teaspoon garlic salt
1 (8-ounce) can tomato sauce with mushrooms
¼ cup Burgundy
1 (10½-ounce) can beef bouillon
1 teaspoon salt
¼ teaspoon pepper
1 cup sour cream
½ cup grated Parmesan cheese

Cook noodles as directed on package; drain and set aside. Sauté onion in margarine; add beef and stir until brown and crumbly. Drain off excess fat. Add flour and stir well. Add garlic salt, tomato sauce, wine, bouillon, salt, and pepper. Blend well and simmer for 10 minutes. Stir in sour cream, and remove from heat.
 Alternate layers of cooked noodles and meat sauce in a greased 2-quart casserole dish, ending with sauce. Sprinkle Parmesan cheese on top. Bake at 375° for 25 to 30 minutes or until bubbly. This freezes well. Yield: 6 servings.

Round Steak Ranchero

½ cup salad oil
½ cup red wine or wine vinegar
2 tablespoons bottled steak sauce
½ onion, sliced
1 clove garlic, crushed
½ teaspoon thyme
½ teaspoon salt
¼ teaspoon pepper
1½ pounds round steak

For marinade combine first 8 ingredients. Marinate steak several hours or overnight. Broil steak, using marinade as basting sauce. Yield: 4 servings.

Steak Siciliano

1 cup Burgundy
1 small clove garlic, minced
1 small onion, grated
1 tablespoon Worcestershire sauce
¼ teaspoon powdered oregano
1 teaspoon salt
¼ teaspoon pepper
2 teaspoons prepared mustard
2 teaspoons minced parsley
2 tablespoons prepared horseradish
1 tablespoon sugar
1 tablespoon margarine
1 (2½-pound) round steak, cut 1 to 1½ inches thick
Seasoned meat tenderizer

Combine first 12 ingredients; heat until margarine melts. Cool to room temperature. Meanwhile, sprinkle all surfaces of meat evenly with tenderizer. Pierce deeply and generously with fork. Place in pan and let stand at room temperature for 1 hour. Pour sauce over steak; chill several hours, turning 2 or 3 times in sauce. Strain sauce, keeping solid material as well as liquid. Broil steak on one side, basting occasionally with liquid. Turn; spread top surface with solid particles. Broil to desired doneness (5 minutes on each side for rare; 7 minutes for medium-rare; 8 minutes for medium). Slice to serve. Yield: 6 servings.

Steak Floridian

1 (2-pound) round steak, cut ½ inch thick
¼ cup all-purpose flour
1 teaspoon salt
¼ teaspoon black pepper
3 tablespoons shortening
1 cup catsup
½ cup water
1 unpeeled orange, thinly sliced
1 medium-size onion, thinly sliced
1 unpeeled lemon, thinly sliced
6 whole cloves

Cut steak into 6 serving-size pieces. Combine flour, salt, and pepper; pound into steak. Brown steak in hot shortening. Arrange steak in baking dish. Combine catsup and water and pour over meat. Place orange slices on top of meat; top with onion slices; then lemon slices. Stick a whole clove in each stack. Cover dish and bake at 350° for 1 hour or until meat is tender. Yield: 6 servings.

Spanish Round Steak

¼ cup all-purpose flour
3 teaspoons salt
¼ teaspoon pepper
2 teaspoons paprika
1 (1-pound) round steak
Salad oil
2 cups sliced onion
1 cup canned or cooked tomatoes

Combine flour and seasonings; pound half of flour mixture into steak; then cut steak into serving-size pieces. Brown steak in hot oil; drain on paper towels, and reserve hot oil. Place steak in a 1-quart casserole dish.
  Brown onions lightly in hot oil; remove and add to meat. Drain tomatoes, reserving 1 cup juice; add tomatoes to steak and onion mixture. Add remainder of flour mixture to hot oil and blend. Add reserved tomato juice; cook until thick, stirring constantly. Pour over meat. Cook, covered, at 375° for 1 hour. Uncover and cook until tender. Yield: 4 servings.

Steak with Olives

1½ pounds round steak (¾ inch thick)
2 tablespoons cooking oil
1 medium onion, chopped
½ medium green pepper, chopped
1 (3-ounce) jar stuffed olives, sliced
1 (10¾-ounce) can condensed tomato soup

Cut steak into serving-size pieces. Heat oil in heavy skillet or Dutch oven; brown steak pieces, onion, and pepper in hot oil. Add olives with their liquid and soup. Cover tightly and cook slowly about 1½ hours or until steaks are fork tender, or bake at 350° for approximately 2 hours. Yield: 6 to 8 servings.

Round Steak Roll-Ups

1½ pounds round steak, cut ½ inch thick
¼ cup finely chopped onion
6 tablespoons bacon drippings or shortening, divided
2 cups day-old bread crumbs
½ cup chopped celery
½ teaspoon salt
¼ teaspoon sage
Dash each of pepper and poultry seasoning
1 tablespoon water
All-purpose flour
1 (10¾-ounce) can condensed cream of mushroom soup
1 soup can water
Salt and pepper

Remove bone from steak. Flatten the steak by pounding with a meat pounder or the edge of a heavy saucer.
    Lightly brown onion in 3 tablespoons hot drippings; add bread crumbs, celery, seasonings, and water. Cut meat into 4 pieces; place a fourth of the bread crumb dressing on each piece. Roll up and fasten with small skewers or toothpicks. Dust with flour and brown in remaining fat. Dilute soup with a soup can of water and pour over meat. Sprinkle with salt and pepper. Cover and simmer over low heat 1½ to 2 hours or until tender, or cover and bake at 300° for 1 hour. Yield: 4 servings.

Round Steak Italia

1½ pounds round steak, ¾ to 1 inch thick
3 tablespoons all-purpose flour
1 teaspoon salt
½ teaspoon oregano
¼ teaspoon pepper
1 tablespoon shortening
1 (15½-ounce) can spaghetti sauce with mushrooms
1 (10-ounce) package frozen Italian green beans
1 (16-ounce) can whole onions, drained

Rub steak with mixture of flour and seasonings; reserve remainder of flour mixture. Cut steak into 6 pieces. In large skillet over medium heat, brown steak in hot shortening. Place in baking dish, 11 x 7 x 1½ inches. Heat sauce and flour mixture to boiling, stirring constantly. Pour over steak; cover. Bake at 375° for 45 minutes. Add vegetables; cover and bake 45 minutes. Yield: 6 servings.

Round Steak Special

1 pound round steak
3 tablespoons olive oil
½ cup chopped tomatoes
½ cup chopped green peppers
½ cup chopped onion
½ cup drained, chopped mushrooms
½ cup Burgundy
Salt and pepper to taste
1 cup tomato sauce
Grated Parmesan cheese

Cut steak into 4 serving-size pieces; brown in hot olive oil. Add tomatoes, peppers, onion, and mushrooms, and cook 4 minutes. Put mixture into a 3-quart casserole dish; add Burgundy, salt, pepper, and tomato sauce, and top with grated Parmesan cheese. Cover dish and bake at 350° for 45 minutes. Yield: 4 servings.

Sirloin and Roquefort

1 (3-to 4-pound) sirloin steak
1 (0.7-ounce) package blue cheese salad dressing mix
Salad oil
Red wine vinegar
¼ cup crumbled Roquefort cheese

Place steak in a large flat pan. Mix salad dressing according to package directions. Spread over both sides of steak. Mix enough salad oil and red wine vinegar, in equal parts, to cover steak. Let steak stand in marinade for 1 hour. Remove from marinade and drain. Cook on grill at high setting for 8 minutes. Turn meat carefully with tongs, and lower heat. Sprinkle cooked side with crumbled Roquefort cheese, and grill for 8 minutes for medium-rare. Yield: about 6 to 8 servings.

Sukiyaki

¼ cup peanut or salad oil
1 pound sirloin steak, diagonally cut into ¼- x 2-inch strips
2 medium-size onions, diagonally sliced
1 cup sliced celery, diagonally cut into ½-inch strips
½ pound fresh, sliced mushrooms or 1 (8-ounce) can sliced mushrooms, drained
½ head Chinese or celery cabbage, diagonally cut into ½-inch slices
1 (10- to 12-ounce) can bamboo shoots, drained
2 (6-ounce) cans water chestnuts, drained and thinly sliced
8 scallions, cut into narrow strips
1 teaspoon monosodium glutamate
½ cup chicken broth or 1 chicken bouillon cube dissolved in ½ cup hot water
½ cup bean curd, cut into ½-inch cubes
1 green pepper, thinly sliced into strips
1 tablespoon brown sugar
1 teaspoon salt
½ cup soy sauce
3 cups fresh spinach, torn into large pieces
Cooked brown rice

Pour oil into wok or skillet; heat at 375° for 4 minutes. Place meat in hot oil and stir-fry for 2 minutes; push meat up sides of wok. Add onion and stir-fry for 2 minutes; push onion up sides of wok. Continue same procedure for celery, mushrooms, and Chinese cabbage, adding more oil if needed; stir-fry each ingredient for 2 minutes; push up sides of wok, and add next ingredient.

Combine bamboo shoots, water chestnuts, scallions, monosodium glutamate, and chicken broth; add to wok, stir once. Cook for 2 minutes, and push up sides of wok. Add bean curd, green pepper, brown sugar, salt, and soy sauce; stir once and cook for 30 seconds. Do not push up sides of wok. Sprinkle spinach over all ingredients in wok, cover, and simmer for 2 minutes. Reduce heat to warm for serving. Serve immediately over cooked brown rice. Yield: 6 to 8 servings.

Note: Precise timing on stir-frying should be followed so vegetables will be cooked *al dente* (firm, but slightly under-cooked). They will be crisp in texture and bright and translucent in color. Spinach or other greens will merely be somewhat wilted after stir-frying.

*Beef Tacos

1 pound ground beef
4 tablespoons bacon drippings
¼ teaspoon garlic salt
1 teaspoon chili powder
Salt to taste
1 dozen tortillas (or taco shells)
Shredded lettuce
Chopped onion
Chopped tomatoes

Cook ground beef in hot bacon drippings until meat turns pale; add garlic salt, chili powder, and salt; cook a few minutes longer.

Use taco shells or prepare your own from tortillas. Fold tortillas in half and fry until crisp in hot fat.

Place a layer of ground beef in bottom of each taco shell and finish filling with shredded lettuce, chopped onion, and chopped tomatoes. Yield: 6 servings (2 tacos per person).

Barbecued Chuck Roast

   3- to 4-pound U.S. choice chuck roast, 2½ to 3¾ inches thick
   4 cloves garlic, minced
  ¼ cup olive oil
   1 teaspoon crushed rosemary
  ½ teaspoon dry mustard
   2 teaspoons soy sauce
  ¼ cup wine vinegar
  ¼ cup sherry (optional)
   2 tablespoons catsup
  ½ teaspoon Worcestershire sauce
 1½ teaspoons steak sauce

Select U.S. Choice chuck roast, 2½ to 3 inches thick. Sauté garlic in olive oil; then add rosemary, mustard, and soy sauce. Remove from heat and add vinegar and sherry if desired. Place roast in a bowl and cover with marinade. Cover and place in refrigerator for 24 hours, turning meat occasionally in marinade.

Remove meat from marinade. Add catsup, Worcestershire sauce, and steak sauce to marinade. Place meat on barbecue grill, 3 to 5 inches from gray coals. Brush marinade over roast as it cooks; cooking time is about 40 minutes, with roast rare in center and browned on outside. Yield: 6 servings.

Individual Swiss Steaks

   1 round steak, cut ¾ inch thick
  ¼ cup all-purpose flour
   2 teaspoons salt
  ⅛ teaspoon pepper
   3 tablespoons shortening
  ⅛ teaspoon thyme
   1 medium onion, sliced
  ½ cup sliced celery
   1 (16-ounce) can tomatoes

Cut steak into 4 to 6 pieces. Combine flour, salt, and pepper. Pound seasoned flour into steaks. Brown in shortening. Pour off drippings. Add thyme, onion, celery, and tomatoes. Cover tightly and cook slowly for 1½ to 2 hours or until meat is tender. Thicken liquid for gravy, if desired. Yield: 4 to 6 servings.

Savory Swiss Steak

   1 round steak, cut 1½ inches thick
   2 tablespoons all-purpose flour
   1 teaspoon salt
  ⅛ teaspoon pepper
   2 tablespoons shortening
   2 medium onions, sliced
   1 teaspoon dry mustard
  ½ teaspoon chili powder
   1 small bay leaf
   2 teaspoons Worcestershire sauce
   1 teaspoon sugar
   2 cups canned tomatoes

Place meat on chopping board. Combine flour, salt, and pepper and pound into meat. Heat shortening in a heavy skillet or Dutch oven and brown meat well on both sides. Top steak with sliced onions. Combine other ingredients and pour over and around steak. Cover and cook slowly over low heat until meat is tender, about 1½ to 2 hours. Add more tomatoes or a little water, if needed, during cooking. Skim off excess fat and serve steak topped with sauce. Yield: 3 to 4 servings.

Filet of Beef Duke of Wellington

   1 (16-ounce) beef tenderloin
  ½ cup butter
     Salt and pepper
   6 ounces pâté de foie gras
   6 mushrooms, chopped finely
   1 package piecrust mix (for 2 crusts)
   1 egg, beaten
   1 cup veal stock
  ¼ cup pâté de foie gras
   2 tablespoons red wine

Trim fat from beef tenderloin; cover generously with butter, and sprinkle with salt and pepper. Use a butcher's steel and make a tunnel through filet lengthwise. Stuff incision with pâté de foie gras and chopped mushrooms. Sauté beef 4 minutes on each side; remove, drain, and chill.

Prepare piecrust as directed on package and roll out ⅛ inch thick. Spread crust with extra pâté and mushrooms. Place beef on crust, and fold dough over steak to cover it completely. Trim off extra dough and set aside. Seal edges with beaten egg. Place on baking sheet, seam side down. Cut designs from trimmed crust, place on top of roll, and brush with beaten egg. Bake at 425° for 15 to 20 minutes or until browned.

To pan drippings, add veal stock, ¼ cup pâté, chopped mushrooms, and red wine. Simmer until sauce thickens. Slice beef and serve with sauce. Yield: 2 servings.

Man-Style Beef Stroganoff

    2 pounds beef sirloin
    ¼ cup salad oil
    2 medium onions, sliced
    ½ pound fresh mushrooms, sliced
    1½ teaspoons salt
    ¼ teaspoon pepper
    1 (7-ounce) bottle lemon-lime carbonated
        beverage
    2 beef bouillon cubes
    Dash of bitters
    ¼ teaspoon ground nutmeg
    2 tablespoons cornstarch
    2 tablespoons cold water
    2 cups commercial sour cream
    Cooked rice or noodles
    Paprika
    Parsley

Cut meat diagonally into strips about ⅛ inch thick. Brown quickly in oil, cooking only enough at one time to cover bottom of skillet. Remove meat and keep warm. Add onion and mushrooms to drippings in skillet. Cook until onion is golden. Add salt, pepper, lemon-lime beverage, bouillon cubes, bitters, and nutmeg. Cover pan and simmer slowly about 10 minutes. Dissolve cornstarch in cold water. Add to mixture. Cook until thickened, stirring constantly. Add sour cream and meat; heat through. Serve immediately over rice or noodles. Garnish with paprika and parsley. Yield: 6 to 8 servings.

*Crescent Creole Meat Pie

    ½ to 1 pound ground pork sausage or
        ground beef
    ¼ cup chopped onion or 1 tablespoon instant
        minced onion
    ¼ cup chopped green pepper
    1 (10¾-ounce) can condensed vegetable beef
        soup
    1 cup whole undrained tomatoes, cut into
        chunks
    ½ teaspoon salt
    ⅛ teaspoon pepper
    1 (8-ounce) can refrigerated crescent dinner
        rolls
    1 cup instant mashed potato flakes
    3 slices pasteurized process American cheese,
        cut into ½-inch strips, or 1 cup
        shredded Cheddar cheese
    Green pepper rings (optional)

Brown sausage, onion, and green pepper in large skillet; drain. Stir in soup, tomatoes, and seasonings. Simmer while preparing crust.

Separate crescent dough into 8 triangles. Place triangles in ungreased 8- or 9-inch piepan, pressing to form a crust. Stir potato flakes into hot meat mixture; spoon into crust. Arrange cheese strips over filling. If desired, garnish with green pepper rings. Bake at 375° for 20 to 25 minutes until crust is golden brown. For easier serving, let stand for 5 minutes before cutting into wedges. Yield: 4 to 6 servings.

Stuffed Sausage Roll

    2 pounds bulk sausage
    2 cups diced raw tart apples
    2 cups bread crumbs
    2 small onions, diced

Pat sausage into a flat, rectangular shape about ½ inch thick. Mix apples, bread crumbs, and onion and spread over meat. Roll like a jelly roll, tucking the edges in. Place in a flat baking dish and bake at 350° for about 45 minutes. Yield: 6 servings.

*Bean 'n Sausage Stir

½ pound bulk sausage
¼ cup sliced celery
2 tablespoons chopped green pepper
1 small clove garlic, minced
¼ teaspoon curry powder
1 (1-pound) can pork and beans with tomato sauce
Chopped peanuts, if desired

Shape sausage into 12 meatballs. Cook in saucepan until done; pour off all but 1 tablespoon drippings. Add celery, green pepper, garlic, and curry; cook until celery is tender. Add beans. Heat; stir now and then. Garnish with nuts. Yield: 2 to 3 servings.

Sausage Loaf

2 eggs, slightly beaten
1 cup bread crumbs
⅓ cup milk
¼ cup chopped fresh parsley
2 pounds highly seasoned bulk pork sausage
2 cups cooked rice
1 cup canned condensed cream of mushroom soup
2 tablespoons orange juice

Mix eggs, bread crumbs, milk, and parsley. Add sausage and rice and mix well. Shape into a loaf and place in a shallow baking dish. Bake at 350° for 1 hour. Remove from oven and spoon off fat. Combine mushroom soup and orange juice; heat. Baste the loaf with this mixture as it bakes for an additional 20 minutes. Yield: 6 servings.

Link Sausage

Sausage links should be steamed first in a little water, then panfried until well browned.

Place sausage links in a cold skillet with about 3 tablespoons water, being careful not to prick the skins. Cover and simmer for about 5 minutes. This ensures thorough cooking of the pork. Uncover the skillet and drain off any water. Then panfry links over low heat, turning often until well browned on both sides (about 10 minutes).

Pizza Supper Pie

1 (5-ounce) stick packaged piecrust mix
1 pound bulk pork sausage
¾ cup chopped onion
4 eggs, beaten
½ cup milk
1 cup shredded sharp cheese
½ teaspoon oregano
¼ teaspoon pepper
1 (8-ounce) can pizza sauce
6 triangles sharp cheese

Make an 8- or 9-inch pie shell from packaged mix, making a high rim. Prick pastry with fork and bake at 425° for 8 to 10 minutes or until lightly browned.

Fry sausage, breaking it up. Add onion and cook until tender. Drain off all fat. Combine eggs, milk, cheese, oregano, and pepper; stir into sausage mixture. Turn into pie shell. Bake at 325° for 30 to 35 minutes or until knife inserted near center comes out clean. Spread top with pizza sauce; arrange cheese triangles over top of pie. Return to oven for 5 minutes. Cut pie into wedges and serve immediately. Yield: 4 to 6 servings.

Choucroute

3 (1-pound) cans sauerkraut or 3 pounds fresh sauerkraut
6 tablespoons bacon drippings
2 cups chopped onion
2 cloves garlic, minced
1 cup grated carrots (optional)
2 cups chicken stock
2 cups dry white wine
¼ cup gin
1 teaspoon freshly ground black pepper
2 pounds assorted uncooked link sausages, fresh or smoked
12 small whole, peeled potatoes
4 tablespoons butter
3 tablespoons chopped parsley

Put sauerkraut in colander and wash thoroughly with cold water to remove some of the salt. Melt bacon drippings in 3-quart casserole or Dutch oven. Add onion, garlic, and carrots. Cook for about 5 minutes, stirring constantly, until onion is wilted but not browned. Add drained sauerkraut, chicken stock, white wine, gin, and black pepper. Cover and place in preheated 325° oven. Bake for 2½ hours. At the end of 2½ hours, prick each sausage link 3 or 4 times and place links over sauerkraut; cover and bake for 1 hour. To serve, remove sausage, place sauerkraut on large platter, and top with sausages, either whole links or cut in 2-inch pieces. Sausages may be peeled, if desired. While sauerkraut is baking, boil potatoes until tender. Melt butter in saucepan and add parsley. Stir in potatoes and gently stir until potatoes are coated. Serve hot with sauerkraut and sausages. Yield: 6 servings.

Sausage and Bean Supper

½ pound dried lima beans
1 pint hot water
2 teaspoons salt
1 (20-ounce) can tomatoes
2 pounds sausage links
2 tablespoons water
1 small onion, sliced
1 tablespoon all-purpose flour
1 teaspoon dry mustard
1 tablespoon sugar
Dash black pepper

Cover beans with water and soak overnight. Drain. Add hot water and salt and cook until just tender, about 1 hour. Add tomatoes and continue cooking for 1 hour. Place sausage links and 2 tablespoons water in a cold frying pan. Cover and cook slowly for 8 to 10 minutes. Remove cover and brown the links. Remove links; pour off all but 2 tablespoons drippings. Brown onion in drippings. Blend in flour and add remaining ingredients. Combine with beans. Add sausage links to mixture and simmer for 10 minutes. Yield: 8 to 10 servings.

Weiner Schnitzel

4 (about ¾ inch thick) thin veal cutlets
1 teaspoon salt
¼ teaspoon pepper
½ cup all-purpose flour
1 egg, lightly beaten
2 tablespoons milk
¾ cup dry bread crumbs
¼ pound butter
Lemon wedges

Season veal with salt and pepper; coat well with flour. Dip in mixture of egg and milk, and roll in bread crumbs. In a large skillet, heat butter and fry schnitzel until brown. Turn only once. To insure tenderness, cover skillet for about 5 minutes at beginning of cooking. Remove to hot serving platter and serve with lemon wedges. Yield: 4 servings.

Veal Chops in Cream

6 (about 6 ounces each) veal chops
Salt and pepper to taste
Flour
6 tablespoons salad oil
2 tablespoons chopped onion
2 cups sliced fresh mushrooms
1 tablespoon all-purpose flour
1 cup half-and-half, divided
2 tablespoons cognac
2 egg yolks

Sprinkle chops generously with salt and pepper. Dip each chop in flour to coat evenly. Heat oil in heavy skillet. Add veal chops and cook until golden brown on one side; turn and brown other side. Cover and cook an additional 3 to 5 minutes. Remove chops and put on a warm platter.

Add onion to hot oil and cook for 1 to 2 minutes. Add mushrooms, cover skillet, and cook for about 5 minutes. Gradually stir in flour and mix well. Add ½ cup half-and-half and bring mixture to boiling. Stir in cognac. Beat egg yolks and stir into the remaining ½ cup half-and-half. Gradually add to hot sauce, stirring constantly. Pour sauce over hot veal chops. Yield: 6 servings.

Veal Milanese for Two

- 2 tablespoons margarine
- 1 small clove garlic, crushed
- 1 (2-ounce) can mushrooms, drained, liquid reserved
- 2 veal steaks (about 1/3 inch thick)
- 1 tablespoon minced onion
- 1/8 teaspoon rosemary
- 1/3 cup dry white wine*
- 1 chicken bouillon cube
- 1/2 cup commercial sour cream

Melt margarine in heavy skillet; add garlic and mushrooms. Sauté until slightly browned. Remove mushrooms and garlic and set aside. Brown veal in same margarine; add onion and cook until onion is transparent.

Add rosemary, reserved mushroom liquid, and wine to skillet containing veal. Add bouillon cube and stir to dissolve. Cover and simmer for 30 minutes or until meat is tender. Push meat to one side of skillet; blend sour cream into pan liquid, add mushroom-garlic mixture, and heat but do not bring to a boil. Serve with rice, creamed potatoes, or noodles. Yield: 2 servings.

*If you do not have wine, dissolve 1 chicken bouillon cube in 1/3 cup hot water and add instead of wine.

Veal Grillades and Grits

- 1/2 cup coarsely chopped celery
- 2 large onions, coarsely chopped
- 4 green peppers, coarsely chopped
- 4 cloves garlic, minced
- 2 bay leaves
- 1/2 cup shortening
- 4 to 6 ripe tomatoes, chopped
- 1 quart beef stock or water
- 2 tablespoons cornstarch
- 3 tablespoons water
- Salt and pepper to taste
- 6 (4 ounces each) veal steaks
- Seasoned all-purpose flour
- 1 tablespoon lard
- 1 cup regular grits

Sauté celery, onion, pepper, garlic, and bay leaves in shortening. Add tomatoes and beef stock and simmer for 20 minutes. Dissolve cornstarch in 3 tablespoons water; gradually stir into sauce mixture. Add salt and pepper and boil mixture until it thickens. Remove from heat.

Coat veal steaks in seasoned flour. Sauté in melted lard until brown. Arrange steaks in a baking dish, cover with sauce, and bake at 350° for 30 minutes or until veal is tender. Cook grits according to package directions and serve with veal. Yield: 6 servings.

Little Veal Pies

Filling:

- 6 boiling-size onions
- 2 cups chicken broth or bouillon, divided
- 1/4 cup all-purpose flour
- 1 teaspoon salt
- 1 cup cooked green peas
- 3/4 cup sliced mushrooms
- 2 1/2 cups diced, boiled, or roasted veal

Crust:

- 1 1/2 cups all-purpose flour
- 1/4 teaspoon baking powder
- 1/2 teaspoon salt
- 1/2 cup vegetable shortening (not oil)
- 5 to 6 tablespoons cold water

Parboil onions for about 10 minutes. Remove from heat and set aside. Heat 1 cup of the chicken broth. Mix together 1/4 cup flour, salt, and the remaining chicken broth; stir to make a smooth paste. Add to hot chicken broth and cook over low heat until thick, stirring constantly. Add peas, mushrooms, and diced veal. Continue cooking for 2 minutes, or until vegetables and meat are heated through.

Place a parboiled onion in each of 6 well-greased (10-ounce) glass deep pie dishes. Finish filling the 6 dishes with veal mixture.

Combine 1½ cups flour, baking powder, and ½ teaspoon salt. Cut in shortening until mixture resembles coarse meal. Add water, a little at a time, mixing only enough to hold ingredients together.

Place dough on a lightly floured surface and roll to about ⅛-inch thickness. Cut 6 circles the size of the top of the deep pie dishes. Slit crust circles to allow steam to escape. Place crust over the veal filling and bake at 425° about 30 minutes, or until crust is browned. Yield: 6 servings.

Mushroom-Stuffed Veal Roll

6 *tablespoons butter or margarine, divided*
¼ *cup chopped onion*
¼ *cup chopped green pepper*
1 *tablespoon chopped parsley*
½ *teaspoon grated lemon rind*
1 *teaspoon salt, divided*
½ *cup (4 livers) chopped raw chicken livers*
2 *egg yolks, slightly beaten*
2 *slices whole wheat bread, soaked in milk and drained*
2 *(3- or 4-ounce) cans chopped mushrooms*
¼ *cup Madeira*
1 *teaspoon dried leaf thyme, divided*
1 *(2-pound) veal cutlet slice, pounded thin*
2 *cups commercial sour cream*
1 *bay leaf*
1 *tablespoon all-purpose flour*
1 *(3- or 4-ounce) can sliced mushrooms*

Melt 2 tablespoons butter in a large skillet. Add onion, green pepper, parsley, lemon rind, and ½ teaspoon salt. Cook until vegetables are tender. Add chicken livers and cook until brown. Add egg yolks, bread, mushrooms with liquid, and Madeira. Simmer 5 minutes.

Sprinkle ½ teaspoon thyme and remaining ½ teaspoon salt over veal slice. Spread vegetable-liver filling on veal and roll loosely. Secure with string or skewers. Melt remaining 4 tablespoons butter in Dutch oven or flameproof casserole and brown veal roll on all sides.

Mix sour cream, bay leaf, and remaining ½ teaspoon thyme; pour over veal. Cover and bake at 325° for 1 hour. Remove from oven and transfer veal roll to heated platter. Blend flour with 2 tablespoons liquid from sliced mushrooms; stir into sauce. Drain remaining liquid from mushrooms; add sliced mushrooms to sauce. Cook, stirring constantly, until sauce thickens and comes to a boil. Serve with veal. Yield: 4 to 6 servings.

Stuffed Veal Birds in Sour Cream Gravy

½ *cup diced celery*
¼ *cup chopped onion*
½ *cup butter, divided*
2 *cups soft bread cubes*
¾ *teaspoon salt, divided*
⅛ *teaspoon sage*
Dash pepper
1 *tablespoon chopped parsley*
¼ *cup milk*
8 *(4 to 5 ounces each) boneless veal cutlets*
⅓ *cup all-purpose flour*
¼ *cup water*
¼ *cup white cooking wine*
½ *pint (1 cup) commercial sour cream*
1 *(4-ounce) can mushrooms, drained*

Sauté celery and onion in ¼ cup butter until onion is tender. Combine with bread cubes, salt, sage, pepper, parsley, and milk; toss lightly. Divide dressing evenly between cutlets, placing dressing in center of each cutlet.

Roll meat around dressing and fasten with tooth picks or skewers. Roll meat in flour, saving leftover flour. Brown meat in remaining ¼ cup butter, turning as necessary to brown on all sides. Add water and wine and cover tightly. Cook slowly until meat is tender, about 45 minutes. Remove meat to serving platter and keep warm.

Blend leftover flour and sour cream. Stir into drippings; add mushrooms and remaining ½ teaspoon salt. Cook, stirring constantly, until gravy is heated and thickened. Serve over veal. Yield: 8 servings.

Veal Marengo

  4 *pounds shoulder of veal*
  3 *tablespoons olive oil*
  1 *clove garlic, minced*
  1 *pound sliced mushrooms*
20 *small white onions*
  3 *tablespoons all-purpose flour*
2½ *teaspoons salt*
½ *teaspoon freshly ground black pepper*
  2 *cups canned tomato sauce or 4 large tomatoes, peeled, seeded, and chopped*
  1 *cup dry white wine*
  2 *cups chicken broth*
     Bouquet garni (celery, parsley, bay leaf, thyme)

This is a large recipe: half is to be served immediately; the remainder is to be frozen. You will need two 3-quart casseroles, not necessarily the same shape. Line them with heavy-duty aluminum foil.

Cut the veal into 1½-inch cubes. Heat olive oil and garlic in a large skillet and brown the veal, placing just enough in the skillet at a time to cover the bottom. Place veal in the 2 casseroles, dividing it equally. Add a little additional oil to the skillet if necessary; brown mushrooms very quickly and lightly, then onions, and arrange over meat. Add flour, salt, and pepper to the skillet, stirring them into remaining oil. Add tomato sauce or chopped tomatoes, wine, and broth. Cook, stirring constantly, until thickened and smooth. Pour over veal mixtures. Add to each casserole a small herb bouquet consisting of a 3-inch celery stalk with leaves, 2 sprigs parsley, 1 bay leaf, and a bit of fresh thyme. Tie together with stem of the parsley.

Cover casseroles (use heavy-duty aluminum foil, if casseroles lack covers). Bake at 325° for 1¼ hours. Remove herb bouquets. One casserole may be put in the freezer.

To reheat, place in oven. Solidly frozen, it will take 1 hour at 325° to cook. It will take less time if taken from freezer early in the day and allowed to stand at room temperature until almost thawed. Yield: 6 servings per casserole.

*Potato 'n Frank Casserole

1 *(12-ounce) package frozen potato patties*
3 *franks, sliced*
2 *tablespoons finely chopped onion*
    Dash salt
    Dash pepper
¾ *cup milk*
1 *tablespoon butter*

Layer the patties, franks, and chopped onion in a greased 1½-quart casserole. Sprinkle with salt and pepper, pour milk over the top, and dot with butter. Cover and bake at 350° until the potatoes are tender, about 1 hour. Stir with fork to break up potato patties after 15 minutes of baking and again 30 minutes later. Yield: 3 or 4 servings.

Chinese Pepper Strips

  1 *(½-pound) package fully cooked all-meat weiners*
  1 *tablespoon salad oil*
  1 *small onion, sliced*
  1 *(2-ounce) jar mushrooms, drained*
  1 *clove garlic, minced*
1½ *tablespoons soy sauce*
  1 *tablespoon cornstarch*
  1 *beef bouillon cube*
½ *cup boiling water*
  1 *green pepper, cut into 1-inch strips*
  1 *tomato, cut into eighths*
  1 *(1-pound) package Chinese mixed vegetables or 1 cup hot cooked rice*

Cut weiners into 4 lengthwise strips. Heat oil in skillet or wok. Add weiners, onion, mushrooms, and garlic. Cook until onion is tender; remove garlic. Gradually stir soy sauce into cornstarch; blend well. Dissolve bouillon cube in boiling water; add to soy sauce mixture and stir into mixture in skillet. Cook, stirring constantly, until sauce is translucent and thickened. Stir in green pepper and tomato. Remove from heat and let stand for several minutes, until vegetables are heated through. Serve over Chinese vegetables or rice. Yield: 2 servings.

*Party Franks

- 3 large shredded wheat biscuits, finely crushed
- ⅓ cup finely chopped green pepper
- ⅓ cup finely chopped onion
- ⅓ cup finely chopped celery
- ⅓ cup catsup
- ⅓ cup melted butter or margarine
- ½ teaspoon salt
- ¼ teaspoon pepper
- 1 pound frankfurters

Measure 1 cup crumbs from shredded wheat biscuits. Combine crumbs with green pepper, onion, celery, catsup, butter, salt, and pepper. Mix well. Slit frankfurters down center, and stuff with cereal mixture. Divide stuffing evenly between all frankfurters. Place on lightly greased baking sheet and bake at 350° for 15 minutes. Yield: 8 to 10 servings.

*Curried Frankfurters

- 1 pound frankfurters
- 2 tablespoons butter or margarine
- 2 small onions, chopped
- 1 clove garlic, minced
- 2 tablespoons curry powder
- 1 teaspoon salt
- 1 (8-ounce) can tomato sauce
- 1 cup beef broth (canned, homemade, or made with 1 beef bouillon cube and 1 cup hot water)
- 3 tablespoons lemon juice
- ½ cup half-and-half
- Rice or noodles
- Chutney (optional)

Cut frankfurters into bite-size pieces. Melt butter in a saucepan. Add onion and garlic and cook until tender. Sprinkle in curry powder and salt; stir to blend. Add tomato sauce and beef broth. Cook over low heat, stirring occasionally, about 30 minutes. Stir in lemon juice, then half-and-half. Add frankfurters and cook just long enough to heat franks. Serve with rice or noodles. Pass chutney if desired. Yield: 4 servings.

Frank Pineapple Kabobs

- 8 frankfurters
- 8 slices bacon
- 1 large green pepper
- 1 (20-ounce) can pineapple chunks, drained
- ¼ cup salad oil
- 2 teaspoons Worcestershire sauce
- 2 tablespoons pineapple syrup
- Liquid smoke (optional)
- 8 frankfurter buns, buttered

Cut each frank into 3 pieces. Cut bacon and green pepper into squares. Alternate franks, green pepper, bacon, and pineapple chunks on skewers. Do not place too close together on skewer or bacon will not cook crisp. Brush kabobs with blend of salad oil, Worcestershire sauce, pineapple syrup, and a little liquid smoke if desired. Broil over glowing coals about 5 inches from heat for 7 to 12 minutes, or until well browned on all sides. Brush with the marinade as you grill. Slide off skewers into buttered frankfurter buns. Yield: 8 kabobs.

*Frank-Corn Muffin Casserole

- ¼ cup margarine or butter
- 1 tablespoon chopped onion
- 3 tablespoons all-purpose flour
- 1 tablespoon prepared mustard
- ½ teaspoon salt
- 2 cups milk
- 1 pound franks, cut into 1-inch pieces
- 1 (10-ounce) package frozen peas or 2 cups canned peas
- 1 (12-ounce) package corn muffin mix

Melt the margarine. Add the onion and brown lightly. Blend in flour, mustard, and salt; slowly add milk. Stir and cook until thickened. Add franks and peas; heat until boiling. Pour into a 13- x 9- x 2-inch baking dish.

Prepare corn muffin batter according to directions on the package. Drop the batter by tablespoonfuls along the edges of the hot frank mixture. Bake at 375° for 30 minutes or until topping is a golden brown. Yield: 6 servings.

Sweet-and-Sour Franks

1 (12- to 16-ounce) jar currant jelly
1 (6-ounce) jar prepared mustard
2 (1-pound) packages frankfurters, cut into 1-inch slices

Melt jelly and combine with mustard; cool. Stir franks into cooled mixture and marinate in refrigerator several hours or overnight. At serving time, warm thoroughly over low heat, stirring constantly. Serve piping hot with toothpicks. Yield: about 100 cocktail franks.

Little Links Teriyaki

2 tablespoons cornstarch
1 teaspoon sugar
2 tablespoons soy sauce
1 (10½-ounce) can condensed beef broth
1 (2-ounce) can mushrooms, drained
3 (5½-ounce) packages little wieners

Combine cornstarch, sugar, and soy sauce in saucepan or chafing dish. Gradually stir in beef broth. Cook over medium heat until mixture thickens. Add mushrooms and little wieners. Cook until heated through, about 5 minutes. Serve with toothpicks. Yield: 48 appetizers.

*Blanketed Franks

1 (10-ounce) package refrigerated biscuits
Prepared mustard
Caraway or celery seeds
1 pound franks
1 egg, beaten

Roll biscuits thin and spread with prepared mustard; sprinkle with caraway or celery seeds. Place 1 frank on each circle and roll up. Place on greased baking sheet with lapped side down. Brush tops with beaten egg, and bake at 400° for about 15 minutes. Yield: 10 servings.

Corn 'n Franks

⅓ cup chopped onion
5 tablespoons butter
⅓ cup sliced green pepper
2 (12-ounce) cans whole kernel yellow corn
⅔ cup pitted black olives
⅓ cup shredded Swiss cheese
6 beef franks
⅓ cup tomato puree
Grated Parmesan cheese

Sauté onion in butter. Add green pepper strips and sauté until tender. Drain liquid from corn and olives. Add corn and olives to onion and pepper. Stir in Swiss cheese. Place in 1½-quart baking dish; place franks, slashed diagonally, over corn mixture. Top with tomato puree and a sprinkling of Parmesan cheese. Bake at 350° for 26 minutes. Yield: 6 servings.

Sweet and Pungent Frankfurters

1 pound frankfurters
1 (8¼-ounce) can sliced pineapple
½ cup firmly packed brown sugar
½ cup vinegar
1 tablespoon soy sauce
1 cup water
3 tablespoons cornstarch
¼ cup water
1 green pepper, cut into strips
1 tomato, cut into wedges
Rice

Cut frankfurters into bite-size lengths. Drain juice from pineapple into saucepan. Cut pineapple slices in half and reserve. Add brown sugar, vinegar, soy sauce, and 1 cup water to pineapple juice. Bring to a boil. Combine cornstarch and ¼ cup water. Add to mixture in pan. Cook, stirring constantly, until thickened. Add green pepper, pineapple, and tomato wedges. Cook 2 minutes. Add frankfurters and cook just long enough to heat frankfurters. Serve with rice. Yield: 4 servings.

*Chip 'n Cheese Wieners

    10 weiners
     1 cup shredded pasteurized process American
         cheese
    ½   cup crushed potato chips
     1 tablespoon minced onion
     1 tablespoon catsup
     1 teaspoon Worcestershire sauce

Slit wieners lengthwise, almost through. Flatten and broil, cut side down, 6 inches from heat for 5 minutes or until heated through. Meanwhile, combine cheese, potato chips, onion, catsup, and Worcestershire sauce. Spread on cut side of wieners. Broil until cheese melts. Yield: 5 to 10 servings.

*Corn Dogs

    1½ cups all-purpose flour
     2 tablespoons sugar
     ¾ teaspoon salt
    1½ teaspoons baking powder
    1½ teaspoons dry mustard
     ¾ cup cornmeal
     1 egg
    1⅓ cups milk
     1 tablespoon salad oil
     1 pound franks
     ½ cup all-purpose flour
         Shortening for deep-fat frying

Sift together 1½ cups flour, sugar, salt, baking powder, and dry mustard. Stir in cornmeal. Beat egg; add milk and salad oil together. Add to flour mixture and stir until blended. Stick wooden skewers into ends of franks. Wipe franks with a dry cloth. Dust with flour; then dip in batter. Drop into hot fat (375°) and fry until golden brown. Drain on paper towels. Serve hot. Yield: 10 to 12 corn dogs.

Marinated Franks

    ½   cup wine vinegar
    ⅓   cup salad oil
     1 tablespoon lemon juice
     1 teaspoon tarragon
     1 clove garlic, minced
    ½   teaspoon salt
    ½   teaspoon white pepper
     1 pound cocktail frankfurters, drained
         Hot bouillon or consommé
         Raw vegetables

Mix vinegar, oil, lemon juice, and seasonings in a jar. Add the frankfurters. Cover tightly and refrigerate for several days. Serve cold with demitasse cups of hot bouillon or clear consommé and colorful raw vegetables. Yield: 6 servings.

Rancho Hot Dogs

    ¾   cup chili sauce
     3 tablespoons corn syrup
     3 tablespoons vinegar
     1 tablespoon Worcestershire sauce
     1 tablespoon prepared mustard
    10 franks
     5 hamburger buns
    1½ cups canned baked beans

Combine first 5 ingredients to make sauce. Score franks halfway through and 1 inch apart (makes them curl as they cook); grill, basting often with sauce. When franks are sizzling hot, put 2 franks on hamburger bun to form a ring; fill center with hot baked beans. Top with more sauce. Yield: 5 servings.

Glorified Pork Suey

1½ pounds pork shoulder
2 tablespoons shortening
½ cup chopped celery leaves
¼ cup soy sauce
2 teaspoons sugar
1 cup water
1 (10-ounce) package frozen green beans, thawed
1 cup sliced celery
2 tablespoons sherry (optional)
Salt and pepper to taste
Hot cooked rice

Cut pork into 1-inch cubes. Brown in hot shortening; drain off any excess fat. Add celery leaves, soy sauce, sugar, and water. Cover and cook over low heat until meat is almost tender, about 1½ hours. Add green beans and celery and cook until beans are tender, adding more water if necessary. Add sherry and season with salt and pepper. Serve over hot rice. Yield: 4 to 6 servings.

Tenderloin Sweet 'n Sour

1 (3- to 4-pound) pork tenderloin
2 cloves garlic, crushed
2 teaspoons salt
¾ cup beef consommé
¾ cup orange marmalade
¼ teaspoon pepper
¼ teaspoon ground ginger
3 tablespoons vinegar

Place pork tenderloin in a shallow glass dish. Combine remaining ingredients and pour over pork. Cover and refrigerate for several hours or overnight. Remove pork from marinade and drain well; place on grill over hot coals. Grill, turning often, for 45 minutes. Baste with marinade and grill for an additional 30 to 45 minutes, or until meat tests done with meat thermometer. For a richly glazed roast, turn meat often and baste each time meat is turned. Yield: 4 to 6 servings.

Baked Pork Tenderloin with Apricot Topping

1 (3-pound) fresh pork tenderloin
Salt and pepper to taste
¼ cup apple brandy
2 tablespoons soy sauce
2 tablespoons firmly packed brown sugar
¾ cup apricot puree (make puree by mashing canned, skinned apricots)
Mustard Sauce

Lightly score the tenderloin fat. Sprinkle very lightly with salt and pepper. Marinate the pork in a mixture made of the brandy, soy sauce, and brown sugar for several hours, turning the meat often. Drain off the marinade and reserve it. Place the pork in a baking dish and spread the top and sides with apricot puree. Bake at 325° for 1 hour and 15 minutes or until meat is tender and topping is browned. Baste the meat with the reserved marinade at frequent intervals. To serve, slice thin and serve with Mustard Sauce. Yield: 3 to 4 servings.

Mustard Sauce:

½ cup mayonnaise
1 tablespoon prepared mustard
1 tablespoon tarragon vinegar
Ground pepper to taste

Mix ingredients well and serve as an accompaniment with the meat.

*Braised Pork Shoulder with Lima Beans

1 cup dried lima beans
2½ cups hot water
1 teaspoon salt
4 pork shoulder steaks
3 tablespoons shortening
1 small onion, chopped
1 teaspoon salt
⅛ teaspoon pepper
1 bay leaf
2 tablespoons firmly packed brown sugar
2 tablespoons vinegar
1 cup hot water

Wash lima beans and remove all imperfect ones. Put in a 2-quart saucepan, add 2½ cups hot water, and boil for 2 minutes. Remove from heat, cover, and let stand for 1 hour. Add 1 teaspoon salt and simmer for 1 hour, or until beans are tender. (Add more water during cooking, if necessary.)

Brown steaks in hot shortening; add onion, and cook until lightly browned. Remove steaks from skillet. To drippings add beans and their liquid, 1 teaspoon salt, pepper, bay leaf, brown sugar, vinegar, and 1 cup hot water. Arrange steaks on beans, cover, and cook on low heat for 1 to 1¼ hours, or until meat is tender. Yield: 4 servings.

Canadian Bacon Wheels with Pineapple Slices

   6 *slices Canadian bacon*
   6 *slices canned pineapple*
   6 *teaspoons brown sugar*

Place Canadian bacon slices in cold skillet. Cook at low heat, browning on both sides. Drain on paper towels. Place pineapple slices on baking sheet, sprinkle with brown sugar, and broil until sugar is melted. Top cooked Canadian bacon slice with pineapple and serve hot. Yield: 6 servings.

Grilled Pork Chops

   2 *cups seedless raisins*
   1 *cup water*
   1 *cup honey*
  ½ *cup margarine, melted*
   2 *lemons, cut into slices*
   2 *tablespoons Worcestershire sauce*
   8 *pork chops, 1 inch thick*

Combine all ingredients except pork chops to make marinade. Pour over pork chops and marinate for 4 to 8 hours in refrigerator. Place pork chops on heavy-duty aluminum foil; pour marinade over chops. Close aluminum foil securely. Cook on grill over medium heat for 1 hour or until pork chops are done. Yield: 8 servings.

Saucy Pork Chops

   6 *pork chops, ½ to ¾ inch thick*
   1 *tablespoon shortening*
   Salt and pepper to taste
   1 *medium onion, thinly sliced*
   1 *(10¾-ounce) can condensed cream of chicken soup*
  ¼ *cup catsup*
   2 *tablespoons Worcestershire sauce*

Brown pork chops in skillet in hot shortening. Season with salt and pepper; top with onion slices. Combine soup, catsup, and Worcestershire sauce; pour over chops. Cover skillet and simmer for 40 to 60 minutes. Remove chops to warm platter and spoon sauce over. Yield: 6 servings.

Pork Chops with Scalloped Potatoes

   2 *cups thinly sliced raw potatoes*
   1 *small onion, sliced*
   1 *teaspoon salt*
   Pepper to taste
   4 *loin or rib pork chops (½ to ¾ inch thick)*
   4 *tablespoons all-purpose flour, divided*
   1 *cup milk*

Arrange potatoes and onion in layers in a greased 3-quart baking dish, seasoning each layer with salt and pepper. Trim fat from pork chops and save for later use. Lightly season each chop with salt and pepper and coat well with 3 tablespoons flour. Brown chops on both sides in some of the pork fat in a skillet. When chops are well browned, remove from pan, and set aside all but 1 tablespoon drippings from skillet. Mix the remaining 1 tablespoon flour with the drippings in the pan. Add milk, blend lightly until smooth, and cook to the consistency of thin white sauce. Pour sauce over potatoes in baking dish. Top with browned chops. Cover the baking dish. Bake at 350° for 50 to 60 minutes or until potatoes are soft and meat is tender. Yield: 4 servings.

Sweet-Sour Pork

1½ pounds boneless pork, cut into 1-inch cubes
Corn oil
Salt and pepper to taste
½ cup bottled barbecue sauce
½ cup pineapple juice
¼ cup vinegar
1 tablespoon cornstarch
1 (20-ounce) can pineapple chunks, drained
1 green pepper, cut into strips
Cooked rice

Brown meat in a small amount of corn oil. Season with salt and pepper; stir in mixture of barbecue sauce, pineapple juice, vinegar, and cornstarch. Cover and simmer for 35 minutes. Add pineapple and green pepper; simmer 10 minutes longer. Serve with hot rice. Yield: 6 servings.

Stuffed Pork Chops

¾ cup croutons (bread cubes browned in butter)
1 tablespoon chopped parsley
½ teaspoon salt
Dash pepper
2 tablespoons melted butter or margarine
2 (1½-inch thick) pork chops, with pocket cut alongside of bone
1 tablespoon shortening
1 (10½-ounce) can consommé
¾ cup water, divided
2 tablespoons all-purpose flour

Mix croutons with parsley, salt, pepper, and butter. Stuff chops with crouton mixture. Place shortening in frying pan and brown chops well on both sides. Add consommé and ½ cup water. Cover and reduce heat to medium low. Cook for about 1 hour or until tender. Remove chops from pan. To make gravy, measure remaining liquid, adding enough water to fill 1 cup. Return liquid to pan. Place ¼ cup water and flour in screw-top jar and shake well. Add flour and water mixture to meat stock and cook over low heat until smooth and thickened, stirring constantly. Yield: 2 servings.

Hawaiian Pork Chops with Dressing

6 lean pork chops, about ¾ inch thick
½ cup chopped green onions
½ cup chopped green pepper
1 cup chopped celery
2 tablespoons butter or margarine
3 cups cooked rice
½ cup crushed pineapple, drained
⅓ cup flaked coconut
1 tablespoon grated orange rind
1 teaspoon salt
¼ cup pineapple juice
¼ cup orange juice
1 tablespoon firmly packed brown sugar
1 teaspoon prepared mustard
1 tablespoon steak sauce

Brown pork chops slowly in lightly greased skillet. Cover and cook until almost tender, about 30 minutes. Sauté onions, pepper, and celery in butter until tender, but not browned. Add rice, pineapple, coconut, orange rind, and salt. Toss lightly. Turn into a shallow casserole and top with pork chops. Mix remaining ingredients for glaze and brush over pork chops. Bake at 375° for 30 minutes, brushing pork chops 2 or 3 times with the glaze mixture. Yield: 6 servings.

Braised Pork Chops

6 or 7 double saltine crackers
⅛ teaspoon salt
⅛ teaspoon ground ginger
⅛ teaspoon grated lemon rind
2 loin pork chops, about 1 inch thick
1 clove garlic, peeled and cut in half
1 egg, beaten
1 tablespoon water
2 tablespoons vegetable oil
¼ cup dry vermouth
1 (3-ounce) can mushrooms, drained

Crush crackers into fine crumbs (there should be about ½ cup). Mix with salt, ginger, and lemon rind; set aside. Trim excess fat from pork chops and rub each chop with cut garlic. Roll chops in mixture of egg and water, then in prepared crumbs. Let stand at room temperature for about 15 minutes to "set" the crumbs. (They may be prepared early in the morning, covered, and placed in refrigerator until needed.)

Heat oil in 10-inch skillet over moderate heat. Add chops and brown on both sides. Lower heat, and add vermouth and mushrooms. Cover skillet and simmer slowly until tender and done, about 45 minutes, turning chops once.

Note: chops may be baked, covered, at 375° for about 45 minutes to 1 hour. Yield: 2 servings.

Spanish Pork Chop Bake

- 6 slices bacon
- 6 pork chops, cut ½ inch thick
- 1 cup uncooked regular rice
- 1 10½-ounce can tomato soup, undiluted
- 2½ cups canned tomato juice
- 1 cup water
- ¼ cup diced green pepper
- 1 small onion, diced
- 1 teaspoon salt
- ¼ teaspoon pepper

Brown bacon until crisp; remove and crumble. Drain all but 1 tablespoon bacon drippings from pan and brown pork chops on both sides; set aside. In a greased 13- x 9- x 2-inch baking dish, combine and mix thoroughly the rice, soup, juice, water, green pepper, onion, and bacon. Cover tightly with foil and bake at 350° for 30 minutes. Remove; arrange pork chops over rice mixture, sprinkle with salt and pepper, and bake an additional 30 to 40 minutes or until rice is tender. Yield: 6 servings.

Spicy Glazed Pork Chops with Apricots

- 2 (17-ounce) cans whole apricots
- 1 tablespoon bottled steak sauce
- 1 teaspoon salt
- 6 rib or loin pork chops, cut ½ inch thick
- 1 teaspoon whole cloves

Drain syrup from apricots into medium-size saucepan; stir in steak sauce and salt. Heat to boiling; cook, uncovered, for 15 minutes or until syrup thickens slightly. Save apricots for later use.

Brush chops on both sides with half of syrup; arrange in single layer in shallow baking pan. Do not cover.

Bake at 400° for 45 minutes; turn chops. Stud apricots with cloves; arrange around chops. Brush with remaining syrup. Bake 30 minutes longer or until chops are tender and richly glazed. Yield: 6 servings.

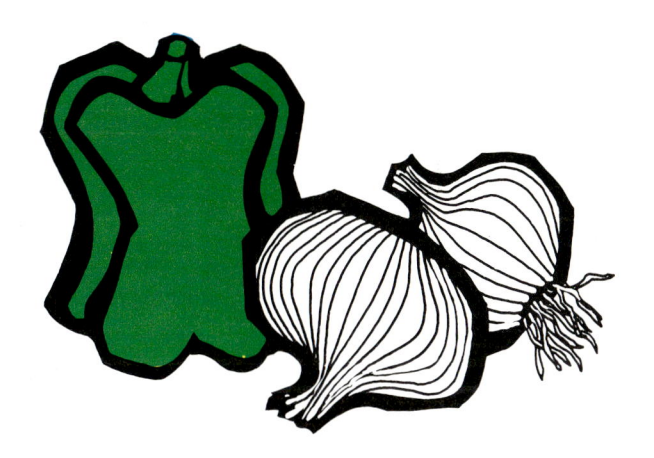

Baked Stuffed Pork Chops

- ½ cup water
- ¼ cup butter
- 1 cup herb-seasoned stuffing
- 2 tablespoons chopped parsley
- 6 thick pork chops, cut with pockets
- 2 tablespoons shortening
- ¼ cup water

Heat water, add butter, and stir until butter melts. Add stuffing and parsley, tossing with fork until crumbs are thoroughly moistened. Fill pockets of chops with stuffing; secure with toothpicks. Brown chops on both sides in melted shortening. Arrange in baking dish. Stir ¼ cup water into skillet drippings; pour over chops. Cover. Bake at 350° for 45 minutes. Uncover; continue baking 15 minutes more or until chops are tender. Yield: 6 servings.

Dixie Pork Chops

    8 pork chops
    2 tablespoons shortening
  ½ teaspoon salt
  ½ teaspoon ground sage
    4 apples, cored and cut into rings
  ¼ cup firmly packed brown sugar
    2 tablespoons all-purpose flour
    1 cup hot water
      Few drops vinegar
  ½ cup seedless raisins

Brown chops in hot shortening. Remove chops and save drippings. Put chops in a shallow baking dish; sprinkle with salt and sage. Top with apple rings and sprinkle with sugar. In skillet blend drippings, flour, water, and vinegar; cook until thick. Add raisins and pour over chops. Bake, uncovered, at 350° for 1 hour. Yield: 8 servings.

Fried Ham with Red-Eye Gravy

Slice ham about ¼ to ½ inch thick. Cut gashes in fat to keep ham from curling. Place slices in a heavy skillet and cook slowly. Turn several times, and cook until ham is brown. Remove from pan and keep warm. To the drippings in the skillet, add about ½ cup hot water; cook until gravy turns red. A little strong coffee might be added to deepen the color. Serve hot with fried ham and hot biscuits.

Molasses Barbecued Ham

    6 slices precooked ham
  ½ cup chopped green pepper
    1 tablespoon salad oil
    1 (6-ounce) can tomato paste
    1 teaspoon cider vinegar
  ½ teaspoon Worcestershire sauce
  1½ teaspoons molasses

Let slices of ham sizzle on the grill for 2 minutes. Sauté green pepper in salad oil; add other ingredients and brush over ham until ham is thoroughly heated. Yield: 6 servings.

Ham Loaf

  ¾ pound ground smoked ham
  ¾ pound ground lean pork
  ¼ cup fine bread crumbs
  ⅛ teaspoon ground cloves
  ½ teaspoon dry mustard
    1 teaspoon Worcestershire sauce
    2 eggs, beaten
  ½ cup tomato juice
  ½ cup milk
  ¼ cup firmly packed brown sugar
    3 slices canned pineapple, drained

Thoroughly mix all ingredients together except brown sugar and pineapple slices. Sprinkle brown sugar evenly on bottom of well-greased loaf baking dish. Cut pineapple slices in half and place on top of sugar. With spoon, spread ham mixture over pineapple. Bake at 350° for 1 hour. Yield: 6 to 8 servings.

Baked Stuffed Ham

  12 -pound fully cooked ham
  ½ cup chopped onion
  ½ cup chopped celery
  ½ cup butter or margarine, melted
    5 cups soft bread crumbs
    2 teaspoons poultry seasoning
  ½ cup light molasses

Place ham in large baking pan. Add about 2 inches boiling water, cover, and simmer on top of range for 1 hour. Cool slightly; trim off rind and fat, leaving about ¼-inch layer of fat. Sauté onion and celery in butter until soft but not brown. Add to bread crumbs in a large bowl. Add poultry seasoning and toss to mix. Place ham, fat-side up, in large shallow pan. Make 2-inch deep cuts in ham, about 1½ inches apart. Press stuffing mixture firmly into cuts. Bake at 325° for about 30 minutes. Brush molasses over ham between rows of stuffing. Continue baking for an additional 45 minutes, brushing ham with molasses every 15 minutes. Yield: 8 to 12 servings.

Stuffed Fresh Ham Merrifield

1 (8- to 10-pound) fresh ham, boned
½ cup bottled Russian dressing
½ cup bourbon
Salt and pepper to taste
1 (9-inch) square corn bread, crumbled, or 5 cups cornbread crumbs
½ pound fresh mushrooms, chopped (or equivalent amount of canned ones, drained)
1 medium-size onion, chopped
1 tablespoon butter
1 pound hot pork sausage
1 (5-ounce) can pimientos, coarsely cut
1 cup boiling water

The day or night before roasting: Cut into, but not through, the thick sides of the boned ham to further open and flatten it. Remove all excess fat. Prepare a marinade of Russian dressing and bourbon. Rub the ham on all cut sides with salt and pepper. Pour the marinade over it and refrigerate overnight. A large plastic bag is ideal for marinating meat, for it keeps liquid in contact with the meat without your having to turn it. Crumble corn bread into a large mixing bowl. Sauté the chopped mushrooms and onion in skillet with butter until soft but not brown. Add to the corn bread crumbs. In the same skillet, sauté the sausage, breaking it up with a wooden spoon, but not browning it. It doesn't have to cook completely at this point. Combine sausage with the crumbs, mushrooms, onion, and pimientos, adding boiling water for consistency, which should be moderately dry; it will take on added moisture from the meat. Drain and reserve marinade from the meat. Spread dressing over cut-side of ham and roll up as tightly as possible. Skewer and/or tie securely with string. Place ham, fat-side up, in open roasting pan and roast 30 minutes per pound or until meat thermometer lodged in meat registers 185°. (If thermometer is lodged in dressing, it will read 165°.) Baste with reserved marinade twice during roasting. Yield: 24 servings.

Note: To keep the dressing corralled during baking, tear a sheet of aluminum foil long enough to reach around circumference of ham; fold twice lengthwise and wrap around bottom half of ham, leaving top half exposed. Fasten with toothpicks. After 2 hours of roasting, you may want to cap the ham with a loose bonnet of foil to prevent overbrowning. Liquor in these recipes is for flavor only. Alcohol itself cooks away at temperatures above 170°, leaving only the essence of flavor.

Grilled Ham

1 center-cut ham, 2 inches thick
2 (8-ounce) cans sweet and sour sauce
1 (15¼-ounce) can pineapple chunks, drained (liquid reserved)

Put ham in a flat, shallow pan. Combine sweet and sour sauce and the juice from the pineapple; pour over ham and let stand for 4½ hours. Remove ham and place on grill set on low heat. Brush with marinade as ham cooks. Grill for at least 2½ to 3 hours. Garnish with pineapple chunks. Yield: 4 to 6 servings.

Polynesian Ham

3 cups chopped cooked ham
2 tablespoons butter
2 small green peppers, cut into strips
1 (13¼-ounce) can pineapple tidbits
½ cup firmly packed brown sugar
2 tablespoons cornstarch
½ cup vinegar
½ cup chicken bouillon
2 teaspoons soy sauce
1 (4-ounce) can sliced mushrooms
3 cups cooked rice

Brown the ham pieces lightly in butter. Add green pepper strips and pineapple with syrup. Cover and simmer for 15 minutes. Mix brown sugar and cornstarch; add vinegar, bouillon, and soy sauce. Add to ham mixture along with mushrooms and liquid, and stir until thickened. Serve over hot cooked rice. Yield: 6 servings.

Party Ham Loaf

  1 *(10¾-ounce) can condensed cream of mushroom soup*
1½ *pounds ground cooked ham*
 ½ *pound ground pork*
 ½ *cup bread cubes*
 ½ *cup finely chopped onion*
  2 *eggs, slightly beaten*
  1 *teaspoon dry mustard*
  3 *pineapple slices, cut in 6 halves*
 ½ *cup commercial sour cream*

Thoroughly mix ⅓ cup soup, meat, bread, onion, eggs, and mustard. Shape into loaf. Press pineapple slices deeply into loaf. Place in shallow baking pan; bake at 350° for 1¼ hours. In saucepan blend remaining soup and sour cream; heat, stirring occasionally, and serve over ham loaf. Yield: 6 to 8 servings.

Upside-Down Ham Loaf

  4 *cups (about 1 pound) ground cooked ham*
  1 *small onion, chopped*
  2 *cups herb-seasoned croutons*
 ½ *cup hot water*
  2 *eggs, slightly beaten*
 ¼ *cup firmly packed brown sugar*
 ½ *teaspoon ground cloves*
  4 *pineapple slices*

Combine ham and onion. Soak croutons in hot water; add eggs and ham mixture, and mix well. Line an 8- x 5-inch loaf pan with foil. Sprinkle brown sugar and cloves over foil in bottom of pan. Arrange pineapple slices in pan. Press meat mixture into loaf pan. Bake at 400° for 1 hour. Turn out of pan; remove foil. Yield: 4 to 6 servings.

Glazed Smoked Ham

10- *to* 13-*pound bone-in ham, fully cooked*
Whole cloves
Orange Glaze

Place ham on rack in shallow roasting pan. Insert meat thermometer so the bulb reaches the center of the thickest part. The bulb should not touch bone or rest in fat. Do not add water. Roast, uncovered, at 325° until thermometer registers 140°. About 20 to 30 minutes before ham is done, decorate with cloves and spread with Orange Glaze. Return to oven to finish cooking and to set glaze. Yield: 10 to 12 servings.

Orange Glaze:

  1 *cup firmly packed brown sugar*
  1 *tablespoon all-purpose flour*
  1 *teaspoon dry mustard*
  1 *tablespoon vinegar*
  3 *tablespoons frozen orange juice, undiluted*

Combine all ingredients and stir until smooth. Yield: ¾ cup.

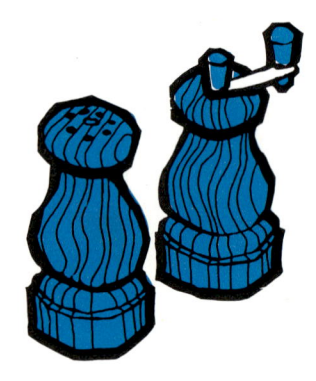

Country-Cured Ham

Scrub ham with a stiff brush and put it in a very large pot (old-fashioned wash boiler or a large lard stand). Cover the ham with cold water and let soak for 18 to 24 hours. Pour off water; place pot on range and add fresh cold water to cover ham. Cover pot. Bring water to a boil; reduce heat immediately to simmer, and let cook for 25 minutes per pound. Be sure that water is always kept below the boiling point. When ham is done, the end bones will protrude and loosen. Turn the ham once or twice during cooking. Let ham cool in the water in which it was cooked. When cool, remove ham and cut off the rind. Score the fat, being careful not to cut into the meat. Glaze and decorate as desired.

Deviled Ham Loaf

  2 *cups dry bread crumbs*
  2 *cups milk*
  3 *cups ground cooked ham*
  2 *eggs, beaten*
  2 *tablespoons grated onion*
  1 *teaspoon prepared mustard*
  2 *tablespoons chopped green pepper*
     Salt and pepper to taste

Soak bread crumbs in milk for 5 minutes. Add ham, eggs, onion, mustard, and green pepper; mix well. Add salt and pepper. Place in a 9- x 5- x 3-inch loaf pan and bake at 350° for about 50 minutes. Yield: 8 to 10 servings.

Creamed Ham and Eggs

  ½ *cup butter or margarine*
  ½ *cup all-purpose flour*
  1 *teaspoon salt*
  1 *teaspoon sugar*
  2 *tablespoons prepared mustard*
  ¼ *cup strong coffee*
     Few drops hot sauce
  1 *quart milk or half-and-half*
  1 *dozen eggs, hard cooked and sliced*
  2 *pounds cooked ham, cut ½ inch thick and cubed*

Melt butter. Smoothly blend in next 6 ingredients. Add milk or half-and-half; cook and stir over medium heat until smooth and thickened. Add eggs and ham. Heat to serving temperature. Yield: 8 servings.

Ham and Cheese Biscuit Pleasers

  1 *(8-ounce) can refrigerated buttermilk or country-style biscuits*
10 *thin slices boiled ham*
10 *(1-inch) cubes Swiss or Cheddar cheese*
  ¾ *cup finely crushed onion cracker crumbs or other seasoned cracker crumbs*
  ¼ *cup butter or margarine, melted*

Separate biscuit dough into 10 biscuits. Pat or roll out each to a 4-inch circle. Wrap ham slice around cheese cube. Wrap biscuit dough around ham and cheese cube, pressing edges to seal. Dip in butter, then in cracker crumbs. Place seam side down on ungreased cookie sheet. Bake at 425° for 10 to 15 minutes until golden brown. Yield: 10 sandwiches.

Special Barbecued Ribs

  1 *tablespoon celery seeds*
  1 *tablespoon chili powder*
  ¼ *cup firmly packed brown sugar*
  1 *tablespoon salt*
  1 *teaspoon paprika*
2½ *pounds loin-back ribs*
  1 *(8-ounce) can tomato sauce*
  ¼ *cup vinegar*

Combine first 5 ingredients and spread a third of this mixture over ribs. To the remaining mixture add tomato sauce and vinegar. Heat mixture and brush over ribs often while they are grilling over a low fire, about 40 minutes to 1 hour. Yield: 3 to 4 servings.

Spit Barbecued Spareribs

  1 *cup barbecue sauce*
  ½ *cup water*
  ¼ *cup molasses*
  ¼ *cup vinegar*
  3 *tablespoons Worcestershire sauce*
  2 *teaspoons salt*
  ½ *teaspoon dry mustard*
  ¼ *teaspoon pepper*
  2 *cloves garlic, minced*
  4 *pounds meaty spareribs*

Mix first 9 ingredients for sauce, and let stand a few hours before using. Lace spareribs on spit. Let ribs rotate over low fire for 1 hour, or until well done. Stir sauce well and baste ribs with sauce during the last 20 minutes of cooking time. Yield: 4 servings.

Herbed Pork Roast

2½ teaspoons salt
1 teaspoon pepper
1 teaspoon ground thyme
½ teaspoon ground nutmeg
1 4- to 6-pound loin of pork
2 carrots, cut in chunks
2 onions, coarsely chopped
2 large cloves garlic, minced
4 whole cloves
Few chopped celery leaves
Few sprigs parsley
2 bay leaves
1 (10½-ounce) can condensed chicken consommé

Combine salt, pepper, thyme, and nutmeg and rub into meat. Bake, uncovered, at 450° for 30 minutes. Reduce temperature to 350° and add remaining ingredients. Cover and bake for 3 hours or until meat is tender, basting often.

Before serving, remove roast to warm platter. Skim fat from gravy, put pan juices and vegetables through a sieve or electric blender, and serve with the meat. Roast may be prepared 1 day ahead. Yield: 8 to 10 servings.

Barbecued Spareribs

1 cup catsup
2 tablespoons firmly packed brown sugar
¼ cup lemon juice
1 medium onion, grated
2 tablespoons vinegar
½ cup water
1 tablespoon Worcestershire sauce
1 teaspoon pepper
½ teaspoon salt
3 pounds meaty spareribs

Combine first 9 ingredients for sauce. Bring to a boil and simmer for about 10 minutes. Place spareribs on grill over low fire and cook for about 20 minutes. Baste with sauce while ribs cook an additional 30 to 40 minutes. Yield: 3 to 4 servings.

Barbecued Spareribs with Herb Sauce

1 medium-size onion, chopped
1 teaspoon dried oregano leaves
1 teaspoon dried rosemary leaves
1 teaspoon thyme leaves
1 clove garlic, minced
1 cup hot water
1 cup dry red wine
⅓ cup catsup
1 tablespoon soy sauce
¼ teaspoon ground ginger
2 tablespoons honey
1 teaspoon salt
6 pounds spareribs

Put onion, herbs, and garlic in a cheesecloth bag. Simmer in 1 cup hot water for 30 minutes. Discard cheesecloth bag; combine water with wine, catsup, soy sauce, ginger, honey, and salt. Place ribs over low fire, meat side up. Cook for 10 minutes; then turn and cook for 10 more minutes. Turn again and baste with sauce until ribs are done, turning occasionally. Yield: 6 to 8 servings.

Dixie Barbecued Spareribs

4 pounds spareribs, cut into 2-inch pieces
½ cup pineapple juice
½ cup dark corn syrup
2 tablespoons soy sauce
1 teaspoon salt

Put ribs in a large kettle, cover with water, and bring to a boil. Cover kettle and cook for 30 minutes. Drain. Combine pineapple juice, corn syrup, soy sauce, and salt in a large pan or bowl. Arrange pieces of ribs in the pan. Cover with aluminum foil or paper; let stand for 45 minutes at room temperature. If desired, prepare ahead and let stand for several hours in the refrigerator. Turn ribs occasionally. Remove ribs from marinade and place in a hinged wire broiler; grill over hot coals until well browned, about 10 minutes. Turn 2 or 3 times and baste with marinade. Yield: 4 to 6 servings.

Pineappled Spareribs

   1 *cup pineapple preserves*
   2 *tablespoons vinegar*
   2 *teaspoons dry mustard*
   1 *teaspoon bottled brown bouquet sauce*
      Salt
   3 *to 4 pounds spareribs*

Combine first 4 ingredients to make a pineapple glaze; set aside. Salt the ribs and place bone-side down on grill over very slow fire. Cook for about 20 minutes, watching carefully. Turn meat side down and cook until meat has browned. Turn meat side up and brush with glaze often; cook an additional 20 to 30 minutes. Yield: 3 to 4 servings.

Barbecued Spareribs with Marinade

   5 *pounds spareribs*
   ½ *cup Cointreau*
   ½ *cup soy sauce*
   ½ *cup honey*
   1 *cup canned crushed pineapple*
   ½ *cup wine vinegar*
   1 *lemon, sliced*
   2 *teaspoons ground ginger*
   2 *cloves garlic, minced*
      Freshly ground black pepper

Marinate spareribs at room temperature for 1 hour in combined Cointreau, soy sauce, honey, pineapple, wine vinegar, lemon slices, ginger, garlic, and pepper. Remove lemon from marinade. Place spareribs on grill; cook 20 to 30 minutes on each side, basting frequently with marinade. Yield: 5 to 6 servings.

Sauerkraut and Ribs Aged in Beer

   3½ *to 4 pounds sauerkraut*
      2 *teaspoons caraway seeds*
   3½ *to 4 pounds lean spareribs*
      Salt and pepper to taste
   1½ *cups (12 ounces) beer*

Rinse sauerkraut in cold water; drain and place in a 3- or 4-quart ovenproof casserole with a tight-fitting cover. Sprinkle caraway seeds over sauerkraut.

Sprinkle ribs with salt and pepper and brown them in a large skillet over medium heat. Brown ribs slowly so as to extract all possible fat. Drain on paper towels and place them over the sauerkraut.

Pour fat from the skillet and add beer, stirring to loosen all the browned bits. Pour beer over the ribs. Cover tightly and bake at 300° for 2½ to 3 hours, or until cooked down and brown. Serve while hot, from the casserole. Yield: 8 servings.

Note: If desired, pared small potatoes may be added during the final hour of baking.

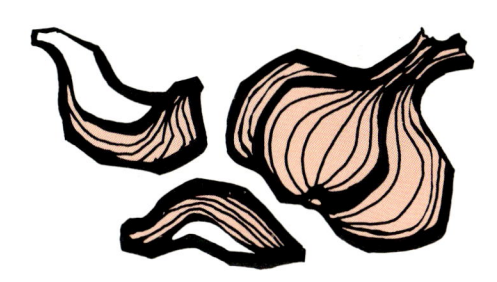

Spareribs and Bohemian Sauerkraut

   2 *pounds spareribs*
   1 *teaspoon salt*
   1 *tablespoon shortening*
   ¼ *cup water*
   1 *(16-ounce) can sauerkraut*
   3 *tablespoons chopped onion*
   ⅛ *teaspoon caraway seeds*
   ⅛ *teaspoon salt*
   3 *tablespoons sugar*
   3 *tablespoons bacon drippings*

Cut ribs into serving pieces. Season. Brown in melted shortening in heavy skillet or kettle. Add water. Cover and cook slowly for 1 hour. Empty kraut into another heavy kettle. (Wash if very tart, drain, and add ¾ cup water.) Add remaining ingredients. Cover and cook slowly for 30 minutes. Pour off drippings from ribs. Add kraut and 3 tablespoons drippings to ribs and cook an additional hour. Yield: 4 servings.

Smoked Spareribs

½ cup Worcestershire sauce
½ cup vinegar
½ cup butter or margarine, melted
½ teaspoon salt
¼ teaspoon hot sauce
2 racks (about 6 pounds) spareribs

Soak wood chips in water about 30 minutes. Combine all ingredients for the sauce. Brush the ribs with this mixture. Arrange hot coals around edge of firebox; place foil drip pan under cooking area. Drain half of chips; add to hot coals. Place meat bone-side down on grill 4 inches from coals; cover grill. Cook for 1½ to 2 hours, or until meat is done. At 30-minute intervals, add drained wood chips and hot coals to maintain smoke and even heat.

During last 40 minutes of cooking, turn and baste spareribs every 10 minutes with vinegar mixture. Yield: 6 servings.

Stuffed Leg of Lamb

7 pound leg of lamb
½ pound ground uncooked veal
½ pound ground cooked ham
½ pound fresh mushrooms, washed, trimmed, and finely chopped
½ cup fine soft bread crumbs
1 egg
1 clove garlic, crushed
1 tablespoon lemon juice
1 tablespoon Worcestershire sauce
¼ to ½ teaspoon oregano
¼ teaspoon pepper

Have lamb boned without breaking surface and without tying it. Mix remaining ingredients thoroughly with hands or spoon. Pack mixture firmly into pocket of lamb. Sew opening with heavy string. Wrap in heavy-duty aluminum foil. Grill 6 to 8 inches from medium coals. Cook 20 to 30 minutes per pound, turning occasionally. Thirty minutes before end of cooking time, remove lamb from foil; place directly on grill, turning to brown all sides. Remove from grill; slice. Yield: 6 to 8 servings.

Roast Lamb Rosemary

1 carrot, sliced
1 stalk celery, chopped
2 leeks, sliced
1 tablespoon butter or margarine
3 cups water, divided
1 (6-pound) leg of lamb
¾ teaspoon ground rosemary, divided
2 teaspoons salt
½ teaspoon freshly ground black pepper
3 tablespoons all-purpose flour

Sauté vegetables in butter for 5 minutes, stirring frequently. Stir in 1 cup of the water. Place lamb in roasting pan. Combine ¼ teaspoon of the rosemary, salt, and black pepper. Rub this into the lamb. Add vegetable mixture. Roast, uncovered, at 325° for 2½ to 3 hours or until tender. Remove roast and keep warm. Skim off excess fat from liquid in pan. Add 1¾ cups of the water and remaining ½ teaspoon rosemary. Bring to a boil; then strain. Add flour, which has been mixed with remaining ¼ cup water. Cook, stirring, until gravy thickens. Serve with gravy. Yield: 10 servings.

Marinated Baby Lamb Racks

4 (1¼ pounds) baby lamb racks, cover fat removed
1¾ cups corn oil
¼ cup lemon juice
¼ cup red wine vinegar
1 teaspoon salt
½ teaspoon cracked black pepper
½ teaspoon crushed oregano
½ teaspoon rosemary
4 cloves garlic, chopped
French fried parsley

Set lamb racks, meat side down, in marinade made by combining other ingredients except parsley. Let sit, covered, in refrigerator for 2 days. Remove from marinade and bake at 450° to desired doneness on meat thermometer. Serve hot, garnished with fried parsley. Yield: 4 servings.

Barbecued Leg of Lamb

  2 *cups dry red wine*
2/3 *cup salad oil*
  2 *cloves garlic, minced*
  2 *small onions, minced*
  1 *teaspoon dry mustard*
  1 *teaspoon salt*
  1 *teaspoon pepper*
1/2 *teaspoon ground nutmeg*
  8 *whole cloves*
  2 *tablespoons chopped parsley*
  1 *(6-pound) leg of lamb, boned and rolled*

Combine all ingredients except the meat. Place leg of lamb in a flat pan and pour marinade over it. Cover, and marinate in refrigerator overnight or for several hours, turning meat occasionally. Place on spit according to manufacturer's directions and place over hot coals when heat registers 350°. Attach the motor and cook lamb at 350° for 1¾ to 2 hours. Baste with marinade frequently while cooking. Remove from spit when done and slice for serving. Yield: 8 to 10 servings.

Lamb Curry with Rice

  1 *cup sliced onions*
1/4 *cup diced green pepper*
  1 *cup diced celery*
  1 *clove garlic, minced*
  4 *tablespoons shortening or oil*
  3 *cups cooked, diced lamb*
  1 *teaspoon curry powder (more if desired)*
1½ *teaspoons salt*
  1 *tablespoon Worcestershire sauce*
  2 *cups lamb gravy or stock*
  1 *cup hot, cooked rice*
    Chutney

Cook onion, green pepper, celery, and garlic in shortening. Add lamb, seasonings, and gravy. Cover and cook about 30 minutes over low heat. (If stock is used, thicken with 2 tablespoons all-purpose flour blended in ¼ cup cold water.) Spoon into a border of the cooked rice; serve with chutney. Yield: 6 servings.

Curried Lamb Burgers

  1 *pound ground lean lamb*
    Onion salt
    Garlic salt
1/4 *cup softened butter or margarine*
1/2 *to ¾ teaspoon curry powder*
  4 *hamburger buns*

Shape ground lamb into 4 patties, ½ inch thick. Sprinkle both sides with onion salt and garlic salt. Cook under broiler until brown, about 15 to 20 minutes, turning to brown on both sides. In the meantime, combine butter with curry powder and spread generously on both sides of the cooked patties. Serve between warm hamburger buns. Yield: 4 servings.

Teriyaki Lamb Shoulder Chops

1/2 *cup soy sauce*
1/4 *cup pineapple juice*
  2 *tablespoons firmly packed brown sugar*
1/2 *teaspoon garlic powder*
1/2 *teaspoon ground ginger*
  4 *lamb shoulder chops, about ¾ inch thick*

Combine all ingredients except lamb chops and mix thoroughly. Marinate lamb chops in soy sauce mixture in covered dish overnight, turning once or twice. Cook on outdoor grill about 4 inches from coals for approximately 8 to 10 minutes per side. (Cook less time if you like them somewhat rare.) Yield: 4 servings.

Rack of Lamb for Two

  1 *(36-ounce) rack of lamb*
    Salt, pepper, and celery salt to taste

Trim rack of lamb and rub with salt, pepper, and celery salt. Place in a roasting pan and roast, uncovered, at 425° about 45 minutes. Especially good served with a variety of garden vegetables. Yield: 2 servings.

Fruited Lamb Kabobs

    2 tablespoons melted butter
    ¼ cup firmly packed brown sugar
    1 to 2 teaspoons curry powder
    2 tablespoons peach syrup
    1½ pounds boneless lamb cubes
    1 (1-pound 13-ounce) can cling peach halves
    1 (8¼-ounce) can pineapple slices
    8 marschino cherries
    2 bananas, each cut into 4 chunks

Combine butter, sugar, curry, and peach syrup; mix well. Arrange lamb on 4 skewers. Grill 4 inches from coals for 20 to 30 minutes, turning and basting with butter mixture. Arrange fruit on 4 skewers. Grill with meat for last 10 to 15 minutes, turning and basting with butter mixture. Yield: 4 servings.

Lamb and Rice Skillet Dinner

    1½ pounds boneless lamb shoulder
    1 clove garlic, halved
    1 tablespoon butter or margarine
    2 tablespoons minced onion
    ½ cup diced celery
    2 medium-sized tomatoes, peeled and diced
    ¾ cup uncooked regular rice
    1½ cups fresh or frozen peas
    2 tablespoons minced parsley
    1½ teaspoons salt
    ¼ teaspoon pepper
    ¼ teaspoon basil
    1¾ cups water

Cut meat into small cubes or slices (be sure all fat is removed). Brown meat and garlic in butter in large skillet. Remove garlic and discard. Add onion and celery; cook 5 minutes or longer, stirring frequently to prevent overbrowning. Add tomatoes and bring to a boil. Lower heat; cover and simmer about 30 minutes or until meat is tender.

Add remaining ingredients in order listed; bring mixture to a boil. Lower heat; cover and simmer about 20 minutes or until rice and peas are tender. Yield: 6 servings.

Lamb Shoulder with Cumberland Sauce

    1 (4-pound) lamb shoulder, boned, rolled, and tied
    Salt and pepper to taste
    1 (10-ounce) jar currant jelly
    ¼ cup orange juice
    1 tablespoon lemon juice
    ¾ teaspoon ground ginger
    ½ teaspoon grated orange rind

Sprinkle lamb with salt and pepper. Place on rotisserie and test for balance. Cook on rotisserie over charcoal for 3 hours, or until meat thermometer registers 175° to 180° for well-done lamb.

Meanwhile, melt jelly and stir in remaining ingredients. Mix well and heat through until sauce is smooth. Serve with lamb shoulder roast. Yield: 8 to 10 servings.

Lamb Shish Kabobs

    Boneless (1½-inch) lamb cubes cut from shoulder or leg
    3 tablespoons vegetable oil
    ¼ cup lemon juice
    1½ teaspoons salt
    1 teaspoon marjoram
    ½ teaspoon oregano
    ⅓ cup chopped onion
    1 clove garlic, crushed
    3 green peppers
    24 cherry tomatoes
    24 canned or fresh mushroom caps

Trim as much fat as possible from lamb. Marinate lamb overnight in refrigerator in mixture of oil, lemon juice, seasonings, onion, and garlic.

When ready to cook, pour enough boiling water over green peppers to cover them. Let stand for 5 minutes; then drain and cut into eighths.

Alternate lamb cubes, green pepper pieces, whole tomatoes, and mushroom caps on metal skewers. Brush with some of remaining marinade.

Broil, turning as needed, until lamb is the desired doneness, about 15 to 20 minutes. Yield: 6 servings.

Honey-Lemon Lamb Spareribs

¼ cup melted butter
¼ cup honey
¼ cup lemon juice
1 teaspoon rosemary, slightly crushed
1 teaspoon minced onion
¼ teaspoon garlic powder
½ teaspoon dry mustard
3 to 3-½ pounds lamb spareribs
Flour
Salt and pepper to taste

Combine butter, honey, lemon juice, rosemary, onion, garlic, and mustard; heat sauce through. Sprinkle spareribs with flour, salt, and pepper; rub in. Grill spareribs 5 to 6 inches from heat about 5 minutes on each side. Then start basting spareribs with honey-lemon sauce; baste and turn frequently for 20 to 25 more minutes. Yield: 4 servings.

Lamb Loin Chops with Herb Butter

¼ cup butter, softened
½ teaspoon ground thyme
8 lamb loin chops, cut 1 inch thick
Salt and pepper to taste

Mix butter and thyme together thoroughly. Cook chops on outdoor grill about 4 inches from heat for 8 to 10 minutes. Sprinkle with salt and pepper. Turn and cook about 8 to 10 minutes longer or to desired degree of doneness. Sprinkle with salt and pepper and spoon some of the herb butter over each chop before serving. Yield: 4 servings.

Chili Lamburgers

1 pound ground lamb shoulder
1 teaspoon salt
1 cup chili sauce
2 tablespoons vinegar
2 teaspoons soy sauce
8 onion rings

Combine lamb and salt; shape into 4 round patties. Combine chili sauce, vinegar, and soy sauce. Brush lamb patties with chili sauce mixture. Broil about 5 minutes 3 to 4 inches from source of heat; turn. Brush with additional chili sauce; top with onion rings. Cook 3 to 5 minutes longer or until lamb is as done as you like it. Yield: 4 servings.

Cajun Duck Supper

4 whole ducks
Bacon drippings
Salt and pepper to taste
2 onions, cut into wedges
1 apple, cut into quarters
Celery
4 bouillon cubes
1 cup red wine, divided
6 green onions, chopped
1 (4-ounce) can mushrooms and juice
1 (6-ounce) can water chestnuts
Cooked rice

Wash and dry ducks. Rub inside and out with bacon drippings. Sprinkle with salt and pepper. Place a piece of onion, an apple quarter, and a rib of celery inside each one. Place ducks in a Dutch oven or roaster and cover with water. Add bouillon cubes and ½ cup red wine. Cook over medium heat until half the water has evaporated. Add rest of wine. Cook until ducks are completely tender. This will take at least 2 hours.

Remove the ducks from the pan; add green onions, mushrooms, and water chestnuts. Simmer until onions are cooked. Halve the ducks and serve on rice. Yield: 8 servings.

Venison Roast

    3- or 4-pound venison roast
    1 large stalk celery
    1 clove garlic, minced
    1 large onion, sliced
    1 large carrot, chopped
    2 bay leaves, crushed or whole
    8 peppercorns
    2 tablespoons soy sauce
    1 teaspoon salt
    ½ cup peanut oil
    4½ cups dry red wine
    ¼ cup oil
    Onion slices
    Salt and pepper to taste

Trim roast and tie securely. Combine celery, garlic, onion, carrot, bay leaves, peppercorns, soy sauce, salt, peanut oil, and red wine in a large pan. Put the roast in the marinade; cover and refrigerate for 12 to 24 hours, turning 3 or 4 times. Remove and blot with toweling.

Heat ¼ cup oil in heavy frying pan and brown the roast on both sides. Then put roast into roasting pan, along with 1 cup marinade, onion slices, and salt and pepper. Cover and cook in 300° oven for about 3 hours. Yield: 6 to 8 servings.

*Venison Recipe

Season chops and steaks with salt and pepper and pan-fry in butter. These cuts also can be broiled or cooked over charcoal and should be brushed with plenty of butter to prevent meat from drying out. Cook venison at the same temperature and for the same length of time as medium-rare beefsteaks.

Prepare larger cuts of venison, such as hams, shoulder, or roasts, as follows: brush with plenty of butter, season with salt and pepper, and wrap in foil before cooking. Add sliced onions, onion salt, and garlic salt if desired. Cooking time should be about 30 minutes per pound over medium heat. Prior to end of cooking time, remove foil and brown meat as desired.

Roast Doves

    4 doves
    Salt and pepper to taste
    4 thin slices lemon, seeded
    4 slices bacon, about 2 inches long
    ¾ cup clear chicken broth
    ¾ cup slightly sour whipping cream
    Parsley jelly

Clean birds very carefully. Rub inside and out with salt and pepper, and place a slice of lemon inside each bird. Tie slice of bacon over the breast of each bird. Arrange in a buttered baking dish, add broth, and bake at 375° for 25 to 30 minutes, basting often. When birds and gravy are a rich brown, pour cream over birds. Return to oven and let cream bubble up in pan for about 1 minute, basting twice with sauce. Serve with gravy from the pan and parsley jelly. Yield: 4 servings.

Wild Duck with Olive Sauce

    6 small ducks
    3 small onions, cut in half
    Salt to taste
    ½ cup vinegar
    Red peppercorns
    Thyme
    Worcestershire sauce
    Bay leaves
    Salt and pepper to taste
    6 slices bacon
    2 tablespoons sugar
    3 tablespoons cornstarch
    1 (6-ounce) can frozen orange juice concentrate
    2 cups water
    ½ cup chopped olives

Clean ducks; put half an onion inside each and salt generously inside and out. Place in a large pot to tenderize, using pot half full of water and adding vinegar. Add peppercorns, thyme, Worcestershire sauce, and bay leaves and boil until ducks are tender, but meat is not falling off bones.

Remove ducks from vinegar solution;

wash, and remove onion. Arrange breast-side down in deep roasting pan. Sprinkle with salt and pepper and put a strip of bacon on each duck.

Mix sugar and cornstarch, and blend in the orange juice. Slowly add water and cook over low heat until mixture is hot. Add olives and pour sauce over ducks.

Bake at 350° in covered roasting pan about 1 hour, basting often. Yield: 4 to 6 servings.

Ranch-Style Creamed Quail

12 *quail*
Salt and pepper to taste
1 *pound butter or margarine*
4 *cups half-and-half*
1 *to 1½ cups toasted bread crumbs*

Clean and dress quail; then salt and pepper. Simmer slowly in butter until tender. Add half-and-half and continue simmering until done. Remove quail to hot platter. Sift toasted bread crumbs over quail. Pour cream gravy from pan over quail. Yield: 12 servings.

*Wild Duck Roasted in Aluminum Foil

1 *(2-pound) duck*
1 *stalk celery (including leaves), chopped*
1 *small onion, chopped*
1 *carrot, chopped*
1 *sprig of parsley, chopped*
Melted margarine
Salt and pepper to taste
Dash mixed herbs
2 *tablespoons currant jelly*
1 *(10½-ounce) can condensed consommé*

Clean duck. Put chopped ingredients into the body cavity of the duck. Place the duck on a piece of strong aluminum foil that is large enough to cover it. Brush the duck with a mixture of margarine, salt, pepper, and mixed herbs. Tie the legs together, and bring the foil up over the duck. Seal all edges with a double, tight fold to make an airtight package. Place the package in a shallow baking pan and roast at 425° for 1 hour and 45 minutes.

When roasting time is over, remove duck from oven and place it on a hot platter. Open the package carefully in order not to spill any of the juices in the foil. Remove all ingredients from body cavity. Pour the juices left in the foil into a small saucepan and cook until a golden brown. To the juices add currant jelly and consommé. Serve as a gravy with the duck. Yield: 1 to 2 servings.

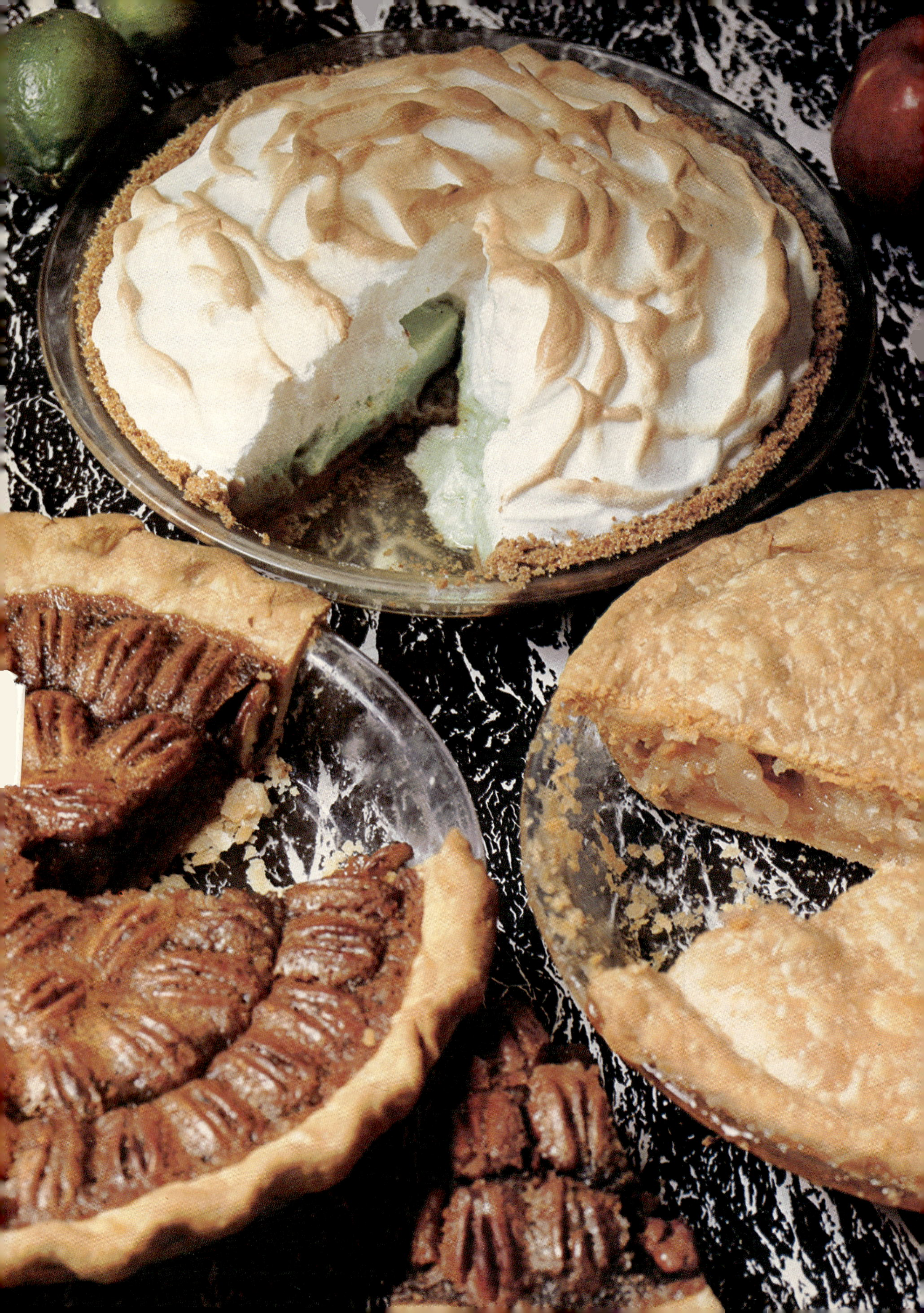

Pies and Pastry

One of the most sought-after pieces of antique furniture these days is the old pie safe, in which baked pies were placed for storage before the advent of refrigeration.

The English passed on their love of pies to us, and several, such as apple, pumpkin, and molasses, are now thought of as particularly American. In early spring, one of the most cherished dishes is fresh blackberry pie, but custard, lemon chess, and pecan pies are year-round favorites. There are almost as many pecan pie recipes as there are cooks; each cook likes to add her own special flavoring.

Calorie counters look unconcerned when a pie, heaped with fluffy white meringue, appears on the table. Luscious in all their sweetness, favorite pies are the grand finale to a typical Southern dinner.

Southern Transparent Pie

- 1 (1-pound) box light brown sugar
- ½ cup butter or margarine, melted
- 5 eggs
- 1 teaspoon vanilla extract
- 2 unbaked 8-inch pie shells

Blend sugar and butter. Add eggs, one at a time, blending well after each addition. Add vanilla. Pour into two unbaked piecrust shells and bake at 400° for 10 minutes. Reduce heat to 300° and bake until firm, about 35 to 40 minutes. Center should be slightly shaky.

Hot Water Pastry:

- ¾ cup shortening
- ¼ cup boiling water
- 1 teaspoon cold milk
- 2 cups all-purpose flour
- ½ teaspoon salt, optional

Scald a mixing bowl with hot water. Put shortening in hot bowl and add boiling water. Beat until blended. Add milk, flour, and salt, and stir until well mixed. Divide into two balls. Roll on floured board and fit into piepans. Yield: two 8- or 9-inch crusts.

Fudge Pie

- ½ cup margarine
- 1 cup sugar
- 2 ounces baking chocolate, melted
- Pinch of salt
- ¼ cup all-purpose flour
- 2 eggs, beaten
- 1 teaspoon vanilla extract
- ½ cup chopped pecans
- Chopped Walnut Pie Shell
- Ice Cream

Cream margarine and sugar. Add chocolate, salt, flour, eggs, and vanilla; blend thoroughly. Fold in nuts. Pour filling into pie shell; bake at 325° for 30 minutes. Serve topped with small scoops of ice cream. Yield: one 9-inch pie.

Chopped Walnut Pie Shell:

- ¼ cup margarine, softened
- 1 tablespoon all-purpose flour
- ¼ cup sugar
- 1 cup finely chopped walnuts

Combine all ingredients; mix well. Press over sides and bottom of a 9-inch pie pan. Yield: one 9-inch pie shell.

*Magic Piecrust

    3 cups all-purpose flour
    1 teaspoon salt
    1¼ cups shortening
    1 egg, slightly beaten
    6 tablespoons water
    1 teaspoon vinegar

Combine flour and salt; cut in shortening with two knives or pastry blender until mixture resembles coarse cornmeal. Combine egg and water; sprinkle over flour mixture. Add vinegar and lightly stir until mixture forms a ball. Wrap in waxed paper and chill until ready to use. Yield: enough crust for 5 single pies.

Standard Piecrust

    2 cups all-purpose flour
    ½ teaspoon salt
    ⅔ cup shortening
    6 tablespoons cold water

Combine flour and salt in a large mixing bowl. Cut in shortening until mixture resembles coarse meal. Sprinkle cold water evenly over surface; stir with a fork until all dry particles are moistened. Shape into a ball; divide into 2 parts. Roll each part into a 12-inch circle. Fit into a 9-inch pieplate and crimp edges. Use other circle for a single piecrust or top of 9-inch pie. Yield: double crust for 9-inch pie.

*Graham Cracker Crumb Shell

    2¼ cups graham cracker crumbs
    1¼ teaspoons ground cinnamon (or to taste)
    2 tablespoons sugar
    ½ cup butter or margarine, softened

Blend together graham cracker crumbs, cinnamon, and sugar. Using butter as a binder, mix together and press firmly and evenly into 10-inch pie plate. Yield: one 10-inch pie shell.

Quiche Pastry

    2¼ cups all-purpose flour
    1 teaspoon salt
    ¾ cup vegetable shortening
    5 tablespoons cold water

Combine flour and salt in large bowl. Cut in shortening with pastry blender until mixture is the size of peas. Blend about ⅓ cup of flour mixture with water; add to the rest of flour mixture and mix until dough holds together. Shape into a flat round. Divide in half and roll to fit a 9- or 10-inch piepan. Yield: pastry for two 9- or 10-inch pies.

*Peanut Butter Cream Pie

    ¾ cup powdered sugar
    ⅓ cup peanut butter
    ⅔ cup sugar
    3 tablespoons cornstarch
    1 tablespoon all-purpose flour
    ½ teaspoon salt
    3 egg yolks
    3 cups milk
    2 tablespoons butter
    1 teaspoon vanilla extract
    Baked 9-inch pie shell
    3 egg whites
    ¼ teaspoon cream of tartar
    ¼ cup sugar

Cream powdered sugar and ⅓ cup peanut butter until crumbly. Set aside. Combine ⅔ cup sugar, cornstarch, flour, salt, egg yolks, milk, butter, and vanilla in a saucepan or in top of double boiler over hot water. Cook over medium heat, stirring constantly, until thick.

Sprinkle two-thirds of the peanut butter mixture in bottom of baked pie shell; pour custard over this. Beat 3 egg whites with cream of tartar until stiff, gradually adding ¼ cup sugar. Spread over custard. Sprinkle remaining crumbly mixture over meringue, and bake at 350° about 20 minutes or until golden brown. Yield: one 9-inch pie.

Fruit Fluff Pie

    1 *(15-ounce) can sweetened condensed milk*
½ *cup lemon juice*
    1 *(9-ounce) carton frozen whipped topping*
    1 *(11-ounce) can mandarin oranges, drained*
    1 *(29-ounce) can sliced peaches, drained*
    1 *(8¼-ounce) can crushed pineapple, drained*
    2 *(9-inch) baked graham cracker crusts*

Beat condensed milk and lemon juice together until well mixed. Fold in whipped topping and well-drained fruits. Spoon mixture into two 9-inch graham cracker crusts and chill. Yield: two 9-inch pies.

Lemon Ice Box Pie

    2 *egg yolks*
    1 *(15-ounce) can sweetened condensed milk*
½ *cup lemon juice*
    1 *teaspoon grated lemon rind*
    1 *unbaked 9-inch vanilla wafer crust*
    3 *egg whites*
½ *cup sugar*

Beat egg yolks until light and fluffy. Add the sweetened condensed milk and beat until fluffy. Mixture will stand in peaks. Stir in lemon juice and grated lemon rind. Spoon filling into crust made of crushed vanilla wafers and melted butter.

Beat egg whites until foamy. Gradually add sugar and beat until mixture is stiff. Spoon on top of lemon filling, being careful to spread to seal all edges. Bake at 350° for 10 minutes. Yield: one 9-inch pie.

Angel Pie

    4 *egg whites*
    1 *teaspoon cream of tartar*
1½ *cups sugar, divided*
    4 *egg yolks*
       Juice and grated peel of 1½ lemons
¾ *cup whipping cream*

Beat egg whites until foamy; add cream of tartar and beat until stiff. Gradually add 1 cup sugar. Spread the meringue into a greased 9-inch pieplate, and bake at 250° for 1½ hours (meringue should not brown). Cool.

Beat egg yolks until light; add lemon juice and grated peel and ½ cup sugar. Stir over hot water until slightly thickened. Cool.

Whip the cream, and add half to the cooled filling. Spread filling in meringue crust, and cover with remaining whipped cream. Chill in refrigerator at least 24 hours. Yield: one 9-inch pie.

*Sweet Potato Pie

1½ *cups mashed, cooked sweet potatoes or 1 (1-pound) can water-packed sweet potatoes, drained and mashed*
    3 *eggs, slightly beaten*
    1 *cup evaporated milk*
½ *cup dark corn syrup*
½ *cup firmly packed brown sugar*
    2 *tablespoons melted margarine*
    1 *teaspoon salt*
    1 *teaspoon ground cinnamon*
½ *teaspoon ground nutmeg*
¼ *teaspoon ground ginger*
    1 *unbaked 9-inch pastry shell*

Beat together first 10 ingredients until smooth and frothy. Pour into pastry shell. Bake at 425° for 15 minutes; reduce heat to 350° and continue baking about 45 minutes or until knife inserted in center comes out clean. Yield: one 9-inch pie.

Variation: For a Pecan Sweet Potato Pie, add 1 cup pecan halves to filling before baking.

Toss pecan halves with 1 tablespoon melted margarine until evenly coated. Arrange over sweet potato mixture. Bake at 350° until knife inserted in center comes out clean, about 55 to 60 minutes. Yield: one 9-inch pie.

Banana Meringue Pie

5 egg whites
Dash salt
1 cup sugar
1 (9-inch) unbaked graham cracker crust
1 cup whipping cream
1 cup flaked coconut
Sugar
2 large bananas, sliced

Combine egg whites and salt; beat until soft peaks form. Add 1 cup sugar slowly, beating until mixture is stiff. Pour into crust and spread evenly. Bake at 200° for 1 hour; cool. Whip cream; add coconut, and sweeten to taste. Alternate layers of bananas and whipped cream over baked meringue. Chill. Yield: one 9-inch pie.

Cheery Cherry Pie

1 cup sugar
3 tablespoons cornstarch
¼ teaspoon salt
1 cup cherry juice
¼ teaspoon red food coloring (optional)
2 (16-ounce) cans red tart pitted cherries
1 baked 9-inch crumb crust
Whipped cream (optional)

Mix sugar, cornstarch, and salt in a saucepan. Add juice and coloring; stir until smooth. Cook until thickened and clear, stirring constantly. Add cherries; simmer 10 to 15 minutes, stirring gently once or twice. Cool. Pour into 9-inch crumb crust; chill. Garnish with whipped cream, if desired. Yield: one 9-inch pie.

*Grated Apple Pie

4 large apples
1 cup sugar
½ teaspoon ground cinnamon
Pastry for double-crust 9-inch pie
2 tablespoons butter or margarine
¼ cup sugar, if desired

Wash apples and grate (do not peel). Add 1 cup sugar and cinnamon; mix well. Spoon mixture into pastry-lined, 9-inch piepan. Cover top with lattice strips. Dot with butter and sprinkle with ¼ cup sugar, if desired. Bake at 350° for 1 hour or until browned. Yield: one 9-inch pie.

Crunchy Apple Pie

2 cups chopped cooking apples
½ cup firmly packed brown sugar
½ cup granulated sugar
½ cup all-purpose flour
1 egg yolk, beaten
½ teaspoon vanilla extract
½ teaspoon freshly squeezed lemon juice
½ cup chopped nuts
1 egg white, beaten until foamy
1 (9-inch) unbaked pie shell

Put chopped apples in a large bowl. Add sugar, flour, egg yolk, vanilla, lemon juice, and nuts; mix well. Add egg white. Stir well and pour mixture into unbaked pie shell. Bake at 350° for 30 to 45 minutes or until apples are tender and brown. Yield: one 9-inch pie.

*Colonial Apple Pie

Pastry for double-crust 9-inch pie
5 to 6 cups pared, sliced apples
2 tablespoons all-purpose flour
1 cup sugar
¼ teaspoon salt
1 teaspoon ground cinnamon
2 tablespoons butter or margarine

Line a 9-inch piepan with half the pastry rolled ⅛ inch thick. Arrange apples in unbaked shell. Combine flour, sugar, salt, and cinnamon; sprinkle over apples. Dot with butter. Roll out remaining pastry. Slash crust to permit steam to escape. Place crust over apples; seal and flute edges. Bake at 375° for 1 hour and 15 minutes or until crust is brown and apples tender. Yield: one 9-inch pie.

Sour Cream Apple Pie

½ cup sugar (or less when using Golden Delicious apples)
1 tablespoon all-purpose flour
¼ teaspoon salt
¼ teaspoon ground cinnamon
¼ teaspoon ground nutmeg
6 cups pared, cored, sliced tart apples
1 (9-inch) unbaked pastry shell
1 cup commercial sour cream
¼ cup firmly packed brown sugar
Ground nutmeg

Combine sugar, flour, salt, cinnamon, and nutmeg. Toss with apples. Arrange in pastry shell. Cover loosely with foil. Bake at 400° for 50 to 55 minutes or until apples are tender. Remove foil. Combine sour cream and brown sugar. Pour evenly over apples. Sprinkle with nutmeg. Bake 2 to 3 minutes longer. Yield: one 9-inch pie.

Caramel-Topped Apple Pie

5½ cups apples, peeled and sliced
¼ cup water
¾ cup sugar
1 tablespoon all-purpose flour
½ teaspoon ground cinnamon
½ teaspoon ground nutmeg
½ cup chopped pecans
¾ cup graham cracker crumbs
¼ teaspoon salt
⅓ cup melted butter or margarine
½ pound caramels
½ cup hot milk

Combine apples and water in saucepan. Cover and steam about 3 minutes. Drain and spread apples on cookie sheet to cool quickly. Arrange slices in 9- or 10-inch pieplate. Combine sugar, flour, cinnamon, nutmeg, pecans, graham cracker crumbs, salt, and melted butter or margarine; sprinkle over apples. Bake at 425° for 10 minutes; then reduce heat to 350° and bake for 20 minutes.

While pie is baking, combine caramels and hot milk in top of a double boiler; cook until caramels are melted. Pour the hot caramel sauce over top of pie and continue baking for an additional 10 minutes. Cool before serving. Yield: one 9- or 10-inch pie.

Fried Apple Pies

2½ cups canned sliced apples
¾ cup firmly packed light brown sugar
1 teaspoon ground cinnamon
½ teaspoon ground nutmeg
¼ teaspoon ground allspice
1 tablespoon all-purpose flour
¼ cup seedless raisins
2 cups sifted all-purpose flour
2 tablespoons sugar
½ teaspoon salt
⅔ cup shortening
About ¼ cup cold water
Powdered sugar

Drain apple slices; dice. Combine first seven ingredients. Let stand until needed.

Combine 2 cups flour, sugar, and salt. Cut in shortening with 2 knives or pastry blender. Add enough water to make a firm dough. Roll out small pieces of dough to ⅛-inch thickness; cut in 5-inch circles. Place apple mixture on half of each circle; moisten edge of pastry with water. Fold over and press edges lightly together with tines of fork. Fry in hot shortening (350°) about 4 minutes or until brown. Drain on paper towels; dust with powdered sugar. Yield: 18 small pies.

*Fresh Blackberry Pie

1 quart blackberries
½ cup sugar
1 baked 9-inch pie shell
Whipped cream

Wash berries and place in a saucepan; add sugar. (If berries are tart, add more sugar.) Boil for 3 minutes. Store in refrigerator until serving time.

When ready to serve, pour berries in pie shell and top with whipped cream. Yield: one 9-inch pie.

Blackberry Meringue Pie

    4   *cups fresh blackberries*
    1   *cup sugar*
    1   *teaspoon lemon juice*
 1½   *teaspoons cornstarch*
  ¼   *cup cold water*
  ⅛   *teaspoon salt*
    2   *tablespoons butter or margarine*
       Baked 9-inch pie shell
    3   *egg whites*
  ¼   *teaspoon cream of tartar*
  ½   *cup sugar*

Wash and drain blackberries. Crush ½ cup of the berries with a fork; add 1 cup sugar and 1 teaspoon lemon juice. Add remaining berries and cook over low heat until berries are soft; stir to prevent sticking. Dissolve cornstarch in cold water and add to cooked berries. Add salt and the butter or margarine; cook and stir until mixture has thickened. Cool.

Place mixture in baked pie shell. Beat egg whites until foamy; add cream of tartar. Continue beating, adding sugar a little at a time, until meringue stands in peaks. Spread over pie and bake at 350° about 15 to 20 minutes or until browned. Yield: one 9-inch pie.

*Old-Fashioned Blackberry Pie

    3   *cups blackberries*
       Pastry for a 9-inch double-crust pie
    1   *cup sugar*
    1   *tablespoon grated lemon rind*
    2   *tablespoons butter*

Place blackberries in the bottom of a 9-inch unbaked pie shell. Dust sugar on top of berries and sprinkle lemon rind over sugar. Dot with butter. Cover top with lattice strips. Bake at 350° for 40 minutes or until the strips are browned. Yield: one 9-inch pie.

Honey-Pecan Pumpkin Pie

    2   *cups cooked or canned pumpkin*
    1   *cup honey*
  ½   *cup firmly packed brown sugar*
  ½   *teaspoon salt*
  ½   *teaspoon ground ginger*
    1   *teaspoon ground cinnamon*
  ¼   *teaspoon ground nutmeg*
    3   *eggs, slightly beaten*
    1   *cup whole milk*
 1¼   *cups evaporated milk*
    2   *unbaked 9-inch pie shells*
    1   *cup chopped pecans*

Mix together pumpkin, honey, sugar, salt, and spices. Add eggs and milk and mix thoroughly. Pour into pie shells and sprinkle generously with chopped pecans. Bake at 450° for 10 minutes; reduce heat to 325° and bake an additional 45 minutes. Yield: two 9-inch pies.

*Blueberry Pie

    1   *teaspoon vinegar*
    1   *cup sugar*
    2   *tablespoons all-purpose flour*
  ⅛   *teaspoon ground nutmeg*
    1   *quart fresh blueberries*
       Pastry for a (9-inch) double crust pie
    2   *tablespoons butter*

Combine vinegar, sugar, flour, and nutmeg. Mix with berries. Put in pastry-lined pan and dot with butter. Cover with top crust. Bake at 425° for 10 minutes; reduce heat to 375° and bake an additional 25 minutes or until brown. Yield: one 9-inch pie.

*Fresh Blueberry Glacé Pie

    1   *(9-inch) baked pie shell, cooled*
    4   *cups fresh blueberries, divided*
    1   *cup sugar*
    3   *tablespoons cornstarch*
  ¼   *teaspoon salt*
  ¼   *cup water*
  ¼   *teaspoon ground cinnamon*
    1   *tablespoon butter or margarine*

Line cooled pie shell with 2 cups well-drained blueberries. Cook remaining 2 cups berries with sugar, cornstarch, salt, and water over medium heat until thickened. Remove from heat; add cinnamon and butter and cool slightly. Pour over berries in shell. Chill until served. Yield: one 9-inch pie.

Refrigerator Cherry Pie

 1 *(15-ounce) can sweetened condensed milk*
 1 *teaspoon vanilla extract*
 1/3 *cup lemon juice*
 1/2 *pint whipping cream, whipped (do not sweeten)*
 1 *(9-inch) baked pie shell*
 1 *(22-ounce) can cherry pie filling*

Mix milk, vanilla, and lemon juice until thick. Fold in whipped cream. Pour into pastry shell. Top with cherry pie filling and chill for 3 or 4 hours. Yield: one 9-inch pie.

Cherry Cream Pie

 1 *cup hot cooked rice*
 3 *tablespoons maraschino cherry juice*
 1 *(3-ounce) package lemon-flavored gelatin*
 1 *cup hot water*
 1 *(8-ounce) package cream cheese*
 1/3 *cup sugar*
 1/2 *cup whipping cream, whipped*
 Baked 9-inch piecrust
 1 *scant tablespoon unflavored gelatin*
 3 *tablespoons maraschino cherry juice*

Combine hot cooked rice and cherry juice. Cool. Dissolve gelatin in hot water. Stir; then chill in refrigerator until thick and syrupy.
 Combine cream cheese and sugar. Beat to a smooth paste. Beat cream cheese mixture into gelatin; stir in rice, and fold in whipped cream. Turn into cooled, baked piecrust; chill. When set about 1 hour, top pie with unflavored gelatin dissolved in cherry juice. Yield: one 9-inch pie.

Chocolate-Butterscotch Pie

 3 *cups firmly packed light brown sugar*
 1/2 *cup butter or margarine*
 3 *eggs*
 1 *teaspoon vanilla extract*
 1/2 *cup half-and-half*
 1 *(1-ounce) square unsweetened chocolate, melted*
 1 *(9-inch) unbaked, chilled pie shell with stand-up edge*
 1 *cup sweetened whipping cream, whipped*
 Chocolate shavings

Beat sugar and butter together until creamy. Add eggs, one at a time, beating well after each addition. Add vanilla and mix well. Beat in the half-and-half; add chocolate, and beat well. Pour into pie shell and bake at 350° for 30 minutes. Reduce heat to 300° and bake 30 to 40 minutes longer or until pie is set. Test for doneness, and cook longer if needed. Let cool; then decorate with whipped cream and chocolate shavings. (Note: The pie puffs up during cooking, then falls as it cools.) Yield: one 9-inch pie.

Chocolate Chip Pie

 1 *(6-ounce) package chocolate morsels*
 2 *tablespoons sugar*
 2 *tablespoons milk*
 1 *teaspoon vanilla extract or rum or mint flavoring*
 4 *eggs, separated*
 1 *(9-inch) baked pie shell*
 Whipped topping
 Chocolate shavings

Combine chocolate morsels, sugar, and milk in top of double boiler and heat over boiling water until chocolate is melted. Add flavoring and cool to lukewarm. Beat egg yolks one at a time into chocolate mixture. Beat egg whites separately and gently fold into chocolate. Pour into baked pie shell and refrigerate. Garnish with whipped topping and chocolate shavings. Yield: one 9-inch pie.

Chocolate Pie

- 3 egg whites
- 1 teaspoon vanilla extract
- ¾ cup sugar
- 1 teaspoon baking powder
- 1 (4-ounce) bar sweet cooking chocolate, grated
- 1 cup fine cracker crumbs
- ½ cup chopped pecans
- 1 cup whipping cream
- 2 tablespoons sugar
- 1 teaspoon vanilla extract

Beat egg whites with 1 teaspoon vanilla to form soft peaks. Combine ¾ cup sugar and baking powder; gradually add to egg whites, beating to stiff peaks. Reserve 2 tablespoons chocolate; fold remainder into whites along with cracker crumbs and pecans. Spread in a greased 9-inch piepan. Bake at 350° for 25 minutes or until done. Cool.

Whip cream; add sugar a tablespoon at a time, beating after each addition. Add vanilla and spread over meringue pie filling. Sprinkle with reserved chocolate and chill 6 to 8 hours. Yield: one 9-inch pie.

Chocolate Rum Pie

- 6 egg yolks
- ⅞ cup sugar
- 2 ounces unsweetened chocolate, melted
- 1 tablespoon unflavored gelatin
- ¼ cup cold water
- 1 pint whipping cream, whipped
- ¼ cup rum
- 1 baked 9-inch pie shell

Beat egg yolks until thick and lemon colored; gradually beat in the sugar. Add melted chocolate along with gelatin that has been softened in cold water and then dissolved over hot water. Stir briskly. Fold in whipped cream and rum. Cool until mixture just begins to congeal and then spoon into pie shell. Refrigerate 3 or 4 hours. If desired, garnish with whipped cream. Yield: one 9-inch pie.

*Never Fail Chocolate Pie

- 3 egg yolks
- 1 cup sugar
- 3 tablespoons cornstarch
- 3 heaping tablespoons cocoa
- Dash salt
- 1 cup boiling water
- 1 baked 9-inch pie shell
- 3 egg whites
- 3 tablespoons sugar

Beat egg yolks until light and lemon colored. Mix together the sugar, cornstarch, and cocoa. Add beaten egg yolks and salt to sugar mixture. Slowly blend in 1 cup boiling water. Cook (preferably in top of a double boiler), stirring constantly, until mixture is thick. Cool.

When filling has cooled, spoon into cooled, baked piecrust. Beat egg whites until light and fluffy, but not dry. Add sugar and beat well. Spread on top of pie and bake at 350° about 15 to 20 minutes or until crust is brown. Yield: one 9-inch pie.

German Chocolate Pie

- ½ cup margarine
- ½ (4-ounce) bar sweet chocolate
- 3 eggs
- 1 cup sugar
- ½ cup all-purpose flour
- ½ cup pecans
- ½ teaspoon vanilla extract

Melt margarine and chocolate in top of a double boiler. Beat eggs; add sugar and flour and mix well. Combine with melted mixture; add pecans and vanilla. Pour mixture into greased 9-inch piepan. Bake at 325° for 40 minutes. Yield: one 9-inch pie.

*Butterscotch Pie

    1 *baked 9-inch pie shell*
    ¾ *cup firmly packed brown sugar*
    ⅓ *cup all-purpose flour*
    ½ *teaspoon salt*
    2 *cups milk*
    3 *egg yolks*
    3 *tablespoons softened butter or margarine*
    1 *teaspoon vanilla extract*
    3 *egg whites*
    6 *tablespoons sugar*

Bake pie shell and let cool. Combine brown sugar, flour, and salt in the top of a double boiler. Mix well. Blend in milk and cook over simmering water, stirring constantly, until thick and smooth.

Beat egg yolks until thick and lemon colored. Add a small amount of hot mixture to egg yolks and mix well. Add yolks to hot mixture. Cook, stirring constantly, for 3 minutes. Remove from heat and add butter and vanilla. Cool slightly; then spoon into cooled baked pie shell.

Beat egg whites until they begin to stiffen. Continue beating while adding sugar, a tablespoon at a time, until whites form stiff peaks. Spread over warm filling; be sure that meringue touches edge of crust. Bake at 325° for 15 minutes or until meringue is lightly browned. Cool; then chill before serving. Yield: one 9-inch pie.

French Silk Pie

    ½ *cup butter or margarine at room temperature*
    ¾ *cup sugar*
    1 *square unsweetened chocolate, melted*
    1 *teaspoon vanilla extract*
    2 *eggs*
    Baked 8-inch pie shell
    Whipped cream
    3 *tablespoons grated chocolate*

Cream butter until quite soft. Gradually add sugar, and cream until mixture is perfectly smooth. Beat in the melted chocolate and vanilla. Add eggs, one at a time, beating 5 minutes after each one is added or until the mixture is quite smooth. Pour into a cooled baked pie shell and chill until serving time. Garnish with whipped cream and grated chocolate. Yield: one 8-inch pie.

Buttermilk Pie

Crust:

    3 *cups all-purpose flour*
    1 *teaspoon salt*
  1¼ *cups shortening*
    1 *egg, well beaten*
    1 *tablespoon vinegar*
    5 *tablespoons water*

Combine flour and salt; cut in shortening. Combine egg, vinegar, and water and add to first 3 ingredients. Divide into 4 parts and roll out on floured surface. (Dough will keep in the refrigerator for 4 weeks and can be rerolled.) Yield: 4 single crusts.

Buttermilk Filling:

    6 *eggs*
    3 *cups sugar*
    1 *cup margarine*
    2 *teaspoons vanilla extract*
    1 *cup buttermilk*
    Pastry for 2 (9-inch) pies

Mix eggs, sugar, and margarine until light. Add vanilla and buttermilk. Pour into 2 unbaked pie shells. Bake at 350° for 10 minutes. Reduce heat to 325° and bake for 30 more minutes or until firm in the middle. Yield: two 9-inch pies.

Dried Fruit Turnovers

Cook dried apples, peaches, or apricots until tender. Mash and add sugar to taste. Prepare pastry, using less shortening than for pies. Roll small balls of pastry one at a time, and cut into 5-inch circles. Spread half the circle with fruit, dampen edges of dough, and fold other half over fruit. Seal edges with tines of fork. Fry in deep hot fat until browned. Serve hot.

*Southern Burnt Cream Pie

1 cup sugar, divided
½ cup boiling water
¼ cup all-purpose flour
⅛ teaspoon salt
1½ cups milk
2 beaten egg yolks
1½ tablespoons margarine
1 teaspoon vanilla extract
One 9-inch baked pie shell

Meringue:

2 egg whites
⅛ teaspoon salt
4 tablespoons sugar

Place ½ cup sugar in a skillet and dissolve over medium heat until sugar turns a light brown. Stir in boiling water and boil mixture for 2 minutes.
Blend together remaining sugar, flour, and salt. Add milk to sugar-flour mixture and mix until smooth. Stir in the burnt sugar syrup. Cook and stir over low heat or over hot water. When the mixture is hot, pour part of it over the beaten egg yolks. Then add yolks to hot mixture. Stir until mixture coats a spoon. Add margarine and vanilla. Cool filling. Fill pie shell.
Beat together egg whites and salt until stiff, but not dry. Gradually beat in the sugar. Pile meringue on pie and bake at 300° for 15 to 20 minutes. Yield: one 9-inch pie.

Coconut Pie

4 eggs, well beaten
½ cup self-rising flour (not regular flour)
1¾ cups sugar
¼ cup butter or margarine, melted
1 teaspoon vanilla extract
2 cups milk
1 (7-ounce) can flaked coconut

Combine all ingredients. Mix well and pour into two 9-inch piepans; bake at 325° for 30 minutes or until brown. This pie makes its own crust. Yield: two 9-inch pies.

One-Step Coconut Custard Pie

1 (15.4-ounce) package vanilla frosting mix
⅓ cup all-purpose flour
¼ teaspoon salt
½ cup milk
2 tablespoons butter or margarine, melted
1 teaspoon vanilla extract
3 eggs
1⅓ cups flaked coconut
2 tablespoons chopped maraschino cherries

Generously grease and lightly flour bottom and sides of 10-inch piepan or 13- x 9- x 2-inch baking pan.
In large mixing bowl, combine all ingredients except coconut and cherries. Beat at medium speed 2 minutes. Stir in coconut and cherries. Pour into prepared pan. Bake at 350° for 30 to 35 minutes until golden brown and center is almost set. (Cover with foil during last 5 to 10 minutes if crust becomes too dark.) Best served warm. Yield: one 10-inch pie.

Hawaiian Pie

2 bananas, sliced
1 (9-inch) graham cracker crust, baked
2 bananas, sliced
1 (15-ounce) can sweetened condensed milk
½ cup lemon juice
1 (20-ounce) can crushed pineapple, drained
½ pint whipping cream
¼ cup sugar
¼ cup flaked coconut
¼ cup chopped nuts
¼ cup chopped maraschino cherries

Put a layer of banana slices in baked graham cracker crust. Top with a layer of sweetened condensed milk which has been mixed with lemon juice. Then add a layer of crushed pineapple, topped with a layer of cream whipped with sugar. Repeat layers until all have been used. Garnish with coconut, nuts, and chopped cherries. Chill before serving (3 or 4 hours). Yield: one 9-inch pie.

Hawaiian Fluff Pie

- 2 *tablespoons softened butter or margarine*
- 1 *(7-ounce) can flaked coconut*
- 1 *tablespoon sugar*
- 1 *envelope unflavored gelatin*
- ¼ *cup cold water*
- 3 *egg yolks*
- 1 *cup sugar, divided*
- 1 *(8¼-ounce) can crushed pineapple*
- 3 *tablespoons lemon juice*
- ¼ *teaspoon salt*
- 3 *egg whites*
- *Whipped cream (optional)*

Spread butter or margarine evenly on bottom and sides of a 9-inch pie pan (one with a cutter bar in it makes removal of pie easier). Sprinkle coconut over butter; press firmly to bottom and sides. Sprinkle 1 tablespoon sugar over coconut. Bake at 350° for 9 minutes or until crust is golden brown. Cool.

Soften gelatin in cold water. Combine egg yolks, ½ cup sugar, undrained pineapple, and lemon juice in top of a double boiler. Cook over hot water, stirring frequently, until mixture thickens, about 10 to 15 minutes. Add softened gelatin and stir until gelatin dissolves; remove from heat. Cool in refrigerator until mixture begins to thicken.

Add salt to egg whites. Beat until stiff, gradually stirring in remaining sugar. Fold egg whites into cooked mixture; spoon into cooled crust. Place in refrigerator to chill until firm (2 to 3 hours). If desired, top with whipped cream. Yield: one 9-inch pie.

Old-Fashioned Cranberry Pie

- 2 *(1-pound) cans whole-berry cranberry sauce*
- 2 *tablespoons butter, melted*
- ¼ *cup firmly packed brown sugar*
- 1 *(9-inch) unbaked pie shell*
- *Additional pastry for lattice topping*

Combine cranberry sauce, butter, and brown sugar. Spoon into unbaked pastry shell. Cover with lattice topping. Bake at 425° for 30 to 40 minutes or until crust is golden brown. Yield: one 9-inch pie.

Tropical Dream Pie

- 1 *(16-ounce) can sour pitted cherries, drained*
- 1 *(20-ounce) can crushed pineapple*
- ⅔ *cup sugar*
- ¼ *cup all-purpose flour*
- 1 *(3-ounce) package orange-flavored gelatin*
- 1 *(3-ounce) package lemon-flavored gelatin*
- 3 *bananas*
- 1 *cup chopped pecans*
- 1 *(9-inch) baked pie shell, cooled*
- 1 *cup whipping cream, whipped*
- 2 *tablespoons powdered sugar*

Combine cherry juice and pineapple juice (from crushed pineapple) to make ½ cup juice. Combine the ⅔ cup sugar with flour; add the juice and cook until thick. Stir in the orange and lemon gelatin and continue stirring (while liquid is still hot) until gelatin is thoroughly dissolved. Add the fruits and pecans. Pour into the baked pie shell and place in the refrigerator until congealed thoroughly. Top with whipped cream to which powdered sugar has been added. Yield: one 9-inch pie.

Ice Cream Pie

- 4 *cups corn flakes*
- 7 *tablespoons butter, melted*
- ⅓ *cup firmly packed brown sugar*
- 4 *ounces unsweetened chocolate, melted*
- 1 *quart French vanilla ice cream*
- *Shaved sweet chocolate*
- ½ *cup coarsely chopped pecans*

Combine corn flakes, butter, sugar, and chocolate. Mix well and pat into a 10-inch piepan. Cool. Fill pie shell with ice cream; sprinkle chocolate shavings and pecans over top. Wrap in aluminum foil; freeze until serving time. Yield: one 10-inch pie.

Grape Juice Pie

    ¾ cup sugar
    ¼ cup cornstarch
  1⅓ cups grape juice
    1 egg, slightly beaten
    2 tablespoons butter or margarine
    2 tablespoons lemon juice
    1 baked 9-inch pie shell
       Whipped cream (optional)

Mix sugar and cornstarch in saucepan. Gradually stir in grape juice. Cook over medium heat, stirring constantly until mixture thickens and starts to boil. Boil for 1 minute. Remove from heat; slowly stir mixture into beaten egg. Return to heat, add butter and lemon juice, and boil 1 minute. Pour into baked pie shell and cool. Serve plain or with whipped cream. Yield: one 9-inch pie.

✓ Lemon Chess Pie

    3 eggs
    1 cup sugar
    ½ cup light corn syrup
    ⅓ cup melted margarine
    ⅓ cup commercial sour cream
    1 tablespoon corn meal
    1 tablespoon lemon juice
    ½ teaspoon vanilla extract
    1 unbaked 9-inch pastry shell
    ⅓ cup flaked coconut (optional)

Beat eggs and sugar in mixing bowl. Add corn syrup, melted margarine, sour cream, corn meal, lemon juice, and vanilla. Blend thoroughly. Pour into pastry shell. Sprinkle with coconut. Bake at 350° for 45 to 50 minutes or until almost set. Yield: one 9-inch pie.

Lemon-Cherry Pie

    1 (15-ounce) can sweetened condensed milk
    ⅓ cup lemon juice
    ½ teaspoon vanilla extract
    ½ teaspoon almond extract
    ½ cup whipping cream, whipped
    1 stick piecrust mix
    ½ cup ground or finely chopped almonds
    1 (22-ounce) can cherry pie filling

Mix first 4 ingredients well. Whip the cream and fold into this mixture. Let sit in refrigerator 2 to 3 hours.

Mix piecrust according to package directions, adding almonds to the mixture. Roll pastry and fit into a 9-inch piepan. Prick pastry and bake at 475° for 8 to 10 minutes. Cool.

Add the chilled mixture to cooled piecrust, and pour the cherry filling over top. Return to refrigerator until ready to serve. Yield: one 9-inch pie.

Lemon Tarts

    1 cup sugar
    ¼ cup cornstarch
  1¼ cups milk
    3 egg yolks, slightly beaten
    1 teaspoon grated lemon rind
    ⅓ cup lemon juice
    ¼ cup margarine
    1 cup commercial sour cream
    6 to 8 baked 3-inch tart shells
       Lemon slices for garnish

Mix sugar and cornstarch in a 2-quart saucepan. Gradually add milk, stirring until smooth. Stir in egg yolks, lemon rind, and lemon juice until blended. Add margarine and cook over medium heat, stirring constantly, until mixture comes to a boil. Boil for 1 minute.

Pour into bowl, and cover with waxed paper or plastic film. Chill. Fold in sour cream. Turn into baked pastry shells. Serve at once or chill until serving time. If desired, garnish with lemon slices. Yield: 6 to 8 servings.

Lemon Cream Cheese Pie

1 (3-ounce) package regular (not instant) lemon pudding and pie filling mix
1 (3-ounce) package cream cheese, softened
¼ cup sugar
1 (9-inch) baked pie shell
Whipped cream (optional)
Ground cinnamon (optional)

Prepare pie filling, but where package directions call for whole eggs, use only egg yolks, reserving the whites. Remove from heat and add cream cheese, beating well. Beat egg whites until stiff; gradually add sugar and beat until stiff peaks form. Fold into lemon mixture. Spoon into baked pie shell and chill until cool. Put whipped cream and a dash of cinnamon on each serving, if desired. Yield: one 9-inch pie.

Lemon Custard Pie

6 eggs, slightly beaten
1½ cups sugar
2 teaspoons grated lemon peel
⅔ cup lemon juice
1½ cups water
Unbaked 9-inch pie shell
Ground nutmeg (optional)

Combine eggs, sugar, grated lemon peel, lemon juice, and water in a large mixing bowl; beat at low speed for 5 minutes. Pour into unbaked pie shell. Bake at 425° for 25 minutes; reduce heat to 250° and bake 10 minutes longer. Sprinkle top with nutmeg, if desired. Cool on rack. Yield: one 9-inch pie.

Lemon Cream Pie

Cream Cheese Pastry:

1⅔ cups all-purpose flour
½ teaspoon salt
1 (3-ounce) package cream cheese, softened
⅔ cup butter, softened

Combine flour and salt in mixing bowl. Mix cream cheese and butter together thoroughly. Blend cheese-butter mixture into dry ingredients until it forms a dough. Shape mixture into flat, round patty. Wrap and chill in refrigerator until firm. Roll about ⅛ inch thick on lightly floured board or pastry cloth. Fit crust into a 9-inch pan and trim 1 inch beyond edge of pan. Fold crust under and flute edge. Prick bottom and sides of crust with fork. Chill. Bake at 425° until crisp and brown, 12 to 15 minutes. Cool and fill with Lemon Cream Filling. Yield: one 9-inch shell.

Lemon Cream Filling:

1 cup sugar
⅓ cup cornstarch
¼ teaspoon salt
2 cups milk, scalded
2 tablespoons butter
3 egg yolks, beaten
⅓ cup lemon juice
1 teaspoon grated lemon peel
1 egg white

Mix sugar, cornstarch, and salt in top of double boiler. Add hot milk slowly, stirring constantly. Add butter, and blend. Cook over boiling water until thick, stirring constantly. Remove from heat and stir a small amount of hot mixture into beaten egg yolks. Add yolks to remaining hot mixture, stirring vigorously. Blend in lemon juice and peel. Return to heat and cook 2 minutes. Remove from heat and fold in stiffly beaten egg white. Cool slightly and pour into baked pastry shell. Make meringue border (recipe below) around edge of pie. Lightly brown meringue at 400° for 5 to 7 minutes. Chill. Yield: one 9-inch pie.

Meringue:

¼ teaspoon salt
¼ teaspoon lemon extract
2 egg whites
¼ cup sugar

Add salt and extract to egg whites; beat until they form soft peaks. Add sugar, 1 tablespoon at a time; beat well after each addition. Continue beating until mixture forms stiff peaks.

Frozen Lemon Pie

  3 *egg yolks, beaten*
½ *cup sugar*
¼ *cup lemon juice*
     Grated rind of 1 lemon
     Pinch of salt
  3 *egg whites*
¼ *cup sugar*
  1 *(5⅓-ounce) can evaporated milk, chilled and whipped*
     Vanilla wafer crumbs

Combine beaten egg yolks, sugar, lemon juice, lemon rind, and salt in top of double boiler and cook until thick. Beat egg whites until stiff, and add ¼ cup sugar. Whip milk and combine with egg whites. Fold cooked mixture into egg whites and whipped milk. Sprinkle bottom of 8-inch piepan with vanilla wafer crumbs. Pour in pie mixture; cover with crumbs and freeze. Yield: one 8-inch pie.

Lemon Meringue Pie

   ½ *cup sugar*
   4 *tablespoons cornstarch*
   ¼ *teaspoon salt*
1½ *cups water*
   3 *egg yolks*
   ½ *cup sugar*
   2 *tablespoons margarine*
   ⅓ *cup lemon juice*
1½ *teaspoons grated lemon rind*
   1 *baked 9-inch pastry shell*
   3 *egg whites*
   6 *tablespoons sugar*

Combine ½ cup sugar, cornstarch, and salt in top of double boiler. Gradually blend in water. Cook over boiling water, stirring constantly until thickened. Cover; cook 10 minutes longer, stirring occasionally. Meanwhile, beat together egg yolks and ½ cup sugar. Blend a little of the hot mixture into egg yolks; then stir yolks into remaining hot mixture. Cook over boiling water 2 minutes; stir constantly. Remove from boiling water. Add margarine, lemon juice, and lemon rind. Cool and pour into baked shell. Beat egg whites until foamy. Add sugar, 1 tablespoon at a time; beat well after each addition. Continue beating until stiff peaks form when beater is raised. First spread meringue around edge of filling to touch crust; then fill in center. Bake for 15 to 20 minutes at 350°. Cool at room temperature away from drafts. Yield: one 9-inch pie.

Macaroon Pie

14 *saltine crackers, finely crushed*
12 *chopped dates*
 ½ *cup chopped pecans*
  1 *generous teaspoon almond extract*
 ¼ *teaspoon salt*
  1 *cup sugar*
  3 *egg whites*

Mix all ingredients except egg whites. Beat egg whites and fold into mixture. Bake in a greased 9-inch piepan at 300° for about 45 minutes. Serve with whipped cream. Yield: one 9-inch pie.

Spicy Mince Pie

1⅓ *cups sugar*
  ½ *teaspoon salt*
  ½ *teaspoon ground cinnamon*
  ¼ *teaspoon ground cloves*
  ¼ *teaspoon ground ginger*
1½ *cups chopped apples*
  1 *cup seedless raisins*
  ½ *cup jellied cranberry sauce*
  ⅓ *cup chopped walnuts*
  1 *teaspoon grated orange peel*
  ½ *teaspoon grated lemon peel*
  ¼ *cup lemon juice*
     Pastry for double crust (9-inch) pie
  1 *tablespoon butter*

Combine sugar, salt, and spices. Add apples, raisins, cranberry sauce, walnuts, orange peel, lemon peel, and lemon juice; mix well. Pour into pastry-lined 9-inch piepan. Dot with butter. Add top crust. Bake at 400° for 30 to 35 minutes. Serve warm. Yield: one 9-inch pie.

Avocado Lime Pie

- 2 cups sugar, divided
- 1/3 cup cornstarch
- 1/4 teaspoon salt
- 1 1/2 cups water
- 4 eggs, separated
- 1 tablespoon grated lime peel
- 1 avocado
- 1/2 cup fresh lime juice (about 5 limes)
- 9-inch baked pie shell
- 1/4 teaspoon cream of tartar
- 1/8 teaspoon salt

Blend 1 1/2 cups sugar, cornstarch, and salt; gradually stir in water. Stir constantly over medium heat and allow to boil 30 seconds. Gradually beat half of hot mixture into beaten egg yolks; then return to saucepan. Stir and boil 1 minute longer. Remove from heat and stir in lime peel. Puree the avocado with lime juice, and blend with egg mixture. Turn into 9-inch baked pie shell.

To make meringue, beat egg whites, cream of tartar, and salt until foamy. Continue beating, gradually adding remaining 1/2 cup sugar; beat until stiff but not dry. Top pie with meringue. Bake at 350° for 10 to 15 minutes until golden brown. Yield: one 9-inch pie.

*Southern Molasses Pie

- 1 1/2 cups all-purpose flour
- 1/2 cup firmly packed brown sugar
- 1/4 teaspoon salt
- 1/4 teaspoon ground cinnamon
- 1/8 teaspoon ground cloves
- 1/8 teaspoon ground ginger (optional)
- 1/8 teaspoon ground nutmeg
- 1/4 cup margarine
- 1 cup boiling water
- 1/2 cup dark molasses
- 1 1/2 teaspoons soda
- 1 egg, slightly beaten
- 1 (10-inch) unbaked pastry shell
- Whipped cream

In large bowl, combine flour, sugar, salt, and spices. Cut in margarine with pastry blender or two knives until mixture resembles coarse meal. Combine water, molasses, and baking soda; blend in egg. Alternate layers of flour mixture and molasses mixture in pastry-lined piepan, beginning and ending with flour mixture. Bake in hot oven at 450° for 10 minutes. Reduce heat to 350° and bake 15 minutes longer. Top with whipped cream. Yield: one 10-inch pie.

Grandma's Molasses Pie

- 5 eggs
- 3 tablespoons all-purpose flour
- 1 cup sugar
- 1/2 cup softened butter or margarine
- 1 teaspoon ground allspice
- 1 teaspoon ground cloves
- Pinch of salt
- 1 1/2 cups unsulphured molasses
- Pastry for two (9-inch) pies

Combine eggs, flour, sugar, butter, allspice, cloves, and salt in mixing bowl and beat until well blended. Put molasses in saucepan; bring to a boil and pour over egg mixture. Stir well; then pour into prepared pie shells. Bake at 300° for 30 to 40 minutes or until mixture is firm in center. Yield: two 9-inch pies.

Persimmon Pie

- 2 cups persimmon pulp
- 1 beaten egg
- 1 cup milk
- 1/2 cup sugar
- Dash salt
- 1 tablespoon cornstarch
- Unbaked 9-inch pie shell

Beat together persimmon pulp, egg, and milk. Combine sugar, salt, and cornstarch; mix well, and stir into persimmon mixture. Spoon filling into pie shell. Bake at 400° for 10 minutes; reduce heat to 350° and bake an additional 50 minutes. Yield: one 9-inch pie.

Millionaire Pie

1 (15-ounce) can sweetened condensed milk
⅓ cup lemon juice
⅓ cup chopped maraschino cherries
⅓ cup chopped pecans
⅓ cup crushed pineapple
1 (8- or 9-inch) baked pie shell
Whipped cream

Blend milk and lemon juice. Stir in cherries, pecans, and pineapple and mix well. Spoon into baked pie shell (pastry or graham cracker crust.) Chill for 2 hours and top with whipped cream before serving. Yield: one 8- or 9-inch pie.

*Oatmeal Pie

¾ cup sugar
6 tablespoons softened margarine
2 eggs
⅔ cup dark corn syrup
⅔ cup regular oats, uncooked
1 teaspoon vanilla extract
Unbaked 9-inch pie shell

Cream together sugar and margarine. Add eggs and beat well. Stir in corn syrup, oats, and vanilla. Pour into unbaked pie shell, and bake at 325° about 40 to 45 minutes or until done. Yield: one 9-inch pie.

Fresh Peach Chiffon Pie

1 envelope (1 tablespoon) unflavored gelatin
¼ cup cold water
3 egg yolks, slightly beaten
¼ cup sugar
1½ cups fresh peaches, slightly mashed
¼ teaspoon salt
1 tablespoon lemon juice
¼ teaspoon almond extract
3 egg whites
¼ cup sugar
1 (9-inch) baked pie shell

Soften gelatin in cold water and set aside. Combine slightly beaten egg yolks, ¼ cup sugar, mashed peaches, salt, and lemon juice in the top of a double boiler. Cook over simmering water until mixture is slightly thickened and coats a metal spoon. Remove from heat and stir in softened gelatin. Cool until mixture begins to set. Add almond extract.

Beat egg whites until stiff but not dry, gradually adding ¼ cup sugar. Fold egg whites into peach mixture. Spoon into baked pie shell and chill until firm. Yield: one 9-inch pie.

Southern Pecan Pie

1 cup pecan halves
1 (9-inch) unbaked pie shell
3 eggs
1 cup dark corn syrup
1 cup sugar
2 tablespoons margarine, melted
1 teaspoon vanilla extract
⅛ teaspoon salt

Place pecan halves in a pattern in bottom of unbaked pastry shell. Beat eggs slightly; mix in corn syrup, sugar, margarine, vanilla, and salt. Gently pour into unbaked shell. Bake at 400° for 15 minutes; lower temperature to 350° and bake an additional 30 to 35 minutes (filling should be slightly less set in center than around edge). Yield: one 9-inch pie.

"Down-Home" Pecan Pie

1 cup sugar
½ cup white corn syrup
¼ cup butter
1 tablespoon vinegar
3 eggs
1 cup pecans (chopped or whole)
¼ teaspoon ground allspice
¼ teaspoon ground nutmeg
1 unbaked 9-inch pie shell

Mix sugar, syrup, butter, and vinegar. Bring to a boil and boil 1 minute. Cool slightly. Stir eggs with a fork and stir into mixture. Add nuts and spices. Pour into unbaked pastry shell. Bake at 350° for 10 minutes; lower temperature to 300° and bake 35 more minutes. Yield: one 9-inch pie.

Date Pecan Pie

 2 tablespoons margarine, melted
 ¼ cup half-and-half
 ¾ cup sugar
 2 tablespoons all-purpose flour
 1 teaspoon salt
 1 cup dark corn syrup
 2 eggs
 1 cup finely chopped dates
 ½ cup pecan halves
 1 teaspoon vanilla extract
 1 unbaked (9-inch) 1-2-3 pastry shell

Combine margarine and cream. Mix sugar, flour, and salt in bowl. Blend in dark corn syrup. Beat in eggs, one at a time. Stir in cream mixture, then dates, pecans, and vanilla. Pour into unbaked pastry shell. Bake at 400° for 15 minutes; reduce heat to 350° and continue baking until pie is set, 30 to 35 minutes longer. (Filling should be slightly less set in center than at outer edge.) Yield: one 9-inch pie.

 1-2-3 Pastry:

 1 cup plus 2 tablespoons all-purpose flour
 ½ teaspoon salt
 ⅓ cup corn oil
 2 tablespoons cold water

Mix flour and salt. Blend in oil thoroughly with fork. Sprinkle the water over mixture; mix well. Press dough firmly into ball with hands. If it's too dry, mix in 1 to 2 tablespoons more oil.

Flatten dough slightly; immediately roll into 12-inch circle between 2 pieces of waxed paper. Wipe counter with damp cloth to keep paper from slipping. Peel off top paper; place pastry in pan, paper-side up. Peel off paper; fit pastry loosely in pan. Trim ½ inch beyond rim of pan. Fold under and flute. Yield: one 9-inch pastry shell.

Praline Pie

 ⅓ cup butter or margarine
 ⅓ cup firmly packed brown sugar
 ½ cup chopped pecans
 1 lightly baked 8-inch pie shell
 1 (3¾-ounce) package butterscotch pudding and pie filling mix (not instant)
 2 cups milk
 1 cup prepared whipped topping
Pecan halves

Combine butter and brown sugar in a saucepan; cook and stir until sugar melts and mixture bubbles vigorously. Remove from heat and stir in pecans. Spread mixture over bottom of pie shell. Bake at 425° for 5 minutes or until bubbly. Remove from oven.

Combine pudding mix and milk in a saucepan; cook and stir over medium heat until mixture comes to a full boil. Remove from heat. Cool 5 minutes, stirring once or twice. Spoon into pie shell over nut layer. Chill until set. Garnish with prepared whipped topping and pecan halves before serving. Yield: one 8-inch pie.

Pineapple Cheese Pie

 2 (8-ounce) packages cream cheese, softened
 ½ cup sugar
 ½ teaspoon vanilla extract
 2 eggs
 1 (13¼-ounce) can crushed pineapple, well drained
 1 (9-inch) graham cracker crust

Combine cream cheese, sugar, and vanilla; mix until well blended. Add eggs, one at a time, mixing well after each addition. Stir in pineapple; pour into graham cracker crust. Bake at 325° for 25 minutes. Cool before serving. Yield: one 9-inch pie.

Pineapple-Lemon Lattice Pie

½ cup sugar
3 tablespoons cornstarch
¼ teaspoon salt
1 (20-ounce) can crushed pineapple, undrained
½ cup canned pineapple juice
2 tablespoons butter or margarine
2 tablespoons lemon juice
1 teaspoon grated lemon peel
⅔ cup flaked coconut
Pastry for 9-inch double crust pie

Blend together sugar, cornstarch, and salt. Stir in undrained crushed pineapple and pineapple juice. Cook, stirring, over moderate heat until mixture boils and thickens. Stir in butter. Remove from heat; add lemon juice, lemon peel, and coconut. Cool about 5 minutes. Pour into pastry-lined 9-inch piepan.

Cut remaining pastry into ½-inch wide strips and lay across filled pie about 1 inch apart. Weave with remaining strips to make lattice effect. Fold lower crust up and over pastry strips. Press to seal; flute edges. Bake, below oven center, at 425° for 30 to 35 minutes. Cool before serving. Yield: one 9-inch pie.

Pineapple Pie

2 egg whites
¼ teaspoon cream of tartar
¾ cup sugar
1 teaspoon almond flavoring
18 soda crackers, crushed
1 cup finely chopped pecans
½ pint whipping cream
1 (12-ounce) jar pineapple or peach preserves
1 (7-ounce) can flaked coconut

To make pie shell, beat egg whites with cream of tartar until stiff. Gradually add sugar as you beat. Add almond flavoring. Fold in cracker crumbs and pecans. Pour into greased pieplate (makes one large pie or two 9-inch pies). Bake at 350° for 25 minutes. Cool. Whip cream and into it fold preserves. Pile on top of cooled pie shell and sprinkle heavily with flaked coconut. Chill before serving. This freezes well. Yield: one 10- to 11-inch pie or two 9-inch pies.

Banana Pumpkin Pie

3 eggs, well beaten
¾ cup sugar
2 teaspoons pumpkin pie spice
½ teaspoon salt
1¾ cups canned pumpkin
1 cup evaporated milk
½ cup water
1 (9-inch) unbaked pie shell
1 cup whipping cream, whipped
1 banana, sliced

Mix together well-beaten eggs, sugar, spice, salt, and pumpkin. Add milk and water; stir until smooth. Pour into pie shell. Bake at 425° for 45 to 55 minutes or until mixture is firm and crust is well browned. Just before serving, spoon whipped cream in a circle on pie. Arrange slices of banana in the whipped cream. Yield: one 9-inch pie.

Pumpkin-Pecan Pie

3 eggs, slightly beaten
1 cup canned or cooked mashed pumpkin
1 cup sugar
½ cup dark corn syrup
1 teaspoon vanilla extract
½ teaspoon ground cinnamon
¼ teaspoon salt
1 unbaked 9-inch pastry shell
1 cup chopped pecans
Whipped cream

Combine eggs, pumpkin, sugar, corn syrup, vanilla, cinnamon, and salt; mix well. Pour into pastry shell. Top with chopped pecans. Bake at 350° for about 40 minutes or until knife inserted in center comes out clean; chill. To serve, top with whipped cream. Yield: one 9-inch pie.

Makes-Its-Own-Crust Raisin Pie

  ¼ *cup butter or margarine*
  ¾ *cup sugar*
  3 *eggs*
  1 *teaspoon vanilla extract*
 1½ *cups seedless raisins*
  ½ *cup chopped walnuts*
  ½ *(9¼-ounce) package piecrust mix*
   Whipped cream

Cream butter and sugar. Add eggs and continue beating until light and fluffy. Add vanilla, raisins, and chopped walnuts. Crumble piecrust mix and add to mixture; stir well and spoon into a well-oiled 9-inch piepan. Bake at 325° about 35 minutes or until pie is firm in center. Cool. Serve with whipped cream. Yield: one 9-inch pie.

Candied Fruit Rum Pie

  1 *envelope (1 tablespoon) unflavored gelatin*
  ¼ *cup water*
  3 *large eggs, separated*
  ½ *cup sugar*
  1 *cup milk*
  ¼ *teaspoon ground mace*
  ¼ *cup light rum*
  ¼ *cup diced candied fruit*
  ⅛ *teaspoon salt*
  1 *cup whipped cream*
  1 *(9-inch) baked pastry shell*
   Whipped cream (optional)
   Candied cherries (optional)

Soften gelatin in water and set aside. Beat egg yolks lightly in top of double boiler. Blend in sugar and milk; cook 10 minutes over hot (not boiling) water until thickened. Remove from heat. Stir in gelatin, mace, and rum. Chill until mixture begins to thicken. Add candied fruit.

 Add salt to egg whites and beat until stiff peaks form; fold into custard along with 1 cup whipped cream. Pour into pastry shell. Chill. Before serving, garnish with additional whipped cream and candied cherries, if desired. Yield: one 9-inch pie.

Best-Ever Rhubarb Pie

   About 1½ pounds unpeeled rhubarb
  2 *egg yolks*
 1⅓ *cups sugar*
  3 *tablespoons quick-cooking tapioca*
  1 *tablespoon grated orange rind*
   Unbaked 9-inch pie shell
  2 *egg whites*
  ¼ *cup sugar*

Cut rhubarb into 1-inch pieces and measure 4 cups. Beat egg yolks; add sugar, tapioca, and orange rind, and add to rhubarb. Stir to mix well.

 Spoon mixture into unbaked pie shell and bake at 450° about 10 minutes. Reduce heat to 350° and bake about 30 to 40 minutes longer or until rhubarb is tender.

 Beat egg whites until stiff, but not dry. Add sugar, beating well to make meringue. Spoon meringue in a ring around edge of pie, leaving center of pie open. Return to oven and bake about 8 to 10 minutes or until meringue is brown. Yield: one 9-inch pie.

*Deep-Dish Strawberry Pie

  ½ *to 1 cup sugar (depending on sweetness of berries)*
  ¼ *cup all-purpose flour*
  ⅛ *teaspoon salt*
  4 *cups washed and hulled strawberries*
  2 *tablespoons butter*
   Pastry for 1 (9-inch) single crust pie
   Plain or whipped cream

Combine sugar with flour and salt. Toss lightly with the berries. Fill a 1-quart baking dish with the fruit mixture and dot with butter. Top with the pastry which has been rolled out on pastry cloth to size 1 inch larger all around than top of baking dish. Fold edges of pastry under and press firmly to rim of dish. Flute edges and cut gashes in pastry to allow steam to escape. Bake at 425° for 25 minutes or until crust is browned. Serve slightly warm with plain or whipped cream. Yield: one 9-inch pie.

Strawberry Glacé Pie

    2 *pints strawberries, divided*
    ¾ *cup sugar*
    3 *tablespoons cornstarch*
    ¼ *cup orange juice*
    1 *(3-ounce) package cream cheese, softened*
    ¼ *teaspoon grated orange peel*
    1 *(9-inch) baked pie shell*
       Sweetened whipped cream

Puree 1 pint of strawberries in blender; strain to remove seeds. Combine sugar and cornstarch in small saucepan. Stir in strawberry puree and orange juice. Cook and stir over medium heat until mixture boils for 1 minute. Cool. Blend cream cheese and orange peel; spread in bottom of pie shell. Add three-fourths of strawberry filling. Arrange remaining whole strawberries on top and glaze them with remaining filling. Chill about 3 hours. Pipe whipped cream around edge of pie. Yield: one 9-inch pie.

Strawberry Chiffon Pie

    1 *pint fresh strawberries*
    ¾ *cup sugar, divided*
  1½ *envelopes unflavored gelatin*
    ¼ *cup cold water*
    ½ *cup boiling water*
    1 *tablespoon lemon juice*
    ½ *cup whipping cream*
    2 *egg whites*
    ⅛ *teaspoon salt*
    1 *(9-inch) baked pie shell*
       Whipped cream (optional)

Reserve a few strawberries for garnish; halve remainder and puree in electric blender with ½ cup of the sugar, or force through food mill and add sugar. Strain thoroughly to remove seeds. Soften gelatin in cold water; stir in boiling water until dissolved. Add to strawberry puree; stir in lemon juice and mix well. Chill until mixture mounds when dropped from a spoon.

  Whip cream and fold into strawberry mixture. Beat egg whites with salt until soft peaks form. Gradually add remaining sugar, beating constantly until whites are glossy and stiff. Fold into strawberry mixture. Spoon into baked pie shell (if mixture isn't stiff enough to mound, chill 10 to 15 minutes before spooning into shell). Chill 4 hours or overnight. Garnish with reserved strawberries and additional whipped cream, if desired. Yield: one 9-inch pie.

Glazed Strawberry Pie

    2 *cups very ripe strawberries*
       Water
    4 *tablespoons cornstarch*
    1 *cup sugar*
    1 *tablespoon butter or margarine*
    2 *tablespoons lemon juice*
       Dash salt
    4 *cups firm whole strawberries*
       Baked 9-inch pie shell
       Whipped cream

Crush 2 cups strawberries in a small saucepan. Heat slowly to boiling point and simmer for 2 to 3 minutes. Strain through a sieve, then through cheesecloth to make a clear liquid. Add enough water to make 1½ cups liquid. Stir the cornstarch in a small amount of the liquid, and mix with remaining liquid. Add sugar. Bring to a boil, stirring constantly, and cook until mixture thickens, about 5 minutes. Remove from heat and add butter, lemon juice, and salt. Cool.

  Arrange 4 cups whole strawberries in the baked pie shell. Spoon cooled sauce over the berries. Chill. Spread whipped cream around outer edge of pie. Yield: one 9-inch pie.

Colorful Glazed Strawberry Pie

1 quart fresh strawberries or 2 pints frozen whole strawberries
1 baked 9-inch pastry shell, cooled
Strawberry Glaze
Whipped cream, sweetened

Wash, drain, and hull fresh strawberries or thaw frozen berries. Place berries in cooled, baked shell. Spoon Strawberry Glaze over all; be sure that all berries are covered. Cool. Just before serving, spread with sweetened cream. Yield: one 9-inch pie.

Strawberry Glaze:

1 pint strawberries
½ cup water
1 cup sugar
2½ tablespoons cornstarch
1 tablespoon butter
Red food coloring

Crush berries well; combine with water and cook about 5 minutes. Strain and add sugar and cornstarch. Bring to a boil, and cook until mixture is clear. Add butter and enough food coloring for an attractive red color. Cool slightly; spoon over strawberries in pie shell.

Strawberry-Rhubarb Pie

2 cups fully ripened strawberries
½ cup sugar
3 tablespoons cornstarch
4 tablespoons cold water
2½ cups diced rhubarb
Pastry for 9-inch double crust pie
1 cup sugar
2 tablespoons butter or margarine

Stem and wash berries. Mix with ½ cup sugar and mash to extract juice. Set aside. Stir cornstarch into cold water and mix well. Add to strawberries in a small saucepan; mix well, and cook on medium heat until juice is clear and thickened. Spread rhubarb on bottom crust of pie shell. Sprinkle with 1 cup sugar and dot with butter. Spoon cooled strawberry mixture over rhubarb. Cover with top crust; slit in several places to allow steam to escape. Bake at 450° for 10 minutes; reduce heat to 350° and bake an additional 30 minutes. Yield: one 9-inch pie.

Strawberry Pineapple Lattice Pie

2 pints strawberries
1 (8¼-ounce) can crushed pineapple, drained
¾ cup sugar
¼ cup cornstarch
¼ teaspoon salt
Pastry for double crust 9-inch pie
1 tablespoon margarine
Milk

Combine strawberries, pineapple, sugar, cornstarch, and salt; set aside. Fit pastry into bottom of pieplate. Add fruit; dot with margarine. Cut remaining pastry into strips to form lattice top; trim and flute edge. Brush pastry with milk. Bake at 400° for 45 minutes or until crust is golden brown. Yield: one 9-inch pie.

Strawberry 'n Cream Pie

1¼ cups graham cracker crumbs
¼ cup butter, softened
¼ cup sugar
1 (10-ounce) package frozen strawberries
1 (10½-ounce) package marshmallows
1 cup whipping cream

Mix graham cracker crumbs with softened butter and sugar. Spoon crumb mixture into 10-inch pieplate. Press mixture firmly against bottom and sides of pieplate. Bake at 375° for 8 minutes. Cool.

Thaw strawberries and drain off juice. Pour juice into top of double boiler; add marshmallows and heat until they dissolve. Cool mixture; then fold in strawberries. Whip cream and fold into strawberry mixture. Pour into crust; chill in refrigerator for 3 to 4 hours. Yield: one 10-inch pie.

Sky-High Pie

- ½ teaspoon vinegar
- 1 teaspoon vanilla extract
- ¼ teaspoon salt
- 4 egg whites
- 1 cup sugar
- ½ cup uncooked regular oatmeal, browned
- 1 pint whipping cream, whipped
- 2 cups fresh or frozen strawberries or peaches

Combine vinegar, vanilla, and salt; stir into egg whites and beat until frothy. Gradually add sugar, beating well after each addition. Continue beating until mixture is stiff and glossy. Lightly fold in browned oatmeal. (To brown oatmeal, place on cookie sheet and brown at 375° for 10 to 15 minutes. This makes it crisp and provides a nutty flavor.)

Put egg white mixture in a mound on well-greased brown paper placed on a baking sheet. With spatula or back of tablespoon, hollow out the center and build up the sides to resemble a pie shell. Bake at 275° for 45 minutes to 1 hour. Cool for a few minutes and remove brown paper. Place the shell on a serving plate and cool thoroughly. Fill the center with sweetened whipped cream to which fruit has been added. Yield: 6 to 8 servings.

Sherry Pie

- 1½ cups graham cracker crumbs
- ¼ cup sugar
- ¼ cup butter or margarine, melted
- ¾ cup miniature marshmallows
- ¾ cup cream sherry
- 1 cup whipping cream, whipped
- Grated chocolate

To make crust, combine graham cracker crumbs and sugar. Stir in melted butter and mix well. Press mixture on bottom and sides of 8- or 9-inch piepan. Bake at 300° for 10 minutes; cool.

Combine marshmallows and sherry in top of double boiler. Place over hot (not boiling) water and cook until smooth. Cool thoroughly. Fold in whipped cream and spoon mixture into prepared crust. Sprinkle grated chocolate on top; chill thoroughly. Yield: one 8- or 9-inch pie.

Marshmallow Prune Pie

- 1 cup graham cracker crumbs
- 1 tablespoon sugar
- ⅓ cup melted margarine
- 2 cups miniature marshmallows
- ½ cup milk
- 1½ cups chopped, cooked dried prunes
- 1 tablespoon lemon juice
- ⅛ teaspoon salt
- ⅔ cup whipping cream, whipped

Combine cracker crumbs, sugar, and melted margarine. Press into a 9-inch piepan. Melt marshmallows in milk in top of a double boiler. Cool. Add prunes, lemon juice, and salt. Fold mixture into whipped cream. Pour into graham cracker crust and chill until set. Yield: one 9-inch pie.

Alsatian Cream Pie

- ½ cup all-purpose flour
- ½ cup cold unseasoned mashed potatoes
- ½ teaspoon salt
- 1 tablespoon shortening
- Cold water
- 1½ cups commercial sour cream
- 1 egg, beaten
- ¼ teaspoon salt
- ½ teaspoon ground allspice

Measure flour into large bowl. Add mashed potatoes, salt, and shortening and mix with pastry blender. Add enough water to make dough easy to handle (1 tablespoon at a time). Roll thin and place in a 9-inch pieplate.

Combine sour cream, beaten egg, salt, and allspice. Mix well and pour into prepared pastry shell. Bake at 350° about 20 to 25 minutes. Serve warm. Yield: one 9-inch pie.

Double Crust Rhubarb Pie

1½ cups sugar
3 tablespoons all-purpose flour
½ teaspoon ground nutmeg
1 tablespoon softened butter or margarine
2 eggs, well beaten
3 cups cut rhubarb
Pastry for a 9-inch double crust pie

Combine sugar, flour, nutmeg, and butter and mix well. Stir into well-beaten eggs and mix well. Place rhubarb, cut into 1-inch pieces, in bottom crust of pie shell. Pour sugar-egg mixture over rhubarb. Cover with top crust that has been cut into strips. Bake at 450° about 10 minutes; reduce heat to 325° and cook an additional 30 minutes. Yield: one 9-inch pie.

✓ Raisin Nut Pie

¾ cup water
2 cups seedless raisins
1 tablespoon cider vinegar
1 tablespoon butter or margarine
½ cup chopped nuts
⅔ cup sugar
1 tablespoon all-purpose flour
¼ teaspoon salt
Pastry for 8-inch double crust pie, unbaked

Add water to raisins and simmer until approximately ¼ cup liquid remains. Add vinegar, butter, and nuts. Cool slightly. Mix sugar, flour, and salt. Stir into raisin-nut mixture and pour into pastry-lined pie-pan. Cover with top crust or lattice strips. Bake at 450° for 10 minutes; then reduce heat to 375° and bake 25 minutes longer. Serve slightly warm. Yield: one 8-inch pie.

* Transparent Pie

½ cup butter
1 cup sugar
3 eggs, separated
1 tablespoon all-purpose flour
1 cup whipping cream
1 teaspoon vanilla extract
1 (10- or 11-inch) unbaked pie shell
6 teaspoons tart jelly
6 tablespoons sugar

Cream butter and 1 cup sugar until light and fluffy. Add egg yolks and flour and beat well. Stir in cream and vanilla; blend mixture. Dot pie shell with jelly, and pour cream mixture over it. Bake at 325° for 1 hour. Remove from oven and allow to cool.
Beat egg whites until foamy; gradually add 6 tablespoons sugar, and continue beating until meringue stands in peaks. Spread over cooled pie and bake at 350° for about 10 minutes or until meringue is brown. Yield: one 10- or 11-inch pie.

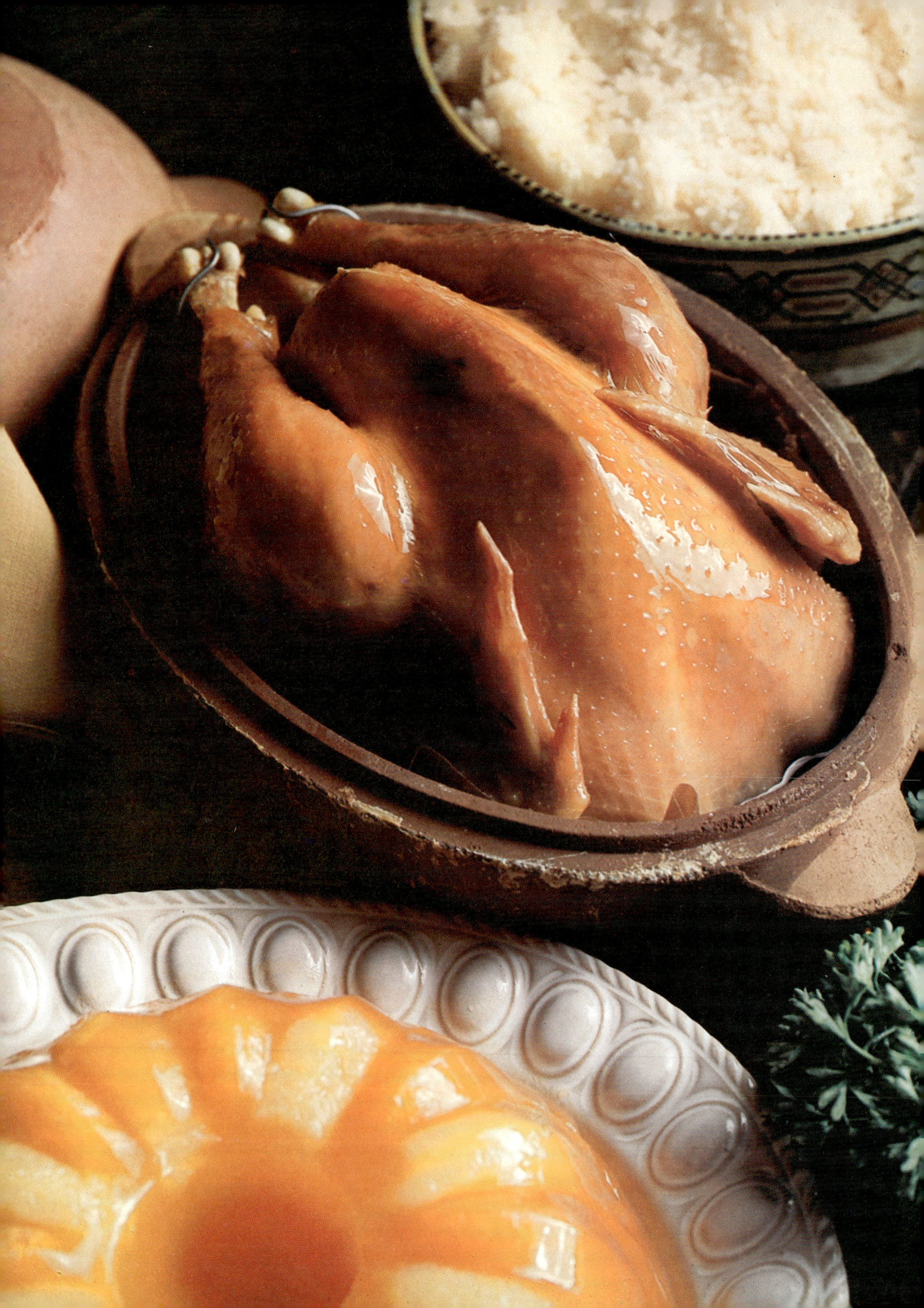

Poultry and Dressing

Mention chicken south of the Mason-Dixon Line and the immediate response is "fried," but just try to get the typical recipe. Every cook has her own secret method of seasoning and frying, although the results are all invariably delicious. Chicken and dumplings is another popular entrée, as is baked chicken, and the number of variations on the chicken casserole theme would stagger the mind.

Thanksgiving would hardly be a holiday without the traditional turkey and dressing. Here, too, there is some controversy about what constitutes the typical dressing, or stuffing, as Southerners prefer to call it. Some loyally swear by the time-honored sage dressing, and others like oyster dressing. Most cooks agree, however, that the basic ingredient should be corn bread and not that "Yankee white stuff."

*Southern Fried Chicken

- 1 (2- to 2½-pound) fryer chicken
- ¾ cup all-purpose flour
- 2½ teaspoons salt
- ¾ teaspoon freshly ground black pepper
- Vegetable shortening

Cut chicken into serving-size pieces. Wash thoroughly under cold running water. Drain, but do not dry.

Combine flour, salt, and pepper in a brown paper bag. Add a few pieces of the chicken at a time, close top of bag, and shake so that pieces are well coated with flour.

Heat shortening (enough for depth of about ½ inch) in a 10- or 11-inch heavy skillet. Be sure that shortening is very hot before dropping in the pieces of chicken, fleshy side down. Cook rapidly for a few minutes until the pieces have a light brown crust on bottom. Turn each piece as it reaches this state and brown other side.

Reduce heat to quite low and cover the skillet. Cook approximately 20 minutes. Remove cover and turn heat up to cook chicken to a golden brown, turning so each side is evenly browned. Remove pieces and drain on paper towels. Yield: 4 servings.

Chicken Kiev

- 4 boned, unskinned chicken breasts
- 4 tablespoons butter or margarine, cut into pats
- Chopped parsley and/or tarragon (optional)
- 2 eggs
- Salt and pepper to taste
- ½ cup bread crumbs
- Salad oil

Put meat between two pieces of waxed paper or two paper plates and pound with mallet or other heavy object until flattened. Set each mashed chicken piece, skin side down, on a separate paper plate. Put butter pat near one end and lightly sprinkle with herbs, if desired. Roll meat, starting at butter end, and fasten with one or two toothpicks. Continue operation for all 4 pieces.

(If you wish to freeze these for later use, do so now, continuing recipe after thawing.)

Beat eggs with salt and pepper. Dip rolled breasts in beaten egg and then in bread crumbs; fry in hot oil, with heat turned down to medium as cooking starts. Turn rolls with tongs as they become golden. Test for doneness. Remove toothpicks before serving. Yield: 4 chicken rolls.

Chinese Fried Chicken

⅓ cup cornstarch
1 teaspoon soy sauce
3 tablespoons cold water
1 pound chicken breasts
Salad oil
Chinese Sauce
Hot cooked rice

Combine cornstarch, soy sauce, and water; mix well to form a thin, creamy paste. Dry chicken breasts thoroughly and dip into this mixture. Heat ½-inch deep oil in skillet; brown chicken in hot oil. Lower heat and cook, turning occasionally, until chicken is tender, about 30 to 45 minutes. Drain on paper towels and arrange on heated platter. Make sauce and pour over chicken. Serve with rice. Yield: 3 to 4 servings

Chinese Sauce:

¾ cup chicken broth
1½ tablespoons cornstarch
2 tablespoons instant minced onion or ½ cup finely chopped raw onion
1 to 3 teaspoons soy sauce
1 (6-ounce) can water chestnuts, drained and sliced
½ (10-ounce) package frozen green peas
2 teaspoons wine vinegar

Combine chicken broth, cornstarch, onion, and soy sauce in saucepan. Cook and stir until mixture is clear and has thickened. Add water chestnuts and peas. Boil gently until peas are barely tender. Stir in vinegar. Yield: 3 to 4 servings.

Everyday Fried Chicken

⅔ cup all-purpose flour
1 teaspoon monosodium glutamate
1 teaspoon salt
1 teaspoon paprika
⅛ teaspoon pepper
1 broiler-fryer chicken, cut in serving-size pieces
Salad oil

Combine flour and seasonings. Rinse chicken in cold running water, but do not dry; immediately roll pieces in seasoned flour. Heat ½-inch deep oil in skillet. Place chicken, skin side down, in skillet. Put larger, meatier pieces in first; add liver last few minutes of cooking time. Cook, uncovered, for 15 to 25 minutes on each side, turning only once. Drain well on absorbent paper. Yield: 4 servings.

Savory-Fried Chicken: Add 1 teaspoon poultry seasoning, savory, or thyme to flour mixture.

Curry-Fried Chicken: Add 1 teaspoon curry powder and ¼ teaspoon ginger to flour mixture.

Parmesan-Fried Chicken: Decrease flour to ½ cup; add ½ cup grated Parmesan cheese and 1 teaspoon oregano to flour mixture.

Crispy-Fried Chicken: Do not rinse chicken. Dip pieces in evaporated milk; then roll in seasoned flour.

Chicken Paella

8 to 10 chicken pieces
¼ cup salad oil
⅛ teaspoon saffron (optional)
1½ cups rice, uncooked
½ pound salami, diced
1 large onion, chopped
2 cups water
2 chicken bouillon cubes
1 (7-ounce) can whole clams and juice
1 teaspoon paprika
1 (5-ounce) can shrimp, drained
1 (1-pound) can tomatoes
1 (10-ounce) package frozen peas
1 (4-ounce) can pimientos

Brown chicken in oil; remove chicken and stir in saffron (if desired) and rice. Sauté until golden; add salami and onion, and sauté for an additional 7 minutes. Add water, bouillon cubes, clams, and paprika. Cover and cook for 10 minutes.

Place chicken in a 3-quart casserole, and cover with rice mixture. Add remaining ingredients. Cover casserole and bake at 325° for 1 hour. Yield: 8 to 10 servings.

Polynesian Chicken

⅓ cup molasses
Juice 2 lemons
2 teaspoons soy sauce
¼ teaspoon ground ginger
¼ teaspoon dry mustard
1 small chopped onion
1 (2½- to 3¼-pound) broiler-fryer, cut up
2 pineapple slices, halved
2 green-topped bananas, halved
1 tablespoon butter or margarine

Blend molasses, lemon juice, soy sauce, ginger, dry mustard, and onion. Place chicken in a shallow dish and pour molasses mixture over chicken. Refrigerate for 1 hour, turning once. Place chicken, skin-side up, in shallow baking pan that has been lined with aluminum foil. Brush chicken with marinade. Cover and bake at 375° for 40 minutes. Arrange fruits with chicken and dot with butter. Place under broiler for 10 to 15 minutes, until flecked with brown. Yield: 4 servings.

*Stewed Chicken and Dumplings

1 (4-pound) stewing hen
Salted water
1½ cups all-purpose flour
½ teaspoon salt
1½ teaspoons baking powder
¼ cup shortening
½ cup milk

Cut hen into serving-size pieces and place in a large saucepan. Cover with salted water. Cover pan, and cook until chicken is tender and meat begins to fall from bones.

While chicken is cooking, combine flour, salt, and baking powder. Cut in shortening until mixture is size of small peas. Add milk and mix well. Turn out on lightly floured board and knead lightly. Roll out to ⅛-inch thickness; cut into strips. When chicken is tender, drop strips into pan. Cover and continue simmering for 20 minutes. Yield: 8 servings.

Herbed Chicken

2 (2½-pound) fryer-broiler chickens
Shortening
½ cup all-purpose flour
1 teaspoon salt
¼ teaspoon white pepper
½ teaspoon thyme
½ teaspoon rosemary
½ teaspoon marjoram
½ teaspoon parsley flakes
½ cup water

Cut each chicken into 4 pieces. Melt shortening to a depth of ¼ inch in a heavy skillet. Combine flour, salt, and pepper in a paper bag. Shake 2 pieces of chicken at a time in flour until well coated. Brown in hot shortening. Remove to large 2-quart casserole. Combine thyme, rosemary, marjoram, parsley flakes, and water and pour over chicken. Cover casserole and bake at 350° for 45 minutes, basting occasionally. Yield: 8 servings.

*Saucy Chicken

2 (2- to 2½-pound) broiler chickens, cut in half
1 cup salad oil
½ cup vinegar
1 tablespoon prepared horseradish
¼ cup chili sauce
½ teaspoon dry mustard
1 teaspoon salt
½ clove garlic, crushed

Wash and dry halves of chicken and arrange in a large flat dish. Combine remaining ingredients for sauce and pour over chicken, completely coating with mixture. Let stand in refrigerator for at least 2 hours. Turn halves once. Remove from marinade and arrange on grill. Adjust grill so that it is not too near fire, as chicken must cook slowly to be thoroughly done. It should not be allowed to get too dry. Grill slowly for about 45 minutes, basting and turning several times while cooking. Yield: 4 servings.

Ginger-Glazed Chicken

 2 broiler chickens, cut in half
 1 (8-ounce) bottle Italian-style salad dressing
 ½ cup orange marmalade
 2 teaspoons ground ginger
 ⅛ teaspoon pepper

Place chicken halves in a single layer in a large baking pan. Pour half of the salad dressing over chicken to coat all sides. Cover and let stand at room temperature for 2 to 3 hours, turning chicken occasionally (chicken may be put in refrigerator overnight).

Combine remaining dressing with the marmalade, ginger, and pepper; brush chicken with this mixture while it cooks on the grill. Cook chicken slowly for about 1 hour, basting often. Yield: 4 servings.

Baked Chicken Puff

 1 (10¾-ounce) can condensed cream of mushroom soup
 ⅓ cup milk
 1 cup cubed cooked chicken
 4 eggs, separated
 ¼ cup shredded pasteurized process American cheese

Combine soup and milk in a 1½-quart casserole; add chicken. Bake at 375° for 10 minutes. Meanwhile, beat egg yolks well; add cheese. Beat egg whites until stiff and fold into egg-cheese mixture. Pile fluffy egg topping on hot chicken; continue baking for 30 minutes. Yield: 6 servings.

Chicken Marinade

 1½ cups salad oil
 ¾ cup soy sauce
 ¼ cup Worcestershire sauce
 2 tablespoons dry mustard
 2½ teaspoons salt
 1 tablespoon freshly ground black pepper
 ½ cup wine vinegar
 1½ teaspoons parsley flakes
 ⅓ cup lemon juice

Combine all ingredients and mix well. Pour over chicken pieces and marinate in refrigerator overnight. (Turn occasionally if possible.) Cook chicken on grill and baste with leftover marinade for 1¼ hours. Yield: enough marinade for 2 chickens.

Chicken Oriental

 1 (4-ounce) package blanched slivered almonds
 3 tablespoons peanut or salad oil
 ½ cup chopped onion
 4 chicken breasts, boned and thinly sliced
 1 (6- to 8-ounce) can bamboo shoots, drained
 1 (6-ounce) can water chestnuts, drained and sliced
 1 cucumber, unpeeled and thinly sliced
 ½ cup chicken stock or broth
 2 teaspoons sherry or dry white wine
 ¼ teaspoon ground ginger
 1 teaspoon soy sauce
 ½ teaspoon cornstarch
 1 tablespoon cold water
 Dash salt and pepper
 Cooked rice or noodles

Place almonds in shallow pan and brown in oven at 400° for 8 to 12 minutes. Pour oil into wok or skillet; heat at 375° for 3 minutes. Add onion and stir-fry for 1 minute; push onion up sides of wok. Add ¼ of chicken and stir-fry for 1 minute; push up sides of wok. Repeat with remaining chicken. Add bamboo shoots and water chestnuts; stir-fry for 1 minute and push up sides of wok. Add cucumber and stir-fry for 1 minute.

Combine chicken stock, sherry, ginger, and soy sauce; add to wok and cook for 1 minute, uncovered. Combine cornstarch and water in small bowl; slowly stir into hot liquid in wok. Add salt and pepper. Stir and heat about 2 minutes until liquid thickens. Reduce heat to warm for serving and gently stir all foods together with sauce. Serve over cooked rice or noodles; sprinkle with the toasted almonds. Yield: 4 to 6 servings.

Chicken Pie with Sweet Potato Crust

- 2 cups diced (or sliced) cooked chicken
- 2 green peppers, thinly sliced
- 1 (20-ounce) can small boiled onions, drained
- 1/3 cup finely chopped parsley
- 2 tablespoons butter
- 2 tablespoons all-purpose flour
- 2 cups chicken broth
- 1 teaspoon grated lemon peel
- Salt and pepper
- Sweet Potato Crust

Put a layer of chicken in a 2-quart casserole; add a layer of green pepper and a layer of onions. Sprinkle generously with parsley. Repeat layers until all ingredients are used.

Melt butter over moderate heat; blend in flour and add chicken broth slowly, stirring until sauce thickens and is smooth. Add lemon peel and salt and pepper to taste; mix well. Pour over chicken mixture. Top with Sweet Potato Crust and bake at 350° for about 40 minutes. Yield: 6 servings.

Sweet Potato Crust:

- 1 cup mashed sweet potatoes (drained canned potatoes may be used)
- 1/4 cup melted butter
- 1 egg, beaten
- 1 tablespoon grated orange peel
- 1 tablespoon orange juice
- 1 cup sifted all-purpose flour
- 1 teaspoon baking powder
- 1/2 teaspoon salt

Mix sweet potatoes with butter, egg, orange peel, and juice. Sift flour with baking powder and salt; combine with potato mixture, beating until smooth. Roll out on lightly floured board to about 1/4-inch thickness; shape to fit top of casserole and crimp edges to seal.

Chicken Napoli

- 4 whole broiler-fryer chicken breasts, cut into halves
- 1 cup butter or margarine
- 2 (0.6-ounce) packages Italian salad dressing mix
- 1/3 cup lime juice

Wash and dry chicken breasts. Melt butter in small saucepan; stir in salad dressing mix and lime juice. Brush sauce on both sides of chicken pieces. Place chicken, skin side down, on barbecue grill, about 10 inches above heat. Grill, turning and basting often with sauce, for about 40 minutes or until chicken breasts are tender and richly glazed. Yield: 8 servings.

Delectable Fried Chicken Breasts

- 4 whole broiler-fryer chicken breasts, halved, boned, and skinned
- 1/4 cup all-purpose flour
- 2 eggs, well beaten
- 1 1/2 cups Italian seasoned bread crumbs
- 1 teaspoon Ac'cent
- 3 tablespoons corn oil
- 3 tablespoons corn oil margarine

Pound chicken breasts between two pieces of aluminum foil to flatten. Dust chicken breasts lightly with flour. Dip into beaten eggs, then into bread crumbs mixed with Ac'cent. Chill chicken for 30 minutes. Heat oil and margarine in 11-inch chicken fryer. Add chicken (4 pieces at a time) and cook 5 minutes on each side, until golden brown and crisp. Keep first batch warm while preparing second batch. Yield: 8 servings.

Chicken Livers Burgundy

 1 pound chicken livers
 2 teaspoons Kitchen Bouquet
 2 tablespoons butter
 1 (4-ounce) can button mushrooms
 3 tablespoons Burgundy
 ½ teaspoon salt
 Dash pepper
 1 teaspoon cornstarch
 2 teaspoons cold water

Place chicken livers in a bowl and sprinkle with Kitchen Bouquet. Toss lightly with a fork until livers are coated. Heat butter over low heat and add livers and mushrooms. Sauté until livers are lightly browned, about 10 minutes. Add Burgundy, salt, and pepper. Dissolve cornstarch in water. Add to livers, stirring constantly. Cover pan and cook 3 minutes longer. Serve over grits or toast points. Yield: 3 to 4 servings.

Chicken Salonika

 4 tablespoons olive oil or butter, divided
 ¼ cup chopped onion
 ¼ cup uncooked brown rice
 ½ cup sliced almonds
 1 (3-pound) chicken, cut for frying
 ⅓ cup all-purpose flour
 1 teaspoon salt
 ⅛ teaspoon black pepper
 1½ cups milk
 ¼ teaspoon thyme
 Dash sugar
 Dash cayenne pepper
 3 tablespoons chopped pimiento
 1½ tablespoons cornstarch
 ½ cup half-and-half

Heat 2 tablespoons olive oil in large heavy skillet. Add onion, rice, and almonds. Sauté slowly, stirring occasionally, until golden brown. Remove from pan and spread over bottom of a 2-quart shallow baking dish.

Put remaining 2 tablespoons olive oil in same pan and heat until sizzling. Dip pieces of chicken in mixture of flour, salt, and black pepper. Fry quickly, just enough to brown chicken. Place chicken on top of rice.

Combine milk, thyme, sugar, cayenne pepper, and pimiento; pour over chicken and rice. Bake at 375° for 1 hour. Remove chicken from rice; keep warm. Mix cornstarch and half-and-half; add to rice mixture. Stir thoroughly and return to oven for 10 minutes. Serve chicken with rice. Yield: 4 to 6 servings.

Mexican Chicken

 1 (3-pound) chicken, boiled, skinned, and boned
 12 crisp tortillas, broken up
 1 (10¾-ounce) can condensed cream of chicken soup
 ½ soup can water
 1 onion, finely chopped
 1 teaspoon chili powder
 ½ teaspoon garlic powder
 1 (16-ounce) can stewed tomatoes
 1 cup shredded Cheddar cheese

Cut up chicken and set aside. Line a 13- x 9- x 2-inch pan with tortillas. Mix soup and water; pour over tortillas. Add cut-up chicken. Combine onion, chili powder, garlic powder, and tomatoes; pour over chicken. Wrap and freeze.

To serve, thaw in refrigerator and sprinkle cheese over top. Bake at 350° for 45 to 55 minutes. Yield: 4 to 5 servings.

Chicken Jubilee

 1 (17-ounce) can dark sweet Bing cherries, pitted
 2 tablespoons kirsch
 ¼ cup all-purpose flour
 ½ teaspoon salt
 ⅛ teaspoon white pepper
 4 chicken breasts, boned, skinned, and halved
 2 tablespoons butter, melted
 1 (1½-ounce) envelope chicken and rice soup mix
 1½ cups boiling water
 ⅓ cup dry white wine

Drain cherries and reserve the juice. Sprinkle cherries with kirsch and turn occasionally.

Combine flour, salt, and white pepper. Dredge chicken in seasoned flour mixture. Sauté chicken in butter until delicately browned on both sides. Combine chicken and rice soup mix, boiling water, and ¾ to 1 cup of reserved cherry juice. Stir and add to sautéed chicken breasts. Cover and simmer until tender, about 20 minutes. Remove chicken breasts to warm platter and keep warm.

Add dry white wine to liquid in skillet. Cook over high heat, stirring until liquid thickens. Add cherries and kirsch. Heat without boiling, and pour over chicken breasts on platter. Serve piping hot with rice. Yield: 8 servings.

Vatapa

1 hen or 2 fryers
Water
2 green peppers, chopped
2 large onions, chopped
1 cup margarine
2 (8-ounce) packages spaghetti
1 (17-ounce) can drained English peas
1 (1-pound) can tomatoes and peppers
1 (4-ounce) can pimientos, chopped
1 pound pasteurized process cheese
Salt and pepper to taste

Cover the hen with water in a large saucepan. Simmer about 3 hours on very low heat. Add water as chicken cooks so that you have 3 cups broth when chicken is done. Let chicken cool in broth; then take out of broth and remove bones.

Sauté green pepper and onion in margarine. Cook the spaghetti in the chicken broth and add water if needed. Do not drain. Add peas, tomatoes, pimientos, cheese, chicken, and sautéed pepper and onion. Add salt and pepper. Put in casseroles and bake at 325° for 30 minutes.

This dish can be made in advance and frozen for later use. To freeze, omit the last 30 minutes in the oven; after thawing, cook it the 30 minutes. Yield: 12 to 15 servings.

*Spaghetti and Chicken Bake

1 (5-pound) chicken
1 cup butter or margarine
¾ cup all-purpose flour
5 cups chicken broth
1 cup milk
1 cup chopped celery
1 (4-ounce) can mushrooms
1 (3-ounce) can tomato paste
1 (4-ounce) can pimientos, cut fine
2 small cloves garlic, minced
1 (8-ounce) package spaghetti

Cover chicken with water; cook until meat is tender and begins to pull away from bones. Remove chicken from broth and cool; remove meat from bones. Cut meat into small pieces; measure 4½ cups and set aside.

Melt butter; add flour and stir until dissolved. Add chicken broth and milk and cook until mixture is thick. Add celery, mushrooms, tomato paste, pimientos, garlic, and cooked chicken. Let stand about 1 hour.

Cook spaghetti according to package directions; drain and cool. Combine spaghetti and chicken mixture. Put into two (2-quart) baking dishes; cover with foil or put into plastic bags. Seal securely and freeze.

To serve, remove from freezer and let stand in refrigerator overnight. Bake at 350° about 30 to 40 minutes. Yield: 10 servings.

Chicken with Apricot Jam

3 to 4 pounds chicken (breasts, thighs, and drumsticks)
Salt and pepper to taste
1 (8-ounce) bottle French dressing
1 (⅞-ounce) package onion soup mix
1 (10-ounce) jar apricot jam or preserves
Dash hot sauce

Remove skin from chicken, if desired. Season chicken with salt and pepper and place in a shallow roasting pan. Combine remaining ingredients and pour over chicken. Bake at 350° for 50 minutes. Yield: 6 to 8 servings.

Baked Broiler Chicken

- 1 (2½-pound) chicken, cut into serving-size pieces
- 1 (¾-ounce) package buttermilk-style salad dressing mix
- 2 cups mayonnaise
- 1 cup buttermilk
- 2 cups crushed corn flakes

Wash chicken and pat dry; set aside. Combine salad dressing mix, mayonnaise, and buttermilk, mixing well.

Dip chicken pieces in buttermilk mixture, then roll in corn flakes. Place chicken, skin side up, in a single layer in a 13- x 9- x 2-inch ungreased casserole. Bake at 325° for 1½ hours or until tender. Do not turn. Yield: 4 to 6 servings.

Chicken Vermouth with Rice

- 3 pounds broiler-fryer parts
- 2½ teaspoons salt
- ½ teaspoon pepper
- 3 medium-size carrots, sliced
- 2 stalks celery, thinly sliced
- 1 medium-size onion, thinly sliced
- 4 cloves garlic
- 2 tablespoons chopped parsley
- ⅓ cup dry vermouth
- ¼ cup commercial sour cream
- Baked rice

Dry chicken. Sprinkle with salt and pepper. Place all ingredients except sour cream and rice in a 2-quart casserole. Cover and bake at 375° for 1½ hours. Remove from oven; discard garlic and stir in sour cream. Serve over Baked Rice. Yield: 6 servings.

Baked Rice:

- 1 cup uncooked regular rice
- 2 cups boiling chicken broth (fat-free)
- ½ teaspoon salt

Combine ingredients in a greased 2-quart casserole. Stir once. Cover with foil or tight-fitting lid. Put in oven with chicken 30 minutes before chicken is done. Yield: 6 servings.

Chicken-Macaroni-Cheese Bake

- 1 (8-ounce) can sliced mushrooms
- 1 tablespoon butter or margarine
- 1 (10¾-ounce) can condensed cream of chicken soup
- 2 cups shredded Cheddar cheese
- 1¼ cups cooked elbow macaroni
- 2¼ cups cooked diced chicken
- 1½ cups cooked or canned peas
- ¼ teaspoon poultry seasoning
- ¼ teaspoon Worcestershire sauce
- ¼ cup fine dry bread crumbs
- 1 tablespoon butter or margarine, melted

Drain mushrooms, reserving liquid. Add enough water to mushroom liquid to make ⅔ cup. Brown mushrooms in 1 tablespoon butter. Combine mushrooms, mushroom liquid, soup, and cheese. Cook over low heat, stirring often, until cheese melts. Remove from heat.

Add macaroni, chicken, peas, and seasonings. Mix lightly. Pour into a greased 2-quart casserole. Combine bread crumbs and melted butter. Sprinkle over mixture in casserole. Bake, uncovered, at 350° for 30 minutes. Yield: 6 servings.

Skillet Chicken Supreme

- 1 (12-ounce) package wide noodles
- 6 whole chicken breasts, split in half and boned
- 4 slices boiled ham, cut into thirds
- ¼ cup butter or margarine
- ¼ cup dry white wine or water
- 1 pint commercial sour cream
- 2 tablespoons all-purpose flour
- 1 teaspoon salt
- ½ cup snipped parsley
- ¼ cup sliced pimiento
- 1 (3-ounce) can whole mushrooms, drained

Cook noodles according to package directions; drain and set aside. Prepare chicken breasts; tuck piece of ham into slit of each chicken breast where breast bone was removed. Secure with toothpicks. Preheat electric skillet to 250°. Melt butter in skillet. Arrange chicken, skin side down, in skillet. Pour wine, or water, over chicken. Cook, covered and with vent closed, for 30 minutes or until chicken is tender. Meanwhile combine sour cream, flour, and salt; then add parsley and pimiento and mix gently.

Remove chicken from skillet. Turn temperature control to 200°. Place noodles in skillet; mix gently with pan drippings. Stir in half of sour cream mixture. Arrange chicken, skin side up, on top of noodles. Top chicken with remaining sour cream mixture. Place 1 mushroom on top of each chicken breast. Yield: 12 servings.

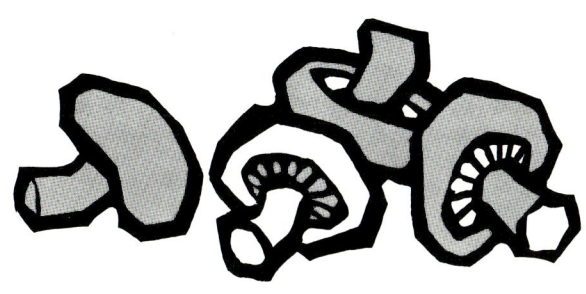

Sweet-Sour Chicken

1 tablespoon cornstarch
1 tablespoon cold water
½ cup sugar
½ cup soy sauce
¼ cup vinegar
1 clove garlic, minced
½ teaspoon ground ginger
¼ teaspoon coarsely ground black pepper
Salt and pepper
2 (2-pound) broiler fryers, cut into halves or into serving-size pieces
1 (20-ounce) can pineapple chunks, drained

Combine cornstarch and cold water in small saucepan. Add sugar, soy sauce, vinegar, garlic, ginger, and pepper. Cook and stir over medium heat until mixture thickens slightly. Salt and pepper chicken pieces, and brush with glaze. Place skin side down in shallow greased baking dish, and bake at 425° for 30 minutes. Brush with glaze every 10 minutes. Turn chicken skin-side up, and bake 30 minutes longer, brushing with glaze occasionally. Add pineapple during last 10 minutes of baking. Yield: 4 to 6 servings.

Thai-Style Chicken

1 (3-pound) frying chicken, cut up
¼ cup salad oil
¼ pound fresh mushrooms, sliced
¼ cup chopped onion
½ teaspoon salt
2 tablespoons finely chopped preserved ginger or 1 to 2 teaspoons ground ginger
¼ teaspoon ground coriander
½ cup water
4 tablespoons lime juice
2 tablespoons soy sauce
2 tablespoons vinegar
½ teaspoon sugar
1½ cups ripe olives, drained and pitted
Cooked rice

Brown chicken slowly in salad oil. Remove chicken; brown mushrooms and onion in drippings. Drain off any excess oil. Return chicken to skillet; sprinkle with salt, ginger, and coriander. Add water; cover and simmer for 10 minutes. Combine lime juice, soy sauce, vinegar, and sugar; sprinkle over chicken. Add ripe olives; cover and cook 10 minutes longer. Serve over rice. Yield: 4 servings.

Chicken with Oysters

1 clove garlic
3 tablespoons olive oil
1 (3-pound) chicken, cut up
2 tablespoons all-purpose flour
1 cup oysters, chopped
½ teaspoon salt
1 bay leaf
Dash hot sauce
¼ cup dry white wine
½ cup chicken stock

Sauté garlic in olive oil until browned. Remove garlic. Dredge chicken with flour; fry in garlic-flavored oil until golden. Add oysters, salt, bay leaf, hot sauce, white wine, and chicken stock. Cover and simmer gently for 30 minutes or until the chicken is tender. Yield: 4 servings.

Stuffed Chicken Breasts Dixie

 4 whole broiler-fryer chicken breasts, boned
 ¼ teaspoon pepper
 ½ teaspoon seasoned salt
 ¼ teaspoon poultry seasoning
 1 (5-ounce) can deviled ham
 2 teaspoons instant minced onion
 1 cup soft bread crumbs
 ½ cup butter or margarine
 1 (0.6-ounce) envelope Parmesan salad dressing mix

Start fire in outdoor grill. Prepare chicken while coals are readying. Place chicken breasts, skin side down, on flat surface. Mix pepper, salt, and poultry seasoning, and sprinkle over meaty surface of chicken. Mix deviled ham, onion, and bread crumbs. Spoon mixture equally along hollows in chicken breasts. Fold edges of chicken over stuffing, covering completely, and secure with toothpicks.

Melt butter in small saucepan; stir in salad dressing mix. Brush chicken with mixture, and place, skin side down, on grill. Cook for 20 minutes, basting now and then with sauce. Turn, baste, and cook 20 minutes longer or until chicken is tender and golden brown. Yield: 4 to 6 servings.

*Southern Upside-Down Dinner

Meat Layer:

 ¼ cup chicken fat
 ½ cup all-purpose flour
 1 teaspoon salt
  Dash pepper and paprika
 3 cups chicken stock
 ½ cup milk
 1 tablespoon lemon juice
 3 cups cooked chicken, cut into 1-inch pieces
 ½ cup sliced stuffed olives

Put chicken fat in skillet; add flour and stir until smooth. Add salt, pepper, paprika, stock, and milk; cook until mixture is fairly thick. Stir in lemon juice, chicken, and olives. Put two thirds of mixture in a greased oven-proof skillet. Cover with Corn Bread Batter. Bake at 400° for 25 minutes. Cut into wedges and serve upside down with remaining hot chicken mixture as a gravy over top. Yield: 6 to 8 servings.

Corn Bread Batter:

 1 cup all-purpose flour
 1 cup cornmeal
 2 tablespoons sugar
 2 teaspoons baking powder
 ¾ teaspoon salt
 ½ teaspoon soda
 3 tablespoons shortening
 1 cup buttermilk

Combine dry ingredients in large bowl. Cut in shortening with pastry blender. Add buttermilk and stir just enough to blend the ingredients. Pour the batter over hot mixture in skillet.

Chicken Bake

 2 (5- to 6-ounce) cans boned chicken, diced
 1¼ cups (8-ounce) packaged seasoned bread dressing
 1 (2-ounce) jar pimientos
 1 cup canned chicken broth
 2 eggs, slightly beaten
  Tasty Mushroom Sauce

Combined diced chicken, bread dressing, and drained, chopped pimientos. Stir in chicken broth and slightly beaten eggs. Press into 6 well-greased custard cups. Bake at 325° for 1 hour or until done. Cool for a few minutes; unmold and serve with Tasty Mushroom Sauce. Yield: 6 servings.

Tasty Mushroom Sauce:

 1 small onion, finely chopped
 2 tablespoons butter or margarine
 1 (10¾-ounce) can condensed cream of mushroom soup
 ¼ cup milk
 ¼ cup chopped parsley

Cook onion in butter. Stir in soup, milk, and parsley; heat. Yield: 1½ cups.

Apple Chicken

- 6 *chicken breasts or* 1 *(4-pound) fryer chicken, cut up*
- ¼ *cup butter or margarine*
- *Salt and pepper to taste*
- ¾ *cup apple juice*
- 2 *small onions, minced*
- 2 *unpeeled apples, cut into chunks*
- 1 *green pepper, cut into strips*
- 1 *(4-ounce) can mushrooms or* ¾ *cup chopped fresh mushrooms*
- ½ *cup water*
- 2 *teaspoons cornstarch*

Brown chicken in butter; season with salt and pepper. Place chicken on paper towels and drain excess fat from pan. Add apple juice and onion to pan; bring to a boil. Return chicken to pan; simmer, covered, for 35 minutes. Remove chicken and keep warm.

Add apples, green pepper, and mushrooms (sauté mushrooms if fresh) to juice mixture. Stir and cook for 2 or 3 minutes. Combine water and cornstarch; add to pan mixture and stir until thickened. To serve, pour sauce over chicken. Yield: 6 servings.

*Chicken-Vegetable Bake

- 1 *3-pound fryer, cut into serving-size pieces*
- ¼ *cup all-purpose flour*
- ½ *teaspoon salt*
- ¼ *teaspoon pepper*
- ¼ *cup salad oil*
- ½ *cup chopped onion*
- ¼ *cup chopped green pepper*
- ¼ *teaspoon garlic powder*
- 3 *carrots, sliced*
- 3 *stalks celery, sliced*
- 1 *cup water*
- 2 *(8-ounce) cans tomato sauce*
- 1½ *cups uncooked elbow macaroni*

Sprinkle chicken with mixture of flour, salt, and pepper. Brown in heated oil in skillet. Remove chicken and sauté onion, green pepper, and garlic powder in the same pan. Add remaining ingredients except chicken and macaroni, and simmer for 10 minutes.

Line a 3-quart casserole with heavy-duty aluminum foil. Place macaroni in bottom of casserole, and cover with the chicken. Pour sauce over all. Cover and bake at 325° for 1 to 1½ hours or until chicken is tender. Cool quickly and freeze until mixture is solid. Remove from casserole and wrap in moistureproof, vaporproof container. Seal, label, and return to the freezer.

To serve, unwrap and return to original casserole; cover and bake at 350° for 1½ hours. Remove cover for the last 15 minutes of baking. Yield: 6 servings.

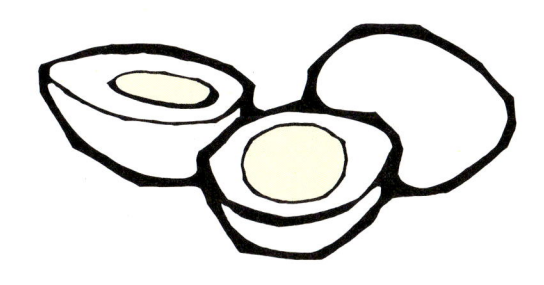

Easy Baked Chicken Breasts in Wine

- 8 *to* 10 *whole broiler-fryer chicken breasts*
- 2 *slices bacon, cut into* 16 *to* 20 *pieces*
- 2 *tablespoons Worcestershire sauce*
- 2 *(10¾-ounce) cans condensed golden mushroom soup*
- ¼ *cup corn oil margarine*
- ½ *cup cooking sherry*
- 1½ *teaspoons Ac'cent*
- 1 *(1⅜-ounce) envelope onion soup mix*

Cut chicken breasts in half. Place one piece of bacon under skin of each half chicken breast. Line an 18- x 12- x 1-inch roasting pan with aluminum foil. Combine Worcestershire sauce and mushroom soup in medium bowl. Heat margarine in saucepan; stir in one-fourth of mushroom soup mixture. Dip chicken breasts in margarine mixture and place skin side up in roasting pan. Pour sherry over chicken; sprinkle with Ac'cent. Spoon remaining mushroom soup mixture over chicken breasts and sprinkle with onion soup mix. Bake at 375° for 1 hour, basting once. Yield: 16 to 20 servings.

Baked Chicken Parmesan

- ½ cup salad oil
- 3 broiler-fryer chickens (about 2 pounds each), cut into serving-size pieces
- 1½ teaspoons oregano, divided
- 1½ teaspoons salt, divided
- Paprika
- 2 (4-ounce) cans sliced mushrooms
- 4 tablespoons grated Parmesan cheese

Line a 15- x 10- x 1-inch pan with aluminum foil. Pour oil into pan and place in a 425° oven to heat for 10 minutes. Remove pan and place chicken, skin side down, in hot oil. Sprinkle lightly with half the oregano and salt and with paprika.

Return pan to oven and bake at 425° for 30 minutes. Turn chicken and sprinkle with remaining oregano and salt; sprinkle lightly with paprika. Bake 15 minutes longer. Remove from oven and spoon drippings over chicken. Pour mushrooms with liquid over chicken and sprinkle with Parmesan cheese. Bake for 5 minutes. Yield: 12 servings.

Barbecued Chicken

- 2 (8-ounce) cans tomato sauce
- ½ cup vinegar
- ½ cup salad oil
- ½ teaspoon liquid smoke
- 1 teaspoon soy sauce
- 1 teaspoon Worcestershire sauce
- 1 teaspoon steak sauce
- 1 teaspoon chili powder
- 1 teaspoon garlic powder
- 1 teaspoon rosemary
- 1 medium-size onion, finely chopped or grated
- 1 teaspoon salt
- 2 fryers, cut into serving-size pieces

Combine all ingredients for sauce. Place chicken in mixture; marinate overnight in refrigerator. Brush marinade over chicken while it is cooking, 45 minutes to 1 hour. Yield: 8 to 10 servings.

Kentucky Barbecued Chicken

- 5 fryer chickens, cut in half
- 2½ cups water
- 1 tablespoon sugar
- 2½ teaspoons pepper
- 2 tablespoons butter
- ¼ cup vinegar
- 2½ teaspoons salt
- 2 tablespoons Worcestershire sauce
- ¼ small onion, grated
- 1 teaspoon dry mustard
- 2 teaspoons chili powder
- ½ teaspoon hot sauce
- 1 clove garlic, mashed

Wash chickens and pat dry. Mix all ingredients for sauce and heat. Place chicken on grill and brush with heated sauce as chicken cooks. Yield: 10 servings.

Chicken Teriyaki Barbecue

- 1 broiler-fryer chicken cut into serving-size pieces
- ½ cup soy sauce
- ¼ cup honey
- 1 clove garlic, minced

Place chicken pieces in shallow pan. Combine other ingredients and pour over chicken. Put in refrigerator and leave for 4 to 5 hours, spooning marinade over chicken occasionally. Remove from marinade. Place chicken, skin side down, on oiled grill. Grill at low setting for 30 minutes or until tender, turning often. Yield: 2 to 3 servings.

*Virginia Barbecued Chicken

- 5 fryer chickens
- 1 cup salad oil, butter, or margarine
- 2 cups vinegar
- ½ cup water
- 4 tablespoons salt
- 1 teaspoon pepper
- 2 teaspoons poultry seasoning

Cut chickens in half; clean and dry well. Combine oil, vinegar, water, salt, pepper, and poultry seasoning. Heat to boiling and set aside. Place chicken on grill over gray coals. Brush with sauce mixture every 5 minutes or as often as necessary to prevent burning. Cook until tender; chicken is done when leg bone turns easily in the socket. Yield: 10 servings.

*Oven-Barbecued Chicken

12 *chicken thighs*
½ *cup all-purpose flour*
1 *teaspoon salt*
Dash pepper
½ *cup salad oil*
1 *cup catsup*
½ *cup cooking sherry*
⅓ *cup water*
2 *tablespoons lemon juice*
1 *medium-size onion, minced*
1 *tablespoon Worcestershire sauce*
2 *tablespoons margarine*
1 *tablespoon firmly packed brown sugar*

Coat chicken pieces with mixture of flour, salt, and pepper. Brown in hot oil. Place chicken pieces in one layer in a shallow pan.

Combine other ingredients and bring to a boil. Pour heated sauce over chicken; cover pan, and bake at 325° about 1½ hours or until chicken is tender. Yield: 6 servings.

*Easy Barbecued Chicken

4 *large broiler chicken halves*
4 *tablespoons Ac'cent*
4 *tablespoons paprika*
4 *tablespoons salt*
1 *tablespoon pepper*
3 *tablespoons salad oil*
1 *tablespoon white vinegar*
1 *teaspoon hot sauce*

Sprinkle both sides of chicken halves with Ac'cent, paprika, salt, and pepper. Place chicken halves on grill at low heat with generous smoke from hickory chips or meal. Cook for 3 to 3½ hours. Combine oil, vinegar, and hot sauce, and brush over chicken the last hour of cooking. Yield: 4 servings.

Backyard Barbecued Chicken

1 *pound margarine*
¾ *cup vinegar*
3½ *tablespoons dry mustard*
2 *teaspoons salt (½ teaspoon per broiler half)*
2 *broiler-fryer chickens*

Combine ingredients for sauce and heat thoroughly. Split fryers in half; wash and dry. Place, skin side down, on grill. Cook slowly over low heat for 1¼ hours, basting often with sauce until all sauce has been used. Yield: 4 servings.

Outdoor Barbecued Chicken

2 *cloves garlic*
1 *teaspoon salt*
½ *cup salad oil*
½ *cup lemon juice or vinegar*
½ *cup water*
4 *tablespoons finely grated onion*
1 *teaspoon pepper*
2 *teaspoons Worcestershire sauce*
2 *broiler-fryer chickens (about 1¾ pounds each)*

Mash garlic with salt; stir in remaining ingredients for sauce. Chill 24 hours before using. Heat and use as basting for barbecued chicken.

Cut fryers in half lengthwise. Tuck the wing tip under and fasten wing close to body with a thin nail. Bring leg close to body and fasten to tail. Let coals in grill burn down to an ashy color, or set gas or electric grill at "low." Place chicken on grill about 6 inches from heat. Brush with sauce as chicken cooks, turning often. Cook until chicken is tender, 30 to 45 minutes. Yield: 4 servings.

*Lemon Broiled Chicken

    1 *(2- to 2½-pound) chicken, halved*
    ½ *cup butter or margarine*
    ¼ *cup salad oil*
    ¼ *cup lemon juice*
    1 *teaspoon salt*
    ½ *teaspoon pepper*
    ¼ *teaspoon thyme*
    1 *clove garlic, crushed*
    1 *small onion, minced*

Place chicken halves, skin side down, in broiler pan. Combine remaining ingredients in saucepan and heat. Brush chicken with heated sauce at 10-minute intervals, turning chicken each time. Broil 40 to 50 minutes, until tender and golden brown. Yield: 2 large servings.

*Chicken Cacciatore for Freezing

    ⅓ *cup all-purpose flour*
    1 *teaspoon paprika*
    1 *teaspoon salt*
    ¼ *teaspoon pepper*
    1 *(3-pound) fryer chicken, cut up*
    1 *cup salad oil*
   1¼ *cups cooked tomatoes*
    ⅓ *cup chopped onion*
    ½ *cup chopped celery*
    2 *teaspoons Worcestershire sauce*
    1 *(10¾-ounce) can condensed cream of mushroom soup (optional)*

Combine flour, paprika, salt, and pepper in plastic bag; add chicken pieces and shake to coat. Heat oil in heavy skillet; add chicken and cook over medium heat until brown; drain on paper towels.

Drain oil from skillet. Return chicken to skillet, and add tomatoes, onion, celery, and Worcestershire sauce. Simmer for 30 minutes or until chicken is tender. Add soup, if desired.

To freeze, transfer to a 4-quart covered casserole and seal securely. To serve, thaw in refrigerator and bake at 350° for 30 minutes or until thoroughly heated. Yield: 4 to 5 servings.

Broiled Chicken with Herbs

    3 *broiler chickens*
   1½ *teaspoons salt*
    ½ *teaspoon pepper*
    1 *cup butter, softened*
    1 *tablespoon finely chopped parsley*
    ½ *teaspoon marjoram*
    ½ *teaspoon chives*
    ½ *teaspoon sage*
    1 *teaspoon finely chopped mint*
    ¼ *teaspoon fennel seeds or ½ teaspoon oil of fennel*
    ¼ *teaspoon ground nutmeg*
    ½ *teaspoon ground cinnamon*
    1 *cup orange juice*

Clean and cut broilers in half; wipe with damp cloth; season with salt and pepper. Blend butter with herbs and spices; rub over inside and outside of broilers. Broil until golden brown. Place in roaster; add orange juice and juice from broiler pan. Cover and bake at 375° for about 45 minutes, basting frequently. Yield: 6 servings.

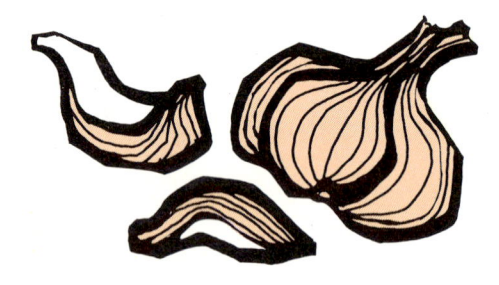

Blue Cheese Chicken

    1 *broiler-fryer chicken, cut into serving-size pieces, or 2½ pounds chicken parts (thighs, drumsticks, or breasts)*
    ½ *cup commercial sour cream*
    ¼ *cup blue cheese*
   1½ *cups fine dry bread crumbs*
    2 *teaspoons paprika*
    1 *teaspoon salt*
    1 *teaspoon Ac'cent*
    ½ *teaspoon pepper*
    ¼ *cup corn oil margarine, melted*

Pat chicken dry on paper towels. Blend sour cream and blue cheese. Mix together bread crumbs, paprika, salt, Ac'cent, and pepper on aluminum foil. Coat each chicken piece thoroughly with the blue cheese mixture; then coat with the crumb mixture. Place coated chicken pieces in a single layer, skin side up, in a 13- x 9- x 2-inch ungreased casserole.

Cover tightly with aluminum foil. Bake at 400° for 45 minutes. Remove foil; increase oven temperature to 450°. Brush chicken pieces with margarine. Bake 15 minutes longer or until golden brown. Yield: 4 servings.

Chicken Breasts with Sauce Béarnaise

6 chicken breasts
¼ cup butter, melted
½ teaspoon salt
1 teaspoon paprika
White and wild rice, cooked
Sauce Béarnaise

Place chicken breasts, skin side up and not touching, in an ungreased shallow baking dish. Combine butter, salt, and paprika; brush over chicken. Bake, uncovered, at 375° for 1 hour or until tender; do not turn. Serve with white and wild rice and Sauce Béarnaise. Yield: 6 servings.

Sauce Béarnaise:

2 egg yolks
2 teaspoons vinegar
½ cup butter, melted
1 teaspoon lemon juice
1 tablespoon minced shallots or green onions
½ teaspoon tarragon, crushed
Salt and pepper to taste

In top of double boiler, beat egg yolks with vinegar until blended. Place over hot, not boiling, water. (Don't let water in bottom pan touch top pan.) Gradually add butter, stirring constantly. Cook and stir only until mixture thickens. Remove from heat; stir in lemon juice, shallots, and tarragon. Add seasonings. Serve warm. Yield: sauce for 6 servings.

Chicken Broccoli Casserole

1 (2½- to 3-pound) chicken, cut into serving-size pieces
2 (10-ounce) packages frozen broccoli spears
1 (8-ounce) package pasteurized process American cheese
½ cup butter or margarine
1 (3-ounce) can sliced mushrooms, drained
1 cup chicken broth
¾ cup cracker crumbs

Cover chicken with water and cook over medium heat about 1½ hours or until tender; cool. Remove meat from bones and reserve 1 cup broth. Measure 2½ cups chopped chicken and set aside.

Cook broccoli according to package directions; drain. Combine cheese, butter, mushrooms, and chicken broth in saucepan; heat until cheese melts. Line bottom of a greased, 8-inch square casserole with cracker crumbs. Layer broccoli and chicken over crumbs; cover with cheese sauce. Wrap securely and freeze.

To serve, thaw in refrigerator and bake at 350° for 20 to 30 minutes. Yield: 6 servings.

Creamed Chicken in Avocado Half Shell

3 tablespoons margarine, melted
3 tablespoons all-purpose flour
1 cup milk
½ teaspoon salt
1½ cups diced cooked chicken
1 (2-ounce) can mushrooms, drained
3 avocados

Combine margarine and flour; blend well. Add milk and salt; cook and stir until mixture boils and is thick. Blend in chicken and mushrooms and heat thoroughly. Keep hot over boiling water. Cut each avocado in half lengthwise and remove seed. Place in shallow pan and pour ¼ inch warm water in bottom of pan. Heat at 300° for 10 to 15 minutes. Remove avocado half shells to serving plate and fill with hot chicken mixture. Serve at once. Yield: 6 servings.

Chicken Curry

- 1 (5- to 6-pound) stewing hen, cut up
- 6 cups water
- 3 medium onions, chopped
- 2 apples, minced
- 8 stalks celery, minced
- ¼ cup olive oil
- ¼ cup curry powder
- ¼ teaspoon pepper
- ½ teaspoon ground ginger
- ½ teaspoon hot sauce
- ¼ cup all-purpose flour
- 2 cups whipping cream
- 3 egg yolks, slightly beaten
- ½ cup sherry
- Salt
- 6 cups hot cooked rice
- Condiments (see below)

Simmer chicken in water in covered pan until tender; reserve 4 cups broth. Bone and dice chicken; set aside.

Cook onion, apple, and celery in olive oil until browned, stirring frequently. Add curry powder and simmer 5 minutes. Add reserved broth and seasonings; simmer 20 minutes. Blend in flour and cook until thickened, stirring constantly. Add chicken to sauce and let stand at least 3 hours in refrigerator.

When ready to serve, add cream, egg yolks, sherry, and salt to taste. Heat thoroughly. Serve over hot rice; accompany with condiments. Yield: 6 to 8 servings.

Condiments:

- 4 hard-cooked eggs, chopped
- 2 cups chutney
- 1 fresh coconut, grated
- 2 green peppers, chopped
- ½ pound bacon, fried and chopped
- ½ cup currant jelly
- ½ cup chopped pickles
- ½ pound salted peanuts, chopped

Country Captain

- 12 chicken pieces (6 chicken breasts, 3 drumsticks, 3 thighs)
- Salt and pepper
- ½ cup all-purpose flour
- 1 tablespoon paprika
- ½ cup butter

Sauce:

- 1 large onion, chopped
- 1 large green pepper, chopped
- 1 clove garlic, chopped
- ½ cup butter
- 1 (16-ounce) can tomatoes
- 1 cup chopped fresh parsley
- 2 teaspoons vinegar
- 2 tablespoons prepared mustard
- 1 tablespoon Worcestershire sauce
- 1 teaspoon curry powder
- 1 teaspoon thyme
- 1 teaspoon salt
- 1 teaspoon pepper
- 1 (4-ounce) can mushrooms, drained
- 1 cup currants
- ½ cup toasted slivered almonds (or more)

Wash and pat chicken pieces dry with paper toweling. Sprinkle each piece with salt and pepper. Dredge in flour mixed with paprika.

Melt butter in skillet and brown chicken pieces. Arrange chicken in an oblong baking dish or pan.

Sauté onion, green pepper, and garlic in butter until onions are transparent but not brown.

Add remaining ingredients except mushrooms, currants, and almonds; simmer about 20 minutes.

Add mushrooms to sauce and pour over chicken. Cover tightly with foil and bake for 1 hour and 15 minutes at 350°. Lift foil and sprinkle currants over chicken; cover and bake another 15 minutes.

Lift chicken onto serving dish so that currants remain on top; pour sauce all around. Top with slivered almonds and serve with rice. Yield: 6 servings.

Chicken à la Newberry

- 4 chicken breasts
- 2 tablespoons butter or margarine, melted
- 1 tablespoon all-purpose flour
- 1 vegetable bouillon cube
- 1 cup hot water
- 1 (3-ounce) can mushroom slices
- 2 tablespoons sherry
- 1 teaspoon Worcestershire sauce

Sauté chicken breasts in butter, turning to brown on all sides. Remove from skillet and drain on paper towels. Add flour, bouillon cube dissolved in hot water, mushrooms with liquid, sherry, and Worcestershire sauce to skillet; mix well.

Arrange chicken breasts in a flat pan, and pour liquid over chicken. Cover and bake at 350° for 45 minutes to 1 hour or until the chicken is tender. Yield: 4 servings.

Chicken Caribbean

- 2 broiler-fryer chickens, quartered
- 1½ teaspoons salt
- ¼ teaspoon pepper
- ½ cup plus 2 tablespoons corn oil margarine, divided
- 2 tablespoons finely chopped onion
- 1 clove garlic, minced
- 6 fresh or canned whole mushrooms, sliced
- 1 avocado, peeled and diced
- ½ cup dry white wine
- 4 tomatoes, peeled and quartered
- 1½ teaspoons Ac'cent
- 1 tablespoon chopped parsley
- Hot cooked rice
- Paprika (optional)
- Parsley sprigs
- Radish roses

Sprinkle chicken with salt and pepper. Heat ½ cup margarine over medium heat in 11-inch chicken fryer. Add chicken, cover, and cook over low heat for 45 minutes or until tender. Remove chicken to serving platter.

Add onion and garlic to fryer and cook until slightly browned. Add mushrooms and avocado and cook about 3 minutes. Slowly add wine, then tomatoes; sprinkle with Ac'cent and cook very gently for 10 minutes. Gradually stir in remaining 2 tablespoons margarine; add parsley.

To serve, spoon rice onto platter or serving dish. Arrange chicken on top and pour sauce over all. Sprinkle lightly with paprika, if desired. Garnish with sprigs of parsley and radish roses. Yield: 8 servings.

*Chicken 'n Dressing

- 1 broiler-fryer chicken, cut into serving-size pieces
- 3 cups water
- 2 teaspoons salt, divided
- 1 stalk celery, chopped
- 1 small onion, chopped
- 1 small green pepper, chopped
- 1 (10-ounce) package frozen mixed vegetables
- 8 tablespoons corn oil margarine, divided
- 1 egg, beaten
- 2½ cups corn bread stuffing mix
- ¼ cup all-purpose flour
- 1½ teaspoons Ac'cent

Place chicken in 3-quart saucepan; add water, 1 teaspoon salt, celery, onion, and green pepper; cover and cook until tender, about 1 hour. Cool; remove chicken pieces; reserve broth. Remove meat from bones; dice.

Cook mixed vegetables according to package directions; stir in 1 tablespoon margarine, and set aside. Melt 5 tablespoons margarine; mix with egg and ¼ cup chicken broth; stir in corn bread stuffing. Line a 9- x 5- x 3-inch loaf pan with stuffing mixture.

To make a sauce, melt remaining 2 tablespoons margarine in saucepan; stir in flour, Ac'cent, and remaining 1 teaspoon salt; stir in chicken broth and cook until thickened, stirring constantly. Add cooked chicken and vegetables to sauce; pour into prepared loaf pan. Bake at 425° for 15 minutes. Yield: 4 to 6 servings.

East India Chicken

⅓ cup vegetable shortening
3 pounds chicken pieces (thighs and breasts)
½ cup all-purpose flour
1 cup thinly sliced onion
1 (28-ounce) can tomatoes
1½ cups buttermilk or sour milk
1 clove garlic, minced
1 teaspoon salt
½ teaspoon ground ginger
⅛ teaspoon pepper
⅛ teaspoon chili powder
All-purpose flour (optional)
½ cup coarsely chopped cashew nuts
Cooked rice

Heat shortening in 12-inch skillet. Coat chicken with flour and brown. When chicken is nearly all browned, add onion and cook until transparent. Add tomatoes, buttermilk, and seasonings. Cover and cook over low heat for 50 to 60 minutes or until chicken is tender. If desired, remove chicken and thicken sauce with a few teaspoons of flour. Stir in nuts. Serve over rice. Yield: 6 servings.

Chicken Florentine

1 pound fresh spinach or 1 (10-ounce) package frozen chopped spinach
3 tablespoons butter or margarine, divided
3 tablespoons all-purpose flour
1 teaspoon Ac'cent
1 teaspoon salt
Dash cayenne pepper
1½ cups milk
½ cup (2-ounces) shredded Swiss cheese
½ cup half-and-half
2 cups diced cooked chicken
⅓ cup dry bread crumbs

Cook spinach and drain well; chop finely and place in a 1½-quart casserole. Preheat broiler. Melt 2 tablespoons butter in a saucepan. Stir in flour, Ac'cent, salt, and cayenne; gradually add milk. Cook, stirring constantly, until mixture thickens and comes to a boil. Add cheese and half-and-half; cook over low heat until cheese is melted. Remove from heat; add chicken. Pour creamed chicken mixture over spinach. Sprinkle with bread crumbs and dot with remaining 1 tablespoon butter. Place under broiler until lightly browned. Yield: 4 servings.

Champagne Chicken

1 broiler-fryer, cut into serving-size pieces
¼ cup all-purpose flour
Salt and pepper to taste
¼ teaspoon ground ginger
¼ cup butter or margarine
1 onion, quartered
1 carrot, sliced into 4 pieces
1 bay leaf
1 cup champagne or dry white wine
1 (6-ounce) package long grain and wild rice
1 cup whipping cream
1 (8-ounce) can white seedless grapes

Shake chicken pieces in flour which has been seasoned with salt, pepper, and ginger. Brown chicken slowly in melted butter. Add onion, carrot, bay leaf, and champagne. Cover pan, and simmer for 25 to 30 minutes or until chicken is tender.
Prepare rice according to package directions. Arrange rice on heated serving platter; place chicken over rice. Discard onion, carrot, and bay leaf; add cream and grapes to sauce, and heat without letting mixture boil. Spoon sauce over chicken and rice. Yield: 4 to 6 servings.

Coq au Vin

3 tablespoons margarine
½ pound unsliced bacon, cut into cubes
½ pound small white onions
1 (3- to 3½-pound) chicken, cut into pieces
½ pound mushrooms, sliced
½ teaspoon salt
½ teaspoon bouquet garni
Dash pepper
2 tablespoons brandy
1 cup Burgundy
1 tablespoon cornstarch
2 tablespoons water
Lemon slices
Fleurons

Melt margarine in skillet; add bacon and onions and cook over low heat, stirring frequently, until lightly browned. Add chicken, mushrooms, salt, bouquet garni, and pepper. Cover and cook over high heat, turning as needed, until chicken is browned on all sides. Skim off fat. Pour brandy over chicken; ignite. Add wine; cover and simmer until chicken is tender, about 45 minutes.

Arrange chicken pieces on hot platter. Blend cornstarch and water; stir into sauce in skillet. Cook until mixture thickens and is clear. Pour over chicken. Garnish with lemon slices and fleurons. Yield: 4 servings.

Fleurons: Prepare pastry for a single crust pie. Roll out to ¼-inch thickness; then cut into half moons with crimped edge cutter. Place on ungreased cookie sheet. While chicken is simmering, bake at 425° for 8 to 10 minutes or until lightly browned.

Baking the Turkey

Thaw frozen turkey completely. Remove giblets, rinse, and place in a pan with desired seasonings and water. Let simmer 2 hours or longer. Use the broth in the dressing; add chopped giblets to the gravy.

Rinse turkey quickly in cool water and pat dry. Rub inside with salt. The cavity may be loosely filled with dressing or the dressing may be cooked in a separate pan. Fold neck skin under back and fasten with a skewer. Tie drumsticks to tail. Twist wing tips onto back, if desired.

Place turkey, breast side up, on a rack in a shallow pan that has been lined with aluminum foil. Brush the skin with butter. Insert meat thermometer so that the bulb is in the center of the inside thigh muscle. Be sure that the bulb does not touch bone.

Place a loose tent of aluminum foil over the legs and breast to prevent excessive browning. Bake at 325° until skin is a light golden brown. When turkey is two-thirds done, cut cord to release the legs and permit heat to reach heavy-meated part.

Roast until thermometer reaches 180° to 185°. An 8- to 12-pound turkey will take approximately 3½ to 4½ hours to cook to this temperature. The traditional "doneness" test when a thermometer is not used is a "feel" test. Turkey is done when the thickest part of the drumstick feels very soft when pressed between protected fingers.

When the turkey is done, remove to a warm platter and keep hot. Cover tightly with foil and allow to stand for 30 minutes. This will let the juices be absorbed into the meat and will make carving easier.

Turkey Casserole

- 2 *cups cooked chopped turkey*
- 1 *(10¾-ounce) can condensed cream of chicken soup*
- 2 *teaspoons chopped onion*
- 1 *cup finely chopped celery*
- ½ *teaspoon pepper*
- ½ *teaspoon salt*
- 1 *cup slivered almonds*
- 1 *teaspoon lemon juice*
- ½ *cup mayonnaise*
- 3 *hard-cooked eggs, chopped*
- ½ *to ¾ cup cracker crumbs*

Combine all ingredients except cracker crumbs in a 2-quart greased baking dish. Spread cracker crumbs over top, and bake at 375° for 25 minutes. Yield: 6 to 8 servings.

*Turkey Gumbo

  2 *small onions, diced*
  2 *tablespoons salad oil*
  4 *cups turkey broth*
  2 *cups canned tomatoes*
  4 *cups cooked okra*
  2 *cups diced cooked turkey*
  2 *tablespoons chopped parsley*
½ *teaspoon paprika*
    Salt and pepper
  2 *cups cooked rice*

Sauté onion in salad oil until tender but not brown. Add broth, tomatoes, okra, turkey, parsley, and paprika. Simmer for 10 minutes. Season to taste with salt and pepper. Add cooked rice. Heat and serve. Yield: 4 to 6 servings.

Roasting a Deep-Basted Turkey

   1. Free legs and tail from tucked position and remove neck from body cavity.
   2. Simmer giblets in salted water: allow 2½ hours for neck, heart, and gizzard; cook liver about 30 minutes. Chop giblets and use in gravy or in the dressing. Rinse turkey well and drain.
   3. Stuff neck and body cavities lightly (allow ¾ cup dressing per pound, based on purchased weight of turkey).
   4. Return tail and legs to tucked position. Secure neck skin to back with skewers.
   5. Insert meat thermometer into center of thigh bone next to body; be sure that thermometer does not touch bone. Set oven at 325°. Place turkey, breast side up, on rack in shallow pan. Do not use water or cover.
   6. Rub skin with shortening to prevent drying. If you are cooking a turkey that is not prebasted, you will need to baste with drippings as turkey bakes.
   7. Shield only skin of neck cavity with a small square of aluminum foil. When turkey is a light golden brown, place lightweight aluminum foil loosely over breast and thighs to prevent over-browning.
   8. Test for doneness. Before removing from oven, be sure that meat thermometer is in original position. The internal temperature of the thigh should be 180° to 185°. Another test is to check the thickest part of the drumstick. Protect thumb and forefinger with paper; pinch drumstick. If turkey is done, the meat should feel soft.
   9. Approximate roasting time in uncovered pan at 325° for a turkey that weighs 8 to 11 pounds is 4½ to 4¾ hours; 11 to 14 pounds, 4¾ to 5½ hours; 14 to 20 pounds, 5½ to 6 hours.

Special Turkey Soufflé

  1 *tablespoon butter*
  7 *slices white bread, cubed and crusts removed*
½ *pound fresh (or 1 cup canned) mushrooms*
  3 *tablespoons butter*
  3 *cups diced cooked turkey (or chicken)*
½ *cup mayonnaise*
  1 *teaspoon dried green onion*
¾ *teaspoon salt*
¼ *teaspoon freshly ground white pepper*
¼ *teaspoon lemon bits or finely grated lemon rind*
½ *teaspoon monosodium glutamate*
  1 *(6-ounce) can water chestnuts, drained and thinly sliced*
  1 *(2-ounce) jar pimientos, drained and finely chopped*
  3 *large eggs, beaten until very light*
1½ *cups milk*
½ *(10¾-ounce) can condensed cream of celery soup*
  1 *(10¾-ounce) can condensed cream of mushroom soup*
¼ *teaspoon paprika*
  1 *cup shredded sharp cheese*

Grease a 3-quart baking dish with 1 tablespoon butter; then line with bread cubes, reserving some for later use.

Sauté the mushrooms in 3 tablespoons butter in a heavy skillet over medium heat for 7 to 10 minutes. Drain on a paper towel and slice.

Combine the diced turkey, mayonnaise, onion, salt, white pepper, lemon bits, and monosodium glutamate in a large bowl. Spread evenly over bread cubes. Place a layer of half the water chestnuts over this, then a layer of pimientos, a layer of mushrooms, and another layer of water chestnuts.

Sprinkle the remaining bread cubes over the mixture.

Add the beaten eggs to the milk and pour over the entire dish. Cover and chill for several hours or overnight.

Before placing in oven, spoon the combined celery and mushroom soups over the top and sprinkle with paprika. Bake 1 hour or until the soufflé "sets." Sprinkle the shredded cheese over the dish the last 10 minutes of cooking. Test with silver knife for doneness; it should come out clean if soufflé is done.

The soufflé will hold in the oven for 30 minutes on warm without affecting its consistency. Serve hot! Yield: 8 to 10 servings.

Note: The soufflé freezes well. Do not add the soup and cheese until time to bake. Thaw completely at room temperature before cooking.

Turkey Tetrazzini

- ¼ cup butter or margarine
- ¼ cup all-purpose flour
- 2 cups milk
- 1½ teaspoons salt
- ⅛ teaspoon pepper
- 1½ cups diced roast turkey
- 1½ cups cooked (¾ cup uncooked) spaghetti
- ½ cup cooked mushrooms
- ¼ cup chopped pimiento
- ¾ cup shredded Cheddar cheese
- ¾ cup dry bread crumbs
- Melted butter or margarine

Melt ¼ cup butter in heavy saucepan. Add flour and stir until blended. Gradually add milk and cook over low heat for 5 minutes, stirring constantly. Add seasonings.

Combine this white sauce with turkey, spaghetti, mushrooms, pimiento, and cheese. Place in buttered 2-quart casserole. Combine bread crumbs and melted butter and sprinkle over top. Bake at 325° for about 25 minutes or until well browned. Yield: 6 servings.

*Turkey Sticks

- 3 tablespoons butter or margarine
- 3 tablespoons all-purpose flour
- 1 cup hot milk
- 1 large egg, well beaten
- 2 teaspoons lemon juice
- 2 teaspoons grated onion or onion puree
- 1 teaspoon Worcestershire sauce
- ¼ teaspoon salt
- ⅛ teaspoon white pepper
- ¼ teaspoon paprika
- 2 tablespoons chopped parsley (dried, fresh, or frozen)
- 1 cup finely chopped celery
- 2 cups finely chopped cooked turkey (or chicken)
- 2 egg whites, unbeaten
- 1½ cups cracker crumbs
- 2 cups salad oil

Melt butter in top of double boiler over rapidly boiling water. Add flour and blend with a wire whisk. Slowly add the hot milk and stir constantly. Cook until mixture begins to thicken; then add well-beaten egg, lemon juice, grated onion, Worcestershire sauce, salt, pepper, and paprika.

Cook sauce until very thick. Add parsley, celery, and turkey. Allow mixture to cool on a large platter. Take a tablespoon of mixture and shape into a finger-length strip. Place on a cookie sheet, cover with foil, and chill overnight. Thirty minutes before serving the next day, dip sticks in the unbeaten egg whites and roll in cracker crumbs, covering completely.

Put oil in heavy skillet over high heat. When oil is hot and bubbling, drop the sticks in very gently; fry on each side, about 6 to 8 minutes, until golden brown. Watch carefully and adjust heat. Drain on paper towels. These will keep on a hot platter in a warm oven for 30 to 40 minutes. Yield: 12 sticks.

Note: If you cannot eat fried food, you may bake the sticks on an ungreased cookie sheet at 400° for 40 minutes or until they are golden brown. Prepared this way they need a sauce to complement them, for oven baking tends to dry them out a little.

Turkey Divan

- ⅓ cup butter
- ⅓ cup all-purpose flour
- 1 teaspoon salt
- ⅛ teaspoon pepper
- 2 cups milk
- 1 cup shredded American cheese
- 12 to 18 stalks fresh asparagus, cooked
- 8 to 10 slices cooked turkey or chicken
- 1 pimiento, cut in strips

Melt butter in saucepan over low heat; blend in flour and seasonings. Add milk, stirring constantly, and cook until sauce is smooth and thickened. Add cheese and stir until melted. Arrange asparagus in shallow baking dish or in 6 individual casseroles. Pour half the sauce over the asparagus. Arrange turkey or chicken over sauce and cover with remaining sauce. Garnish with pimiento strips. Bake at 375° about 25 minutes or until lightly browned. Yield: 6 servings.

Turkey Newburg

- ⅓ cup butter
- 3 tablespoons all-purpose flour
- 2 teaspoons salt
- ⅛ teaspoon pepper
- ¼ teaspoon ground nutmeg
- 2 cups milk or half-and-half
- 2 cups diced cooked turkey
- 4 egg yolks, beaten
- Toast points or pastry shells
- Parsley or paprika

Melt butter in saucepan over low heat; blend in flour and seasonings. Add milk, stirring constantly. Cook and stir until sauce is smooth and thick. Add turkey and heat through. Add some of the hot sauce to the beaten egg yolks, stirring well. Stir egg mixture back into turkey mixture. Cook over low heat, stirring gently but continually until mixture thickens. Transfer to a chafing dish and serve on toast points or in pastry shells. Garnish with parsley or paprika. Yield: 6 servings.

Turkey Tetrazzini Sauce

- 3 cups diced celery
- 2 cups diced green pepper
- ½ cup chopped onion
- 1 cup sliced mushrooms (fresh or canned)
- 1½ cups butter or margarine
- ½ cup all-purpose flour
- 4 cups milk
- 1 pound sharp Cheddar cheese, shredded
- 4 teaspoons salt
- ½ teaspoon pepper
- 4 tablespoons Worcestershire sauce
- 3 cups diced cooked turkey
- ¼ cup lemon juice
- Cooked spaghetti

Cook celery, green pepper, onion, and mushrooms in butter until onion is just transparent. Add flour and blend well. Add milk all at once; cook, stirring constantly, until mixture thickens. Blend in remaining ingredients except for spaghetti. Stir until cheese is melted.

Cool mixture immediately and put into dishes for the freezer. Seal securely so that wrapping is moisture- and vaporproof. To serve, remove from freezer to refrigerator overnight. Put into saucepan and heat thoroughly. Serve over cooked spaghetti. Yield: 5 pints.

Scalloped Turkey

- ½ cup chopped celery
- ¼ cup chopped green pepper
- 3 tablespoons butter, divided
- 2 tablespoons all-purpose flour
- ¼ teaspoon salt
- 1½ cups milk
- 2 cups diced cooked turkey
- 1 tablespoon chopped pimiento
- 2 cups crushed potato chips, divided

Sauté celery and green pepper in 1 tablespoon butter; remove from pan. Add remaining butter to pan; blend in flour and salt. Remove from heat. Gradually add milk; cook until mixture thickens, stirring constantly. Add turkey, celery, green pepper, and pimiento.

Place 1½ cups potato chips in a greased 1½-quart baking dish. Add turkey mixture. Sprinkle remaining potato chips on top. Bake at 350° for 30 to 40 minutes. Yield: 4 servings.

Turkey Soufflé

- ½ cup shredded Swiss cheese
- 1 (10¾-ounce) can condensed cream of chicken soup
- 1 teaspoon chopped green onion
- 1 teaspoon chopped parsley
- ¼ teaspoon dry mustard
- ⅛ teaspoon pepper
- 6 eggs, separated
- 1 cup diced cooked turkey

Combine cheese, soup, onion, parsley, mustard, and pepper in a large saucepan; place over very low heat and stir just until cheese melts. Beat in egg yolks one at a time; stir in turkey. Beat egg whites until stiff but not dry; fold into cheese mixture.

Pour into a well-greased 2-quart soufflé dish. Bake at 375° about 30 minutes. Serve at once. Yield: 4 or 5 servings.

*Cream of Turkey Soup

- 1 cup finely diced celery
- ¼ cup minced onion
- 3 tablespoons butter or margarine
- ¼ cup all-purpose flour
- 2 cups turkey broth
- 2 cups milk
- 1 cup grated carrot
- ½ cup chopped cooked turkey
- Salt and pepper to taste
- 2 tablespoons chopped parsley (optional)

Sauté celery and onion in butter until vegetables are softened but not browned, about 5 minutes. Remove from heat. Add flour and blend thoroughly; add broth and milk. Return to heat and cook, stirring constantly, until thickened. Add carrot and turkey; heat to serving temperature. Season with salt and pepper. Garnish with parsley, if desired. Yield: 4 to 6 servings.

Turkey Dinner-in-a-Dish

- ¼ cup margarine, melted
- ¼ cup all-purpose flour
- 1 teaspoon salt
- Dash pepper
- 2½ cups milk
- 1 (4-ounce) can mushrooms, drained
- ¼ cup diced pimientos
- 1 (10-ounce) package frozen mixed vegetables
- 1 (16-ounce) package frozen French fries
- 1⅓ cups cooked boned turkey pieces

Combine margarine, flour, salt, and pepper. Stir over low heat until bubbly. Add milk; continue to stir over low heat until mixture is smooth and thick. Add remaining ingredients. Pour into 2-quart shallow baking dish. Bake at 400° for 20 minutes. Yield: 4 servings.

Asparagus and Turkey Casserole

- 15 asparagus spears, cooked and drained
- 1 pound cooked turkey, sliced
- 1 (10¾-ounce) can condensed cream of mushroom soup
- ½ cup shredded Cheddar cheese
- 1 tablespoon dry sherry or white wine

Arrange asparagus in shallow greased casserole. Cover with turkey slices. Combine soup, cheese, and wine; heat until cheese melts. Pour sauce over turkey and asparagus: broil until well browned. Serve immediately. Yield: 4 servings.

Corn Bread-Sausage Dressing

- 1 cup finely chopped celery
- ¾ to 1 cup finely chopped onion
- ½ cup finely chopped green pepper (optional)
- ½ cup margarine
- 6 chicken bouillon cubes
- 4 cups hot water
- 5 cups toasted white bread cubes
- 7½ to 8 cups crumbled corn bread
- ½ pound bulk pork sausage
- 1 teaspoon poultry seasoning
- ½ teaspoon salt
- ¼ teaspoon pepper
- 4 eggs, slightly beaten
- 1 cup finely chopped pecans

Cook celery, onion, and green pepper until tender in melted margarine in a heavy skillet. Dissolve bouillon cubes in hot water and pour over the white bread cubes and corn bread, which have been combined in a large bowl. Add celery, onion, and green pepper. Cook sausage until browned; add to bread mixture, along with seasonings, eggs, and chopped pecans. Toss lightly to mix well.

Dressing may be cooked in an uncovered 13- x 9- x 2-inch pan at 325° for about 45 minutes. Yield: 15 to 20 servings or enough to stuff an 18 to 20 pound turkey.

Oyster Stuffing

- 1 pint oysters
- ½ cup chopped celery
- ½ cup chopped onion
- 4 tablespoons butter
- 4 cups day-old bread cubes
- 1 tablespoon chopped parsley
- 1 teaspoon salt
- ⅛ teaspoon poultry seasoning
- ⅛ teaspoon pepper

Drain oysters, reserving liquor, and chop. Cook celery and onion in butter until tender. Combine oysters, cooked vegetables, bread cubes, and seasonings, and mix thoroughly. If stuffing seems dry, moisten with oyster liquor. Yield: enough stuffing for a 4- to 6-pound hen.

Turkey-Time Sausage Dressing

- 1 pound bulk pork sausage
- ½ pound ground veal
- ½ pound ground pork
- ¾ cup chopped onion
- 1¼ cups chopped celery and leaves
- ¼ cup chopped parsley
- 4 eggs
- 1 (10-ounce) package frozen chopped spinach, cooked according to package directions (optional)
- 1 cup grated Parmesan cheese
- 1 (8-ounce) package stuffing
- ½ teaspoon rubbed sage
- 1 clove garlic, chopped
- 1 cup turkey broth
- 2 tablespoons olive oil
- 1 tablespoon butter

Fry sausage until thoroughly cooked; break apart and add ground veal and pork; cover and cook 15 minutes. Add onion, celery, and parsley; cook, covered, 20 minutes longer. Stir to mix thoroughly.

Meanwhile, beat eggs lightly; add spinach and Parmesan cheese. Place packaged stuffing in bowl; add meat mixture, egg mixture, sage, garlic, broth, olive oil, and butter. Mix carefully with fork. Spinach may be omitted and additional celery added. Yield: stuffing for a 15- to 20-pound turkey.

Oldtime Dressing

10 cups stale dry bread crumbs (mostly corn bread mixed with a few stale biscuits and toast)
   Cold water or stock to moisten
1 or 2 onions, finely minced
1 cup precooked celery, finely minced
½ cup butter or melted turkey fat
½ teaspoon pepper
   Salt to taste
½ teaspoon sage, or more if desired
1 or 2 eggs
   Stock
2 dozen oysters (optional)

Sprinkle crumbs with cold water or stock and let stand 30 minutes to 1 hour to fluff. Sauté onion and celery in butter. Combine all ingredients, adding stock last and using just enough to moisten it sufficiently so that a few crumbs pressed between fingers will hold together. Stuff lightly into turkey.

To make oyster stuffing, add 2 dozen oysters with a little of their liquid to the above recipe. Yield: enough for a 10-pound turkey.

Clam Stuffing for Poultry or Fish

2 tablespoons finely chopped green pepper
1 medium onion, finely chopped
1 large stalk celery, finely chopped
¼ cup butter
1 pint shucked soft-shell clams with liquor
1 teaspoon lemon juice
2 to 3 dashes garlic powder
⅛ teaspoon oregano
½ teaspoon parsley flakes
1 teaspoon salt
⅛ teaspoon pepper
8 slices day-old bread, cubed

Cook vegetables in butter until tender. Add clams and liquor; cook just until edges curl. Add lemon juice and seasonings; mix in bread. Mix well. Yield: about 4 cups stuffing.

Orange-Prune Dressing

3 cups toasted bread cubes
½ cup melted butter or margarine
1 tablespoon grated orange peel
½ cup diced orange sections
1½ cups diced celery
1½ cups chopped cooked prunes
1 teaspoon salt
½ teaspoon poultry seasoning

Combine bread cubes and butter; add orange peel, orange sections, celery, prunes, salt, and poultry seasoning; toss together lightly to blend. Stuff turkey lightly with dressing. Yield: dressing for a 10- to 12-pound turkey.

Toasted Rice-Oyster Dressing

1½ cups uncooked regular rice
3 cups water
1½ teaspoons salt
⅓ cup chopped onion
1 cup chopped celery
3 tablespoons minced parsley
½ cup butter or margarine
1½ quarts oysters
3 cups toasted fine dry bread crumbs
3 teaspoons poultry seasoning
   Salt and pepper
3 eggs, well beaten

Spread rice in shallow baking pan. Roast until golden brown in 400° oven about 20 minutes, shaking pan occasionally so rice will brown evenly. Combine rice, water, and salt in a 4-quart saucepan. Bring to a boil; lower heat. Cover and cook slowly about 14 minutes or until rice is tender. Cook onion, celery, and parsley in butter until soft. Add oysters and cook them until the edges begin to curl. Remove from heat, and stir in bread crumbs, poultry seasoning, salt and pepper to taste, eggs, and rice. Toss lightly with fork until combined. Spread in shallow pan and bake at 350° for 20 minutes. Dressing may be used to stuff a 12- to 16-pound turkey. Yield: 24 servings.

Rice Stuffing for Turkey

   1 *large onion, chopped*
   1 *tablespoon shortening*
  ½ *pound bulk sausage*
   1 *cup soft bread crumbs*
   1 *cup milk*
   4 *cups cold cooked rice*
  ½ *teaspoon ground sage*
   1 *teaspoon thyme*
   1 *teaspoon salt*
  ⅛ *teaspoon pepper*

Brown onion in shortening; add sausage and cook until brown. Soak bread crumbs in milk. Combine all ingredients and stuff turkey for baking. Yield: 6 cups.

*Corn Bread Dressing

 1½ *cups crumbled corn bread*
   3 *slices dry toast, diced*
   1 *stalk celery, chopped*
   1 *small onion, diced*
   2 *or 3 sprigs parsley, chopped*
 1½ *to 1¾ cups orange juice*
  3- *to 5-pound hen*

Mix ingredients for dressing together in a large mixing bowl. The amount of orange juice is determined by preference for a dry or moist dressing. Stuff hen and bake at 325° for 30 to 40 minutes per pound. As a side dish, dressing may be baked in a buttered casserole at 350° for 30 minutes or until crust forms on top. Yield: 6 servings.

*Sage Dressing

 1½ *cups finely chopped onion*
 1½ *cups finely chopped celery*
  ⅓ *cup butter or margarine*
   8 *cups crumbled cornbread*
 1½ *teaspoons salt*
  ⅛ *teaspoon pepper*
  ½ *teaspoon poultry seasoning*
  ½ *teaspoon ground sage*
  ¼ *cup water*
   1 *egg well beaten*

Cook onion and celery until tender in melted butter in a large Dutch oven. Add crumbled corn bread. Sprinkle with seasonings. Add water and egg; toss together to mix well. Stuff turkey lightly or place in a greased 4-quart casserole and bake at 325° for 25 minutes or until lightly browned. Yield: 8 to 10 servings or enough to stuff a 10- to 12-pound turkey.

Pineapple Glazed Cornish Hens

   4 *Cornish hens*
  ¼ *cup dry white wine*
    Salt
    Cracked pepper
    Wild Rice Stuffing
  ¼ *cup butter, melted*
   2 *(8¼-ounce) cans pineapple slices*
  ½ *cup chicken broth*
   2 *tablespoons sugar*
  ¼ *teaspoon ground ginger*
   1 *teaspoon cornstarch*

Season inside of hens with wine, salt, and pepper. Fill loosely with Wild Rice Stuffing. Skewer openings. Brush hens with part of butter; place breast side up in shallow roasting pan. Drain pineapple, reserving juice. Combine ¼ cup pineapple juice and chicken broth; pour over hens. Bake at 350° about 1 hour, basting every 15 minutes with rest of butter and pan drippings.

Top each bird with a pineapple slice. Mix sugar, ginger, and cornstarch with remaining ¼ cup pineapple juice; spoon over hens. Place rest of pineapple slices in pan with hens. Increase temperature to 400° and bake about 15 minutes, basting occasionally, until skin looks glazed. Serve pan liquid as sauce. Yield: 4 servings.

Wild Rice Stuffing:

- 1 *cup wild rice*
- *Hot water*
- ¼ *cup butter, melted*
- 1½ *cups chicken broth*
- 1 *teaspoon salt*
- 6 *green onions, chopped*
- 1 *cup chopped celery*
- ½ *cup chopped toasted almonds*
- 1 *(8-ounce) can mushrooms, sliced*
- ½ *teaspoon ground marjoram*
- ⅛ *teaspoon ground nutmeg*

Soak wild rice in hot water to cover for 1 hour. Drain; dry on paper towels. Sauté rice in butter until golden brown. Add chicken broth and salt; cover tightly and simmer until tender, about 25 minutes. Add green onions, celery, toasted almonds, mushrooms, marjoram, and nutmeg. Mix well. Stuff hens lightly with stuffing. Yield: enough stuffing for 4 Cornish hens.

Cornish Game Hens Veronique

- 8 *ounces chicken or duck liver*
- 1 *ounce bacon bits*
- 1 *teaspoon chopped shallots*
- 2 *tablespoons butter*
- 2 *ounces wild rice, cooked*
- *Salt and pepper to taste*
- 6 *(1-pound) Cornish game hens*
- 1½ *pints demiglace (a commercial sauce)*
- 1 *cup canned white seedless grapes*
- ½ *lemon, cut into slivers*
- 2 *lumps sugar*
- *Several drops vinegar*
- 1½ *ounces rum*

Brown liver, bacon bits, and shallots in butter; add wild rice and season. Stuff hens with this mixture; tie closures. Brown hens quickly in small amount of fat. Pour off fat, cover pan, and bake at 400° about 45 minutes or until done. Moisten often with demiglace. When hens have cooked, skim off fat and strain sauce. Add grapes, lemon, caramel (made by browning sugar and dissolving in vinegar), and rum. Arrange hens on a dish and cover with sauce. Serve remaining sauce on side. Yield: 6 to 12 servings.

Crumb-Coated Cornish Hens

- 2 *Cornish hens*
- ¼ *cup garlic-flavored commercial sour cream or* ¼ *cup commercial sour cream and* ¼ *teaspoon garlic powder*
- 1¼ *cups crushed cheese crackers*
- ¼ *teaspoon thyme*
- ¼ *teaspoon pepper*
- 1 *teaspoon salt*

Cut hens in half; wash and pat dry. Rub hens with sour cream. Combine cheese crackers, thyme, pepper, and salt; roll hens in crumb mixture. Place hens, skin side up in foil or baking dish. Bake at 350° for 45 to 60 minutes or until tender. Yield: 4 servings.

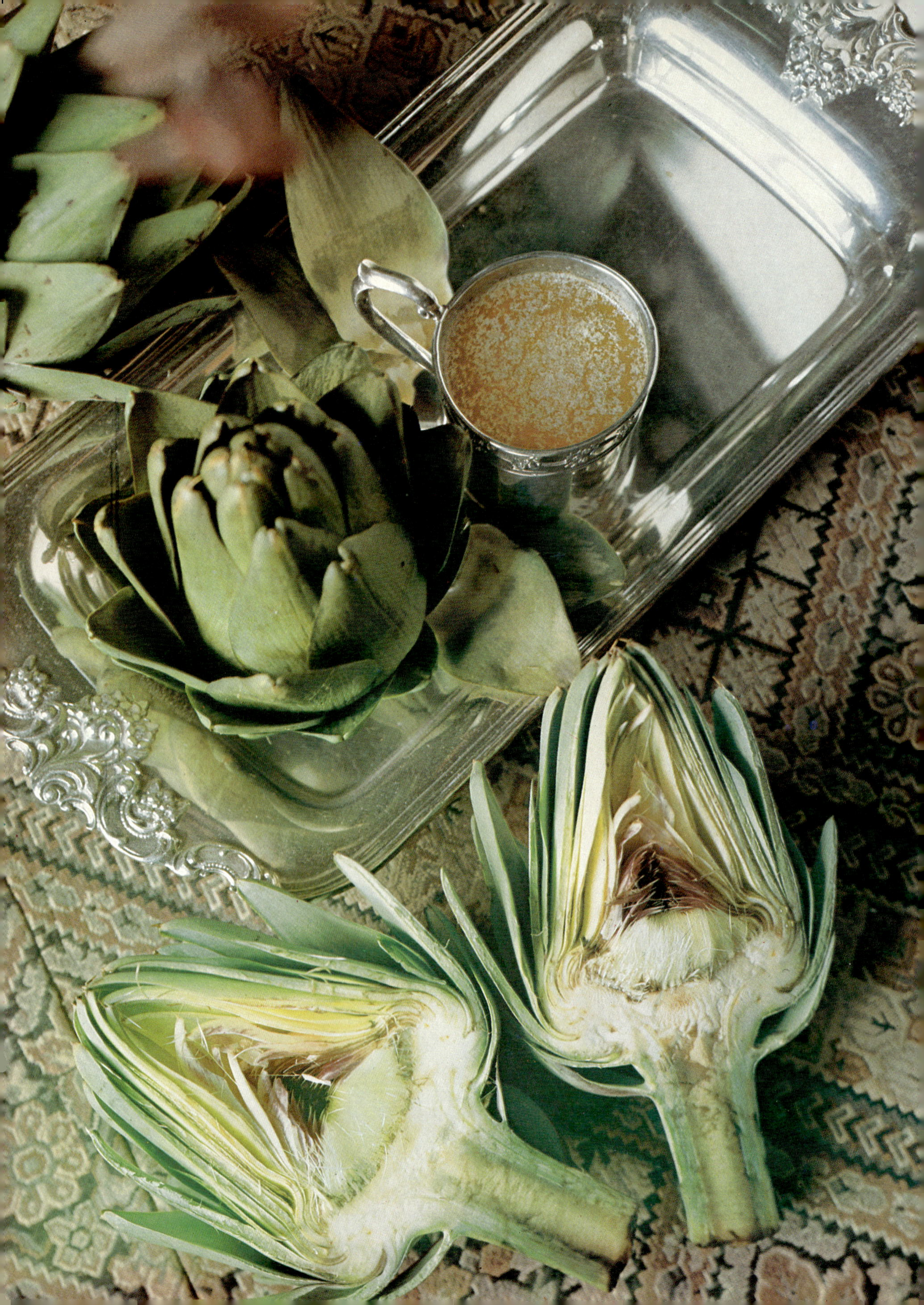

Salads and Salad Dressing

A salad may be as simple as chopped lettuce or cabbage tossed with a dressing of vinegar and oil. Or, it may be as complex as a molded concoction of combined fruits, gelatin, nuts, and whipped cream. Many vegetables, and almost all fruits, which are high in vitamin content, are excellent in a salad combination.

Meat salads often serve as the main dish for a light luncheon; a salad plus a bowl of hot soup with crisp rolls or crackers will make a complete meal. Seafood, cheese, and eggs are often used in main dish salads.

The success of a salad may depend on the type of dressing selected for it. Remember that the dressing should be added, in most cases, just before serving. Many recipes are interchangeable for fruit and vegetable salads. We offer a selection for your choice.

Apricot Cream

- 1 (1-pound 13-ounce) can apricot halves
- 1 (3-ounce) package cherry-flavored gelatin
- ½ cup cold water
- ¼ teaspoon salt
- 1 tablespoon lemon juice
- 1 cup whipping cream, whipped

Drain apricots (reserve the syrup); force through sieve and measure 1 cup pulp. Bring 1 cup apricot syrup to boil and dissolve gelatin in it; add cold water, salt, lemon juice, and apricot pulp. Chill until slightly thickened. Fold in whipped cream. Pour into 1½-quart mold and chill until firm. Unmold on serving plate. Yield: 8 servings.

*Ambrosia

- 4 large navel oranges
- 6 tablespoons powdered sugar
- 1 (3½-ounce) can flaked coconut
- 3 tablespoons orange juice

Peel oranges, being careful to remove all outer white membrane. Cut oranges crosswise into slices about ⅛ inch thick, or cut into sections. Layer a third of the orange slices in a serving bowl. Sprinkle with 2 tablespoons powdered sugar, a third of the coconut, and 1 tablespoon orange juice. Repeat layers. Cover and refrigerate for at least 1 hour. Yield: 6 servings.

Black Cherry Salad

- 1 (3-ounce) package black cherry-flavored gelatin
- ⅓ cup sugar
- 1 cup water
- 1 cup shredded pasteurized process American cheese
- 1 (8¼-ounce) can crushed pineapple
- 1 cup whipping cream, whipped

Mix gelatin, sugar, and water; cook until gelatin and sugar are dissolved. Cool and add cheese and pineapple. Chill until partially set. Add whipped cream and chill until firm. Yield: 6 servings.

Apricot Nectar Salad

    1 *envelope (1 tablespoon) unflavored gelatin*
    2 *tablespoons sugar*
   1/4 *teaspoon salt*
    1 *(12-ounce) can apricot nectar*
   1/2 *cup water*
    8 *whole cloves*
    1 *tablespoon lemon juice*
 1 1/2 *cups drained fruit cocktail*

Mix gelatin, sugar, and salt in a saucepan; add apricot nectar, water, and cloves. Place over heat and stir until gelatin is dissolved. Simmer for 5 minutes. Remove from heat; strain to remove cloves. Add lemon juice. Place in a bowl of ice and chill to the consistency of unbeaten egg white. Fold in fruit cocktail. Pour into a 3-cup mold or individual molds. Chill until firm. Yield: 6 servings.

Shimmering Cherry Salad

    1 *(1-pound) can red, sour, pitted cherries*
    1 *(20-ounce) can crushed pineapple*
   1/2 *cup sugar*
    1 *orange*
    1 *lemon*
       Water
    1 *envelope (1 tablespoon) unflavored gelatin*
   1/2 *cup cold water*
    1 *(3-ounce) package cherry-flavored gelatin*
       Lettuce
       Commercial sour cream

Drain cherries and pineapple, reserving syrup. Pour sugar over cherries and stir gently. Grate orange and lemon rinds; squeeze juices. Combine juices and reserved syrup; add water to make 2 1/2 cups liquid. Soften unflavored gelatin in 1/2 cup cold water. Heat 1 cup of the liquid to boiling and combine with cherry gelatin; add softened gelatin and stir until dissolved.

    Add remainder of juice mixture; stir. Then add cherries, pineapple, and grated rind. Pour into 6-cup molds or 8 individual molds. Chill. Unmold onto lettuce. Top with mounds of sour cream. Yield: 8 servings.

Cherry Mallow Salad

Red Layer:

    1 *(3-ounce) package red raspberry-flavored gelatin*
    1 *cup boiling water*
   1/2 *cup cold water*
   1/2 *cup cooking claret*
    1 *(17-ounce) can pitted dark sweet cherries, drained and cut into halves*

Dissolve gelatin in boiling water. Add cold water and claret and chill until partially set. Add cherries; pour into a 9- x 9- x 2-inch pan and chill until almost firm. Top with Green Layer.

Green Layer:

    1 *(20-ounce) can crushed pineapple*
    1 *(3-ounce) package lime-flavored gelatin*
    1 *(3-ounce) package cream cheese, softened*
   1/2 *cup mayonnaise*
   1/2 *cup cold water*
   1/2 *cup miniature marshmallows*
   1/2 *cup whipping cream, whipped*

Drain pineapple. Measure 1 cup pineapple juice and bring to a boil. Dissolve gelatin in boiling juice. Cool slightly; then add cream cheese and mayonnaise. Beat until smooth; then stir in cold water, pineapple, and marshmallows. Chill until partially set. Fold whipped cream into mixture. Spread over Red Layer and chill until firm. Yield: 9 servings.

White Fruit Salad

    1 *envelope unflavored gelatin*
    2 *tablespoons sugar*
   1/2 *cup cold water*
    1 *(17-ounce) jar Royal Anne cherries*
    1 *(8 1/4-ounce) can crushed pineapple*
    1 *cup milk*
   1/2 *pound blanched slivered almonds*
    1 *cup mayonnaise*

Soften gelatin and sugar in water. Drain cherries and pineapple and measure 1 cup juice from the fruits. Bring juice to a boil and stir in gelatin mixture, continuing to stir until gelatin is dissolved. Cool. Add milk and let chill until mixture thickens slightly. Fold in pineapple, cherries, and almonds. Stir in mayonnaise, beat slightly, and spoon into individual molds. Chill until firm. Yield: 8 servings.

Cherry Avocado Salad

Cherry Layer:

- 1 (17-ounce) can pitted Bing cherries
- 1 (3-ounce) package cherry-flavored gelatin
- ½ cup port
- ¼ cup chopped nuts

Drain juice from cherries and add water to make 1½ cups liquid. Bring juice to a boil; add gelatin and stir until dissolved. Add port; cool until slightly set. Fold in nuts and cherries. Spoon into a lightly greased 1-quart mold. Chill until firm. Top with Avocado Layer.

Avocado Layer:

- 1 (3-ounce) package lime-flavored gelatin
- 1 cup boiling water
- 1 tablespoon lemon juice
- 1 small avocado, cut into cubes
- 1 cup small curd cottage cheese

Place lime gelatin in blender container. Add boiling water, cover container, and blend for about 3 seconds to dissolve gelatin. Add lemon juice, avocado, and cottage cheese; blend until smooth. Carefully spoon on top of Cherry Layer; chill until firm. Yield: 6 servings.

Frosty Cranberry Salad

- 1 (16-ounce) can whole-berry cranberry sauce
- 1 (8¼-ounce) can crushed pineapple, drained
- 1 cup commercial sour cream
- ¼ cup sifted powdered sugar

Combine cranberry sauce and pineapple. Combine sour cream and powdered sugar; add to fruit mixture and mix thoroughly. Line an 8- or 9-inch piepan with aluminum foil; pour in fruit mixture. Freeze until firm. To serve, turn out salad and let stand for a few minutes. Remove aluminum foil and cut salad into 6 wedges. Yield: 6 servings.

Molded Cranberry Relish

- 1 (3-ounce) package raspberry-flavored gelatin
- ¼ teaspoon ground nutmeg
- 1 cup boiling water
- 1 cup pineapple juice
- 1½ cups fresh cranberries, ground
- ¾ cup diced celery
- ⅓ cup slivered almonds

Mix together the gelatin and nutmeg. Add boiling water. Stir until gelatin has dissolved. Add pineapple juice. Chill until thickened. Stir in remaining ingredients. Pour into a 5-cup mold or individual molds. Chill until firm. Unmold to serve. Yield: 8 to 10 servings.

Ruby Red Salad Mold

- 2 cups cranberry juice cocktail
- 1 (6-ounce) package raspberry-flavored gelatin
- 1 cup pineapple tidbits
- ½ cup port
- ½ cup water
- 1 avocado, peeled and sliced
- 1 cup diced, pared apple
- ½ cup finely chopped celery

Heat cranberry juice to boiling. Add gelatin, stirring to dissolve. Add undrained pineapple tidbits, port, and water. Arrange avocado slices in bottom of 5-cup mold. Pour enough gelatin mixture over slices to cover. Chill until almost set; fold apple and celery into gelatin mixture. Pour over avocado layer. Chill until firm. Yield: 8 to 10 servings.

Cranberry Gelatin Salad

    1 *(6-ounce) package raspberry- or cherry-flavored gelatin*
    1 *cup boiling water*
    1 *(20-ounce) can crushed pineapple, drained, liquid reserved*
 1½ *tablespoons lemon juice*
    1 *(14-ounce) jar cranberry-orange relish*
    1 *cup diced apples*
   ½ *to ¾ cup broken pecans*
   ½ *to 1 cup chopped celery, if desired*

Dissolve gelatin in 1 cup boiling water. Add enough water to liquid from drained pineapple to make 1 cup; stir into gelatin mixture. Add lemon juice; chill until slightly thickened. Fold in pineapple, cranberry-orange relish, apples, pecans, and, if desired, celery. Chill 24 hours before serving. Yield: 10 to 12 servings.

Cranberry Salad

 1½ *cups crushed pineapple*
       Hot water
    1 *(3-ounce) package raspberry-flavored gelatin*
    1 *(1-pound) can whole-berry cranberry sauce*
    1 *(11-ounce) can mandarin oranges, drained*
   ½ *cup chopped nuts*
    2 *tablespoons frozen orange juice, undiluted*
    1 *cup whipping cream, whipped*

Drain pineapple. Measure juice and add enough hot water to make 1¼ cups. Bring to a boil; add gelatin and stir until it is dissolved. Chill until mixture begins to set.
    Stir in pineapple, cranberry sauce, mandarin oranges, nuts, and orange juice. Fold in whipped cream. Put in an 8-cup mold and let sit in refrigerator until firm. Yield: 8 to 10 servings.

Crown Jewel Salad

    1 *envelope (1 tablespoon) unflavored gelatin*
   ¾ *cup cold water*
   ¾ *cup salad dressing or mayonnaise*
    1 *(3-ounce) package cream cheese, softened*
    2 *(3-ounce) packages lemon-flavored gelatin*
    2 *cups boiling water*
 1½ *cups ginger ale*
    1 *cup sliced seedless grapes*
    1 *cup banana slices*
   ½ *cup sliced maraschino cherries*

Soften gelatin in cold water; stir over low heat until dissolved. Combine salad dressing or mayonnaise and cream cheese, mixing until well blended. Stir in gelatin and blend well. Pour into a 2-quart mold; chill until firm.
    Dissolve lemon-flavored gelatin in boiling water; add ginger ale. Chill until slightly thickened. Fold in grapes, banana slices, and cherries. Pour over molded gelatin layer. Chill until firm. Yield: 8 to 10 servings.

Blueberry Salad

    1 *(1-pound) can blueberries*
    2 *(3-ounce) packages black cherry-flavored gelatin*
 1½ *cups cold water*
    1 *(8¼-ounce) can crushed pineapple, undrained*
    1 *(4½-ounce) carton non-dairy whipped topping*
    1 *(3-ounce) package cream cheese, softened*
   ½ *cup chopped nuts*

Drain blueberries; add enough water to blueberry juice to make 2 cups liquid. Bring juice to boil and stir in gelatin until dissolved. Add 1½ cups cold water, pineapple, and blueberries. Pour into a 13- x 9- x 1½-inch pan and refrigerate until firm.
    Blend whipped topping with softened cream cheese and nuts. Spread over congealed salad and chill for 2 hours before serving. Yield: 8 to 10 servings.

Cola Fruit Salad

    1 envelope (1 tablespoon) unflavored gelatin
    2 tablespoons sugar
  ¼ cup water
      Juice of 1 lemon
1½ cups cola or ginger ale
1½ cups mixed diced fruit, fresh, frozen, or canned
      Crisp salad greens
      Salted nuts
      Whipped cream

Combine gelatin and sugar in saucepan. Add water and lemon juice. Place over low heat, stirring constantly, until gelatin and sugar are dissolved. Remove from heat. Add cola or ginger ale. Chill until mixture is the consistency of an unbeaten egg white. Fold in fruit. Turn into 6 individual molds and chill until firm. Unmold on crisp salad greens. Garnish with nuts and serve with whipped cream. Yield: 6 servings.

Frozen Fruit Cheese Salad

2 cups cottage cheese, sieved
1 cup commercial sour cream
3 tablespoons powdered sugar
¾ teaspoon salt
1 cup drained pineapple tidbits
1 cup drained mandarin oranges
1 cup fresh blueberries
1 large banana, sliced
½ cup quartered maraschino cherries
½ cup chopped blanched almonds
   Creamy Pink Dressing

Combine cottage cheese, sour cream, sugar, and salt; blend well. Fold in fruit and almonds. Pour into 2-quart mold and freeze until firm. Serve with Creamy Pink Dressing. Yield: 12 servings.

Creamy Pink Dressing:

2 tablespoons maraschino cherry juice
1 cup commercial sour cream

Combine cherry juice and sour cream. Serve over salad. Yield: about 1 cup.

Florida Dessert Salad

1 (14½-ounce) can pineapple tidbits
3 egg yolks
2 tablespoons cider vinegar
2 tablespoons sugar
1 tablespoon butter
   Dash salt
2 cups miniature marshmallows
2 cups orange segments
1 cup diced mango (when available)
1 cup diced papaya (when available)
1 cup whipping cream

Drain pineapple, reserving 2 tablespoons juice. In top of double boiler beat egg yolks; add vinegar, sugar, pineapple juice, butter, and salt. Cook over hot (not boiling) water and stir until thickened. While still warm, fold in marshmallows. When cool, add fruit. Orange segments should be drained and free of membrane. Beat cream until it holds shape. Fold into salad. Spoon into bowl, cover, and refrigerate overnight. Yield: 8 servings.

Note: You can substitute other fruit, such as peaches, cherries, or sweet melon for the mango or papaya.

Frozen Fruit Nut Salad

2 (3-ounce) packages cream cheese, softened
2 tablespoons lemon juice
½ cup mayonnaise
¼ cup sugar
1 teaspoon salt
1 (1-pound 13-ounce) can fruit cocktail, drained
½ cup coarsely chopped nuts
1 cup whipping cream, whipped
   Watercress or other greens for garnish

Blend cream cheese, lemon juice, and mayonnaise until smooth. Add sugar and salt; mix well. Stir in fruit cocktail and nuts. Fold in whipped cream. Pour into mold or freezing tray and freeze until firm. Dip mold in hot water and quickly unmold on serving plate. Garnish with watercress or other greens. Cut into slices and serve. Yield: 10 servings.

Frozen Salad

1 (15-ounce) can condensed milk
Juice of 2 lemons
1 (8¼-ounce) can crushed pineapple, drained
1 (22-ounce) can cherry pie filling
2 cups prepared non-dairy whipped topping

Combine first 4 ingredients; mix thoroughly. Fold in prepared whipped topping. Pour into 13- x 9- x 2-inch pan; cover and freeze. Cut into squares to serve. Yield: 10 servings.

Frosty Date-Sour Cream Mold

2 (3-ounce) packages lime-flavored gelatin
2 cups boiling water
1 cup commercial sour cream
1 (20-ounce) can crushed pineapple, drained
⅓ cup chopped pecans
1 (8-ounce) package diced dates

Mix gelatin and water until gelatin is dissolved. Chill until thick but not completely set. Whip with electric mixer or hand beater until frothy and light. Add sour cream and mix well. Fold in pineapple, pecans, and dates. Pour into lightly greased 6-cup mold. Chill until firm. Yield: 8 to 10 servings.

Creamy Frozen Fruit Salad

1 (1-pound 14-ounce) can fruit cocktail
1 teaspoon unflavored gelatin
2 tablespoons lemon juice
1 (3-ounce) package cream cheese
¼ cup mayonnaise
¼ teaspoon salt
⅔ cup whipping cream, chilled
½ cup sugar
½ cup nuts, chopped

Drain fruit cocktail. Soften gelatin in lemon juice; then dissolve over hot water in double boiler. Blend cream cheese with mayonnaise and salt. Stir in gelatin. Whip cream until stiff, adding sugar gradually during last stages of beating. Stir in cheese mixture, nuts, and fruit cocktail. Pour into refrigerator tray that has been lined with waxed paper. Freeze for about 4 hours or until firm. Turn out onto platter, remove paper, and cut into thick slices. Let the salad stand at room temperature for a few minutes just before serving to improve the flavor and texture. Yield: 8 servings.

Golden Fruit Salad

2 (3-ounce) packages orange-flavored gelatin
2 cups boiling water
1½ cups cold water
1 (11-ounce) can mandarin oranges
1 (8¾-ounce) can apricot halves
1 cup seedless white grapes, fresh or canned
2 large bananas, sliced
Fluffy Topping
¼ cup shredded pasteurized process American cheese

Dissolve gelatin in boiling water. Add cold water; chill until mixture begins to thicken. Drain canned fruits and reserve liquid for Topping. Add fruits to gelatin mixture; place in 2½-quart mold and refrigerate overnight. To serve, add Fluffy Topping and cheese. Refrigerate for 1 additional hour to set Topping. Yield: 12 servings

Fluffy Topping:

6 tablespoons sugar
2 tablespoons cornstarch
1 egg, slightly beaten
1 cup reserved liquid drained from canned fruits
2 tablespoons butter or margarine
1 tablespoon lemon juice
½ pint whipping cream, whipped, or non-dairy whipped topping

Combine sugar and cornstarch in heavy saucepan. Blend in egg and liquid. Cook over low heat, stirring constantly, until mixture thickens. Stir in butter and lemon juice; cool. Fold in whipped cream or topping.

Fresh Fruit Salad

1 fresh pineapple
1 fresh cantaloupe
1 pint fresh blueberries
4 large peaches
4 large nectarines
1 large banana
1 (2-ounce) jar maraschino cherries
Lemon juice or commercial ascorbic-citric mixture

Peel, core, and cut pineapple into cubes. Cut cantaloupe in half, remove seeds, and scoop out center with melon ball cutter. Wash and drain blueberries. Peel and slice peaches, nectarines, and banana. Combine all fruits and add lemon juice or commercial ascorbic-citric mixture to prevent fruit from turning brown. Yield: 8 to 10 servings.

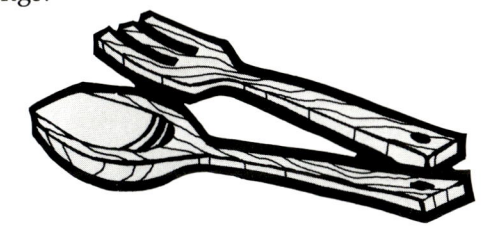

Fruit Salad with Cooked Dressing

½ cup sugar
2 tablespoons all-purpose flour
1 egg, beaten
½ cup pineapple juice
Juice of 1 orange
2 tablespoons butter or margarine
1 cup sliced bananas
1 cup coarsely chopped apples
1 cup drained pineapple tidbits
1 cup sliced fresh strawberries or cherries

Combine sugar and flour in saucepan. Combine egg and fruit juices; gradually blend with flour-sugar mixture. Cook over low heat until mixture thickens, stirring constantly. Remove from heat; add butter and cool. Fold in bananas, apples, and pineapple. Put into a dish, garnish with strawberries or cherries, cover, and chill. Yield: 4 to 6 servings.

Luncheon Salad

1 (1-pound) can grapefruit sections, syrup reserved
3 cups grapefruit juice, canned, fresh, or frozen
2 envelopes unflavored gelatin
¼ cup sugar
¼ teaspoon salt
1½ cups cooked shrimp
¼ cup diced pimiento
½ cup finely diced celery
Salad greens

Drain grapefruit sections, reserving ½ cup of the syrup. Combine syrup with grapefruit juice. Mix together gelatin, sugar, and salt in saucepan; add 1 cup of the grapefruit juice mixture. Place over low heat, stirring constantly, until gelatin and sugar are dissolved. Remove from heat. Add remaining 2½ cups grapefruit juice mixture.

Place several whole grapefruit sections, shrimp, and pimiento in a design in the bottom of a 6-cup mold. Cover with small amount of clear gelatin and chill until almost firm. At the same time, chill remaining gelatin until it is the consistency of unbeaten egg white. Halve remaining grapefruit sections and cut shrimp into small pieces. Fold into gelatin along with pimientos and celery. Spoon over almost-firm first layer; chill until firm. Unmold on salad greens. Garnish wih additional grapefruit sections and shrimp. Yield: 8 to 10 servings.

Mandarin Orange Salad

1 (3-ounce) package lemon-flavored gelatin
1 (3-ounce) package orange-flavored gelatin
2 cups boiling water
1 (11-ounce) can mandarin oranges
1 pint orange sherbet
1½ cups crushed pineapple

Dissolve gelatins in boiling water. Drain oranges and reserve juice. Add enough water to juice from oranges to make 1 cup; stir into gelatin mixture. Chill until thickened. Fold in sherbet and sliced fruit. Chill until firm. Yield: 12 servings.

Mandarin Orange Dessert Salad

    1 *medium-size orange*
    3 *teaspoons green tea leaves*
1½ *cups boiling water*
    1 *(3-ounce) package orange-flavored gelatin*
    2 *tablespoons lemon juice*
    1 *(11-ounce) can mandarin orange sections, drained*
    1 *cup white seedless grapes or seeded grapes, halved*

Squeeze orange, reserving ⅓ cup of juice. Put orange shell into a bowl with tea leaves; pour in boiling water and cover; allow to steep for 5 minutes. Strain; dissolve gelatin in hot tea. Add reserved orange juice and lemon juice; mix well. Chill until mixture is slightly thick. Add mandarin oranges and grapes; mix thoroughly. Pour into 1-quart mold. Chill until firm. Yield: 6 servings.

Psychedelic Salad

1 *cup crushed pineapple or pineapple tidbits*
1 *cup red raspberries, frozen or canned*
1 *cup mandarin orange sections, canned*
1 *cup miniature marshmallows*
1 *cup flaked coconut*
1 *cup commercial sour cream*

Drain pineapple, raspberries, and oranges. Mix all ingredients carefully. Make this salad the day before serving and store, covered, in refrigerator. Yield: 6 to 8 servings.

Tropical Salad and Ice Cream Dressing

4 *cups coarsely shredded lettuce*
1 *cup cubed pineapple, drained*
¼ *cup chopped dates*
¼ *cup chopped nuts*
   Ice Cream Dressing

Put lettuce in a large bowl; add pineapple, dates, and nuts. Mix lightly. Add Ice Cream Dressing and toss lightly. Yield: 4 to 6 servings.

Ice Cream Dressing:

4 *tablespoons vanilla ice cream*
2 *tablespoons salad dressing*
2 *tablespoons crunchy peanut butter*
   Pineapple juice

Thoroughly mix ice cream, salad dressing, and peanut butter. Thin with pineapple juice. Yield: ¾ cup.

*Surprise Salad

    1 *(3-ounce) package lime-flavored gelatin*
1½ *cups boiling water*
    1 *(8¼-ounce) can crushed pineapple, drained*
    1 *cup diced celery*
2¼ *tablespoons prepared horseradish*

Dissolve gelatin in boiling water; cool thoroughly. Stir in pineapple, celery, and horseradish. Spoon into a large mold or individual molds; chill until firm. Yield: 6 to 8 servings.

Twenty-Four Hour Salad

2 *eggs, beaten*
4 *tablespoons vinegar*
4 *tablespoons sugar*
2 *tablespoons butter*
1 *pint whipping cream, whipped*
2 *cups white cherries, halved*
2 *cups pineapple chunks, drained*
2 *cups orange slices, drained*
2 *cups marshmallows, quartered*

Put eggs in top of double boiler; add vinegar and sugar and beat constantly until mixture is thick and smooth. Remove, add butter, and cool. When mixture is cold, fold in whipped cream, fruit, and marshmallows. Pour into a 2-quart mold and place in the refrigerator for 24 hours.

    To serve, unmold on large serving platter. Yield: 12 to 14 servings.

Salad Supreme

- 2 (3-ounce) packages orange-flavored gelatin
- 1 (20-ounce) can crushed pineapple
- 1 cup chopped walnuts, divided
- 1 (4½-ounce) carton non-dairy whipped topping
- 1 (8-ounce) package cream cheese, softened
- 1 tablespoon lemon juice
- ¾ cup sugar
- 2 tablespoons all-purpose flour
- 2 eggs, beaten

Prepare gelatin according to package directions; chill until mixture begins to congeal. Drain pineapple, reserving juice. Add pineapple to chilled gelatin; pour into an oiled 13- x 9- x 2-inch pan. Sprinkle with ½ cup walnuts; chill until mixture is completely congealed.

Blend whipped topping and cream cheese. Spread this mixture on congealed gelatin; cover and chill.

Add enough water to reserved pineapple juice to make 1 cup. Combine lemon juice, sugar, flour, and eggs; add to pineapple juice. Cook over low heat until thick; chill thoroughly. When this mixture is cool, spread over cream cheese mixture. Sprinkle remaining walnuts on top. Yield: 12 to 15 servings.

Tangy Lemon-Lime Salad

- 1 (3-ounce) package lemon-flavored gelatin
- 1 (3-ounce) package lime-flavored gelatin
- 1 cup boiling water
- 1 cup mayonnaise or salad dressing
- 1 cup commercial sour cream
- 1 cup small curd cottage cheese
- ¾ cup finely diced celery
- 1 (8¼-ounce) can crushed pineapple
- 2 teaspoons prepared horseradish
- ½ cup chopped pecans
- ¼ cup chopped pimientos

Dissolve gelatins in boiling water. Combine remaining ingredients in a large bowl; mix well. Stir in hot gelatin, blending throughly. Pour into 2-quart mold or 8 to 10 individual molds. Chill until set. Unmold. Yield: 8 to 10 servings.

Lemon Cheese Salad

- 2 (3-ounce) packages lemon-flavored gelatin
- 3¾ cups boiling water
- 1 (8-ounce) package cream cheese
- 1 teaspoon salt
- 1 (8¼-ounce) can crushed pineapple
- 1 cup chopped nuts
- 1 cup chopped celery
- ½ pint whipping cream, whipped

Dissolve gelatin in boiling water; cool. Blend cream cheese and salt together; stir into gelatin. Add next 3 ingredients; fold in whipped cream. Pour into 2-quart mold. Chill until firm. Yield: 8 to 10 servings.

Yum Yum Salad

- 1 (3-ounce) package lemon-flavored gelatin
- 1 cup boiling water
- ½ cup creamed cottage cheese
- ½ pint whipping cream, whipped
- ½ cup chopped pecans
- ½ cup quartered maraschino cherries
- 1 cup drained crushed pineapple

Dissolve gelatin in boiling water; chill until partially set. Fold in remaining ingredients. Pour into 5-cup mold and chill until firm. Yield: 6 to 8 servings.

Wine Berry Spray

- 1 (6-ounce) package raspberry-flavored gelatin
- 1½ cups boiling water
- ⅔ cup red wine vinegar and oil dressing
- 1 (16-ounce) can stewed tomatoes
- 2 (1-pound) cans whole cranberries
- Commercial sour cream

Dissolve raspberry gelatin in boiling water; add vinegar and oil dressing. Chill until syrupy. Cut tomatoes into bits; add tomatoes and cranberries to gelatin. Pour into a 2-quart mold. Chill until firm. Unmold; serve with sour cream as topping. Yield: 10 to 12 servings.

Frozen Pineapple Salad

1 cup pineapple juice
2 tablespoons all-purpose flour
½ cup butter or margarine
2 tablespoons sugar
¼ teaspoon salt
1 egg, slightly beaten
2 tablespoons lemon juice
4 slices pineapple, cut into cubes
2 (11-ounce) cans mandarin oranges, drained
¼ cup chopped nuts
10 large mashmallows
8 maraschino cherries, cut into halves
1 pint whipping cream, whipped

Make a paste with a small amount of the pineapple juice and flour; gradually add the rest of pineapple juice. Add butter, sugar, and salt and transfer to top of a double boiler. Cook over simmering water for about 10 minutes, stirring often.

Add egg and continue to cook for a few minutes, stirring constantly. Cool and add lemon juice, pineapple, oranges, nuts, marshmallows, and cherries. Fold in whipped cream. Freeze in a tray or in a can. Yield: 8 servings.

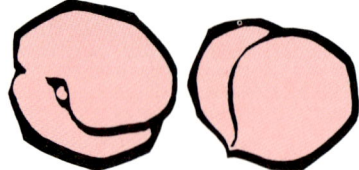

Port Wine Salad

2 (3-ounce) packages raspberry-flavored gelatin
2 cups boiling water
1 (18-ounce) can crushed pineapple
1 (15-ounce) can whole berry cranberry sauce
½ cup chopped nuts
1 cup chopped celery
1 cup port

Mix gelatin with boiling water; stir until gelatin is dissolved. Stir in other ingredients and chill until mixture is firm; stir often until mixture begins to set. Yield: 8 to 10 servings.

Chicken and Carrot Salad

1 tablespoon lemon juice
1 cup mayonnaise
2 cups cooked diced chicken
1 cup shredded carrot
¾ cup diced celery
½ cup slivered almonds
2 tablespoons finely chopped onion
Salt to taste
Lettuce

Stir lemon juice into mayonnaise. Toss with chicken, carrot, celery, almonds, onion, and salt. Chill and serve on lettuce. Yield: 4 servings.

*Macaroni and Chicken Salad

¾ cup cooked diced chicken
2 cups cooked macaroni
1½ tablespoons grated onion
¾ cup chopped mushrooms
1 teaspoon salt
¼ teaspoon pepper
¾ to 1 cup mayonnaise or salad dressing
Lettuce leaves
6 tomatoes, quartered

Combine all ingredients except lettuce and tomatoes; place in refrigerator for about 2 hours to chill. To serve, spoon salad mixture onto lettuce leaves; garnish with tomatoes. Yield: 6 servings.

Chicken Salad Hawaiian

2 cups cooked diced chicken
3 hard-cooked eggs, chopped
¼ teaspoon salt
½ cup sliced celery
1 cup pineapple cubes
¼ cup stuffed sliced olives
¼ cup diced sweet pickle
French dressing
Lettuce leaves
Mayonnaise

Combine first 7 ingredients and mix with French dressing to taste. Chill and serve in lettuce leaves. Serve with additional French dressing or mayonnaise. Yield: 6 servings.

*Spicy Chicken Salad Mold

   3 envelopes unflavored gelatin
   1 cup cold chicken bouillon
   1 cup hot chicken bouillon
   2 cups cooked chopped chicken
   1 cup diced celery
   ¼ cup pickle relish
   ¼ cup finely diced green pepper
   ½ cup mayonnaise
   ½ cup French dressing
   1½ teaspoons salt
      Dash black pepper
      Dash cayenne pepper
   3 tablespoons lemon juice
      Lettuce
      Coleslaw

Soften gelatin in cold bouillon. Dissolve in hot bouillon. Chill until syrupy; then add remaining ingredients. Pour into 1¼-quart ring mold. Chill until firm. Garnish with lettuce and fill center with coleslaw. Yield: 6 servings.

*Chicken Rice Salad

   ⅔ cup packaged precooked rice
   ¼ teaspoon salt
   ¾ cup boiling water
   1 cup mayonnaise
   1½ tablespoons diced pimiento
   1 teaspoon salt
   ¼ teaspoon pepper
   1½ cups cooked diced chicken
   1½ cups diced celery
   1½ cups cooked peas
      Crisp lettuce

Add rice and ¼ teaspoon salt to boiling water in saucepan. Mix just to moisten all rice. Cover and remove from heat. Let stand for 13 minutes; then uncover and let cool to room temperature.

About 1 hour before serving, combine mayonnaise, pimiento, salt, and pepper, mixing well. Combine chicken, celery, and peas in bowl. Stir in the mayonnaise mixture. Then add the rice and mix lightly with a fork. Chill. Serve on lettuce. Yield: 5 or 6 servings.

Curried Chicken Salad

   3 cups cooked diced chicken
   2 cups diced celery
   ½ cup chutney
   1 teaspoon salt
   ¾ cup Curry French Dressing
      Salad greens
      Orange and grapefruit sections
      Apples
      Cherries
      Pear halves
      Ground ginger

Combine chicken, celery, chutney, salt, and Curry French Dressing. Chill for several hours. Serve on salad greens surrounded with fruit. Sprinkle pear halves with ginger. Yield: 6 servings.

Curry French Dressing:

   ⅔ cup salad or olive oil
   3 tablespoons vinegar
   ¼ teaspoon salt
   ⅛ teaspoon white pepper
   1 teaspoon curry powder

Beat ingredients together until well blended. Yield: ¾ cup.

*Chicken Salad

   2 cups cooked diced chicken
   1 cup chopped celery
   ¼ cup blanched almonds
      Salt and white pepper
   2 tablespoons grated onion (optional)
   2 hard-cooked eggs, diced
   1 tablespoon chopped pimiento
   1 cup mayonnaise
   3 tablespoons lemon juice
      Lettuce leaves
      Pickle slices

Chill all ingredients. Combine chicken, celery, almonds, salt and pepper, onion, eggs, and pimiento. Add mayonnaise and lemon juice and stir lightly. Serve on lettuce leaves with pickle slices as garnish. Yield: 6 to 8 servings.

Chicken Cocktail Salad

    2   whole chicken breasts
    1   teaspoon salt
    1   quart water
  1/2 cup mayonnaise or salad dressing
    1   tablespoon cream or milk
    1   teaspoon lemon juice
  1/4 teaspoon ground nutmeg
  1/8 teaspoon curry powder
    1   (17-ounce) can fruit cocktail, drained, reserving 1 teaspoon of liquid
  1/4 cup slivered toasted almonds
       Lettuce leaves

Cook chicken in boiling, salted water over medium heat for 35 to 45 minutes, or until tender when pierced by a fork.

Meanwhile, mix together the next 6 ingredients. Debone cooked chicken and cut into 1/2-inch chunks. Add dressing mixture and toss lightly until all chicken is coated. Chill for 30 minutes. When ready to serve, add fruit cocktail and almonds. Toss lightly; serve on lettuce leaves. Yield: 4 to 5 servings.

Molded Chicken Loaf

    1   envelope unflavored gelatin
  1/2 cup cold chicken stock or bouillon
  3/4 cup hot chicken stock or bouillon
  1/2 teaspoon salt
    2   tablespoons lemon juice
  1/4 cup pineapple syrup
 1 1/4 cups cooked diced chicken
  1/2 cup canned crushed pineapple, drained
  1/2 cup diced celery
       Toasted slivered almonds

Soften gelatin in chicken stock or bouillon. Add hot stock and salt and stir until dissolved. Add lemon juice and pineapple syrup. Chill until consistency of unbeaten egg whites. Fold in chicken, pineapple, and celery. Turn into loaf pan or individual molds and chill until firm. Unmold and garnish with slivered almonds. Yield: 6 servings.

Tropical Chicken Salad

    2   envelopes unflavored gelatin
  1/2 cup cold milk
 1 1/2 cups scalded milk
    2   chicken bouillon cubes
    1   teaspoon salt
    1   cup commercial sour cream
  1/2 cup salad dressing
    1   cup cooked cubed chicken
  1/2 cup finely chopped cooked ham
  1/2 cup cold cooked rice (optional)
  1/3 cup coarsely chopped chutney
  1/3 cup flaked coconut
  1/4 cup chopped pimiento, drained
       Salad greens
       Pineapple and tomato slices
       Toasted slivered almonds

Soften gelatin in 1/2 cup cold milk. To scalded milk, add bouillon cubes, gelatin, and salt; stir until gelatin is dissolved. Chill mixture until partially set. Blend sour cream and salad dressing into gelatin mixture. Fold in next 6 ingredients. Pour into greased 1 1/2-quart melon or ring mold. Chill until firm. Unmold on salad greens. Garnish with pineapple and tomato slices and serve with toasted slivered almonds. Yield: 8 to 10 servings.

Chicken and Ham Salad with Mustard Dressing

 1 1/2 cups cooked diced chicken
 1 1/2 cups cooked diced ham
  1/2 teaspoon minced onion
  1/2 cup chopped celery
  1/4 cup French dressing
    6   medium-size tomatoes
  1/2 teaspoon salt
  1/2 cup mayonnaise or salad dressing
    1   tablespoon prepared mustard
       Lettuce

Combine chicken, ham, onion, celery, and French dressing. Place in refrigerator for 1 hour; drain. Peel tomatoes and scoop out centers. Sprinkle tomato shells with salt and invert on plate. Place in refrigerator to chill.

Combine mayonnaise or salad dressing with mustard; add to chilled mixture and blend lightly. Place tomato shells on lettuce; fill with chicken and ham mixture. Yield: 6 servings.

Chicken Salad Supreme

- 2 (2- to 2½-pound) chickens
- 1 hard-cooked egg, diced
- ½ cup diced pineapple, fresh or canned
- Mayonnaise to moisten
- ½ bunch celery, diced
- ½ cup chopped nuts
- 2 apples, diced
- ½ cup chopped sweet pickles
- Salt and pepper to taste

Cook chicken over low heat in salted water until meat is tender, about 1 hour. Take chicken from stock; cool, remove bones, and dice. Combine with remaining ingredients. Chill before serving. Yield: 8 to 10 servings.

Curried Chicken Salad in Tomato Petals

- 1 (3-pound) chicken, cooked
- ½ cup diced celery
- 1 tart apple, peeled and diced
- 2 teaspoons grated onion
- ½ cup seedless grapes, halved
- ⅓ cup toasted slivered almonds
- 2 teaspoons curry powder
- 1 cup mayonnaise
- 1 teaspoon salt
- Dash pepper
- 6 tomatoes

Remove meat from bones; dice. Add celery, apple, onion, grapes, and almonds. Combine curry, mayonnaise, and seasonings and add to chicken mixture. Chill. Cut tomatoes in sixths, almost but not quite through, to form petals. Fill with salad. Yield: 6 servings.

Chef's Salad with Ham

- 1 quart torn iceberg lettuce leaves
- 1 quart torn endive leaves
- 3 cups (about ¾ pound) cooked julienne ham strips
- 2 cups (about ½ pound) julienne Swiss cheese strips
- 2 cups small cauliflower flowerets
- 1 cup thinly sliced carrots
- 8 large ripe olives
- 1 (3-ounce) jar mushrooms
- Chopped fresh parsley
- Tangy Dressing

Place greens in salad bowl. Arrange ham, cheese, cauliflower, carrots, olives, and mushrooms in a decorative pattern over the salad greens. Garnish with parsley. Top with Tangy Dressing. Yield: 4 servings.

Tangy Dressing:

- ½ cup mayonnaise
- ¼ cup chili sauce
- 2 tablespoons bottled Italian dressing
- 1 teaspoon prepared horseradish
- ¼ cup drained sweet pickle relish

Combine mayonnaise, chili sauce, Italian dressing, and horseradish; stir in pickle relish. Chill. Stir well before serving. Yield: about 1 cup.

Ham and Celery Salad

- 2 cups cooked diced ham
- 1 cup chopped celery
- 3 whole sweet pickles, chopped
- ½ green pepper, chopped
- Mayonnaise or salad dressing

Mix ham with celery, pickles, and green pepper. Add enough mayonnaise or salad dressing to moisten. Yield: 3 to 4 servings.

Ham and Egg Rice Salad

- 2 cups cooked rice
- 6 hard-cooked eggs, chopped
- 1 cup cooked diced ham
- 3 tablespoons finely chopped green pepper
- 1 tablespoon minced onion
- 1 teaspoon salt
- 1/8 teaspoon pepper
- 1/2 teaspoon prepared mustard
- 1/2 cup mayonnaise
- 1/2 cup diced Swiss cheese
- 8 to 12 slices bologna
- Crisp greens
- Tomato wedges

Combine rice, eggs, ham, vegetables, and seasonings. Add mustard and mayonnaise and mix well. Toss lightly with cheese. Roll some of mixture in bologna slices and arrange around edge of bowl. Fill center with remaining salad mixture. Chill. Serve plain, with crisp greens, or with tomato wedges. Yield: 5 to 6 servings.

Ham Loaf Salad

- 4 cups ground cooked ham
- 1 cup chopped celery
- 1 cup crushed crackers
- 1/2 cup salad dressing
- 4 envelopes unflavored gelatin
- 1/2 cup cold water
- 1 (4-ounce) can pimientos, chopped
- 1 medium-size green pepper, chopped
- 1 tablespoon lemon juice
- 3 hard-cooked eggs, chopped
- Salad greens

Combine ham, celery, crackers, and salad dressing. Sprinkle gelatin over cold water and heat until gelatin dissolves. Stir into ham mixture. Add pimientos, green pepper, lemon juice, and eggs. Blend well and press mixture into a 1½-quart oblong dish; chill until firm. Slice and serve on salad greens. Yield: 8 to 10 servings.

*Ham and Macaroni Toss

- 1 (10¾-ounce) can condensed cream of chicken soup, undiluted
- 1/4 cup chopped celery
- 1/4 cup chopped onion
- 2 tablespoons chopped green pepper
- 1/2 teaspoon prepared mustard
- Dash hot sauce
- Dash pepper
- 2 cups cooked macaroni
- 1 cup cooked diced ham
- 3 tomatoes, cut into wedges

Combine soup, celery, onion, green pepper, mustard, hot sauce, and pepper. Stir in macaroni and ham and mix well. Chill. Serve with tomato wedges. Yield: 4 to 6 servings.

Beef Salad

- 2 cups chopped cold roast beef
- 1 cup diced celery
- 1/4 cup chopped sweet pickles
- 2 hard-cooked eggs, diced
- 1/2 teaspoon salt
- 1 cup diced tart apples (optional)
- 1/3 cup mayonnaise
- Crisp lettuce

Combine beef, celery, pickles, eggs, salt, and apples. Stir in mayonnaise and mix lightly. Serve on lettuce. Yield: 4 to 6 servings.

Corned Beef Salad

- 1 (3-ounce) package lemon-flavored gelatin
- 1¾ cups boiling water
- 1 cup salad dressing
- 1 tablespoon sugar
- 1 (12-ounce) can corned beef
- 3/4 cup diced celery
- 1/2 green pepper, chopped
- 1/2 onion, grated
- 1 tablespoon lemon juice
- 1 cup chopped pecans
- 1/2 teaspoon salt
- 3 hard-cooked eggs, diced

Dissolve lemon gelatin in boiling water. Chill. When set, beat until foamy. Blend in salad dressing and beat well. Add sugar. Fold in other ingredients. Pour into mold and chill. Cut into squares when congealed. Yield: 6 to 8 servings.

Two-Toned Corn Beef Salad

Vegetable Layer:

 1 (3-ounce) package lemon-flavored gelatin
 1 cup boiling water
 ¼ cup vinegar
 ½ cup cold water
 ½ teaspoon salt
  Sliced stuffed olives
 1 teaspoon finely minced onion
1½ cups finely shredded cabbage
 ½ cup finely minced celery
 2 tablespoons diced pimiento
 2 tablespoons finely minced green pepper

Dissolve gelatin in boiling water. Add vinegar, cold water, and salt. Pour 1 or 2 tablespoonfuls into bottom of 1½-quart salad mold and arrange design of olives in bottom. Chill in refrigerator until firm. Chill remaining gelatin in refrigerator until consistency of uncooked egg white. Fold in vegetables; pour carefully into salad mold and chill in refrigerator until firm. Top with Corn Beef Layer.

Corn Beef Layer:

 1 envelope unflavored gelatin
 ¼ cup cold water
 1 cup chicken stock, or 1 cup boiling water
   and 2 chicken bouillon cubes
 ½ teaspoon grated onion
  Dash hot pepper sauce
 2 tablespoons lemon juice
 ½ teaspoon prepared mustard
  Salt to taste
 1 cup commercial sour cream
 ½ cup diced celery
 1 (12-ounce) can corn beef, diced
 ¼ cup finely chopped sweet pickle
  Cucumber slices
  Parsley

Soak gelatin in cold water for 5 minutes. Heat chicken stock to boiling. Add gelatin; stir until dissolved. Cool to room temperature. Add onion, pepper sauce, lemon juice, mustard, and salt. Blend in sour cream; chill in refrigerator until consistency of uncooked egg white. Fold in celery, corn beef, and pickle. Pour carefully on top of firm Vegetable Layer. Chill in refrigerator until firm. Unmold on plate; garnish with cucumber slices and parsley. Yield: 8 servings.

Crabmeat Salad

 1 pound crabmeat, preferably backfin
 ¾ cup (2 or 3 stalks) chopped celery
 2 tablespoons lemon juice
 1 teaspoon salt
 ⅛ teaspoon pepper
 3 tablespoons mayonnaise
 1 teaspoon capers

Remove all bones from crabmeat. Put celery in bowl; mix in lemon juice, salt, pepper, mayonnaise, and capers. Add crabmeat and mix gently but thoroughly. Keep refrigerated until served. Yield: 3 to 4 servings.

Crab Salad in Avocado

 1 pound lump crabmeat
 2 tablespoons minced onion
 3 tablespoons chopped celery
 1 tablespoon Worcestershire sauce
 1 teaspoon salt
 3 tablespoons lemon juice
  White pepper to taste
 3 tablespoons mayonnaise
 4 avocados
  Sliced stuffed olives

Chill crabmeat. Combine with onion, celery, Worcestershire sauce, salt, lemon juice, white pepper, and mayonnaise. Mix lightly, but well. Peel avocados and cut into halves just before serving. Spoon crabmeat mixture into halves and garnish with sliced olives. Yield: 8 servings.

Gulfport Salad

1 cup lump crabmeat
½ cup chopped celery
4 tablespoons mayonnaise
2 crisp lettuce leaves
2 hard-cooked eggs, quartered
8 shrimp, stuffed with chopped olives and capers.

Combine crabmeat, celery, and mayonnaise, and mix lightly. Place crab mixture on lettuce leaves and garnish with eggs and stuffed shrimp. Yield: 2 servings.

Seafood Salad

2 (7½-ounce) cans crabmeat
1 cup chopped celery
¼ cup chopped sweet pickle
2 tablespoons chopped onion
3 hard-cooked eggs, chopped
½ teaspoon salt
Dash pepper
½ cup mayonnaise
Lettuce
Tomato wedges

Drain crabmeat; remove any shell or cartilage. Combine all ingredients except lettuce and tomato, being careful not to break seafood into pieces that are too small. Serve on lettuce and garnish with tomato wedges. Yield: 6 servings.

Seafood-Avocado Salad

1 (6½-ounce) can (about 1 cup) lobster meat
2 (6-ounce) packages (about 2 cups) quick-frozen crabmeat
2 cups cooked shrimp, fresh, quick-frozen, or canned
Bottled French dressing
3 ripe avocados
½ cup mayonnaise
½ cup commercial sour cream
1 tablespoon cut chives
Cucumber and tomato slices

Remove any bits of shell from lobster and crabmeat and break meat into bite-size pieces. Reserve claw meat of lobster and a few whole shrimp for garnish. Cut remaining shrimp into pieces. Combine lobster, crabmeat, and shrimp. Add just enough French dressing to coat generously; chill. Just before serving, cut avocados in halves, remove pits, and fill with seafood mixture. Combine mayonnaise, sour cream, and chives for dressing and top each avocado with a generous spoonful. Garnish with lobster claw meat and whole shrimp. Arrange on platter or chop plate and surround with overlapping alternate slices of cucumber and tomato. Yield: 6 servings.

*Tuna Salad

1 (7-ounce) can tuna fish, drained
1 tart apple, peeled and diced
½ cup chopped celery
1 tablespoon chopped sweet pickles
Dash salt
½ cup chopped almonds
2 tablespoons sliced stuffed olives
¼ cup mayonnaise
2 tablespoons lemon juice
Crisp lettuce

Combine first 9 ingredients. Mix well and serve on crisp lettuce. Yield: 4 to 6 servings.

Tuna Louis

⅔ cup mayonnaise
2 tablespoons lemon juice
1 teaspoon dry mustard
⅓ cup chili sauce or catsup
¼ cup chopped pimiento-stuffed olives
1 tablespoon instant minced onion
1 tablespoon capers (optional)
1 head lettuce
2 (7-ounce) cans tuna fish, chilled

To make dressing, combine first 7 ingredients; chill. To serve, shred lettuce and put into salad bowl; add tuna fish. Spoon dressing over salad and toss well before serving. Yield: 4 servings.

Molded Tuna Ring

2 (7-ounce) cans tuna fish
2 hard-cooked eggs, chopped
½ cup chopped stuffed green olives
½ cup chopped celery
1 envelope (1 tablespoon) unflavored gelatin
¼ cup cold water
1 cup mayonnaise or salad dressing
1 cup commercial sour cream
1 tablespoon minced onion
1 teaspoon salt (or more, to taste)
¼ cup lemon juice
2 tablespoons finely minced parsley
Salad greens
Salad dressing
Tomato and cucumber slices

Drain tuna fish and flake, if necessary. Combine with eggs, olives, and celery. Soften gelatin in cold water for at least 5 minutes; then dissolve over hot water and stir into mayonnaise or salad dressing. To this mixture add sour cream, onion, salt, lemon juice, and parsley; combine with the tuna fish. Spoon into a 1-quart mold or 6 individual molds and chill until firm. Unmold on chilled salad plate; garnish with greens and salad dressing or with tomato and cucumber slices. Yield: 6 servings.

*Fish Salad Mold

Salmon Layer:

1 tablespoon (1 envelope) unflavored gelatin
½ teaspoon salt
½ cup cold water
1½ cups boiling water
2 tablespoons lemon juice
1 (1-pound) can salmon or 2 cans solid-pack tuna, drained and flaked

Combine gelatin and salt and add cold water; let stand for 5 minutes. Add gelatin mixture to boiling water and stir until clear. Cool. Blend in lemon juice and salmon or tuna. Pour into fish mold or 9- x 5- x 3-inch loaf pan that has been rinsed in cold water. Chill until set while preparing Cheese Layer.

Cheese Layer:

2 tablespoons unflavored gelatin
1 teaspoon sugar
1 teaspoon salt
½ cup cold milk
2 cups hot milk
1 cup cottage cheese
⅓ cup mayonnaise
1 tablespoon lemon juice
¾ teaspoon grated onion
½ cup diced cucumber
¾ cup diced celery
Lettuce
Sliced tomatoes and cucumbers
Mayonnaise or sour cream dressing

Combine gelatin, sugar, and salt. Soak 5 minutes in cold milk. Gradually add hot milk, stirring until gelatin is dissolved. Cool until thick and syrupy. Blend in cottage cheese and mayonnaise; add lemon juice. Fold in onion, cucumber, and celery. Pour onto fish layer. Chill until firm. Unmold on crisp lettuce leaves and garnish with tomatoes and cucumbers. Serve with additional mayonnaise or sour cream dressing. Yield: 10 servings.

*Hearty Tuna Salad

1 (10-ounce) package frozen green beans
1 (7-ounce) can tuna fish, drained and flaked
1 cup thinly sliced celery
½ cup mayonnaise or salad dressing
1 tablespoon lemon juice
1½ teaspoons soy sauce
Dash garlic powder
1 cup chow mein noodles
Lettuce

Cook green beans according to package directions; drain and cool. Combine green beans, tuna, celery, mayonnaise or salad dressing, lemon juice, soy sauce, and garlic powder; chill. Before serving, add chow mein noodles to tuna mixture; toss lightly. Serve on lettuce. Yield: 4 servings.

Buffet Tuna-Avocado Loaf

 2 envelopes (2 tablespoons) unflavored gelatin
 2 cups cold water
 1 teaspoon grated lemon rind
 ¼ cup lemon juice
 1 large ripe avocado, peeled and mashed
 ¾ cup mayonnaise
 ½ teaspoon salt
 ½ teaspoon chili powder
 1 (7-ounce) can tuna fish, flaked
 ½ cup chopped celery
 ½ cup tomato juice
   Salad greens
 1 lemon, sliced

Sprinkle gelatin over cold water in saucepan. Place over low heat; stir constantly until gelatin dissolves. Remove from heat; add lemon rind and juice; chill until syrupy. Divide mixture into 2 bowls. In one bowl, stir in avocado, mayonnaise, salt, and chili powder. Pour this mixture into a 9- x 5- x 3-inch loaf pan; chill until almost firm.

Stir tuna fish, celery, and tomato juice into remaining gelatin mixture. Pour over almost firm avocado mixture. Chill until firm. To serve, unmold on salad greens and garnish with lemon slices. Yield: 8 servings.

*Tuna-Macaroni Salad

 2 (7-ounce) cans tuna fish
 2 cups cooked shell macaroni
 1 cup chopped raw cauliflower
 1 cup sliced celery
 ¼ cup chopped parsley
 ¼ cup chopped sweet pickle or drained pickle relish
 ½ cup mayonnaise or salad dressing
 3 tablespoons bottled garlic French dressing
 1 tablespoon lemon juice
 1 teaspoon grated onion
 1 teaspoon celery seeds
 ½ teaspoon salt
 ¼ teaspoon pepper
   Salad greens
 1 hard-cooked egg, sliced

Drain tuna fish; break into large pieces. Combine macaroni, cauliflower, celery, parsley, pickle, and tuna. Combine mayonnaise or salad dressing, French dressing, lemon juice, onion, and seasonings; mix thoroughly. Add mayonnaise mixture to tuna fish mixture and toss slightly; chill. Serve on salad greens. Garnish with egg slices. Yield: 6 servings.

Shrimp Salad

 2 cups cooked cleaned shrimp
 2 hard-cooked eggs, diced
 2 tablespoons chopped pimientos
 1 cup chopped celery
 1 tablespoon chopped green pepper
 1 tablespoon chopped onion
 ½ cup mayonnaise
 1½ teaspoons salt
 ½ teaspoon white pepper
 3 tablespoons lemon juice
   Lettuce leaves
   Pickle slices
   Lemon wedges
   Stuffed olives

Combine shrimp, eggs, pimientos, celery, green pepper, and onion in a large bowl. Mix mayonnaise, salt, pepper, and lemon juice; add to shrimp mixture and toss lightly. Serve on lettuce leaves with pickle slices, lemon wedges, and stuffed olives. Yield: 4 to 6 servings.

Shrimp Deluxe Salad

 1 cup elbow macaroni
 ½ cup commercial sour cream
 ⅓ cup bottled French dressing
 ¾ teaspoon salt
 ¼ teaspoon garlic salt
 ⅛ teaspoon curry powder or seafood seasoning
   Dash pepper
 2 cups cooked shrimp, chilled
 ¼ cup chopped onion

Cook macaroni according to package directions; rinse in cold water. Combine sour cream, French dressing, salt, garlic salt, curry powder or seafood seasoning, and pepper. Fold in shrimp, onion, and macaroni. Chill. Yield: 6 servings.

Shrimp Chef's Salad

1 pound fresh shrimp
1 large avocado
Juice of 1 lemon
1 quart torn Bibb lettuce leaves
1 quart torn endive leaves
1 (7½-ounce) can Alaska king crab, drained and flaked
1 (11-ounce) can mandarin oranges, drained
1 cucumber, thinly sliced
Honey Dressing

Devein and cook shrimp; chill thoroughly. Peel and slice avocado; brush with lemon juice. Place greens in salad bowl. Arrange shrimp, crab, avocado, oranges, and cucumber in a decorative pattern over salad greens. Serve with Honey Dressing. Yield: 4 servings.

Honey Dressing:

½ cup salad oil
1 teaspoon grated lemon peel
¼ cup lemon juice
2 tablespoons water
1 teaspoon garlic salt
2 tablespoons honey
½ teaspoon savory leaves

Combine all ingredients in a jar; cover tightly. Shake well to blend before serving. Yield: 1 cup.

Gulf Shrimp Salad

3 (4½- or 5-ounce) cans shrimp
2 cups cooked rice
1 cup sliced celery
½ cup chopped parsley
¼ cup sliced ripe olives
½ cup mayonnaise or salad dressing
2 tablespoons bottled French dressing
2 tablespoons lemon juice
1 teaspoon curry powder
Salad greens

Drain shrimp. Cover shrimp with ice water and let stand for 5 minutes; drain. Cut large shrimp in half. Combine shrimp, rice, celery, parsley, and olives. Combine mayonnaise or salad dressing, French dressing, lemon juice, and curry powder; mix thoroughly. Add mayonnaise mixture to shrimp mixture; toss lightly. Chill. Serve on salad greens. Yield: 6 servings.

Coastal Shrimp Salad

2 cups all-purpose flour
1 teaspoon salt
½ cup shortening
1 cup shredded sharp Cheddar cheese
4 to 7 tablespoons cold water
¼ cup mayonnaise or salad dressing
¼ cup commercial sour cream
4 teaspoons lemon juice
1 teaspoon salt
¼ teaspoon dry mustard
Dash hot sauce
2 cups (1 pound fresh or frozen or two 4½-ounce cans) cooked chopped shrimp
2 cups chopped celery
1 medium-size unpeeled apple, chopped
½ cup chopped pecans
¼ pound seedless green grapes, halved
¼ cup finely chopped green onions
Paprika

Combine flour and 1 teaspoon salt in mixing bowl. Cut in shortening until mixture resembles coarse crumbs; stir in cheese. Sprinkle with water, a little at a time, mixing lightly until dough begins to stick together. Turn out onto lightly floured surface or pastry cloth and press together. Divide into 6 equal portions; roll out each to fit ungreased aluminum baking shells or 5-inch tart pans. Fit dough into shells or pans. Trim pastry 1 inch beyond rim of pans; turn under and flute edge. Prick bottom and sides with fork to allow steam to escape. Bake at 450° for 12 to 15 minutes or until lightly browned. Remove from pans immediately and cool.

While shells are cooling, blend together mayonnaise or salad dressing, sour cream, lemon juice, 1 teaspoon salt, mustard, and hot sauce; set aside. Combine shrimp, celery, apple, pecans, grapes, and green onions. Pour dressing over shrimp mixture; toss lightly. Spoon into cooled pastry shells and sprinkle with paprika. Yield: 6 servings.

*Salmon and Rice Dinner Salad

1 envelope (1 tablespoon) unflavored gelatin
1 cup cold water, divided
1 cup mayonnaise
1 tablespoon lemon juice
1 teaspoon salt
1 (1-pound) can red salmon
2 cups cold cooked rice
1/3 cup chopped stuffed olives
2 tablespoons minced onion
2 tablespoons capers (optional)
Parsley
Lemon slices

Soften gelatin in 1/2 cup of the cold water. Dissolve in top of double boiler over boiling water. Slowly stir dissolved gelatin into mayonnaise. Stir in remaining water, lemon juice, and salt. Chill until set enough to mound when dropped from a spoon.

Drain salmon; remove skin and bones. Flake salmon with a fork. Fold salmon, rice, olives, onion, and capers into partially set mayonnaise mixture. Pour into a 1-quart mold. Chill until firm. Unmold onto chilled platter; garnish with parsley and lemon slices. Yield: 6 servings.

Salmon Mousse

1 envelope (1 tablespoon) unflavored gelatin
1/4 cup cold water
1/4 cup vinegar
1 tablespoon sugar
1 1/4 teaspoons salt
1 teaspoon prepared mustard
2 cups flaked canned salmon
1 cup finely diced celery
1 tablespoon capers (optional)
1/2 cup whipping cream, whipped
Sliced cucumbers
Mayonnaise or Cucumber Dressing

Soften gelatin in cold water and vinegar. Place over boiling water and stir until dissolved. Add sugar, salt, and mustard; stir until blended. Cool. Stir in salmon, celery, and capers. Fold in whipped cream. Turn into 6-cup mold or individual molds and chill until firm. Unmold and garnish with cucumbers. Serve with mayonnaise or Cucumber Dressing. Yield: 6 servings.

Cucumber Dressing:

1/2 cup well-drained finely chopped cucumber
1/2 cup whipping cream, whipped
1/2 teaspoon salt
1 tablespoon vinegar

Do not peel cucumber, but wash and chop very finely; drain well. Combine all ingredients. Yield: 6 servings.

Sour Cream Salmon Salad

2 envelopes (2 tablespoons) unflavored gelatin
1/2 cup cold water
1/4 cup lemon juice
2 cups commercial sour cream
1/2 cup mayonnaise or salad dressing
1 teaspoon seasoned salt
1/2 teaspoon salt
1 (1-pound) can salmon, drained, boned, and flaked
1 cup finely chopped pared cucumber
1 cup finely chopped celery
2 tablespoons chopped pimientos
1/2 cup shredded Cheddar cheese
Salad greens

Soften gelatin in cold water. Dissolve over low heat. Combine with lemon juice and add to sour cream, mayonnaise or salad dressing, and salt; stir. Add salmon, cucumber, celery, and pimientos; stir. Pour into a greased 1 1/2-quart casserole. Sprinkle with shredded cheese. Chill until firm. Cut in squares and serve on salad greens. Yield: 6 to 8 servings.

Creamy Aspic Salad

1 (10¾-ounce) can tomato soup, undiluted
3 (3-ounce) packages cream cheese, softened
1 envelope (1 tablespoon) unflavored gelatin
½ cup cold water
1 cup mayonnaise or salad dressing
½ cup chopped green pepper
½ cup chopped celery
½ cup chopped cucumber
1 teaspoon salt

Put soup in a small saucepan and bring to a boil. Remove from heat, add cream cheese, and beat until melted. Soak gelatin in cold water, add to hot soup mixture, and stir until gelatin is dissolved. Cool. Stir in mayonnaise or salad dressing, vegetables, and salt. Pour into a 4-cup mold and chill until firm. Yield: 6 servings.

Aspic à la Blue

1½ cups tomato juice
¼ cup chopped celery
¼ cup chopped onion
¼ cup chopped green pepper
1 teaspoon lemon juice
1 bay leaf
½ teaspoon salt
Dash pepper
⅓ cup cold tomato juice
2 tablespoons vinegar
1 envelope (1 tablespoon) unflavored gelatin
1 (2-ounce) package blue cheese, crumbled
Salad greens

Combine 1½ cups tomato juice, celery, onion, green pepper, lemon juice, bay leaf, salt, and pepper. Simmer, uncovered, for 10 minutes. Remove bay leaf.

Combine ⅓ cup cold tomato juice and vinegar; sprinkle with gelatin to soften. Add gelatin mixture to hot mixture and stir until gelatin is dissolved. Pour into a 4-cup mold and refrigerate. When mixture is partially set, fold in blue cheese. Refrigerate until firm. Unmold on salad greens. Yield: 4 servings.

Broccoli Salad

2 (10-ounce) packages frozen chopped broccoli
1 cup beef consommé
2 envelopes (2 tablespoons) unflavored gelatin
¾ cup mayonnaise
1 (3-ounce) package cream cheese, softened
¼ cup lemon juice
2 tablespoons Worcestershire sauce
1½ teaspoons hot sauce
½ teaspoon salt
1 teaspoon pepper
4 hard-cooked eggs, chopped
1 (3-ounce) jar pimientos, chopped

Cook broccoli according to package directions. Drain and chill. Put consommé in small saucepan. Sprinkle gelatin over consommé; heat and stir until gelatin is dissolved. Chill until thickened; then stir in broccoli and other ingredients. Spoon mixture into a 6-cup mold and chill until firm. Yield: 8 servings.

Avocado-Buttermilk Salad

1½ packages unflavored gelatin
½ cup cold water
1½ cups mashed and sieved avocado
2 cups buttermilk
½ cup mayonnaise
1½ teaspoons salt
Dash celery salt
1 tablespoon grated onion
1 teaspoon prepared horseradish (optional)
2 tablespoons lemon juice
Dash hot sauce
Green food coloring
Grapefruit sections
Avocado slices

Soften gelatin in cold water; dissolve over hot water. Cool slightly; then add to avocado and mix well. Add all other ingredients except grapefruit sections and avocado slices. Put into greased 8-cup ring mold and chill until firm. Unmold on salad greens and fill center with grapefruit sections and avocado slices. Yield: 8 servings.

Cheese and Vegetable Salad

- 1 firm head lettuce, cut into wedges
- 4 tomatoes, cut into quarters
- 1 medium-size onion, finely diced
- 1 cup diced celery
- ½ cup sliced radishes
- 1 cucumber, sliced
- ½ cup bottled French dressing
- ⅓ pound cubed Cheddar cheese
- 3 hard-cooked eggs

Place lettuce wedges in a large salad bowl. Add tomatoes, onion, celery, radishes, and cucumber. Mix lightly and add French dressing to coat. Garnish with cheese cubes and sliced eggs. Yield: 6 servings.

*Congealed Beet Salad

- 1 (3-ounce) package lemon-flavored gelatin
- 1 cup boiling water
- 1 (16-ounce) can or jar of sliced beets, drained, juice reserved
- ½ teaspoon salt
- 3 tablespoons vinegar
- 2 tablespoons onion juice

Dissolve gelatin in boiling water. Cut beets into cubes; set aside. Add ¾ cup beet juice to gelatin mixture. Add salt, vinegar, and onion juice and chill until mixture is syrupy. Add beets and chill until firm. Yield: 6 servings.

Marinated Beans

- ½ cup salad oil
- ½ cup vinegar
- ½ cup sugar
- ½ teaspoon salt
- ½ teaspoon pepper
- ½ cup chopped onion
- ½ cup chopped green pepper
- 1 pimiento, chopped
- 2 (16-ounce) cans cut green beans, drained

Mix all ingredients together; cover and let sit in refrigerator overnight, stirring occasionally. Yield: 8 to 10 servings.

*Molded Beet Salad

- 1½ cups cooked sliced beets
- 1 cup beet juice
- 1 (3-ounce) package lemon-flavored gelatin
- ¼ lemon, peeled and seeded
- 1 teaspoon salt
- ¼ small onion
- 3½ teaspoons prepared horseradish
- 2 or 3 drops hot sauce
- 2 carrots, cut into 1-inch pieces

Add enough water to beet juice to make 1 cup. Heat to boiling, and pour into blender along with gelatin. Cover and run on low speed until gelatin is dissolved. Add lemon, salt, onion, horseradish, and hot sauce; cover blender and run at high speed until smooth. Add carrots; run blender at low speed just until carrots are coarsely chopped. Add beets; run at low speed just until beets are chopped. Pour into a 1-quart mold or individual molds and chill until set. Yield: 6 servings.

Caesar Salad

- 1 clove garlic
- Freshly ground black pepper
- Salt
- 4 anchovies
- 6 tablespoons oil
- 2 tablespoons vinegar
- Dash dry mustard
- Dash Worcestershire sauce
- 1 coddled egg
- 1 crisp head romaine lettuce
- Grated Parmesan cheese
- Croutons

Crush garlic in wooden bowl; remove remaining pulp. Add pepper and salt. Add anchovies to garlic and mince with fork. Add oil, vinegar, mustard, Worcestershire sauce; stir well. Add egg and mix thoroughly. Add whole romaine leaves and sprinkle generously with cheese. Add croutons and toss lightly.

Caesar Salad should be served on a chilled plate. Yield: 2 servings.

Cucumber Mousse

- 1 (3-ounce) package lime-flavored gelatin
- 1 cup boiling water
- 1 cup grated cucumber, leave part of the rind on
- 1 tablespoon minced onion
- 1 (3-ounce) package cream cheese, softened
- 1 tablespoon vinegar
- ⅛ teaspoon cayenne pepper
- ½ teaspoon salt
- 1 cup diced celery
- ½ cup diced green pepper

Dissolve gelatin in boiling water. Chill until the consistency of egg white. Meanwhile, combine other ingredients and mix well. Stir into gelatin and chill until firm. Yield: 6 to 8 servings.

*Calico Slaw

- 3 cups shredded green cabbage
- 3 cups shredded red cabbage
- 1 large sweet pepper, shredded
- Salt and pepper to taste
- 3 tablespoons sweet pickle relish
- ½ cup mayonnaise

Shred cabbage into large bowl. Add green pepper, salt, pepper, relish, and mayonnaise. Toss with a fork. Yield: 6 to 8 servings.

Great Bean Salad

- 2 (16-ounce) cans cut green beans
- 2 (16-ounce) cans kidney beans
- 2 (16-ounce) cans cut yellow wax beans
- 2 green peppers, chopped
- 2 onions, sliced
- 1 (4-ounce) jar pimientos, drained and chopped
- 1½ cups sugar
- ⅔ cup vegetable oil
- 1⅓ cups tarragon vinegar
- 1 teaspoon black pepper
- 2 teaspoons seasoned salt

Combine first 6 ingredients and drain well. Place in a large bowl. Combine sugar, vegetable oil, vinegar, pepper, and salt; pour over bean mixture. Mix well and place in a refrigerator dish with a tight-fitting cover. Keep cool until ready to serve. Yield: about 12 servings.

Bean Sprout Salad

- 1 (1-pound) can drained bean sprouts
- 1 (6-ounce) can water chestnuts, drained and minced
- 1½ tablespoons finely chopped green onions and tops
- 2 tablespoons soy sauce
- 2 tablespoons sesame seeds, toasted and crushed
- 1 tablespoon salad oil
- ½ teaspoon sugar
- ¼ teaspoon garlic salt
- Dash cayenne pepper
- Lettuce leaves

Rinse bean sprouts in cold water and chill. Chill water chestnuts. Combine all ingredients and chill. Drain and serve on lettuce leaves. Yield: 6 to 8 servings.

*Shamrock Salad

- 2 (3-ounce) packages lime-flavored gelatin
- 1⅔ cups boiling water
- 1 teaspoon salt
- 1 cup cold water
- ¼ cup vinegar
- ¼ cup chopped green pepper
- 1 cup finely sliced celery
- 1 cucumber, pared and chopped
- ½ cup chopped or shredded cabbage
- 1 cup shredded carrots

Dissolve gelatin in hot water. Add salt, cold water, and vinegar. Cool until gelatin is the consistency of egg whites, stirring occasionally; add vegetables. Spoon into a 9-inch square pan and chill until firm. To serve, cut into squares. Yield: 8 to 10 servings.

*Four-Bean Salad

1 (16-ounce) can kidney beans, drained
1 (16-ounce) can cut wax beans, drained
1 (16-ounce) can cut green beans, drained
1 (16-ounce) can black-eyed peas, drained
½ cup sugar
½ cup white wine vinegar
½ cup salad oil
1 teaspoon salt
½ teaspoon dry mustard
¼ teaspoon tarragon
¼ teaspoon basil
1 tablespoon parsley
1 medium-size onion, thinly sliced into rings
Lettuce

Place beans and peas in large bowl. Combine all remaining ingredients except onion rings and lettuce; pour over beans. Cover and chill for several hours or overnight. Add onion rings before serving; toss lightly and drain. Transfer to large lettuce-lined salad bowl. Yield: 12 servings.

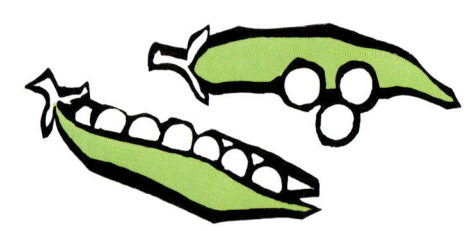

Cucumber-Lime Salad

1 (3-ounce) package lime-flavored gelatin
1 cup boiling water
2 cups grated cucumber
1 teaspoon grated onion
1 (3-ounce) package cream cheese, softened
½ cup mayonnaise
½ to 1 teaspoon salt
1 teaspoon lemon juice
1 teaspoon vinegar

Dissolve gelatin in boiling water. Chill thoroughly. Combine cucumber, onion, and cream cheese; blend well. Stir in mayonnaise; add salt, lemon juice, and vinegar; mix well. Stir into chilled gelatin mixture. Spoon into 3-cup mold or individual molds; chill until firm. Yield: 6 to 8 servings.

Zippy Pineapple Slaw

2 cups shredded cabbage
1 cup shredded carrots
½ cucumber, grated
½ teaspoon salt
1 cup mayonnaise
1 (15¼-ounce) can crushed pineapple, drained

Combine all ingredients and mix well. Cover and chill for at least 1 hour before serving. Yield: 8 to 10 servings.

Strassburg Salad

3 cups chopped cabbage
Water
1 cup crushed pineapple
2 bananas, sliced
½ cup nuts
¼ cup mayonnaise
½ cup whipping cream, whipped

Put about 1 cup cabbage at a time in blender container. Cover with water and process on chop. Remove and strain through sieve. Continue until all cabbage has been chopped. Drain well and discard water.
 Put other ingredients except cream in blender and blend. Add to cabbage and stir well. Chill. Fold in whipped cream at serving time. Yield: 6 servings.

Old-Fashioned Cold Slaw

1 (3-ounce) package lemon-flavored gelatin
1 cup boiling water
½ cup cold water
½ cup salad dressing or mayonnaise
½ cup commercial sour cream
½ teaspoon salt
 Grated onion to taste
¼ teaspoon prepared mustard
1 teaspoon sugar
2 cups chopped or shredded cabbage

Dissolve gelatin in boiling water; add cold

water and stir into mixture of salad dressing or mayonnaise and sour cream. Add salt, onion, mustard, and sugar. Put in refrigerator until mixture is the thickness of unbeaten egg whites. Stir in the cabbage and spoon into a greased mold. Chill until firm. Yield: 8 to 10 servings.

Fruited Cabbage Salad

  1 *cup chopped fresh cranberries*
¼ *cup sugar*
  2 *cups finely shredded cabbage*
½ *cup orange juice*
¼ *cup finely diced celery*
¼ *cup diced green pepper*
  1 *cup green or red grapes, seeded*
¼ *teaspoon salt*
¼ *cup mayonnaise*

Mix the cranberries with sugar. Moisten the cabbage with orange juice. To cabbage, add the sugared cranberries, celery, green pepper, and grapes. When ready to serve, add salt and toss lightly with mayonnaise. Yield: 4 to 6 servings.

Asparagus Salad

1½ *cups cold water, divided*
¾ *cup sugar*
½ *cup white vinegar*
½ *teaspoon salt*
2½ *envelopes (2½ tablespoons) unflavored gelatin*
  1 *(10½-ounce) can asparagus spears*
  1 *(2-ounce) jar pimientos, chopped*
¾ *cup chopped celery*
  1 *teaspoon grated onion*
½ *cup nuts (optional)*

Combine 1 cup water, sugar, vinegar, and salt; boil over medium heat. Dissolve gelatin in ½ cup cold water; add to hot mixture, stirring until gelatin is completely dissolved. Chill until gelatin mixture is slightly thick. Add asparagus, pimientos, celery, onion, and nuts; mix well. Pour into 5-cup mold. Chill until firm. Unmold and serve. Yield: 6 to 8 servings.

Gold and Green Salad Mold

  1 *(3-ounce) package lime-flavored gelatin*
  2 *cups boiling water*
¼ *to ½ teaspoon salt*
¾ *cup grated carrots*
  1 *cup cooked rice*
½ *cup crushed drained pineapple*
¼ *cup slivered toasted almonds*
⅓ *cup mayonnaise*
   Crisp salad greens

Add lime gelatin to boiling water and stir until dissolved. Remove from heat, add salt, and chill until slightly thickened. Stir in carrots, rice, pineapple, and almonds. Fold in mayonnaise. Pour into 1-quart mold or individual molds. Chill until firm. Unmold and serve on salad greens. Garnish with additional mayonnaise. Yield: 5 to 6 servings.

Garlic Garden Salad

  4 *cloves garlic*
   Salt
  1 *lemon*
  3 *ounces salad oil*
  1 *head lettuce*
  1 *ripe avocado*
  1 *cucumber*
12 *radishes*
  2 *tomatoes*

Cut up garlic and place in a covered container. Sprinkle with salt; allow garlic to absorb salt; sprinkle again with salt and allow garlic to absorb it. Continue this process until garlic no longer absorbs salt. Squeeze lemon; pour juice over garlic and salt mixture. Cover and let sit for 45 minutes. Add twice as much oil as lemon juice. Shake and let sit until ready to use. Shake again before using.
  Wash lettuce, avocado, cucumber, radishes, and tomatoes. Tear lettuce into small pieces and place in salad bowl. Peel avocado, cucumber, radishes, and tomatoes; cut into bite-size pieces; add to lettuce and toss lightly. Strain dressing over salad; toss lightly and serve. Yield: 6 to 8 servings.

Refrigerator Slaw

    3 pounds cabbage, shredded
    2 medium-size onions, diced
    2 green peppers, diced
    ¼ cup diced pimiento
    1 cup vinegar
    1 cup sugar
    1 cup salad oil
    2 tablespoons salt
    3 tablespoons prepared mustard
    2 teaspoons celery seeds

Put cabbage, onion, and pepper into a very large bowl. Combine remaining ingredients and bring to a boil. Pour over cabbage mixture and mix thoroughly. Refrigerate overnight to blend flavors. This slaw keeps indefinitely in sealed containers in the refrigerator. Yield: about 1 gallon.

Grandma's Southern Slaw

    2 cups chopped cabbage
    1 medium-size onion
    ½ cup canned tomato wedges, drained and chopped
    3 tablespoons tomato juice
    ¼ cup sugar
    1½ tablespoons vinegar
    1 teaspoon salt
    ¼ teaspoon pepper

Put cabbage into large bowl. Cut onion in quarters and add to cabbage. Add tomatoes, tomato juice, sugar, vinegar, salt, and pepper. Mix well, cover bowl, and store in refrigerator until flavors blend. Yield: 6 servings.

Guacamole

    2 medium-ripe large avocados
    1 tablespoon lemon juice
    2 medium-size tomatoes, peeled and finely chopped
    1 cup finely chopped onion
    1½ teaspoons seasoned salt
    ½ teaspoon seasoned pepper
    Tostados or corn chips

Mash the avocados with a fork. Add the lemon juice and blend well. Add remaining ingredients and combine thoroughly. Serve with warm tostados or kingsize corn chips. Yield: about 3 cups.

*Molded Eggs and Vegetables

    1 envelope (1 tablespoon) unflavored gelatin
    ½ cup cold water
    1 teaspoon salt
    2 tablespoons lemon juice
    ¼ teaspoon hot sauce
    ¾ cup mayonnaise or salad dressing
    1½ teaspoons grated onion
    ½ cup finely diced celery
    ¼ cup finely diced green pepper
    ¼ cup chopped pimientos
    4 hard-cooked eggs, chopped
    Sliced hard-cooked eggs for garnish

Soften gelatin in cold water. Place over boiling water and stir until gelatin is dissolved. Add salt, lemon juice, and hot sauce. Cool. Add mayonnaise or salad dressing; mix in remaining ingredients. Turn into a 6-cup mold or individual molds; chill until firm. Unmold and garnish with sliced eggs. Yield: 6 servings.

Cauliflower Mold

    1 (3-ounce) package lemon-flavored gelatin
    2 cups boiling water
    Juice of 1 lemon
    ⅛ teaspoon salt
    ½ cup diced celery
    1 cup broken cauliflowerets
    ½ cup diced carrots
    ¼ cup broken walnut meats
    Lettuce
    Mayonnaise

Dissolve gelatin in boiling water. Add lemon juice and salt and chill until slightly congealed. Add celery, cauliflower, carrots, and walnuts. Chill until firm and serve on lettuce with mayonnaise. Yield: 4 to 6 servings.

Health Salad Special

- 2 tablespoons cranberry juice cocktail
- ½ cup mayonnaise
- 2 cups coarsely grated raw carrots
- 3 cups shredded iceberg lettuce
- 1 (6-ounce) can water chestnuts, drained and sliced
- ½ cup seedless raisins
- Salt to taste
- ¼ cup salted peanuts, chopped

Stir cranberry juice into mayonnaise and mix well. In a large salad bowl, lightly toss together the carrots, lettuce, water chestnuts, raisins, salt, and mayonnaise. Sprinkle top with peanuts. Yield: 6 servings.

Green Wonder Salad

- 1 (1-pound) can French-style green beans
- 1 (1-pound) can small English peas
- 1 (1-pound) can fancy Chinese vegetables, without meat
- 1 (6-ounce) can water chestnuts, thinly sliced
- 1½ cups thinly sliced celery
- 3 medium-size onions, thinly sliced
- 1 cup sugar
- ¾ cup cider vinegar
- 1 teaspoon salt
- Pepper to taste

Drain and discard liquid from all canned vegetables. Mix all ingredients in a large bowl. Cover and refrigerate for several hours or overnight before serving. This will keep several weeks in the refrigerator if container is tightly covered. Yield: 3 pints.

Wilted Lettuce

- 1 large head lettuce
- 6 slices crisp bacon
- ¼ cup bacon drippings
- ¼ cup tarragon vinegar
- ⅛ teaspoon salt
- ¼ teaspoon freshly ground black pepper
- ¼ teaspoon sugar

Wash lettuce, pat dry, and tear into bite-size pieces. Place in a salad bowl. Break bacon into 1-inch pieces and add to lettuce. Heat together the remaining ingredients. Pour over lettuce, tossing as poured. Serve at once. Yield: 6 servings.

Golden Nugget Salad

- 4 cups cooked diced potatoes
- 4 hard-cooked eggs, chopped
- 1 cup diced celery
- ½ cup chopped green pepper
- ¼ cup chopped green onion
- ¼ cup chopped dill pickle
- 1½ cups mayonnaise
- 2 tablespoons prepared mustard
- 2 tablespoons dill pickle juice
- 2 teaspoons salt
- Salad greens

Combine potatoes, eggs, celery, pepper, onion, and pickle. Mix mayonnaise, mustard, pickle juice, and salt; toss lightly with potato mixture. Serve in bowl lined with salad greens. Yield: 6 to 8 servings.

Mexican Fiesta Salad

- 1 head lettuce
- ½ cup fresh spinach
- 1 ripe avocado
- 1 cup corn chips
- ½ cup shredded Cheddar cheese
- ¼ cup sliced green onion
- 1 (12-ounce) can corned beef, chilled
- 1 cup bottled Green Goddess dressing
- ⅓ cup commercial sour cream
- 1½ tablespoons lemon juice
- Few drops hot sauce

Tear lettuce and spinach into pieces. Cut half the avocado into slices. Combine greens, avocado slices, corn chips, cheese, and onion. Cut chilled corned beef into cubes; add to salad. For dressing, mash remaining avocado with fork and blend in remaining ingredients. Yield: 4 to 5 servings.

Pimiento Cheese-Avocado Salad

 4 *ripe firm avocados*
 1 *(7-ounce) can or jar whole pimientos, drained*
 1 *(8-ounce) package cream cheese*
 ½ *cup minced black olives*
 1 *tablespoon minced parsley*
  Dash cayenne pepper
  Salt and pepper to taste
  Lemon juice
  Commercial sour cream (optional)
  Salad greens
  Salad dressing

Halve avocados and remove pits. Enlarge pit cavity, reserving the meat. Roughen cavity surface with a fork. Line hollow with opened-out whole pimientos and trim around edges, reserving bits of pimiento for filling.

To make filling, combine the cream cheese, olives, parsley, seasonings, reserved avocado meat, and pimiento bits. Add lemon juice and, if desired, sour cream.

Fill avocado cavity with cheese mixture. Brush avocado with lemon juice, wrap tightly, and chill. Just before serving, halve each shell; arrange on crisp salad greens and top with your favorite dressing. Yield: 8 servings.

*Refreshing Pea Salad

 1 *(16-ounce) can peas*
 2 *tablespoons chopped green pepper*
 1 *teaspoon chopped pimiento*
 2 *tablespoons chopped celery*
 2 *tablespoons diced sharp Cheddar cheese*
 1 *tablespoon chopped onion*
 1 *tablespoon pickle relish*
 1 *hard-cooked egg, diced*
 1½ *tablespoons mayonnaise*

Drain peas and set aside. Combine next 6 ingredients and mix well. Add peas, egg, and mayonnaise; toss gently. Chill thoroughly. Yield: 4 to 6 servings.

*Molded Macaroni and Cheese

 1 *envelope (1 tablespoon) unflavored gelatin*
 ½ *cold water*
 ¾ *cup hot water*
 1 *cup shredded pasteurized process American cheese*
 1 *tablespoon lemon juice*
 1 *teaspoon salt*
 2 *teaspoons grated onion*
 2 *tablespoons chopped parsley*
 1 *tablespoon chopped pimiento*
 ½ *cup diced celery*
 1½ *cups broken cooked macaroni*
 ½ *cup mayonnaise or salad dressing*
  Sliced stuffed olives

Soften gelatin in cold water. Add hot water; stir constantly until gelatin is dissolved. Add shredded cheese. Stir until cheese has softened. Stir in lemon juice, salt, and onion. Chill until mixture is consistency of unbeaten egg whites. Stir in parsley, pimiento, celery, macaroni, and mayonnaise or salad dressing. Turn into a 6-cup mold or individual molds, and chill until firm. Unmold; garnish with olives. Yield: 6 servings.

*Easy Perfection Salad

 2 *(3-ounce) packages lemon-flavored gelatin*
 1¾ *cups boiling water*
 1 *tablespoon vinegar*
 12 *to 15 ice cubes*
 6 *or 7 small green onions*
 1 *pimiento, chopped*
 1 *(1-pound) can chopped sauerkraut, drained*
  Crisp salad greens
 1 *teaspoon prepared horseradish*
 1 *cup mayonnaise*

Place the gelatin in a 9- x 5- x 3-inch loaf dish. Add boiling water and stir to dissolve gelatin. Add vinegar and ice cubes; stir constantly until gelatin begins to thicken, about 3 minutes. Remove any ice cubes that are not melted.

Snip the tops of the green onions into gelatin mixture. Stir in pimiento. Add sauerkraut to gelatin; stir mixture gently. Chill until mixture is firm, about 4 hours. Unmold onto salad greens. Combine horseradish and mayonnaise and serve as a topping for salad. Yield: 8 servings.

*Vegetable Trio Salad

   1 *(3-ounce) package lemon-flavored gelatin*
   1 *cup boiling water*
1½ *tablespoons vinegar*
    Cold water
1½ *teaspoons salt*
    Dash pepper
 ¼ *teaspoon paprika*
    Dash cayenne pepper
   1 *cup shredded raw cabbage*
   2 *tablespoons grated onion*
 ¾ *cup chopped raw spinach*
 ¾ *cup grated raw carrot*
    Lettuce
    Cottage cheese

Dissolve gelatin in boiling water. Place vinegar in a measuring cup and add enough cold water to make ¾ cup. Add vinegar mixture to dissolved gelatin and stir in seasonings. Chill until syrupy. Add cabbage and onion to one-third of this mixture. Pour into 1-quart ring mold and chill until set. Add spinach and carrot to remainder of gelatin; pour over set mixture. Chill until firm. Unmold onto a bed of crisp lettuce and serve with cottage cheese in the center. Yield: 6 servings.

*Jade Ring Salad

   1 *(3-ounce) package lime-flavored gelatin*
   2 *cups hot water*
   1 *tablespoon vinegar*
   1 *cup cottage cheese*
 ¼ *cup mayonnaise*
 ⅓ *cup green pepper strips*
 ½ *cup diced carrots*
 ½ *teaspoon grated onion*
   1 *teaspoon salt*
 ⅛ *teaspoon pepper*

Dissolve gelatin in hot water; add vinegar. Pour a thin layer (about ¾ cup) into 3-cup ring mold and chill until firm. Chill remaining gelatin until slightly thickened; set container in a bowl of ice water and whip until gelatin mixture is fluffy and thick like whipped cream. Combine cottage cheese, mayonnaise, green pepper, carrots, onion, salt, and pepper. Fold into whipped gelatin. Spoon over firm gelatin in mold; return to refrigerator and chill until firm. Yield: 4 to 6 servings.

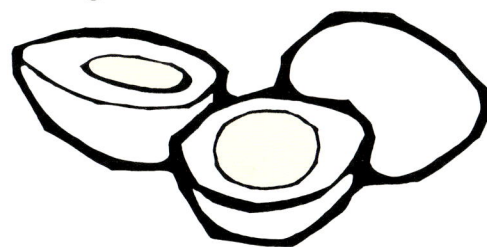

Spinach Salad

   4 *slices bacon*
   4 *cups torn spinach leaves*
   1 *(8¼-ounce) can pineapple tidbits, chilled and drained*
 ½ *cup sliced onion*
    Bottled French dressing

Cook bacon until crisp; drain and crumble. Place spinach in large salad bowl. Top with pineapple tidbits and onion slices. Sprinkle crumbled bacon over top. Just before serving, add dressing and toss lightly. Yield: 4 servings.

Dutch Spinach Salad

   3 *cups (about 6 ounces) fresh spinach, washed and cut into bite-size pieces*
   5 *slices crisp bacon, crumbled*
   1 *medium-size carrot, shredded*
   1 *tablespoon minced onion*
 ¼ *cup commercial Italian dressing*
 ⅛ *teaspoon dry mustard*
    Dash pepper

Combine spinach, bacon, carrot, and onion in a medium-size bowl. Heat Italian dressing with mustard and pepper in a small saucepan; pour over spinach and toss. Yield: about 4 servings.

Fresh Spinach Salad

⅔ cup salad oil
¼ cup wine vinegar with garlic
2 tablespoons white wine
2 teaspoons soy sauce
1 teaspoon sugar
1 teaspoon dry mustard
½ teaspoon curry powder
1½ teaspoons salt
½ teaspoon seasoned pepper
1 bunch (about 2 to 3 cups) fresh spinach
5 slices bacon
2 hard-cooked eggs

Combine first 9 ingredients in a jar and set aside until ready for use. Wash and dry spinach; tear into bite-size pieces and place in refrigerator to keep crisp. Fry bacon until crisp. Chop hard-cooked eggs and crumble bacon; combine.

Arrange the spinach in individual salad dishes or a large bowl. Pour dressing over spinach and top with crumbled bacon and chopped eggs. Yield: 4 to 6 servings.

Jellied Vegetable Salad

1 (3-ounce) package lemon-flavored gelatin
1 cup hot water
2 tablespoons lemon juice
1 tablespoon sugar
½ teaspoon salt
½ cup mayonnaise
½ cup commercial sour cream
1 tablespoon prepared mustard
1 cup finely shredded cabbage
½ cup grated carrots
1 cup finely chopped celery
2 tablespoons grated onion
1 tablespoon chopped parsley

Pour gelatin into hot water. Add lemon juice, sugar, and salt, stirring until gelatin is dissolved. Chill until syrupy. Fold in mayonnaise, sour cream, and mustard. Chill until slightly thickened; stir in vegetables. Put salad in a greased quart mold or individual molds. Chill until firm. Yield: 10 to 12 servings.

Deviled Potato Salad

8 hard-cooked eggs
2 tablespoons vinegar
1 tablespoon prepared horseradish
2½ tablespoons prepared mustard
1 cup mayonnaise or salad dressing
1 cup commercial sour cream
½ teaspoon celery salt
1 teaspoon salt
6 medium-size (4½ cups) potatoes, cooked, peeled, and cubed
1 cup chopped celery
¼ cup chopped onion
2 tablespoons chopped green pepper
2 tablespoons chopped pimiento
Tomato wedges
Cucumber slices

Cut eggs in half and remove yolks. Mash and blend yolks with vinegar, horseradish, and mustard. Add mayonnaise or salad dressing, sour cream, celery salt, and salt; mix well. Chop egg whites and combine with potatoes and chopped vegetables. Fold in egg yolk mixture; chill. Garnish with tomatoes and cucumbers. Yield: 6 to 8 servings.

Sour Cream Potato Salad

⅓ cup bottled French or Italian dressing
7 medium-size (6 cups) potatoes, cooked in jackets, peeled and sliced
¾ cup sliced celery
⅓ cup sliced green onions and tops
4 hard-cooked eggs, yolks and whites separated
1 cup mayonnaise
½ cup commercial sour cream
1½ teaspoons prepared horseradish mustard
Salt and celery seeds to taste
⅓ cup pared diced cucumber
Sliced green onion tops

Pour dressing over warm potatoes and chill for 2 hours. Add celery, onion, and chopped egg whites. Sieve yolks, reserving some for garnish. Combine remaining sieved yolks with mayonnaise, sour cream, and horseradish mustard. Fold into salad.

Add salt and celery seeds. Chill salad for 2 hours. Add cucumber and mix well. Garnish with reserved sieved yolk and onion tops. Yield: 8 to 10 servings.

German Potato Salad

 6 to 8 slices bacon, cooked and diced
 6 medium-size potatoes, unpared
 1 onion, finely chopped
 1 teaspoon salt
 ⅛ teaspoon pepper
 1 teaspoon dry mustard
 ¼ cup sugar
 ½ cup water
 ¼ to ½ cup vinegar
 1 egg, slightly beaten
  Onion rings (optional)
  Crisp bacon (optional)

Cook bacon until crisp, reserving drippings. Cook the potatoes until tender; remove the skins while hot and slice. Combine the bacon, potatoes, and onion. To the bacon drippings add salt, pepper, dry mustard, sugar, water, vinegar, and beaten egg. Cook the mixture only until the egg thickens; pour it over the bacon-potato mixture and heat until the liquid is absorbed. Garnish, if desired, with onion rings and additional pieces of crisp bacon. Yield: 6 to 8 servings.

*Fire and Ice Tomatoes

 ¾ cup vinegar
 1½ teaspoons celery salt
 1½ teaspoons mustard seeds
 ½ teaspoon salt
 6 teaspoons sugar
 ⅛ teaspoon red pepper
 ⅛ teaspoon black pepper
 ¼ cup cold water
 6 large ripe tomatoes, peeled and quartered
 1 green pepper, sliced into rings
 1 onion, sliced into rings
 1 cucumber, peeled and sliced

Mix vinegar, celery salt, mustard seeds, salt, sugar, red and black pepper, and water. Bring to a boil; boil hard for 1 minute. Pour hot mixture over tomatoes, green pepper, and onion. Cover and place in refrigerator to chill. Before serving, add cucumber. Serve very cold as a salad on lettuce or as a relish. Yield: 8 to 10 servings.

Herbed Tomatoes

 6 large ripe tomatoes
 1 teaspoon salt
 ¼ teaspoon coarsely ground pepper
 ½ teaspoon thyme
 ½ teaspoon marjoram
 ¼ cup finely snipped parsley
 ¼ cup chopped chives
 ⅔ cup salad oil
 ¼ cup tarragon vinegar

Peel tomatoes and cut into halves crosswise. Place by layers in a deep bowl, sprinkling each layer with mixture of seasonings and herbs. Combine oil and vinegar and pour over tomatoes. Cover and chill for 1 hour or longer, occasionally spooning dressing over tomatoes. Drain and serve cold. Yield: 6 servings.

*Zesty Stuffed Tomatoes

 6 large firm tomatoes
 ¼ cup chopped green pepper
 1 small onion, minced
 2 tablespoons chopped stuffed olives
 ½ cup chopped celery
 ½ cup mayonnaise
 2 cups creamed cottage cheese
 ¼ teaspoon Worcestershire sauce
  Salt and pepper to taste
  Paprika

Wash and hollow center of each tomato; save the pulp. Turn tomatoes upside down to drain. Chill. Dice drained tomato pulp; combine pulp with other ingredients except paprika. Fill tomatoes with mixture and sprinkle tops with paprika. Chill thoroughly, so flavors are well blended. Yield: 6 servings.

*Quick Tomato Aspic

1 (3-ounce) package lemon-flavored gelatin
1 cup boiling water
1 (8-ounce) can tomato sauce with onions
¼ cup cold water
Salt to taste
Lettuce
Cucumber-Mayonnaise Dressing

Dissolve gelatin in boiling water; add tomato sauce. Rinse out tomato sauce can with cold water and add to gelatin mixture. Add salt. Pour into ring mold and chill until firm.

Unmold onto lettuce and fill center with Cucumber-Mayonnaise Dressing. Yield: 6 servings.

Cucumber-Mayonnaise Dressing:

½ cup mayonnaise
¼ cup chopped cucumber
1 tablespoon chopped parsley

Combine ingredients and serve with Quick Tomato Aspic.

Warehouse Blue Cheese Dressing

4 ounces blue cheese
1 cup mayonnaise
¼ cup salad oil
¼ cup commercial sour cream
¼ cup buttermilk
1 tablespoon white vinegar
¼ teaspoon salt
1 teaspoon garlic powder
Salt and pepper to taste (optional)

Crumble blue cheese into a large mixing bowl. Add mayonnaise and salad oil and blend thoroughly. Add sour cream. Blend thoroughly again. Then add buttermilk, vinegar, salt, and garlic powder. Blend well and add more salt and pepper, if desired. Store covered in refrigerator for at least 24 hours before serving. Yield: 2 cups.

Blue Cheese Dressing

1 cup cottage cheese
½ cup crumbled blue cheese
½ cup milk
1 tablespoon lemon juice
¼ teaspoon salt

Beat together cottage cheese and blue cheese until fairly smooth. Blend in milk, lemon juice, and salt. Cover and chill. Yield: 1½ cups.

Sour Cream-Blue Cheese Dressing

3 ounces blue cheese
1 teaspoon garlic salt
½ cup salad oil
¼ cup vinegar
1 cup commercial sour cream

Mash blue cheese with a fork; blend with garlic salt. Beat into the oil and vinegar. Fold in sour cream. Cover and chill. Serve on tossed greens. Yield: 2 cups.

Creamy Avocado Dressing

1 ripe avocado
¼ cup salad oil
¼ cup vinegar
¼ cup commercial sour cream
½ cup blue cheese
Salt and pepper to taste
Dash hot sauce
Lettuce

Mash avocado. Combine oil and vinegar; combine all ingredients. Serve on lettuce. Yield: 2 cups.

Avocado Dressing

½ cup mayonnaise
½ cup commercial sour cream
2½ tablespoons powder sugar
2 tablespoons lemon juice
1 medium-size avocado, mashed

Blend all ingredients. Chill for about 1 hour before serving; serve with fruit or vegetable salads. Yield: about 1½ cups.

Avocado Dressing for Fruit

1 cup whipping cream, whipped
½ cup powdered sugar
⅛ teaspoon salt
¾ cup sieved ripe avocado
3 drops green food coloring

Combine cream and sugar; mix well. Add salt and avocado and mix well. Stir in food coloring. Serve over fruit salads. Yield: 1¼ cups.

*Buttermilk Salad Dressing

1 tablespoon cornstarch
1 tablespoon dry mustard
Dash paprika
¼ teaspoon onion salt
Salt and ground white pepper to taste
1 cup buttermilk
2 eggs, beaten
½ cup vinegar
¼ cup lemon juice
Sugar to taste

Combine cornstarch, dry mustard, paprika, onion salt, salt, and white pepper in the top of a double boiler. Gradually stir in buttermilk and eggs. Stir constantly while cooking over hot, not boiling, water until mixture begins to thicken. Remove from heat.

In a separate bowl, combine remaining ingredients. Add gradually to the hot, creamy buttermilk mixture, beating well after each addition. Chill before serving. Good on peach and cottage cheese salad. Yield: 2 cups.

French Dressing

1 (10¾-ounce) can tomato soup, undiluted
1 soup can corn oil
½ soup can cider vinegar
⅓ cup sugar
1 teaspoon garlic salt
Dash monosodium glutamate (optional)
Dash oregano

Combine ingredients in a jar and mix well. Store in refrigerator several hours or overnight to blend flavors. Shake well before using. Use on green salad. Yield: 1½ pints.

*Celery Seed Dressing

1 teaspoon salt
1 teaspoon dry mustard
1 teaspoon paprika
1 teaspoon celery seeds
½ cup light corn syrup
¼ to ⅓ cup vinegar
1 cup corn oil
1 tablespoon grated onion

Combine all ingredients. Beat with rotary beater until well blended and thick. Place in a covered container in the refrigerator and chill for several hours. Shake thoroughly before serving. Yield: about 1¾ cups.

Note: For variety, substitute poppy seeds or sesame seeds for celery seeds.

Creamy Celery Seed Dressing

½ cup commercial sour cream
2 tablespoons milk
1 teaspoon dried chives
¾ teaspoon celery seeds
¼ teaspoon salt
¼ teaspoon coarsely ground pepper
1 tablespoon vinegar

Combine sour cream, milk, chives, celery seeds, salt, and pepper in a small bowl; mix well. Blend in vinegar. Serve with molded vegetable salads, cucumbers, tomatoes, or tossed mixed greens. Yield: ½ cup.

*Blender Salad Dressing

½ cup sugar
2 tablespoons salt
1 tablespoon white pepper
1 large onion
1 cup salad oil
1 cup water
1 cup cider vinegar
1 clove garlic, if desired
¼ cup chopped celery, if desired
¼ cup chopped green pepper, if desired

Put all ingredients in blender and mix well. Store in refrigerator; mix well before using. Yield: about 4 cups.

*Cooked Salad Dressing

1 teaspoon dry mustard
Few grains cayenne pepper
2 tablespoons sugar
2 beaten egg yolks or 1 whole egg
1 cup undiluted, evaporated milk
¼ cup lemon juice

Combine dry ingredients and add egg yolks. Mix well; then add evaporated milk. Cook in double boiler, stirring constantly until thick. Cool and add lemon juice. Yield: about 1½ cups dressing.

Famous Salad Dressing

4 egg yolks, well beaten
4 tablespoons tarragon vinegar
1 tablespoon sugar
1 tablespoon butter
¼ teaspoon salt
1 teaspoon dry mustard mixed with a little water
Dash red pepper
1 pint whipping cream, whipped

Cook the first 7 ingredients in the top of a double boiler, stirring constantly until thick. Let cool; then fold whipped cream into the cooked mixture just before serving. Serve with fruit salads. Yield: 2 cups.

*Curry French Dressing

⅔ cup salad or olive oil
3 tablespoons vinegar
¼ teaspoon salt
⅛ teaspoon white pepper
1 teaspoon curry powder

Beat ingredients together until well blended. Serve on salad greens. Yield: ¾ cup.

*Creamy French Dressing

1 teaspoon salt
½ teaspoon dry mustard
3 to 4 tablespoons sugar
3 tablespoons catsup
¼ cup undiluted evaporated milk
½ cup corn oil
3 tablespoons vinegar

Combine all ingredients except vinegar in mixing bowl. Beat with rotary beater until smooth and well blended. Add vinegar all at once, beating until thoroughly mixed. Dressing will be creamy thick. Yield: about 1¼ cups.

Sweet 'n Spicy French Dressing

1½ cups corn oil
¾ cup tarragon vinegar
½ cup light corn syrup
1 teaspoon salt
½ teaspoon curry powder
¼ teaspoon pepper
Dash cayenne pepper
1 teaspoon finely chopped onion
1 clove garlic

Combine all ingredients except garlic; beat with rotary beater until well blended and thick. Add garlic and chill in covered container for several hours; then remove garlic. Shake thoroughly before serving on green salad. Yield: 2 cups.

French Dressing for Shrimp

 1 *cup olive oil or salad oil*
 1 *cup vinegar*
 1 *(10¾-ounce) can tomato soup, undiluted*
 ¼ *cup sugar*
 3 *tablespoons Worcestershire sauce*
 ½ *teaspoon salt*
 ½ *teaspoon pepper*
 1 *medium-size onion, grated*

Combine all ingredients and mix well. Serve on shrimp salad. Yield: 2 cups.

*Dressing for Green Salad

 1 *small clove garlic, crushed*
 ¼ *teaspoon salt*
 ⅔ *cup salad oil*
 ⅓ *cup red wine vinegar*
 ¼ *teaspoon dry mustard*
    Freshly ground pepper to taste
 1 *teaspoon Worcestershire sauce*

Combine garlic with salt and a few drops of oil. Add salad oil, vinegar, mustard, pepper, and Worcestershire sauce. Beat with rotary beater until mixture is well blended. Keep in covered jar in refrigerator until ready to use. Yield: 1 cup.

Lemon-Honey Dressing

 1 *egg, well beaten*
 ¼ *cup lemon juice*
 ½ *cup honey*
 3 *tablespoons milk*
 1 *cup small curd cottage cheese*
    Dash salt
    Dash ground mace

Combine egg, lemon juice, and honey in top of double boiler and cook over hot water, stirring constantly, until mixture thickens. Cool. Stir milk into cottage cheese and beat until smooth. Add salt and mace to cottage cheese and blend with cooked mixture. This is delicious over fruit salad. Yield: 1½ cups.

Lemon-Honey Cream Dressing

 1 *cup commercial sour cream*
 3 *tablespoons honey*
 3 *tablespoons lemon juice*
 ½ *teaspoon grated lemon rind*
 ½ *teaspoon salt*

Combine all ingredients and chill for 30 minutes to blend flavors. Serve over fruit salads. Yield: 1 cup dressing.

Louis Dressing for Crab Salad

 1 *cup mayonnaise*
 ¼ *cup whipping cream*
 ¼ *cup chili sauce*
 1 *teaspoon Worcestershire sauce*
 ¼ *cup chopped green pepper*
 ¼ *cup chopped green onion*
 2 *tablespoons lemon juice*
    Salt (optional)

Combine all ingredients and refrigerate for about 2 hours before serving. Add salt and more lemon juice, if desired. Spoon over lump crabmeat on shredded lettuce. Yield: 2 cups.

Pineapple Dressing for Fruit Salad

 ⅓ *cup sugar*
 4 *teaspoons cornstarch*
 ¼ *teaspoon salt*
 1 *cup unsweetened pineapple juice*
 ¼ *cup orange juice, fresh, frozen, or canned*
 2 *eggs, beaten*
 2 *(3-ounce) packages cream cheese, softened*

Combine sugar, cornstarch, and salt in saucepan. Blend in pineapple juice and orange juice, and cook, stirring constantly, until mixture is clear (about 5 to 8 minutes). Slowly stir mixture into beaten eggs. Return to saucepan and cook over low heat, stirring constantly, until mixture thickens. Let cool for 5 minutes. Beat into cream cheese. Chill. Yield: 2 cups.

Mexicali Dressing

 1 *hard-cooked egg yolk*
 ¾ *cup French dressing*
1½ *tablespoons Worcestershire sauce*
 ½ *teaspoon chili powder*
 1 *clove garlic, peeled*

Sieve the egg yolk into the French dressing. Blend Worcestershire sauce and chili powder together and stir into dressing. Jab a toothpick into the garlic clove and drop into the dressing. This dressing is best made several hours in advance. Remove the garlic before serving. Serve on green salad. Yield: 4 servings.

Lime Dressing

 ½ *cup salad oil*
 ½ *cup lime juice*
 ½ *teaspoon salt*
 2 *tablespoons honey or sugar*
  Dash cayenne pepper

Combine all ingredients and shake well. Serve on fruit or green salad. Yield: 1 cup.

Dressing for Lettuce Salad

2¼ *tablespoons salad dressing*
 2 *teaspoons olive oil*
  Dash wine
 1 *teaspoon sugar*
 1 *teaspoon poppy seeds*
  Paprika

Combine all ingredients and mix well. Spoon over shredded lettuce salad and sprinkle with paprika. Yield: 2 servings.

Strawberry-Sour Cream Dressing

 ½ *cup mayonnaise*
 ½ *cup commercial sour cream*
 ½ *cup sugar*
 ½ *cup chopped fresh strawberries*

Combine all ingredients and mix well. If frozen strawberries are used, add berries and taste for amount of sugar to add. Serve on fruit salad. Yield: 2 cups.

Poppy Seed Dressing

1½ *cups sugar*
 2 *teaspoons dry mustard*
 2 *teaspoons salt*
 ⅔ *cup vinegar*
 3 *tablespoons onion juice*
 2 *cups salad oil*
 3 *tablespoons poppy seeds*

Mix the first 4 ingredients. Then add onion juice and stir thoroughly. Add salad oil slowly, beating constantly. Continue to beat until thick. Add poppy seeds and mix well. Store in refrigerator. Serve with fruit or vegetable salads. Yield: about 3½ cups.

Honey-Poppy Seed Dressing

 ⅓ *cup honey*
 ⅓ *cup vinegar*
 1 *cup salad oil*
 1 *teaspoon dry mustard*
 1 *teaspoon salt*
 2 *teaspoons fresh onion juice*
 1 *tablespoon poppy seeds*

Blend honey, vinegar, oil, mustard, salt, and onion juice in blender. After this mixture is well blended, add poppy seeds and put into jar with tightly sealed lid. Serve on fruit salad. Yield: about 1 cup.

*Lemon-Poppy Seed Dressing

 2 *tablespoons poppy seeds*
 ¼ *cup honey*
 ½ *cup salad oil*
 ½ *teaspoon ground cinnamon*
 ¼ *teaspoon ground coriander*
 ¾ *teaspoon salt*
 ⅓ *cup lemon juice*

Put poppy seeds in blender; blend on high

speed for 1 minute or until seeds are crushed. Add honey, salad oil, cinnamon, coriander, and salt. Blend until well mixed. Add lemon juice and blend until creamy. Store in a tightly covered jar in refrigerator until ready to use. Yield: 1 cup.

Curry-Poppy Seed Dressing

½ cup sugar
½ cup honey
1 teaspoon grated onion
6 tablespoons tarragon vinegar
3 tablespoons lemon juice
1 cup salad oil
1 teaspoon dry mustard
1 teaspoon paprika
¼ teaspoon salt
2 teaspoons poppy seeds
1 teaspoon curry powder

Put all ingredients in a jar and shake thoroughly. Keeps indefinitely in the refrigerator. Pour sufficient dressing to marinate over chopped fresh fruits that have been tossed with thawed frozen coconut. Serve on lettuce and garnish with selected fruits. Serve with crackers or finger cheese sandwiches. Yield: about 3 cups.

*Low-Calorie Dressing for Potato Salad

2 tablespoons all-purpose flour
1 tablespoon sugar
1 teaspoon dry mustard
1 teaspoon salt
Dash cayenne pepper
1 cup milk
1 egg, slightly beaten
1 tablespoon salad oil
⅓ cup vinegar or lemon juice

Combine flour, sugar, mustard, salt, and cayenne in the top of a double boiler. Gradually stir in milk. Cook over boiling water, stirring constantly, until mixture begins to thicken. Cover and cook for 10 minutes, stirring often.

Beat egg slightly and stir a little of the hot mixture into the egg; then add this to the rest of the mixture. Cook for 3 minutes, stirring constantly. Add salad oil and remove from heat. Slowly blend in vinegar or lemon juice. Yield: about 1½ cups.

*Yogurt Thousand Island Salad Dressing

1 cup plain yogurt
1 tablespoon finely chopped stuffed olives
¼ teaspoon grated onion
¼ teaspoon salt
¼ cup chili sauce
1 hard-cooked egg, finely chopped

Combine all ingredients and mix well. Chill for several hours before using. Yield: 1¼ cups.

Stockman Salad Dressing

4 hard-cooked eggs, finely chopped
4 cloves garlic, minced
5 sprigs parsley, finely chopped
4 whole green onions, finely chopped
3 stalks celery, finely chopped
¼ cup lemon juice
¼ cup vinegar
1 quart mayonnaise

Put eggs, garlic, parsley, onion, celery, lemon juice, and vinegar in a large container. Add mayonnaise and mix well. Put mixture into jar, cover, and keep in refrigerator. Serve over tossed salad. Yield: 4½ cups.

Thousand Island Salad Dressing

1 teaspoon grated onion
½ cup mayonnaise
3 tablespoons catsup
2 tablespoons sweet pickle relish
Dash seasoned salt
½ hard-cooked egg, sieved

Combine all ingredients and chill. Serve on green salads. Yield: ¾ cup.

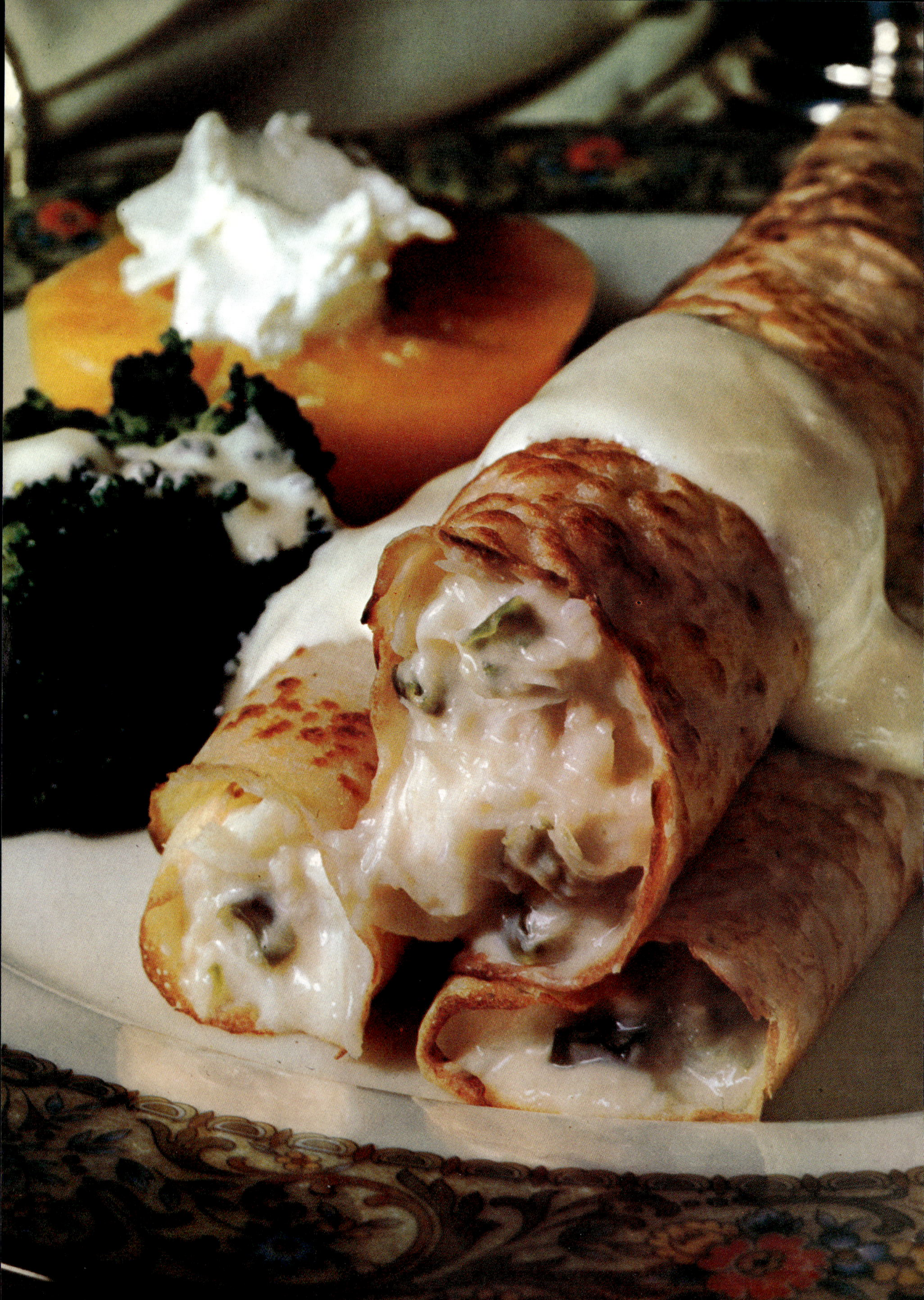

Sauces

A sauce has often been the making of a great dish. Sauces, which were brought to perfection by the French, may be divided into several categories, such as cream, emulsified, and vinaigrette. However, one popular sauce that does not fit into any category and is considered an American invention is barbecue sauce.

A cream sauce, whether simple or elaborate, will greatly enhance the overall taste of many vegetables. And everyone has a favorite dessert sauce; plain custard, fruit, chocolate, mint, butterscotch, and hard sauces are all delicious.

Sauces are not difficult to prepare and once you master the few basic ones, you will be able to make many.

Sour Cream Sauce

½ cup chopped onion
3 tablespoons butter or margarine
3 tablespoons all-purpose flour
2 cups commercial sour cream
½ teaspoon salt

Sauté onion in melted butter until wilted. Stir in flour and cook until mixture thickens. Add sour cream and salt. Heat slowly, but do not boil. Serve with chicken or leftover meat. Yield: 2 cups.

Hollandaise Sauce

4 egg yolks
2 tablespoons lemon juice
1 cup butter, melted
¼ teaspoon salt
Dash pepper

Beat egg yolks in top of a double boiler. Stir in lemon juice. Cook very slowly over low heat, never letting water in bottom of pan come to a boil. Add butter, a small amount at a time, stirring constantly with a wooden spoon. Add salt and pepper; continue cooking until mixture has thickened. Excellent on vegetables. Yield: 1 cup.

Easy Hollandaise Sauce

½ cup butter
3 egg yolks
3 tablespoons lemon juice

Combine all ingredients in top of double boiler; let stand at room temperature for 30 minutes. Just before serving, place over simmering water (do not let water reach boiling point). Cook, stirring briskly (a wire whisk works well), 1½ to 2½ minutes or until mixture thickens. Serve on vegetables. Yield: ¾ cup.

*Cheese Sauce

2 tablespoons butter or margarine
2 tablespoons all-purpose flour
1 cup milk
¼ teaspoon salt
½ cup shredded Cheddar cheese

Combine butter and flour in top of double boiler. Mix well. Gradually add milk, stirring constantly until mixture thickens. Add salt and cheese, stirring until cheese is melted. Serve on eggs or vegetables. Yield: 1½ cups.

*Barbecue Sauce

- 2 (8-ounce) cans tomato sauce
- 2 tablespoons firmly packed brown sugar
- ¼ cup vinegar
- 2 tablespoons Worcestershire sauce
- 1 teaspoon salt
- 1 teaspoon dry mustard
- 1 teaspoon chili powder
- 1 tablespoon paprika
- ⅛ teaspoon cayenne pepper
- 2 tablespoons chopped green onion tops

Combine all ingredients except green onion tops. Simmer 15 minutes, stirring occasionally. Serve hot with onion sprinkled on top. Yield: 2½ cups sauce.

*Fiesta Barbecue Sauce for Chicken

- 1 cup salad oil
- 1 cup chili sauce
- 2 tablespoons Worcestershire sauce
- Juice of 2 lemons
- 1 tablespoon sugar
- ½ teaspoon dry mustard
- ⅛ teaspoon hot sauce
- 1 small onion, finely chopped
- 1 clove garlic, minced (optional)

Combine all ingredients in saucepan; heat. Brush on chicken while it cooks. Yield: 2¾ cups, or enough to barbecue 4 broiler-fryers.

Quick Barbecue Sauce

- 1 cup butter or margarine
- 1 (6-ounce) jar prepared mustard
- ½ cup catsup
- Dash salt
- 1 tablespoon dehydrated onion
- Dash pepper, parsley, and thyme

Melt butter and add mustard and catsup. Add salt, onion, pepper, parsley, and thyme. Stir thoroughly and use for basting beef or chicken on grill. Yield: about 2 cups.

Hawaiian Barbecue Sauce

- ½ cup salad oil
- ¾ cup pineapple juice
- ¼ cup unsulphured molasses
- ¼ cup lemon juice
- ⅓ cup soy sauce
- 1 teaspoon ground ginger

Combine all ingredients and brush on chicken during the last 15 minutes on the grill. Yield: 2 cups (enough to barbecue 3 broiler-fryers).

Butter Barbecue Sauce

- ½ cup butter
- ½ cup finely chopped onion
- ½ cup catsup
- ¼ cup firmly packed brown sugar
- 3 tablespoons Worcestershire sauce
- 1 teaspoon salt
- ⅛ teaspoon pepper
- 1½ teaspoons chili powder, (if desired)

Melt butter in small saucepan. Add onion and sauté until tender; stir in remaining ingredients. Simmer 5 minutes. Use as basting sauce for turkey or chicken. Yield: 1½ cups.

Best Barbecue Sauce

- ½ cup butter or margarine
- ½ cup catsup
- ⅓ cup vinegar
- 1 tablespoon Worcestershire sauce
- 1 tablespoon prepared mustard
- 2 tablespoons aromatic bitters
- 1 tablespoon salt (if using on chicken)

Slowly melt butter. Add all other ingredients and mix well. If using on steaks, omit the salt. Marinate meat in sauce at least 4 hours or overnight if possible. Baste meat with sauce while cooking. Meat may get a burned look. Grill chicken 1½ hours over medium heat; grill steaks to suit individual tastes. Yield: 2½ cups sauce.

Herb Barbecue Sauce

½ cup salad oil
¾ cup lemon juice or vinegar
½ cup water
2 tablespoons sugar
2 teaspoons salt
½ teaspoon dried leaf rosemary
½ teaspoon dried basil
1 medium onion, chopped
1 clove garlic, minced

Combine all ingredients; let stand at least 2 hours to develop flavor. Yield: 2 cups (enough to barbecue 3 broiler-fryers).

Hamburger Barbecue Sauce

1 (8-ounce) can tomato sauce
½ cup catsup
¼ teaspoon hot sauce
1 tablespoon Worcestershire sauce
⅓ cup wine vinegar
2 tablespoons sugar
2 tablespoons prepared mustard
1 teaspoon celery salt
¼ teaspoon pepper
½ teaspoon ground thyme
½ teaspoon oregano

Combine ingredients. Cover meat patties with sauce and marinate in a covered glass dish in refrigerator for 24 hours. Remove meat; baste with sauce during cooking. Yield: 1½ cups sauce.

Old-Fashioned Hot Barbecue Sauce

1¼ pounds butter
1 small onion, minced
1 cup hot sauce
1 teaspoon pepper
2 tablespoons molasses

Melt butter, and sauté onion until wilted. Remove from heat and add other ingredients. Pour mixture in a quart jar and keep in refrigerator until ready to use for beef, pork, or chicken. Yield: 1½ cups.

* Pit Barbecue Sauce

2 cups catsup
1 cup butter or margarine
2 cups vinegar
1 tablespoon hot sauce
1 (4-ounce) bottle Worcestershire sauce
1 tablespoon firmly packed brown sugar
1 tablespoon onion juice
1½ cloves garlic, minced
2 tablespoons salt
2 tablespoons pepper

Combine all ingredients in a saucepan and bring to a boil. Remove from heat, cool, and store in jars for use as needed to brush on beef, chicken, or pork while grilling. Yield: 2 quarts.

Barbecue Sauce for Chicken

1 pound margarine
Juice of 3 lemons
1 cup white vinegar
1 (3-ounce) jar prepared mustard
4 tablespoons Worcestershire sauce

Melt margarine; add other ingredients. This sauce may be refrigerated in a jar until ready to use. Brush heated sauce on chicken while grilling. Yield: enough sauce for 8 chickens.

* Easiest Barbecue Sauce

3 tablespoons catsup
2 tablespoons vinegar
1 teaspoon lemon juice
2 tablespoons Worcestershire sauce
4 tablespoons water
2 tablespoons salad oil
3 tablespoons firmly packed brown sugar
1 teaspoon salt
1 teaspoon dry mustard
1 teaspoon chili powder
1 teaspoon paprika
½ teaspoon cayenne pepper

Combine all ingredients in a quart jar; shake well and refrigerate until ready to use as a basting sauce for barbecued chicken, beef, or pork. Yield: 1 cup.

Spicy Barbecue Sauce

2 (14-ounce) bottles catsup
1 quart plus 10 ounces water
1 lemon, sliced
1 large or 2 small onions, chopped
2 cloves garlic, chopped
¾ cup cider vinegar
¾ cup firmly packed dark brown sugar
½ cup Worcestershire sauce
1 tablespoon chili powder
1 tablespoon celery seeds
1 tablespoon paprika
1 tablespoon cayenne pepper
1 tablespoon ground cinnamon
1 tablespoon prepared mustard
1 tablespoon hot sauce
1 tablespoon pickled pepper sauce (optional)

Combine all ingredients in a large saucepan. Simmer about 40 minutes and strain. This sauce may be used for ribs and chicken as well as for turkey. For ribs, have sauce hot and dip ribs in it. Use just enough to moisten and dip ribs before serving to keep them from turning too dark. Yield: about 2 quarts.

Texas Barbecue Sauce

1 pound butter
2 tablespoons dry mustard
1 (4-ounce) bottle Worcestershire sauce
¼ cup strong garlic vinegar
3 tablespoons lemon juice
Salt
2 teaspoons hot sauce
Cayenne pepper (optional)

Soften butter at room temperature. With a wooden spoon stir in the mustard. Blend in other ingredients adding salt and pepper to taste; cover and refrigerate for about 2 days. Warm and brush over meat when barbecueing; good for beef, pork, or chicken. Yield: 2 cups.

Chicken Liver Sauce for Ravioli or Spaghetti

4 to 8 chicken livers, dried with paper towels
2 to 3 tablespoons olive oil
8 fresh mushrooms, wiped clean and sliced
1 teaspoon instant beef bouillon or 1 bouillon cube
1 cup water
1 (1-pound) can cooked tomatoes
½ cup red wine
4 large fresh basil leaves, cut up, or ¼ teaspoon dried basil
2 teaspoons chopped fresh chives or 1 teaspoon dried chives
Salt and pepper
2 teaspoons cornstarch
½ cup cold water
Cooked ravioli or spaghetti
Grated Parmesan cheese

Sauté livers in oil until lightly browned. Remove to a separate dish. Sauté mushrooms in same oil. When mushrooms are browned, add bouillon and water, tomatoes, wine, herbs, and salt and pepper to taste. Simmer, uncovered, for 30 to 45 minutes. If mixture seems extremely dry, add more water or wine.

Mix cornstarch in ½ cup cold water and add to the simmering sauce while stirring rapidly. Simmer 5 minutes or until cornstarch loses "raw" taste. Correct seasoning. Reheat livers in sauce and serve over cooked ravioli or spaghetti. Sprinkle with grated cheese. Yield: 4 to 5 servings.

*Jiffy Butterscotch Sauce

1½ cups firmly packed brown sugar
⅔ cup corn syrup
⅔ cup evaporated milk

Put brown sugar and corn syrup into a heavy 1-quart saucepan. Cook and stir until mixture comes to a full rolling boil, about 5 minutes. Remove from heat and cool. Stir in milk. Serve warm or cold over ice cream. Yield: 1⅔ cups.

Chocolate-Peanut Butter Sauce

1⅓ cups sweetened condensed milk
2 (1-ounce) squares unsweetened chocolate
⅛ teaspoon salt
½ to 1 cup hot water
¼ cup peanut butter
½ teaspoon vanilla extract

Combine sweetened condensed milk, chocolate, and salt in top of double boiler. Cook over hot water, stirring frequently, until thickened. Remove from heat. Slowly stir in hot water and peanut butter until sauce is of desired thickness. Stir in vanilla. Serve hot or chilled over ice cream. Yield: about 2 cups.

Grape-Orange Tropical Sauce

2 tablespoons butter or margarine
2 tablespoons all-purpose flour
⅓ cup sugar
1 (6-ounce) can frozen orange juice concentrate, thawed and undiluted
1¼ cups water
2 cups halved and seeded red grapes
Vanilla ice cream

Melt butter; stir in flour and sugar. Gradually stir in orange juice and water. Cook over low heat, stirring constantly, until sauce bubbles and thickens. Cool. Fold in grapes. Chill. Spoon sauce over individual servings of vanilla ice cream. Yield: 4 cups.

* Lemon Sauce

1 egg
1 cup sugar
Juice of 2 lemons
Grated rind of 1 lemon
1 tablespoon butter or margarine

Beat egg slightly; add sugar, lemon juice, and rind. Cook in top of double boiler until slightly thickened. Add butter and remove from heat. Serve on puddings or gingerbread. Yield: 1 cup.

* Mint Sauce

¼ cup vinegar
¾ cup water, divided
¼ cup flaked dried mint leaves, divided
1 tablespoon lemon juice
1 to 2 tablespoons sugar
¼ teaspoon salt

Simmer vinegar, half the water, and half the mint for 4 to 5 minutes until reduced to about half; strain. Add remaining water and mint, lemon juice, sugar, and salt; bring to a boil. Serve chilled over ice cream. Yield: ⅔ cup.

* Double Fudge Sauce

¾ cup sugar
⅓ cup cocoa
3 tablespoons water
2 tablespoons white corn syrup
½ cup evaporated milk
¾ teaspoon vanilla extract

Mix sugar and cocoa in a 1-quart saucepan. Stir in water; then add corn syrup. Boil until a few drops form a soft ball when dropped into cold water. Stir in milk and vanilla. Serve warm or cold over ice cream. Sauce can be stored in a covered jar in the refrigerator. Yield: about 1¼ cups.

French Chocolate Sauce

2½ ounces unsweetened chocolate, grated
½ cup water
¾ cup sugar
Dash salt
1 teaspoon vanilla extract
½ cup whipping cream, whipped

Combine chocolate and water; cook over direct heat for 4 minutes, stirring constantly. Beat with mixer until smooth. Add sugar, salt, and vanilla; cook 4 minutes longer, stirring constantly. Cool. Fold in whipped cream. Serve over ice cream. Yield: 1 pint.

Hot Fudge Sauce

    3 *(1-ounce) squares unsweetened chocolate*
1⅓ *cups sweetened condensed milk*
  ½ *cup hot water*
  ¼ *teaspoon salt*
  ¼ *cup sugar*
  1 *teaspoon vanilla extract*

Melt chocolate in top of double boiler over hot water. Stir in sweetened condensed milk. Cook until very thick, stirring constantly. Add hot water, salt, and sugar; continue to cook until mixture is very smooth and of desired thickness. Remove from heat and stir in vanilla. Serve hot over ice cream. Yield: about 2 cups.

*Lemon-Molasses Ice Cream Sauce

  1 *cup molasses*
  2 *tablespoons butter*
  ⅓ *cup freshly squeezed lemon juice*

Heat molasses to boiling point, stirring; add butter and boil 1 minute. Remove and add lemon juice, mixing thoroughly. Yield: 1 cup sauce.

White Raisin Sauce

  1 *cup sugar*
  ¾ *cup water*
  ½ *cup white corn syrup*
    Few grains salt
  1 *cup white seedless raisins, chopped*
  1 *to 2 teaspoons chopped crystallized ginger*
  2 *tablespoons lemon juice*
1½ *teaspoons grated lemon rind*
  ½ *cup coarsely chopped walnuts*

Combine sugar, water, corn syrup, salt, and cook over medium heat, stirring until mixture boils. As soon as sugar dissolves add chopped raisins, ginger, lemon juice, and rind. Cook until mixture thickens slightly, about 5 to 7 minutes. Add nuts and blend thoroughly. Serve hot or cold over ice cream. Yield: 6 to 8 servings.

Marshmallow Sauce

16 *marshmallows*
 ⅓ *cup evaporated milk*
 ⅓ *cup light corn syrup*
   Few grains salt

Place all ingredients in a 1-quart saucepan and cook over medium heat, stirring constantly, until marshmallows are melted. Chill thoroughly and serve over ice cream. Yield: 1 cup.

Lemon-Parsley Sauce

½ *cup butter or margarine, melted*
1 *teaspoon grated lemon rind*
3 *tablespoons lemon juice*
1 *tablespoon chopped parsley*

Combine all ingredients. Serve hot over broiled or baked fish. Yield: about ½ cup.

Curry Sauce

1 *cup commercial sour cream*
½ *cup mayonnaise*
1 *tablespoon chopped fresh parsley*
2 *teaspoons curry powder*
1 *teaspoon lemon juice*
½ *teaspoon Worcestershire sauce*
½ *clove garlic, crushed*
¼ *teaspoon salt*

Blend all ingredients until smooth; chill. Serve as dip for cooked beef, chicken, or shrimp. Yield: 1½ cups sauce.

Taco Cheese Sauce

1 *(8-ounce) container sharp Cheddar cheese spread*
1 *(4-ounce) can taco sauce*
3 *(5½-ounce) packages little wieners*

Allow cheese spread to reach room temperature. Combine with taco sauce, blending well. Heat little wieners in a small amount of water. Use sauce as a dip for wieners. Yield: 1⅓ cups sauce; 48 appetizers.

*Creole Sauce

¼ cup minced onion
⅓ cup chopped green pepper
2 tablespoons butter or margarine, melted
¼ cup chopped stuffed green olives
1½ cups finely chopped tomatoes
¼ teaspoon salt
1 teaspoon sugar
Dash cayenne pepper

Sauté onion and green pepper in butter until onion is a light brown. Add remaining ingredients; simmer 10 to 15 minutes. Serve over broiled or baked fish. Yield: about 2 cups.

Island Kabob Sauce for Beef

1 cup salad oil
¾ cup soy sauce
½ cup lemon juice
¼ cup Worcestershire sauce
¼ teaspoon garlic juice
¼ cup prepared mustard
½ teaspoon pepper
½ teaspoon salt
About 1½ pounds round steak

Mix salad oil, soy sauce, lemon juice, Worcestershire sauce, garlic juice, mustard, pepper, and salt. Cut steak into chunks. Marinate beef in sauce for several hours (at least 4 hours, but overnight is better). Grill or broil with vegetables of your choice. Yield: 2 cups sauce.

*Cocktail Sauce for Fish

1 cup catsup
1 tablespoon grated horseradish
1 tablespoon grated onion
Few drops hot sauce
2 tablespoons vinegar
1 tablespoon minced celery
½ teaspoon salt
1 teaspoon Worcestershire sauce

Blend all ingredients. Pour into a jar, cover, and chill. Yield: 1¼ cups.

Raisin Sauce for Ham

¼ cup sugar
1½ teaspoons dry mustard
1½ tablespoons cornstarch
¼ teaspoon salt
1½ cups water
½ cup dark corn syrup
¼ cup orange marmalade
½ cup seedless raisins
¼ cup cider vinegar
1 tablespoon butter

Combine sugar, mustard, cornstarch, and salt in a small saucepan. Gradually stir in water, corn syrup, marmalade, and raisins. Cook over medium heat until mixture thickens and comes to a boil. Remove from heat; stir in vinegar and butter. Serve over ham. Yield: 2 cups.

Red Devil Sauce

1 (15-ounce) can or 2 (8-ounce) cans tomato sauce with tomato bits
4 teaspoons sugar
2 tablespoons thinly sliced green onions (tops included)
2 tablespoons red wine vinegar
1 clove garlic, crushed
Few drops red pepper sauce, if desired

Combine all ingredients; chill. Serve as dip for cooked beef, chicken, or shrimp. Yield: about 2 cups sauce.

Beefeater Mushroom Sauce

3 tablespoons chopped onion
1 tablespoon lemon juice
1 tablespoon butter
Fresh mushrooms, sliced
2 cups brown sauce (bottled or made from a mix)

Sauté the onion in lemon juice and butter; add the sliced fresh mushrooms, and cook gently. Add brown sauce and bring to a boil; serve on steak. Yield: 4 servings.

Tomato Sauce for Fish

  2 cups tomato sauce
  1 teaspoon Worcestershire sauce
  2 tablespoons chopped fresh parsley
  ¼ cup chopped stuffed olives
  ½ cup cooked or canned shrimp
  ½ cup canned sliced mushrooms
  ¼ cup diced celery

Combine all ingredients in saucepan and heat to the boiling point. Taste and add more seasoning, if desired. Serve with baked or broiled fish (it is best served from a platter that can be placed under the broiler for just a few minutes). Yield: 3½ cups sauce.

Marchand De Vin Sauce

  ¾ cup butter
  ⅓ cup finely chopped fresh mushrooms
  ½ cup minced ham
  ⅓ cup finely chopped shallots
  ½ cup finely chopped onion
  2 tablespoons minced garlic
  2 tablespoons all-purpose flour
  ½ teaspoon salt
  ⅛ teaspoon black pepper
  Dash cayenne pepper
  ¾ cup beef stock
  ½ cup red wine

Melt butter in a 9-inch skillet; add mushrooms, ham, shallots, onion, and garlic. Sauté until lightly browned. Add flour, salt, black pepper, and cayenne; cook until browned. Blend in beef stock and wine and simmer over low heat for 35 to 45 minutes. Yield: 2 cups.

Dill Butter Sauce for Lobster

  ½ cup melted butter
  ¼ cup finely chopped fresh dill
  ¼ cup lemon juice
  2 tablespoons tomato paste

Combine all ingredients and stir well to blend. Brush mixture on lobster while it is broiling. Yield: about 1 cup.

Tartar Sauce

  ½ cup chopped dill pickles (not kosher)
  ¼ cup chopped onion
  ¼ cup capers
  Mayonnaise or salad dressing

Put pickles and onion in blender with capers and blend briefly. Drain excess liquid if necessary. Measure blended ingredients and add slightly less than an equal quantity of mayonnaise or salad dressing. Serve with fish. Yield: about 1 cup.

Cucumber Cream Sauce

  ¼ teaspoon salt
  ½ cup whipping cream, whipped
  2 tablespoons vinegar
  ½ cup diced or grated cucumber (pared)

Add salt to cream. Gradually add vinegar, beating constantly until thick, not stiff. Fold in cucumbers. Serve with asparagus, cold fish, or vegetable salads. Yield: approximately 1 cup.

Cranberry Wine Sauce

  3 tablespoons sugar
  Dash ground nutmeg
  1 teaspoon ground cinnamon
  ¼ teaspoon ground cloves
  Grated rind of 1 lemon
  ½ cup port
  1 (1-pound) can whole-berry cranberry sauce

Combine dry ingredients with wine; mix well. Place in a saucepan over low heat and simmer for 5 minutes. Add cranberry sauce; stir with a fork or wire whisk until mixture is smooth and thoroughly heated. Serve with game, pork, or lamb. Yield: 2 cups.

Spaghetti Sauce

  1 *large onion, chopped*
⅓ *cup chopped green pepper*
  2 *cloves garlic, minced*
⅓ *cup chopped celery*
  2 *tablespoons olive oil*
  2 *pounds ground chuck*
  1 *(6-ounce) can tomato paste*
  1 *(10¾-ounce) can condensed tomato soup*
  1 *soup can water*
  1 *teaspoon salt*
¼ *teaspoon pepper*
  1 *chicken thigh*
  1 *pork chop*
½ *cup sliced pepperoni sausage*
  1 *carrot, grated*

Cook onion, green pepper, garlic, and celery in olive oil until tender. Add ground chuck, and cook until brown. Add remaining ingredients; simmer about 2 hours. Remove chicken thigh and pork chop; cool. Remove meat from bones and add meat to mixture. Freeze in freezer cartons.

To serve, thaw and heat. Serve over hot, cooked spaghetti. Yield: 2 quarts sauce.

Bordelaise Sauce

  2 *medium carrots, chopped*
  2 *medium onions, chopped*
  2 *sprigs parsley, chopped*
¼ *cup butter*
  2 *tablespoons all-purpose flour*
  1 *cup dry white wine*
1½ *cups consommé*
½ *teaspoon salt*
½ *teaspoon pepper*
¼ *teaspoon thyme*
  1 *bay leaf*
  1 *cup dry red wine*
  1 *teaspoon lemon juice*

Sauté carrots, half the chopped onion, and parsley in butter in medium saucepan until golden brown. Add flour and cook until slightly brown, stirring constantly. Add white wine, consommé, and seasonings. Bring to a boil; cover and simmer 15 minutes.

Meanwhile, put remaining onion and red wine in an 8-inch skillet. Bring to a boil and cook about 10 minutes until 2 tablespoons of liquid remain. Drain liquid from carrot mixture into red wine. Add lemon juice and cook 10 to 15 minutes until reduced to about 1 cup. Serve warm over vegetables. Yield: 1 cup sauce.

Sweet-Sour Sauce

  4 *slices bacon, diced*
  2 *tablespoons all-purpose flour*
1½ *cups boiling water*
⅓ *cup lemon juice*
  2 *tablespoons sugar*
¾ *teaspoon salt*
  2 *tablespoons prepared mustard*
  1 *egg, slightly beaten*

Brown bacon; remove from skillet. Blend flour with bacon drippings. Slowly add water, lemon juice, sugar, salt, and mustard. Cook over low heat until thick and smooth. Remove from heat and cool slightly. Stir in egg and cook 2 minutes longer. Add cooked bacon. Serve on cooked or raw shredded greens. Yield: 2 cups.

Sherry Cream Sauce

  2 *tablespoons butter*
  2 *tablespoons all-purpose flour*
  1 *cup hot milk*
½ *teaspoon salt*
⅛ *teaspoon white pepper*
⅛ *teaspoon paprika*
  4 *tablespoons Parmesan cheese*
  3 *tablespoons sherry*
Parsley

Melt butter in top of double boiler over rapidly boiling water. Add flour and blend in with wire whisk. Slowly add the hot milk and stir constantly. Add salt, pepper, and paprika. Cook and stir until it is smooth and boiling. Add Parmesan cheese and stir until melted. Add sherry as you remove from heat. Garnish with parsley. Serve as dip for appetizers. Yield: 1¼ cups.

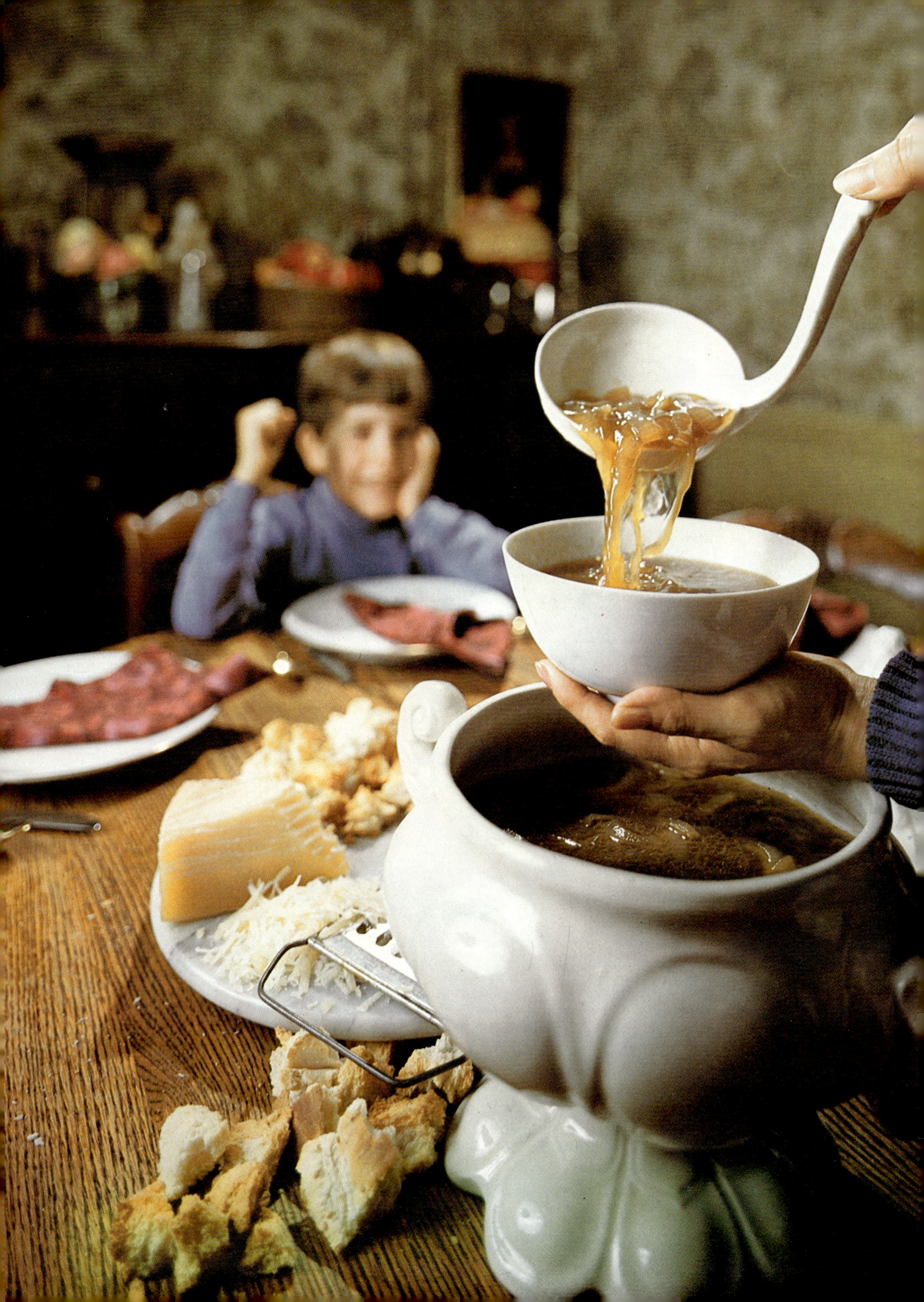

Soups, Stews and Chowders

Soups, stews, and chowders share one common element, their liquid base. But each derives it own unique flavor and consistency from the type liquid used and the solid food which cooks in it. The speciality food of a region will almost always give you a clue as to the favorite soup, stew, or chowder of the area.

From the Louisiana bayous we get our good fish soups, and stews. The cattle country of Texas and other cattle producing states has given us our many beef-based soups and stews. And from the Southwest comes our chili which is probably somewhere between a soup and a stew.

Chowder, a thick, hearty soup that usually consists of seafood and vegetables cooked in milk, probably originated in New England, but we Southerners seem to have a special way with it since we have an abundance of seafood on our shores.

Quick Onion Soup

6 medium onions, thinly sliced
½ cup butter or margarine, melted
1 teaspoon sugar
3 dashes ground nutmeg
8 rounded teaspoons beef stock base
7 cups boiling water
¼ to ½ cup cooking sherry
Salt
Big croutons
Grated Parmesan cheese

Sauté sliced onions in melted butter with sugar and nutmeg. Cook just until onions are transparent, but not browned.

Dissolve beef stock base in boiling water in a large saucepan. Add onions and simmer for about 20 minutes. Add sherry during the last 2 minutes of cooking. Taste, and add salt if needed. Spoon into serving dishes; add croutons and top with grated Parmesan cheese. Put under broiler for about 10 minutes. Yield: about 6 to 8 servings.

Meatball Vegetable Soup

1 egg
½ cup fresh bread crumbs
2 tablespoons chopped onion
2 tablespoons snipped parsley
1 tablespoon chopped green pepper
1 teaspoon salt
Few grains freshly ground black pepper
1 pound ground beef
Salad oil
1½ cups cooked mixed vegetables
1½ cups boiling water
1 (10¾-ounce) can condensed cream of chicken soup

Beat egg; mix in bread crumbs, onion, parsley, green pepper, salt, and pepper. Add ground beef and mix well. Shape into 24 meatballs. Brown in a small amount of heated oil; remove and set aside. In same skillet, stir in mixed vegetables, water, and soup. Heat to boiling point, stirring constantly. Add meatballs; simmer, covered, 10 minutes. Yield: 6 to 8 servings.

Artichoke Soup

1 (10¾-ounce) can condensed cream of mushroom soup
1 (10¾-ounce) can condensed cream of celery soup
2½ soup cans milk
1 (5-ounce) can shrimp, drained
1 cup finely shredded carrots
1 (14-ounce) can artichoke hearts, drained and coarsely snipped
½ teaspoon curry powder
Dash seasoned pepper
Dash ground allspice
¼ teaspoon onion powder
½ teaspoon Ac'cent

About 30 minutes before serving combine all ingredients in deep saucepan and simmer, uncovered, for 15 minutes. Yield: 8 to 9 servings.

Canadian Cheese Soup

¼ cup butter or margarine
2 tablespoons minced onion
½ cup thinly sliced carrot
¾ cup finely chopped celery
1 cup chicken stock
¼ cup all-purpose flour
3 cups milk, divided
2 cups (½ pound) shredded pasteurized process American cheese
Finely minced parsley or additional shredded cheese

Melt butter in a heavy saucepan; add onion, and cook and stir until yellow. Add carrot, celery, and chicken stock. Cover and simmer gently until vegetables are tender, about 15 minutes.
Combine flour with 1 cup milk and add to vegetable mixture, stirring constantly until smooth and thickened. Add cheese, and stir over low heat until melted. Gradually add remaining milk, stirring briskly. Heat only to serving temperature. Serve in warm soup bowls with a garnish of minced parsley or shredded cheese. Yield: 5 to 6 servings.

*Cheese Soup

1 cup grated carrots
1 cup minced celery
½ cup minced onion
1½ quarts chicken stock
2 cups milk
1 cup butter
1 cup all-purpose flour
¾ pound shredded sharp Cheddar cheese
1 teaspoon salt
½ teaspoon white pepper
3 tablespoons Worcestershire sauce

Boil carrots, celery, and onion in chicken stock until tender. Add milk and set aside. Melt butter in large skillet or saucepan; add flour and cook and stir until well blended. Add stock mixture and cook to make a smooth sauce. Add shredded cheese, salt, pepper, and Worcestershire sauce and stir until cheese is melted. Serve hot. Yield: 1 gallon.

Cool Avocado Bisque

1 (10-¾-ounce) can condensed cream of chicken soup
1 soup can milk
½ cup chopped celery
1 tablespoon chopped onion
1 ripe medium avocado, peeled and cut up
Additional milk

Combine soup, milk, celery, and onion in saucepan. Heat, stirring occasionally. Chill 6 hours or longer. Blend soup mixture and avocado in blender until smooth. Thin to desired consistency with additional milk. Serve immediately. Yield: about 4 cups.

Cold Avocado Soup

1 large avocado
1 (10-ounce) can condensed consommé
Several dashes hot sauce
3 tablespoons lemon juice
1 pint commercial sour cream
Chopped parsley or chives

Peel and pit avocado; cut into small pieces. Put avocado into blender container along with consommé, hot sauce, and lemon juice. Blend well. Add sour cream and blend just to mix well.

Chill in refrigerator for several hours, and serve cold. Garnish with chopped parsley or chives. Yield: 8 servings.

* Senate Bean Soup

- 2 *cups navy or great northern beans*
- 1 *meaty hambone*
- 3 *quarts water*
- ½ *cup mashed potatoes*
- 3 *onions, finely chopped*
- 1 *whole bunch celery tops, chopped*
- ¼ *cup finely chopped parsley*
- 1 *teaspoon salt*
- *Freshly ground pepper*

Put the beans and hambone in 3 quarts water and soak overnight. The next day, simmer beans (and hambone) 2 hours in water in which they were soaked. At the end of the first hour add mashed potatoes. Stir in well. Then add onions, celery tops, parsley, salt, and pepper. Let simmer the second hour. Take hambone from soup and remove meat from bone. Chop meat into slivers. Return to soup and reheat. Yield: 8 servings.

Easy Summer Borsch

- 1 *(16-ounce) can beets*
- 1 *teaspoon minced onion*
- 1 *(10½-ounce) can condensed bouillon*
- 1 *cup cold water*
- ½ *teaspoon salt*
- 1 *tablespoon lemon juice*
- ¼ *cup commercial sour cream*
- 4 *teaspoons minced dill pickle*

Drain beets and reserve juice; dice beets and combine with juice, onion, bouillon, and water. Heat well; do not boil. Add salt and lemon juice. Chill; pour into 4 soup bowls. Top each with sour cream and minced pickle. Yield: 4 servings.

* Old-Fashioned Bean Soup

- 1 *pound (2 cups) dried red kidney or pinto beans soaked in 3 quarts water*
- *Meaty ham bone or ham hocks*
- 1 *cup finely chopped onion*
- 2 *cloves garlic, minced*
- 1 *small bay leaf*
- 1 *cup thinly sliced celery*
- 1 *cup diced raw carrots*
- 1 *cup cooked instant mashed potatoes*
- *Salt and pepper to taste*
- *Half-and-half or undiluted evaporated milk (optional)*

Soak beans in 3 quarts water for 2 hours. In heavy cooking pot or Dutch oven combine the beans and water, ham bone, onion, garlic, and bay leaf. Bring to boiling point; reduce heat to simmer. Cover tightly and cook about 2 hours or until beans are quite tender.

Add celery and carrots. Stir in the prepared mashed potatoes to thicken the soup. Add salt and pepper to taste. Simmer, covered, about 1 hour. Remove ham bone and cut off the meat; dice it and add to the soup. Reheat to just boiling, stirring to prevent scorching. Half-and-half or undiluted evaporated milk may be stirred into soup just before serving. Yield: 10 servings.

Cream of Chicken Soup

- 2 *tablespoons butter or margarine*
- ¼ *cup all-purpose flour*
- 3 *cups chicken broth*
- 1 *cup half-and-half*
- ½ *cup shredded, cooked chicken*
- *Salt*
- *Pepper*
- *Chives or apple cubes*

Melt butter in top of double boiler over direct heat; stir in flour. Slowly stir in broth and cream; cook over boiling water until smooth and thickened. Add chicken, and salt and pepper to taste. Serve topped with chives or apples. Yield: 5 to 6 servings.

Asparagus Cheese Soup

¼ cup butter
¼ cup all-purpose flour
1 tablespoon salt
Dash ground nutmeg
Dash pepper
1½ quarts milk
2 (10-ounce) packages frozen asparagus, cooked, drained, and diced
3 cups shredded Cheddar cheese
Paprika
Shredded Cheddar cheese or grated Parmesan cheese

Melt butter and blend in flour, salt, nutmeg, and pepper. Gradually add milk and cook, stirring constantly, until slightly thickened. Add asparagus and cheddar cheese and continue to stir until cheese melts. To serve, garnish with paprika and a little more shredded Cheddar cheese or grated Parmesan cheese. Yield: 6 servings.

Soup Continental

¼ cup butter or margarine
1 cup chopped cooked turkey
2 tablespoons finely chopped onion
2 cups diced raw potatoes
1 cup diced celery
2 cups turkey broth
2½ cups cream-style corn
1 (13½-ounce) can evaporated milk
1 teaspoon salt
¼ teaspoon paprika
¼ teaspoon ground ginger
⅛ teaspoon pepper
2 tablespoons chopped parsley

Melt butter over low heat. Add turkey and onion. Cook until onion is transparent. Add potatoes, celery, and turkey broth. Simmer until vegetables are tender. Add corn, milk, and seasonings. Heat thoroughly, stirring occasionally. Season to taste with additional salt and pepper. Serve hot. Garnish with parsley and serve with crackers, hard rolls, or toast. Yield: 2 quarts.

Fruit Soup

1 (12-ounce) package mixed dried fruit
6 cups water
½ cup sugar
1 cinnamon stick
Grated rind of half lemon
2 tablespoons tapioca
Juice of half lemon

Mix all ingredients except the lemon juice; cover and cook slowly until the fruit is tender and tapioca is clear, about 30 to 40 minutes. Chill. Add lemon juice. Serve with almond rusks. Yield: 6 servings.

Cream of Corn Soup

1 teaspoon finely chopped onion
2 tablespoons butter or margarine
2 to 3 tablespoons all-purpose flour
1 teaspoon salt
⅛ teaspoon pepper
1 (1-pound) can cream-style corn
4 cups milk or half-and-half

Sauté onion in butter. Blend in flour, salt, and pepper. Cook over low heat, stirring constantly, until smooth and bubbly. Stir in cream-style corn; bring to a boil and boil 1 minute.

Remove from heat and stir in milk. Heat to serving temperature, but do not boil. Put in blender and blend until smooth, if desired. Add additional seasoning, if needed. Yield: 6 servings.

Cucumber Soup

1 to 1½ cups grated cucumber
1 quart buttermilk
2 tablespoons chopped green onion
1 teaspoon salt
Cucumber slices
Chives

Combine grated cucumber, buttermilk, onion, and salt; mix well. Cover and chill at least 2 or 3 hours. Mix again before serving in chilled cups. Garnish with cucumber slices and chives. Yield: 6 to 8 servings.

Note: Scoop out and discard seeds before grating cucumber.

Creole Court-Bouillon

Use fish with firm flesh which will hold up under long cooking. Creole cooks prefer a redfish (channel bass) from the Gulf of Mexico or a freshwater catfish or gaspergou. The fish should have head, fins, and tail removed when it is cleaned and scaled. You will have to decide about the bones. If you don't use fillets, cut the fish into 2-inch sections.

¾ cup shortening or cooking oil
1 cup all-purpose flour
3 cups finely chopped onions
1 (16-ounce can) whole tomatoes
1 (6-ounce) can tomato paste
2½ quarts warm water
10 pounds fish, seasoned well with salt, black pepper, and cayenne pepper
2 lemons, sliced
4 cloves garlic, finely chopped
1 teaspoon thyme
¾ cup finely chopped celery
3 bay leaves
1 teaspoon ground allspice
1 green pepper, finely chopped
1 (4-ounce) can button mushrooms
Salt, black and cayenne pepper to taste
Hot sauce to taste
¼ cup dry wine, if desired
Creole rice
6 tablespoons chopped parsley

Heat the shortening or oil in a Dutch oven or cast iron pot. Add the flour when the oil is hot and resign yourself to stirring continuously until the roux is dark brown. Add the onions and keep stirring until they are clear and tender. This must be done over low heat.

Stir in tomatoes and tomato paste and cook until fat comes to the surface and the mixture is a smooth pulp. Add 2½ quarts of warm water, seasoned fish, lemon, garlic, thyme, celery, bay leaves, allspice, and green pepper. Boil for 15 minutes. Lower heat and simmer for 20 minutes. The fish should be tender and the liquid should thicken. Add mushrooms and season with salt, black and red pepper, and hot sauce at least 20 minutes before serving. If desired, add wine at the last moment.

Serve over Creole rice and garnish with parsley. Yield: 12 servings.

Gazpacho with Shrimp

½ pound or more fresh shrimp, cooked (rinse before cooking, but not after) or 2 (5-ounce) cans shrimp
6 tablespoons lemon juice
3 cups finely chopped tomatoes (about 6 tomatoes, peeled and seeded)
2 cups tomato juice
2 cups finely chopped cucumber (about 2 large cucumbers, peeled and seeded)
½ cup finely minced onion
½ cup finely diced green pepper
¼ cup minced parsley
2 tablespoons chopped chives
4 teaspoons salt
1 teaspoon hot sauce
⅓ cup olive oil
2 cloves garlic, chopped

Prepare shrimp and cool. Pour the lemon juice over the shrimp; let chill in refrigerator while you prepare remaining ingredients. Combine everything but the garlic. Rub the garlic around the sides of a large glass bowl. Add shrimp and lemon juice to the bowl. Then add vegetables and seasonings to the shrimp and mix thoroughly. Chill until serving time. May be served over ice. Yield: about 10 cups.

Old-Fashioned Potato Soup

- 4 medium potatoes, diced
- 1 large onion, diced
- ½ cup diced celery
- 1¼ cups water
- 3 cups milk
- 1 tablespoon salt
- ¼ teaspoon pepper
- 8 slices bacon, diced
- 2 tablespoons minced parsley

Combine potatoes, onion, celery, and water. Cover and simmer 45 minutes or until done. Put vegetables through a coarse sieve, and return to the water in which they were cooked. Add milk, salt, and pepper. Reheat. Cook bacon until crisp. Just before serving, float parsley and crisp bacon pieces on soup. Yield: 6 servings.

Tomato-Cream Cheese Soup

- 1 (3-ounce) package cream cheese or cream cheese with chives, softened
- 2 (10¾-ounce) cans condensed tomato soup
- 2 soup cans water
- ¼ teaspoon celery seeds
- Celery seeds, sliced stuffed olives, sliced mushrooms, or grated lemon rind

Put cream cheese in a saucepan and beat until smooth. Gradually add soup, mixing well. Add water and celery seeds and beat with rotary beater until blended. Heat, but do not boil; stir occasionally. Garnish each serving with celery seeds, olives, mushrooms, or lemon rind. Yield: 5 to 6 servings.

*Lentil Soup

- ½ pound lentils
- Salted water
- 2 medium onions, chopped
- 2 or 3 carrots, diced
- 1 (10¾-ounce) can condensed tomato soup
- 3 or 4 sliced frankfurters
- 1 (10¾-ounce) can condensed cream of celery soup

Cook lentils for 30 minutes in salted water to cover. Add remaining ingredients and simmer for 1 hour. Yield: 8 servings.

Oyster Soup

- ¼ pound butter or margarine
- 1½ cups finely chopped onions
- ¼ cup finely cut parsley
- 2 tablespoons finely chopped fennel (optional)
- 2 tablespoons finely chopped celery
- 1 pint oysters and liquid
- 4 teaspoons salt
- ½ teaspoon freshly grated black pepper
- 1½ quarts hot soup stock

Heat butter or margarine in large frying pan; add onions and sauté until transparent. Add parsley, fennel, and celery; sauté until onions are golden. Drain oysters, saving liquid. Cut oysters as fine as possible with scissors and add to sautéed vegetables. Add salt and pepper and oyster liquid and let cook 5 minutes; add stock and simmer a few minutes, but do not boil. Yield: 8 to 10 servings.

*Onion Soup au Gratin

- 6 medium-size onions, chopped
- 3 cups meat broth (or make your own with bouillon cubes or beef flavoring)
- 1½ teaspoons salt
- 4 tablespoons all-purpose flour
- 2 tablespoons cold water
- Toast rounds or croutons
- ½ cup grated Cheddar cheese

Simmer onions in a small amount of water until tender. Add 2 tablespoons fat from the meat broth or the same quantity of butter and let the onions cook until they are yellow. Mix salt and flour with cold water; then add to broth. Add onions and let simmer for a few minutes.

Pour into earthenware or pottery bowls. Add toast rounds and sprinkle grated cheese over all. Place in a 350° oven until cheese is melted. Yield: 4 servings.

Occidentally Oriental Vegetable Soup

- 2½ pounds beef soupbones
- 2 quarts cold water
- 1 medium onion, chopped
- 1 carrot, slivered
- 1 tablespoon beef-flavored instant bouillon
- 1 tablespoon browning sauce
- ½ teaspoon pepper
- 1 (1-pound) can chow mein vegetables, drained
- Salt to taste

Put soupbone, water, onion, and carrot in a deep saucepan. Bring to a boil, lower heat, cover pot, and simmer for 2 hours. Remove bone and cut off all meat. Return meat to pot. Add remaining ingredients and mix well. Heat to boiling and serve hot. Yield: 5 servings.

Note: 2 cups chopped, canned tomatoes may be added to vary flavor.

*Vegetable Soup

- 1 ham bone
- 3 quarts boiling water
- 2 cups sliced carrots
- 1 cup sliced celery
- 1 cup sliced okra
- 1 cup chopped onion
- 1 (16-ounce) can mixed vegetables
- 1 (12-ounce) can whole kernel corn
- 1 small cabbage, coarsely shredded
- 1 (16-ounce) can tomatoes
- 2 cups cooked, diced potatoes
- 2 cups cooked macaroni

Simmer ham bone in boiling water for 20 minutes to make broth. Add all ingredients except potatoes and macaroni. Simmer about 3 hours. Add potatoes and macaroni. Heat and serve. Yield: 8 to 10 servings.

Note: To freeze this soup, omit potatoes and macaroni. When ready to use, allow soup to thaw and add potatoes and macaroni. Heat and serve.

*Peanut Butter Soup

- 2 tablespoons margarine
- ⅔ cup finely chopped celery
- ¼ cup finely chopped onion
- ¼ cup all-purpose flour
- 1 cup peanut butter
- 2 cups milk, divided
- 4 cups chicken stock
- ¼ teaspoon salt
- Dash pepper

Melt margarine in skillet. Add celery and onion; cook over low heat, stirring frequently until tender. Stir in flour, mixing until smooth. Blend peanut butter with 1 cup milk. Stir into mixture in skillet along with remaining milk, stock, salt, and pepper. Cook over medium heat, stirring constantly, until slightly thickened. Serve hot. Yield: about 7 servings.

Hearty Soup

- 1 pound bacon
- 1 pound ham
- 1 (17-ounce) can whole kernel corn
- 1 (16-ounce) can tomatoes
- 1 (17-ounce) can peas
- 1 (4-ounce) can mushrooms
- 1 cup cooked spaghetti noodles
- Salt and pepper

Fry bacon until crisp, and cut into small pieces. Dice ham into small cubes and fry. Combine all ingredients and season to taste. Simmer over medium heat for 30 to 45 minutes. Freezes well. Yield: 8 servings.

Elegant Beef Stew

- 3½ to 4 pounds beef chuck
- ½ cup all-purpose flour
- 1½ teaspoons ground cloves
- ½ teaspoon ground allspice
- ½ teaspoon ground cinnamon
- 1½ teaspoons salt
- ¼ teaspoon pepper
- 6 tablespoons butter or margarine
- 1 (10½-ounce) can condensed beef consommé
- 1 teaspoon sugar
- ½ cup dry red wine
- 8 carrots, sliced
- 3 cups cubed potatoes
- ½ cup coarsely chopped onion

Cut beef in 1½-inch cubes. Combine flour, cloves, allspice, cinnamon, salt, and pepper. Put flour mixture in a paper bag; add a few pieces of meat at a time and shake to coat each piece.

Melt butter in a heavy skillet or Dutch oven; add beef cubes and cook over medium heat until meat is lightly browned. Add consommé; cover and simmer for 1½ hours. Combine sugar and wine and pour over meat. Simmer 15 minutes. Add carrots and potatoes; simmer, covered, for 1 hour.

Add chopped onion and cook 15 minutes longer or until vegetables are tender. Skim off fat, and serve hot. Yield: 8 to 10 servings.

Cold Cream of Spinach Soup

- 1 (10-ounce) package frozen chopped spinach
- 2 teaspoons finely chopped onion
- 2 tablespoons melted butter or margarine
- ¼ cup all-purpose flour
- 1 teaspoon salt
- ⅛ teaspoon white pepper
- 1 quart milk, divided
- 3 tablespoons lemon juice

Cook spinach according to package directions; drain well and set aside.

Sauté onion in butter; stir in flour, salt, and pepper. Cook over low heat, stirring constantly, until smooth and bubbly. Gradually stir in 2 cups milk; heat until mixture is thick.

Blend cream sauce and spinach; add remaining milk and lemon juice, and blend well. Cover and refrigerate at least 4 hours. Stir gently. Serve in chilled bowls or mugs. Yield: 6 to 8 servings.

*Spinach Soup

- 2 (10-ounce) packages frozen chopped spinach
- ¼ cup peanut oil
- ¼ cup finely chopped onion
- ⅓ cup all-purpose flour
- 1 tablespoon salt
- ¼ teaspoon pepper
- Dash ground nutmeg
- 6 cups milk

Cook spinach in unsalted water according to package directions; drain. Heat oil in large saucepan. Add onion and sauté until transparent, about 5 minutes. Remove from heat; blend in flour, salt, pepper, and nutmeg. Gradually add milk, stirring constantly; then add spinach and cook over medium-high heat about 15 minutes. Stir often to prevent scorching. Yield: 6 to 8 servings.

Gazpacho

- 4 medium tomatoes, quartered
- ½ cucumber, peeled and sliced
- 2 stalks celery, sliced
- 3 sprigs parsley or 3 tablespoons parsley flakes
- 2 cloves garlic, peeled
- ¼ cup dry red wine
- 2 tablespoons olive oil
- ½ teaspoon Worcestershire sauce
- ½ green pepper, sliced
- ½ cup diced onion
- 3 scallions, sliced
- ¼ cup cold water
- 2 tablespoons wine vinegar
- 1 teaspoon salt
- ¼ teaspoon pepper (optional)

Combine all ingredients in blender. Using setting marked "grate" or "low," blend about 15 seconds. Refrigerate to chill thoroughly. Serve cold. Yield: 6 servings.

Easy Gazpacho

½ cup diced celery
½ cup diced green pepper
½ cup diced onion
½ cup thinly sliced cucumber
1 cup diced tomatoes
1 (10¾-ounce) can condensed tomato soup
1 soup can water
1½ cups cocktail vegetable juice
1 tablespoon wine vinegar
1 tablespoon commercial Italian dressing
Garlic salt to taste
¼ teaspoon salt
⅛ teaspoon pepper
4 dashes hot sauce
Dash Worcestershire sauce

Combine all ingredients in a large bowl. Cover and refrigerate at least 4 hours. Stir gently. Serve in chilled bowls or mugs. Yield: 6 to 8 servings.

Vichyssoise

¼ cup diced green onions
1 white onion, sliced
2 tablespoons butter or margarine
2 cups chicken consommé
3 cups diced potatoes
Salt and white pepper
½ cup whipping cream
2 cups milk, divided
Chopped chives

Sauté onion in butter until soft; do not brown. Combine consommé, potatoes, and seasonings in saucepan; add onion and simmer until potatoes are soft. Put through a food mill or in blender until smooth; cool.

Add cream and 1 cup milk. Bring to a boil over medium heat; blend in remaining milk. Chill thoroughly and serve garnished with chives. Yield: 6 to 8 servings.

*Brunswick Stew

1 (3-pound) stewing chicken or hen
3 cups water
1½ teaspoons salt
1 cup diced potatoes
1¾ cups frozen or canned lima beans, drained
1¾ cups tomato sauce
⅔ cup chopped onion
1¾ cups corn, fresh or frozen
1 teaspoon sugar
Salt to taste
⅛ teaspoon pepper
⅛ teaspoon oregano
⅛ teaspoon poultry seasoning
Few grains cayenne pepper

Simmer chicken in salted water until tender, about 2 to 2½ hours. Drain off the broth and set it aside. Separate the meat from the skin and bones and cut into small pieces. Skim the fat from the broth. Boil the broth to concentrate it to about 2 cups.

Add potatoes to broth and simmer for 10 minutes. Add lima beans, tomato sauce, and onion. Cook 20 minutes longer. Add chicken, corn, and seasonings. Cook 15 to 20 minutes longer or until vegetables are tender. Yield: 6 servings.

Creole Beef Stew

2 pounds beef stew meat, cut in cubes
⅓ cup all-purpose flour
3½ teaspoons salt
½ teaspoon pepper
2 tablespoons vegetable shortening
1 cup hot water
1 cup sliced onion rings
1 cup sliced okra
1 cup drained canned corn
2 cups drained canned tomatoes
1 cup diced potatoes

Cut beef into 1-inch cubes. Mix flour with salt and pepper. Sprinkle over beef cubes to coat. Brown meat in hot shortening. Add hot water; cover and simmer for 2 hours or until meat is tender. Add vegetables about 30 minutes before cooking time is up. Serve hot. Yield: 6 servings.

352 soups, stews, and chowders

*Grits-Beef Stew

2½ pounds stewing beef
1 cup all-purpose flour
2 tablespoons salt
½ teaspoon pepper
6 tablespoons shortening
2 cloves garlic, minced
4 cups boiling water
3 cups cooked tomatoes
1 teaspoon Worcestershire sauce
18 small white onions, peeled and quartered
7 carrots, peeled and cut into 2-inch strips
2 cups cooked green peas
1 cup uncooked grits

Cut meat into 1½-inch cubes. Combine flour, salt, and pepper; coat meat well with this mixture. Melt shortening in Dutch oven; add meat and brown. Add garlic, boiling water, tomatoes, and Worcestershire sauce. Cover and simmer for about 2 hours or until meat is tender. Add onions and carrots and cook an additional 20 minutes. Add more salt, if needed. Add peas and uncooked grits; cook for 15 minutes. Yield: 8 servings.

*Chili for a Crowd

15 pounds ground beef
4 pounds chopped onion
4 cups chopped celery
1 cup soy sauce
1¼ to 2½ cups chili powder
1 tablespoon thyme
1 tablespoon oregano
3 tablespoons celery seeds
4 bay leaves
5 gallons canned tomatoes
5 gallons kidney beans
2 gallons tomato juice
Salt to taste

Brown meat with onion and celery. Add soy sauce and spices (vary chili powder according to how hot you like it), and mix well. Then add tomatoes, beans, tomato juice, and salt to taste. Simmer mixture for about 2 hours. Add ¼ to 1 cup water, if necessary. Yield: 230 cups.

*Chili Con Carne

½ cup coarsely chopped onion
½ cup coarsely chopped green pepper
2 cups tomato sauce
2 tablespoons tomato paste
½ teaspoon salt
1 teaspoon sugar
⅛ teaspoon pepper
2 to 3 teaspoons chili powder
1 tablespoon olive oil
½ pound ground beef
1 (1-pound) can red kidney beans

Put onion, green pepper, tomato sauce, tomato paste, and seasonings in blender container. Blend until vegetables are finely cut and thoroughly mixed. Melt oil in a large frying pan. Add beef and cook until crumbly. Add blended mixture and cook slowly until sauce is thick. Add beans, and heat through. Yield: about 5 cups.

Chili Italexico

1 pound dried pinto beans
1 teaspoon salt
1 teaspoon garlic powder
1 teaspoon cayenne pepper
3 pounds ground round
3 tablespoons salad oil
2 (1-pound) cans tomatoes, chopped
2 tablespoons chili powder
2 tablespoons cayenne pepper
1 tablespoon garlic powder
2 large onions, finely chopped
1 cup water
2 tablespoons dry celery flakes
2 (15-ounce) cans tomato sauce
Grated Parmesan cheese

Cover pinto beans with water, and cook until tender (about 2 hours). When beans begin to get soft, add salt, garlic powder, and cayenne pepper.

Cook ground round in heavy skillet with salad oil until meat is slightly browned (about 10 minutes).

Add chopped tomatoes, chili powder, cayenne pepper, garlic powder, chopped onions, and water. Bring to a boil; then reduce heat, cover, and simmer for 1 hour.

Add cooked beans, celery flakes, and tomato sauce and simmer for 45 minutes. Serve hot and sprinkle with Parmesan cheese. Yield: 12 to 18 servings.

Flemish Stew

       3 tablespoons butter or margarine, divided
       3 medium onions, chopped
       2 to 2½ pounds boneless beef, cut in 1½-inch cubes
    1½ tablespoons all-purpose flour
       ½ (10½-ounce) can beef bouillon, undiluted
       1 cup beer
       1 tablespoon wine vinegar
       1 clove garlic, crushed
       1 tablespoon minced fresh (or 1½ teaspoons dried) parsley
       1 bay leaf
       ¼ teaspoon ground thyme
       ½ teaspoon paprika
       1 teaspoon salt
       1 teaspoon Kitchen Bouquet
         Pepper

Heat 2 tablespoons butter in a heavy skillet, and sauté onions until golden. Remove and set aside; add remaining butter to skillet. Add beef cubes and brown well on all sides. Sift flour into pot; stir until thoroughly absorbed. Gradually add bouillon, then beer and all other ingredients. Return onions to pot; cover tightly and simmer over low heat for 2½ to 3 hours.

Any vegetables desired may be stirred into the stew during the last 45 minutes of cooking. Or the stew may be served over noodles, rice, or any "foundation" desired. Yield: 6 servings.

Hot Chili

      ¼ pound chopped beef suet
      1 cup chopped onion
    1½ teaspoons minced garlic
    2½ pounds coarsely chopped or ground beef
      1 tablespoon salt
      ½ pod dried red pepper
      1 teaspoon cumin
      ¼ cup chili powder
      3 cups boiling water

Fry beef suet in frying pan until it cooks to cracklings; remove cracklings, and add onion and garlic to oil remaining in pan. Cook until onion is a deep yellow, stirring frequently. Add beef and cook until gray. Stir in salt, hot pepper, cumin, chili powder, and boiling water.

Bring mixture to a boil over very low heat. Cook at low heat for 1½ hours or until meat is tender and flavors are thoroughly blended. Stir occasionally. If mixture becomes too thick, add more boiling water. Yield: about 8 cups.

* Family Beef Stew

    1½ pounds boneless beef stew meat
      ⅓ cup all-purpose flour
    1½ teaspoons salt
      ⅛ teaspoon pepper
      2 tablespoons salad oil
    2¼ cups water
      3 medium onions, sliced
      4 medium potatoes, cut in cubes
      5 medium carrots, quartered
    1½ cups frozen peas

Cut beef into 1½-inch cubes. Combine flour, salt, and pepper, and coat cubes of beef with mixture. Brown meat thoroughly in oil in a large heavy skillet or Dutch oven. Sprinkle remaining seasoned flour over meat; stir well. Add water, cover skillet, and simmer for 2 to 3 hours or until meat is tender. Add onions, potatoes, and carrots; simmer, covered, for 15 minutes. Add peas, and simmer until vegetables are tender, stirring occasionally. Yield: 6 servings.

New Year's Eve Oyster Stew

    5 tablespoons butter
    3 dozen oysters, shucked and with liquid
    2 tablespoons Worcestershire sauce
    1 teaspoon salt
    ¼ teaspoon seasoned pepper
    6 cups half-and-half
    ½ bunch parsley, minced
      Paprika to taste
      Butter

Heat the butter in a deep, heavy kettle. When it bubbles, add oysters, Worcestershire sauce, salt, and seasoned pepper. Cook gently until the edges of the oysters begin to curl (about a minute). Heat the half-and-half until hot but not boiling; combine with the oysters and simmer briefly but do not boil. Let stand to blend the flavors. When ready to serve, heat until hot but not boiling. Pour into a warm tureen and top with minced parsley, paprika to taste, and dots of butter. Yield: 8 servings.

Brown Stew

    1½ pounds beef chuck, shank, or round, cut in large cubes
    1½ pounds lamb shoulder, cut in small cubes
    3 tablespoons all-purpose flour
    2 teaspoons salt
    ½ teaspoon pepper
    ¼ teaspoon ground ginger
    3 tablespoons olive or salad oil
    1 cup chopped onion
    2 cloves garlic, minced
    4 cups cocktail vegetable juice
    1 (1-inch) stick cinnamon
    4 medium carrots, scraped and quartered
    1 medium eggplant, cut in large cubes (do not pare)
    4 stalks celery, cut in 3-inch sticks
    8 large dried pitted prunes, split
    8 large dried apricot halves

Trim all fat from beef and lamb. Combine flour, salt, pepper, and ginger in a paper bag; add meat, a few cubes at a time, and shake to coat evenly. Brown meat quickly in oil in large heavy skillet or Dutch oven. Stir in onion, garlic, vegetable juice, and cinnamon.

Arrange carrots, eggplant, and celery around meat. Cover and simmer for 1 hour.

Stuff each prune with an apricot half. Place on top of stew. Cover and simmer about 1 hour or until meat is tender. Yield: 6 to 8 servings.

Meatball Stew

    1½ pounds ground chuck
    ½ teaspoon salt
    ½ teaspoon pepper
    ¾ cup dry bread crumbs
    ¼ cup vegetable oil
    1 clove garlic, minced
    1 (6-ounce) can tomato paste
    ¾ cup Burgundy wine
    2 cups water
    1 teaspoon salt
    ½ teaspoon thyme
    1 bay leaf
    ¾ cup cubed potatoes*
    ¾ cup sliced carrots*
    ½ cup chopped celery*
    ½ cup small canned onions
    1 (3-ounce) can sliced mushrooms
    1 tablespoon chopped parsley
    1 tablespoon chopped pimiento

Combine ground chuck, ½ teaspoon salt, pepper, and bread crumbs. Shape into small balls (1½ inches in diameter), and brown in hot oil. Add garlic, tomato paste, wine, water, 1 teaspoon salt, thyme, and bay leaf. Simmer for 30 minutes, or transfer to 3-quart casserole dish and bake at 325° for 30 minutes.

Add potatoes, carrots, celery, onions, and mushrooms and cook an additional 15 minutes or until vegetables are tender. To serve, sprinkle top with chopped parsley and pimiento. Yield: 8 servings.

*You may substitute 1 (1½-pound) package frozen vegetables.

Bake-A-Roux

    8 *cups all-purpose flour*
    4 *cups cooking oil*

Mix flour and oil together in a heavy ovenproof container. Place on center shelf in oven.

Bake at 400° for 1½ to 2 hours. Set timer, and stir roux every 15 minutes. Roux should be a caramel color when done. Remove from oven, cool, transfer to containers with tight-fitting lids, and store in refrigerator until needed. Roux may also be frozen. Yield: enough roux for 4 to 6 pots of gumbo.

Southern Gumbo

    1 *cup cooking oil*
    1 *cup all-purpose flour*
    8 *stalks celery, chopped*
    3 *large onions, chopped*
    1 *green pepper, chopped*
    2 *cloves garlic, minced*
    About ½ *cup chopped parsley (optional)*
    1 *pound sliced okra*
    2 *tablespoons shortening*
    2 *quarts chicken stock*
    2 *quarts water*
    ½ *cup Worcestershire sauce*
    Hot sauce to taste
    ½ *cup catsup*
    1 *large ripe tomato, chopped*
    2 *tablespoons salt*
    4 *slices bacon, or large slice ham, chopped*
    1 *or 2 bay leaves*
    ¼ *teaspoon thyme*
    ¼ *teaspoon rosemary*
    Red pepper flakes to taste (optional)
    2 *cups cooked, chopped chicken*
    1 *or 2 pounds cooked crabmeat*
    4 *pounds boiled shrimp*
    1 *pint oysters (optional)*
    1 *teaspoon molasses or brown sugar*
    Lemon juice (optional)
    Cooked rice

Heat oil in heavy iron pot over medium heat (or use oven method for cooking roux). Add flour very slowly, stirring constantly with a wooden spoon until roux is medium brown. This will take from 30 to 40 minutes. Add celery, onion, green pepper, garlic, and parsley; cook an additional 45 minutes to 1 hour, stirring constantly. (You may cut cooking time at this stage, but the gumbo won't be as good.)

Fry okra in 2 tablespoons shortening until brown. Add to gumbo and stir well over low heat for a few minutes. (At this stage the mixture may be cooled, packaged, and frozen or refrigerated for later use.)

Add chicken stock and water, Worcestershire sauce, hot sauce, catsup, tomato, salt, bacon or ham, bay leaves, thyme, rosemary, and red pepper flakes. Simmer for 2½ to 3 hours.

About 30 minutes before serving time, add cooked chicken, crabmeat, and shrimp; simmer for 30 minutes. Add oysters during last 10 minutes of simmering period. Add molasses or brown sugar. Check seasonings and add more, if needed. A bit of lemon juice may be added at the very last, if desired. Put a generous amount of hot, cooked rice in soup bowls; spoon gumbo over the rice and serve at once. Yield: 12 large servings.

Florida Brunswick Stew

    3 *pounds beef*
    3 *pounds pork*
    3 *pounds chicken*
    3 *medium onions*
    3 *(17-ounce) cans cream style corn*
    3 *(16-ounce) cans tomatoes*
    1 *pound butter*
    Salt and pepper

Boil the beef, pork, and chicken together until tender. Cool and remove meat from bones. Save meat stock. Then grind meat with the onions, using coarse blade on chopper or grinder. Add corn, tomatoes, butter, and salt and pepper to taste. Simmer mixture 3 to 4 hours, gradually adding meat stock, after having skimmed off fat. Yield: 30 servings.

*Ranch Stew

- 1 tablespoon shortening
- 1 pound ground beef
- 1 medium onion, chopped
- 1 green pepper, diced
- 1 (12-ounce) can whole kernel corn
- 1 (15½-ounce) can kidney beans
- 1 (16-ounce) can tomato wedges
- 2 teaspoons chili powder
- ¾ teaspoon salt
- Pepper to taste

Melt shortening in heavy saucepan. Cook beef, onion, and green pepper in shortening until meat is brown and onion and pepper are tender. Drain corn, beans, and tomatoes; add this liquid to meat and simmer until liquid is reduced to about half, about 15 minutes. Add corn, beans, and tomatoes, chili powder, salt, and pepper. Simmer, stirring occasionally, for about 10 minutes. Yield: 6 servings.

Italian Meat Stew

- 1 pound lean beef stew meat
- 1 pound lean lamb stew meat
- ¼ cup olive oil
- 1 (28-ounce) can tomatoes
- 1½ cups boiling water
- ⅓ cup onion flakes
- 1 cup diced celery
- 2 teaspoons salt
- ½ teaspoon pepper
- 5 medium potatoes, quartered
- 8 carrots, quartered
- 2 tablespoons parsley flakes
- 1 teaspoon crushed dried basil leaves
- ¼ teaspoon garlic powder

Cut meat into 1½-inch cubes; sauté in hot oil until brown on all sides. Add tomatoes, water, onion flakes, celery, salt, and pepper. Cover and cook slowly 1½ to 2 hours or until meat is tender.

Add potatoes, carrots, parsley flakes, basil, and garlic powder 30 minutes before cooking time is up. Serve hot. Yield: 4 servings.

Savory Lamb Stew with Parsley Dumplings

- 1½ pounds lamb shoulder, cubed
- Seasoned all-purpose flour
- 2 tablespoons shortening
- 2 cups water
- 4 medium-size onions, sliced
- 6 medium-size carrots, sliced
- 6 medium-size potatoes, diced
- ½ teaspoon rosemary
- Salt and pepper
- 2 cups all-purpose flour
- 3 teaspoons baking powder
- 1 teaspoon salt
- 2 tablespoons chopped parsley
- ¼ cup shortening
- 1 cup milk

Coat lamb with seasoned flour. Heat shortening; add lamb and cook until lightly browned on all sides. Add water. Cover and cook over low heat for 45 minutes. Add onions, carrots, potatoes, rosemary, and salt and pepper. Cover; cook until vegetables are tender, stirring occasionally.

Combine flour, baking powder, and 1 teaspoon salt. Add parsley. Cut in shortening; add milk and blend. Drop by tablespoonfuls into lamb mixture. Cook, uncovered, for 10 minutes. Then cover and cook another 10 minutes. Yield: 6 servings.

Baked Beef Stew

- 1½ pounds round steak, cut in 1-inch cubes
- 2 tablespoons shortening
- 2 (10½-ounce) cans condensed golden mushroom soup
- ½ cup water
- ½ cup sliced onion
- ¼ teaspoon savory
- 3 medium carrots, halved lengthwise and cut in 2-inch pieces
- 1 (17-ounce) can peas, drained
- 1½ cups commercial biscuit mix
- ½ cup milk
- ½ cup chopped parsley
- 2 tablespoons melted butter or margarine

Brown steak in hot shortening in heavy skillet; pour off drippings. Add soup, water, onion, and savory. Pour into a 2-quart casserole. Cover; bake at 350° for 1 hour. Add carrots. Cover; bake 1 hour longer. Add peas.

Combine biscuit mix and milk. Stir 20 times; knead on floured surface 10 times. Roll dough into a 12- x 8-inch rectangle; sprinkle with parsley. Then roll in jelly roll fashion, starting at long edge. Seal ends; cut into 7 slices. Top stew with biscuit slices; brush with melted butter. Bake, uncovered, 20 minutes or until biscuits are brown. Yield: 6 servings.

*Short Rib Stew

   3 *pounds beef short ribs*
 ½ *cup seasoned all-purpose flour*
   3 *tablespoons shortening*
      Boiling water
   6 *medium potatoes, cut in halves*
   6 *medium onions, cut in halves*
   6 *medium carrots, cut in halves*
   6 *long pieces celery, cut in halves*

Coat short ribs with flour that has been seasoned to taste with salt and pepper. Brown in hot shortening in a heavy skillet or Dutch oven. Add enough boiling water to almost cover ribs, and simmer for 1 hour. Add potatoes, onions, and carrots. Continue cooking, covered, an additional 15 minutes. Add celery and cook 15 minutes longer. Yield: 6 servings.

Olive Minestrone

   1 *(10½-ounce) can condensed beef bouillon*
   1 *(1-pound) can French-cut green beans*
   1 *(1-pound) can mixed vegetables*
   1 *(20-ounce) can tomatoes*
 ⅓ *cup chopped onion*
 ⅓ *cup chopped pimiento-stuffed green olives*
   2 *cups water*
 ½ *teaspoon celery salt*
 ¼ *cup egg pastina**
   1 *tablespoon vinegar*
      Salt and pepper

Combine beef bouillon, green beans, mixed vegetables, tomatoes, onion, olives, water, and celery salt. Heat to boiling point. Simmer 20 minutes, stirring occasionally. Gradually add pastina so that mixture continues to boil. Cook 5 minutes or until tender. Add vinegar, and salt and pepper to taste; mix well. Yield: about 2½ quarts.

*If you cannot get pastina (a rice-shaped macaroni), you may substitute vermicelli broken into short lengths.

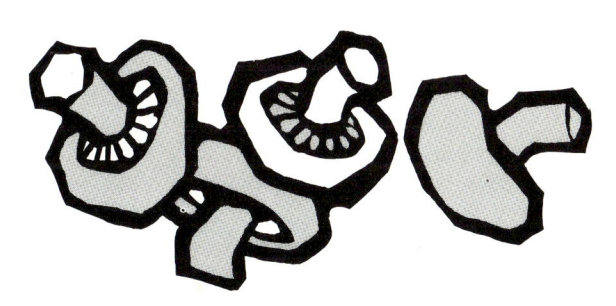

Iron Pot Stew

   2 *pounds beef stewing meat*
 ⅔ *cup all-purpose flour*
   2 *tablespoons bacon drippings*
   2 *teaspoons salt*
 ½ *teaspoon pepper*
 ½ *teaspoon thyme*
      Water
   8 *medium potatoes*
   8 *medium carrots*
   8 *small onions*
   1 *green pepper, cut in eighths*
 ¼ *cup cold water*

Roll stew meat in flour to coat all sides. Reserve any leftover flour. Brown meat thoroughly in hot bacon drippings in heavy iron kettle. Sprinkle meat with salt, pepper, and thyme. Add water just to cover the meat.

Cover kettle tightly and cook over low heat about 2 hours or until meat is almost tender. Add whole potatoes, carrots, onions, and green pepper. Cover kettle and simmer until vegetables are tender, about 20 to 30 minutes.

Dissolve leftover flour in ¼ cup cold water and add to stew; cook until mixture thickens slightly. Add more flour if needed, and adjust seasonings, adding more salt and pepper if needed. Yield: 4 servings.

358 soups, stews, and chowders

Venison Stew

- 2 pounds venison, cut in 1-inch cubes
- 4 tablespoons bacon drippings
- 1 teaspoon garlic salt
- 1 teaspoon Worcestershire sauce
- 1½ teaspoons salt
- ½ teaspoon pepper
- ¾ cup chopped onion
- 4 medium potatoes, cut in cubes
- 6 medium carrots, sliced
- 1 green pepper, chopped
- 2 cups sliced celery
- 3 tablespoons all-purpose flour
- ¼ cup cold water

Brown venison cubes in hot bacon drippings in heavy Dutch oven. Add water to cover, seasonings, and onion. Cover and simmer for about 2 hours. Add potatoes, carrots, pepper, and celery and cook about 20 minutes or until vegetables are tender. Taste and add more seasonings, if desired.

Dissolve flour in ¼ cup cold water and stir into stew. Cook about 5 minutes, and serve hot. Yield: 8 servings.

Crab Stew Monteleone

- 1 cup olive oil
- 1½ cups all-purpose flour
- ½ pound green peppers, chopped
- 1 large clove garlic, minced
- 1 pod red pepper, crushed
- 3 pounds onions, chopped
- 3 stalks celery, chopped
- 1 dozen large lake crabs
- Salt
- Chopped parsley
- Chopped green onion tops
- Hot cooked rice

Put olive oil in large iron pot; heat thoroughly, and stir in flour. Cook over very low heat for about 30 minutes, stirring constantly so flour does not brown. Add green pepper, garlic, red pepper, onion, and celery; cook slowly for about 20 minutes, stirring once or twice. Add crabs, which have been cleaned and cut into halves (do not discard the crab fat). Stir well; add salt to taste and cover pot.

Do not add water at any time; cook slowly for 30 minutes; add crab fat and meat from crab claws. Simmer, covered, 15 minutes longer. When ready to serve, sprinkle with chopped parsley and green onion tops. Serve with hot cooked rice. Yield: 8 servings.

Hungarian Goulash

- 2 pounds boneless beef, cut into 1½-inch cubes
- ¼ cup flour
- 2 large or 3 medium onions, sliced
- 2 tablespoons oil or shortening
- ½ cup (1 medium) chopped green pepper
- 1 clove garlic, minced
- 1 to 2 tablespoons paprika
- 2 teaspoons salt
- 1 teaspoon caraway seeds (optional)
- ½ teaspoon ground marjoram (optional)
- ¼ teaspoon pepper
- 2 cups undrained canned tomatoes
- 1½ cups water
- 3 tablespoons all-purpose flour
- ½ cup water

Coat beef cubes with ¼ cup flour. Brown beef and onions in hot oil in a Dutch oven. Add green pepper, garlic, paprika, salt, caraway seeds, marjoram, pepper, tomatoes, and 1½ cups water. Simmer, covered, for 2 hours or until meat is tender. Combine 3 tablespoons flour with ½ cup water. Blend into meat mixture. Bring to boil, stirring constantly. Serve goulash over noodles or potatoes. Yield: 6 to 8 servings.

*Salmon Chowder

- 1 (1-pound) can salmon
- ¼ cup chopped onion
- ¼ cup chopped celery
- ¼ cup peanut oil
- 2 tablespoons flour
- 4 cups milk
- 1 cup diced raw potato
- 1 cup tomato juice
- 1½ teaspoons salt
- Chopped parsley

Drain salmon (reserving liquid), bone, and flake. Set aside the liquid and salmon.

In large heavy saucepan, sauté chopped onion and celery in oil over low heat until tender, about 10 minutes. Blend in flour; then gradually stir in milk. Add diced potatoes and continue cooking over low heat, stirring occasionally, until potatoes are tender, about 20 minutes.

Heat tomato juice with salt until hot; very gradually add to milk mixture, stirring constantly. And salmon and reserved liquid.

Heat over low heat about 5 minutes. Serve topped with chopped parsley. Yield: 6 to 8 servings.

Maryland Clam Chowder

- 3 quarts water
- 1 whole chicken breast
- 3 tablespoons chicken stock base
- 1 teaspoon salt
- 2 stalks celery, with tops
- 1½ cups minced, Chesapeake Bay soft-shell clams (about 3 dozen), liquor reserved
- 1 tablespoon freeze-dried chopped chives
- 2 tablespoons minced onion
- ½ teaspoon celery salt
- ¼ teaspoon thyme leaves
- ¼ teaspoon white pepper
- 1 cup sliced carrots
- 1 cup diced potatoes
- 1 (10-ounce) package frozen corn
- 1 (10-ounce) package frozen peas
- 1 whole pimiento, minced
- 1 cup clam juice
- 1 teaspoon parsley flakes

Combine water, chicken, chicken stock base, salt, and celery in a large saucepan; simmer for 1 hour. Discard celery, remove chicken, and finely chop the meat; set aside. To the stock add remaining ingredients except the clam juice, parsley flakes, and chopped chicken. Simmer for 20 minutes; then add remaining ingredients. Continue cooking for 5 minutes. Yield: 4 quarts.

Note: For an especially elegant version, add 1 dozen shucked, Chesapeake Bay soft-shell clams along with the chicken, clam juice, and parsley flakes.

Fish Chowder

- ¼ cup butter
- 1 cup thinly sliced onion
- 1 cup cubed raw potatoes
- 1 cup sliced raw carrots
- 1 cup water
- 2 teaspoons salt, divided
- ⅛ teaspoon pepper
- 1 (1-pound) package frozen haddock, defrosted and cut into 1-inch cubes
- 3 cups milk
- ½ teaspoon leaf rosemary
- ¼ teaspoon leaf thyme
- 1 cup half-and-half
- 2 tablespoons all-purpose flour

Melt butter; add onion, potato, carrot, water, 1 teaspoon salt, and pepper. Cover and simmer until carrot is almost tender, about 15 minutes. Add fish, milk, herbs, and remaining 1 teaspoon salt; heat to simmering and cook until fish flakes easily. Blend together half-and-half and flour; add to chowder and heat thoroughly. Yield: 8 to 10 servings.

The Warehouse's Clam Chowder

- 1 cup chopped clams
- 2 cups boiling water
- ½ cup chopped onion
- 1 medium carrot, chopped
- 2 cups tomatoes, put through food mill
- ½ teaspoon salt
- ½ teaspoon pepper
- Dash paprika
- 1 teaspoon minced parsley
- 2 tablespoons all-purpose flour
- Hot water
- ½ cup half-and-half

Add clams to 2 cups boiling water and cook for 35 minutes. Add chopped onion and carrot. Cook for 8 minutes.

Add tomatoes, salt, pepper, paprika, and parsley. Beat flour with enough hot water to make a thin batter. Add batter slowly to clams, stirring constantly, until soup thickens. Add half-and-half, stirring constantly, and let simmer for 5 more minutes. Yield: 4 to 6 servings.

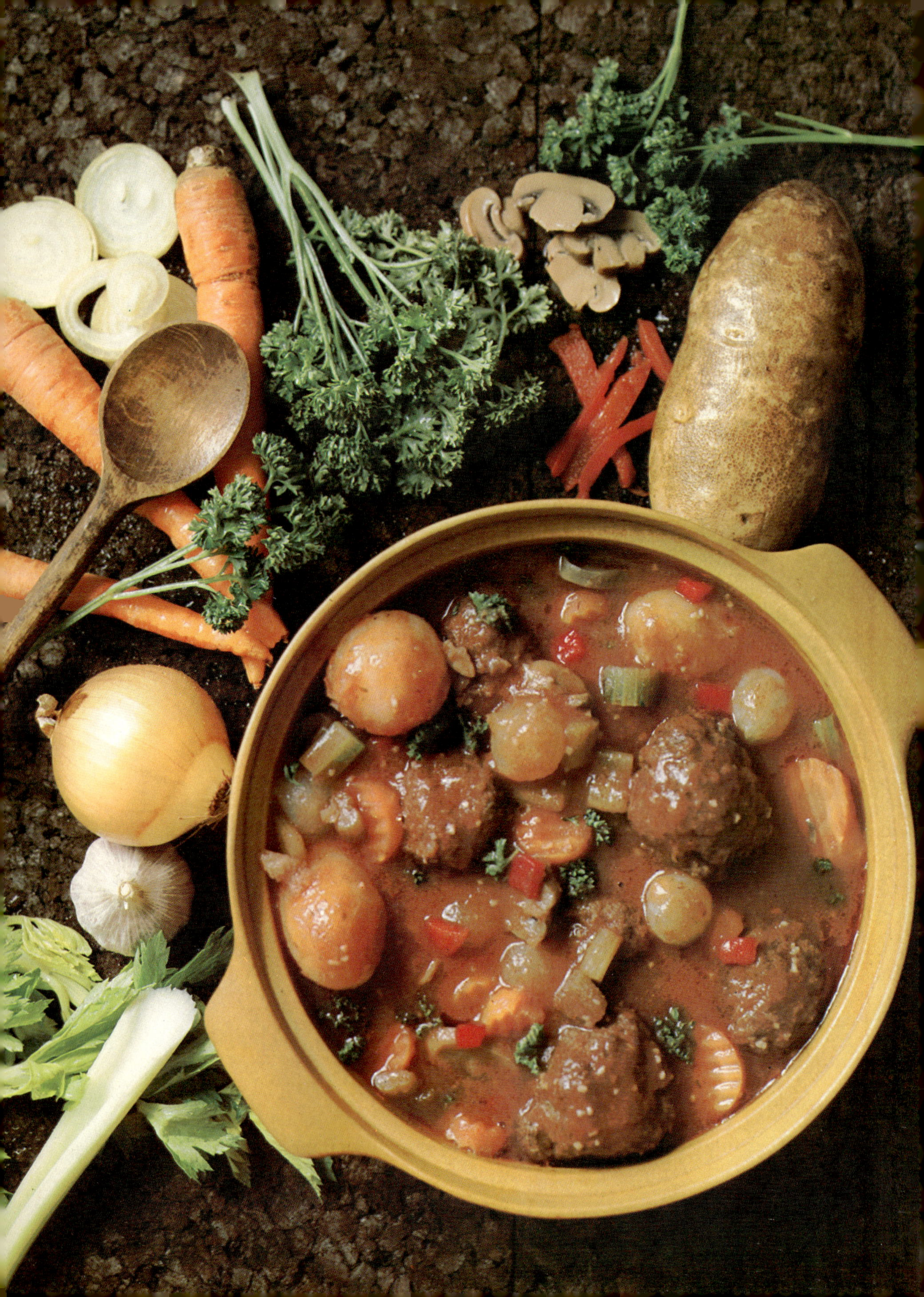

Vegetables

The South has always been a veritable vegetable garden, and housewives have served a variety of vegetables since colonial days. In fact, the vegetable garden, along with the herb and spice garden, was planned along with the construction of a home. It was early recognized that from this class of foods came our most essential vitamins and minerals, long before they were identified as such.

Before the days of food preservation, gardens were planned to provide year-round fresh vegetables of some kind. Today we have methods for home-freezing of vegetables as well as for canning. Frozen and canned foods are commonly found on grocery shelves and methods of preservation have been improved to the extent that loss of vitamins and minerals is minimal in the preservation process.

It is essential that vegetables be cooked in as little water as possible, so that vitamins and minerals are not lost in liquid which is not used. (Saving this vegetable liquid for soups, stews, or cooking other vegetables is a nutritious trick every homemaker should know.) For basic good health everyone should have at least one serving of a green and yellow vegetable each day as well as a serving of citrus, tomatoes, or raw cabbage, and a serving of potatoes.

Stuffed Artichokes

6 *fresh artichokes*
Lemon juice
2 *quarts boiling water*
2 *teaspoons salt*
½ *cup olive oil*
1 *cup chopped mushrooms*
2 *cloves garlic, crushed*
1 *small onion, minced*
½ *cup melted butter*
¼ *cup chopped parsley*
½ *pound ground ham, cooked*
1 *cup grated Parmesan cheese*
2 *cups bread crumbs*

Cut tips from fresh artichokes and brush with lemon juice. Cook until tender in boiling water, to which salt and olive oil have been added. Drain; remove centers of artichokes.

Sauté mushrooms, garlic, and onion in butter until browned. Stir in parsley, ham, cheese, and bread crumbs and mix well. Spoon into artichoke shells and bake at 325° about 15 minutes. Serve hot. Yield: 6 servings.

Artichoke Delight

½ *cup butter or margarine*
1 *(3-ounce) package Roquefort cheese, cut into small pieces*
¼ *teaspoon lemon juice*
Dash paprika
Salt to taste
1 *(14-ounce) can artichoke hearts, drained*

Melt butter in top of double boiler over rapidly boiling water; add cheese, lemon juice, paprika, and salt. Serve hot as a dip for artichoke hearts. Yield: 4 servings.

Artichoke Stuffed with Crabmeat Louis

    6 artichokes
    1 teaspoon salt
    1 teaspoon olive oil
    1 pound crabmeat
    Louis Sauce

Wash artichokes in cold water. Place enough water in a large saucepan to half cover the artichokes. Add salt and olive oil and bring to a boil. When the water is boiling, add the artichokes; cover and simmer 25 to 30 minutes or until a leaf pulls out easily; drain. When cool, gently spread the leaves to allow room for the fingertips to reach down and pull out the choke at the center of the artichoke.

At serving time, fill the artichokes with Crabmeat Louis. Serve extra sauce with the meal. Yield: 6 servings.

Louis Sauce:

    1 cup mayonnaise
    ¼ cup whipping cream
    ¼ teaspoon Worcestershire sauce
    ¼ cup chopped green pepper
    ¼ cup chopped green onion
    2 tablespoons lemon juice

Combine all ingredients. Mix well and set aside for an hour or two before use. At serving time, mix desired amount with crabmeat. Yield: 2 cups.

Hearts of Artichoke Supreme

    6 fresh artichoke hearts
    Lemon juice
    2 quarts water
    2 tablespoons salt
    ½ teaspoon lemon-pepper marinade
    1 lemon, juice and rind
    4 cups Madeira wine, or enough to cover the hearts
    3 or 4 drops green food coloring for deeper color (optional)
    1 (2¾-ounce) can pâté de foie gras

To prepare the artichoke hearts, begin with the outermost leaves of the artichoke. Bend each leaf back until it snaps; pull off and discard. Continue to do this until the bottom of the leaves reaches the curve of the base. Cut off the top of the remaining leaves a full ½ inch from their base. Cut off the stem even with the base. This leaves the choke and the base with a rim. Trim base portion of leaves until only white is showing. Rub with lemon juice as you cut to prevent discoloration of artichoke. Place the artichoke hearts in seasoned boiling water as soon as possible.

Combine the water, salt, lemon-pepper marinade, lemon juice and rind in a large pan. Bring to a boil and add fresh artichoke hearts. Cook 20 minutes; drain.

Place artichoke hearts, Madeira wine, and food coloring, if desired, in a smaller saucepan. Simmer another 20 minutes or until tender. Test with fork. Take from pan and gently remove choke with small spoon.

These hearts may be prepared several days in advance and refrigerated, but reheat before serving. Place the hot artichoke hearts on a warm serving platter and spread the cold pâté de foie gras on each one. Yield: 6 servings.

Note: Canned artichoke hearts may be used, but they will not make as flavorful a dish. Do not cook these, but soak them in hot Madeira wine for 30 minutes before using.

Fresh Artichokes with Horseradish Dip

    4 fresh artichokes
    4 cloves garlic
    4 tablespoons salad oil
    4 slices lemon
    1 cup mayonnaise
    ½ cup whole milk
    1 tablespoon lemon juice
    ¼ cup horseradish
    ¼ teaspoon freshly ground black pepper

Wash artichokes thoroughly. Trim about ⅓ inch off the top, using a very sharp knife. Cut off stem end about 1 inch from base, leaving a stub. Pull off any loose leaves around the bottom. Cut off the tip of each leaf with scissors.

Drop artichokes into boiling, salted water to cover. Add garlic, salad oil, and lemon slices. Cover tightly and boil until a leaf can be pulled easily from the stalk, or the stem can be easily pierced with a fork (20 to 45 minutes). Remove carefully from water; drain, and cut off stub.

Combine mayonnaise, milk, lemon juice, horseradish, and pepper. Blend well and serve with hot or chilled artichokes. Yield: 4 servings.

Artichoke Hearts with Sauce Winifred

- 2 tablespoons finely chopped onion
- 3 tablespoons pureed or finely diced carrots
- 2 tablespoons butter or margarine
- 2 cups chicken stock
- 6 peppercorns
- 3 sprigs parsley
- 1 bay leaf
- 4 tablespoons butter or margarine
- 4 tablespoons all-purpose flour
- 1½ cups scalded milk
- ¼ teaspoon salt
- ⅛ teaspoon white pepper
- 2 cups cooked chicken or turkey, cut into chunks
- ½ (2-ounce) jar pimientos, drained and finely chopped
- 1 teaspoon dried green parsley
- 1 pound large fresh mushrooms or 2 (4-ounce) cans sliced mushrooms
- 6 fresh artichoke hearts, cooked

Sauté onion and carrots in 2 tablespoons butter, using a heavy skillet. When the onion is transparent and golden, add chicken stock, peppercorns, parsley, and bay leaf. Simmer for 30 minutes, uncovered. Strain and chill.

To complete sauce, melt 4 tablespoons butter in top of double boiler; add flour slowly and stir with wooden spoon until mixture is bubbly. Slowly add scalded milk, using a wire whisk for blending.

When sauce is the consistency of thick cream, stir in salt, pepper, and chilled broth; heat. Stir in hot chicken, pimientos, parsley, and mushrooms. Cook for 10 minutes; taste to see if more salt is needed. Serve over very hot artichoke hearts. Yield: 6 servings.

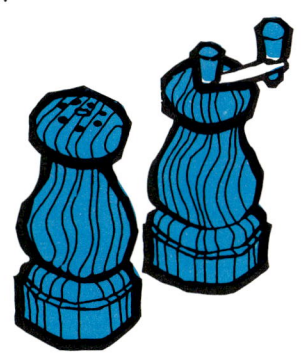

Artichoke Rollino

- ½ cup olive oil or salad oil
- 2 tablespoons vinegar
- 1 teaspoon salt
- ½ teaspoon pepper
- 1 clove garlic, minced
- 1 cup finely diced boiled potatoes
- ½ cup finely diced cooked carrots
- ½ cup cooked French peas, well drained
- ¼ cup cooked beets, well drained and finely diced
- 1 (6-ounce) can artichoke bottoms, well drained
- 1 cup mayonnaise
- 2 hard-cooked eggs, finely chopped
- 1 (2-ounce) can anchovy filets
- 1 (2-ounce) jar pimientos

Combine oil, vinegar, salt, pepper, and garlic. Combine potatoes, carrots, peas, and beets in a second bowl. Pour dressing over vegetables, mix well, and marinate for at least 30 minutes.

Drain the artichokes and pat dry. Drain marinated vegetables and mound the mixture on the artichoke bottoms. Ice each artichoke bottom with mayonnaise. Sprinkle the surface generously with finely chopped egg.

Garnish with anchovy filets and pimiento. Serve cold. Yield: 8 to 10 servings.

Asparagus Spears with Shrimp Sauce

 2 *small bunches fresh asparagus*
 ¼ *cup butter*
 ¼ *cup all-purpose flour*
 1 *teaspoon salt*
 Dash pepper
 Dash hot sauce
 2 *cups milk*
 1½ *cups cooked, peeled, and deveined shrimp*
 2 *hard-cooked eggs, sliced*
 6 *slices buttered toast*
 Pimiento
 Parsley sprigs

Break off tender asparagus spears from woody base and remove sandy scales. Wash thoroughly. Cook, covered, in boiling salted water until tender; drain. Melt butter in saucepan over low heat and blend in flour and seasonings. Add milk slowly, stirring constantly, until sauce is smooth and has thickened. Carefully fold shrimp and eggs into sauce. Allow shrimp to heat through. Place hot buttered toast slices on serving dish. Cover slices with well-drained asparagus spears. Top with shrimp sauce or pour sauce in separate dish to be served with asparagus. Garnish with pimiento and parsley sprigs. Yield: 6 servings.

Dilled Asparagus

 2 *pounds fresh asparagus, cooked, or 2 (14½-ounce) cans asparagus spears*
 ½ *cup olive oil*
 ⅓ *cup chopped dill pickles*
 ½ *cup dill pickle liquid*
 1 *clove garlic, crushed*
 Lettuce

Place drained asparagus spears in a flat casserole with a cover. Combine olive oil, pickles, pickle liquid, and garlic; pour over the asparagus. Cover and let marinate for at least 1 hour; drain. Serve on lettuce. Yield: 4 to 6 servings.

Asparagus Amandine

 2 *(16-ounce) cans asparagus spears*
 1 *(10¾-ounce) can condensed cream of mushroom soup*
 ½ *teaspoon salt*
 ¼ *teaspoon pepper*
 1 *cup shredded Cheddar cheese*
 4 *tablespoons melted margarine*
 1 *cup bread crumbs*
 ½ *cup whole almonds*

Drain asparagus, reserving ½ cup liquid. Arrange asparagus in oblong casserole. Combine soup, reserved asparagus liquid, salt, and pepper; pour over asparagus, and sprinkle with cheese. Combine margarine and bread crumbs; sprinkle over cheese. Garnish with almonds. Bake at 300° for 45 minutes. Yield: 5 to 6 servings.

Company Asparagus

 1 *(14½-ounce) can asparagus*
 1 *(11-ounce) can condensed Cheddar cheese soup*
 2 *hard-cooked eggs, chopped*
 ½ *cup toasted slivered almonds*
 1 *cup buttered bread crumbs, divided*

Combine asparagus, soup, chopped eggs, almonds, and ½ cup bread crumbs in a greased 1-quart casserole. Spread remaining ½ cup bread crumbs over mixture and bake, uncovered, at 375° for 20 minutes. Yield: 4 to 6 servings.

Asparagus with Cashew Butter

 3 *pounds fresh or 3 (10-ounce) packages frozen asparagus*
 ½ *cup butter or margarine*
 2 *tablespoons lemon juice*
 ½ *teaspoon marjoram*
 ½ *cup salted cashews, coarsely chopped*

Cook fresh asparagus in simmering salted water in large covered skillet until tender, about 18 minutes. If using frozen asparagus, cook according to package directions.

Meanwhile, melt butter in a small saucepan; add lemon juice, marjoram, and cashews. Simmer over low heat for 3 minutes. Drain asparagus and arrange on heated platter. Pour sauce over asparagus. Yield: 10 servings.

Asparagus and Fresh Mushrooms

> 2 *pounds fresh asparagus*
> ¾ *pound fresh mushrooms, sliced*
> 1 *tablespoon finely chopped onion*
> 2 *tablespoons butter or margarine*
> 3 *tablespoons all-purpose flour*
> 1 *teaspoon salt*
> ¼ *teaspoon white pepper*
> 1 *cup milk*
> ½ *cup half-and-half*
> 1 *tablespoon dry sherry*

Cook asparagus in boiling salted water just until spears are crisp-tender. Sauté mushrooms and onion in 2 tablespoons butter until tender. Sprinkle mushrooms with flour, salt, and pepper. Slowly stir in milk and half-and-half. Cook and stir until thickened. Add sherry and pour sauce over hot drained asparagus. Yield: 6 to 8 servings.

Asparagus with Parmesan

> 1 *pound fresh asparagus*
> 3 *tablespoons butter or margarine*
> 3 *tablespoons all-purpose flour*
> 1½ *cups milk*
> ¾ *teaspoon salt*
> ¼ *teaspoon pepper*
> ½ *teaspoon dry mustard*
> 2 *egg yolks, slightly beaten*
> ⅓ *cup grated Parmesan cheese*

Cook asparagus until tender; drain. Melt butter; add flour and blend well. Slowly add milk and cook until thickened and bubbling, stirring constantly. Add salt, pepper, and mustard. Add a small amount of the sauce to egg yolks; return to sauce, and stir well to blend.

Arrange drained asparagus spears in a shallow baking pan; spoon sauce over spears and sprinkle with Parmesan cheese. Broil until cheese melts and mixture is hot. Yield: 4 servings.

Asparagus with Sour Cream Sauce

> 1 *pound fresh asparagus spears*
> 3 *tablespoons salad oil*
> ¼ *cup water*
> ½ *teaspoon salt*
> ½ *cup commercial sour cream*
> 2 *tablespoons mayonnaise*
> ¼ *teaspoon salt*
> 1 *tablespoon lemon juice*

Break off tender asparagus spears from woody base and remove scales; wash carefully. Put salad oil, water, and salt in a large skillet with a tight cover. Add asparagus and cook, covered, about 5 minutes. Add more water if needed.

In a small saucepan, combine remaining ingredients; heat slowly (do not boil). Arrange asparagus spears in serving dish; pour sauce over and serve hot. Yield: 3 to 4 servings.

Asparagus Milano

> 1 *(16-ounce) can asparagus, drained*
> ½ *cup margarine, melted*
> 1 *(1⅜-ounce) envelope onion soup mix*
> 1 *cup shredded mozzarella cheese*
> 2 *tablespoons grated Parmesan cheese*

Pour asparagus into greased baking dish. Combine margarine and onion soup mix; pour over asparagus. Top with cheese. Bake at 350° for 10 minutes or until cheese melts and browns lightly. Yield: 4 servings.

Asparagus Pacifico

2 pounds fresh asparagus
Boiling salted water
1 (10¾-ounce) can condensed cream of shrimp soup
½ cup commercial sour cream
½ teaspoon tarragon
1 (4½-ounce) can shrimp
Paprika

Wash asparagus and break off each stalk as far down as it will snap easily; leave stalks whole. Cook, covered, in 1 inch of boiling salted water for 10 to 20 minutes or until stalks can be pierced easily with a fork.

While the asparagus is cooking, put soup in a saucepan and heat slowly until smooth, stirring occasionally. Stir in sour cream and tarragon, blending well; heat thoroughly. Pour over hot asparagus and garnish with shrimp and paprika. Yield: 4 servings.

Green Beans with Special Sauce

1 medium-size onion
1 tablespoon bacon bits
4 cups cut green beans
2 cups water
Salt and pepper to taste
Special Sauce

Cook onion, bacon bits, and green beans in boiling water for about 20 minutes or until beans are tender. Add salt and pepper. Drain beans and cover with Special Sauce. Yield: 6 to 8 servings.

Special Sauce:

Juice of 1 lemon
1 cup salad dressing
2 hard-cooked eggs, chopped
1 tablespoon parsley flakes
½ teaspoon celery seeds or celery salt
½ cup slivered almonds

Combine all ingredients and serve over beans. Yield: 2 cups.

*Fresh Green Beans with New Potatoes

1½ pounds fresh green beans
6 cups water
¼ pound diced salt pork or ham hock
Salt to taste
Dash sugar
1 pound small new potatoes, pared

String the beans, cut into 1½-inch pieces, and wash. Put water in a 3-quart saucepan and add diced salt pork or ham hock. Cover and cook about 20 minutes. Add beans, salt, and sugar. Cook about 20 minutes. Place pared potatoes on top of beans and continue cooking until potatoes are tender. Yield: 4 to 6 servings.

*Dilly Beans

1 pound fresh green beans
2 tablespoons butter or margarine
¼ teaspoon dillseed

Cook green beans in ½ inch boiling salted water in a covered saucepan over low heat for 15 to 30 minutes or until tender. Cook for 10 minutes more, stirring occasionally; drain. Melt butter over medium heat; add dillseed and cook until butter is browned. Toss dill butter with beans. Yield: 4 to 6 servings.

Green Beans Supreme

4 slices bacon
2 tablespoons bacon drippings
¼ cup chopped onion
1 (10¾-ounce) can condensed cream of celery soup
⅓ cup milk
1 pound green beans, cooked and drained

Fry bacon until crisp; crumble. Cook onion in bacon drippings until tender. Blend in soup, milk, and beans. Heat slowly, stirring occasionally. Place in serving dish; sprinkle bacon over top. Yield: 4 to 6 servings.

Green Beans Polonaise

  2 (10-ounce) packages frozen French-style green beans
  4 tablespoons margarine, divided
  2 tablespoons water
  2 tablespoons fine bread crumbs
  1 hard-cooked egg, finely chopped
  2 tablespoons chopped parsley

Place green beans in a saucepan with 2 tablespoons margarine and water. Bring to a boil; cover and cook until tender, 20 to 25 minutes. Meanwhile, brown bread crumbs in 2 tablespoons margarine. Combine chopped egg and chopped parsley. Place green beans in a serving dish; top with egg mixture, then bread crumbs. Yield: 7 servings.

*Grilled Green Beans

  1 (16-ounce) can green beans
  1 small onion, chopped
  2 tomatoes, sliced
  ¼ cup margarine
  3 teaspoons prepared mustard with horseradish
  1 teaspoon salt
  1 tablespoon firmly packed brown sugar
  ⅛ teaspoon pepper

Drain green beans well and place on a large square of heavy-duty aluminum foil. Arrange chopped onion and tomato slices over beans. Combine margarine, mustard, salt, sugar, and pepper until blended. Spoon over the beans and fold foil tightly; seal edges. Cook 30 to 35 minutes over medium-hot coals. Yield: 4 servings.

Savory Green Beans

  4 cups cooked fresh green beans
  1 teaspoon summer savory
  2 tablespoons finely chopped pimiento
  ⅓ cup butter or margarine
  ½ teaspoon salt
     Dash pepper

Drain cooked beans. Add remaining ingredients and heat slowly, stirring often. Yield: 6 servings.

Green Beans Mornay

  1 tablespoon butter or margarine
  1 tablespoon all-purpose flour
  ¼ teaspoon dry mustard
  ½ teaspoon salt
  1 teaspoon instant minced onion
  ⅔ cup half-and-half
  ¼ cup grated Parmesan cheese
  1 (16-ounce) can cut green beans

Melt butter in a saucepan over low heat. Blend in flour, mustard, salt, and onion. Stir in half-and-half and cook over medium heat, stirring constantly, until mixture thickens and comes to a boil. Stir in cheese and heat about 1 minute longer. Drain beans; add to sauce and heat but do not boil. Yield: 4 or 5 servings.

*Deviled Brussels Sprouts

  3 (10-ounce) packages frozen Brussels sprouts
  ½ cup butter or margarine
  2 teaspoons prepared mustard
  ¾ teaspoon salt
  1 teaspoon Worcestershire sauce
     Dash cayenne pepper

Cook Brussels sprouts according to package directions; drain. Melt butter in a saucepan; add remaining ingredients. Place the sprouts in a hot vegetable dish and pour sauce over all. Serve hot. Yield: 6 servings.

Brussels Sprouts Oriental

- 2 pounds Brussels sprouts, washed and trimmed
- 1 teaspoon soy sauce
- ½ teaspoon seasoned salt
- 1 tablespoon butter or margarine
- 1 (6-ounce) can water chestnuts, drained and sliced

Simmer Brussels sprouts, covered, in a small amount of salted water, 8 to 10 minutes or until tender; drain. Add remaining ingredients and heat. Serve hot. Yield: 6 servings.

Souffléed Broccoli

- ⅓ cup chopped onion
- 1 tablespoon salad oil
- 1 (1-pound) bunch fresh broccoli spears, cooked and drained
- 6 eggs, beaten
- ¼ cup milk
- ½ teaspoon garlic salt
- Dash pepper
- ½ cup grated Parmesan cheese

Cook onion in oil in an 8-inch skillet until tender; cover with broccoli. Combine eggs, milk, garlic salt, and pepper. Pour over broccoli. Sprinkle with cheese; cover and cook over low heat for 15 minutes. Cut into wedges; serve immediately. Yield: 6 servings.

Sicilian Broccoli

- 1 medium-size onion, thinly sliced
- 1 clove garlic, minced
- 2 tablespoons olive oil
- 1½ tablespoons all-purpose flour
- 1 cup chicken stock or chicken bouillon cube dissolved in 1 cup water
- 4 anchovies, chopped
- ½ cup sliced black olives
- ⅛ teaspoon pepper
- 2 cups shredded mozzarella or pasteurized process American cheese
- 1¾ pounds fresh broccoli, cooked

Sauté onion and garlic in olive oil; blend in flour. Add chicken stock; stir and cook until sauce begins to thicken, 5 to 6 minutes. Add anchovies, olives, pepper, and cheese. Mix well and serve over hot broccoli. Yield: 6 servings.

Broccoli-Peas Casserole

- 2 (10-ounce) packages frozen chopped broccoli, divided
- 1 (17-ounce) can green peas
- 1 (10¾-ounce) can condensed cream of mushroom soup
- 1 cup mayonnaise
- 1 teaspoon salt
- ½ teaspoon pepper
- 1 cup shredded sharp Cheddar cheese
- 1 medium-size onion, chopped
- 2 eggs, beaten
- ½ cup crushed buttery crackers

Cook broccoli according to package directions; drain. Arrange 1 package cooked broccoli in a greased 2-quart casserole. Cover with peas. Combine mushroom soup, mayonnaise, salt, pepper, cheese, onion, and eggs to make sauce. Pour half of sauce over broccoli and peas. Add remaining broccoli and top with remaining sauce. Sprinkle cracker crumbs on top. Bake at 350° for 30 minutes. Yield: 8 servings.

Broccoli with Shrimp Sauce

- 2 (10-ounce) packages broccoli spears frozen in butter sauce
- ¼ cup chopped celery
- 1 (10¾-ounce) can condensed cream of shrimp soup
- ½ cup commercial sour cream
- ½ teaspoon salt
- ¼ teaspoon pepper

Cook broccoli according to package directions. Open plastic bags and drain all butter sauce into saucepan. Sauté celery in butter sauce over high heat until all liquid is gone. Celery should be tender. Add soup; slowly stir in sour cream. Add salt and pepper. Heat well. Serve over broccoli. Yield: 6 servings.

Broccoli Surprise

¾ cup uncooked macaroni
1 (10-ounce) package frozen broccoli
1 (12-ounce) can luncheon meat, cut into bite-size pieces
¼ cup margarine, melted
1 cup shredded Cheddar cheese
1 cup milk
2½ tablespoons commercial sour cream

Cook and drain macaroni. Cook broccoli according to package directions; drain. Brown luncheon meat in melted margarine until brown and crisp. Combine macaroni, broccoli, luncheon meat, and cheese in casserole; pour in milk. Gently stir in sour cream. Bake at 350° until bubbly, about 20 minutes. Serve at once. Yield: 6 servings.

Fresh Broccoli with Sour Cream Dressing

1 pound broccoli
1 cup commercial sour cream
2 tablespoons firmly packed brown sugar
2 tablespoons lemon juice
¼ teaspoon salt
½ teaspoon prepared mustard

Wash broccoli and trim off tip ends of stems. If any stems are more than 1 inch in diameter, make lengthwise slices through them almost to the flowerets. Drop prepared broccoli into a small amount of boiling, salted water; cover and cook about 10 to 15 minutes or until just tender.

Combine remaining ingredients for dressing and mix well. Carefully remove broccoli from boiling water, place in serving dish, and cover with dressing. Yield: 4 servings.

Company Cabbage

6 cups shredded cabbage
1 cup commercial sour cream
½ teaspoon caraway or dillseed
Salt and pepper to taste

Cook cabbage in a small amount of boiling salted water in a covered pan just until tender, about 4 minutes; drain well. Combine sour cream, caraway or dillseed, salt, and pepper. Add to cabbage, tossing to mix. Heat well. Yield: 4 servings.

Scalloped Cabbage and Apples

2 quarts shredded cabbage
1 quart tart sliced apples
2 teaspoons salt
2 to 4 tablespoons melted butter or margarine
4 tablespoons sugar
1 cup buttered bread crumbs

Place alternate layers of cabbage and apples in a greased 2-quart baking dish. Season each layer with salt and butter and sprinkle sugar on the apples. Over the last layer, spread buttered bread crumbs. Cover and bake at 350° for 45 minutes or until cabbage and apples are tender. Near the end of cooking time, remove cover so crumbs can brown. Serve from baking dish. Yield: 6 servings.

* Stuffed Cabbage Leaves

12 large cabbage leaves
1 cup lean ground beef
2 cups ½-inch bread cubes
1½ teaspoons salt
¼ teaspoon pepper
¼ teaspoon garlic salt
½ cup chopped onion
2 eggs
1 (10¾-ounce) can condensed tomato soup

Parboil cabbage leaves for 5 minutes. Handle carefully so that leaves are not broken.

Combine beef, bread cubes, salt, pepper, garlic salt, onion, and eggs. Form meat mixture into 12 oblong patties. Place a meat patty on each of the cabbage leaves. Roll patty in cabbage leaf and fasten with toothpicks. Place stuffed cabbage leaves in skillet. Pour undiluted soup over cabbage rolls. Cover and cook over low heat for 45 minutes. Yield: 6 servings.

Cabbage Supreme

- 1 medium-size head cabbage
- 4 tablespoons butter or margarine
- 4 tablespoons all-purpose flour
- ½ teaspoon salt
- ¼ teaspoon pepper
- 2 cups milk
- ½ green pepper, chopped
- ½ medium-size onion, chopped
- ⅔ cup shredded cheese
- ½ cup mayonnaise
- 3 tablespoons chili sauce

Cut cabbage into small wedges and cook in boiling salted water until tender, about 15 minutes. Drain cabbage and place in a 13- x 9- x 2-inch pan.

To prepare white sauce, melt butter in saucepan. Blend in flour, salt, and pepper. Cook over low heat, stirring until mixture is smooth and bubbly. Stir in milk and boil for 1 minute, stirring constantly. Spread white sauce over cabbage in baking dish. Bake at 375° for 20 minutes.

To prepare topping, combine green pepper, onion, cheese, mayonnaise, and chili sauce. Spread over top of casserole and bake at 400° for an additional 20 minutes. Yield: 8 to 10 servings.

*Baked Cream Cabbage

- 1 medium-size head cabbage
- ½ cup boiling salted water
- 3 tablespoons butter or margarine
- 3 tablespoons all-purpose flour
- ½ teaspoon salt
- 1½ cups milk
- ¼ cup bread crumbs

Shred cabbage finely and cook 9 minutes in boiling salted water. Remove cabbage, drain well, and place in a buttered 1½-quart casserole. Melt butter in saucepan; stir in flour and salt until smooth. Add milk gradually. Continue stirring until mixture thickens. Pour sauce over cabbage and sprinkle bread crumbs over top. Bake at 325° about 15 minutes or until crumbs are browned. Yield: 6 servings.

Cabbage Rolls

- 1 pound lean lamb or beef
- 1 cup regular rice, uncooked
- ¼ cup butter
- Salt and pepper to taste
- 1 medium-size head cabbage
- 8 cloves garlic, halved
- Juice of 2 lemons

Grind meat, using a coarse blade, mixing fat with lean. Combine meat, rice, butter, salt, and pepper to make stuffing. Mix thoroughly.

Cut out the core of the cabbage and place the head in a pan of boiling water to loosen the leaves. Cut out the rib of the cabbage leaves and cut each leaf in two. Line a pan with all of the ribs.

Spread about 1 tablespoon of meat filling on the edge of each leaf and roll up. Stack the rolls in layers over the ribs.

Sprinkle garlic cloves over cabbage rolls. Add enough water to just cover rolls. Bring to a boil and simmer until stuffing is done. When the rolls are almost done, add lemon juice and cook about 5 minutes longer. Yield: about 3 dozen cabbage rolls.

Cabbage-Noodle Bake

- 5 slices bacon
- 1 tablespoon sugar
- 1 teaspoon salt
- 1 medium-size head cabbage, chopped
- 1 (5-ounce) package noodles, cooked and drained
- 1 cup commercial sour cream
- Paprika

Fry bacon until crisp; remove from pan, drain, crumble, and set aside. Stir sugar and salt into drippings in pan. Add cabbage and stir until coated. Cover and cook over medium heat for about 10 minutes. Combine cabbage, noodles, and bacon in a 1½-quart casserole. Cover and bake at 325° for 30 minutes. Spoon sour cream into mixture, sprinkle with paprika, and bake an additional 15 minutes. Yield: 6 servings.

*Cabbage Chop Suey

   3 *cups shredded cabbage*
   1 *large sweet onion, thinly sliced*
   1 *large green pepper, thinly sliced*
   1 *cup sliced celery*
 ½ *teaspoon salt*
 ¼ *cup water*
   2 *tablespoons butter or margarine*

Combine cabbage, onion, green pepper, celery, and salt; toss lightly. Place in skillet with water and butter; cover and let steam 10 to 12 minutes, stirring lightly twice during the cooking period. Mixture will be slightly crisp and still green. Yield: 6 to 8 servings.

Cabbage with Caraway Seed Butter

   1 *medium-size head cabbage*
 ½ *teaspoon salt*
 ¾ *teaspoon whole marjoram leaves, crushed*
   3 *tablespoons butter or margarine*
   1 *teaspoon caraway seeds*

Shred cabbage. Place in saucepan with ½ inch boiling water and salt. Cover and cook quickly until tender, lifting lid 3 or 4 times to allow steam to escape. Drain; add marjoram, butter, and caraway seeds. Yield: 6 servings.

*Tex-Mex Cabbage

   1 *head cabbage*
   1 *tablespoon sugar*
   2 *tablespoons butter or margarine*
   1 *onion, sliced*
   1 *green pepper, sliced*
   2 *cups canned tomatoes, drained*
      Salt and pepper to taste
 ¾ *cup shredded Cheddar cheese*

Cut cabbage into 6 slices and cook in boiling salted water for about 10 minutes, or until tender-crisp. Place in a greased 2-quart casserole.

Sauté sugar, butter, onion, and green pepper. Add tomatoes and salt and pepper. Pour mixture over cabbage and sprinkle with cheese. Bake at 350° until heated through. Yield: 8 servings.

Marinated Carrots

   5 *cups sliced carrots*
   1 *medium-size sweet onion*
   1 *small green pepper*
   1 *(10 ¾-ounce) can condensed tomato soup*
 ½ *cup salad oil*
   1 *cup sugar*
 ¾ *cup vinegar*
   1 *teaspoon prepared mustard*
   1 *teaspoon Worcestershire sauce*
   1 *teaspoon salt*
   1 *teaspoon pepper*

Cook carrots; drain and cool. Cut onion and green pepper in round slices and mix with cooled carrots. Combine remaining ingredients and pour over vegetables. Cover and marinate for 12 hours or more. Drain to serve. This will keep for two weeks in the refrigerator. Yield: 8 to 10 servings.

*Lemon-Glazed Carrots

      Carrots (enough for 3 servings)
      Dash salt
1½ *tablespoons butter or margarine*
   2 *tablespoons firmly packed brown sugar*
      Juice of 1 lemon

Scrape carrots and cut into thin, short pieces. Place in saucepan, add salt, and cover with boiling water (about 1½ cups). Cover pan and simmer until carrots are just tender. Do not overcook.

While carrots cook, melt butter in small saucepan over low heat; blend in sugar; add lemon juice.

When carrots are done, drain thoroughly, pour sauce over them, return to low heat, and reheat, uncovered, until thoroughly glazed, stirring constantly. Serve in heated bowl. Yield: 3 servings.

Glazed Carrots

- 2 tablespoons chopped onion
- 1 tablespoon chopped parsley
- 3 tablespoons butter or margarine
- 8 medium-size carrots, cut into 1-inch pieces
- 1 (10½-ounce) can condensed consommé
- ¼ teaspoon ground nutmeg
- ¼ teaspoon sugar
- Hot sauce to taste

Sauté onion and parsley in butter for about 5 minutes. Add carrots, consommé, nutmeg, sugar, and hot sauce. Cover and cook about 15 minutes. Uncover and cook additional 15 minutes or until carrots are tender and sauce is slightly thickened. Yield: about 4 servings.

Baked Pineapple and Carrots

- 1 cup sliced carrots
- 1 cup canned crushed pineapple, drained, liquid reserved
- 1 teaspoon cornstarch
- 1 tablespoon water
- 1 teaspoon butter or margarine

Cook carrots, tightly covered, in reserved pineapple liquid. If necessary, add water to make ¼ cup liquid. When carrots are tender, remove from liquid. Make a paste of the cornstarch and water to thicken liquid; return carrots to liquid and add crushed pineapple and butter. Place in a 1-quart baking dish and bake at 350° for 30 minutes. Yield: 4 to 6 servings.

Carrots with Celery Seed Sauce

- 4 medium-size carrots
- ¼ cup water
- 2 tablespoons butter or margarine
- 1 teaspoon all-purpose flour
- ½ teaspoon celery seeds
- ¼ teaspoon salt

Scrape carrots and cut into ⅛-inch crosswise slices. Cook carrots with water in a tightly covered 2-quart saucepan over low heat for 12 to 15 minutes. Brown butter in a small skillet. Stir in flour, liquid from the carrots, celery seeds, and salt. Cook over low heat for 1 minute, stirring constantly. Mix sauce with carrots. Yield: 2 servings.

Glazed Carrots and Onions

- 8 small onions
- 4 carrots
- 1 teaspoon salt
- ¼ teaspoon ground nutmeg
- 2 tablespoons butter
- 2 tablespoons sugar
- 2 tablespoons water

Peel onions, making deep cross in stem end. Scrape carrots and cut into quarters. Place in a 10- x 16-inch cooking bag with salt, nutmeg, butter, sugar, and water. Close bag and make six ½-inch slits in top. Cook at 300° to 325° for 1½ hours. Yield: 8 servings.

Crisp Candied Carrots

- 1½ cups cooked shredded carrots, drained
- ½ cup sliced water chestnuts
- ¼ cup butter or margarine
- ¼ cup powdered sugar

Combine carrots and water chestnuts in a 1-quart casserole. Dot with butter and sprinkle with sugar. Bake, uncovered, at 350° for 30 minutes or until casserole is hot and bubbly. Yield: 4 to 6 servings.

Sweet and Sour Carrots

8 medium-size carrots, cut into 3-x ½-inch strips
2 tablespoons butter or margarine
½ cup apple cider vinegar
¾ cup sugar

Cover carrot strips with ½ inch boiling salted water and cook for about 15 minutes or until tender. Drain; add butter, vinegar, and sugar and cook over low heat until carrots are transparent. Serve hot. Yield: 6 to 8 servings.

Hugo's Carrots

8 to 10 baby carrots
1 tablespoon butter
2 teaspoons sugar
3 to 4 tablespoons white wine
Juice of 1 orange
Salt to taste

Cook carrots in boiling water until tender; drain. Melt butter in skillet; add sugar and let brown slightly. Add white wine, orange juice, and salt. Cook carrots in this mixture until they are glazed. Yield: 2 servings.

Cauliflower Oriental

1 medium-size head cauliflower
1 meduim-size onion, finely chopped
½ cup diced celery
3 sprigs parsley, finely chopped
1 tablespoon butter or margarine
1 beef or chicken bouillon cube
1 cup hot water
1 tablespoon cornstarch
1 tablespoon soy sauce
Dash pepper

Wash cauliflower and remove outer green stalks. Cook, covered, in a small amount of boiling, salted water until just tender, about 20 minutes.

Sauté onion, celery, and parsley in butter until tender. Dissolve bouillon cube in hot water and blend in cornstarch; add soy sauce and pepper. Add to onion and celery mixture and cook over low heat, stirring constantly, until mixture thickens. Place hot cooked cauliflower in a serving dish and pour hot sauce over all. Yield: 4 servings.

* Parmesan Cauliflower

1 head cauliflower
About 2 tablespoons butter
Dash grated Parmesan cheese

Cook cauliflower in boiling water about 15 minutes. Remove from water and drain. Heat butter until light brown. Divide cauliflower into flowerets, top with Parmesan cheese and browned butter; serve hot. Yield: 3 to 4 servings.

Batter-Fried Cauliflower

1 (10-ounce) package frozen cauliflower
2 eggs, beaten
½ cup all-purpose flour
Salt and pepper to taste
¼ cup salad oil

Cook cauliflower according to package directions; drain well. Dip cauliflower in egg, then in flour seasoned with salt and pepper, then in egg again. Fry in hot oil until golden brown. Yield: 4 to 6 servings.

* Spanish Eggplant

2 cups cubed eggplant
½ cup chopped onion
½ cup chopped celery
¼ cup chopped green pepper
¼ cup butter or margarine
½ teaspoon salt
¼ teaspoon pepper
1 cup cubed fresh tomatoes

Soak eggplant in salted water for 10 minutes. Sauté onion, celery, and green pepper in butter; add salt, pepper, tomatoes, and well-drained eggplant. Cook, covered, for 20 to 25 minutes over medium heat. Yield: 6 servings.

Eggplant Parmesan

- 2 tablespoons tomato paste
- 4 cups diced fresh tomatoes
- ½ cup olive or salad oil, divided
- 1 teaspoon sugar
- 1¾ teaspoons salt
- ¼ teaspoon freshly ground black pepper
- 1 clove garlic, quartered
- 1 medium-size eggplant
- 2 cups soft bread crumbs
- 2 tablespoons chopped fresh parsley
- ½ cup grated Parmesan cheese
- ¼ pound mozzarella cheese, thinly sliced

Combine tomato paste, tomatoes, 2 tablespoons oil, sugar, salt, pepper, and garlic. Simmer 15 minutes or until thickened; set aside.

Pare eggplant and cut into ½-inch slices. Heat remaining oil in a large skillet. Add a few slices of eggplant at a time and brown on both sides. Place fried eggplant in a 9- x 5- x 3-inch baking dish. Combine bread crumbs, parsley, and Parmesan cheese; sprinkle half the mixture over eggplant. Cover with tomato sauce. Top with remaining crumb-cheese mixture, and place mozzarella cheese slices over top. Bake at 350° for 30 minutes or until cheese is melted. Serve hot. Yield: 8 servings.

Eggplant à la Caribe

- 1 medium-size eggplant, peeled and cut into small pieces
- 2 large onions, sliced
- 1 tablespoon salad oil
- 1½ cloves garlic, diced
- 7 peppercorns, ground
- 1 tablespoon vinegar
- 1 teaspoon salt
- ½ teaspoon seasoned salt
- ½ teaspoon seasoned pepper
- 4 tablespoons water

Sauté eggplant and onion in salad oil for about 5 minutes. Add remaining ingredients, cover saucepan, and cook for 15 minutes or until mixture is very soft. Chill and serve as a dip. Yield: about 1½ cups.

Eggplant Scallop

- 2 large onions, chopped
- 1 large eggplant, pared and cut into ½-inch cubes
- 4 tablespoons salad oil
- 1 (1-pound) can whole kernel corn, drained
- ½ cup shredded Cheddar cheese
- ¼ cup chopped ripe olives
- 3 tomatoes, peeled and cubed
- 2 eggs, beaten
- 1½ teaspoons salt
- ½ teaspoon basil
- Pepper to taste

Sauté onions and eggplant cubes in oil, half at a time, just until golden. Combine remaining ingredients and stir into onion and eggplant mixture. Spoon into a 10-cup baking dish. Cover and bake at 350° for 1 hour. Yield: 8 servings.

Eggplant Patrice

- 1 small eggplant
- 4 medium-size tomatoes, sliced
- 2 medium-size green peppers, chopped
- 2 medium-size onions, chopped
- ½ teaspoon salt
- ¼ teaspoon pepper
- ¼ teaspoon garlic salt
- Dash Ac'cent
- ¾ pound sharp Cheddar cheese, sliced ⅛ inch thick

Slice unpeeled eggplant about ¼ inch thick. Parboil until partially tender. Place a layer of eggplant slices in a 13- x 9- x 2-inch pan. Add a layer of sliced tomatoes. Fill spaces with a mixture of chopped pepper and chopped onion. Sprinkle with salt, pepper, garlic salt, and Ac'cent. Add a layer of cheese. Repeat layers until casserole is filled, ending with a layer of cheese.

Cover and bake at 400° until mixture is steaming. Remove cover; reduce heat to 350° and bake about 30 to 45 minutes or until eggplant is tender and sauce is thick and golden brown. Yield: 6 servings.

Stuffed Eggplant with Shrimp and Crabmeat

 2 *medium-size eggplant*
 1 *pound fresh river shrimp (small)*
 1 *large onion, finely chopped*
 1 *tablespoon butter*
 1 *pound lump crabmeat*
1½ *cups dry bread crumbs, divided*
 2 *eggs, well beaten*
¼ *teaspoon Ac'cent*
 1 *teaspoon crumbled dry oregano*
 2 *tablespoons chopped parsley*
½ *teaspoon salt*
¼ *teaspoon white pepper*
  Paprika
 4 *tablespoons melted butter*

Parboil eggplant until tender. Remove from water and let cool. Partially cook shrimp until pink; drain, and reserve liquid. Sauté onion in butter until tender. Set aside.

Cut cooked eggplant in half, lengthwise, and scoop out pulp. Put pulp in a large mixing bowl; add onion, cooked shrimp, crabmeat, 1 cup bread crumbs, beaten eggs, Ac'cent, oregano, parsley, salt, and white pepper. Mix well and add liquid from shrimp if needed. Fill eggplant shells with mixture; arrange in a shallow baking dish, sprinkle with bread crumbs, then sprinkle lightly with paprika and top with melted butter. Bake at 350° for 35 to 45 minutes or until topping is browned. Yield: 4 servings.

Baked Eggplant with Shrimp

 1 *large (or 2 small) eggplant*
 1 *slice bread, crust removed*
 1 *egg, well beaten*
½ *teaspoon salt*
⅛ *teaspoon pepper*
 1 *tablespoon shortening*
 1 *small onion, chopped*
 1 *stalk celery, chopped*
¼ *medium-size green pepper, chopped*
½ *pound raw shrimp, peeled, deveined, and cut into pieces*

Cut eggplant lengthwise; scrape out pulp and cut into pieces. Parboil until tender; drain, mash, and combine with slice of bread which has been wet with water and squeezed until no water remains. Add beaten egg, salt, and pepper. Melt shortening; add onion, celery, green pepper, and chopped shrimp. Remove from pan when cooked but not browned. Add to eggplant mixture and mix well. Pack this mixture into eggplant shells; bake in a small pan at 375° for 20 minutes. Yield: 2 to 4 servings.

*Italian Eggplant

 2 *cups cooked noodles*
 2 *cups chopped fresh tomatoes*
 1 *cup thinly sliced green peppers*
¼ *cup all-purpose flour*
  Salt and pepper to taste
 1 *medium-size eggplant, sliced and chopped*
½ *cup beef broth or bouillon*
½ *cup shredded sharp Cheddar cheese*
 2 *tablespoons butter or margarine*
½ *cup cracker crumbs*

Layer noodles, tomatoes, and green peppers in a greased 2-quart casserole. Sprinkle flour, salt, and pepper on each layer. Cover with chopped, sliced eggplant. Pour beef broth over mixture and sprinkle top with shredded cheese. Dot with butter and top with cracker crumbs. Bake at 300° about 1 hour. Yield: 6 servings.

*Panfried Eggplant

 1 *medium-size eggplant*
 1 *egg, beaten*
 2 *tablespoons milk*
  All-purpose flour or fine dry bread crumbs
  Salt and pepper to taste
  Salad oil

Pare eggplant and cut into ½-inch slices. Combine egg and milk. Dip eggplant slices in flour or bread crumbs, then in egg mixture; dip again in flour or bread crumbs and season with salt and pepper. Fry slowly in a small amount of hot oil until browned on one side and slightly transparent. Turn and brown on other side. Serve hot. Yield: 4 servings.

Eggplant Stuffed with Oysters

- 1 (2-pound) eggplant
- ¼ cup minced onion
- 1 clove garlic, minced
- 2 tablespoons minced celery
- ½ cup butter or margarine
- 1 pint oysters, drained and chopped
- ¼ cup soft bread crumbs
- ¼ cup minced parsley
- ½ teaspoon thyme

Cut eggplant in half lengthwise; scoop out center, leaving shell about ½ inch thick. Chop eggplant that was scooped from center. Sauté chopped eggplant, onion, garlic, and celery in butter until onion is golden. Combine oysters and remaining ingredients and add to hot eggplant mixture. Spoon into eggplant shells and place in a greased 2-quart baking dish. Cover and bake at 375° for 30 minutes. Yield: 6 servings.

Eggplant Caviar

- 1 large eggplant
- ½ cup olive oil
- 1 teaspoon salt
- 2 tablespoons grated onion
- Dark pumpernickel bread
- Lettuce
- Tomato and cucumber slices

Choose a firm, smooth, shiny eggplant. Broil under open flame or over flame or top burner, turning so all sides are broiled and eggplant is tender and skin is well charred; let cool.

Dip fingers in cold water; peel the eggplant until pulp is very clean. Do not leave black spots as it darkens the eggplant.

Place in wooden bowl; chop with stainless steel chopper (other metals will blacken eggplant). Chop, adding oil slowly until a firm paste is obtained; add salt. Chill. Just before serving, add grated onion. Serve on dark pumpernickel bread as an appetizer. Garnish with lettuce and sliced tomatoes and cucumbers. Yield: about 1½ cups.

Scalloped Eggplant

- 1 large eggplant, peeled and chopped
- 1 tablespoon minced onion
- 2 medium-size tomatoes, cut into cubes
- ¼ cup chopped celery
- Salt and pepper to taste
- ¼ cup butter or margarine
- 1 egg, slightly beaten
- ½ cup milk
- ½ cup cracker crumbs
- 1 cup shredded sharp Cheddar cheese

Cook eggplant in boiling salted water about 8 minutes; drain. Combine onion, tomatoes, and celery. Place a layer of eggplant in a greased 1-quart casserole. Add a layer of uncooked vegetables. Sprinkle each layer with salt and pepper. Dot with butter. Combine egg and milk and pour over vegetables. Cover with cracker crumbs and sprinkle top with shredded cheese. Bake at 350° for 30 minutes or until well browned. Yield: 6 servings.

* Barbecued Corn

- 12 ears corn
- 1 cup butter or margarine
- 6 tablespoons barbecue sauce
- ½ teaspoon salt
- Dash hot sauce
- ¼ to ½ teaspoon pepper

Remove husks and silks from corn. Place each ear on heavy-duty aluminum foil (allow enough foil for sealing). Melt butter; add barbecue sauce, salt, hot sauce, and pepper. Brush sauce generously over each ear of corn. Seal foil firmly and place on grill over hot coals. Cook about 30 minutes, turning packets often. Yield: 12 servings.

Blue Ribbon Corn Rarebit

1½ cups grated fresh corn or canned corn
3 tablespoons butter or margarine
3 tablespoons all-purpose flour
1 teaspoon salt
⅛ teaspoon pepper
¼ teaspoon dry mustard
1 cup milk
¾ cup shredded sharp Cheddar cheese
8 slices toast
12 slices bacon, diced and fried crisp

To prepare grated corn, cut off cob about one-half the depth of kernel. Scrape cob to remove the remaining corn (not any of the cob).

Melt butter in a skillet; blend in flour and seasonings. Add milk and corn. Cook, stirring constantly, until thickened. Stir in cheese and heat only until cheese is melted. Spread over toast and sprinkle with crisp bacon pieces. Yield: 8 servings.

Fresh Corn Rarebit with Bacon

2 ears fresh corn
3 tablespoons bacon drippings
3 tablespoons all-purpose flour
Salt to taste
¼ teaspoon dry mustard
⅛ teaspoon freshly ground black pepper
1 cup half-and-half
½ cup shredded sharp Cheddar cheese
6 slices toast
12 slices crisp bacon

Remove husks and silks from corn. Split kernels lengthwise with a sharp knife. Cut a thin layer of corn from the cob; repeat, cutting two more layers. Scrape cob with bowl or a tablespoon to extract all the milk. Measure; there should be 1½ cups of corn.

Pour bacon drippings into a saucepan. Blend in flour, salt, mustard, and pepper. Add cream and corn. Stir and cook for 4 minutes or until medium thick. Add cheese. Heat only to melt cheese. Serve on toast topped with crisp bacon. Yield: 6 servings.

Southwestern Corn Scallop

2 eggs, slightly beaten
1 (17-ounce) can cream-style corn
¾ cup milk
½ cup coarsely crushed crackers
1 cup shredded sharp Cheddar cheese
1 tablespoon chopped, canned green chili peppers
1 teaspoon sugar
1 teaspoon salt
⅛ teaspoon pepper

Combine all ingredients and place in a greased 1-quart casserole. Bake at 350° for 60 minutes. Yield: 8 servings.

Corn Fritters

1½ cups all-purpose flour
1½ teaspoons baking powder
¾ teaspoon salt
⅔ cup milk
1 egg, beaten
1½ cups fresh corn cut from cob
Cooking oil

Combine flour, baking powder, and salt. Blend milk and egg; add gradually to dry ingredients. Stir in corn; mix well. Drop by tablespoonfuls into deep hot oil; cook from 2 to 5 minutes or until fritters are browned. Yield: 4 to 6 servings.

*Corn Custard for Two

1 egg
½ cup milk
1 cup cream-style corn
¼ teaspoon salt
⅛ teaspoon pepper
¼ teaspoon Worcestershire sauce
Buttered bread crumbs

Combine egg and milk; beat slightly. Stir in corn. Add salt, pepper, and Worcestershire sauce. Pour into a greased 2- or 3-cup casserole. Sprinkle top with buttered bread crumbs. Bake at 350° for 35 to 40 minutes or until custard is set and bread crumbs are browned. Yield: 2 servings.

Corn and Asparagus with Sour Cream

- 1 (10-ounce) package frozen corn
- 1 (10-ounce) package frozen asparagus spears
- 1 cup commercial sour cream
- ¼ cup crumbled blue cheese
- 1 tablespoon chopped onion
- 1 teaspoon white vinegar
- 1 teaspoon salt
- 1 tablespoon butter or margarine

Cook corn and asparagus separately in unsalted water according to package directions. Meanwhile, blend sour cream, cheese, onion, vinegar, and salt in a heavy 1½-quart saucepan; stir over low heat until hot. Drain vegetables thoroughly; arrange on warm platter. Dot with butter; pour hot sauce over vegetables. Serve immediately. Yield: 4 to 6 servings.

Foil-Baked Corn on the Cob with Herb Butter

- 12 ears of corn
- Salt and pepper to taste
- ½ cup butter or margarine
- ½ teaspoon rosemary
- ½ teaspoon marjoram

Remove husks and silks from corn. Combine salt and pepper, butter, rosemary, and marjoram to make the herb butter. Spread the butter over the corn. Wrap tightly in foil and bake at 450° for about 25 minutes or until done. Turn several times. Yield: 12 servings.

*Corn on the Grill

Remove dry outer shucks from corn. Remove silks, but do not cut ends of shuck from corn. Soak about 2 hours in water. Wrap in foil and place on grill. Turn about every 15 minutes and cook about 1½ hours over hot coals.

*Elegant Scalloped Corn

- 1 (17-ounce) can cream-style corn
- 1 cup cracker crumbs
- ½ cup diced celery
- ¼ cup diced onion
- ¾ cup pasteurized process American cheese, cut into small pieces
- 1 teaspoon salt
- 2 eggs, well beaten
- 2 tablespoons melted butter or margarine
- 1 cup milk
- Parsley
- ¼ teaspoon paprika

Combine corn, cracker crumbs, celery, onion, cheese, salt, eggs, melted butter, and milk. Pour into a greased 2-quart casserole and bake at 350° for 50 minutes. Garnish with parsley; sprinkle paprika on top. Yield: 8 servings.

Top Hat Cheese and Corn Soufflé

- ¼ cup butter or margarine
- ¼ cup all-purpose flour
- 2 cups yellow cream-style corn
- ⅓ cup milk
- ¼ teaspoon salt
- ⅛ teaspoon garlic salt
- ½ teaspoon Worcestershire sauce
- 1½ cups shredded Cheddar cheese
- ½ cup shredded provolone cheese
- 5 large egg yolks, slightly beaten
- 5 large egg whites, stiffly beaten

Melt butter in a saucepan and blend in flour until smooth. Add corn, milk, salt, garlic salt, and Worcestershire sauce; cook, stirring constantly, until thickened. Add cheeses and stir until melted. Blend egg yolks into sauce. Cool slightly. Gently stir one-fourth of egg whites into cheese sauce. Carefully fold remaining egg whites into sauce until just blended. Pour into ungreased 2-quart casserole and bake at 350° for 45 to 50 minutes. Serve immediately. Yield: 4 to 6 servings.

*Fresh Corn Fritters

    ¼ cup all-purpose flour
    1 teaspoon salt
    ½ teaspoon baking powder
    2 egg yolks
  1½ cups fresh corn cut from cob
    ¼ teaspoon pepper
    1 tablespoon salad oil
    2 egg whites
        Shortening

Combine flour, salt, and baking powder. Beat egg yolks in a medium-size bowl; stir in corn, pepper, and flour mixture. Blend in salad oil, beat egg whites until they stand in soft peaks; fold into mixture. Drop by tablespoonfuls into skillet with 1 inch of hot shortening. Cook until golden brown, turning once. Yield: 1½ dozen.

Fried Cucumbers

    1 teaspoon salt
    1 teaspoon pepper
    ½ cup all-purpose flour
    2 cucumbers, peeled and sliced
    ½ cup chopped onion
    1 cup shortening

Salt, pepper, and flour the cucumber slices. Fry with chopped onion in shortening until browned. Yield: 4 servings.

Cucumbers in Sour Cream

    1 cup commercial sour cream
    2 tablespoons cider vinegar
    ½ teaspoon salt
    ½ teaspoon ground dill or dillseed
    2 tablespoons chopped onion
        Paprika
    2 medium-size cucumbers

Combine all ingredients except cucumbers in a quart container; mix well. Peel cucumbers, slice thin, and add to sour cream mixture. Let sit in refrigerator 3 or 4 hours before serving. Yield: 4 to 6 servings.

Cucumbers in Sour Cream with Fresh Dill

    2 (8-inch) cucumbers
    1 cup thinly sliced onion rings
    ¼ cup commercial sour cream
    1 tablespoon cider vinegar
    1 tablespoon water
    ½ teaspoon salt
    ¼ teaspoon ground white pepper
    2 tablespoons finely chopped fresh dill
    2 hard-cooked eggs, sliced

Wash cucumbers, wipe dry, and score down the sides with a fork. Slice thin and combine with onion rings, sour cream, cider vinegar, water, salt, ground white pepper, and fresh dill. Toss lightly. Turn into a serving bowl. Garnish with hard-cooked egg slices. Yield: 6 servings.

Savory Baked Beans

    1 (28-ounce) can pork and beans
    ⅓ cup catsup
    2 tablespoons firmly packed brown sugar
    1 teaspoon prepared mustard
    ½ to 1 cup diced Monterey Jack cheese
    2 strips bacon, diced

Combine beans, catsup, brown sugar, mustard, and diced cheese in a 1½-quart casserole. Scatter diced bacon over top; bake at 350° about 30 minutes or until bubbly hot. Yield: 4 servings.

Dixie Lima Beans

    2 (10-ounce) packages frozen lima beans
    1 cup diced celery
    4 slices bacon
    2 tablespoons finely chopped onion
    1 tablespoon diced pimiento

Cook lima beans with celery according to package directions; drain. Fry bacon; reserve 3 tablespoons bacon drippings. Sauté onion in drippings; mix with hot lima beans. Add pimiento and top with crumbled bacon. Yield: 6 servings.

*Grandma's Baked Beans

    1 *pound (2 cups) dried peas or navy beans*
    2 *quarts water*
    1 *chopped onion*
  ¼ *pound salt pork*
  ¾ *cup light molasses*
    1 *teaspoon salt*
    1 *teaspoon dry mustard*

Rinse beans in cold water; drain. Place in a large saucepan and add 2 quarts water. Bring to a boil and boil for 2 minutes. Remove from heat, cover loosely, and let stand for 1 hour. (This takes the place of soaking.)

Return to heat and bring to a boil; cover and simmer gently over low heat for 1 hour or until beans are tender. Drain beans and reserve liquid.

Turn beans into a 2½-quart casserole; add onion and mix lightly. Cut through surface of salt pork every ½ inch, making cuts about 1 inch deep. Bury pork in beans. Mix 2 cups reserved bean liquid with molasses, salt, and dry mustard; pour over beans. Cover and bake at 300° for 5 to 6 hours.

Check beans about once an hour and add additional bean liquid or water if the beans become dry. At the beginning of the cooking, the beans should be covered with liquid; at the end of the cooking, the beans should be very moist and coated with syrup liquid. Yield: 8 servings.

Southern Dried Lima Beans

    1 *pound large dried lima beans*
  ¼ *to ½ pound cubed ham, chopped bacon, or salt pork*
    1 *(13-ounce) can evaporated milk*
      Salt and pepper to taste

Wash beans, place in a saucepan, and cover with cold water. Add ham and cook until beans are well done and most of the water has been absorbed. Add evaporated milk and heat thoroughly, but do not boil or the milk will curdle. Remove from heat and add seasonings. Yield: 6 to 8 servings.

Calico Baked Beans

    1 *(16-ounce) can pork and beans*
  ¼ *cup chopped green pepper*
    1 *cup sliced unpeeled cucumber*
  ¼ *cup sliced green onion*
    2 *tablespoons chopped pimiento*
    1 *teaspoon crushed garlic*
    1 *teaspoon dried dill*
    1 *tablespoon prepared mustard*
    1 *tablespoon firmly packed brown sugar*
    2 *strips bacon, diced*

Combine all ingredients except bacon in a 1½-quart casserole. Place bacon over beans and bake at 350° for 30 to 40 minutes, or until bubbly and brown. Yield: 6 servings.

Refried Beans (Frijoles Refritos)

    2 *cups cooked pinto beans*
  ½ *cup bacon drippings*
  ¼ *pound sharp Cheddar cheese, shredded (optional)*
  ¼ *cup finely chopped green onions and tops*

Mash beans, or put through a food mill. Melt bacon drippings in heavy skillet; add beans and cook and stir until beans have turned dark and are crisp and brown around the edges.

Turn heat to low, spread beans over bottom of skillet, and add shredded cheese, if desired. Stir gently until cheese melts. Serve with chopped green onion. Yield: 6 to 8 servings.

Beef-Baked Beans

    1 *pound ground beef*
  ½ *cup finely chopped onion*
    1 *tablespoon shortening*
  ½ *teaspoon salt*
  ¼ *teaspoon pepper*
    2 *tablespoons vinegar*
    2 *tablespoons sugar*
    1 *(16-ounce) can pork and beans*
  ½ *cup catsup*
  ½ *teaspoon hot sauce*

Cook ground beef and onion in shortening in a heavy skillet. Cook very slowly until the meat has been thoroughly cooked. Drain off accumulation of oil. Add remaining ingredients and mix well. Spoon and bake at 350° for 30 minutes. Yield: 6 servings.

Baked Beans with Cheese Swirls

   2 (16-ounce) cans pork and beans, divided
   1 small onion, minced
  ⅓ cup finely chopped celery
  ⅓ cup milk
   1 cup commercial biscuit mix
  ⅔ cup shredded sharp Cheddar cheese
   2 tablespoons diced pimiento

Empty one can of baked beans into a shallow casserole. Sprinkle with minced onion and celery; add second can of beans. Bake at 400° while preparing cheese swirls.

Add milk to biscuit mix; mix and knead lightly. Roll out into an oblong about 6 x 8 inches. Sprinkle with cheese and pimiento; roll up in jelly roll fashion, sealing edge. Cut into 6 or 8 slices and arrange over beans. Continue baking for 25 minutes or until swirls are done. Yield: 6 to 8 servings.

*Baked Lima Beans

   1 pound dried lima beans
   1 teaspoon salt
   1 cup firmly packed brown sugar
  ¼ cup butter or margarine

Wash beans well; place in a large saucepan and cover with water; soak overnight. Drain; add fresh water to cover. Add salt; cover saucepan and simmer for 1 hour or until beans are tender. Drain, reserving 1 cup liquid.

Combine bean liquid, brown sugar, and butter. Place beans in a 2-quart casserole; pour sugar mixture over beans and cover casserole. Bake at 325° for 2 hours. Uncover the last 30 minutes of baking. Yield: 6 to 8 servings.

Lima-Cheese Bake

   1 (10-ounce) package frozen baby lima beans
   1 (11-ounce) can condensed Cheddar cheese soup
  ½ cup milk
  ½ cup chopped celery
   1 tablespoon chopped parsley
   1 (3½-ounce) can French fried onions, divided

Pour boiling water over frozen lima beans to thaw, breaking beans apart. Combine soup and milk. Add limas, celery, parsley, and half the French fried onions. Mix well and place in a 1-quart casserole. Bake at 350° for 35 minutes. Sprinkle remaining French fried onions over top and bake at 350° for 10 more minutes. Yield: 6 servings.

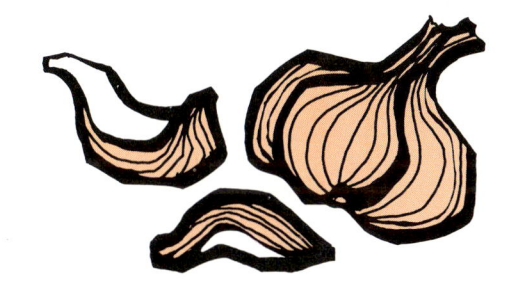

*Red Beans and Rice

   1 pound red beans
  ¼ pound salt pork or ham, cut in small pieces
   1 medium-size onion, chopped
   1 clove garlic, minced
    Salt to taste
    Hot cooked rice

Wash beans thoroughly, removing all stones and imperfect beans. Place in a large kettle, cover with water, and let soak overnight. The next day, add ham or salt pork and more water, if needed. Simmer for several hours. It may be necessary to add more water as beans cook; be sure that only boiling water is added. When beans are tender, add onion and garlic and cook until beans are tender enough to mash. Add salt. Beans may be mashed or served whole. Serve with hot rice. Yield: 4 to 6 servings.

Onion-Bean Bake

2 (16-ounce) cans pork and beans
4 frankfurters, sliced
1 cup shredded Cheddar cheese
2 tablespoons firmly packed light brown sugar
2 teaspoons parsley flakes
¼ teaspoon seasoned salt
1 (3½-ounce) can French fried onions, divided

Combine all ingredients except onions. Stir in half of onions and spoon mixture into a lightly greased 1½-quart casserole. Bake at 325° for 25 minutes. Before serving, sprinkle with remaining onions. Serve hot. Yield: 6 to 8 servings.

*Pickle Relish Baked Beans

1 (28-ounce) can pork and beans
½ cup pickle relish
½ cup cubed sharp Cheddar cheese
½ teaspoon dry mustard
1 teaspoon Worcestershire sauce
1 tablespoon firmly packed brown sugar

Combine all ingredients. Mix well and spoon into a greased 1-quart casserole. Bake at 375° for 30 minutes. Yield: 4 to 6 servings.

*Texas Frijoles (Pinto Beans)

1 pound pinto beans
2 medium-size onions
2 or 3 cloves garlic
About ¼ pound diced salt pork
1 to 3 teaspoons chili powder (optional)
Salt to taste

Wash beans thoroughly, removing all stones and imperfect beans. Place in a large kettle, cover with water, and soak overnight. The next day, add more water if needed to cover beans. Add whole onions, garlic, and diced salt pork.

Bring beans quickly to a boil; reduce heat and simmer for 3 to 4 hours, adding more boiling water if necessary. Do not add cold water as this will toughen beans. Add chili powder after beans are soft; add salt. (A few of the beans may be mashed to thicken beans; some Mexican restaurants mash all beans after they have been cooked to the soft stage.) Yield: 6 to 8 servings.

Frijoles (Pinto Beans)

1 pound dry pinto beans
4 cups water
1 bay leaf
½ teaspoon oregano
1 to 2 teaspoons chili powder
½ cup minced onion
1 clove garlic, minced
1 teaspoon salt
½ pound ground beef (optional)

Wash beans thoroughly, removing all stones and imperfect beans. Place in a 4-quart Dutch oven and cover with water. Cover and let soak overnight. The next day, bring to a boil. Add bay leaf and oregano and simmer for 3 hours. Add chili powder, onion, garlic, salt, and ground beef, if desired, and simmer an additional hour. Taste and add more seasonings, if needed. Yield: 8 to 10 servings.

Kentucky Wonder Beans and Tomatoes

1 pound fresh Kentucky Wonder beans
2 tablespoons chopped onion
2 tablespoons salad oil
2 cups chopped fresh tomatoes
1 teaspoon fresh sweet basil
1 teaspoon oregano

Wash beans thoroughly and cut into 1-inch lengths. Brown onion in hot salad oil; add tomatoes and herbs and cook about 15 minutes. Add beans, cover pan, and cook until beans are tender. Yield: 4 servings.

Fried Green Beans

1 *pound fresh Kentucky Wonder beans*
About 1 *cup all-purpose flour*
2 *eggs, well beaten*
About 1 *teaspoon salt*
About 1 *cup finely ground cracker crumbs*
Oil
Tartar sauce or catsup

Remove ends from beans and wash carefully. Roll the damp beans in flour, then in beaten eggs to which salt has been added. Roll in cracker crumbs. Beans may be set aside until ready to fry. Heat 2 inches oil very hot in deep pan. Place a handful of beans in a wire basket and drop into hot oil; fry until golden brown, 1 or 2 minutes. Drain on absorbent paper; serve hot with tartar sauce or catsup. Yield: about 6 servings.

Baked Black-eyed Peas

1 *cup dried black-eyed peas*
1½ *cups boiling water*
1 *teaspoon salt*
½ *to 1 cup chopped ham*
1 *medium-size onion, chopped*
1 *green pepper, chopped*
2 *cups cooked, drained tomatoes*

Add peas to boiling salted water and boil until peas are almost tender. Add more water, if needed. Add remaining ingredients. Mix well; spoon into a 1-quart casserole. Bake at 350° about 30 minutes. Yield: 4 servings.

*Black-eyed Peas with Ham Hock

1 *pound dry black-eyed peas*
5 *to 6 cups water*
1 *small ham hock*
1 *to 3 teaspoons salt*
1 *large onion*

Place dry peas in a colander in sink and wash well under cold running water; remove faulty peas. Drain and place in a heavy 6- to 8-quart kettle. Cover with water and soak 12 hours or overnight.

The next day, add ham hock to kettle (add more water if water does not cover peas) and bring to a boil. Reduce heat and add 1 teaspoon or more salt (it is better to start with a smaller amount if salty ham hock is used). Add whole onion. Cover kettle and simmer about 1 hour or until peas are tender. To avoid excessive breaking of peas, do not stir during cooking. Add more salt if needed. Yield: 6 (¾ cup) servings.

Orange Beets

1 *teaspoon grated orange rind*
½ *cup orange juice*
2 *tablespoons lemon juice*
¼ *cup sugar*
1 *tablespoon cornstarch*
½ *teaspoon salt*
2 *tablespoons butter or margarine*
3 *cups diced, cooked or canned beets, drained*

Heat grated orange rind, orange and lemon juices in top of double boiler. Combine sugar, cornstarch, and salt; add all at once; stir until thickened and clear. Add butter and beets and heat 15 to 20 minutes. Yield: 4 to 6 servings.

*Harvard Beets

1 *tablespoon cornstarch*
½ *cup sugar*
½ *cup mild vinegar*
¼ *teaspoon salt*
⅓ *cup beet liquid*
2 *tablespoons butter or margarine*
3 *cups diced or sliced, cooked or canned beets*

Combine cornstarch, sugar, vinegar, and salt; mix well. Slowly stir in beet liquid; blend to a smooth mixture. Cook, stirring constantly, over medium heat until sauce is clear and thickened; add butter and beets, stirring well to coat beets. Keep warm for 10 to 15 minutes before serving. Yield: 6 servings.

*Pickled Beets

- ½ teaspoon dry mustard
- 1 tablespoon sugar
- ½ teaspoon salt
- ½ teaspoon ground cloves
- ½ clove garlic
- 6 tablespoons vinegar
- ¼ cup water
- 2 cups cooked or canned beets, sliced and drained

Combine mustard, sugar, salt, cloves, and garlic. Slowly stir in vinegar and water. When mixture is smooth, pour over beets. Refrigerate until well chilled. Remove garlic clove. Serve with meat or fish. Yield: 6 servings.

Sauced Beets and Onions

- 2 tablespoons firmly packed brown sugar
- 2 teaspoons cornstarch
- ¼ teaspoon salt
- 2 teaspoons grated orange rind
- ½ cup orange juice
- 2 tablespoons butter or margarine
- 1 (16-ounce) can or jar sliced beets
- 1 (16-ounce) can or jar whole onions

Combine brown sugar, cornstarch, and salt in a saucepan. Add grated orange rind and juice; cook until thickened and clear, stirring frequently. Add butter, along with drained beets and onions; mix gently and heat. Yield: 6 to 8 servings.

Beets in Sour Cream Sauce

- 2 bunches fresh young beets
- ¼ cup boiling water
- ¼ teaspoon salt
- 1 tablespoon butter or margarine
- 1 tablespoon all-purpose flour
- ½ teaspoon salt
- ¼ teaspoon pepper
- 2 tablespoons lemon or orange juice
- ½ cup water
- ⅔ cup commercial sour cream

Scrub beets with vegetable brush under cold water. Pare; cut into thick slices, then into ½-inch cubes. Place in saucepan; add boiling water and ¼ teaspoon salt. Cover pan tightly; bring to a boil over high heat; reduce heat and cook until beets are tender-crisp, about 20 minutes. Shake saucepan two or three times as beets cook.

Melt butter in another saucepan. Blend in flour; cook, stirring constantly, until mixture bubbles. Remove from heat. Add seasonings; then gradually add fruit juice and water, stirring to smooth mixture. Bring to a boil over medium heat; then add cooked beets. Stir in sour cream; heat thoroughly, but do not allow to boil or cream will curdle. Serve hot. Yield: 6 servings.

Beets with Pineapple

- 2 tablespoons firmly packed brown sugar
- 1 tablespoon cornstarch
- ¼ teaspoon salt
- 1 (13¼-ounce) can pineapple tidbits or chunks
- 1 tablespoon lemon juice
- 1 tablespoon margarine
- 1 (1-pound) can sliced beets, drained

Combine brown sugar, cornstarch, and salt in a saucepan. Stir in pineapple (with syrup). Cook, stirring constantly, until mixture thickens and bubbles. Add lemon juice, margarine, and beets. Cook over medium heat until heated thoroughly. Yield: 4 to 6 servings.

*Fresh Turnip, Mustard, or Collard Greens

1 large bunch greens (about 2 to 2½ pounds)
¼ pound salt pork, diced
About ½ cup boiling water
Salt to taste

Check leaves of fresh greens carefully; remove pulpy stems and discolored spots on leaves. Wash thoroughly in several changes of warm water; add a little salt to the last water. Place greens in colander to drain.

Cook diced salt pork about 10 minutes in boiling water in covered saucepan. Add washed greens a few at a time, cover pot, and cook slowly until greens are tender. Do not overcook. Add additional salt, if needed. Yield: 6 to 8 servings.

Note: An alternate method is to wash greens carefully and place in a large cooking pot with only the water that clings to the leaves. Chopped turnip roots may be added when the greens are almost done. Add salt and bacon drippings after greens are tender. Serve with vinegar or hot sauce.

Fried Okra

Fresh okra
Cornmeal
Salt to taste
Shortening

Wash and slice fresh okra ¼ to ½ inch thick. Shake in plastic or brown paper bag with cornmeal and salt to taste. Place okra in a wire basket with handle; lower into a deep pot with several inches of melted shortening brought to frying temperature. Fry okra to golden brown, shaking to brown evenly. Serve with more salt if needed.

Note: Okra may be cut and mealed several weeks ahead and frozen in large freezer bags. Thaw and fry as needed.

*Grilled Okra

1 pound okra
½ to 1 cup cornmeal
Salt to taste
½ cup butter or margarine, divided

Wash okra and slice in ½-inch slices. Combine cornmeal and salt. Add okra and stir until each slice is well coated. Melt butter. Place individual servings of okra on squares of heavy-duty aluminum foil. Divide melted butter between packets; seal and cook over hot coals about 30 minutes, turning the packets often. Yield: 4 to 6 servings.

Stuffed Mushrooms

12 large fresh mushrooms
1 cup fresh lump crabmeat
1 tablespoon butter
½ cup Hollandaise Sauce
2 tablespoons whipping cream
2 teaspoons commercial sour cream

Remove stems from mushrooms; wash, poach, and dry well. Place on fireproof plate. Combine remaining ingredients; heat and stir until mixture is fluffy. Remove from heat and spoon mixture into mushrooms. Broil until lightly browned; serve immediately. This can be an appetizer or entrée. Yield: 6 to 12 servings.

Hollandaise Sauce:

2 egg yolks
1 tablespoon lemon juice
½ cup butter, melted
⅛ teaspoon salt
Dash pepper

Beat egg yolks in top half of double boiler and stir in lemon juice. Cook very slowly over low heat, never allowing water in bottom of pan to come to a boil. Add butter a little at a time, stirring constantly with a wooden spoon. Add salt and pepper. Continue cooking slowly until thickened. Yield: ½ cup.

Creamed Celery Continental

6 celery hearts
1 cup chicken stock or bouillon
1 tablespoon finely chopped onion
2 tablespoons melted butter or margarine
2 tablespoons all-purpose flour
½ cup half-and-half
1 teaspoon lemon juice
1 cup halved green grapes
Salt and white pepper to taste

Cut celery hearts in half lengthwise; place in a saucepan with chicken stock. Cover and cook for 5 minutes. Remove celery and keep warm; reserve broth.

Sauté onion in butter until transparent; blend in flour. Gradually add half-and-half and reserved broth. Bring to a boil; reduce heat and cook until thickened, stirring constantly. Blend in lemon juice, grapes, and seasonings. Add warm celery hearts and simmer for 5 minutes. Remove to serving dish and serve hot. Yield: 6 servings.

Marinated Vegetables

1 large head cauliflower
1 bunch broccoli
1 stalk celery or 25 thin asparagus spears
3 cups whipping cream
1 tablespoon buttermilk
3 to 6 tablespoons wine vinegar
½ to 1 teaspoon salt

Cut off cauliflower and broccoli flowerets 1 inch from top of stalks; cut into bite-size pieces. Cut celery into 2-inch strips (if using asparagus, cut off tender portion 3 inches from top). Steam vegetables for 2 to 3 minutes until partially done but still crunchy; chill.

To make marinade, combine whipping cream and buttermilk in saucepan; blend and heat until slightly warm. Place in a glass container and let sit overnight or until cream thickens. Add vinegar and salt.

Arrange vegetables on a platter and pour marinade over all. Serve with toothpicks. Yield: 50 servings.

Dill Marinated Vegetables

1 (10-ounce) package frozen cauliflower
1 (10-ounce) package frozen sliced green beans
2 tablespoons olive oil
2 tablespoons wine vinegar
1 teaspoon dillseed
½ teaspoon instant minced garlic
½ teaspoon salt
1/10 teaspoon freshly ground black pepper
Crisp bacon bits

Cook vegetables according to package directions; drain. Combine oil, vinegar, dillseed, minced garlic, salt, and pepper. Pour over cauliflower and beans. Toss gently. Serve either hot or cold, garnished with crisp bacon bits. Yield: 6 servings.

Note: Frozen peas, carrots, waxed or Italian beans, mixed vegetables, or Brussels sprouts may be used in place of cauliflower and green beans.

Seafood Stuffed Peppers

12 green peppers
1 pound ground pork
1 pound boiled shrimp, chopped
½ pint fresh oysters, chopped
1 pound crabmeat
¼ cup butter or margarine
6 slices fresh bread
2 eggs, beaten
Salt and black pepper to taste
1 tablespoon Ac'cent
¼ to 1 teaspoon cayenne pepper
1 tablespoon sherry
Seasoned, buttered bread crumbs

Slice top from peppers and remove seeds. Boil for a short time until peppers are limp. Drain and set aside.

Combine pork, shrimp, oysters, and crabmeat. Fry in butter until pork is browned. Add bread which has been soaked in water and squeezed dry, eggs, salt and pepper, Ac'cent, cayenne pepper, and sherry. Mix thoroughly.

Stuff peppers with meat mixture and top with seasoned, buttered bread crumbs.

Bake at 350° until crumbs are browned. Yield: 12 servings.

Variation: To substitute eggplant for the green peppers, cut in half, boil, remove centers, and fill with meat mixture.

Tasty Stuffed Green Peppers

 2 *large green peppers*
 ½ *cup minced cooked meat*
 ½ *cup moistened bread crumbs*
 ½ *teaspoon salt*
 Dash pepper
 1 *tablespoon melted margarine*
 ½ *teaspoon onion flakes*
 ½ *cup tomato sauce or beef stock*

Cut a slice from stem end of each pepper. Remove seeds and parboil peppers for 10 minutes. Combine meat, bread crumbs, salt, pepper, margarine, and onion flakes. Stuff peppers with meat mixture and place in a baking dish. Add tomato sauce or beef stock and bake at 350° for 30 minutes. Yield: 2 servings.

Southern Stuffed Peppers

 6 *large green peppers*
 ½ *pound chopped chicken livers*
 6 *slices bacon, diced*
 1 *cup chopped onion*
 1 *cup sliced celery*
 1 *clove garlic, crushed*
 ½ *cup canned sliced mushrooms*
 2 *cups cooked regular rice*
 1 *teaspoon salt*
 ¼ *teaspoon black pepper*
 Dash cayenne pepper

Wash peppers, cut slice from stem end and remove seeds. Cook peppers about 5 minutes in a small amount of boiling salted water; drain. Cook chicken livers, bacon, onion, celery, and garlic until vegetables are tender. Add mushrooms, rice, and seasonings. Stuff peppers with liver mixture. Arrange in baking dish; seal and freeze. To serve, thaw, and add ½ inch water to the pan, cover, and bake at 375° for 20 to 25 minutes. Yield: 6 servings.

Stuffed Peppers

 6 *green peppers*
 2 *cups cooked rice or bread crumbs*
 2 *cups cooked ground beef*
 1 *small onion, finely chopped*
 Salt to taste
 ½ *cup chili sauce, catsup, or meat gravy*
 1 *cup buttered bread crumbs*

Cut off stem ends of peppers; remove seeds. Boil peppers for 5 minutes in lightly salted water; drain. Combine 2 cups rice or bread crumbs, ground beef, onion, salt, and chili sauce, catsup or meat gravy. Stuff peppers with meat mixture, cover with buttered bread crumbs, and place in a greased flat casserole. Bake at 325° about 30 minutes or until peppers are tender and bread crumbs are browned. Yield: 6 servings.

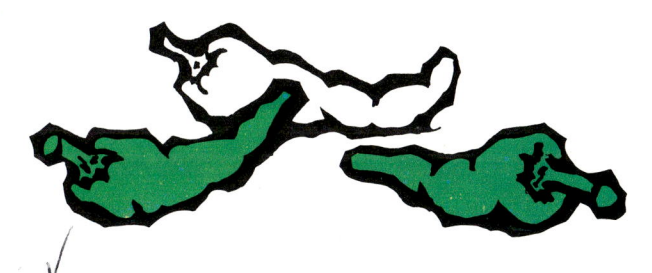

Rice-Stuffed Green Peppers

 4 *medium-size green peppers*
 ¼ *cup chopped celery*
 2 *tablespoons salad oil*
 1 *cup cooked rice*
 ¼ *cup chili sauce*
 ½ *cup shredded Cheddar cheese*
 ¼ *teaspoon salt*
 ¾ *cup buttered bread crumbs*

Cut off stems and remove seeds from peppers. Parboil peppers for 5 minutes; drain. Cook celery in hot salad oil until tender. Combine rice, chili sauce, cheese, and salt; add to celery. Fill peppers with rice mixture and top with buttered bread crumbs. Place in baking dish, seal, and freeze. To serve, thaw and add ½ inch water to baking dish. Bake at 350° for 30 minutes. Yield: 4 servings.

Poultry-Stuffed Peppers

 4 *firm green peppers*
 2 *eggs, beaten*
 1 *cup milk*
 1 *teaspoon salt*
  Pepper to taste
 1 *small onion, grated*
 1 *teaspoon parsley flakes*
 ½ *teaspoon curry powder*
1½ *cups diced, cooked chicken*
 4 *tablespoons shredded pasteurized process American cheese*
 1 *cup boiling water*

Cut tops from stem ends of green peppers. Remove seeds and fibers. Parboil for 5 minutes; drain.

Combine eggs, milk, salt, pepper, onion, parsley, and curry powder. Add chicken. Stuff peppers to within ½ inch of top. Sprinkle with cheese. Place in a baking dish with boiling water. Bake at 350° for about 35 minutes or until peppers are tender and filling is set. Yield: 4 servings.

Chinese Vegetables

 ¾ *cup green beans, sliced*
 1 *(6-ounce) can water chestnuts, sliced*
 ½ *cup bean sprouts*
 1 *chicken bouillon cube*
 ½ *cup water or vegetable liquid*
 1 *teaspoon salt*
 ¾ *teaspoon sugar*
 ⅛ *teaspoon pepper*
 1 *teaspoon soy sauce*
1½ *cups sliced celery*
 2 *teaspoons cornstarch*
 1 *tablespoon cold water*

Drain vegetables and reserve liquid. Dissolve bouillon cube in water over low heat. Stir in salt, sugar, pepper, and soy sauce. Add celery and drained vegetables; cover and steam 5 minutes. Blend cornstarch with cold water. Add to vegetables and cook just until broth thickens and becomes transparent. Yield: 4 servings.

Oriental Peas

 2 *(10-ounce) packages frozen peas*
 1 *(11-ounce) can mandarin oranges, liquid reserved*
 1 *tablespoon cornstarch*
 ½ *teaspoon dried mint*
 3 *tablespoons margarine*
 1 *tablespoon lemon juice*

Cook peas as directed on package; drain. Drain oranges and measure juice; add water to make ¾ cup. Combine cornstarch and mandarin orange juice in a saucepan. Add mint; heat until sauce thickens. Simmer for 2 minutes. Add margarine and lemon juice; stir into hot peas. Add mandarin oranges; heat gently. Yield: 6 servings.

*Spanish Potato Dish

 6 *medium-size potatoes*
 3 *tablespoons shortening*
 3 *eggs*
1½ *tablespoons chili powder*
 ¼ *teaspoon salt*
 1 *(16-ounce) can tomatoes*
 1 *(8-ounce) can tomato sauce*
 ½ *cup water*

Dice potatoes and cook in hot shortening until softened; drain off shortening. Add eggs; stir and cook until eggs are done. Add chili powder, salt, tomatoes, tomato sauce, and water. Cook for about 5 minutes. Yield: 6 to 8 servings.

*Parsley New Potatoes

 1 *pound small new potatoes*
 2 *cups water*
  Salt to taste
 ¼ *cup melted butter or margarine*
 2 *tablespoons minced parsley*

Cook peeled potatoes in boiling salted water until tender. Melt butter or margarine, stir in parsley, and serve over hot, drained potatoes. Yield: 3 servings.

Sausage Fried Potatoes

4 large potatoes
1 large onion
Salt and pepper to taste
1 pound pork link sausage
2 tablespoons salad oil

Dice potatoes and onion; add salt and pepper. Cut pork links into small chunks. Heat oil; add potatoes, onion, and sausage and cook over low heat until potatoes and onion are tender. Pour off grease before serving. Yield: 6 servings.

* Mexican Potato Cakes

2 cups cooked mashed potatoes
¼ cup shredded pasteurized process American cheese
1 egg, slightly beaten
1 egg yolk, slightly beaten
¼ cup dry bread crumbs
1 teaspoon minced onion
½ teaspoon salt
¼ teaspoon chili powder
Vegetable oil or shortening

Combine mashed potatoes, cheese, egg, egg yolk, bread crumbs, onion, salt, and chili powder. Mix until well blended. Pour oil into medium-size skillet to a depth of ⅛ inch. Heat oil over moderate heat. Drop mashed potato mixture by rounded teaspoonfuls into the hot oil; flatten slightly with a spatula. Cook over moderate heat for 3 to 5 minutes on each side, or until cakes are lightly browned. Yield: 12 to 15 cakes.

Cowboy Potatoes

6 large potatoes
4 tablespoons bacon drippings
2 medium-size onions, chopped
Salt and pepper to taste
Grated Parmesan cheese

Peel potatoes and split in half lengthwise; cut into thin half-rounds. Melt drippings in a heavy skillet with a cover. Add potatoes and chopped onion; season with salt and pepper. Cover and cook for 10 minutes. Turn potatoes with spatula; cook an additional 10 minutes. Potatoes should be tender but not completely browned. Uncover and brown potatoes on each side. Sprinkle with Parmesan cheese and serve hot. Yield: 6 to 8 servings.

Creole Potatoes

3 cups peeled, cubed potatoes
1 green pepper, sliced
1 small onion, chopped
1 cup tomato juice
Salt and pepper to taste

Simmer potatoes in boiling salted water for 5 minutes; drain. Add green pepper, onion, and tomato juice. Simmer 10 minutes longer or until potatoes are tender. Add salt and pepper. Yield: 6 servings.

Stuffed Potatoes Creole

6 baking potatoes
1 medium-size green pepper, diced
⅓ cup butter or margarine, divided
2 tablespoons minced onion
1 medium-size tomato, diced
1 to 2 tablespoons milk
2 teaspoons salt
¼ teaspoon freshly ground white pepper
1 teaspoon paprika
¼ teaspoon crumbled whole rosemary leaves
Paprika

Bake potatoes at 425° for 1 hour or until tender. Sauté green pepper in 3 tablespoons butter until limp. Add onion and tomato; cook 1 minute longer. Cut potatoes in half lengthwise and scoop out centers, leaving shells intact. Add milk and seasonings to potato mixture and mash well. Blend in sautéed vegetables. Fill shells with mixture and dot tops with remaining butter. Bake at 400° for 20 minutes. Serve at once. Garnish with paprika. Yield: 6 servings.

Creamed Vegetable Sauce with New Potatoes

12 small new potatoes
¼ cup butter
¼ cup all-purpose flour
1½ teaspoons salt
Dash pepper
¼ teaspoon onion salt or grated fresh onion
2 cups milk
1 cup cooked peas
¾ cup sliced, cooked celery
Parsley or watercress

Scrub potatoes and peel skin from a ½-inch strip around center of each potato. Steam potatoes, or cook covered in boiling salted water, until tender.

Melt butter in a saucepan over low heat. Blend in flour and seasonings. Add milk slowly, stirring constantly. Cook and stir until sauce is smooth and thickened. Arrange hot potatoes on heated serving dish. Stir three-fourths of the peas and celery into sauce. Pour sauce over potatoes. Top with remaining vegetables. Garnish with sprigs of parsley or watercress. Yield: 4 servings.

Pimiento Potatoes

6 medium-size cooked potatoes, sliced and chilled
1 (4-ounce) jar pimientos, cut into pieces
1 whole canned chili pepper, very finely cut
1 tablespoon all-purpose flour
Salt and pepper to taste
1 cup half-and-half
1½ cups shredded sharp Cheddar cheese

Combine all ingredients except cream and cheese. Place in a greased 2½- to 3-quart shallow baking dish. Pour cream over potatoes and top with shredded cheese. Cover with foil and bake at 350° for 30 minutes or until cheese is melted and potatoes are bubbly hot. Remove foil and return to oven for approximately 15 minutes more. Yield: 8 to 10 servings.

Vegetable Puffs

1 cup cooked mashed potatoes
2 eggs, well beaten
½ cup all-purpose flour
1 teaspoon baking powder
1 teaspoon salt
Pepper to taste
Dash ground nutmeg
1 cup cooked corn, peas, or carrots
1 tablespoon grated onion
1 tablespoon chopped parsley
Shortening

Combine potatoes with eggs and blend thoroughly. Combine flour, baking powder, salt, pepper, and nutmeg and sift over potatoes; blend well. Add remaining vegetables and parsley and mix well. Drop by spoonfuls into deep hot shortening (375°). Fry until golden brown. Yield: 2 to 4 servings.

*New Potatoes Rissole

1½ pounds small new potatoes
1 teaspoon salt
¼ cup butter or margarine, divided
2 tablespoons all-purpose flour
1 cup milk
¾ teaspoon salt
Dash pepper
Fresh parsley

Wash potatoes; pare or, if desired, cook in the jackets. Place in a saucepan with 1 inch boiling water; add 1 teaspoon salt. Cover and bring to a boil. Boil until partially tender, 10 to 15 minutes; drain. Place potatoes in a shallow baking dish and dot with 2 tablespoons butter. Bake, uncovered, at 425° for 15 minutes or until tender, turning once.

Melt remaining butter in a small saucepan; blend in flour and gradually stir in milk. Cook over medium heat, stirring constantly, until mixture thickens. Add ¾ teaspoon salt and pepper. Pour sauce over potatoes. Garnish with parsley. Yield: 6 servings.

Pumpkin Soufflé

2½ cups canned or cooked mashed pumpkin
¼ cup melted butter or margarine
½ teaspoon salt
3 tablespoons firmly packed brown sugar
½ cup hot milk
3 egg yolks, beaten
3 egg whites, stiffly beaten
1 teaspoon grated lemon rind
½ cup seedless raisins or flaked coconut

Combine pumpkin, butter, salt, brown sugar, milk, and beaten egg yolks; beat until fluffy. Fold stiff egg whites into pumpkin mixture along with lemon rind and raisins or coconut. Spoon into an ungreased 1½-quart casserole and bake at 350° for 1 hour or until lightly browned. Yield: 6 to 8 servings.

French Fried Rutabaga

1 medium-size rutabaga
1 teaspoon sugar
½ cup cornmeal
1 teaspoon salt
1 egg, slightly beaten
Salad oil

Cut rutabaga into ¼-inch slices; peel slices and cut into ¼-inch strips. (If strips are too long, cut crosswise once.) Parboil strips for 5 minutes in a small amount of boiling water with sugar added; drain well and cool.
 Combine cornmeal and salt. Dip rutabaga strips in egg; roll in cornmeal. Fry strips in hot oil; drain. Keep strips warm in oven while remaining strips cook. Yield: 4 to 6 servings.
 Note: Leftover rutabaga fries will freeze well. To reheat, spread in a shallow pan and bake at 350° until warmed through.

Honeyed Rutabaga

1 pound rutabaga (about 2½ cups sliced)
1 cup honey
⅓ cup melted butter

Slice rutabaga, pare, and cook in boiling salted water until tender. Drain and place in a shallow, greased 4-cup baking dish. Cover with a mixture of honey and melted butter and bake at 350° for 20 to 30 minutes. Turn rutabaga slices once; baste several times. Yield: 6 to 8 servings.

Glazed Rutabagas

2 medium-size rutabagas
1 cup firmly packed brown sugar
½ cup water
1½ tablespoons butter
Parsley

Cut rutabagas into ¼-inch slices; peel slices and cut into ½-inch strips. Parboil rutabaga in a small amount of boiling salted water for 5 minutes. Drain and place in a shallow baking dish. Combine brown sugar, water, and butter; pour over rutabaga. Bake at 350° for 45 to 60 minutes or until rutabaga is tender, basting frequently. Garnish with parsley. Yield: 6 to 8 servings.

Exotic Spinach Dish

2 (10-ounce) packages frozen whole spinach
3 cups commercial sour cream
1 (1-ounce) package dry onion soup
2 tablespoons sherry
Bread crumbs (optional)

Cook spinach in unsalted water according to package directions. Drain and chop finely. Add sour cream, onion soup, and sherry. Sprinkle bread crumbs over top, if desired. Place in a 1½-quart casserole; bake at 325° for 15 to 20 minutes. Yield: 8 to 10 servings.
 Note: Fresh spinach may be used if you increase the cooking time.

Au Gratin Spinach Ring

 3 *tablespoons all-purpose flour*
 1 *teaspoon salt*
 1/8 *teaspoon pepper*
 1 *teaspoon dry mustard*
 1/4 *cup butter or margarine*
 1 *cup milk*
 1 *cup shredded Cheddar cheese*
 1 *teaspoon Worcestershire sauce*
 1 *(27-ounce) can spinach, drained*
 4 *eggs, beaten*

Blend flour and seasonings into melted butter. Add milk and cook until thickened, stirring constantly. Add cheese, Worcestershire sauce, and well-drained spinach. Stir in beaten eggs. Pour into a well-greased and floured 6-cup ring mold. Set mold in a pan of hot water and bake at 350° about 45 minutes or until set. Cool 5 to 10 minutes. Carefully loosen ring and invert onto serving plate. Yield: 6 to 8 servings.

Mozzarella-Spinach Bake

 8 *slices bread, crusts removed, divided*
 8 *(1-ounce) slices mozzarella cheese, divided*
 1 *(10-ounce) package frozen, chopped spinach*
 1/4 *cup pizza sauce*
 2 *cups milk*
 1/2 *teaspoon salt*
 3 *eggs, beaten*
 1/4 *teaspoon paprika*

Place 4 bread slices in an 8-inch square baking dish. Arrange 4 cheese slices over bread. Heat spinach in a small amount of boiling, salted water just until thawed; drain. Spread spinach evenly over cheese slices. Top with pizza sauce and remaining cheese and bread slices. Cover dish tightly and chill until ready to cook.
 Combine milk and salt with beaten eggs; pour over spinach and cheese layers. Sprinkle paprika over top. Bake at 350° about 45 minutes or until browned. Yield: 4 servings.

*Spinach au Gratin

 1 1/2 *tablespoons all-purpose flour*
 1/4 *teaspoon dry mustard*
 1/4 *teaspoon salt*
  Dash pepper
 2 *tablespoons margarine, melted*
 2/3 *cup milk*
 2/3 *cup shredded Cheddar cheese*
 1 *(15-ounce) can spinach, drained*

Combine flour and seasonings with margarine. Add milk and cook until thickened, stirring constantly. Add cheese and heat until melted; stir well. Add spinach; heat. Yield: 4 servings.

Spinach Custard

 2 *eggs*
 1 *cup hot milk*
 1 *cup chopped cooked spinach*
 1 *teaspoon butter or margarine*
 1/2 *teaspoon salt*
 1/2 *teaspoon pepper*
 2 *hard-cooked eggs, chopped*
  Double pastry for 9-inch pie shell, divided

Beat eggs in a medium-size bowl. Add milk, spinach, butter, salt, and pepper; mix well. Add chopped eggs, stirring carefully through mixture. Line a deep 9-inch dish with half the pastry. Spoon spinach mixture into pastry. Cover top with remaining pastry, leaving about 1 inch open in the center. Bake at 350° for 35 to 40 minutes. Yield: 6 to 8 servings.

Stuffed Yellow Squash

 3 *small firm, yellow crookneck squash*
 3 *tablespoons dry bread crumbs*
 2 *tablespoons shredded sharp Cheddar cheese*
  Salt, pepper, and onion salt to taste
 2 *tablespoons shredded sharp Cheddar cheese*

Wash squash and simmer until tender; drain and cool slightly. Slice in two lengthwise pieces; scoop out centers and mash.

Stir in bread crumbs, 2 tablespoons cheese, salt, pepper, and onion salt. Mix lightly and return to squash shells. Top with 2 tablespoons cheese and bake at 350° about 8 minutes or until cheese melts and browns slightly. Yield: 2 generous servings.

Fluffy Squash Soufflé

- 2 pounds small yellow squash
- 1 tablespoon onion, chopped
- ½ teaspoon salt
- 2 eggs, beaten
- ¼ pound sharp Cheddar cheese, shredded
- ½ cup cracker crumbs
- 2 tablespoons butter
- Paprika
- Pepper

Cook squash and onion in salted water until tender; drain and cool squash. Add beaten eggs and mix well. Place in a casserole and add cheese. Sprinkle cracker crumbs over top; dot with butter and sprinkle with paprika and pepper. Bake at 350° about 20 minutes or until browned. Yield: 6 servings.

Squash Eudora

- 2 pounds tender yellow squash
- 3 tablespoons butter
- ½ teaspoon salt
- 1 teaspoon dried green onion
- ¼ teaspoon freshly ground black pepper
- ¼ teaspoon paprika
- ¾ pound chicken livers
- 3 tablespoons butter
- 4 teaspoons Worcestershire sauce
- ½ teaspoon salt
- ¼ teaspoon freshly ground black pepper
- ¼ teaspoon celery seeds
- ⅛ teaspoon curry powder
- 1 egg, lightly beaten
- Grated Parmesan cheese

Wash squash; do not peel. Slice as thinly as possible and place slices in a saucepan with 3 tablespoons butter, ½ teaspoon salt, dried green onion, ¼ teaspoon pepper, and paprika. Simmer over low heat about 25 minutes or until squash is tender when tested with a fork.

Wash chicken livers and cut in halves. Melt 3 tablespoons butter; place in a baking dish and add Worcestershire sauce, ½ teaspoon salt, and ¼ teaspoon pepper. Marinate livers in this mixture for 20 minutes. Place in an uncovered 2-quart baking dish and bake at 350° for 20 minutes. Turn livers after 10 minutes.

Add cooked squash, celery seeds, curry powder, and lightly beaten egg. Mix lightly, and taste to see if more salt is needed. Sprinkle top with Parmesan cheese and bake at 350° for about 25 minutes. Yield: 6 to 8 servings.

Baked Acorn Squash

- 3 acorn squash
- Butter
- 6 tablespoons firmly packed brown sugar, divided

Cut each squash in half lengthwise; remove seed. Place in a baking dish, cut side down, and bake at 400° for 35 to 40 minutes. Turn over; brush inside with butter, and add 1 tablespoon brown sugar to center of each squash half. Continue baking for 20 to 25 minutes. Yield: 6 servings.

Squash Soufflé

- 1½ pounds yellow squash, sliced
- 1 small onion, minced
- 1 tablespoon minced parsley
- 1 egg, slightly beaten
- ¼ cup milk
- ½ cup cottage cheese
- ½ teaspoon salt
- ½ teaspoon pepper
- 1 teaspoon sugar
- ¼ cup finely chopped pecans

Parboil squash; mash. Add remaining ingredients except nuts. Place in a greased 2-quart casserole and sprinkle pecans over the top. Bake at 350° about 25 minutes or until top is browned. Yield: 6 to 8 servings.

Zucchini Delicious

- 3 slices bacon, chopped
- 1 cup chopped onion
- 3½ cups unpeeled sliced zucchini
- 1 (8-ounce) can tomato sauce
- ¾ teaspoon salt
- ⅛ teaspoon pepper

Fry bacon slightly; add onion and cook until golden. Add remaining ingredients and cook, covered, until tender and most of the sauce is absorbed, 20 to 25 minutes. Yield: 6 servings.

South American Zucchini

- 2 pounds zucchini squash
- 2 slices bacon, diced
- 3 tablespoons minced onion
- ⅓ cup chopped green pepper
- 1 (8-ounce) can tomato sauce
- ½ tablespoon bottled condiment sauce
- 1 tablespoon sugar
- ½ teaspoon salt
- ¼ teaspoon pepper

Wash zucchini and cut into ⅛-inch slices. Cook, covered, in 1 inch boiling salted water about 15 minutes or until tender.

Sauté bacon, onion, and green pepper until bacon is lightly browned. Add zucchini and remaining ingredients and simmer, uncovered, for 10 minutes. Serve hot. Yield: 6 servings.

Zucchini Parmesan

- 4 or 5 zucchini squash, thinly sliced (about 3 cups)
- 2 tablespoons butter or margarine
- ½ teaspoon salt
- Dash pepper
- 2 tablespoons grated Parmesan cheese

Combine zucchini, butter, and seasonings in a skillet. Cover and cook slowly for 5 minutes. Uncover and cook, turning slices, until barely tender, about 5 minutes more. Sprinkle with cheese; toss. Yield: 4 servings.

*Oriental-style Zucchini and Onions

- 4 zucchini squash
- 2 to 4 tablespoons shortening
- 1 to 2 large onions, sliced
- 2 tablespoons all-purpose flour
- 2 bouillon cubes dissolved in 1 cup water, divided
- ½ teaspoon salt
- 1 teaspoon soy sauce

Wash zucchini and slice ½ inch thick; do not pare. Heat shortening in a skillet; add zucchini and onions. Fry over medium heat until golden brown.

Make a paste of flour and 1 tablespoon bouillon. Add remaining bouillon, salt, and soy sauce. Pour mixture over vegetables. Cover and simmer 15 to 20 minutes or until zucchini is tender. Yield: 4 servings.

Baked Stuffed Sweet Potatoes

- 8 medium-size sweet potatoes
- 6 tablespoons margarine, melted
- 3 tablespoons sugar
- ¾ cup diced orange sections
- ¼ cup flaked coconut
- ½ teaspoon salt
- 8 teaspoons margarine, divided

Scrub potatoes and bake at 350° for 1 hour or until tender. Remove from oven and cut a thin slice from one side of each potato; spoon out all pulp, being careful not to break skin. Mash pulp; add 6 tablespoons melted margarine, sugar, oranges, coconut, and salt; mix well. Spoon into shells. Dot each with 1 teaspoon margarine. Bake at 450° for 15 minutes or until tops are lightly browned. Yield: 8 servings.

Louisiana Sherried Sweet Potatoes

- 1 cup sugar
- ¾ cup water
- ½ teaspoon salt
- 5 sticks cinnamon
- 10 whole cloves
- 8 whole allspice berries
- 6 medium-size sweet potatoes, cooked, peeled, and cut into 2-inch slices
- ¼ cup sherry

Combine sugar, water, salt, cinnamon, cloves, and allspice; heat to boiling over medium heat and cook 15 minutes. Remove spices and add sweet potatoes and sherry; heat. Yield: 6 servings.

* Baked Sweet Potatoes

Scrub medium-size sweet potatoes with a brush until clean; dry. Rub potatoes with oil or vegetable shortening. Arrange on a baking sheet and bake at 350° for 45 to 50 minutes.

Brandied Sweet Potatoes

- 3 to 4 oranges, peeled, divided
- ¼ cup firmly packed brown sugar
- 1 tablespoon grated orange rind
- ½ cup brandy
- ¼ cup half-and-half
- ¼ cup melted butter or margarine
- 1 teaspoon salt
- 4 cups mashed, cooked sweet potatoes
- Brown sugar (optional)

Slice 1 peeled orange into cartwheels; set aside. Cut remaining oranges into very small pieces to yield 2 cups drained fruit. Sprinkle orange pieces with brown sugar; set aside. Heat together grated orange rind, brandy, half-and-half, melted butter, and salt. Beat mixture into mashed sweet potatoes until well blended. Stir in drained, sweetened orange pieces. Spoon mixture into a well-greased 1½-quart casserole; top with orange slices. Sprinkle lightly with additional brown sugar, if desired. Bake uncovered at 350° for 35 to 40 minutes. Yield: 8 servings.

Note: Casserole may be made in advance and chilled until ready to bake.

* Sweet Potato-Apple Casserole

- 4 medium-size sweet potatoes
- 4 medium-size apples
- ½ cup sugar
- 1 cup water
- Butter
- ½ cup firmly packed brown sugar
- Bread crumbs

Wash sweet potatoes thoroughly; boil until tender. Meanwhile, pare, core, and slice apples and place in a saucepan with sugar and water. Boil slowly until the potatoes are ready. Drain apples, reserving liquid.

Peel sweet potatoes and cut lengthwise into slices. Place a layer of sweet potato slices in a greased, 1-quart casserole. Dot with butter and sprinkle with brown sugar. Add a layer of apples. Repeat layers until all ingredients are used. Add reserved apple liquid. Sprinkle with bread crumbs; add a few dots of butter. Bake at 400° for 15 minutes. Yield: 6 servings.

Orange Sweet Potatoes

- 6 medium-size sweet potatoes
- ¾ cup sugar
- ¼ cup butter
- ½ teaspoon salt
- ⅓ cup water
- Dash ground nutmeg or cinnamon
- Peel of ½ orange, dried and cut into small slivers

Boil potatoes whole until the peel slips easily but potatoes are not cooked through. Peel and leave whole. Combine sugar, butter, salt, water, nutmeg or cinnamon, and orange peel in a heavy skillet with a lid. Heat until butter and sugar are melted; add sweet potatoes. Cover and cook until syrup is thickened and potatoes are tender. Yield: 6 servings.

Cranberried Yams

2½ cups cooked, mashed sweet potatoes
Dash salt
1 (16-ounce) can cranberry sauce
2 tablespoons firmly packed brown sugar
1 teaspoon grated orange rind
2 tablespoons melted butter or margarine
½ cup chopped pecans or walnuts

Add salt to mashed sweet potatoes and spoon into a greased 4-cup casserole. Combine cranberry sauce, brown sugar, orange rind, and melted butter; spread over sweet potatoes. Top with chopped nuts. Bake at 350° for 25 to 30 minutes. Yield: 8 servings.

Sweet Potato Crisp

6 medium-size or 1 (29-ounce) can sweet potatoes
½ cup margarine
¼ cup all-purpose flour
½ cup firmly packed brown sugar
1½ teaspoons freshly ground black pepper
¼ cup evaporated milk
¼ cup ground pecans

Cook sweet potatoes; peel and slice crosswise, about ⅜ inch thick. Spread in a greased shallow 1½-quart casserole. Cut margarine into flour and brown sugar as you would in making pie crust. Add pepper, milk, and ground nuts; mix well. Spread over potato slices. Broil about 6 inches from heat until bubbly and caramelized, about 7 minutes. Yield: 6 servings.

Tomatoes Provençale en Salade

4 large, ripe, firm tomatoes
1 teaspoon salt
Large bunch parsley
2 cloves garlic
3 tablespoons olive oil, divided
Salt and white pepper to taste
1 tablespoon lemon juice
Lettuce

Do not peel tomatoes, but slice stem off, removing any green or white center pulp. Soften the pulp by jabbing with tines of fork several times. Sprinkle pulp with salt and set tomatoes upside down to drain.

Remove stems from parsley and chop leaves very fine. Put garlic cloves through garlic press. Pound parsley and garlic with 1½ tablespoons olive oil, salt, pepper, and lemon juice in a mortar. (If you do not have a mortar, try a small flat-bottomed glass in a small wooden bowl.) Add remaining olive oil and mix.

Turn tomatoes over and wipe outside dry with a paper towel. Cut a very thin slice from bottom, if necessary, to make them rest squarely on the salad plate. Spoon proportionate amounts of dressing on and into the tops of the tomatoes, using fork tines gently to get the mixture well into the pulp. Chill well and serve on lettuce. Yield: 4 servings.

* Spinach-Stuffed Tomatoes

6 large firm tomatoes
2 pounds fresh spinach or 2 (10-ounce) packages frozen spinach
4 tablespoons minced onion
4 tablespoons butter
4 tablespoons all-purpose flour
½ teaspoon salt
Freshly ground black pepper
¼ teaspoon ground nutmeg
4 tablespoons half-and-half
6 tablespoons buttered bread crumbs

Slice top off each tomato. Scoop out pulp and discard; stand tomatoes upside down to drain. Cook spinach until just wilted; drain and squeeze out all water; chop very finely.

Sauté onion in butter in a heavy skillet. Stir in flour, seasonings, spinach, and half-and-half; simmer over low heat until smooth and thickened, stirring constantly. Fill tomatoes with spinach mixture; top with bread crumbs. Wrap tomatoes in heavy-duty aluminum foil. Grill over moderate heat for 20 to 30 minutes or until tender and browned. Yield: 6 servings.

*Scalloped Tomatoes

 6 *large tomatoes*
 1 *tablespoon grated onion*
1½ *cups soft bread cubes*
 ¼ *cup melted butter*

Peel tomatoes and cut into quarters. Place in a saucepan and mash slightly to press out some of the juice. Cook over very low heat about 10 minutes, stirring constantly. Add grated onion.

 Alternate layers of tomatoes and bread cubes in a greased 1-quart casserole. Pour melted butter over top of casserole and bake at 375° for 20 to 30 minutes. Yield: 4 to 6 servings.

Tomatoes and Okra

 3 *slices bacon*
 2 *pounds okra, cut into ½-inch slices*
 1 *medium-size green pepper, finely chopped*
 1 *small onion, chopped*
 2 *cloves garlic, minced (optional)*
 2 *pounds fresh tomatoes, peeled and cubed*
  Salt and pepper to taste

Fry bacon until crisp; drain. Cook okra in bacon drippings. Add green pepper, onion, and garlic, if desired; stir in tomatoes and cooked bacon. Add salt and pepper. Cover skillet and cook an additional 15 minutes. Yield: 8 servings.

Fried Green Tomatoes

 4 *medium-size or 3 large green tomatoes*
 ¼ *cup fine dry bread crumbs*
 ½ *teaspoon salt*
  Dash pepper
  Bacon drippings

Cut each tomato into about 4 thick slices. Combine bread crumbs, salt, and pepper. Coat tomato slices on both sides with bread crumb mixture. Fry in hot bacon drippings, about ¼ inch deep, turning carefully to brown each side. Remove to a hot platter and serve hot. Yield: 6 servings.

Spicy Stuffed Tomatoes

 4 *medium-size tomatoes*
 1 *(4½-ounce) can deviled ham*
 ½ *cup chopped celery*
 2 *scallions, chopped*
 ¼ *cup chopped green pepper*
  Salad greens
  Curried Mayonnaise Dressing

Scoop centers from tomatoes and cut tulip-like edges on tomatoes. Combine deviled ham, celery, scallions, and green pepper. Stuff tomatoes with this mixture; chill. Serve on salad greens with Curried Mayonnaise Dressing. Yield: 4 servings.

Curried Mayonnaise Dressing:

 ½ *teaspoon curry*
 ½ *cup mayonnaise*

Combine curry with mayonnaise and serve with the stuffed tomatoes. Yield: ½ cup.

*Baked Tomatoes and Corn

 6 *large ripe, firm tomatoes*
 ½ *cup all-purpose flour*
  Salt and pepper to taste
 1 *clove garlic, cut into halves*
 ⅓ *cup olive oil*
 10 *ears corn*
 1 *large onion, sliced*
 ¾ *cup fresh bread crumbs*
 ¼ *cup butter*

Slice tomatoes into ½-inch slices; dredge in flour seasoned with salt and pepper. Cook garlic in olive oil in a large skillet until browned; discard garlic. Add tomato slices to the oil and sauté on both sides until slices are slightly golden.

 Scrape kernels from corn. Arrange alternate layers of tomatoes, corn, and onion slices in a 2-quart casserole; season the layers with salt and pepper.

 Sauté bread crumbs in butter until golden brown; sprinkle over vegetable layers. Bake at 350° for 35 to 40 minutes. Yield: 8 servings.

Southern Scalloped Tomatoes

    4   *tablespoons butter or margarine*
    1   *cup bread cubes*
    1   *small onion, minced*
 2½   *cups canned tomatoes*
    4   *tablespoons or more sugar*
        Salt and pepper to taste
        Dash sweet basil
        Fine bread crumbs
        Shredded Cheddar cheese (optional)

Melt butter; add bread cubes and brown lightly. Remove bread cubes, add more butter if necessary, and lightly brown the minced onion. Combine bread cubes, onion, tomatoes, sugar, salt, pepper, and basil. Spoon into a 2-quart casserole, cover with bread crumbs, and bake at 350° for 30 or 40 minutes. Add shredded cheese the last 15 minutes of baking time, if desired. Yield: 6 servings.

Swiss Mushroom-Stuffed Tomatoes

    8   *tomatoes*
    2   *tablespoons butter or margarine*
 ¼   *cup chopped onion*
 ¼   *cup chopped parsley*
    1   *cup soft bread crumbs*
    1   *teaspoon dried basil leaf*
 1½   *teaspoons salt*
 ¼   *teaspoon hot sauce*
    2   *(3- or 4-ounce) cans sliced mushrooms, drained*
    1   *cup shredded Swiss cheese*
    1   *cup cooked green peas*

Cut out stem-end core of tomatoes and discard. Scoop out pulp, leaving shells intact; reserve pulp. Melt butter in a large skillet, add onion and parsley; cook until onion is tender. Add reserved tomato pulp, bread crumbs, basil, salt, hot sauce, and drained mushrooms. Simmer 5 minutes. Add Swiss cheese and stir until melted. Stir in peas. Spoon into tomatoes, place in a 13- x 9- x 2-inch baking dish and bake at 350° for 15 to 20 minutes. Yield: 8 servings.

Scalloped Tomatoes and Zucchini

 1½   *cups sliced zucchini squash*
    2   *cloves garlic, minced*
 ¼   *cup butter or margarine*
    2   *(1-pound) cans tomatoes*
 ¾   *cup saltine cracker crumbs*
    1   *teaspoon seasoned salt*

Cook zucchini and garlic in butter until zucchini is almost tender. Add tomatoes, cracker crumbs, and seasoned salt; mix and place in a casserole. Bake at 375° about 40 minutes. Yield: 6 to 8 servings.

Extra-Special Onions

  12   *small onions*
    1   *(10¾-ounce) can condensed cream of mushroom soup*
 ¼   *cup pimiento strips*
 ¼   *cup shredded Cheddar cheese*

Boil onions in salted water until tender. Combine onions, soup, and pimiento strips. Pour into baking dish and sprinkle top with cheese. Bake at 350° for 30 minutes or until cheese is melted. Yield: 4 to 6 servings.

*Creamed Spring Onions

    4   *bunches spring onions, shallots, or leeks*
    3   *tablespoons butter or margarine*
 ½   *cup all-purpose flour*
 ½   *cup evaporated milk*
    1   *cup water*
 ¾   *teaspoon salt*
    1   *cup shredded Cheddar cheese*
        Toast, corn bread squares, or muffins

Trim roots and ends of tops from onions. Wash thoroughly, chop coarsely, and cook in boiling salted water until tender.
    Melt butter in a skillet. Stir in flour; add milk and water and cook until mixture thickens. Add salt and grated cheese; stir until mixture is blended. Drain onions and place on toast, corn bread squares, or muffins. Pour sauce over all. Yield: 5 servings.

*Stuffed Onions

    5 large mild onions
    2 tablespoons butter or margarine
  ½ cup chopped celery
    2 tablespoons chopped parsley
    1 tablespoon butter or margarine
    2 cups bread crumbs
    1 teaspoon salt
        Pepper to taste
        Shredded Cheddar cheese

Skin the onions, cut in half crosswise, and simmer in salted water until almost tender; drain. Remove the centers without disturbing the outer layers and chop fine. Melt 2 tablespoons butter in a skillet; add chopped onion, celery, and parsley and cook until tender but not brown.

Push the vegetables to one side of the skillet. Melt the remaining 1 tablespoon butter and add bread crumbs, salt, and pepper. Mix well with cooked vegetables to make stuffing.

Fill onion shells with stuffing; place in baking dish, cover, and bake at 350° about 30 minutes, or until onions are tender. Remove cover from baking dish, sprinkle onions with cheese, and continue baking until cheese melts. Yield: 4 servings.

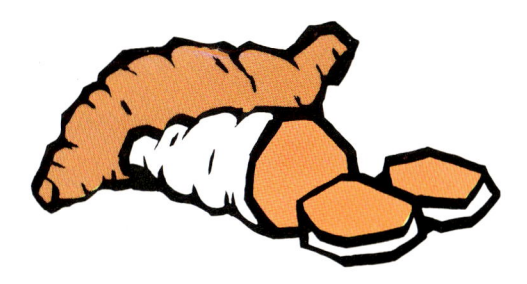

Golden Herbed Onions

    6 cups thinly sliced onion rings
  ¼ cup butter
  ¼ cup flour
    1 (13-ounce) can evaporated milk
  ⅓ cup water
    1 teaspoon dried parsley flakes
  ½ teaspoon salt
  ¾ teaspoon marjoram
        Dash pepper
    2 cups shredded Cheddar cheese

Place onion rings in ungreased 1½-quart casserole. Melt butter in a medium-size saucepan. Remove from heat; blend in flour. Slowly stir in evaporated milk and water. Cook over medium heat, stirring constantly, until thickened. Add parsley, salt, marjoram, pepper, and shredded cheese. Stir until cheese has melted and sauce is smooth. Pour cheese sauce over onions in casserole. Bake at 350° until onions are tender. Yield: 6 to 8 servings.

French Fried Onion Rings

    2 large Bermuda onions
        Milk
  ½ cup cornmeal
  ½ cup all-purpose flour
    1 teaspoon salt
  ¼ teaspoon pepper
    1 egg
  ¾ cup milk
        Shortening
        Salt (optional)

Peel onions; cut into ¼-inch slices. Separate to form rings and place in a bowl. Cover with milk and let stand for 15 minutes.

Combine cornmeal, flour, 1 teaspoon salt, and pepper. Add egg and ¾ cup milk, and blend well. Drain onion rings and dip into batter. Fry in deep hot shortening (375°) for 2 or 3 minutes or until golden brown. Drain on paper towels and sprinkle with salt, if desired. Yield: 4 to 6 servings.

INDEX

A

Acorn Squash. See Squash
Almond(s)
  Almond Paste, 82
  Cakes, 133
  * Casserole, Chicken-Noodle-Almond, 102
Appetizers and Snacks
  Ball(s)
    Cheese Ball, 10
      Merry Cheese Ball, 10
      Party Cheese Ball, 10
      * Zippy Cheese Ball Appetizers, 10
    Sausage Balls, 10
  Beef
    Fondue, Beef, 20
    Nuggets, Curried Beef, 19
    Roll-Ups, Bacon-Beef, 18
  Burgers, Western, 12
  Canapés, Hot Crabmeat, 14
  * Celery Fingers, 19
  Celery Sticks, Zippy Stuffed, 13
  Cheese
    Beer Cheese, 11
    and Egg Appetizer, Cheese, 11
    * Hounds, Cheese, 11
    * Log, Cheese-and-Beef, 10
    Logs, Cheese, 11
    Puffs, Cheese, 12
    Puffs, Parmesan, 11
    Spreads
      Beer, Cheese-, 8
      Blue-Cheddar Appetizer Spread, 8
      Blue Cheese Spread, 9
      Blue Cheese Spread, Tangy, 9
      * Cottage Cheese Spread, Crunchy, 8
      Sherry-Cheese Spread, 9
    Straws, Cheese, 11
    * Tuna Cheesies, 12
    Wafers, Cheese, 13
  Clams Casino, Appetizer, 14
  Corned Beef Spread Puff, 12
  Dips
    Anchovy-Cheese Dip, 15
    * Bean Dip, Hot, 18
    * Chili-Cheese Dip, 15
    Chili Dandy Dip, 14
    Clam Appetizer Dip, 15
    Clam Chip Dip, 14
    Cottage Cheese Dip, 16
    * Cottage Cheese Dip, Curried, 15
    Cucumber Dip, 15
    Green Dragon Dip, 17
    Oyster Dip, Smoked, 17
    * Pea Dip, Tasty Black-Eyed, 14
    * Peanut Butter-Cheese Dip, 17
    Shrimp Dip, 17
      French Fried Shrimp with Coral Dip, 15
      Indonesian Shrimp Dip, 17
    * Tuna Dip, 16

    * Spicy Tuna Dip, 16
    * Tuna Cream Dip, 16
    * Zippy Dip, 18
  * Franks, Crispy Crust, 13
  * Ham Mousse-Pâté, 19
  Ham Pinwheels, 20
  Links in Oriental Sauce, Little, 19
  Links Teriyaki, Little, 224
  Livers
    Chicken Liver Pâté, 20
    Easy Chicken Liver Pâté, 20
    Liver Pâté, 20
    Rumaki, 18
  Meatballs, Party, 21
  Meatballs, Tangy, 21
  Peanuts
    Hot Chili Nuts, 21
    Party Mix, 18
    Smoky Peanuts, 21
  Pizzas, Miniature, 7
  Spreads
    * Corned Beef Spread, Mini-Reuben, 8
    Guacamole Cocktail Spread, 9
    Guacamole Spread, 9
    * Liver Spread, Chopped, 9
    * Tuna Canapé Spread, 8
  * Sticks, Peanut Butter, 13
  * Sticks, Turkey, 287
  * Tamale Teasers, 13
  Teriyaki Steak for Fondue, 21
  * Wieners in Butter and Beer Sauce, 12
Apples
  Apples-on-a-stick, 81
  Baked Apples, Cinnamon, 147
  Baked Apples and Figs, 147
  Brown Betty, Apple, 148
  Cakes. See also Cakes, Apple
    Apple-Coconut Coffee Cakes, 78
    Apple Coffee Cake, 79
    Apple Dapple Cake, 72
    Apple Loaf Cake, 72
    Applesauce Cake, 72
  Casseroles
    * Scalloped Rutabaga and Apple Casserole, 110
    * Sweet Potato-Apple Casserole, 395
  Chicken, Apple, 277
  * Fried Apples, Southern, 147
  * Marshmallow Apple Crisp, 148
  Pancakes, German Apple, 47
  Pies
    Caramel-Topped Apple Pie, 247
    * Colonial Apple Pie, 246
    Crunchy Apple Pie, 246
    Fried Apple Pies, 247
    * Grated Apple Pie, 246
    Sour Cream Apple Pie, 247
  Pudding Soufflé, Apple, 150
  Scalloped Cabbage and Apples, 369
Apricots
  Bread, Apricot Nut, 45
  Coffee Cake, Quick Apricot, 39
  Pork Chops with Apricots, Spicy Glazed, 229

  Rice Pudding, Apricot, 144
  Salad. See Salads
  Sticks, Apricot, 120
  Sundaes, Butterscotch-Apricot, 155
Artichokes
  Delight, Artichoke, 361
  Hearts of Artichoke Supreme, 362
  Hearts with Sauce Winifred, Artichoke, 363
  with Horseradish Dip, Fresh Artichokes, 362
  Rollino, Artichoke, 363
  Soup, Artichoke, 344
  Stuffed, Artichokes, 361
  Stuffed with Crabmeat Louis, Artichoke, 362
Asparagus
  with Cashew Butter, Asparagus, 364
  Casserole(s)
    Asparagus Amandine, 364
    Asparagus Casserole, 114
    Asparagus, Peas, and Mushroom Casserole, 114
    Asparagus Pinwheel Casserole, 114
    Asparagus and Turkey Casserole, 289
    * Company Asparagus, 364
    Dilled Asparagus, 364
    Greenpea and Asparagus Casserole, 115
    Ham and Asparagus Casserole, 94
  Corn and Asparagus with Sour Cream, 378
  Milano, Asparagus, 365
  Mushrooms, Asparagus and Fresh, 365
  Pacifico, Asparagus, 366
  with Parmesan, Asparagus, 365
  Salad, Asparagus, 319
  Soup, Asparagus Cheese, 346
  with Sour Cream Sauce, Asparagus, 365
  Spears with Shrimp Sauce, Asparagus, 364
Avocados
  Bisque, Cool Avocado, 344
  Green Dragon Dip, 17
  Pie, Avocado Lime, 257
  Salad
    Avocado-Buttermilk Salad, 315
    Buffet Tuna-Avocado Loaf, 312
    Cherry Avocado Salad, 297
    Crab Salad in Avocado, 309
    Crab-Stuffed Avocados, 174
    Pimiento Cheese-Avocado Salad, 322
    Seafood-Avocado Salad, 310
  Soup, Cold Avocado, 344

B

Bananas
  Baked Bananas, 148
  Beverages. See also Beverages
    * Banana Milk Smoothee, 32

* Asterisks indicate budget recipes.

Banana-Strawberry Float, 27
* Chocolate Banana Nog, 31
Bread. *See also* Breads
   * Banana Bran Muffins, 40
   Banana Bran Nut Bread, 44
   * Banana Breakfast Loaf, 42
Cakes. *See also* Cakes
   Banana Nut Cake, 75
   Banana Nut Layer Cake, 73
   Sour Cream Banana Cake, 73
* Ice Cream, Banana-Orange, 138
Pie, Banana Meringue, 246
Pie, Banana Pumpkin, 260
* Pudding, Banana, 141
Barbecue
   Chicken
      Backyard Barbecued Chicken, 279
      Barbecued Chicken, 278
      Chicken Napoli, 271
      Chicken Teriyaki Barbecue, 278
      * Easy Barbecued Chicken, 279
      Kentucky Barbecued Chicken, 278
      Outdoor Barbecued Chicken, 279
      * Oven-Barbecued Chicken, 279
      Saucy Chicken, 269
      Stuffed Chicken Breasts Dixie, 276
      * Virginia Barbecued Chicken, 278
   * Meat Patties, Barbecue, 193
   Sauces
      * Barbecue Sauce, 334
      Barbecue Sauce for Chicken, 335
      Best Barbecue Sauce, 334
      Butter Barbecue Sauce, 334
      * Easiest Barbecue Sauce, 335
      * Fiesta Barbecue Sauce for Chicken, 334
      Hamburger Barbecue Sauce, 335
      Hawaiian Barbecue Sauce, 334
      Herb Barbecue Sauce, 335
      Old-Fashioned Hot Barbecue Sauce, 335
      * Pit Barbecue Sauce, 335
      Quick Barbecue Sauce, 334
      Spicy Barbecue Sauce, 336
      Texas Barbecue Sauce, 336
Beans
   Baked
      Baked Beans with Cheese Swirls, 381
      * Baked Beans Deluxe, 112
      Beef-Baked Beans, 380
      Calico Baked Beans, 380
      * Grandma's Baked Beans, 380
      * Pickle Relish Baked Beans, 382
      Savory Baked Beans, 379
   * Bean 'n Sausage Stir, 218
   Beans Hawaiian Style, 111
   Casseroles
      Onion-Bean Bake, 382
      Texas Bean Casserole, 111
   Green, Snap, String
      Dilly Beans, 366
      Fresh Green Beans with New Potatoes, 366
      Fried Green Beans, 383
      Green Beans Mornay, 367
      Green Beans Polonaise, 367
      Green Beans with Special Sauce, 366
      Green Beans Supreme, 366
      * Grilled Green Beans, 367
      Kentucky Wonder Beans and Tomatoes, 382

      Savory Green Beans, 367
   * Hot Bean Dip, 18
   Limas
      * Braised Pork Shoulder with Lima Beans, 226
      Casseroles
         * Baked Lima Beans, 381
         Lima Bean and Mushroom Casserole, 111
         Lima-Cheese Bake, 381
         Sausage-Bean Casserole, 111
         Sausage and Bean Supper, 219
      Dixie Lima Beans, 379
      Southern Dried Lima Beans, 380
   Pinto
      * Frijoles (Pinto Beans), 382
      * Red Beans and Rice, 381
      Refried Beans (Frijoles Refritos), 380
      * Texas Frijoles (Cooked Pinto Beans), 382
   Salads
      Bean Sprout Salad, 317
      * Four-Bean Salad, 318
      Great Bean Salad, 317
      Marinated Beans, 316
   * Soup, Senate Bean, 345
   * Soup, Old-Fashioned Bean, 345
Beef
   Bacon-Beef Roll-Ups, 18
   Beef and Beans Paprikash, 208
   * Bologna, Rotisserie, 193
   Bourguignon, Beef, 196
   * Brisket, Beef, 209
   Casseroles
      Baked Beef and Rice, 96
      Beef-Noodle Casserole, 98
      Burgundy Beef, 195
      * Chili con Carne Casserole, 100
      * Corn Casserole, Beef-, 98
      * Eggplant Meat Casserole, 109
      * Enchilada Casserole, 97
      * Favorite Casserole, 97
      * German Meat Casserole, 97
      * Ground Beef Casserole, 99
      * Ground Beef in Sour Cream, 95
      * Hamburger-Corn Casserole, 98
      * Hamburger-Noodle Bake, 99
      * Italian Meat Casserole, 96
      Johnny Marzetti, 100
      * Mañana Beef Dinner, 96
      * Meatball Casserole, 96
      Mexican Casserole, 97
      * Potato Patch Casserole, 107
      * Ranch-Style Lentil Casserole, 110
      * South's Favorite Casserole, 100
      * Spanish Delight Casserole, 92
      * and Squash Casserole, Beef, 98
      Tasty Casserole, 113
      * Zucchini Casserole, Beef-, 99
   * Crescent Creole Meat Pie, 217
   Curried Beef Nuggets, 19
   * East Indian Beef, 196
   Enchiladas, 210
   Filet of Beef Duke of Wellington, 216
   * Florentine Beef with Rice, 195
   Fondue, Beef, 20
   Fondue Bourguignon, 194
   Franks
      * Blanketed Franks, 224
      * Casserole, Frank-Corn Muffin, 223

      * Corn Dogs, 225
      Corn 'n Franks, 224
      * Crispy Crust Franks, 13
      * Curried Frankfurters, 223
      Frank Pineapple Kabobs, 223
      Little Links Teriyaki, 224
      Marinated Franks, 225
      * Party Franks, 223
      Rancho Hot Dogs, 225
      Sweet and Pungent Frankfurters, 224
      Sweet-and-Sour Franks, 224
      * Wieners in Butter and Beer Sauce, 12
      * Wieners, Chip 'n Cheese, 225
   Hamburgers
      Beefburger Special, 197
      Blue Cheese Hamburgers, 194
      Home on the Range Burgers, 194
      * Polynesian Hamburgers, 194
      Smoke-Flavored Burgers, 194
      Western Burgers, 12
   * Hash, Hamburger, 197
   Kabobs
      Beef Kabobs Waikiki, 198
      Beef Teriyaki Kabobs, 199
      Charley-Bobs, 199
      Kabobs, Kyoto, 198
      Shish Kabobs, 199
      Sirloin Kabobs, 198
   Livers
      Casserole, Liver and Rice, 101
      French-Fried Liver, 204
      Liver Piquant, 205
      * Spread, Chopped Liver, 9
   * Log, Cheese-and-Beef, 10
   Meatballs
      * Cheese Meatballs with Spaghetti Sauce, 205
      * Deviled Meatballs, 204
      Party Meatballs, 21
      * Saucy Meatballs, 204
      Sherried Spaghetti and Meatballs, 206
      Swedish Meatballs, 206
      Sweet and Sour Meatballs, 205
      Tangy Meatballs, 21
   Meat Loaf
      Beef and Potato Loaf, 203
      * Cheeseburger Loaf, 199
      Cheese-Stuffed Meat Loaf, 200
      Creole Meat Loaf, 200
      Favorite Meat Loaf, 204
      Frosted Meat Loaf, 201
      Gourmet Meat Loaf, 202
      Hamburger and Sausage Loaf, 200
      Layered Meat Loaf, 201
      Mainly-Meat Loaf, 200
      * Meat Loaf Delight, 201
      Meat Loaf with Orange Slices, 202
      Meat Loaf in the Round, 201
      Meat Loaf with Zesty Topping, 203
      Triple Meat Loaf with Mustard Sauce, 203
      Triple-Treat Meat Loaf, 202
   * Meat Patties, Barbecue, 193
   * Mexican Dinner, 208
   Noisettes of Beef, 209
   Roasts
      Chuck Roast, Barbecued, 216
      * Chuck Roast, Marinated, 208
      Grilled Beef Roast, Savory, 209

* Asterisks indicate budget recipes.

index

Pot
    Daube of Beef with Fruit (Hot Pot Roast), 207
    Deviled Pot Roast, 207
    Fruited Spiced Pot Roast, 210
    Sirloin of Beef (Rare), Roast, 209
Sandwiches
    Beefy Spread Sandwiches, 3
    Hot Burger-Cheese Sandwiches, 3
    The Trail Driver, 6
Short Ribs
    * Braised Short Ribs with Vegetables, 206
    Pineapple Beef Short Ribs, 208
* Spanish Rice with Meat, 165
Steaks
    Bonanza Steak Broil, 193
    Chef's Grilled Steak, 197
    * Chuck Steak, Lemon Barbecued, 197
    Country Steak à la Sonora, 198
    Round
        Beef Almond Supreme, 210
        Chicken Fried Steak, 212
        * Grillades with Gravy, 210
        Oriental Celery Steak, 211
        Oven Barbecued Round Steak, 210
        Paprika Beef, 211
        Round Steak Italia, 214
        Round Steak Ranchero, 213
        Round Steak Roll-Ups, 214
        Round Steak Special, 214
        Spanish Round Steak, 213
        Steak Floridian, 213
        Steak with Olives, 214
        Steak Siciliano, 213
        Swiss Steak
            Individual Swiss Steaks, 216
            Savory Swiss Steak, 216
    Sirloin and Roquefort, 215
    Sukiyaki, 215
    Teriyaki Steak, 212
    Teriyaki Steak for Fondue, 21
Stew. See Soups and Stews
Stroganoff, Hamburger, 212
Stroganoff, Man-Style Beef, 217
* Tacos, Beef, 215
* Tamale Pie, Hot, 212
Wieners. See Franks
Beets
    Beets with Pineapple, 384
    Beets in Sour Cream Sauce, 384
    * Harvard Beets, 383
    Orange Beets, 383
    * Pickled Beets, 384
    * Red Beet Eggs, 161
    * Salad, Congealed Beet, 316
    * Salad, Molded Beet, 316
    Sauced Beets and Onions, 384
Beverages
    * Buttermilk, Pink, 28
    Champagne Punch, 23
    Chocolate
        * Chocolate Banana Nog, 31
        Chocolate-Peppermint Shakes, 33
        Hot and Ready Chocolate, 28
        Hot Tarry Chocolate, 28
        Spanish Egg Chocolate, 30
    Coffee
        Cafe Brûlot, 30
        Cafe Mexicano, 29
        Luscious Coffee Frosted, 30

        * Spiced Coffee Vienna, 29
    Eggnog
        Eggnog Deluxe, 30
        Eggnog for Thirty, 30
        Eight-Egg Nog, 31
        George Whitfield's Eggnog, 32
        Holiday Eggnog, 31
        Hot Almond Eggnog, 31
        Orange Eggnog, 31
    Fruit
        * Banana Milk Smoothee, 32
        Banana-Strawberry Float, 27
        Cranberry Brunch Float, 24
        Frozen Daiquiri, 24
        * Lemonade, Buttermilk, 29
        Lemonade, Old-Fashioned, 24
        Limeade, 24
        Lime Delight, 24
        Orange-Lime Fizz, 26
        * Orange Milk Shake, 33
        Pineapple Tea Fizz, 26
    Punch
        * Citrus Punch, 25
        Cranberry, 24
            Cranberry-Champagne Punch, 23
            Cranberry Christmas Punch, 23
            Sparkling Cranberry Punch, 23
            Tangy Orange-Cranberry Punch, 26
        * Fruit Punch, 25
        Fruit Punch Cooler, 25
        * Fruit Shake Cooler, 29
        * Orange-Grape Harvest Punch, 26
        Planters Punch, 25
        Punch for a Crowd, 27
        Ruby Red Frost, 28
        Strawberry Punch, 26
        Summertime Cooler, 27
        Three-Fruit Punch, 27
        Tropical Pineapple Punch, 26
    South Seas Sparkler, 28
    * Spicy Lemon Tingle, 25
    * Strawberry Cooler, 29
    Strawberry-Lemon Freeze, 27
    Hot Tom and Jerry, 33
    * Palm Springs Cooler, 29
    Tea
        Backyard Cooler, 24
        * Hot Spiced Afternoon Tea, 32
        * New Twist Iced Tea Cooler, 32
        Vegetable-Clam Juice Cocktail, 33
        Wine, Mulled, 32
Biscuits. See also Breads
    * Baking Powder Biscuits, 38
    Cheese Biscuits, 38
    Easy Buttermilk Biscuits, 38
    * Stir 'n' Roll Biscuits, 38
    * Whole Wheat Biscuits, 38
Blackberries
    Blackberry Meringue Pie, 248
    * Fresh Blackberry Pie, 247
    * Old-Fashioned Blackberry Pie, 248
Blueberries
    Fresh Blueberry Cream, 153
    * Muffins, Blueberry, 41
    * Pie, Blueberry, 248
    * Pie, Fresh Blueberry Glacé, 248
    Salad, Blueberry, 298
Bourbon Balls, 89
Breads

Biscuits
    * Baking Powder Biscuits, 38
    Buttermilk Biscuits, Easy, 38
    Cheese Biscuits, 38
    * Stir 'n' Roll Biscuits, 38
    * Whole Wheat Biscuits, 38
* Buttermilk Puffs, 46
* Carrot-Orange Bread, 44
Cheese
    Basil Cheese Bread, 39
    * Batterway Cheese and Herb Bread, 48
    Cheese Bread, 48
    * Cheese Crown, 49
    Skillet Cheese Bread, 39
* Chewy Dumplings, 39
Cinnamon Buns, 44
Coffee-Bran Küchen, 52
Coffee Cake, Quick Apricot, 39
Corn
    * Buttermilk Corn Bread, 35
    * Casserole, Chicken-Corn Bread, 101
    * Corn Kernel Corn Bread, 37
    * Country Corn Bread, 36
    Deluxe Corn Bread, 35
    * Dressing, Corn Bread, 292
    Dressing, Corn Bread-Sausage, 290
    * Florida Hoe Cake, 36
    * Florida Hush Puppies, 37
    * Hot Water Corn Bread, 38
    * Hush Puppies with Onions, 37
    Jalapeño Corn Bread, 36
    Mexican Corn Bread, 36
    * Southern Corn Dodgers, 37
    * Southern Corn Pones, 37
    * Tennessee Corn Bread, 36
    * Yeast Corn Bread, 49
Crêpes, Basic, 42
* Danish Pastry, 50
Doughnuts
    Chocolate Surprise Doughnuts, 42
    Doughnut Wonder Balls, 44
    * Drop Doughnuts, 43
    Japanese Doughnuts, 43
    * Pumpkin Doughnuts, 43
* Loaf, Banana Breakfast, 42
* Lost Bread, 41
Muffins
    * Banana Bran Muffins, 40
    * Blueberry Muffins, 41
    Butterfly Orange Muffins, 41
    Cheese Corn Muffins, 40
    * Corn Muffins, 41
    Molasses Muffins, 40
    * Oatmeal Muffins, 40
    * Sweet Potato Muffins, 41
    * Whole Wheat Muffins, 40
Nut
    Apricot Nut Bread, 45
    Banana Bran Nut Bread, 44
    Date Nut Bread, 48
    Pineapple Nut Bread, 45
Pancakes
    Eggcellent Pancakes, 47
    German Apple Pancakes, 47
    Soufflé Pancakes, 46
Pudding, Pineapple Upside Down Bread, 143
Pumpkin Bread, 45
Rolls
    Cheesy Biscuit Finger Rolls, 46
    * Onion Rolls, 45

* Asterisks indicate budget recipes.

Yeast
  * Orange-Cinnamon Yeast Rolls, 55
  Pecan Yeast Rolls, 56
  * Refrigerator Rolls, 55
  Sixty-Minute Rolls, 56
  * Sweet Potato Rolls, 56
  * Sweet Potato Yeast Rolls, 55
Spoonbread, Cheese, 46
* Spoonbread, Plain, 46
* Waffles, Cornmeal, 47
* Waffles, Pecan, 47
Yeast
  * Basic Sweet Dough, 50
  Basic Yeast Dough, 53
  Christmas Küchen, 51
  Dutch Batter Bread, 49
  * Old-Country Tomato Bread, 57
  Old-Fashioned Raisin Bread, 54
  * Onion Bread, 54
  * Orange-Cinnamon Yeast Rolls, 55
  Pecan Yeast Rolls, 56
  * Pumpernickel, 53
  * Sally Lunn, 54
  Swedish Rye Bread, 57
  * Sweet Brioche, 52
  * Sweet Potato Yeast Rolls, 55
  * Yeast Corn Bread, 49
  * Yeast White Bread, 56
Broccoli
  Casseroles
    Broccoli-Peas Casserole, 368
    Broccoli Surprise, 369
    Chicken Broccoli Casserole, 281
    Ham, Macaroni, and Broccoli Casserole, 112
    Rice-Broccoli Casserole, 108
    Tuna-Broccoli Almondine, 190
  Fresh Broccoli with Sour Cream Dressing, 369
  Salad, Broccoli, 315
  Shrimp Crisp, Broccoli-, 182
  with Shrimp Sauce, Broccoli, 368
  Sicilian Broccoli, 368
  Souffléed Broccoli, 368
Brownies. See Cookies
Brussels Sprouts
  Brussels Sprouts Oriental, 368
  * Deviled Brussels Sprouts, 367
Buttermilk
  Avocado-Buttermilk Salad, 315
  * Buttermilk Lemonade, 29
  Buttermilk Pie, 251
  * Buttermilk Puffs, 46
  * Pink Buttermilk, 28
Butterscotch
  * Bars, Butterscotch, 123
  Brownies, Butterscotch, 119
  Pie, Butterscotch, 251
  * Rice Pudding, Butterscotch, 144
  * Sauce, Jiffy Butterscotch, 336
  Sundaes, Butterscotch-Apricot, 155

C

Cabbage
  Cabbage Chop Suey, 371
  Cabbage with Caraway Seed Butter, 371
  Casseroles

* Asterisks indicate budget recipes.

  * Baked Cream Cabbage, 370
  Cabbage-Noodle Bake, 370
  Cabbage Supreme, 370
  * Tex-Mex Cabbage, 371
  Company Cabbage, 369
  Rolls, Cabbage, 370
  Salad, Fruited Cabbage, 319
  Scalloped Cabbage and Apples, 369
  Stuffed Cabbage Leaves, 369
Cakes
  Apple
    Apple Dapple Cake, 72
    Apple Loaf Cake, 72
    Applesauce Cake, 72
    Date and Applesauce Cake, 61
  Banana
    Banana Nut Cake, 75
    Banana Nut Layer Cake, 73
    Sour Cream Banana Cake, 73
  Bohemian Cake, 74
  Chantilly Cake, 75
  Cheesecake, 78
    Berry-Glazed Cheesecake, 78
    Sour Cream Cheesecake, 67
  Chocolate
    Cream Cake, Chocolate, 66
    Different Chocolate Cake, 67
    Fudge Cake, Double, 66
    Fudge Cake, Oldtime, 66
    Nut Cake, Chocolate, 74
    Oatmeal Cake, Chocolate, 74
    * Sauerkraut Chocolate Cake, 76
    Sweet Chocolate Cake, 76
  Christmas Pecan Cake, 71
  Coffee Cakes
    Apple-Coconut Coffee Cakes, 78
    Apple Coffee Cake, 79
    Berry Patch Coffee Cake, 60
    Elizabeth's Easy Coffee Cake, 60
    * German Streusel Coffee Cake, 61
    Sour Cream Coffee Cake, 59
  Cola Cake, 64
  Date, 61
    Date and Applesauce Cake, 61
    Date-Nut Loaf Cake, 62
  Dump Cake, 61
  Fruitcakes
    Christmas Nut Fruitcake, 60
    Easy-Do Fruitcake, 63
    Favorite Fruitcake, 63
    Kentucky Fruitcake, 62
    Light Fruitcake, 62
    Mardi Gras Fruitcake, 63
  * Gingerbread, 68
  * Gingerbread, Plantation, 69
  Kentucky Jam Cake, 70
  Lady Baltimore Cake, 64
  Man on the Moon Cake, 68
  * Marble Cake, 65
  Mississippi Mud Cake, 63
  * Molasses Pound Cake, 59
  * Nutmeg Cake, 68
  * Oatmeal Cake, 70
  Orange
    Orange-Nut Butter Cake, 65
    Orange Rum Cake, 69
    Orange Slice Cake, 69
  * Peanut Butter Cake, 70
  Pineapple Ambrosia Upside-Down Cake, 77
  * Red Velvet Cake, 79
  * Silver Cake, 71
  Strawberry Cream Roll, 72

  Symphony Cake, 71
  Tutti-Frutti Cake, 77
Canapés. See Appetizers and Snacks
Candies and Confections
  Almond Paste, 82
  Apples-on-a-Stick, 81
  Bourbon Balls, 89
  Chocolate Crunchies, 82
  Date Nut Fondant, 85
  Divinity, 84
  * Divinity, Ripple, 81
  Filbert Sweetmeats, 84
  Fudge
    Caramel Fudge Roll, 83
    * Fudgies, 83
    Old-Fashioned Chocolate Fudge, 82
    10-Minute Fudge, 83
    * Quick Peanut Butter Fudge, 87
  Glazed Nuts, 85
  Heavenly Delight, 84
  * Molasses Coconut Chews, 82
  Peanut
    Chocolate-Covered Peanut Balls, 86
    Chocolate Peanut Logs, 86
    Molasses Peanut Crunch, 85
    Peanut Brittle, 86
    Peanut Brittle, Dixie, 86
    Raisin Peanut Clusters, 85
  Pecan Brittle, 83
  Pecans, Orange, 84
  Penuche, 87
  Pralines, 88
    Louisiana Yam Pralines, 87
    Pecan Pralines, 88
    Plantation Pralines, 88
    Southern Pralines, 87
  * Taffy, Molasses, 88
  * Taffy, Vanilla, 88
  Walnut Clusters, 84
  Walnuts, Minted, 83
Carrots
  Baked Pineapple and Carrots, 372
  * Carrot-Orange Bread, 44
  Carrots with Celery Seed Sauce, 372
  Crisp Candied Carrots, 372
  Chicken and Carrot Salad, 304
  Glazed Carrots, 372
  Glazed Carrots and Onions, 372
  Hugo's Carrots, 373
  * Lemon-Glazed Carrots, 371
  Marinated Carrots, 371
  Sweet and Sour Carrots, 373
Casseroles
  Beef. See Beef
  * Caballero Casserole, 112
  Cheese. See Cheese
  Chicken. See Chicken
  Fish and Shellfish. See also Shrimp, Tuna, Oysters
    Seafood Casserole, 180
  Ham. See Pork
  Macaroni. See Macaroni
  Noodles. See Noodles
  Pork. See Pork
  Rice. See Rice
  Turkey. See Turkey
  Vegetable. See Specific Vegetable
Catfish
  Cajun Catfish, 169
  Continental Catfish, 170
  Crispy Catfish, 170

* Dixieland Catfish, 170
* Grilled Sesame Catfish, 170
New Orleans Catfish, 171
* Smoky Broiled Catfish, 169
* Southern Fried Catfish, 170
Cauliflower
    Batter-Fried Cauliflower, 373
    Cauliflower Mold, 320
    Cauliflower Oriental, 373
    * Parmesan Cauliflower, 373
Celery
    * Celery Fingers, 19
    Creamed Celery Continental, 386
    Ham and Celery Salad, 307
    Zippy Stuffed Celery Sticks, 13
Cheese
    Baked Fish and Cheese, 171
    * Baked Trout and Cheese, 188
    Balls. See Appetizers and Snacks
    Blue Cheese Chicken, 280
    Breads. See also Breads, Cheese
    Basil Cheese Bread, 39
        * Batterway Cheese and Herb Bread, 48
        Cheese Bread, 48
        * Cheese Crown, 49
        Cheese Spoonbread, 46
        Cheesy Biscuit Finger Rolls, 46
        Skillet Cheese Bread, 39
    Casseroles
        Cheddar Chops Casserole, 95
        * Cheese Grits Casserole, 163
        Cheese Rice, 181
        * Corn-Cheese Casserole, 109
        Crab and Cheese Casserole, 114
        Elegant Cheese Puff, 113
        * Joseph Harris Cheese Casserole, 113
        Macaroni and Cheese, 94
        * Okra and Cheese Casserole, 109
        * Skillet Macaroni and Cheese, 94
        * Squash-Cheese Casserole, 110
    Coeur à la Crème, 154
    Cottage
        Cottage Cheese Blintzes, 153
        * Cottage Cheese Cookies, 127
        Cottage Cheese Scrambled Eggs, 162
    Cream Cheese Frosting, 73
    Deviled Eggs with Cheese, 159
    Dips
        Cottage Cheese Dip, 16
        * Curried Cottage Cheese Dip, 15
        * Peanut Butter-Cheese Dip, 17
    Eggs, Cheese-Stuffed, 162
    Pineapple Cheese Pie, 259
    Salads. See also Salads, Cheese
        Cheese and Vegetable Salad, 316
        Cherry Avocado Salad, 297
        Frozen Fruit Cheese Salad, 299
        Lemon Cheese Salad, 303
        * Molded Macaroni and Cheese, 322
        Pimiento Cheese-Avocado Salad, 322
    Sandwiches. See also Sandwiches
        * Cheese and Egg Sandwich Filling, 4
        Cheese Salad Sandwich Filling, 4
        Cheese and Turkey Melt, 4
        * Cream Cheese Sandwich Filling, 4
        * Cucumber-Cheese Sandwiches, 4

    Ham 'n Cheese French Toast, 5
    Hot Burger-Cheese Sandwiches, 3
    Tuna-Cheese Soufflé Sandwiches, 7
Sauces. See Sauces, Cheese
* Soup, Cheese, 344
Spreads. See Appetizers and Snacks
Cherries
    * Cherries à la Mode, 151
    Cherries in the Snow, 150
    Cherry Delight Dessert, 150
    Cherry Whirl, 152
    Pie. See also Pies, Cherry
        Cheery Cherry Pie, 246
        Cherry Cream Pie, 249
        Lemon-Cherry Pie, 254
        Refrigerator Cherry Pie, 249
    Salad. See also Salads, Cherry
        Black Cherry Salad, 295
        Cherry-Avocado Salad, 297
        Cherry Mallow Salad, 296
        Shimmering Cherry Salad, 296
Chicken
    Apple Chicken, 277
    Baked Chicken Parmesan, 278
    Barbecued, 278
        Backyard Barbecued Chicken, 279
        Chicken Napoli, 271
        Chicken Teriyaki Barbecue, 278
        * Easy Barbecued Chicken, 279
        Kentucky Barbecued Chicken, 278
        Outdoor Barbecued Chicken, 279
        * Oven-Barbecued Chicken, 279
        * Saucy Chicken, 269
        Stuffed Chicken Breasts Dixie, 276
        * Virginia Barbecued Chicken, 278
    Breasts
        à la Newberry, Chicken, 283
        Apple Chicken, 277
        Chicken Jubilee, 272
        Chicken Kiev, 267
        Chicken Oriental, 270
        with Sauce Béarnaise, Chicken Breasts, 281
        Stuffed Chicken Breasts Dixie, 276
        Skillet Chicken Supreme, 274
        in Wine, Easy Baked Chicken Breasts, 277
    Broiled Chicken with Herbs, 280
    * Broiled Chicken, Lemon, 280
    Casseroles
        Baked Broiler Chicken, 274
        Baked Chicken Puff, 270
        Blue Cheese Chicken, 280
        Chicken Broccoli Casserole, 281
        * Chicken-Corn Bread Casserole, 101
        * Chicken Enchilada Casserole, 101
        Chicken Florentine, 284
        * Chicken-Green Noodle Casserole, 104
        Chicken-Macaroni-Cheese Bake, 274
        * Chicken-Noodle-Almond Casserole, 102
        * Chicken Noodle Casserole, 104
        Chicken Paella, 268
        Chicken-Shrimp Tetrazzini, 104
        * Chicken Spaghetti, 103
        * Chicken-Vegetable Bake, 277
        Chicken Vermouth with Rice, 274
        Chicken-Wild Rice Casserole, 103
        * Continental Chicken Casserole, 104

    Herbed Chicken, 269
    * Party Chicken Casserole, 102
    Sherried Chicken, 102
    * Swiss-Chicken Casserole, 103
    Vatapa, 273
Champagne Chicken, 284
Chicken with Apricot Jam, 273
Chicken Bake, 276
* Chicken Cacciatore for Freezing, 280
Chicken Caribbean, 283
Chicken Curry, 282
* Chicken 'n Dressing, 283
Chicken Marinade, 270
Chicken with Oysters, 275
Chicken Pie with Sweet Potato Crust, 271
Chicken Salonika, 272
* Chicken Spaghetti, 103
Coq au Vin, 284
Country Captain, 282
Creamed Chicken in Avocado Half Shell, 281
East India Chicken, 284
Fried
    Chinese Fried Chicken, 268
    Delectable Fried Chicken Breasts, 271
    Everyday Fried Chicken, 268
    * Southern Fried Chicken, 267
Ginger-Glazed Chicken, 270
Livers
    Chicken Liver Pâté, 20
    Chicken Livers Burgundy, 272
    Easy Chicken Liver Pâté, 20
    Liver Pâté, 20
    Sauce. See Sauces, Chicken Liver
    Rumaki, 18
Mexican Chicken, 272
Oriental Chicken, 270
Polynesian Chicken, 269
Spaghetti Chicken Bake, 273
Salad. See Salads
* Sandwiches, Crunchy Chicken, 4
* Southern Upside-Down Dinner, 276
* Stewed Chicken and Dumplings, 269
Sweet-Sour Chicken, 275
Thai-Style Chicken, 275
Chili
    * Casserole, Chili con Carne, 100
    * Chili for a Crowd, 352
    Chili Italexico, 352
    * Chili-Rice Dish, 166
    * Dip, Chili-Cheese, 15
    Dip, Chili Dandy, 14
    Hot Chili, 353
    Louisiana Chili Rice, 166
Chocolate
    Beverages
        * Chocolate Banana Nog, 31
        Chocolate-Peppermint Shakes, 33
        Hot and Ready Chocolate, 28
        Hot Tarry Chocolate, 28
        Spanish Egg Chocolate, 30
    Cakes. See also Cakes, Chocolate
        Cream Cake, Chocolate, 66
        Different Chocolate Cake, 67
        Fudge Cake, Double, 66
        Fudge Cake, Oldtime, 66
        Nut Cake, Chocolate, 74
        Oatmeal Cake, Chocolate, 74

* Asterisks indicate budget recipes.

* Sauerkraut Chocolate Cake, 76
Sweet Chocolate Cake, 76
Candy. *See also* Candies and Confections
   Chocolate Crunchies, 82
   * Fudgies, 83
   Old-Fashioned Chocolate Fudge, 82
   * Quick Peanut Butter Fudge, 87
   10-Minute Fudge, 83
Chocolate Angel Food Dessert, 149
Chocolate Bavarian, 149
Cookies. *See also* Cookies
   * Baked Chocolate Fudge Squares, 124
   Chocolate Chip Cookies, 132
   Chocolate-Nut Puffs, 131
   Chocolate Toffee Squares, 124
   Choco-Nut Brownies, 119
Doughnuts, Chocolate Surprise, 42
Frosting
   Chocolate Cream Cheese Frosting, 76
   Chocolate Frosting, 63, 75
   Easy Chocolate Frosting, 77
   German Chocolate Frosting, 78
Ice Cream, Chocolate, 137
Ice Cream, Chocolate Custard, 137
Meringue au Chocolate, 153
Pies
   Chocolate-Butterscotch Pie, 249
   Chocolate Chip Pie, 249
   Chocolate Pie, 250
   Chocolate Rum Pie, 250
   Fudge Pie, 243
   German Chocolate Pie, 250
   * Never Fail Chocolate Pie, 250
   Pudding, Chocolate Fudge, 142
Pudding Cups, Double-Chocolate, 142
Sauce. *See* Sauces
Soufflé, Chocolate, 149
Clam
   Appetizer Clams Casino, 14
   Chowder, Maryland Clam, 359
   Chowder, The Warehouse's Clam, 359
   Dip, Clam Appetizer, 15
   Dip, Clam Chip, 14
   Stuffing for Poultry or Fish, 291
Coconut
   Coffee Cake, Apple-Coconut, 78
   * Coconut-Noodle Custard, 141
   Coconut Torte, 151
   Cookies
      Bars, Coconut, 122
      * Bars, Coconut Cherry, 122
      Bars, Coconut Pecan, 121
      Brownies, Upside-Down Coconut, 119
      * Coconut Jumbles, 133
      * Coconut Puffs, 127
      * Crisp Coconut Cookies, 128
   Pie, Coconut, 252
   Pie, One-Step Coconut Custard, 252
Coffee Cake. *See* Cakes
Coffee. *See* Beverages
Cola Cake, 64
Cola Fruit Salad, 299
Cookies
   Almond Cakes, 133
   Apricot Sticks, 120
   Bars and Squares

* Asterisks indicate budget recipes.

Baked Chocolate Fudge Squares, 124
* Butterscotch Bars, 123
Chocolate-Toffee Squares, 124
Coconut Bars, 122
* Coconut Cherry Bars, 122
Coconut Pecan Bars, 121
Date Nut Bar Cookies, 121
Fruit and Nut Bars, 119
Fruit 'n' Nut Squares, 120
* Lemon Bars Deluxe, 124
* Lemon Squares, 122
Marzipan Bars, 120
Molasses Date-Nut Bars, 122
Orange Slice Bars, 120
* Peanut Brittle Delights, 117
Penuche Bars, 123
Taffy Bars, 123
Brownies
   Best Brownies, 118
   Brownies Deluxe, 118
   Butterscotch Brownies, 119
   Choco-Nut Brownies, 119
   Upside-Down Coconut Brownies, 119
Chocolate Chip Cookies, 132
Chocolate-Nut Puffs, 131
Coconut. *See also* Coconut
   * Coconut Jumbles, 133
   Coconut Macaroon Cookies, 128
   * Coconut Puffs, 127
   * Crisp Coconut Cookies, 128
Coffee Crescents, 135
* Corn Flake Macaroons, 131
* Cottage Cheese Cookies, 127
Crisp Buttery Cookies, 131
Date Nut Cookies, 125
Date Sticks, 121
Fruitcake Cookies, 129
Fruit Cookies, 125
* Gingerbread Men, 118
"Hello Dolly" Cookies, 123
Holiday Fruit Cookies, 125
Holiday Lizzies, 129
Koulourakia (Cookie Twists), 133
* Meringue Cookies, 128
* Molasses Cookies, Crisp Rolled, 133
Molasses Oatmeal Cookies, 126
* Oatmeal Cookies, Old-Fashioned, 127
* Oatmeal Delights, 127
Oldtime Jumbles, 117
Orange
   Orange Date Cookies, 130
   Orange Oatmeal Cookies, 128
   * Orange Sugar Cookies, 134
Peanut
   * Peanut Butter Cookies, 130
   * Peanut-Oatmeal Cookies, 131
   Salted Peanut Cookies, 129
Pecan Cookies, 131
Raisin Cookies, Jumbo, 126
Rocky Road Cookies, 130
* Sesame Seed Wafers, 124
Smackeroons, 125
Sour Cream
   Sour Cream Cookies, 126
   Sour Cream Nut Cookies, 126
   Sour Cream-Nutmeg Sugar Cookies, 134
   * Sour Cream Twists, 132

Sugar
   Brown Sugar Refrigerator Cookies, 135
   * Favorite Sugar Cookies, 129
   * Orange Sugar Cookies, 134
   * Powdered Sugar Cookies, 134
   Sour Cream-Nutmeg Sugar Cookies, 134
   * Sugar Cookies, 135
* Yogurt Cookies, 132
Yum Yum Cookies, 132
Corn
   and Asparagus with Sour Cream, Corn, 378
   * Barbecued Corn, 376
   Casseroles
      * Baked Tomatoes and Corn, 397
      * Beef-Corn Casserole, 98
      * Corn-Cheese Casserole, 109
      * Corn Custard for Two, 377
      * Corn and Oyster Scallop, 178
      Creamed Fresh Corn, 91
      * Elegant Scalloped Corn, 378
      * Hamburger-Corn Casserole, 98
      Southwestern Corn Scallop, 377
      * and Tomato Casserole, Corn, 109
      Top Hat Cheese and Corn Soufflé, 378
   Corn Bread. *See* Breads
   Corn and Crab Imperial, 173
   Corn 'n' Franks, 224
   * Corn on the Grill, 378
   Foil-Baked Corn on the Cob with Herb Butter, 378
   Fritters, Corn, 377
   * Fritters, Fresh Corn, 379
   Rarebit with Bacon, Fresh Corn, 377
   Rarebit, Blue Ribbon Corn, 377
Corned Beef
   * Corned Beef 'n Eggs, 196
   Corned Beef Spread Puff, 12
   * Hot Corned Beef Sandwiches, 5
   * Mini-Reuben Corned Beef Spread, 8
Cornish Hens. *See* Game
Crabmeat
   Casseroles
      Crab and Cheese Casserole, 114
      Crab Imperial, 173
      Crab and Shrimp au Gratin, 92
      Corn and Crab Imperial, 173
   Crab Burgers, 172
   Crab Cakes, 172
   Crab Ravigote, 173
   Crabmeat Louis, Artichoke Stuffed with, 362
   Crabmeat Royale, 173
   Crab Stew Monteleone, 358
   Crab Stuffed Avocados, 174
   Deviled Crabs, 172
   Deviled Crab, Gulf, 172
   Fried Soft-Shell Crabs, 172
   Hot Crabmeat Canapés, 14
   Salad in Avocado, Crab, 309
   Salad, Crabmeat, 309
   Sandwich, Grilled Crab, 5
   Stuffed Eggplant with Shrimp and Crabmeat, 375
Cranberries
   Cranberry Brunch Float, 24
   Cranberry Wine Sauce, 340
   Pie, Old-Fashioned Cranberry, 253

index 407

Punches
  Cranberry-Champagne Punch, 23
  Cranberry Christmas Punch, 23
  Cranberry Punch, 24
  Sparkling Cranberry Punch, 23
Salads
  Cranberry Gelatin Salad, 298
  Cranberry Salad, 298
  Frosty Cranberry Salad, 297
  Molded Cranberry Relish, 297
Crayfish
  Crayfish Jambalaya, 174
  Crayfish or Shrimp Étouffée, 174
Crust, Graham Cracker, 78
Cucumbers
  * Dip, Cucumber, 15
  Fried Cucumbers, 379
  Salads
    Cucumber-Lime Salad, 318
    Cucumber Mousse, 317
  Sandwiches, Cucumber, 5
  * Sandwiches, Cucumber-Cheese, 4
  Soup, Cucumber, 347
  in Sour Cream, Cucumbers, 379
  in Sour Cream with Fresh Dill, Cucumbers, 379
Curried
  Beef Nuggets, Curried, 19
  Chicken Curry, 282
  Chicken Salad, Curried, 305
  Chicken Salad in Tomato Petals, Curried, 307
  * Dip, Curried Cottage Cheese, 15
  Eggs in Rice Ring, Curried, 158
  * Frankfurters, Curried, 223
  * French Dressing, Curry, 328
  Lamb Burgers, Curried, 237
  Lamb Curry with Rice, 237
  * Rice, Curried, 165
  Rice, Elegant Curried, 164
  Shrimp, Curried, 184
  of Shrimp Suzanne, Curry, 183
Custards
  * Baked Custard, 140
  * Baked Peach Custard, 141
  * Coconut Noodle Custard, 141
  Custard Sauce, 150
  Peach Custard, Baked, 141

D

Dates
  Cake, Date, 61
  Cookies
    Date Nut Bar Cookies, 121
    Date Nut Cookies, 125
    Date Sticks, 121
    Molasses Date-Nut Bars, 122
    Orange Date Cookies, 130
  Date Nut Fondant, 85
  Filling, Date Cream, 75
  Filling, Date Pecan, 76
  Frosty Date-Sour Cream Mold, 300
  Mocha Date Dessert, 148
  Nut Bread, Date, 48
  Pie, Date Pecan, 259
  Pudding, Date, 141
Desserts. *See* Specific Kind
Doughnuts. *See* Breads
Dove. *See* Game

* Asterisks indicate budget recipes.

Dressings and Stuffings
  Oyster Dressing, Toasted Rice-, 291
  Oyster Stuffing, 290
  Poultry
    Clam Stuffing for Poultry or Fish, 291
    * Corn Bread Dressing, 292
    Corn Bread-Sausage Dressing, 290
    Oldtime Dressing, 291
    Orange-Prune Dressing, 291
    Rice Stuffing for Turkey, 292
    * Sage Dressing, 292
    Turkey-Time Sausage Dressing, 290
    Wild Rice Stuffing, 293
  Salad. *See* Salad Dressings
Duck. *See* Game

E

Eggs
  Baked Eggs, French-Style, 157
  Baked Eggs with Rice and Cheese Sauce, 159
  Casseroles
    Baked Deviled Egg Casserole, 106
    Baked Eggs New Orleans, 106
    * Company Casserole, 105
    Egg Casserole, 106
    * Ham and Egg Casserole, 95
  Cheese and Egg Appetizer, 11
  * Corned Beef 'n Eggs, 196
  Creamed Eggs Diable, 158
  Creamed Ham and Eggs, 233
  Creole, Baked Eggs, 157
  Creole, Eggs, 160
  Croquettes with Mushroom Sauce, Egg, 160
  * Curried Eggs in Rice Ring, 158
  Deviled Eggs, Beefy, 157
  Deviled Eggs with Cheese, 159
  Egg and Tuna Toss, 189
  * Eggs Germaine, 158
  Eggs Hussarde, 159
  * Molded Eggs and Vegetables, 320
  Omelets
    Herb Omelet, 161
    * Plain Omelet, 161
    Poultry or Meat Omelet, 161
    Swiss Omelet, 161
    * Ten-Minute Omelet, 161
  Pancakes, Eggcellent, 47
  Poached Egg on Ham Toast, 160
  * Red Beet Eggs, 161
  Scrambled
    Cottage Cheese Scrambled Eggs, 162
    Parsley Scrambled Eggs, 162
    * Scrambled, 162
    Swiss Scrambled Eggs, 162
  Stuffed
    Caper Stuffed Eggs, 163
    Cheese-Stuffed Eggs, 162
    * Peanutty Stuffed Eggs, 162
Eggnog. *See* Beverages
Eggplant
  à la Caribe, 374
  Baked Eggplant with Shrimp, 375
  Casseroles
    * Eggplant Casserole, 108
    Eggplant Patrice, 374

    Italian Eggplant, 375
    * Meat Casserole, Eggplant, 109
    Scalloped Eggplant, 376
  Caviar, Eggplant, 376
  * Panfried Eggplant, 375
  Parmesan, Eggplant, 374
  Scallop, Eggplant, 374
  * Spanish Eggplant, 373
  Stuffed Eggplant with Shrimp and Crabmeat, 375
  Stuffed with Oysters, Eggplant, 376

F

Figs, Baked Apples and, 147
Fish. *See also* Names of Fish and Seafood
  Anchovy-Cheese Dip, 15
  Bacon-Barbecued Fish, 171
  Baked Fish and Cheese, 171
  * Baked Fish, Savory, 171
  * Fish Salad Mold, 311
Flounder, Stuffed, 176
Franks
  Blanketed Franks, 224
  * Casserole, Frank-Corn Muffin, 223
  Casserole, Potato 'n Frank, 222
  Chinese Pepper Strips, 222
  * Chip 'n Cheese Wieners, 225
  * Corn Dogs, 225
  Corn 'n Franks, 224
  * Crispy Crust Franks, 13
  * Curried Frankfurters, 223
  Kabobs, Frank Pineapple, 223
  Little Links Teriyaki, 224
  Marinated Franks, 225
  * Party Franks, 223
  Rancho Hot Dogs, 225
  Sweet and Pungent Frankfurters, 224
  Sweet-and-Sour Franks, 224
  * Wieners in Butter and Beer Sauce, 12
Frostings and Fillings
  Frostings
    Caramel Frosting, 71, 73
    Chocolate Cream Cheese Frosting, 76
    Chocolate Frosting, 63
    Chocolate Frosting, Easy, 77
    Chocolate Marshmallow Frosting, 130
    Cream Cheese Frosting, 73
    German Chocolate Frosting, 78
    Kentucky Jam Cake Frosting, 70
    Mocha Whipped Cream Frosting, 76
    Seven Minute Frosting, 64
  Fillings
    Cottage Lemon Filling, 153
    Date Cream Filling, 75
    Date Pecan Filling, 76
    Lady Baltimore Filling, 64
    Lemon Cream Filling, 255
    Tutti-Frutti Filling, 77
  Glazes
    Berry Glaze, 78
    Orange Glaze, 69, 130
    Strawberry Glaze, 263
  Icing, Deluxe, 118
  Icing, Mystery, 79

Sauce, Hard, 152, 68
Sauce, Orange, 62
Toppings
    Cola Topping, 65
    Lunar Landing Topping, 68
    Whipped Orange Topping, 65
Fruits. *See also* Specific Fruit
    Dried Fruit Turnovers, 251
    Fruit Cocktail Mint Delight, 154
    Pie, Fruit Fluff, 245
    Salad. *See* Salads
    Sherry Fruit Cup, 149
    Soup, Fruit, 346
Fruitcake. *See* Cakes

G

Game
    Cornish Hens
        Cornish Game Hens "Veronique," 293
        Crumb-Coated Cornish Hens, 293
        Pineapple Glazed Cornish Hens, 292
    Doves, Roast, 240
    Duck
        Cajun Duck Supper, 239
        with Olive Sauce, Wild Duck, 240
        * Roasted in Aluminum Foil, Wild Duck, 241
    Quail, Ranch-Style Creamed, 241
    * Venison Recipe, 240
    Venison Roast, 240
Gingerbread. *See* Cakes
Glazes. *See* Frostings and Fillings
Grapes in Cognac, Green, 155
Grape Juice Pie, 254
Greens, Fresh Turnip, Mustard, or Collard, 385
Grits
    Casseroles
        * Cheese Grits Casserole, 163
        Quenelle de Grits, 92
        * Southern Grits Casserole, 105
        * True Grits Casserole, 105
    * Soufflé, Grits, 163
    * Stew, Grits-Beef, 352
    Veal Grillades and Grits, 220

H

Hamburgers. *See* Beef
* Hominy and Tomato Casserole, 106

I

Ice Cream
    * Banana-Orange Ice Cream, 138
    Butter Pecan Ice Cream, 139
    Chocolate Custard Ice Cream, 137
    Chocolate Ice Cream, 137
    Custard Ice Cream, Old-Fashioned, 137
    Parfait, Hawaiian, 154
    * Peach Ice Cream, 139
    Peach Ice Cream, Easy, 138
    Pie, Ice Cream, 253

* Asterisks indicate budget recipes.

* Pineapple-Lemon Ice Cream, 138
* Strawberry Ice Cream, 139
Strawberry Ice Cream, Rich, 140
Sundaes, Butterscotch-Apricot, 155
Tia Maria Marble Ice Cream, 139
* Vanilla Ice Cream, 140
Vanilla Ice Cream, Marshmallow-, 140

L

Lamb
    Burgers
        Chili Lamburgers, 239
        Curried Lamb Burgers, 237
    Casserole, Lamb Risotto, 100
    Chops with Herb Butter, Lamb Loin, 239
    Chops, Teriyaki Lamb Shoulder, 237
    Curry with Rice, Lamb, 237
    Kabobs, Fruited Lamb, 238
    Kabobs, Lamb Shish, 238
    Lamb and Rice Skillet Dinner, 238
    Leg of Lamb, Barbecued, 237
    Leg of Lamb, Stuffed, 236
    Roast
        Marinated Baby Lamb Racks, 236
        Rack of Lamb for Two, 237
        Roast Lamb Rosemary, 236
    Shoulder with Cumberland Sauce, 238
    Spareribs, Honey-Lemon Lamb, 239
Lemon
    Chicken, Lemon Broiled, 280
    * Chuck Steak, Lemon Barbecued, 197
    * Ice Cream, Pineapple-Lemon, 138
    * Lemon Bars Deluxe, 124
    * Lemon-Glazed Carrots, 371
    Lemon-Molasses Ice Cream Sauce, 338
    Lemon-Parsley Sauce, 338
    Lemon Squares, 122
    Pies
        Cherry Pie, Lemon-, 254
        Cream Cheese Pie, Lemon, 255
        Cream Pie, Lemon, 255
        Custard Pie, Lemon, 255
        Frozen Lemon Pie, 256
        Ice Box Pie, Lemon, 245
        Meringue Pie, Lemon, 256
        Pineapple-Lemon Lattice Pie, 260
        Tarts, Lemon, 254
    Salad, Lemon Cheese, 303
    Salad, Tangy Lemon-Lime, 303
    * Spicy Lemon Tingle, 25
Lemonade. *See* Beverages
Lettuce, Wilted, 321
Lime
    Lime Delight, 24
    Orange-Lime Fizz, 26
    Pie, Avocado Lime, 257
    Salad, Cucumber-Lime, 318
    Salad, Tangy Lemon-Lime, 303
Limeade. *See* Beverages
Lobster
    Boiled Lobster, 176
    Broiled Florida Lobster, 175
    Broiled Lobster, 176
    Gourmet Rock Lobster, 175
    Lobster Newberg, 175

M

Macaroni
    Casseroles
        Ham, Macaroni, and Broccoli Casserole, 112
        Macaroni and Cheese, 94
        * Skillet Macaroni and Cheese, 94
    Salads
        * Ham and Macaroni Toss, 308
        * Macaroni and Chicken Salad, 304
        * Molded Macaroni and Cheese, 322
        * Tuna-Macaroni Salad, 312
Meat. *See* Specific Kind
Meatballs
    * Cheese Meatballs with Spaghetti Sauce, 205
    * Deviled Meatballs, 204
    Party Meatballs, 21
    * Saucy Meatballs, 204
    Sherried Spaghetti and Meatballs, 206
    Swedish Meatballs, 206
    Sweet and Sour Meatballs, 205
    Tangy Meatballs, 21
Mint Delight, Frosted, 154
Mint Delight, Fruit Cocktail, 154
Mint Sauce, 337
Molasses
    Bars, Molasses Date-Nut, 122
    * Cookies, Crisp Rolled Molasses Cookies, 133
    Cookies, Molasses Oatmeal, 126
    Molasses Barbecued Ham, 230
    * Molasses Coconut Chews, 82
    * Molasses Peanut Crunch, 85
    Muffins, Molasses, 40
    Pies
        Grandma's Molasses Pie, 257
        Southern Molasses Pie, 257
    Pound Cake, Molasses, 59
    * Taffy, Molasses, 88
Muffins
    * Banana Bran Muffins, 40
    * Blueberry Muffins, 41
    Butterfly Orange Muffins, 41
    Cheese Corn Muffins, 40
    * Corn Muffins, 41
    Molasses Muffins, 40
    * Oatmeal Muffins, 40
    * Sweet Potato Muffins, 41
    * Whole Wheat Muffins, 40
Mushrooms
    Asparagus and Fresh Mushrooms, 365
    Casserole, Lima Bean and Mushroom, 111
    Casserole, Pork and Mushroom, 113
    Mushroom Sauce, 160
    Mushroom Sauce, Beefeater, 339
    Mushroom-Stuffed Veal Roll, 221
    Stuffed Mushrooms, 385
    Swiss Mushroom-Stuffed Tomatoes, 398

N

Noodles
    Casseroles
        Beef-Noodle Casserole, 98
        * Chicken-Green Noodle Casserole, 104

index 409

* Chicken-Noodle-Almond Casserole, 102
* Chicken Noodle Casserole, 104
* Hamburger-Noodle Bake, 99

Nuts
See also Names of Nuts
  Cakes
    Banana Nut Cake, 75
    Banana Nut Layer Cake, 73
    Chocolate Nut Cake, 74
    Christmas Nut Fruitcake, 60
    Date-Nut Loaf Cake, 62
    Orange-Nut Butter Cake, 65
  Candies. *See* Candies and Confections
  Casserole, Sweet Potato-Nut, 107
  Cookies. *See* Cookies

O

Oatmeal
  Cake, Chocolate Oatmeal, 74
  * Cake, Oatmeal, 70
  Cookies
    Molasses Oatmeal Cookies, 126
    * Oatmeal Delights, 127
    * Old-Fashioned Oatmeal Cookies, 127
    Orange Oatmeal Cookies, 128
    * Peanut-Oatmeal Cookies, 131
  * Muffins, Oatmeal, 40
  * Pie, Oatmeal, 258
Okra
  * Casserole, Okra and Cheese, 109
  Fried Okra, 385
  * Grilled Okra, 385
  Tomatoes and Okra, 397
Onions
  * Bread, Onion, 54
  * Creamed Spring Onions, 398
  Extra-Special Onions, 398
  Glazed Carrots and Onions, 372
  Golden Herbed Onions, 399
  * Oriental-Style Zucchini and Onions, 394
  Rings, French Fried Onion, 399
  * Rolls, Onion, 45
  Sauced Beets and Onions, 384
  Soup
    * Onion Soup au Gratin, 348
    Quick Onion Soup, 343
  * Stuffed Onions, 399
Oranges
  * Ambrosia, 148, 295
  Beverages
    Orange Eggnog, 31
    Orange-Lime Fizz, 26
    * Orange Milk Shake, 33
    * Punch, Orange-Grape Harvest, 26
    Punch, Tangy Orange-Cranberry, 26
  Breads
    Butterfly Orange Muffins, 41
    * Carrot-Orange Bread, 44
    * Orange-Cinnamon Yeast Rolls, 55
  Cakes
    Orange-Nut Butter Cake, 65
    Orange Rum Cake, 69
    Orange Slice Cake, 69
  Cookies
    Orange Date Cookies, 130

Orange Oatmeal Cookies, 128
Orange Slice Bars, 120
Dressing, Orange-Prune, 291
Frostings and Fillings
  Orange Glaze, 69
  Whipped Orange Topping, 65
* Ice Cream, Banana-Orange, 138
Orange Pecans, 84
Pudding, Orange Sponge, 145
* Rice, Orange, 167
Salad, Mandarin Orange, 301
Salad, Mandarin Orange Dessert, 302
Sauce, Orange, 62
Sherbet, Orange-Pineapple, 138
Sweet Potatoes, Orange, 395
Oysters
  Baked Trout with Oyster Stuffing, 187
  Broiled Oysters, 179
  Chicken with Oysters, 275
  Corn and Oyster Scallop, 178
  Creole Oyster Pie, 178
  Dip, Smoked Oyster, 17
  Dressing, Toasted Rice-Oyster, 291
  Eggplant Stuffed with Oysters, 376
  Fried Oysters, 179
  Loaf, Low Country Oyster, 177
  Oyster Mario, 176
  Oyster Surprise, 177
  Oysters Parmesan, 178
  Panned Oysters, 177
  Scalloped Oysters, 179
  Soufflé, Oyster, 177
  Soup, Oyster, 348
  Stuffing, Oyster, 290

P

Pancakes
  Eggcellent Pancakes, 47
  German Apple Pancakes, 47
  Soufflé Pancakes, 46
Peaches
  * Custard, Baked Peach, 141
  * Ice Cream, Easy Peach, 138
  Ice Cream, Peach, 139
  Peach Crisp, 152
  Peach Freeze, 152
  Peaches-and-Cream Rice Dessert, 152
  Pie, Fresh Peach Chiffon, 258
  Pudding, Tappy Peach, 145
Peanuts
  Candy
    Chocolate-Covered Peanut Balls, 86
    Chocolate Peanut Logs, 86
    * Molasses Peanut Crunch, 85
    Peanut Brittle, 86
    Peanut Brittle, Dixie, 86
    Raisin Peanut Clusters, 85
  Chili Nuts, Hot, 21
  * Cookies, Peanut-Oatmeal, 131
  Cookies, Salted Peanut, 129
  Party Mix, 18
  Smoky Peanuts, 21
Peanut Butter
  * Cake, Peanut Butter, 70
  * Cookies, Peanut Butter, 130
  * Dip, Peanut Butter-Cheese, 17
  * Peanut Butter Sticks, 13
  Peanutty Stuffed Eggs, 162
  * Pie, Peanut Butter Cream, 244

* Soup, Peanut Butter, 349
Peas
  Black-Eyed
    Baked Black-Eyed Peas, 383
    Casserole, Black-Eyed Pea, 110
    * Dip, Tasty Black-Eyed Pea, 14
    With Ham Hock, Black-Eyed Peas, 383
  Casseroles
    Asparagus, Peas, and Mushroom Casserole, 114
    Broccoli-Peas Casserole, 368
    Green Pea and Asparagus Casserole, 115
  Oriental Peas, 388
  * Salad, Refreshing Pea, 322
Pecans
  Breads
    Waffles, Pecan, 47
    Yeast Rolls, Pecan, 56
  Cake, Christmas Pecan, 71
  Candy
    Orange Pecans, 84
    Pecan Brittle, 83
    Pecan Pralines, 88
  Cookies
    Coconut Pecan Bars, 121
    Pecan Cookies, 131
  Pie
    Date Pecan Pie, 259
    "Down-Home" Pecan Pie, 258
    Pumpkin-Pecan Pie, 260
    Southern Pecan Pie, 258
Peppers
  Poultry-Stuffed Peppers, 388
  Rice-Stuffed Green Peppers, 387
  Seafood Stuffed Peppers, 386
  Southern Stuffed Peppers, 387
  Stuffed Peppers, 387
  Tasty Stuffed Green Peppers, 387
Pies and Pastries
  Alsatian Cream Pie, 264
  Apple
    Caramel-Topped Apple Pie, 247
    * Colonial Apple Pie, 246
    Crunchy Apple, 246
    Fried Apple Pies, 247
    * Grated Apple Pie, 246
    Sour Cream Apple Pie, 247
  Avocado Lime Pie, 257
  Banana Meringue Pie, 246
  Banana Pumpkin Pie, 260
  Blackberry
    Blackberry Meringue Pie, 248
    * Fresh Blackberry Pie, 247
    * Old-Fashioned Blackberry Pie, 248
  Blueberry
    * Blueberry Pie, 248
    * Fresh Blueberry Glacé Pie, 248
  Buttermilk Pie, 251
  * Butterscotch Pie, 251
  Cherry
    Cheery Cherry Pie, 246
    Cherry Cream Pie, 249
    Lemon-Cherry Pie, 254
    Refrigerator Cherry Pie, 249
  Chess Pie, Lemon, 254
  Chocolate, 250
    Chocolate-Butterscotch Pie, 249
    Chocolate Chip Pie, 249
    Chocolate Rum Pie, 250
    Fudge Pie, 243

* Asterisks indicate budget recipes.

German Chocolate Pie, 250
* Never Fail Chocolate Pie, 250
Coconut Custard Pie, One-Step, 252
Coconut Pie, 252
Cranberry Pie, Old-Fashioned, 253
French Silk Pie, 251
Fruit Fluff Pie, 245
Grape Juice Pie, 254
Hawaiian Fluff Pie, 253
Hawaiian Pie, 252
Ice Cream Pie, 253
Lemon
   Angel Pie, 245
   Cream Cheese Pie, Lemon, 255
   Cream Pie, Lemon, 255
   Custard Pie, Lemon, 255
   Frozen Lemon Pie, 256
   Ice Box Pie, Lemon, 245
   Lemon-Cherry Pie, 254
   Lemon Meringue Pie, 256
   Tarts, Lemon, 254
Macaroon Pie, 256
Marshmallow Prune Pie, 264
Millionaire Pie, 258
Mince Pie, Spicy, 256
Molasses
   Grandma's Molasses Pie, 257
   * Southern Molasses Pie, 257
* Oatmeal Pie, 258
Pastry
   Chopped Walnut Pie Shell, 243
   * Graham Cracker Crumb Shell, 244
   Hot Water Pastry, 243
   * Magic Piecrust, 244
   1-2-3 Pastry, 259
   Quiche Pastry, 244
   Standard Piecrust, 244
Peach Chiffon Pie, Fresh, 258
* Peanut Butter Cream Pie, 244
Pecan
   Date Pecan Pie, 259
   "Down-Home" Pecan Pie, 258
   Pumpkin-Pecan Pie, 260
   Southern Pecan Pie, 258
Persimmon Pie, 257
Pineapple, 260
   Pineapple Cheese, 259
   Pineapple-Lemon Lattice Pie, 260
Praline Pie, 259
Pumpkin Pie, Honey-Pecan, 248
Raisin Nut Pie, 265
Raisin Pie, Makes-Its-Own-Crust, 261
Rhubarb
   Rhubarb Pie, Best-Ever, 261
   Rhubarb Pie, Double Crust, 265
   Strawberry-Rhubarb Pie, 263
Rum Pie, Candied Fruit, 261
Sherry Pie, 264
Sky-High Pie, 264
* Southern Burnt Cream Pie, 252
Southern Transparent Pie, 243
Strawberry
   Chiffon Pie, Strawberry, 262
   * Deep-Dish Strawberry Pie, 261
   Glacé Pie, Strawberry, 262
   Glazed Strawberry Pie, 262
   Glazed Strawberry Pie, Colorful, 263
   Strawberry 'n Cream Pie, 263
   Strawberry Pineapple Lattice Pie, 263

* Sweet Potato Pie, 245
* Transparent Pie, 265
Tropical Dream Pie, 253
Turnovers, Dried Fruit, 251
Pineapple
   Baked Pineapple and Carrots, 372
   Beets with Pineapple, 384
   Cake, Pineapple Ambrosia Upside-Down, 77
   Frank Pineapple Kabobs, 223
   * Ice Cream, Pineapple-Lemon, 138
   Pie, 260
      Pineapple Cheese Pie, 259
      Pineapple-Lemon Lattice Pie, 260
   Pineapple Cream, 155
   Pineapple Nut Bread, 45
   * Pineapple Puff, 151
   Pineapple Tea Fizz, 26
   Pudding, Pineapple Upside Down Bread, 143
   Punch, Tropical Pineapple, 26
   Salad, Frozen Pineapple, 304
   Sherbet, Orange-Pineapple, 138
   * Sherbet, Quick Pineapple Milk, 138
   Slaw, Zippy Pineapple, 318
   Soufflé, Unbaked Pineapple, 151
   Spareribs, Pineappled, 235
Pizza Supper Pie, 218
Pizzas, Miniature, 7
Pompano en Papillote, 191
Pork
   Bacon
      Bacon-Barbecued Fish, 171
      Bacon-Beef Roll-Ups, 18
      Bacon-Cheese Special, 13
      Canadian Bacon Wheels with Pineapple Slices, 227
   Baked Pork Tenderloin with Apricot Topping, 226
   * Braised Pork Shoulder with Lima Beans, 226
   Casseroles
      Cheddar Chops Casserole, 95
      Hearty Bacon Casserole, 94
      Pork and Mushroom Casserole, 113
      Vegetable-Pork Chop Casserole, 95
   Chops
      Baked Stuffed Pork Chops, 229
      Braised Pork Chops, 228
      Dixie Pork Chops, 230
      Grilled Pork Chops, 227
      Hawaiian Pork Chops with Dressing, 228
      Saucy Pork Chops, 227
      with Scalloped Potatoes, Pork Chops, 227
      Spanish Pork Chop Bake, 229
      Spicy Glazed Pork Chops with Apricots, 229
      Stuffed Pork Chops, 228
   Franks
      * Blanketed Franks, 224
      * Casserole, Frank-Corn Muffin, 223
      * Corn Dogs, 225
      Corn 'n Franks, 224
      * Crispy Crust Franks, 13
      * Curried Frankfurters, 223
      Kabobs, Frank Pineapple, 223
      Little Links Teriyaki, 224
      Marinated Franks, 225
      * Party Franks, 223
      Potato 'n Frank Casserole, 222

      Rancho Hot Dogs, 225
      Sweet and Pungent Frankfurters, 224
      Sweet-and-Sour Franks, 224
      * Wieners in Butter and Beer Sauce, 12
      * Wieners, Chip 'n Cheese, 225
   Glorified Pork Suey, 226
   Ham
      Casseroles
         Ham and Asparagus Casserole, 94
         * Ham and Egg Casserole, 95
         Ham, Macaroni, and Broccoli Casserole, 112
         * Ham and Spaghetti Casserole, 112
         Scalloped Potatoes and Ham, 107
      Country-Cured Ham, 232
      Creamed Ham and Eggs, 233
      Fried Ham with Red-Eye Gravy, 230
      Glazed Smoked Ham, 232
      Grilled Ham, 231
      * Ham Mousse-Pâté, 19
      Ham Pinwheels, 20
      Loaf, 230
         Deviled Ham Loaf, 233
         Party Ham Loaf, 232
         Upside-Down Ham Loaf, 232
      Molasses Barbecued Ham, 230
      Poached Egg on Ham Toast, 160
      Polynesian Ham, 231
      Salad. See Salads
      Sandwiches
         Ham and Cheese Biscuit Pleasers, 233
         Ham 'n Cheese French Toast, 5
         * Ham Salad Sandwiches, 5
      Stuffed Fresh Ham Merrifield, 231
      Stuffed Ham, Baked, 230
   * Liverwurst and Egg Sandwich, 6
   Meatballs
      Cheese Meatballs with Spaghetti Sauce, 205
      Swedish Meatballs, 206
   Meat Loaf
      Hamburger and Sausage Loaf, 200
      Layered Meat Loaf, 201
      Triple Meat Loaf with Mustard Sauce, 203
      Triple Treat Meat Loaf, 202
   Roast, Herbed Pork, 234
   Sausage
      Balls, Sausage, 10
      * Bean 'n Sausage Stir, 218
      Casserole, Sausage-Bean, 111
      Choucroute, 218
      * Crescent Creole Meat Pie, 217
      Dressing, Corn Bread-Sausage, 290
      Dressing, Turkey-Time Sausage, 290
      Little Links in Oriental Sauce, 19
      Link Sausage, 218
      Loaf, Hamburger and Sausage, 200
      Loaf, Sausage, 218
      Stuffed Sausage Roll, 217
      Supper, Sausage and Bean, 219
   Spareribs
      Barbecued, 234
         Dixie Barbecued Spareribs, 234
         with Herb Sauce, Barbecued Spareribs, 234

* Asterisks indicate budget recipes.

index   411

with Marinade, Barbecued Spareribs, 235
Special Barbecued Ribs, 233
Spit Barbecued Ribs, 233
Pineappled Spareribs, 235
Sauerkraut and Ribs Aged in Beer, 235
Sauerkraut, Spareribs and Bohemian, 235
Smoked Spareribs, 236
Sweet-Sour Pork, 228
Tenderloin Sweet 'n Sour, 226
Weiners. *See* Franks
Potatoes
  Casseroles
    Potato 'n Frank Casserole, 222
    * Potato Patch Casserole, 107
    Scalloped Potatoes and Ham, 107
  Cowboy Potatoes, 389
  Creole Potatoes, 389
  * Mexican Potato Cakes, 389
  New
    Creamed Vegetable Sauce with New Potatoes, 390
    Fresh Green Beans with New Potatoes, 366
    * New Potatoes Rissole, 390
    * Parsley New Potatoes, 388
  Pimiento Potatoes, 390
  Pork Chops with Scalloped Potatoes, 227
  Salad
    Deviled Potato Salad, 324
    German Potato Salad, 325
    Sour Cream Potato Salad, 324
  Sausage Fried Potatoes, 389
  Soup, Old-Fashioned Potato, 348
  * Spanish Potato Dish, 388
  Stuffed Potatoes Creole, 389
  Vegetable Puffs, 390
Poultry. *See* Names of Individual Birds
Poultry Dressing. *See* Dressings
Puddings
  * Banana Pudding, 141
  * Bread
    * Bread Pudding, 143
    * Old-Fashioned Bread Pudding, 144
    Pineapple Upside Down Bread Pudding, 143
    with Whiskey Sauce, Bread Pudding, 143
  Chocolate Fudge Pudding, 142
  Date Pudding, 141
  Double-Chocolate Pudding Cups, 142
  * Indian Pudding, 146
  Orange Sponge Pudding, 145
  Peach Pudding, Tappy, 145
  Persimmon Pudding, 146
  Queen of Puddings, 146
  * Rice, 142
    Apricot Rice Pudding, 144
    * Butterscotch Rice Pudding, 144
    Chantilly Raisin Rice Pudding, 144
    * Rice Pudding with Raisins, 145
  Rhubarb Surprise Pudding, 145
  Strawberry Pudding, French, 146
Pumpkin
  Bread, Pumpkin, 45
  * Doughnuts, Pumpkin, 43
  Pie
    Banana Pumpkin Pie, 260
    Honey-Pecan Pumpkin Pie, 248
    Pumpkin-Pecan Pie, 260

Soufflé, Pumpkin, 391
Punch. *See* Beverages

Q

Quail. *See* Game

R

Raisin
  Bread, Old-Fashioned Raisin, 54
  Cookies, Jumbo Raisin, 126
  Pie, Makes-Its-Own Crust, 261
  Pie, Raisin Nut, 265
  Rice Pudding, Chantilly Raisin, 144
  * Rice Pudding with Raisins, 145
  Sauce for Ham, Raisin, 339
  White Raisin Sauce, 338
Redfish, Baked, 191
Red Snapper, Broiled, 187
Red Snapper Mozart, 187
Rhubarb
  Pie
    Best-Ever Rhubarb Pie, 261
    Double Crust Rhubarb Pie, 265
    Strawberry-Rhubarb Pie, 263
  Rhubarb Surprise Pudding, 145
Rice
  Baked Eggs with Rice and Cheese Sauce, 159
  Beefeater Wild Rice, 166
  Casseroles
    * Baked Beef and Rice, 96
    Cheese Rice, 181
    Chicken-Wild Rice Casserole, 103
    Creole Rice Casserole, 191
    Creole Rice and Shrimp, 182
    * Delmonico Rice, 167
    Giralda Rice, 115
    Liver and Rice Casserole, 101
    Olive-Rice Casserole, 164
    Rice-Broccoli Casserole, 108
    Romany Rice, 167
  * Chili-Rice Dish, 166
  Chili Rice, Louisiana, 166
  * Chinese Rice, 163
  * Curried Eggs in Rice Ring, 158
  * Curried Rice, 165
  Curried Rice, Elegant, 164
  Dessert, Peaches-and-Cream Rice, 152
  Dessert, Rice Florentine, 155
  Far East Fruited Rice, 165
  * Florentine Beef with Rice, 195
  Green Goddess Rice, 165
  * Green Rice, 166
  * Herb Fried Rice, 164
  Lamb and Rice Skillet Dinner, 238
  * Orange Rice, 167
  Pudding
    Apricot Rice Pudding, 144
    * Butterscotch Rice Pudding, 144
    Chantilly Raisin Rice Pudding, 144
    Rice Pudding with Raisins, 145
  Rice Almandine, 164
  * Salad, Chicken Rice, 305
  * Soufflé, Rice, 164
  * Spanish Rice with Meat, 165
  Stuffing for Turkey, Rice, 292
  * Tarragon Rice, 167

Toasted Rice-Oyster Dressing, 291
Rolls. *See* Breads
Rum
  Cake, Orange Rum, 69
  Pie, Candied Fruit Rum, 261
Rutabagas
  * Casserole, Scalloped Rutabaga and Apple, 110
  French Fried Rutabaga, 391
  Glazed Rutabagas, 391
  Honeyed Rutabaga, 391

S

Salads
  * Ambrosia, 295
  Apricot Cream, 295
  Apricot Nectar Salad, 296
  Asparagus Salad, 319
  Aspic
    Aspic à la Blue, 315
    Creamy Aspic Salad, 315
    * Quick Tomato Aspic, 326
  Avocado
    Avocado-Buttermilk Salad, 315
    Cherry Avocado Salad, 297
    Pimiento Cheese-Avocado Salad, 322
    Seafood-Avocado Salad, 310
  Bean
    Bean Sprout Salad, 317
    * Four-Bean Salad, 318
    Great Bean Salad, 317
    Marinated Beans, 316
  Beef Salad, 308
  * Beet Salad, Congealed, 316
  * Beet Salad, Molded, 316
  Blueberry Salad, 298
  Broccoli Salad, 315
  Cabbage Salad, Fruited, 319
  Caesar Salad, 316
  Cheese
    Cheese, Molded Macaroni and, 322
    Cheese Salad, Frozen Fruit, 299
    Cheese Salad, Lemon, 303
    Cheese and Vegetable Salad, 316
    Pimiento Cheese-Avocado Salad, 322
  Cherry
    Black Cherry Salad, 295
    Cherry Avocado Salad, 297
    Cherry Mallow Salad, 296
    Shimmering Cherry Salad, 296
  Chicken
    * Chicken Salad, 305
    Chicken and Carrot Salad, 304
    Chicken Cocktail Salad, 306
    Chicken and Ham Salad with Mustard Dressing, 306
    * Chicken Rice Salad, 305
    Chicken Salad Hawaiian, 304
    Chicken Salad Supreme, 307
    Curried Chicken Salad, 305
    Curried Chicken Salad in Tomato Petals, 307
    * Macaroni and Chicken Salad, 304
    Molded Chicken Loaf, 306
    * Spicy Chicken Salad Mold, 305
    Tropical Chicken Salad, 306
  Corn Beef Salad, 308
  Corn Beef Salad, Two-Toned, 309
  Crabmeat Salad, 309

* Asterisks indicate budget recipes.

Crab Salad in Avocado, 309
Cranberry, 298
   Cranberry Gelatin Salad, 298
   Frosty Cranberry Salad, 297
   Molded Cranberry Relish, 297
Crown Jewel Salad, 298
Cucumber-Lime Salad, 318
Cucumber Mousse, 317
Dressings. *See* Salad Dressings
* Easy Perfection Salad, 322
Florida Dessert Salad, 299
Frozen Salad, 300
Fruit. *See also* Specific Fruit
   Cola Fruit Salad, 299
   Creamy Frozen Fruit Salad, 300
   Fresh Fruit Salad, 301
   Frozen Fruit Cheese Salad, 299
   Frozen Fruit Nut Salad, 299
   Fruit Salad with Cooked Dressing, 301
   Golden Fruit Salad, 300
   White Fruit Salad, 296
Garlic Garden Salad, 319
Golden Nugget Salad, 321
Green Wonder Salad, 321
Guacamole, 320
Gulfport Salad, 310
Ham
   Chef's Salad with Ham, 307
   Chicken and Ham Salad with Mustard Dressing, 306
   Ham and Celery Salad, 307
   Ham and Egg Rice Salad, 308
   Ham Loaf Salad, 308
   * Ham and Macaroni Toss, 308
Health Salad Special, 321
* Jade Ring Salad, 323
Lemon-Lime Salad, Tangy, 303
Lemon Cheese Salad, 303
Lettuce, Wilted, 321
Luncheon Salad, 301
Macaroni
   * Ham and Macaroni Toss, 308
   Macaroni and Chicken Salad, 304
   Molded Macaroni and Cheese, 322
   * Tuna-Macaroni Salad, 312
Mexican Fiesta Salad, 321
Molded
   Cauliflower Mold, 320
   * Fish Salad Mold, 311
   Frosty Date-Sour Cream Mold, 300
   Gold and Green Salad Mold, 319
   Molded Chicken Loaf, 306
   * Molded Eggs and Vegetables, 320
   * Molded Macaroni and Cheese, 322
   Ruby Red Salad Mold, 297
   * Spicy Chicken Salad Mold, 305
Orange Dessert Salad, Mandarin, 302
Orange Salad, Mandarin, 301
* Pea Salad, Refreshing, 322
Pineapple Salad, Frozen, 304
Port Wine Salad, 304
Potato
   Deviled Potato Salad, 324
   German Potato Salad, 325
   Sour Cream Potato Salad, 324
Psychedelic Salad, 302
Salad Supreme, 303
Salmon
   Salmon Mousse, 314
   * Salmon and Rice Dinner Salad, 314

Sour Cream Salmon Salad, 314
Seafood Salad, 310
* Shamrock Salad, 317
Shrimp, 312
   Coastal Shrimp Salad, 313
   Gulf Shrimp Salad, 313
   Shrimp Chef's Salad, 313
   Shrimp Deluxe Salad, 312
Slaw
   * Calico Slaw, 317
   Grandma's Southern Slaw, 320
   Old-Fashioned Cold Slaw, 318
   Refrigerator Slaw, 320
   Zippy Pineapple Slaw, 318
Spinach, 323
   Dutch Spinach Salad, 323
   Fresh Spinach Salad, 324
Strassburg Salad, 318
* Surprise Salad, 302
Tomatoes
   * Fire and Ice Tomatoes, 325
   Herbed Tomatoes, 325
   * Quick Tomato Aspic, 326
   * Zesty Stuffed Tomatoes, 325
Tropical Salad and Ice Cream Dressing, 302
Tuna
   Buffet Tuna-Avocado Loaf, 312
   * Hearty Tuna Salad, 311
   Molded Tuna Ring, 311
   Tuna Louis, 310
   * Tuna-Macaroni Salad, 312
   * Tuna Salad, 310
Twenty-Four-Hour Salad, 302
Vegetable Salad, Jellied, 324
* Vegetable Trio Salad, 323
Wine Berry Spray, 303
Yum Yum Salad, 303
Salad Dressings
   Avocado, 327
      Avocado Dressing, Creamy, 326
      Avocado Dressing for Fruit, 327
   * Blender Salad Dressing, 328
   Blue Cheese Dressing, 326
   Blue Cheese Dressing, Warehouse, 326
   * Buttermilk Salad Dressing, 327
   * Celery Seed Dressing, 327
   Celery Seed Dressing, Creamy, 327
   * Cooked Salad Dressing, 328
   Cucumber Dressing, 326
   * Dressing for Green Salad, 329
   Dressing for Lettuce Salad, 330
   Famous Salad Dressing, 328
   Fluffy Topping, 300
   French, 327
      * Creamy French Dressing, 328
      * Curry French Dressing, 328
      French Dressing for Shrimp, 329
      Sweet 'n' Spicy French Dressing, 328
   Honey, 313
      Lemon-Honey Cream Dressing, 329
      Lemon-Honey Dressing, 329
   Ice Cream Dressing, 302
   Lime Dressing, 330
   Louis Dressing for Crab Salad, 329
   * Low-Calorie Dressing for Potato Salad, 331
   Mexicali Dressing, 330
   Pineapple Dressing for Fruit Salad, 329

   Poppy Seed, 330
      Curry-Poppy Seed Dressing, 331
      Honey Poppy Seed Dressing, 330
      * Lemon-Poppy Seed Dressing, 330
   Sour Cream-Blue Cheese Dressing, 326
   Sour Cream Dressing, Strawberry-, 330
   Stockman Salad Dressing, 331
   Tangy Dressing, 307
   Thousand Island Salad Dressing, 331
   * Thousand Island Salad Dressing, Yogurt, 331
Salmon
   Casseroles, Salmon-Macaroni, 180
   * Chowder, Salmon, 358
   * Croquettes with Celery Sauce, Salmon, 179
   Loaf, Salmon, 179
   * Pie, Country Salmon and Cracker, 180
   * Salad, Salmon and Rice Dinner, 314
   Salad, Sour Cream Salmon, 314
   Salmon Mousse, 314
Sandwiches
   Bacon-Cheese Special, 13
   Beef
      Beefy Spread Sandwiches, 3
      Hot Burger-Cheese Sandwiches, 3
      The Trail Driver, 6
   Cheese
      * Cheese and Egg Sandwich Filling, 4
      Cheese Salad Sandwich Filling, 4
      Cheese and Turkey Melt, 4
      * Cream Cheese Sandwich Filling, 4
   * Chicken Sandwiches, Crunchy, 4
   * Corned Beef Sandwiches, Hot, 5
   Crab Sandwiches, Grilled, 5
   *Cucumber-Cheese Sandwiches, 4
   * Cucumber Sandwiches, 5
   Ham 'n Cheese French Toast, 5
   * Ham Salad Sandwiches, 5
   Hot Sardine-Egg Sandwich, 6
   Lemon Butter Party Sandwiches, 6
   Liverwurst and Egg Sandwich, 6
   Po' Boy Sandwiches, 6
   Sausage Balls, 10
   Shrimp Party Sandwiches, 6
   Tuna
      Little Hero Sandwiches, 7
      Tuna-Cheese Soufflé Sandwiches, 7
   Turkey Melt, Cheese and, 4
Sauces
   Barbecue
      * Barbecue Sauce, 334
      Best Barbecue Sauce, 334
      Butter Barbecue Sauce, 334
      for Chicken, Barbecue Sauce, 335
      * for Chicken, Fiesta Barbecue Sauce, 334
      * Easiest Barbecue Sauce, 335
      Hamburger Barbecue Sauce, 335
      Hawaiian Barbecue Sauce, 334
      Herb Barbecue Sauce, 335
      Old-Fashioned Hot Barbecue Sauce, 335
      * Pit Barbecue Sauce, 335

* Asterisks indicate budget recipes.

Quick Barbecue Sauce, 334
Spicy Barbecue Sauce, 336
Texas Barbecue Sauce, 336
Bordelaise Sauce, 341
* Butterscotch Sauce, Jiffy, 336
Cheese
   * Cheese Sauce, 333
   Taco Cheese Sauce, 338
Chicken Liver Sauce for Ravioli or Spaghetti, 336
Chocolate
   Chocolate-Peanut Butter Sauce, 337
   * Double Fudge Sauce, 337
   French Chocolate Sauce, 337
   Hot Fudge Sauce, 338
* Cocktail Sauce for Fish, 339
Cranberry Wine Sauce, 340
* Creole Sauce, 339
Cucumber Cream Sauce, 340
Curry Sauce, 338
Custard Sauce, 150
Dill Butter Sauce for Lobster, 340
Grape-Orange Tropical Sauce, 337
Hard Sauce, 152
Hollandaise Sauce, 333
Hollandaise Sauce, Easy, 333
Ice Cream Sauce, 147
Island Kabob Sauce for Beef, 339
Lemon
   * Lemon Sauce, 337
   * Lemon-Molasses Ice Cream Sauce, 338
   Lemon-Parsley Sauce, 338
Marchand de Vin Sauce, 340
Marshmallow Sauce, 338
* Mint Sauce, 337
Mushroom Sauce, 160
Mushroom Sauce, Beefeater, 339
Orange Sauce, 62
Raisin Sauce for Ham, 339
Red Devil Sauce, 339
Sherry Cream Sauce, 341
Sour Cream Sauce, 333
Spaghetti Sauce, 341
Sweet-Sour Sauce, 341
Tartar Sauce, 340
Tomato Sauce for Fish, 340
Turkey Tetrazzini Sauce, 288
Whiskey Sauce, 143
White Raisin Sauce, 338
Sauerkraut
   * Sauerkraut Chocolate Cake, 76
   Sauerkraut and Ribs Aged in Beer, 235
   Spareribs and Bohemian Sauerkraut, 235
Seafood. *See also* Fish and individual kinds
   Casserole, Seafood, 180
   Salad, Seafood, 310
   Salad, Seafood-Avocado, 310
   Stuffed Peppers, Seafood, 386
Shad Bake, Outdoor Style, 180
Sherbet, Orange-Pineapple, 138
* Sherbet, Quick Pineapple Milk, 138
Sherry
   Sherry Cream Sauce, 341
   Sherry Tuna Scallop, 93
Shrimp
   Bisque, Shrimp, 184
   Broccoli-Shrimp Crisp, 182
   Broiled Barbecued Shrimp, 181

Casseroles
   Chicken-Shrimp Tetrazzini, 104
   Crab and Shrimp au Gratin, 92
   Creole Rice and Shrimp Casserole, 182
   Golden Shrimp Casserole, 93
   Happy Accident Shrimp Casserole, 93
   Shrimp, 185
   Shrimp Casserole to Freeze, 184
   Shrimp de Jonghe Casserole, 182
   Shrimp and Olive Casserole, 181
Crayfish or Shrimp Étouffée, 174
Creole with Cheese Rice, Shrimp, 181
Creole, Shrimp, 183
Curried Shrimp, 184
Curry of Shrimp Suzanne, 183
Dressing for Shrimp, 329
Dip, 17
   French Fried Shrimp with Coral Dip, 15
   Indonesian Shrimp Dip, 17
Eggplant with Shrimp, Baked, 375
Eggplant with Shrimp and Crabmeat, Stuffed, 375
Grilled Shrimp, 182
Jambalaya, Classic, 174
Marinated Hibachi Shrimp, 184
Salad, 312
   Coastal Shrimp Salad, 313
   Gulf Shrimp Salad, 313
   Shrimp Chef's Salad, 313
   Shrimp Deluxe Salad, 312
Sandwiches, Shrimp Party, 6
Shrimp à la King, 183
Shrimp de Jonghe, 183
Shrimp Mull, 185
Shrimp Rockefeller, 186
Shrimp Supreme, 185
Shrimp Tempura, 185
Shrimp Wiggle in Toast Cups, 186
Snacks. *See* Appetizers and Snacks
Sole Marguery, Filet of, 186
Soufflés
   Apple Pudding Soufflé, 150
   Broccoli, Souffléed, 368
   Chocolate Soufflé, 149
   * Grits Soufflé, 163
   Oyster Soufflé, 177
   Pineapple Puff, 151
   Pineapple Soufflé, Unbaked, 151
   Pumpkin Soufflé, 391
   * Rice Soufflé, 164
   Squash Soufflé, 393
   Squash Soufflé, Fluffy, 393
   Turkey Soufflé, 289
   Turkey Soufflé, Special, 286
Soups
   Artichoke Soup, 344
   Asparagus Cheese Soup, 346
   Avocado Bisque, Cool, 344
   Avocado Soup, Cold, 344
   * Bean Soup, Old-Fashioned, 345
   * Bean Soup, Senate, 345
   Bisque, Shrimp, 184
   * Cheese Soup, 344
   Cheese Soup, Canadian, 344
   Chicken Soup, Cream of, 345
   Chowders
      Clam Chowder, Maryland, 359
      Clam Chowder, The Warehouse's, 359

      Fish Chowder, 359
      * Salmon Chowder, 358
   Corn Soup, Cream of, 346
   Creole Court-Bouillon, 347
   Cucumber Soup, 347
   Easy Summer Borsch, 345
   Fruit Soup, 346
   Gazpacho, 350
      Gazpacho, Easy, 351
      Gazpacho with Shrimp, 347
   Gumbo, Turkey, 286
   Hearty Soup, 349
   * Lentil Soup, 348
   * Onion Soup au Gratin, 348
   Onion Soup, Quick, 343
   Oyster Soup, 348
   * Peanut Butter Soup, 349
   Potato Soup, Old-Fashioned, 348
   Shrimp Bisque, 184
   Soup Continental, 346
   * Spinach Soup, 350
   Spinach Soup, Cold Cream of, 350
   Tomato-Cream Cheese Soup, 348
   * Turkey Soup, Cream of, 289
   Vegetable
      * Vegetable Soup, 349
      Meatball Vegetable Soup, 343
      Occidentally Oriental Vegetable Soup, 349
   Vichyssoise, 351
Sour Cream
   Apple Pie, Sour Cream, 247
   Asparagus with Sour Cream Sauce, 365
   Beets in Sour Cream Sauce, 384
   Cakes
      Sour Cream Banana Cake, 73
      Sour Cream Cheesecake, 67
      Sour Cream Coffee Cake, 59
   Cookies, 126
      Sour Cream Nut Cookies, 126
      Sour Cream-Nutmeg Sugar Cookies, 134
      * Sour Cream Twists, 132
   Corn and Asparagus with Sour Cream, 378
   Cucumbers and Sour Cream, 379
   Cucumbers and Sour Cream with Fresh Dill, 379
   Fresh Broccoli with Sour Cream Dressing, 369
   Frosty Date-Sour Cream Mold, 300
   Gravy, Stuffed Veal Birds in Sour Cream, 221
   * Ground Beef in Sour Cream, 95
   Salad, Sour Cream Potato, 324
   Salad, Sour Cream Salmon, 314
Spinach
   * au Gratin, Spinach Ring, 392
   Casserole
      Exotic Spinach Dish, 391
   Custard, Spinach, 392
   Mozzarella-Spinach Bake, 392
   Salad, 323
      Dutch Spinach Salad, 323
      Fresh Spinach Salad, 324
   Soup
      Cold Cream of Spinach Soup, 350
      * Spinach Soup, 350
   * Spinach-Stuffed Tomatoes, 396
Spoonbread. *See* Breads
Squash
   Acorn Squash, Baked, 393

* Asterisks indicate budget recipes.

index

Summer
  Casseroles
    *Beef and Squash Casserole, 98
    Soufflé, Fluffy Squash, 393
    Soufflé, Squash, 393
    *Squash-Cheese Casserole, 110
  Squash Eudora, 393
  Stuffed Yellow Squash, 392
Zucchini
  Casseroles
    *Beef-Zucchini Casserole, 99
    Royal Zucchini Parmesan, 108
    Scalloped Tomatoes and Zucchini, 398
    *Oriental-Style Zucchini and Onions, 394
  South American Zucchini, 394
  Zucchini Delicious, 394
  Zucchini Parmesan, 394
Stews
  Beef
    Baked Beef Stew, 356
    Creole Beef Stew, 351
    Elegant Beef Stew, 350
    *Family Beef Stew, 353
    *Grits-Beef Stew, 352
    Iron Pot Stew, 357
    *Short Rib Stew, 357
  Brown Stew, 354
  *Brunswick Stew, 351
  Brunswick Stew, Florida, 355
  Chili
    *Chili con Carne, 352
    *Chili for a Crowd, 352
    Chili Italexico, 352
    Hot Chili, 363
  Crab Stew Monteleone, 358
  Flemish Stew, 353
  Hungarian Goulash, 358
  Italian Meat Stew, 356
  Lamb Stew with Parsley Dumplings, Savory, 356
  Meatball Stew, 354
  Olive Minestrone, 357
  Oyster Stew, New Year's Eve, 354
  *Ranch Stew, 356
  Southern Gumbo, 355
  Venison Stew, 358
Strawberries
  Beverages
    Banana Strawberry Float, 27
    *Strawberry Cooler, 29
    Strawberry Lemon Freeze, 27
    Strawberry Punch, 26
  Fresh Strawberries and Cream, 154
  Ice Creams
    Rich Strawberry Ice Cream, 140
    *Strawberry Ice Cream, 139
  Pies
    *Deep-Dish Strawberry Pie, 261
    Glazed Strawberry Pie, 262
    Glazed Strawberry Pie, Colorful, 263
    Strawberry Chiffon Pie, 262
    Strawberry 'n Cream Pie, 263
    Strawberry Glacé Pie, 262
    Strawberry Pineapple Lattice Pie, 263
    Strawberry-Rhubarb Pie, 263
  Pudding, French Strawberry, 146
  Strawberry Cream Roll, 72
Stuffings. See Dressings and Stuffings

Sweet Potatoes
  *Baked Sweet Potatoes, 395
  Baked Stuffed Sweet Potatoes, 394
  Casseroles
    *Brandied Sweet Potatoes, 395
    *Sweet Potato-Apple Casserole, 395
    *Sweet Potato Casserole, 107
    Sweet Potato Crisp, 396
    *Sweet Potato and Marshmallow Casserole, 92
    Sweet Potato-Nuts Casserole, 107
  Louisiana Sherried Sweet Potatoes, 395
  *Muffins, Sweet Potato, 41
  Orange Sweet Potatoes, 395
  *Pie, Sweet Potato, 245
  *Rolls, Sweet Potato, 56
  *Rolls, Sweet Potato Yeast, 55
  Yams, Cranberried, 396

T

Tomatoes
  Casseroles
    *Baked Tomatoes and Corn, 397
    Corn and Tomato Casserole, 109
    Hominy and Tomato Casserole, 106
    Scalloped Tomatoes and Zucchini, 398
  Fried Green Tomatoes, 397
  Kentucky Wonder Beans and Tomatoes, 382
  and Okra, Tomatoes, 397
  Salads
    *Fire and Ice Tomatoes, 325
    Herbed Tomatoes, 325
    *Quick Tomato Aspic, 326
    *Zesty Stuffed Tomatoes, 325
  *Scalloped Tomatoes, 397
  Scalloped Tomatoes, Southern, 398
  Stuffed
    Spicy Stuffed Tomatoes, 397
    *Spinach-Stuffed Tomatoes, 396
    Swiss Mushroom-Stuffed Tomatoes, 398
  Tomatoes Provencale en Salade, 396
Toppings. See Frostings and Fillings
Trout
  *Baked Trout and Cheese, 188
  Baked Trout with Oyster Stuffing, 187
  Barbecued Trout, 188
  *Barbecued Trout Filets, 188
  *Trout Treat, 188
  Trout Veronique, 189
Tuna
  Casseroles
    *One-Dish Tuna Dinner, 190
    Sherry Tuna Scallop, 93
    Tuna Bake, 93
    Tuna-Broccoli Almondine, 190
    Tuna Tetrazzini, 189
    *Tuna-Water Chestnut Casserole, 191
  Dips
    *Spicy Tuna Dip, 16
    *Tuna Cream Dip, 16
    *Tuna Dip, 16
  *Egg and Tuna Toss, 189

  *Grilled Tuna Burgers, 189
  Salad
    Buffet Tuna-Avocado Loaf, 312
    *Hearty Tuna Salad, 311
    Molded Tuna Ring, 311
    Tuna Louis, 310
    *Tuna-Macaroni Salad, 312
    *Tuna Salad, 310
  Sandwiches
    Little Hero Sandwiches, 7
    Tuna-Cheese Soufflé Sandwiches, 7
  Sweet-Sour Tuna, 190
  *Tuna Canapé Spread, 8
  *Tuna Cheesies, 12
Turkey
  Baking the Turkey, 285
  Casserole
    Asparagus and Turkey Casserole, 289
    Individual Turkey Casseroles, 285
    Turkey Casserole, 285
    Turkey Divan, 288
    Turkey Tetrazzini, 287
  *Gumbo, Turkey, 286
  Roasting a Deep-Basted Turkey, 286
  Sandwiches
    Cheese and Turkey Melt, 4
  Scalloped Turkey, 288
  Soufflé, Turkey, 289
  Soufflé, Special Turkey, 286
  *Soup, Cream of Turkey, 289
  Turkey Dinner-in-a-Dish, 289
  Turkey Newburg, 288
  *Turkey Sticks, 287
  Turkey Tetrazzini Sauce, 288
Turnip, Mustard, or Collard Greens, Fresh, 385

V

Veal
  Chops in Cream, Veal, 219
  Grillades and Grits, Veal, 220
  Little Veal Pies, 220
  Mushroom-Stuffed Veal Roll, 221
  Stuffed Veal Birds in Sour Cream Gravy, 221
  Swedish Meatballs, 206
  Triple Meat Loaf with Mustard Sauce, 203
  Triple-Treat Meat Loaf, 202
  Veal Marengo, 222
  Veal Milanese for Two, 220
  Wiener Schnitzel, 219
Vegetables. See also Names of Specific Vegetables
  *Braised Short Ribs with Vegetables, 206
  Casseroles
    *Baked Ratatouille Casserole, 108
    *Chicken-Vegetable Bake, 277
    Vegetable-Pork Chop Casserole, 95
  Chinese Vegetables, 388
  Creamed Vegetable Sauce with New Potatoes, 390
  Dill Marinated Vegetables, 386
  Marinated Vegetables, 386
  Salads
    Cheese and Vegetable Salad, 316

*Asterisks indicate budget recipes.

Jellied Vegetable Salad, 324
*Molded Eggs and Vegetables, 320
*Vegetable Trio Salad, 323
Soups
 Meatball Vegetable Soup, 343
 Occidentally Oriental Vegetable Soup, 349
 *Vegetable Soup, 349
Vegetable Puffs, 390
Venison. *See* Game

W

Waffles. *See* Breads, Pancakes and Waffles

---

* Asterisks indicate budget recipes.